Andrew Edgar

The Bibles of England

A Plain Account for Plain People of the Principal Versions of the Bible in English

Andrew Edgar

The Bibles of England
A Plain Account for Plain People of the Principal Versions of the Bible in English

ISBN/EAN: 9783337097493

Printed in Europe, USA, Canada, Australia, Japan

Cover: Foto ©Lupo / pixelio.de

More available books at **www.hansebooks.com**

THE BIBLES OF ENGLAND:

A PLAIN ACCOUNT FOR PLAIN PEOPLE

OF

THE PRINCIPAL VERSIONS OF THE BIBLE IN ENGLISH.

BY

ANDREW EDGAR, D.D.,

Author of "Old Church Life in Scotland."

ALEXANDER GARDNER,

Publisher to Her Majesty the Queen,

PAISLEY; AND PATERNOSTER ROW, LONDON.

MDCCCLXXXIX.

PREFACE.

THIS work is not a scholastic work, nor is it intended for scholastic readers. It is meant for plain people who have no knowledge of either Hebrew or Greek. Many questions, therefore, are ignored, which scholastic persons may think should, in a review of English versions of the Bible, be brought to the front; and some trivialities are introduced which scholastic persons may think should have been excluded.

The special subject to which most space in this volume is devoted, is that to which in many published works on English versions of the Bible least space is given; namely, the differentiations of successive versions, and the literary peculiarities that in each translation may be supposed most readily to attract the notice of common English readers. It is attempted in this way to shew how dissatisfaction with one version led to the publication of another; and there is set forth as much of the history of each version as will indicate the persistent labour that for five hundred years has been spent on the perfection of the English Bible.

One thing that calls for explanation, if not apology, is that while the book is professedly non-scholastic it contains a considerable number of Latin words and even Latin sentences. It will be found, however, that in many cases the Latin words are self-explanatory, and serve to shew the source from which particular expressions in the several English versions were derived. In all cases, too, the Latin quotations are of simple construction, and will be understood and appreciated by many readers who do not reckon themselves classical scholars. And if in any instance the Latin interpolation should prove a stumbling-block, it may be passed over without causing a breach in the continuity of the narrative.

It will be observed that at the head of each chapter there is a note of the special editions from which examples of the translation under discussion have been obtained. Such a note was necessary. Through misprints and corrections, there are scarcely two editions of any one English version of the Bible, except modern issues of the authorised and revised, that are absolutely identical. If the editions, therefore, from which quotations are taken had not been specified, some of these quotations might, on reference to a different edition, have been pronounced inaccurate. It is not to be supposed, however, that the editions specified at the heads of chapters in this volume are those that are most highly prized by book-hunters. They are simply those that I either happen to possess, or to which I have had most convenient access. But they are all sufficiently authentic for indicating the salient features of each version.

It can scarcely be expected that in a work like this, which abounds in details, there will not be some slips and oversights, misjudgments and mistakes. One mistake that may be thought inexcusable will be found on pages 215-216, in a note on a Hebrew word which an old Catholic controversialist alleges to be the original of the Church term *Mass*. That note was inserted without much consideration as the proofs were passing through the press. To undo the evil of misstatement in that note, a correction, to which the reader's attention is requested, is made in the Appendix, under letter D. Another passage that from awkwardness of expression is open to misconstruction, will be found on page 187. To prevent misapprehension on the subject to which that passage refers—the Theocracy established at Geneva in the days of Calvin—a brief account of Christian theories of Theocracy held by the Reformers is given under letter C in the Appendix.

Both for advice on special points of dubiety, and for access to valuable copies of old versions of the Bible, in Latin as well as in English, I have gratefully to acknowledge my obligations to the courtesy and kindness of friends and others that, although personally unknown to me, I take the liberty of counting friends.

A. E.

THE MANSE, MAUCHLINE,
13th MAY, 1889.

CONTENTS.

CHAPTER I.

THE LOLLARDS' BIBLE (Commonly called WYCLIF'S BIBLE). First version by John Wyclif and Nicholas de Hereford, about 1380. Revised version by John Purvey, about 1388.

Popular interest in the Bible, 1—No Bible in English long after Christianity established in England, 2—Early English versions of parts of Bible, 2—Publication before invention of printing, 4—Wyclif's reasons for translating the Bible, 4—Wyclif's first version, 5—Wyclif's career and end, 7—Wyclif's Bible condemned, 8—Earliest printed copies of Wyclif's Bible, 9—First and revised versions of Wyclif's Bible compared, 9—Wyclif's and Purvey's English, 12—Peculiar words in Wyclif's Bible, 14—Obsolete words in Purvey's revised version, 14—In earlier version, 18—Words used in a sense that is now obsolete, in Purvey's version, 20—In earlier version, 23—Saxon compounds, 25—Translation of proper nouns, 26—Ecclesiastical terms, 27—Phrases in Wyclif's Bible, quaint and apt, 31—Crude and inapt, 33—Peculiar readings and renderings in Wyclif's Bible, 36—Use of articles by Wyclif, 39—Readings and renderings of Wyclif revived in revised version, 41—Homeliness of Wyclif's diction, 42—Anachronisms in Wyclif's Bible, 45—Merits of Wyclif's Bible, 47—Wyclif's order of readers and preachers, 47.

CHAPTER II.

THE REFORMERS' BIBLES.
TYNDALE'S TESTAMENT, 1526; Revised, 1534.

The fundamental doctrine of Protestantism, 49—New translation of the Bible needed at the Reformation, 50—William Tyndale, 51—Resolves to translate the Bible, 53—Goes to London, 54—Meets with Humphrey Monmouth, 55—Goes abroad, 56—Proceeds with translation of the New Testament, 56—Prints his translation, 57—Publishes his translation, 57—His translation denounced, 58—His translation confuted by Sir Thomas More, 62—His other publications, 63—Encouraged to return to England, 65—His apprehension resolved on, 66—Seized and charged with venting heresies, 68—His martyrdom, 69—The advantages he had over Wyclif in translating the Testament, 69—His qualifications for translating the Testament, 71—Editions of Tyndale's Testament, 72—Tyndale's English, 74—Obsolete words in Tyndale's Testament, 75—Common words used in an archaic sense, 76—Ecclesiastical terms used or misused, 79—Proper names translated and untranslated, 83—Expressions and phrases of Tyndale's still surviving in the authorised version of the Testament, 83—Some of Tyndale's phrases that are not retained in authorised version good and forcible, 85—Paraphrastic renderings, 87—Tyndale's Germanisms, 88—Infelicitous renderings, 88—Homely phrases, 89—Use and misuse of articles, 91—Renderings of Tyndale's restored in revised version (1881), 92—Points of discordance between Tyndale's and the authorised version, 93—Causes of these discordances, 96—Other translations of Scripture by Tyndale, 98.

CHAPTER III.

THE REFORMERS' BIBLES (Continued).

    COVERDALE'S BIBLE, 1535.
    MATTHEW'S BIBLE, 1537.
    TAVERNER'S BIBLE, 1539.
    THE GREAT BIBLE or CROMWELL'S BIBLE, 1539; Revised edition, with prologue by Cranmer, and therefore called Cranmer's Bible, 1540.

Miles Coverdale, 100—Publishes a translation of the whole Bible, 101—The text from which he translated, 101—His translation partly original and partly based on Tyndale's, 101—Account of the part that was original, 101—Account of the part based on Tyndale's translation, 106—The Latin and Dutch inspirations in Coverdale's Bible, 110—Dedication of Coverdale's Bible, 114.

Matthew's Bible, 114—Specimens of its annotations, 115.

Taverner's Bible, 117.

The Great Bible, 119—Its printing and publication, 120—Its different designations, 120—Steps taken to promote its circulation, 121—A plethora of Bibles, 122—The three constituent parts of the Great Bible, 123—New Testament in Great Bible follows Tyndale's more than Coverdale's translation, 125—Follows Coverdale's version in some passages, 125—Old Testament, from Genesis to Chronicles, follows Tyndale's more than Coverdale's translation, 127—Antique renderings in Reformers' versions of the Old Testament from Genesis to Chronicles, 128—Old Testament, from Ezra to Malachi, not much changed from Coverdale's, 131—Points of difference between Great Bible and Coverdale's Bible in second part of Old Testament, 134—Great Bible compared with the authorised, 136—Bracketed readings, 138—End of Coverdale, 139.

CHAPTER IV.

THE PURITANS' AND PEOPLE'S BIBLE (Otherwise termed the GENEVA or BREECHES BIBLE).

    First Geneva translation of New Testament, 1557.
    Second Geneva translation of New Testament, with translation of Old Testament, 1560.
    Third, or Tomson's revised translation of New Testament, 1576.

From 1540 to 1557, 140—Sir John Cheke's translation, 140—Its Saxon words, 141—Its Archaisms, 141—Its marginal notes, 142—Reign of Mary in England, 142—Persecution of Reformers, 143—Flight of Reformers to Geneva, 143—First Geneva version of the New Testament, 144—Its peculiarities, 144—Its relation to previous versions, 145—The Geneva Bible in whole, 148—Authors of that translation, 149—Characteristics of that translation, 150—Its popularity, 150—Its interest to Scotsmen, 151—The first Bible in English printed in Scotland, 151—Hart's edition of Geneva Bible, 154—Popular designation of Geneva Bible, 154—Three Geneva versions of New Testament, 155—Only one Geneva version of Old Testament, 156—Second Geneva version of the New Testament compared with the first, 156—Inspired by Beza's Latin translation, 156—Its variations of two kinds, 157—The larger changes, 157—The lesser changes, 159—All the changes not improvements, 161—Majority improvements, 162—Third Geneva version of Testament, by Laurence Tomson, 162—Compared with the second version, 162—Accentuation of Articles, 163—Other amendments, 164—Geneva version of the Old Testament, 165—How framed, 165—Its sources of inspiration, 166—Compared with Great Bible, 166—Correction of renderings in Great Bible, 167—Refinement of renderings in Great Bible, 170—Changes that were not improvements, 173—The language of Geneva Bible, 176—Antiquated forms of words, 177—Obsolete words, 177—Current words in obsolete sense, 178—Ecclesiastical terms, 180—Phrases well chosen, 181—Renderings that are not good, 182—Marginal notes, 184—Anti-papal, 184—Calvinistic, 185—Puritanical, 186—Political, 187—Quaint and curious, 188—Good specimens of sound exposition, 189.

CHAPTER V.

THE BIBLES OF THE CHURCHES. No. 1. BIBLE OF THE CHURCH OF ENGLAND (Commonly called the BISHOPS' BIBLE).

First translation, 1568. Revised translation, 1572.

Need for a new version for public use in Church of England, 191—Resolution to revise the Great Bible, 193—Work of revision and its distribution, 195—Issue of the Bishops' Bible, 195—Bishops' Bible not licensed by Queen for use in Churches, 196—Successive editions, 196—Bishops' Bible a failure, 197—Crotchets of some of the Episcopal translators, 198—Limited and temporary circulation of Bishops' Bible, 199—Close correspondence between Bishops' Bible and Great Bible, 199—In Old Testament the text in some books in Bishops' Bible little, and in others much changed from the text in Great Bible. 200—Points of correspondence between the two texts in Old Testament more striking than points of difference, 205—Incorrect readings in Great Bible retained in Old Testament, 205—Imperfect renderings in Great Bible retained by Bishops, 207—Unapproved readings and imperfect renderings taken by Bishops from Geneva version, 208—Original renderings in Old Testament by Bishops, 210—Adoption in authorised version, 210—Not adopted, 211—Bishops' version of New Testament, 212—Incorrect readings and renderings in Great Bible retained, 213—Infelicitous renderings in Great Bible retained, 214—Infelicitous amendments in Geneva Bible rejected by Bishops, 217—Geneva amendments adopted by Bishops, 218—Wisely, 219—Unwisely, 219—Original renderings by Bishops, 220—Good, 221—Not good, 222—Received into authorised version, 223—Diction of Bishops' Bible, 224—Archaisms in Bishops' Bible, 227—Marginal notes in Bishops' Bible, 228—Interpolations, 231.

CHAPTER VI.

THE BIBLES OF THE CHURCHES. No. 2. BIBLE OF THE CATHOLIC CHURCH (Commonly called the DOUAY BIBLE.)
NEW TESTAMENT, printed at Rhemes, 1582.
OLD TESTAMENT, printed at Douay, 1609-1610.
Modern revisions, by Challoner and others.

Necessity for a Catholic version of the Scriptures in English, 234—Issue of a Catholic version of the Bible in English, 237—The translators, 237—Source from which the Catholic version drawn, 237—Principles according to which the translation was made, 241—Character of the Catholic translation, 242—Latin words too frequently translated by their English derivatives, 243—Excessive literalness in translation, 246—Renderings that bear on controverted points, 248—Three alleged specially sacred terms, 252—The Douay Bible from a literary point of view, 254—Words used, 255—Phrases, 255—Catholic readings and Catholic renderings, 257—Rhemes readings and renderings in revised Testament (1881), 259—Annotations in Rhemes Testament, 260.

Douay version of the Old Testament, 261—Ecclesiastical terms in Douay Bible, 262—Latin words and Latin-English words, 262—Archaisms and colloquialisms, 265—Odd and queer readings, 269—Proper names translated as common nouns, 270—Readings different in meaning from the authorised, 271—The notes in the Douay Bible, 275—Merits of the Rhemes-Douay version, 276—Imperfections, 277.

Revisions of Douay Bible, 278—Catholic opinions on these revisions, 279—No authentic Catholic text of Scriptures in English, 279—Challoner's versions, 280—Inkhorn terms, 280—Inapt terms, 281—Challoner's conformity with diction of the authorised version, 281—Douay phrases retained by Challoner, 282—Challoner's freedom with Catholic terms, 283—Annotations in modern editions of Catholic versions of the Bible, 283.

CHAPTER VII.

THE NATIONAL BIBLE (Sometimes called the KING'S TRANSLATION, more frequently termed the AUTHORISED VERSION, 1611).

Bibles in England in 1600, 286—Still another translation wanted, 286—The King takes the matter in hand, 287—Some churchmen not in favour of the project, 289—The work planned and commenced, 289—The new version published and dedicated to the King, 290—The preface to the new version, 291—The declared aim of the new version, 291—The qualifications of the translators, 292—Helps used in the translation, 293—Principles on which the translation was made, 293—The new version not adopted everywhere at once, 295—Strange misprints in different editions, 296—Deviations from the text of the first edition, 299—Relation of the new version to former versions, 300—Inaccuracies in Bishops' Bible corrected, 305—Diction in Bishops' Bible improved,

305—Renderings appropriated from Geneva version, 306—Renderings appropriated from the Rhemes Testament, 308—Each English version an improvement on previous versions, 309—The true meaning of passages brought out better, 309—Happier words chosen and smoother phrases, 312—Importance of these improvements, 316—Archaic words and expressions that still remain in the authorised version, 317—Headings of chapters, 321—Marginal references and notes, 323.

CHAPTER VIII.

THE INTER-NATIONAL BIBLE (Commonly called the REVISED VERSION).

NEW TESTAMENT, 1881.   OLD TESTAMENT, 1885.

The King's translation not adopted at once, nor expected by the translators to be, 326—Rise and progress of dissatisfaction with the authorised version, 327—A revision proposed, 328—Project abandoned, 329—Demand for revision heard again, 330—Attempts in revision, 331—Doddridge's Expositor, 332—Macknight's translation of Epistles, 334—Thomson's translation of New Testament, 335—An international revision of the English Bible proposed, 337—Work of revision undertaken, 338—Time spent in revision, 339—Issue of new version and demand for copies, 339—Character of revised version, 340—New readings in Greek Testament adopted, 341—Amount of change on English text from adoption of these readings, 342—Ground on which these readings were adopted, 344—Amount of correspondence between new Greek text of Testament and the Vulgate, 344—Amended renderings in the English New Testament, 348—Stricter rendering of the Greek article, 352—Stricter rendering of Greek prepositions, 355—Stricter rendering of the different parts of the Greek verb, 357—Uniformity of rendering, 359—Diction of Revised New Testament, 363—New readings in Hebrew text of Old Testament adopted, 368—Diction of revised version of Old Testament, 370—Dissimilar English readings in authorised and revised versions of Old Testament, 373—Archaisms in authorised version removed or retained in revised, 380—Benefits derived from revision of English Bible, 382.

APPENDIX.

A.	Early Scottish Renderings of Scripture, ...	385
B.	Modern Scottish Versions of Scripture, ...	391
C.	Theocracy in Geneva and Scotland, in explanation of a statement open to misconstruction on page 187, ...	393
D.	The word Mass—correction of note on page 215-216, ...	399

ERRATUM—Pages 144, 347—*For* "Stephen," *read* "Stephens."

BIBLES OF ENGLAND.

The Lollards' Bible, commonly called Wyclif's Bible.

Editions consulted and quoted from :—
    First version, by John Wyclif and Nicholas de Hereford, 1380.—Forshall and Madden's edition.
    Song of Solomon, in Adam Clarke's "Commentary."
    Second version, revised by John Purvey, 1388.—Forshall and Madden's edition.
    New Testament in Bagster's "Hexapla."

THERE is no book that, in respect of either its practical value or its historical interest, can, in the estimation of Christians, be put in comparison with the Bible. The Bible is regarded by Christians as the Word of God, in which may be found all the spiritual truth, indiscoverable by reason, that God has been pleased to reveal to men for their guidance and comfort. The knowledge communicated in the Bible has the special distinction of making men wise unto salvation. The English Bible, moreover, is one of the most notable books of literature, which every student of English literature requires to read and study; and a comparison of ancient and modern versions of the Bible in English gives the careful reader considerable insight into the structure and history of the English language itself. All information, therefore, on the history of the Bible, and especially on its presentation to the people of England and Scotland in their native tongue, should be both interesting and useful to English-speaking people, and particularly to English-speaking Christians.

On every occasion of public worship in Protestant Churches at the present day the Bible is produced, and a part of it is audibly read by the officiating minister, or his assistant, for the edification of the worshippers. It is on some verse or passage of the Bible, too, that, Sabbath after Sabbath, every Christian preacher, in our Protestant Churches, builds his discourses. In view of these facts, it cannot but seem strange that the Christian religion was established in this country several hundred years before there was a Bible either read to, or written for, the people in a language they could understand. Yet such is the case. Christianity was introduced into England more than 1200 years ago (some historians say about 1800 years ago), and long before the year 1000 A.D., the land was overspread with Christian Churches, and a Christian ministry was maintained by the tithes of the land's produce. But in those early times there was no version of the Bible, or at least of the whole Bible, in English. Knowledge of the Bible was then, by those that could read Latin, usually sought in the Latin translation known as the Vulgate; and to those that could not read Latin, it was sparingly conveyed by the lips of the priest, in homilies and paraphrases, which were not remarkable for accurate representation of Scripture truth.

To John Wyclif belongs the honour of having given to his countrymen the first complete version of the Bible in English. This was in, or about, the year 1380. Long prior to that date, however, portions of the Bible had been transcribed both in English and in Anglo-Saxon. About the end of the seventh, or beginning of the eighth century, the Psalter was rendered into Anglo-Saxon by Aldhelm, Bishop of Sherborne. In 735, the venerable Bede bequeathed, "for the advantage of the Church," an Anglo-Saxon translation of the gospel by St. John. Among other portions of Scripture translated into Anglo-Saxon may be mentioned four chapters in Exodus (xx-xxiii), by King Alfred (about 890); the four gospels, by Aldred, a priest of Holy Isle (about 950); and the books of Moses, Joshua, and Judges, by Aelfric,[1] Abbot of Peterborough, and

---

[1] "The work of Aelfric is by no means a complete version of the above-mentioned books. His object was to furnish his countrymen with a translation of those parts of the Scripture only, which he conceived to be most important for them to know; and, in the execution of his purpose . . . he has, for the most part,

afterwards Archbishop of York (about 1000). Of the Old-English versions of portions of Scripture, previous to 1380, it will suffice to mention a metrical paraphrase of the Gospels and Acts, by Orm or Ormin, a monk, who is supposed to have lived in the latter half of the twelfth century; a prose version of the Psalms, by Richard Rolle of Hampole (about 1349); and a gloss of a considerable part of the New Testament (the gospels by St. Mark and St. Luke, and the Epistles of St. Paul), supposed to have been written about the same time as Rolle's Psalter. These excerpts, as they might be aptly enough termed, were not widely circulated; and, although they furnished devotional reading for people of rank and education, they did little to enlighten the community in the knowledge of Scripture. Some of them have to this day been preserved; and not only may old manuscript copies of them be seen in college and other libraries, but printed copies of them (or of parts of them), may be found in books that are quite accessible to the public.[1] In such a popular work, for instance, as Clarke's *Commentary on the Bible*, many curious and interesting extracts are given from an old English annotated manuscript psalter, which, from its archaic phraseology, is evidently of an earlier date than Wyclif's translation.[2]

---

stated in his own words only the substance of the precepts inculcated, and the history recorded by the sacred penmen."—*Baber.*

[1] The following are curious samples of old translation:—Gen. ii., v. 23, "Tha cwaedh Adam, Heo is ban of minum banum, and flaesc of minum flaesce: beo hire name *Uirago*, thaet is faemne." Aelfric: Mark i. v. 6, "And Jhone was kladde wir heris of cameyls, and a gerdel of askyne aboute his lendis, and he ete honysokyls and honye of ye wood; and he prechyde seyande, a stallworthier yane I shal come aftr me, of whom I am not worthe downfallande or knelande to louse ye thonges of his chawcers."—*Gloss on St. Mark about 1350.*

[2] A comparison of the 23rd Psalm in this old Psalter, and in Rolle's Psalter, indicates that Dr. Clarke's manuscript is either a copy of Rolle's translation or a very slight amendment of it. The second clause of Ps. ciii. v. 5, is in Dr. Clarke's manuscript rendered

"Newed sal be als of aeren thi youthed,"

and appended to this translation is a curious note explanatory of the way in which science accounted for the eagle's rejuvenescence. "The arne (eagle), when he is greved with grete elde, his neb waxis so gretely, that he may nogt open his mouth and take mete: bot then he smytes his neb to the stane, and has away the slogh, and than he gaes til mete, and he commes yong agayne."

In saying that an English translation of the Bible was in, or about, 1380 *published* by Wyclif, a word of explanation must be added. At the present day the publication of a book means the printing and issuing for public sale of a large number of copies. In the days of Wyclif there was no printing. Books were all hand-written, and copies of books were transcribed, singly and separately, as occasion required. But although it was with so much labour that copies of Wyclif's Bible were produced, it is certain that soon after its publication, a goodly number of copies was issued and disposed of. It is commonly alleged that 170 copies, written previous to 1430, are still in existence. It is not unlikely, too, that transcripts of parts, as well as of the whole, of the Bible were made and sold. In Dr. Clarke's *Commentary* there is inserted, as a great curiosity, a translation of the Book of Canticles, or Song of Solomon, from a manuscript of the 14th century; and this fragment has now been identified as part of the first edition of Wyclif's Bible.

For more reasons than one, it may be said that, in Wyclif's day, the time had come for the English people to have a Bible in their own language. The people of other countries had that privilege. In a speech attributed to

"Old John of Gaunt, time honoured Lancaster,"

there was a demand expressed, therefore, that in a matter of such high concern, England should be abreast of her neighbours. "We will not be the dregs of all," shouted the speaker, "seeing other nations have the law of God, which is the law of our faith, written in their tongue." To the same effect, John Purvey wrote in his prologue to the revised edition of Wyclif's Bible, 1388: "Freenshe men, Beemers and Britons (*i.e.*, Belgians and Normans) han the Bible . . . translatid in here modir language: whi shulden not English men have the same in here modir language, I can not wite." It was the controversies, however, which Wyclif had with the Romish Church, that were the immediate occasion of his publishing the Bible in English. In those days, corruption had reached its climax in the Church of Rome. The cup of scandal and iniquity was full. There was corruption in doctrine, corruption in ritual, corruption in discipline, and enormous corruption in the patronage of Church livings. At many of the things he saw and heard in the Church, Wyclif was scandalised and shocked. For thirty years he was a trenchant and vehement assailant of ecclesiastical abuses. With voice and pen, he laboured incessantly to effect a Reform in the Church. He derided the doctrine of transubstantiation, ridiculed the worship of images, denounced the sale of indulgences, scoffed at pilgrimages, and had the hardihood not only to call the Pope Anti-Christ, but to accuse his holiness of being "the most cursed of clippers and purse-kervers." And maintaining, as he did, that the doctrines and practices he assailed had no warrant nor foundation in Scripture, Wyclif said that the surest way to put an end to ecclesiastical superstition and presumption was to acquaint the people with the Bible. He resolved, therefore, to publish the Bible for the people in their mother tongue. That, he concluded, would be the true cure for corruption, and would give to the men of England what John the Baptist was appointed to teach the palsied nation of Israel—"the science of health."[1]

It need scarcely be said that it is from the original tongues in which it was written that the Bible should be translated. That would be going to the fountain head. But, in the days of Wyclif, there was not in all England scholarship enough for such an achievement. Instead, therefore, of translating the Old Testament from its original Hebrew, and the New Testament from its original Greek, Wyclif was content to give to his countrymen a translation of the Vulgate, that is of the Latin version of the Bible, which was virtually accepted in the Church of Rome as the true canonical Scriptures. How long he was actually engaged in the work of translation cannot be confidently stated. It is generally admitted that in 1378 he had commenced his work, and the date commonly assigned to its completion is 1380.

Although it is customary to say that Wyclif gave to his

---

[1] Wyclif may be said to have anticipated a modern phrase by rendering "knowledge of salvation" (Luke, i. 77) "the science of health."

countrymen an English version of the entire Bible, we are not to suppose that all the translation was his own work. He had a collaborateur, in the person of Nicholas de Hereford, who translated the Old Testament from Genesis to the middle of Baruch. The remainder of the Old Testament (from Ezekiel to Malachi), and the whole of the New Testament, are believed to have been rendered into English by Wyclif personally.

That Wyclif's Bible, in its first form, was a work of much merit, and that it supplied a great want in England, is universally conceded; but it had many imperfections nevertheless. Probably no one was more alive to that fact than Wyclif himself, and we may presume that if he had lived a few years longer, in health and strength, he would have issued a new and a revised edition, with corrections and amendments. But he was denied the opportunity. In 1379, he had a stroke of paralysis; and in 1384, he died. After his death, however, there rose up in England another anti-papalist of eminent scholarship. This was John Purvey,[1] who set himself to the task of revising Wyclif's translation, and, in (or about) 1388, gave to the world the fruits of his labours. All critics concur in according to Purvey's revision[2] very high commendation.

---

[1] In some books, *e.g.*, "Mombert's English Versions of the Bible," he is called Richard Purvey.

[2] In the translation of poetical passages, such as the Psalms, Purvey was less stately in his diction than Hereford. The latter made large use of "congenial inversions" in the structure of his sentences, which Purvey, in his revision, discarded. Some people will probably consider Hereford's taste in this matter more correct than Purvey's. The following passage will illustrate the respective styles of the two men, in the rendering of poetical pieces:—

HEREFORD.	PURVEY.
Psalm ciii., 7-10.—Knowen he made his weies to Moises, and to the sones of Jacob his willis. Reewere and merciful the Lord, long abidende and myche merciful. In to evermore he shal not wrathen, ne in to withoute end he shal threte. Aftir our synnes he dide not to us, ne aftir oure wickednessis he zelde to us.	Psalm ciii., 7-10.—He made hise weies knowun to Moises: hise willis to the sones of Israel. The Lord is a merciful doer, and merciful in wille: long abidinge and myche merciful. He schal not be wrooth with-outen ende: and he schal not thretne with-outen ende. He dide not to us aftir oure synnes: nether he zeldide to us aftir oure wickednessis.

As a piece of scholastic workmanship, it is characterised by great carefulness. It was prefaced, also, by a long and an interesting prologue, explaining the principles on which "the simple creature" proceeded in his revision, and shewing the pains he was at to make the translation as good as loving labour could. "With comune charite to saue alle men in our rewme (realm), which God wole haue sauid, a symple creature," he said, "hath translated the bible out of Latyn into English. First, this symple creature hadde myche trauaile, with diuerse felawis and helperis, to gedere manie elde biblis, and othere doctouris, and comune glosis,[1] and to make oo Latyn bible sumdel trewe: thanne to studie it of the newe, the text with the glose and othere doctouris, as he might gete: . . . the thridde tyme to counseile with elde gramariens and elde dyuynes, of harde wordis and hard sentencis, hou tho mighten best be understonden and translatid: the fourth tyme to translate as cleerli as he coude to the sentence, and to haue manie gode felawis and kunnynge at the correcting of the translacioun."

As a matter of course, when Wyclif quarrelled with the ecclesiastical powers he had to reckon with his host. Both at home and at Rome he was regarded as a heretic; and although he did not attain to the honours of martyrdom, he had the privilege of enduring some persecution.[2] More than once, he was taken to book for venting erroneous opinions; and on one occasion the Pope directed the king of England "to retain the said John in sure custody and in chains." But he never was actually prevented from going at large; and he died in the enjoyment of both his priestly functions and his

---

[1] The word gloss is commonly used to signify an explanatory statement. In early times it was used differently. Glosses, says Dr. Eadie, were interlinear vernacular translations, "neither free nor yet literal translations, but the interlinear insertion of the vernacular, word against word of the original."—*History of English Bible*, Vol. I., p. 14.

[2] Both Hereford and Purvey suffered for their opinions also. Hereford was excommunicated and imprisoned, and seems to have regained his liberty by renouncing his Lollardism. Purvey was imprisoned in 1390; in 1400 he was frightened into recantation; and in 1421, having recovered his courage, he was thrown into prison again.—See Moulton's "History of the English Bible."

ecclesiastical benefice. Forty years after his burial, however, his remains were disinterred by ecclesiastical order; and, in the presence of a distinguished assemblage of prelates and priests, they were burned on the bridge of a stream close by his grave. And, to make his ignominy complete, his calcined ashes were disallowed either honoured urn or quiet tomb to rest in, but were thrown from the bridge, and committed to the current of the underflowing waters.

After Wyclif's death, his Bible was judicially condemned. In 1408, a Convocation at Oxford, proceeding on the preamble that "it is a dangerous thing to translate the Holy Scripture, it being very difficult in a version to keep close to the sense of the inspired writers," decreed and ordained that "from henceforward no unauthorised person shall translate any part of the Holy Scripture into English or any other language, under any form of book or treatise; neither shall any such book, treatise, or version, made either in Wyclif's time or since, be read, either in whole or in part, publicly or privately, under the penalty of the greater excommunication, till the said translation shall be approved either by the bishop of the diocese or a provincial council, as occasion shall require."[1] Considering that, long before Wyclif's time, there had been many translations of different parts of the Bible made both in English and in Anglo-Saxon; that these translations, before being issued to the public, had never to pass any official scrutiny; that they were read, apparently with ecclesiastical approval, and certainly without ecclesiastical remonstrance, by persons of quality, and in fact by all people that could read, and could afford to purchase such costly manuscripts; this decree of the Oxford Convocation, in 1408, may well excite our astonishment.[2] Its

---

[1] Temporal pains seem to have been subsequently added to spiritual anathemas. Dr. Eadie states that, about 1414, the law inflicted on all Englishmen that were guilty of reading the Scriptures in their mother tongue the forfeiture of their "land, catel, lif, and goods from theyr heyres for ever."—"Hist. of English Bible," Vol. I., p. 89.

[2] "The fact stated by Archbishop Arundel in his funeral sermon on Anne of Bohemia, wife of Richard II., that she habitually read the Gospels in the vulgar tongue, with divers expositions, was probably true of many others of high rank." —Smith's "Dict. of Bible," Article Version authorised, p. 1066.

rigour is doubtless to be accounted for by the fact that, rightly or wrongly, the Popish priests imagined that Wyclif's translation was, by the countenance it seemed to give to un-churchly doctrines, a dangerous source of heresy and schism. This is what Sir Thomas More, writing a hundred and fifty years after Wyclif's death, averred. "The great arch heretike," said that Catholic apologist, "did, in his translation, purposely corrupt the holy text; maliciously planting therein such words as might, in the reader's ears, serve to the proof of such heresies as he went about to sow; which he not only set forth with his own translation of the Bible, but also with certain prologues and glosses which he made thereupon."

It was not till 1850 that English readers had the privilege of seeing the whole of Wyclif's Bible in print. Portions of it had been printed and published long before that date. In 1823, the Song of Solomon, from Wyclif's original version, was published in Dr. Clarke's "Commentary on the Old Testament." The whole of the New Testament, from Purvey's revision, was published as far back as 1731, and has several times been reprinted since. And, strange to say, this Wyclifite Testament was supposed by its successive editors to be the original version of 1380, instead of the revised version of 1388. Even in Bagster's "Hexapla" that mistake is made. The first appearance in print of Wyclif's own version of the New Testament seems to have been in 1848. But in 1850 the whole text of both versions—the original and the revised—Wyclif's and Hereford's own, 1380, and Purvey's amended one, 1388—was published under the editorial care of the Rev. Josiah Forshall and Sir Frederic Madden. The two versions are there given side by side, in parallel columns: the older on the left hand column, and the later on the right hand column of each page. And not only are both versions printed with great care from two of the best extant copies in manuscript, but a large number of different readings found in other manuscripts are appended in footnotes.

To give the reader some idea of the alterations made by Purvey on Wyclif and Hereford's version of the Bible, one or two sentences, printed in parallel columns, shall here be cited from the original (1380) and the revised (1388) versions respectively. And, as the later version of the New Testament had long been mistaken for the earlier, it may be premised that one means of determining the question of priority is furnished in the prologue prefixed by Purvey to the version of 1388. The true principle of translation, Purvey says, is "to translate after the sentence, and not oneli after the wordis, so that the sentence be as open (or openere) in English as in Latin, and go not fer fro the lettre: and if the lettre mai not be suid (*i.e.*, followed) in the translating, let the sentence euere be hool and open." Many Latin forms of expression he accordingly thought should be resolved into their equivalent English forms, even although a change of grammatical structure should be necessitated. He would not, for instance, always render a Latin participle by an English participle, or a relative pronoun in Latin by a relative pronoun in English. "A participle of a present tens . . . may be resolved into a verb of the same tens, and a conjunccioun copulatif. . . and a relatif may be resolved into his antecedent with a conjunccioun copulatif." Purvey's version of Wyclif's Bible may thus be distinguished from the original version by its freer rendering of Latin participles and Latin relatives. To bring out this distinction there shall be given, in a separate column between the earlier and later renderings, the corresponding passages from the Vulgate as now commonly printed. The words italicised will indicate the distinctive phraseology of the two versions:—

WYCLIF AND HEREFORD, 1380.	VULGATE.	PURVEY'S REVISION, 1388
Acts xxi., v. 2.—And whanne we founden a schip passinge over into Fenyse, wi *stizynge* up, schippiden (or *seiliden*).*	Acts xxi., v. 2.—Et cum invenissemus navem transfretantem in Phoenicen, *ascendentes* navigavimus.	Acts xxi., v. 2.—And whanne we founden a schip passynge ouer to fenyce we *wenten* up *into it, and* saileden forth.
v. 5.—And the days *fulfilled*, we *goinge forth wenten*, alle men with wyues and fre children *ledinge* forth us til to withoute the citee; and the knees *putt* in the see brynke, we preieden.	v. 5.—Et *expletis diebus, profecti ibamus, deducentibus* nos omnibus cum uxoribus et filiis usque foras civitatem: et *positis* genibus in littore, oravimus.	v. 5.—And *whanne* the dayis *weren filled*: we zeden forth, and alle men with wyues and children *ledden* forth us withouten the citee, and we *kneliden* in the sea brynke *and* preiden.
Gen. xli., v. 43.—And	Gen. xli., v. 43.—Fecit-	Gen. xli., v. 43.—And

* The letter z in Wyclif's Bible is either silent or pronounced like *y*, and *u* is often pronounced like *v*.

made him steyz upon his secound chaar, *cryinge a bedel*, that alle men shoulden bifore hym knele, and they shoulden wite hym to be prouest to all the loond of Egypte. Numbers xxiv., v. 1.—And whanne Balaam hadde seen that he shulde plese to the Lord for to bless to Ysrael, he wente not as he wente bifore, for to seke dyuininge, but *dressinge* his chere agens the deseert, and *arerynge* the eyen, saw Israel in the tentis dwellynge bi her lynagis. And the spirit of God *fallynge* into hym, *takun to* a parable, seith,	que eum ascendere super currum suum secundum, *clamante praecone*, ut omnes coram eo genu flecterent, et praepositum esse scirent universae terrae Aegypti. Num. xxiv., v. 1.—Cumque vidisset Balaam quod placeret Domino ut benediceret Israel nequaquam abiit ut ante perrexerat, ut augurium quaereret: sed *dirigens* contra desertum vultum suum, et *elevans* oculos, vidit Israel in tentoriis commorantem per tribus suas: et *irruente* in se spiritu Dei, *assumpta* parabola, ait,	Farao made Joseph to stie on his secounde chare, *while a bidele criede*, that alle men schulden knele bifore hym, and schulden knowe that he was souereyn of al the lond of Egypt. Numbers xxiv., v. 1.—And whanne Balaam siz that it pleside the Lord that he schulde blesse Israel, he gede not as he hadde go bifore, that he schulde seke fals dyvynyng, bi chiteryng of briddis, but *he dresside* his face agens the desert, and *reiside* izen, *and* siz Israel dwellynge in tentis bi hise lynagis, And *whanne* the spirit of God felde on hym, And *whanne* a parable *was taken*, he saide,

The above passages shew that both the original version of the Bible by Wyclif and Hereford, and the version revised by Purvey are written in very antiquated English.[1] It is not the oldest form of English, however, but what is technically termed Middle English.

Even in the later of the two versions, which is the one that specially claims our consideration, because it was the ultimate

---

[1] In both editions of Wyclif's Bible, notes or explanations are here and there incorporated with the text, but printed with different type. In the first edition, few notes are found in the part translated by Hereford, but a considerable number in the New Testament, which was translated by Wyclif himself. Purvey rather high-handedly reversed this arrangement, inserting notes where previously there had been none, and abolishing the notes where they had formerly been. The following two examples will give the reader a general notion of the nature of the glosses inserted by Purvey. "If he cometh to me, *that is bi his grace.* Y schal not see hym: if he goith awey, *that is, in withdrawynge his grace.* Y schall not undirstonde."—Job, ix., 11. "Fatnesse, *that is, pride comyng forth of temporal aboundance,* hilide his face, *that is, the knowynge of undirstandyng,* and outward fatnesse hangith doun of his sidis."—Job., xv., 27. The following quotations will shew on the other hand what kind of glosses in the first edition were expunged from the second. "Forsothe in the oon of the saboth, *that is, of the woke,* mary mawdeleyn cam erly, whanne derknessis weren zit, at the grave. And she syz the stoon turned azen ,fro the grave."—John, xx., 1. "Therefore god schal sende to hem a worching of errour, that thei bileue to leesyng, *or gabbyng,* that all be demyd, *or dampyned,* the whiche bileuden to treuthe, but consentiden to wickidnesse."

form that Wyclif's Bible assumed, and it superseded the earlier edition, the grammatical structure of the language is very peculiar. Both verbs and nouns are differently inflected from what they are now. Prepositions are used in unfamiliar senses, and in strange combinations. Interrogations are indicated in ways we are not accustomed to; and inexperienced readers are as much bewildered as amused by the eccentric spelling and the still more eccentric applications of pronouns. At the present day most nouns end with *s* in the plural. A few, however, such as *men, women, children, oxen,* have their plural number indicated by the termination *en.*[1] In the days of Wyclif and Purvey, *en* was a more common sign of the plural. In Purvey's version of the Bible we find *been* for *bees; kien* for *cows; izen* for *eyes;* and *lambren* for *lambs.* And *en* was a much more frequent termination of verbs, than of nouns, in the plural. It was, in fact, the usual termination of verbs that followed a plural nominative. The verbs *did, seide, found, fled, went, blamed, believed,* were all, when attached to a plural nominative, changed into *diden, seiden, founden, fledden, wenten, blameden, believeden.* A passage that exhibits this peculiarity in the inflexion of verbs very clearly and fully, is the account by St. Matthew of our Lord's triumphal entry into Jerusalem : " The disciplis *zeden* and *didden* as Jesus commanded hem, and thei *brouzten* an asse and the fole, and *leiden* her clothis on hem, and *maden* hym sitte aboue, and ful myche puple *streweden* her clothis in the way, other *kittiden* braunchis of trees, and *strewen* in the wey, and the puple that *wenten* before and that *sueden, crieden* and *seiden,* osanna to the sone of Dauith." Of frequent occurrence, also, are such verbal inflexions as the following :—" mai not be *undo* " (undone) ; " hath *bore* (born) a son " ; " thei han *take* (taken) away my Lord " ; " Moses *fley* " (was afraid) ; " wolde haue *slawe* "[2]

---

[1] In the earlier version of Wyclif's Bible we find *kneen* for *knees* (Gen. xxx., v. 3) ; and, on the other hand, *oxis* for *oxen*; " I shall offre to thee *oxis* with buckis of geet " (Ps. lxvi., v. 15).

[2] Other inflexions similar to *fley* and *slawe* may be found in the earlier (1380) version of Wyclif's Bible. In Isaiah, xliv. 19, we read, " I *book* (baked) upon his coles loeues " (loaves), and in 2 Sam., xxii. 8, " smyten and *squat*" (squeezed).

(slain); "what art thou *to doynge?*" (Acts, xxii. 26,—" quid acturus es?"—(Vulg.) "what are thou going to do?"); "if thou haddest *be* (been) here, my brother hadde not *be* (been) dead." Very odd, again, appears[1] to be the sense in which some of the commonest prepositions are used:—" In the bigynnynge was the word and the word was *at* god." . . . "Dare ony of zou that hath a cause azens another be demed *at* wicked men, and not *at* holi men." . . . "Have pacience *in* me, and I schal zelde to thee alle thingis." . . . "If we to day be demed *in* the gode deed *of* a sike man, *in* whom this man is made saaf." . . . "In that tyme, ihesus wente *bi* cornes *in* the Saboth dai." . . . "The word of the Lord was sowun *bi* (throughout) all the countrey." . . . " It bihofte him to passe *bi* samarie." . . . "Thei schuln dampne hym *bi* deeth." . . . "We stonen thee not *of* gode werke, but *of* blasfemy." . . . "This is the werke of god that ye bileue *to* hym whom he sente." Some prepositions, too, appear to be used interchangeably, and without any regard to rhythm or reason. In one sentence we read, "thou schalt loue thi lord god *of* al thin herte and *in* al thin soule;" and in another sentence, "whoeuer swerith *bi* the temple of god it is nothing, but he that swerith *in* the gold of the temple is dettour." In a verse already quoted in this paragraph, it would be noticed how oddly some of the pronouns are spelt. *Their* is uniformly spelt *her*, and *them*, *hem*. We find such combinations, too, as *hem silf* for *themselves*, and *us silf* for *ourselves*.

---

[1] I only say "*appears* to be the sense," because in almost all the cases referred to in this and the following sentences, the seemingly odd prepositions used by Wyclif and Purvey are literal translations of the Latin words in the Vulgate:— "The word was *at* God," (John, i. 1) *apud* Deum; "*In* the good deed *of* a sick man," (Acts, iv. 9) *in* benefacto *hominis* infirmi; "Stone thee not *of* gode werke, but *of* blasphemy," (John, x. 33) *de* bono opere non lapidamus te, sed *de* blasphemia; "*Of* all thine heart, and *in* all thine soul," (Mat., xxii. 37) *ex* toto corde tuo, et *in* tota anima; etc. In Beza's Latin translation of the New Testament most of these prepositions are changed. "Apud Deum" remains; but "in benefacto hominis" is turned into "super beneficio in hominem;" "de bono opere," and "de blasphemia" are altered into "ob bonum opus" and "ob blasphemiam;" and in Mat., xxii. 37, the preposition "ex" is continued all through the sentence.

But the application of the pronouns is more remarkable. At the present day there are many anomalies in the use of pronouns. Sailors, from a feeling of affection to the frail vessel in which they skim the main, speak endearingly of a *ship* or boat as *she* or *her*; and west highlanders may occasionally be heard applying *it* and *itself* to a venerated laird or a respected minister of the gospel. In Wyclif's Bible, *he* and *it*, and *him* and *it*, are used very indiscriminately: the one pronoun in a verse, say, of St. Matthew's Gospel, and the other in the corresponding verse of St. Mark's or St. Luke's Gospel. And some applications of pronouns, which in Wyclif's day were reckoned quite orthodox in the guild of letters, have a somewhat ludicrous effect now. In St. Matthew's Gospel we read, "if thy rizt ize sclaundre thee, pull *hym* out and cast fro thee . . . and if thi rizt hond sclaundre thee kitte *hym* awey and cast fro thee, for it spedith to thee that oon of thi membris perische, thanne that al thi bodi go in to helle." The gospel of St. John concludes in like manner:—" there ben also many other thingis that ihesus dide, whiche if thei ben writun bi eche bi *hym* silf, I deme that the world *hym* silf schal not take tho bokis that ben to be writun."

As might be expected, there occur in both of the Wyclifite versions many words that are widely different from those we find in the same passages in our modern translations. In some instances we meet with words that are now obsolete, and in other instances we find words whose meaning has undergone considerable change. Sometimes proper names are translated by their English equivalents, and sometimes they are left untranslated; occasionally ecclesiastical terms of technical meaning are introduced, as if to furnish Scriptural authority for certain foregone conclusions.

Of obsolete words the store in both versions of Wyclif's Bible is inexhaustible. To begin with Purvey's version: a word that meets our eye in the first chapter of St. Matthew's Gospel is *clepid*, which means called or named, and in the course of the New Testament this word occurs times without number. We read of "ihesus that is clepid Crist" . . "poul the seruant of ihesus Crist, clepid an apostle," . . . "thilke that he bifor ordeyned to bliss, hem he clepid, and whiche he clepid hem he justified." For "mill" the word *querne* is used, as in the passage, "twein wymmen schulen ben gryndynge in o querne, oon schal be taken and the tother left." For "ascendeth" we find *stieth*; as in the verse,—"No man stieth into heaven but he that cam doun from heaven." An archaic expression that stands for "this deceiver" is *thilk gilour*, and an obsolete Anglo-Latin substitute for "the river Jordan" is *the flum Jordan*. More than once the expression "ful wood" occurs:—"Two men metten hym that hadden deuils, and camen out of graves full wood (exceeding fierce), so that no man might go bi that way." "Poul, thou maddist, many letters turn thee to woodnesse." A strange word that we meet with in the parable of the prodigal son is *croude*:—"Whanne he (the elder son) cam and nized to the hous, he herde a symfonye and a croude." This does not mean that along with the players on instruments there was a roaring rabble at the house. The *croude* was a kind of guitar or violin, or rather a combination of both, with four bow strings and two thumb strings. Another word that has long passed out of Queen's English is *birle*, in the sense of "cause to drink" or "ply with drink." In the authorised version of the prophecies of Jeremiah we read : "Thus saith the Lord God of Israel unto me : Take the wine cup of this fury at my hands, and cause all the nations to whom I send thee to drink it." The latter clause of this command is concisely and pithily rendered by Purvey "thou schal *birle* thereof to alle hethene men." Another obsolete word in the later version of Wyclif's Bible is "chepynge," which means marketplace :—" He seide to hem in his techyng, be ze ware of scribis, that wolen wandre in stolis (long robes) and be salutid in chepynge." And this incidental use of the word *wander* suggests another passage, which for its quaintness as well as the obsoleteness of some of its terms, may well be quoted. It is the account of the cure of the cripple who sat at the gate of the temple begging alms :—" In the name of ihesus of nazareth, (said Peter) rise thou up and go : and he took him by the rizt hond and *heued* him up, and anoon his leggis and his feet weren *soudid* to gidre, and he leppid and stode and *wandrid*, and he entrid with hem in to the temple and *wandrid*, and *leppid*, and *heried* God." The common designation now-a-days of those that devote themselves to the cure of the sick and infirm is physician, but in the days of Wyclif and Purvey another word, apt to be misapprehended by modern readers, was in use. This was leech.[1] We read, accordingly, in one passage of Purvey's Bible:—" Leche, hele thi silf," and in another, " hoole men han no nede to a leche, but thei that ben yuel at ease." This is very primitive diction, but still more quaint, both in its tenderness and alliteration, is the announcement,—"luk the leche, moost deare, and demas, greet you wel." A word that has a place in Wyclif's vocabulary, and still survives in some of the local dialects of Scotland is *shog*. It is not a very refined term, and would be voted out of place in the House of Commons. It is introduced, however, with considerable effect into the narrative of Christ's walking on the sea: —" Whanne the euenynge was come he was there (on the hill) alone, and the boot in the myddil of the see was *schoggid*[2] with wawis." Another antiquated expression, very concise, but not very precise, that we find in Purvey's version is " dalf,[3] a lake." This is what our modern translators with more regard for details have rendered " digged a place for the wine fat." Some of the obsolete words in Purvey's Bible are words whose desuetude is much to be lamented, and others are words that can be spared, without either loss or regret, from the vocabulary of living English. For the long, cumbrous adjective, *unleavened*, we have in Purvey's Bible the neat, tidy little term *therf*, as in Luke xxii., v. 1,—" the halidai of the therf looues, that is seide (called) pask nyzed ;" and in Acts xx., v. 6,

---

[1] The physician did not, because of his penchant for blood-letting, get the cognomen of *leech* from the reptile, but the reptile got its name of *leech* from the physician, because, like him, it healed those that were "yuel at ease." The English word leech or leche is derived from the Anglo-Saxon *laéce*, one who heals. —*Skeat's Dict.*

[2] Shog is often used as an intransitive verb, in the sense of move off, by English writers of no great antiquity. More than once it occurs in Shakespeare's play of Henry V. "Will you shog off? . . . I would have you solus."—*Act 2, scene 1.*

[3] A literal translation of the words in the Vulgate, " fodit lacum."

"we schippiden aftir the daies of therf looues fro filippis."
But, on the other hand, the word *leaven*, suggestive of spiritual influences, and interesting on that account, is personated in Purvey's Bible by the vile, realistic compound "sourdough," so that we read of "the kyngdom of heuene (being) like to sourdough, which a womman took and hid in thre mesuris of mele til it were al sourid." A very sorry and unhappy account, surely, of the effects of Christianity on the world!

A small class of obsolete words found in both editions of Wyclif's Bible are verbs derived from adjectives. These often enabled a writer to express his meaning very briefly and tersely, and sometimes very happily and daintily. The word *nigh*, for instance, is often used as a verb in Wyclif's Bible. "Whanne he *nyzed*, he siz the cite and wepte on it, and seide, for if thou haddist knowen thou schuldist wepe also."—Luke, xix., 41. A similar use was made of the words *high* and *low*. "Eche that enhauncith hym schal be *lowed*, and he that *mekith* hym shall be *hizid*."—Luke, xiv., 11.

The following among other obsolete words will also be found in Purvey's edition of Wyclif's Bible :—*Alie*, father-in-law (A. V.)—Exodus, xviii., 5, (ally) ; *aseeth*, contentment or satisfaction.—Mark, xv., 15 ; *arerid*, lifted up.—Mark, i., 31 ; *atwynny*, asunder.—Acts, xv., 39 ; *biclippid*, embraced.—Acts, xx., 10 ; *biggeris*, buyers.—Mark, xi., 15 ; *bouge*, bottle.—Ps., lxxviii., 13 ; *stonen cannes*, pitchers. —John, ii., 6 ; *bie*, a necklace.—Prov., i., 9 ; *buriowne*, to germinate, "buriowne at the odour of water and . . make heer" (hair, foliage).—Job viii., 9 ; *calue*, bald, "a man whos heed heeris fleter awei is calu and clene."—Lev., xiii, 40 ; *cardue*, thistle.— 2 Kings, xiv., 9 ; *chaffare*, trade.—Luke, xix., 13 ; *colle*, embrace, "tyme to colle, and tyme to be far fro collyngis."—Eccles., iii. 5 ; *critouns*, "refuse of frying pan.' Skeat,—Ps., cii., 3 ; *cosynes*, kinsmen.—Acts, x., 24 ; *clerenesse*, praise or honour. —John, v., 41 ; *cacchepollis*, serjeants.—Acts, xvi., 35 ; *culuer*, dove.—John, i., 32 ; *coddis*, husks.—Luke, xv., 16 ; *cracche*, manger.—Luke, ii., 7 ; *deidli men*, mortal.—Acts, xiv. 15 ; *disciplesse*, a woman that believed in Jesus Christ,—Acts, ix., 36 ; *fardels*, baggage.—1 Sam., xvii,, 22 ; *felli*, craftily, "thei thouzten felli." Josh., ix., 4 ; *fonned*, foolish.—1 Cor., i., 20 ; *grees*, stairs.—Acts, xxi., 40 ; *hoose*, hoarse, "my cheekis weren maad hoose."—Ps., lxix., 3 ; *irchons*, hedgehogs. —Ps., civ., 18 ; *jewlich*, as the Jews.—Gal., ii., 14 ; *lesewis*, pasture.—John, x., 9 ; *male ese*, sickness.—Mat. iv., 24 ; *mynutis*, mites.—Mark, xii., 42 ; *moistide*, watered.—1 Cor., iii., 6 ; *mysturne*, pervert.—Gal., i., 7 ; *neisch*, soft or slack, (mollis, Vulgate) "he that is neisch and unstedfast in his werk."—Prov., xviii., 9 ; *peyned*, punished.—Acts, xxii., 5 ; *purpuresse*, woman that sells purple.—Acts, xvi., 14 ; *rue*, repent, "The Lord swoor and it schal not *rewe* him.—Heb., vii., 21 ; *snapere*, to stumble.—Prov., iii., 23 ; *seyn*, pleasant or agreeable.—Acts, xv., 28 ; *sege*, seat or throne.—Mat., xxv., 31 ; *soler*, upper room.—Acts, i., 13 ; *sopun*, swallowed.—1 Cor., xv., 54; *sort*, lot.—Acts, viii., 21; *souking fere*, foster brother.—Acts, xiii., 1; *sweuenes*, dreams,—Acts, ii., 17; good *thewis*, good manners or resolutions.—1 Cor., xv., 33; *thirsten*, press or throng.—Mark, iii., 9; *tristili*, boldly.—Acts, xviii., 26; *unbileful*, incredible.—Acts, xxvi., 8; *unconuenable*, profane.—1 Tim., iv.. 7; *underfongen*, received.—Gal., i., 9; *ver*, cup or glass.—Prov., xxiii., 31; *yrene*, spider, "His trist schal be as a web of yrene."—Job viii., 14.

Most of the foregoing obsolete words, which are taken from Purvey's edition of Wyclif's Bible, are doubtless to be found in the earlier version also, although not always in the same book and chapter. For instance, where we read in the later version, "*chaffare* ye till I come," we read in the earlier, "merchaundise ye till I come." Instead of being called "the *alie*," Jethro, in the earlier version, is designated the "cosyne" of Moses. Most of the obsolete words, however, that have been quoted in the foregoing paragraphs, from the later version of Wyclif's Bible, will be found somewhere in the earlier version. And there are many very antiquated words in the first version which do not appear in the corresponding passages of the second. An expression that may often be heard at the present day, and which probably is used by many people who are ignorant of its meaning, is *scot free*. It is perhaps not necessary to say that *scot* in this connection has nothing to do with Scotsman, but there are probably some persons who reckon themselves not ill-educated, that need to be told it means assessment or contribution. In olden times, when people sat together in a tavern, they had to give their *scot* to the reckoning. And in this sense the word is used in the earlier version of Wyclif's Bible.[1] "Thei tendende to drinkis, and zivende scot shul ben wastid." Another word that may still be heard, where slang is spoken, is *buffer*. What its precise import is in modern speech need not be discussed, but it doubtless conveys a vague idea of reproach and contempt. Although, however, it is only in degenerate speech that the word is heard now, it had once a place in the English Bible. Its ancient meaning was stutterer or stammerer, and it occurs in the earlier of the Wyclif versions, at the fourth verse of the thirty-second chapter of Isaiah:—"The tunge of bufferes swiftli shal speke." A quaintly expressed verse in

---

[1] In later version, "zyuynge mussels togedre," (giving morsels together).

Hereford's translation is 2 Sam. xiv. 26—" The more that he (Absolom) *doddied* the heeris, so mych more thei wexen, forsothe onys in the year he was *doddied*, for the heere heuyde hym." Very graphic and plain-spoken, too, although somewhat coarse, is the title that Hereford bestows on enchanters, and persons of a kindred order, " deuel-cleperes," or invokers of Satan. Two things he represents the prophets to say shall come on the destroyers of Israel, in one moment—widowhood and loss of children—" They shall come upon thee, O Babylon and Chaldea, for the multitude of thy sorceries, and for 'the huge hardness of thi *deuel-cleperes,*'"—Is., xlvii., 9. And speaking of coarse, or so-called coarse expressions, it may here be remarked that while indirect and allusive language is one of the forms in which modern refinement displays its delicacy of feeling, that art does not seem to have been mastered, if even studied, by Wyclif and Hereford. These reformers spoke bluntly, and called things by their proper names.[1] And we may be quite certain that their moral and religious sentiments were as pure and exalted as are those of men who now talk with greater excellency of speech and wisdom.

Among other obsolete words in the earlier version of Wyclif's Bible, the following may be mentioned :—*amyte*, vesture.—Heb., i., 12 ; *armaries*, chronicles. Ezra, iv., 15 ; *biys*, white silk.—Luke, xvi., 19 ; *bob*, to jeer, "I am afraid of the Jews . . . lest . . . thei bobbe to me."—Jer. xxxviii., 19 ; *bugle*, a wild ox.—Deut., xiv., 5 ; *childide*, brought forth a child, "she childide her firste born sone."—Luke, ii., 7 ; *cleen*, hoofs or heels, "bitynge the cleen of an hors."—Gen., xlix., 17 ; *crockere*, potter.—Ps., ii., 9 ; *costrils*, vessels for holding water.—Ruth, ii., 9 ; *croote*, what Purvey terms *critouns*.—Ps., cii., 3 ; *cultre*, knife, "set a cultre in thi throte."—Prov., xxiii., 2 ; *dymes*, tenths or tythes.—Gen., xiv., 20 ; *eggiden*, provoked.—Deut., xxxii., 16 ; *em*, uncle's son (A. V.), "ananeel the sone of myn em."—Jer., xxxii., 9 ; *festu*, a small piece of wood. a twig, "seest thou a festu in the eize of thi brother."—Mat. vii., 3 ; *flotereth*, "flotereth and wagereth," rock and stagger.—Is., xxix., 9 ; *fulfattid*, *fulgresid*, fat and gross, (incrassatus, impinguatus, Vulg.)—Deut., xxxii., 15 ; *garringe*, chiding, "garringe to us with yuale wordis."—3 John, 10 ; *gab*, "before God I lie not, or gabbe not."—Gal. i., 20 ; *keetling*, whelp, "Dan, keetling of a lyon."—Deut., xxxiii., 22 ; *loute*, bow down.—Gen., xxxvii., 7 ; *obite*, death.—Gen., xxvi., 11 ; *oker*, give on loan for interest, "he shal oker to thee."—Deut., xxviii., 44 ; *plaag*, district, "the

---

[1] One sentence of even more than Doric plainness in the earlier version of Wyclif is 1 Samuel, v., 9 :—" He smoot the men of ech cytee fro litil unto more, and the arsroppis of hem goynge out stonken : and gethey wenten into counseil and maden to hem letheran seetis."

eest plage of Eden."—Gen., iv., 16; *poos*, peacocks.—2 Chron., ix., 21; *routeth*, snoreth, (sterlit, Vulg., snorteth, Donay Bible) " he that '*routeth in somer*' is a son of confusion."—Prov., x., 5; *raskeyl*, the common people, "of the puple ¹ seuenti men, and fifti thousandis of the raskeyl," (*porail*, Purvey)—1 Sam., vi., 19; *sparlyvers*, calves of legs.—Deut., xxviii., 35; *stellion*, "a stellion, *that is*, a werme depeynted as with sterris."—Lev., xi., 30; *stithie*, an anvil, "streyned as the stithie of an hamer betere."—Job., xli., 24; *twisil*, double, "the mouth of the twisil tunge I wlate."—Prov,, viii., 13; *tretable*, (ad *tractabilem* montem, et accensibilem igneum, Vulgate), "ze han not come to the tretable fyer."—Heb., xii., 18; *walkere*, fuller.—Mark, ix., 3; *withies*, willows, (seven green *withs*.—Judges, xvi., 7, A. V.), "In withies in the myddes of it, wee heengen up our instrumens."—Ps. cxxxvii., 2; *wonyng*, habitation, "cite of wonyng."—Ps., cvii., 7; *warnysshit*, protected (munitum, Vulg.)—2 Samuel, xxiii., 5.

Of words not strictly obsolete, but used in an obsolete sense, many interesting examples might, without difficulty, be culled from both versions of Wyclif's Bible. Confining ourselves in the mean time to the later of the two versions, we find the word *chimney*, which in modern parlance means the flue or vent of a fire place, used by Purvey for furnace:—" In the endynge of the world, aungelis schulen goen out, and schulen departen yuel men fro the myddil of just men, and schulen sende hem in to the *chymeney* of fier." It will be seen, too, that in the sentence just quoted the word *departen* is used in the peculiar sense of separate or divide. This is a very common usage in Wyclif's Bible:—" Eche kyngdom *departid* azens itself schal be desolat, and eche citie or hous *departid* azens itsilf schal not stonde." And so also the word "avoid" is used, not in the sense of shun or evade, but in the sense of make void or destroy:—" It is good to me," Paul writes, " rather to die thanne that ony man *avoid* my glorie." The word "defamed," which at the present day means slandered or reviled, is by Purvey employed in the harmless sense of published or proclaimed:—" Se ye " (said Jesus) " that no man wite; but thei zeden out and *defameden* hym thoruz all that land." This untoward generation is, in like manner, strangely described as " this *schrewid* generacioun ": unlearned and ignorant men are termed "unlettered and *lewid* men ": nations are designated *folks;* Bethany, the town of

---

¹ The word rendered " puple " is in the Vulgate, *populus*, and the word rendered "raskeyl " or " porail " is *plebs*.

Mary and her sister Martha, is dignified into "bethanie, the *castel* of marie and martha": and the fields into which the prodigal son was sent to feed swine are called a *town*. The word "sad," again, is used repeatedly in the sense of strong or sure, as in the verses :—"We *sadder* men owen to susteyne the feblenesse of sike men": and—"We han a *sadder* word of profecie." The adverb "rather" occurs as the comparative of an old adjective *rathe*, which meaut early or soon, as in the statement: "If the world hatith you, wite ye that it hadde me in hate *rather* thanne zou." And so, also, the composite term "fulfilled" is, with a somewhat odd effect, substituted for "filled full," as in the oft-quoted verse: "Eche man settith first good wyne, and whanne men ben *fulfilled*, thanne that that is worse." Another word frequently used in an odd connection is "science," in the sense of knowledge; as in Luke i. 77—"the science of helth," instead of "the knowledge of salvation"; and in Eph. iii. 19—"the charite of Crist more excellent thanne science," instead of "the love of Christ which passeth knowledge." In several places again, where in modern translations of the Bible the term *goods* occurs, the word "catel" appears in Wyclif's version; as in Luke xv. 11-12—"a manne hadde tweie sones, and the yunger of hem seide to the fadir, fadir geve me the porscioun of *catel* that falleth to me, and he departid to hem the *catel*;" and in Luke viii. 43—"a womman hadde a fluxe of blood twelve yeer, and had spendid al her *catel* in lecchis, and she myght not be curid of ony." Incurable disease is, of course, suggestive of death; and closely associated to us with death is *coffin*. This is a word by which Englishmen at the present day mean and signify the chest in which a corpse is enclosed and conveyed to burial. Etymologically, however, it simply means a basket; and in this sense it occurs more than once in the later version of Wyclif's Bible.[1] In the account of the miracle of the loaves and fishes, as related in the fourteenth chapter of St. Matthew's Gospel, it is said that "alle eten and weren fulfilled, and thei token the relefis of brokun

---

[1] "He turnede awei his bak fro birthens: hise hondis serueden in a *coffyn*." Ps. lxxxi. 6—" had served in *baskets* "—Douay Bible; " were freed from the basket "
—*Revised Version*, 1885.

gobeitis twelve *cofyns* ful." But, although coffins were baskets, all baskets were not coffins. In the Greek language there are two words for basket, *kophinos* and *spuris*. In the Latin Vulgate these words are translated respectively *cophinus* and *sporta;* and these Latin words are by Wyclif and Purvy rendered in English *coffin* and *lepe*. Strange to say, *kophinos* is the name given by all the evangelists to the baskets that were filled after the feeding of the five thousand men; and *spuris* to the baskets that were filled after the feeding of the four thousand. In Purvey's version of Wyclif's Bible, we, therefore, read, Mat. xvi. 9-10,—" Undirstonden not ze nether han mynde of fyue loues in to fyue thousand of men, and hou many *cofyns* ze token. Nether of seuene looues in foure thousand of men, and hou many *lepus* ze token?" In the hasty and secret deposition of St. Paul from the wall of Damascus, it was a *spuris*, and not a *kophinos* that was employed; and he is said, therefore, to have been let down "in a lepe." One other word of which a very curious use is made by Wyclif and Purvey, and, it may be added, by Tyndale and Coverdale, also, is the word *minister*. In Scotland, the common ecclesiastical meaning of "minister" is priest or pastor; and although Scots ministers have ever, since the days of Knox and Melville, laid claim to the exclusive power of what are termed *the keys*, the innocent public never surmised that it was the keys of the jail they insisted on wearing at their belts. To the simple reader, Wyclif and Purvey may seem to throw doubt on this matter, for in their version of the Sermon on the Mount it is said: "Be thou consentynge to thin adversarie sone, while thou art in the weye with hym, leest perauenture thin adversarie take thee to the domesman, and the domesman take the to the *mynystre*, and thou be sent into prisoun."

The following are a few more of the words used by Purvey in an obsolete sense: *abood*, waited for, "he abood the rewme of God "—Mark xv. 43; *borde*, bank, (which etymologically is *bench*), as in the parable of the talent, "why hast thou not zouun my money to the *borde*, and I comynge schulde haue axed it with usuris" —Luke xix. 23; *briggid*, shortened, "the lord schal make a word briggid on alle the erthe."—Rom. ix. 28; *diese*, care, "disese of the world . . . entrith and stranglith the word."—Mark iv. 19; *duyk*, governor, Mat. ii. 6; *feteh*, fix, "in his hondis the fetching of tha nailis."—John xx. 25; *foond*, maintained or supported, "resceyued us bi thre dayes benyngli and foond us."—Acts xxviii. 7; *knighthood*, host (militiae, Lat. Vulg.) "serue to the *knyzhthood* of heuene."—Acts vii. 42; *medelid*, mingled,—Mark xv. 23; *mysels*, lepers,—Mat. x. 8; *ostler*, innkeeper, "he brouzte forth tweie pens and zaf to the ostler, and seide, haue the cure of hym." —Luke x. 35; *profession*, census or taxing. "alle men wenten to make *profession* eche into his owne citee."—Luke ii. 3; *sermon*, treatise, "first I made a *sermoun* of alle thingis that ihesus began to do and to teche."—Acts i. 1; *studyes* (studia, Vulgate) ways or works, "telle ye hise studyes among hethen men."—Ps. ix. 11; *wed*, pledge,—Job. xxii. 6; *worschip*, honour, "my fadir schal worschip hym."— Johu xii. 26.

From the earlier edition of Wyclif's Bible other instances of familiar words used in senses that are now obsolete might with little difficulty be selected. The word *fable*, for instance, is generally considered to mean a story without any foundation in fact. But this is more than it means etymologically. The word literally signifies a spoken narrative, and in that original sense it is used in the first version of Wyclif's Bible. In our Church Testaments, we are accustomed to read, Luke xxiv. 15, —"it came to pass, that, while they *communed* together." In the Vulgate, from which Wyclif made his translation, this is latinised, "factum est, dum *fabularentur*," which Wyclif renders, "it was don the while thei talkiden or *fableden*." The word *comfort* is a word that at the present day is largely used as a verb, both in religious writings and in religious speeches; and, when so used, it invariably means to cheer or console. It is derived, however, from the same root as *force*, and it literally signifies to strengthen. In many passages where the word *strengthen* occurs in modern English Bibles (as in Luke i. 80, Acts ix. 19, Phil. iv. 13, Col. i. 11, 2 Tim. iv. 17), *confortare* is the corresponding term in the Latin Vulgate; and *confortare* is usually in Wyclif's Bible and Purvey's revision rendered by its English derivative *comfort*. We read, for instance, Luke i. 80, "the child wexed and was counfortid in spirit;" Acts ix. 19, "whanne he hadde take mete he was counfortid;" Phil. iv. 13, "I may alle thingis in hym that counfortith me." But, in the earlier edition of Wyclif's Bible the word *comfort* is used in a much more remarkable connection than any of those now instanced. It is said, in our authorised version of the Scriptures, Isaiah xli. 6-7 —" They helped every one his neighbour; and every one said to his brother, Be of good courage. So the carpenter encouraged the goldsmith, and he that smootheth with the hammer him that smote the anvil, saying, It is ready for the sodering; and he fastened it with nails that it should not be moved." Barring one clause, which is changed and made more relevant to the context in the Revised Version, 1885, this statement is very simply and clearly expressed. But the verse as originally rendered by Wyclif presents difficulties of interpretation that to plain English readers might seem well nigh insurmountable: " Eche to his nezhebore shal helpen, and to his brother seyn, Tac counfourt. Counforten shal the metal smyth smytende him with an hamer that forgede that tyme, seiende to the glyu, It is good : and he *counfortide* hym *with nailes* that it shulde not be moved."[1] The word "stable," again, is a word that by long usage has been restricted to a house for horses. In the Latin language, *stabulum* generally bears the same meaning, but is sometimes used for an inn, or a place of entertainment for travellers. In the Vulgate, *stabulum* occurs in Luke x. 34, and *stabularius* in the verse following; and in the Rhemes Testament these words are rendered respectively *inn* and *host;* while in Purvey's edition of Wyclif's Bible they are translated *ostrie* and *ostler.* But in the original version of Wyclif's Bible they are rendered *stable* and *kepere of the stable;* and the passage reads—" He puttynge on his hors ledde in to a *stable*, and dide the cure of hym.[2] And another day he brouzte forth twey pens, and zaf to the *kepere of the stable*, and scide, Have thou the cure of him."

The following are also curious examples of common words used in a sense that is now obsolete. *Cristendom,* baptism, " buried with him bi cristendom in to deeth," Rom. vi. 4 ; *side,* long, " thei nakiden hym the *side* coote to the hele," Gen. xxxvii. 23 ; *waardropis,* privies (Purvey), jakes (Douay), draught house (Authorised), 2nd Kings x. 27.

---

[1] How literally Wyclif in this instance translated will be seen from the words in the Latin Vulgate, which are, " Unusquisque proximo suo auxiliabitur, et fratri suo dicet : *confortare. Confortavit* faber aerarius percutiens malleo eum, qui cudebat tunc temporis, dicens : Glutino bonum est : et *confortavit* eum clavis, ut non moveretur."

[2] The word *cure,* as used by Wyclif in this passage, is the representative of *cura* in the Vulgate, and means *care,* not restoration to health.

In Wyclif's Bible there is also to be found a large number of Saxon compounds, which have now gone out of date, and have for the most part been supplanted by words of Latin origin. The usual designation of husbandman, for instance, is *erthe tilier;* the term applied, Ex. xxi. 29 (first edition), to an ox that is "wont to push with his horn," is *horn-putter;* and in at least one verse, Gen. iii. 14, *cattle* are described by the curious phrase "*soul-hauers*," possessors of souls. We might possibly, or probably, commit a mistake, however, if we inferred from this incidental expression that Wyclif or Hereford believed that the lower animals have souls the same as human beings. The word in the Vulgate which they have translated *soul hauers* is *animantia*, which, strictly speaking, means *things with life;* and thus what we call "life" Hereford called "soul." Very many combinations are made by Wyclif and his coadjutors with the prefix *azen* (back, against) ; as, *azenbier*, redeeming ; *azenrysynge*, resurrection ; *azenclepe*, recall ; *azenbowid*, recurved ; *azenfrusshiden*, became stiff ; *azenseie*, contradict ; *azenstood*, resisted. The preface *bi* is much used, also, in the formation of compound terms ; as in *biclippe*, to embrace ; *bihete*, to promise ; *bimowe*, to mock ; *bisprenge*, to sprinkle ; *bispete*, to spit upon ; *bi se*, to look to ; *biweep*, to weep for ; *bithenke*, to meditate. *Under* is employed, too, in a similar way ; so that we have *underputtiden*, laid down or laid under ; *underfongen*, received ; *underloute*, bent under or subjected ; *undertakere*, support. One prefix whose meaning might be misunderstood by an inexperienced reader is *to;* as in the words, *to-draw*, pull in pieces ; *to-bite*, gnaw in pieces ; *to-stere*, move all together. Quaint uses are made of *un;* as, "it is sowun in *unnobley*," 1 Cor. xv. 43, and "whanne this deedli thing schal clothe *undeedlynesse* thanne schal the word be don that is writun, deeth is sopun up in victorie."[1] 1 Cor. xv. 54.

---

[1] The following are curious applications of some of the above-mentioned compound terms : "Azenclepe thou not me in the myddil of my daies," Ps. cii. 25 ; " Alle the dwellers of Chanaan azenfrusshiden for ferde," Ex. xv. 15 (first edition); " I am giltles of the blood of this rightful man, bi se you," Mat. xxvii. 24 ; " Thei smyten his heed with a rehed (reed) and bispatten hym," Mark xv. 19 ; " I schal sey to God, Myn undertakere thou art," Ps. xl. ii. 9. Another prefix used in

Translators, as might be expected, are sometimes at a loss whether to treat a word as a proper name and present it to their readers in the form in which it appears in the original tongue, or to give its equivalent in English, as if it were a common term. A very notable instance of this dubiety may be found in the authorised and revised renderings of Judges xv. 19. In the authorised translation the verse reads:—" God clave an hollow place that was in *the jaw* (presumably of the ass) and water then came thereout." The statement in the revised translation is:—"God clave an hollow place that was in *Lehi*," that is, in the field or district called Lehi. And so, for "Solomon" and "Baalhamon," Song vii. 2., we find in the first edition of Wyclif's Bible, *peaceable* and *populous*:—" vyne sche was to *pesyble* in hir that *hath peplis*." In Purvey's revision, too, there are many instances of words' being translated, which in other English versions are left untranslated. The line, " In *Salem* also is his tabernacle"—Ps lxxvi. 2.—is rendered, "his place is made in *pees*"; "I will mete out the valley of *Succoth*"—Ps. cviii. 7.—" I schal mete the grete valei of *Tabernaclis*"; "Over Philistia will I triumph"—Ps. cviii. 9.—"*Aliens* been maad frendis to me"; and, "In *Rama* was there a voice heard"—Mat. ii. 18.—" A voyce was herd on *hiz*."[1] So also, for " Simeon that was called *Niger*"—Acts xiii. 1.—we find— " Symount that was clepid *blak*": for, "driven up and down in *Adria*"—Acts xxvii. 27.—"seilinge in the *stony see*": for, "whosoever shall say to his brother, *Raca*"—Mat. v. 22.—" he that seith to his brother, *fy*." On the other hand, several words that are Englished in our church bibles are even in the late edition of Wyclif's version left untranslated. For "cursed," Job xxxiv. 18., we read *apostata*; for " governor of the feast,"

Wyclif's Bible is *for*, as in *for*-do, to destroy (dissolvo, Vulgate); and *for*-think, to repent or change mind : "Eche spirit that *for doith* ihesus is not of God," 1 John, iv. 3; "Afterwarde he *for thouzt* and wente forth," Mat. xxi. 29.

[1] In some of those cases, Wyclif and Purvey, while appearing to have translated proper names, have only Englished words that are given in the Vulgate as common terms. These mistakes in the Vulgate, for they are obviously mistakes, are for the most part corrected in the Latin translations of the Bible issued during the progress of the Reformation.

John ii. 9., *architriclyn*; for "feast of tabernacles," John vii. 2, *senofegia*; for "place that is called the pavement," *place that is seid licostratos* (Lithostrotos, Vulgate): and for "street that is called straight," Acts ix. 11., *street that is clepid Rectus*. This last instance of non-translation is a little remarkable. Rectus is not the name given to street in the Greek Testament, but the Latin translation of that name; so that in treating Rectus as a proper noun which was not to be Englished, Wyclif and Purvey unconsciously contravened the example set by St. Jerome. Had Wyclif translated from the original Greek, and not from the Latin Vulgate, he would not have said a street that is clepid Rectus, but a street that is clepid Eutheia.

There are certain technical terms so frequently used by ecclesiastical writers, and so much founded on for support of high doctrines, that we should expect to find them figure largely in Scripture; and we should naturally like to hear what Scripture has to say about them. There is the word *clergy*, for instance, as commonly used to designate the pastors of congregations, or "the stewards of the mysteries of God." This term has never been received into the ecclesiastical vocabulary of any of the Presbyterian Churches of Scotland. James Melville said it smelled of Papistry; George Gillespie averred it to be "full of pride and vain glory"; and in such a modern, prosaic book as "Cook's Styles of Writs" it is declared to be "unpresbyterian." And it is a somewhat notable fact that the word does not occur anywhere in our authorised English Bible. But in Wyclif's Bible it will be found. In the exhortation, 1 Peter v. 2-3, ("feed the flock of God, which is among you, taking the oversight thereof, not by constraint but willingly, not for filthy lucre, but of a ready mind, neither as being lords over God's heritage, but being ensamples to the flock"), Wyclif uses the word *clergy* instead of God's heritage. "Purueye ye not," he translates, "as hauynge lordschip in the *clergie*." This looks like a good stone to fling at Popery and Prelacy. But it does not seem to have been so considered by Catholics themselves, for it is given in the Rhemes, or Catholic version of the Testament, as the proper rendering of St. Peter's meaning. In the Testaments of Tyndale and Cranmer the passage is translated, "Se that ze fede Christe's flocke which is among you . . . not as though ze were lords over the *parishes*." The word in the original Greek which thus seems to be so discordantly translated is *klēros*, which means "lot" or "allotment." Heritage may be considered, therefore, quite a warrantable translation; and so may parish or ministerial charge, as the office allotted or appointed to a Christian pastor. In the Latin Vulgate the word used for the Greek *klēros* is *clerus*, which is used by ecclesiastical writers as equivalent to *ordo clericorum* (Facciolati Lexicon), or clergy. Wyclif's translation, therefore, made from the Vulgate, was quite literal; but, having regard to the context, most people will probably consider that the best rendering of the passage is that which is given in the revised version of the New Testament, 1881. "Feed the flock of God which is among you . . . not as lording it over the *charges allotted* to you."

The word *clergy* is suggestive of *priests*; although in the Presbyterian Churches of Scotland there are no officers designated priests. Those ordained to preach the word and administer sacraments are termed ministers or pastors. But both in the Church of Rome and in the Church of England, priest is the recognised designation of one of the three orders of clergy. In our authorised version of the Bible, we frequently meet with the word priest. It is the name given to the members of the house of Aaron, whose duty it was to serve in the temple. It is the name given, also, to the ministers of heathen deities; and all Christians are said to have been through Christ made kings and priests unto God. The word in the Greek Testament which is so translated, *priest*, is *hierus*. But, it is remarkable that in the authorised version of the New Testament the word *priest* never occurs as the designation of any officer in the Christian Church. This fact is all the more wonderful from the circumstance, that the word *presbyteros* from which both *Presbyter* and *Priest* are derived, occurs frequently in the Greek Testament. But that word is never, in our authorised version, translated by its English derivative, *priest*. It is always rendered by its English equivalent, *elder*. We read of "the apostles and *elders* and brethren," Acts xv. 23, instead of the apostles and *priests* and brethren, and Wyclif very often uses the word *elders* or *elder men* where *presbyteroi* appears in the Greek ; as in Rev. iv. 4,—" aboue the trones foure and twenti elder men sittynge, hilid aboute with whizt clothis, and in the heedis of hem goldun crownes." It must be kept in mind, however, that Wyclif translated from the Latin Vulgate; and the author of the Vulgate translation, St. Jerome, rendered the Greek word *presbyteroi* sometimes one way and sometimes another. When it meant elders of the city (that is civil rulers), or senior members of a congregation, Jerome translated it *seniores* ; and when it meant officers of the Church, he gave it the Latin form of *presbyteri*. When Wyclif, therefore, found *seniores* in the Vulgate he translated it *elders* or *elder men* ; and when he found *presbyteri* he translated it priests. Paul is thus, in Wyclif's Bible, made to say to Titus, i. 5,—" I lefte thee at Crete that thou . . . ordeyne preestis bi citees "; and to Timothy, 1st Epis. v. 17,—" the preestis that ben wel governouris, be thei hadde worthi to double honour, moost thei that traueilen in worde and techynge." St. James is, in like manner, represented as writing,—" If ony of you is sike, lede ye ynne preestis of the chirche, and preie thei for hym, and anoynte with oile in the name of the Lord."[1] And every one will see the bearing of these translations on sundry questions that have been subjects of ecclesiastical controversy. A semblance of authority is found for priestly unction in certain cases ; and for double honour to those priests, of whom Wyclif was one, that not only read the prayers of the Church in public, and ministered sacraments, but preached the word and taught the people knowledge.

Other ecclesiastical terms that we might be curious to know how Wyclif used are Church, Sacrament, Penance, and Conversion. The first-mentioned of these, church, is of frequent

---

[1] On the principle, apparently, that the Levites of old stood to the Jewish priests in much the same relationship as Deacons stand to priests in the Christian Church, Wyclif has in some places translated *levitae*, in the Vulgate, *deacons* : " This is the witnessynge of joon whanne jewis senten fro jerusalem preestis and *dekenes* to hym." John i. 19 ; "It bifelle that a preest cam doun the same weie . . . also a *dekene*."—Luke x. 31-32.

occurrence in the authorised version of the English Bible. It is the translation given, in certain places, to *ecclesia*, which means an assembly or congregation. But it is not always in the authorised version given as the translation of that word. Etymologically, it means pertaining to the Lord; and it is used, therefore, as a rendering of *ecclesia*, only in cases where *ecclesia* refers to a congregation of Christians. Wyclif was not so particular in that matter. He translated *ecclesia* " Church," even although the *ecclesia* referred to was not a Christian gathering. The " congregation of evil doers," Ps. xxvi. 5, is styled by him " the chirche of yuele men." The word church is applied by him, also, to the uproarious assembly at Ephesus, when the populace shouted for two hours, " Great is Diana of the Ephesians." And, as if confounding civil and spiritual jurisdiction, he gives the name of church to the courts of Cæsar: " If ze seken ouzt of ony other thing, it may be asoilid in the lawful chirche," Acts xix. 39.

In the authorised version of the English Bible the word "sacrament" does not appear at all; but in Wyclif's Bible it does more than once. And the reason of this apparent anomaly is evident. In the Greek Testament there is a word *mysterion*, which is sometimes in the Latin Vulgate translated *sacramentum*. The authors of our received version, translating directly from the Greek, have been content to render *mysterion* by its English derivative *mystery;* and Wyclif, translating from the Vulgate, has rendered *sacramentum* by its English derivative *sacrament*. The statement, " Great is the mystery of godliness," 1 Tim. iii. 16, reads accordingly in Wyclif's Bible—" It is a great sacrament of pitee"; and a seeming countenance is given by Wyclif to the sacramentarian doctrine of marriage by his rendering of Eph. v. 31-32—" A man schal forsake his fadir and modir, and he schal draw to his wiif, and thei schulen be tweyne in o fleisch: this sacrament is greet."

Penance, like sacrament, is a word that has no place in the authorised English Bible; but, like sacrament, it is used repeatedly in Wyclif's translation. John the Baptist, for instance, is represented by Wyclif as crying in the desert, " do ze penaunce, for the kyngdom of heuenes schal nyz."

Jesus, too, is represented as apostrophising Chorazin and Bethsaida, and saying to these graceless cities, "Woe unto you, for if the mighty works that have been done in you had been done in Tyre and Sidon, they would have 'don penaunce in heire and aisch.'" And the Apostles, also, are made by Wyclif to bear testimony to the efficacy of penance. On hearing the report of Peter's visit to Cornelius they are said to have exclaimed, in wonder and delight: "To hethen men God hath given penaunce to leif!"

The words *convert* and *conversion*, the last of the ecclesiastical terms we have here to consider, are in the authorised version applied, mostly, if not exclusively, to things spiritual. "If any of you do err from the truth," we read in Jas. v. 19, 20, "and one *convert* him, let him know that he which *converteth* the sinner from the error of his way shall save a soul from death." And so, also, in Acts xv. 3, we read that Paul and Barnabas "passed through Phenice and Samaria, declaring the *conversion* of the Gentiles." But in Wyclif's Bible the word convert is used much less restrictedly: not as a technical term in theology at all, but as the equivalent of *turn*, which might be used in reference to all sorts of persons and to all sorts of things. A prayer that sounds very strange in our ears occurs in Ps. vi. 5, "Lord be *thou convertid*, and delyuere my soul:" and a statement equally at variance with modern forms of expression appears in Job xlii. 10: "The Lord was *convertid* to the penance of Joob, whanne he priede for hise frendis."[1]

Passing now from words to phrases, it may be said that some phrases and expressions in Wyclif's Bible are notable for their aptness, some for their inaptness, and some for their homeliness. Although in point of clearness and precision of language, easy continuity of statement, and richness of rhythm, the versions of Wyclif are far inferior to our authorised translation of the Scriptures, they nevertheless, particularly the later version as amended by Purvey, contain many singularly happy phrases, which whether strictly accurate or not as renderings of the

---

[1] In the first version of Wyclif's Bible, 1380, the rendering of John xx. 16, is, "she, *conuerted*, saith to hym, Rabbony."

original Bible, and whether equal or not equal in force and beauty to those that have superseded them, we cannot read without delight and admiration. And it may be here remarked that, although it is the same Bible that Wyclif and Tyndal, the divines at Geneva, and the divines of the Church of England in King James' reign, have translated, there are in the style and diction of each version distinguishing features which bear the image of the translator, and reflect the culture of the times in which he lived. Very charming is the simplicity of the following passages in Wyclif's version (Purvey's amended): "If any man serve me, *sue he me*,"[1] John xii. 26; "Men, ye ben britheren, *whi noien ze eche other*," Acts vii. 26; "Nyle ze deme after the face, but *deme* ze a *riztful dome*," John vii. 24. So far as sound goes, there is about as much liquid sweetness as the ear could wish in the opening verse of the thirty-fifth Psalm—"Lord, deme thou hem that anoien me;" and at the same time there is about as much pungency of expression as piety could allow a good man to vent. There is not only simplicity, again, but graphic conciseness in the phrase—"passe we ouer the sea," which in the authorised version of the Scriptures is prolixly drawn out into "let us go over unto the other side of the lake." A similar remark may be made on the statement of the man whom Jesus cured of blindness at the pool of Siloam: "I wente, and waischid, and sai."[2] And although we may consider the expression "brother tite" to compare unfavourably with "Titus, my brother," it will scarcely be disputed that there is a tenderness of Christian feeling in the phrase, "Persida, moost dereworthe womman," which is entirely lost in in its modern substitute, "The beloved Persis." Occasionally, too, we meet with pleasant plays, or what look like pleasant plays on words, and have no uneasy feeling that the solemnity of the passage has been marred by

---

[1] The same form of expression as this will be found in many parts of Wyclif's Bible: "Light be maad, and light was made," Gen. i. 3; "He that hath eeris of herynge, here he," Mat. xi. 15.

[2] A clause in Wyclif's Bible that is made very misleading by means of peculiar spelling occurs in 1 Cor. ii. 9—"I saie not." This does not mean "I say not," but *eye saw not*. The transcriber or printer must surely have been at fault here.

the allusions. One of these pleasantries occurs in Ps. v. 7—
"Thou schalt *leese* (destroy) alle that speken *leesyng*" (falsehood). Another occurs in Ps. cvi. 6—"That thou be *heried*
(praised) with thin *eritage*." There is a fine antithesis, again,
in the following statements: "Alle thingis ben *nedeful* to me,
but not alle thingis ben *spedeful*," 1 Cor. vi. 12; "I have *takun*
of the Lord that thing which I have *bitakun* to zou," 1 Cor. xi.
23; "If ony man *unknowith* he schal be *unknowen*," 1 Cor. xiv.
38.[1] In some cases Wyclif's words (or Purvey's) convey a
clearer meaning than those that have replaced them in the
authorised version, *e.g.*, "The scruant is not gretter thanne his
lord, nether an *apoostle* is gretter thanne he that sente hym," John
xiii. 16; "I schal putte my spirit on hym, and he schal *telle
doom to hethen men*," Mat. xii. 18; "Nyle ye be conformed to
this world, but be ye *reformed in newnesse of youre wit*," Rom.
xii. 2. There is sometimes a grand rhythm, again, in his
words, as in Acts xiii. 25—"I am not he whom ye demen me
to be, but lo, he comith aftir me, and I am not worthi to don
of the schoon of his feet." At other times there is a weird and
ghastly picturesqueness in the repulsive terms he uses: as in
Matt. xxiii. 33—"ze eddris and eddris briddes"; and in Rev.
xxii. 15—"Withouten forth are *houndis* and *wicchis*, and un-
chast men, and manquellers, and servynge to idols, and ech
that loueth and makith leesynge."[1]

Not only, however, is Wyclif's Bible as a translation much
inferior, all through, to our common authorised version—
less accurate, less clear, less concise, less rhythmical—but
it abounds in clauses and sentences that are positively
feeble, obscure, and clumsy. And this is not to be wondered
at, considering that the English tongue was only in process of
formation, and was neither perfected, established, nor settled,
when Wyclif and Purvey wrote. "How long dost thou make
us to doubt" (John x. 24), appears in Wyclif's Bible, *how long*

---

[1] There is a very ingenious euphemism, also, which reflective readers will not fail to perceive and appreciate, in the phrase, Ps. lx. 9, "Moab is the pot of my hope." But Wyclif can scarcely be called the inventor of the euphemism. The words in the Vulgate are, "Moab olla spei meae." The Douay translators give the same rendering as Wyclif.

takist thou awei oure soule; " he groaned in the spirit " (John xi. 33), *he made noise in spirit;* " he breathed on them " (John xx. 22), *he blewe on hem;* " children, have ye any meat " (John xxi. 5), *children, where ze han ony soupinge thing;* " sufficient unto the day is the evil thereof " (Mat. vi. 34), *it sufficith to the dai his owne malice;* " there was a great calm " (Mat. viii. 26), *a greet pesiblenesse was made;* " hold thy peace " (Mark i. 25), *wexe doumbe;* " all men glorified God for that which was done " (Acts iv. 21), *alle men clarifieden that thing that was don in that that was bifalle;* " count I my life dear unto myself " (Acts xx. 24), *make my liif prechour thanne my liif;* " I was in a trance " (Acts xxii. 17), *I was made in rauyschynge of soule;* " I do the more cheerfully answer for myself " (Acts xxiv. 10), *I schal do inouz for me with good resoun;* " why should it be thought a thing incredible with you that God should raise the dead " (Acts xxvi. 8), *what unbileful thing is demed at zou if God reisith deed men;* " worshipped, leaning upon the top of his staff (Heb. xi. 21), *honourede the hiznesse of his zerd;* " think it not strange concerning the fiery trial, which is to try you " (1 Peter iv. 12), *nyle ze go in pilgrimage in feruour that is made to zou to temptacioun.*[1]

The following are a few other specimens of crude diction in the later and revised edition, 1388 (Purvey's), of Wyclif's Bible :—

Ps. xiv. 1—The unwise man seide in his herte, God is not. Thei ben corrupt, and ben maad abhomynable in her studies; noon is that doith good, *noon is til to oon* (non est usque ad unum—Vulgate).

Ps. xc. 2—Fro the world and into the world thou art God (a seculo et usque in seculum—Vulgate).

---

[1] Some of the sentences which are quoted as samples of crude diction are very literal translations of the Vulgate, and might be called Latinisms. How closely Wyclif and Purvey sometimes stuck to the letter of St. Jerome's Latin, may be seen from the subjoined expressions: " For wille lith to me " (Rom. vii. 18), *nam velle adjacet mihi* (Vulgate); " The prudence of fleisch is deeth (Rom. viii. 6), *prudentia carnis mors est* (Vulgate); " And there was made as a space of thre ouris " (Acts v. 7), *factum est autem quasi horarum trium spatium* (Vulgate); " For whiche thing I hauyng myche trist in crist ihesus to comaunde to thee, that that perteyneth to profete " (Philemon 8), *propter quod, multam fiduciam habens in Christo Jesu imperandi tibi quod ad rem pertinat.*

Ps. cxxxvi. 13—Whiche departide the reed sea in to departyngis (Qui divisit mare rubrum in divisiones—Vulgate).

Mat. xxii. 34—And pharisees herde that he hadde putte silence to saduceis camen to gidre.

Mark iii. 14—And he made that there weren twelue with hym, to sende hem to preche.

Luke xii. 58—Lest the domesman bitake thee to a *maistirful axer* (exactori, Vulgate), and the maistirful axer send thee in to prisoun.

Acts xxvi. 2—Of alle thingis of whiche I am accused of the Jewis, thou kyng egrippa, I gesse me blessid at thee, whanne I schal defende me this day.

Rom. ii. 28—He that is in opene is not a jew, nether it is circumcisioun that is openli in the fleisch.

2 Cor. i. 17-18—But whanne I wolde this thing, whether I uside unstidfastnesse? ether tho thingis that I thenke, I thenke aftir the fleische, that at me, be it is and it is not, but god is trewe, for oure word that was at zou is and is not, is not therinne, but is in it.

Eph. i. 9—To make knowe to us the sacrament of his wille bi the good pleasaunce of hym the whiche sacrament he purposid in hym.[1]

The diction of the earlier of the Wyclif versions, 1380, is still cruder than that of the later, as the following examples will shew :—

First Version, 1380.	Second Version, 1388.
Gen. xxix. 13.—The which whanne he had herd, Jacob, his sister sone, comen, zede azens metynge with hym, and clippynge hym and fallynge in cossis, ladde hym in to his hows.	Gen. xxix. 13.—And whanne he had herde that Jacob, the sone of his sister, cam, he ran azens hym, and he biclippid Jacob, and kisside hym, and ledde hym into his hows.
Gen. xl. 23.—And neuerthelater aftir fallynge welsum thingis, the prouest of botelers forzete of his dreem reder.	Gen. xl. 23.—And netheless whanne prosperitees bifelden the souereyn of botelers forgat his expownere.
Isa. xlviii. 3-4.—The rathere thingis fro thanne I told out, and of my mouth thei wenten out, and herd I made them; feerli I wrozte and thei camen. I knez forsothe for thou art hard, and an irene senew thin haterel and thi frount brasene.	Is. xlviii. 3-4.—Fro that time I telde the former thingis, and tho zeden out of my mouth, and I made tho knowun; sudenlie I wrouzte and tho things camen. For I wist that thou art hard, and thi nol is a senewe of irun, and thi forhed is of bras.
Luke xxii. 55.—Sothli a fyer kyndlid in the myddil greet hous and hem sittinge aboute, Petre was in the myddel of hem.	Luke xxii. 55.—And whanne a fier was kyndled in the myddil of the greet hous, and thei saten aboute, petir was in the myddil of hem.

---

[1] The following odd expressions may be quoted as samples of ambiguity, as well as of oddity :—

Prov. iv. 3- I was the sone of my fadir, a tendir sone, and oon gendride *bifore* my modir.

Prov. vi. 15—His perdicioun schal come to hym anoon, . . . and he *schal no more haue medecyn.*

John xix. 42.—Therefore, there, for the makyng redy of Jewis, for the graue was nyz, thei puttiden ihesu.
3 John 2.—Moost dere, of alle thingis I make preyer, thee for to entre and fare welsumly, as thi soule doth welsumly.

John xix. 42.—Therfor, there thei putten ihesus, for the vigile of jewis feest, for the sepulcre was nyz.
3 John 2.—Moost dere brother, of alle thingis I make preier, that thou enter and fare wilfulli, as thi soule doith wilfulli.

In Wyclif's Bible there are, as might be expected, some words and clauses that are not found in the authorised version, and there are some words and clauses in the authorised version that are not found in Wyclif's. This is easily explained. Wyclif and Purvey translated from the Latin tongue, or rather from a Latin text—" sumdel trewe "—a text as correct as they could put together by collating all manuscript copies of the Vulgate they could lay hands on. Their adopted version of the Vulgate varied in many places from that which, after more extensive and skilful collation, has now been attested by the Catholic Church as the authentic Scripture. The Vulgate, again, differs from the most ancient manuscripts of the Bible that have as yet been found in the Hebrew and Greek originals. And, last of all, these old manuscript Bibles in Hebrew and Greek do not correspond with each other in every word and letter. In the process of copying, slips of the pen occurred. Sometimes marginal notes, which were meant as explanations, or appropriate reflections, were, by mistake, transferred into the text. On the issue of the revised version of the New Testament, in 1881, great surprise was expressed in some quarters that the "doxology," or conclusion, annexed to the Lord's prayer, was left out. That omission was no novelty. The doxology is awanting in Wyclif's Bible, and, what to some people may be more surprising, in all the old copies of the English Prayer-Book.[1] The second clause of the sixth petition in the Lord's Prayer—" but deliver us from evil "—is, in Wyclif's version of Luke xi. 4, omitted also. On the other

---

[1] One of the novations in the obnoxious Service Book of Scotland, 1637, commonly called Laud's Liturgy, was the addition of this Doxology to the Lord's Prayer. It may be supposed, however, that this novation was not objected to by the Presbyterians. In his "Alliance of Divine Offices," L'Estrange says that "Learned men conjecture, it (the Doxology) was transplanted out of the liturgies of the Greek Church, or some such solemn usage, into the text of the Gospel."

hand, there are words inserted in Wyclif's version which are not found in the authorised translation. For instance, the three italicised words in the following sentence have no place in the English *textus receptus* :—" Wherfor, britheren, be ze more bisie, that *bi good werkis* ze make zoure clepynge and chesynge certeyn." Another clause in Wyclif's Bible, which is not in the authorised version, occurs in Acts xxiii. 24:—"Make ze redi a hors for poul to ride on, to lede hym saaf to felix the president, *for* the tribune dredde lest the jewis wolden take hym bi the weye and sle hym, and aftirwarde he myzte be chalengid as he hadde take money."

The number of cases in which Wyclif's Bible presents a different reading from what we find in the authorised translation is legion. To select samples out of such a multitude of instances is no easy task. What must strike people unacquainted with any English version of the Bible except the authorised, as a very strange reading, is the first clause of Gen. xli. 45—" And he turnede the name of Joseph, and clepide him bi Egipcian langage, *the sauyour of the world."* Another curious reading occurs in Deut. xxxiv. 7—" Moises was of an hundrid and twenti zeer whanne he diede, his ize dasewide not, nether *hise teeth weren stirid."* In the book of Job there is a sentence that might be adopted as a text by a lecturer on the principles of modern geology—" Watris maken stoonys holowe, and the erthe is wastid litil and litil bi waischyng awey of watir," xiv. 19. A very odd reading appears in Ps. lxxix. 1— " Thei defouledin thin hooli temple, thei settiden Jerusalem into *the keping of applis."* A still greater departure from the words of the authorised version will be found in Prov. xxi. 16, where it is said of those that turn aside from good doctrine, that they " schal dwelle in the cumpany of *giauntis,"* as if some promotion were in store for them.[1] Passing on to the New Testament, we find a very strange and not very relevant answer put into the mouth of our Saviour by Wyclif, as a reply to the

---

[1] The words in the Vulgate are, " in coetu gigantum commorabitur." In many other places the word *gigantes* is used in the Vulgate, where *mortui* (the dead) is used in other Latin versions of the Bible, as in Is. xxvi. 14 and 19.

question from John the Baptist, "Art thou he that should come, or do we look for another?"—"Go ze and telle azen to Jon thoo thingis that ze han herd and seyn, blinde men seen, crokid men gon, mysels ben made clene, deef men heren, deed men risen azen, and *pore men ben taken to prechynge of the Gospel.*" The saying "I will draw all men unto me" appears in Wyclif's version, "*I will draw all thingis to myself;*" the prayer of the legion of demons that they should not be sent into the deep reads that they should not be sent *into helle;* "give alms of such things as ye have" is improved (shall we say?) into *that that is ouerplus geue ze almes;* and the historical statement, Acts xix. 16, that "the man in whom was the evil spirit leaped on them" is certainly not improved by its being made to read "the man in whiche was the worst deuil lipped on hem, and hadde victorie of bothe." A rendering of Wyclif's that many people, scholastic and unscholastic, will doubtless consider preferable to the authorised translation is, John xi. 26, —"Eche that lyueth and bileueth in me schal *not die withouten ende,*" instead of "shall never die." In Wyclif's version of St. James' Epistle, again, there is a small variation from the authorised English reading, which, could it be accepted as the true and authentic Scripture, would be very consolatory to devout people that lack musical gifts: "If ony of zou is sorwful, preye he with paciente soule, and *seye* he a salm."[1]

The following are a few more cases in which it will be seen that Wyclif's version differs in its readings or renderings from the authorised translation:—

---

[1] In most of the cases above cited, Wyclif's version is a literal rendering of the Vulgate as printed at the present day; and Wyclif's translations are substantially the same as those of the Douay divines. Wyclif's version of James v. 13 is remarkable in this respect that it is founded on a peculiar punctuation of his Latin original. The verse as commonly printed in the Vulgate is—"Tristatur aliquis vestrum? oret. Aequo animo est? psallat;" and is accordingly translated in the Rhemes (Catholic) Testament substantially the same as in our authorised version. In Wyclif's copy of the Vulgate there had apparently been no stop after *oret*, but a comma after *animo*, and what is now printed *est* had been written *et*. The phrase "say a psalm" occurs elsewhere in Wyclif's Bible, "I schal synge, and I schal *scie salm* to the Lord." Ps. xxvi. 6.

WYCLIF'S VERSION, 1388.	AUTHORISED VERSION, 1611.
Job v. 6-7.—No thing is doon in erthe without cause, and sorewe schal not go out of the erthe. A man is borun to labour and a brid to flizt.	Job v. 6-7.—Although affliction cometh not forth of the dust, neither doth trouble spring out of the ground. Yet man is born unto trouble, as the sparks fly upwards.
Job vi. 16.—Snow schal come on hem that dreden frost.	Job vi. 16.—Which are blackish by reason of the ice, and wherein the snow is hid.
Job xix. 28.—Whi therfor seien ze now, Pursue we hym, and fynde we the roote of a word azens hym?	Job xix. 28.—But ye should say, Why persecute we him, seeing the root of the matter is found in me?
Job xxxviii. 36.—Who zaf undurstondyng to the cok? [1]	Job xxxviii. 36.—Who hath given understanding to the heart?
Ps. viii. 5.—What is a man, that thou art myndeful of hym: ethir the sone of a virgyn for thou visitist hym?	Ps. viii. 5.—What is man, that thou art mindful of him, and the son of man, that thou visitest him?
Ps. xvi. 5.—The Lord is part of myn eritage and of my *passion*.	Ps. xvi. 5.—The Lord is the portion of mine inheritance and of my cup.
Ps. lv. 13-14.—But thou art a man of o wille: my leeder and my knowun, which tokist togidre swete meetis (dulces cibos, Vulgate) with me : we zeden with consent in the hous of God.	Ps. lv. 13-14.—But it was thou, a man mine equal, my guide, and mine acquaintance. We took sweet counsel together, and walked into the house of God in company.
Ps. lxxxviii. 10.—Whethir thou schalt do merueils to deed men: ether leechis schulen reise, and thei schulen knouleche to thee?	Ps. lxxxviii. 10.—Wilt thou shew wonders to the dead, shall the dead arise and praise thee?
Ps. xc. 9.—Oure zeris schulen bithenke as an yreyn (spider).	Ps. xc. 9.—We spend our years as a tale that is told.
Rom. x. 19.—Moises seith I schal lede zou to enuye that ze be not folk, that ze be an unwise folk I schal sende zou in to wrathe.	Rom. x. 19.—Moses saith, I will provoke you to jealousy by them that are no people, and by a foolish nation will I anger you.
1 Cor. i. 20.—Where is the purchasour of this world?	1 Cor. i. 20.—Where is the disputer of this world?

Sometimes a considerable difference of meaning is produced on a statement by the insertion or omission of the article *a* or *the*, or the substitution of one of these articles for the other. A noted instance of this occurs in the revised version of the New Testament, where the love of money is said to be *a* root, instead of *the* root, of all evil. In Wyclif's Bible there are many phrases that are made to read differently from what they do in the authorised version, from a slight difference of articulation. In the Latin language, from which Wyclif's translation was made, there are no articles. Wyclif was left free, therefore, to insert a definite or an indefinite article in his transla-

---

[1] The Douay rendering is the same as Wyclif's, and in some editions of that version there is subjoined to the passage the following explanatory note :—" Understanding. To distinguish the hours of the night " !

tion, wherever an innate sense of literary propriety prompted him. Sometimes he has done this judiciously, and sometimes injudiciously. One rendering of his that has found its way into the revised version of the New Testament is, "settid hym on *the* pynacle of the temple," Mat. iv. 5. Another peculiar rendering of his, which is not at variance with the original Greek, and admits of something being said in its favour, is, "I came not to send pees but *swerde*," Mat. x. 34.[1] One sentence which reads so well in Wyclif's Bible, that we have a feeling of great disappointment in finding that it lacks the merit of a true translation of the Greek original, is John x. 11—"I am *a* good scheepherde; *a* good scheepherde geueth his liif for his scheep; but *an* hired hyne . . . seeth *a* wolf cometh, and he leuith the scheep and fleeth." It will be noticed that in this verse Wyclif makes a very frequent and very happy use of the *indefinite* article. And this he has done in many other places, with the effect of giving to sober narrative a somewhat quaint and lively colouring. For instance, Job is made to say, chap. xxxi. 40: "If my lond crieth azens me, and hise forewis wepen with it: if I eet fruytis thereof without money, and I turmentide the soule of erthe-tileris of it: *a* brere growe to me for wheete, and *a* thorn for barli." And so also in Ps. cv. Wyclif translates: (ver. 31) "He seide, and *a* fleische flie cam: and gnattis in alle the coostis of hem; (v. 34) He seide, and *a* locust cam: and *a* bruk of which was noon noumbre; (v. 40) Thei axiden, and *a* curlew cam: and he fillide hem with the breed of heuene. He brak *a* stoon, and watris flowiden." At other times, Wyclif is not so happy in his use of the indefinite article. The beneficence of Job is much shorn of its bounteousness by the following rendering of chap. xxix. 11-13—"*An* eere herynge blesside me, and *an* ize seynge zeldide witnessyng to me: for Y had delyueride *a* pore man criynge, and *a* fadirles child that hadde noon helpere. The blessyng of *a* man to

---

[1] Sword is at the present day used as an abstract noun in such phrases as "fire and sword." Wyclif uses the word in an abstract way in other parts of his Bible: "In hungur he schal delyuere thee fro deeth, and in batel fro the power of swerd.' —Job v. 20.

perische cam on me, and Y coumfortide the herte of *a* widowe." And so also the point of the question submitted to Jesus by the Samaritan woman is very much obscured in Wyclif's translation, by the introduction of the article indefinite, where the article definite should have been used:—"Oure fadris worschipiden in this hille, and ze seien that at ierusalem is *a* place where it bihoueth to worschip." An entirely different meaning, affecting what many people will consider a very vital point of doctrine, is, in like manner, by the same small verbal alteration, made on a noteworthy saying of our Lord's, recorded in Luke xi. 13:—"If ze whanne ye ben yuel, kunne zeue gode ziftis to zoure children, hou myche more zoure fadir of heuene schal zeue *a* good spirit to men that axith him."

It is not unworthy of remark that some of Wyclif's readings and renderings, after having been shelved for three hundred years, have been again revived and adopted in the new version of the English Bible. This is not to say that Wyclif's research and scholarship were so remarkable as to be three hundred years in advance of the age in which the authorised translators lived. It only means that the text of the Vulgate has been found to be less corrupt than was once supposed; and, consequently, that in rendering the Vulgate faithfully Wyclif has in many places, where his version varies from the authorised, given accidentally the true teaching of Scripture. Every one knows that the time-honoured phrase, "Almost thou persuadest me to be a Christian," Acts xxvi. 28, is in the revised version displaced by the cynical remark, "With but little persuasion thou wouldest fain make me a Christian." Wyclif's rendering in this passage is not very explicit, but it at least points in the direction of the revisers': " In litil thing thou counceilist me to be made a cristen man." By simply changing *of* into *for*, the revisers have given an entirely new aspect to the Apostolic assurance in James iii. 18—" The fruit of righteousness is sown in peace *of* them that make peace." But in this matter they were forestalled by Wyclif, who translates the latter part of the verse, "*to* men that maken peace." For the words in the authorised version, "All went to be taxed," Luke ii. 3, we find in the revised version, "All went to enrol themselves," and in

Wyclif's, "Alle wenten to make professioun," or (in verse 1) to be "discryued." In Wyclif's version, again, we meet with the revised rendering of John xiii. 18—"he that eateth *my bread*," instead of "eateth bread *with me;*" as also the revised rendering of 2nd Peter i. 5, "*in* your faith supply virtue, and *in* your virtue knowledge," &c.

The following are instances of coincidence between Wyclif's version and the revised translation of the Old Testament:—

Wyclif's Version, 1388.	Authorised Version, 1611.	Revised Version, 1885.
Job iii. 8.—Curse thei it, that cursen the dai, that ben redi to *reise Leuyathan*.	Job. iii. 8.—Let them curse it that curse the day, who are ready to raise up their mourning.	Job iii. 8.—Let them curse it that curse the day, who are ready to *rouse up Leviathan*.
Job xxxvii. 22.—*Gold* schal come fro the north and ferdful preisyng of God.	Job xxxvii. 22.—Fair weather cometh out of the north: with God is terrible majesty.	Job xxxvii. 22.—Out of the north cometh *golden splendour:* God hath upon him terrible majesty.
Ps. lxviii. 30.—Blame thou the *wielde beestis of the reheed*, the gaderyng togidere of bolis is among the kien of puplis.	Ps. lxviii. 30.—Rebuke the company of spearmen, the multitude of the bulls with the calves of the people.	Ps. lxviii. 30.—Rebuke the *wild beast of the reeds,* the multitude of the bulls, with the calves of the people.
Prov. vii. 20.—He took with hym a bagge of money, he schal turne azen in to his hous in the *dai of ful moone*.	Prov. vii. 20.—He hath taken a bag of money with him, and will come home at the day appointed.	Prov. vii. 20.—He hath taken a bag of money with him: he will come home at the *full moon.*
Prov. viii. 30.—I was *making all thingis* with him.	Prov. viii. 30.—I was by him as one brought up with him.	Prov. viii. 30.—I was by him, as a *master workman.*
Prov. xi. 12.—He that dispisith his freend, is nedi in herte.	Prov. xi. 12.—He that is void of wisdom despiseth his neighbour.	Prov. xi. 12.—He that despiseth his neighbour is void of wisdom.
Prov. xvii. 27.—He that mesurith his wordis is wiis and prudent.	Prov. xvii. 27.—He that hath knowledge spareth his words.	Prov. xvii. 27.—He that spareth his words hath knowledge.
Prov. xix. 18.—Teche thi sone, and dispeire thou not : but *sette thou not thi soule to the sleyng of hym*.	Prov. xix. 18.—Chasten thy son while there is hope, and let not thy soul spare for his crying.	Prov. xix. 18.—Chasten thy son, seeing there is hope : and *set not thy heart on his destruction.*
Prov. xxi. 4.—Enhaunsyng of izen is alargyng of the herte : *the lanterne* of wicked men is synne.	Prov. xxi. 4.—An high look and a proud heart, and the plowing of the wicked, is sin.	Prov. xxi. 4.—An high look and a proud heart, even *the lamp* of the wicked is sin.
Eccles. ii. 25.—Who schal deuoure so, and *schal flowe in deliciis*, as I did?	Eccles. ii. 25.—For who can eat, or who else can hasten hereunto more than I?	Eccles. ii. 25.—For who can eat, or who *can have enjoyment* more than I?

The most outstanding feature of Wyclif's Bible, however, is the graphic homeliness of its diction. It was for the common people that Wyclif translated the Scriptures ; and he wished the common people to have the Scriptures set before them in the language of their every-day life. Hence the rustic plainness of his phraseology, which at times is very quaint and delightful, and at other times is deficient in both dignity and delicacy. Very graceful, for instance, in its apostolic affection, is the salutation that St. Paul is made (Rom. i. 7) to address to his fellow Christians in the great city of the Gentiles :—" To alle that ben at rome, *derlyngis of god and clepid holy."* Very simply and very touchingly, again, is it said of Epaphras, who sent his greeting to the brethren at Colosse, that he was "euer bisie for them in preiers." In the phrase, "ihesus *zede aboute al galilee* techynge in the synagogis" (Mat. iv. 23), there is a fine air of leisureliness, in striking and instructive contrast to the high pressure and the forced pace of modern religious life. Very primitive, too, but very graphic withal, is the narrative (Acts xii. 8) of the angel's interview with Peter in the prison at Jerusalem :—" The aungel seide to hym : girde thee, and do on thi hoosis, and he dide so ; and he seide to hym, do aboute thee thi clothis, and sue me, and he zede out and sued hym." In the authorised version of the Bible, we read that when "the Lord turned the captivity of Job," all his friends and acquaintances paid him a visit of congratulation, and "every man also gave him a piece of money, and an ear-ring of gold." As described by Wyclif, the gifts had a more pastoral aspect :— "Thei zauen to hym ech man *o scheep*, and o goldun eerering." More vividly, too, than in the authorised version, is brought out in Wyclif's translation, the self-importance of Sarah's handmaid, on discovering herself in a condition her mistress had never attained. The damsel "dispisede *hir ladie."*

It must be admitted, however, that while the old-fashioned homeliness of Wyclif's phrases is sometimes pathetic, the associations awakened by them are more frequently of a ludicrous tendency. In the story of the legion's dispossession (Luke viii. 33), it is said that "the deuelis wenten out fro the man, and entriden in to the swyn, and *with a birre* the flok wente heedlynge in to the pool." Instead of the stately expression, "consider the ravens" (Luke xii. 24), we find in Wyclif's Bible, *biholde the crowis ;* instead of the grave charge, ' occupy till I come," *chaffare ye till I come ;* and instead of the high misdemeanour of "perverting the nation," the Apostles are accused of *turnynge upso doun oure folk*. The dread solemnity of the declaration "their damnation slumbereth not," disappears entirely in Wyclif's rendering, *the perdicioun of hem nappeth not*. The semi-regal magnificence of Felix, too, is divested of much of its dignity by the statement, "he cam doun with *drussel* his wif." So also is the pomp of Pilate, in being styled "pounce pilat;" and in another place, "pilat of pounce, justice." Even St. Paul is made to appear ridiculous in having "clippid his heed"; and much more so is Bartimaeus, who, in response to the call of Christ, "castid aweie his *cloth*, and *skippid*, and cam." Sometimes Wyclif's diction, when most vigorous, verges on coarseness of expression. The designation given to those that separate themselves from the Church is (Jude 19), "beestli men, not hauynge spirit"; and (2 Peter ii. 1), "maistir lieris that brynge in sectis of perdicioun." It has to be borne in mind, however, that so changed since Wyclif's days are our modes of speech, that many words and phrases of his that would now be counted vulgar colloquialisms, had once an admitted place in the vocabulary of the best English. Of these degraded expressions, it may here suffice to mention two, "certis," and "the toon and the tother." In Wyclif's Bible the words attributed to Jesus regarding John the Baptist are :—"*Certis*, I seie to zou ther is no man more profete." And so, likewise, the words attributed to Jesus in regard to a man's serving two masters, are :—" Ether he schal hate *the toon* and loue *the tother*, eithere he schal susteyne *the toon* and dispise *the tother*."[1]

The following other verses may be quoted as specimens of Wyclif's homeliness of expression :—

Wyclif's Version, 1388.	Authorised Version, 1611.
Gen. xxix. 17.—Lya was blere ized.	Gen. xxix. 17.—Leah was tender eyed.
Judges xviii. 19 (first edition).—To whom they answeriden, *Whist*.	Judges xviii. 19.—And they said unto him, Hold thy peace.
Job xix. 20.—Oneli lippis ben left aboute my teeth.	Job. xix. 20.—I am escaped with the skin of my teeth.

---

[1] A title very commonly given to Jesus by his disciples, in Wyclif's Bible, is commander; a fact for members of the Salvation Army to note. "Petir seide to ihesus, commander, it is good that we be here."—Luke ix. 33.

Job xxxiv. 9.—For he seide. A man schal not plese God, zhe, thouz he renneth with God.

Job xl. 5.—Y spak o thing, which thing y wold that y had not seid: and y spak anothir thing, to which y schal no more adde.

Ps. lxxviii. 45.—He sent a paddock and it loste hem.

Ps. cxxix. 4.—The just Lord schal beete the nollis of synneris.

Ps. cxlvii. 1.—Heriyng be myrie and fair to oure God.

Prov. xx. 23.—Abhomynacioun at God is weizte and weizte.

Prov. xxii. 29.—Thou hast seyn a man smert in his werk: he schal stonde bifore kyngis.

Isaiah xix. 14.—The Lord mengde in his myddel the spirit of *turnegidy* (1st version, 1380).

Mat. x. 16.—Be ze slize as serpentis.

Mat. xii. 44.—Fyndith it uoide, and clensid with bisoms and made faire.

Mark ix. 47.—It is bettir to thee to entre gogil ized in to the rewme of God, thanne haue tweie izen and be sente into helle of fier.

John iv. 49.—The *litil kyng* seith to hym. Lord come doun, bifor that my sone die.

Acts xiv. 8.—A man at listris was *sike* in the feet.

Rom. ix. 10.—Rebecca hadde tweye sones, *of o liggynge*, bi of Isaac our fadir.

2 Cor. xii. 3.—Whether in bodi, or out of bodi *I noot, God woot.*

Rev. xii. 5.—Sche bare a man (*knaue*) child that was to rulinge alle folkis in an irun zerd.

Job xxxiv. ix.—For he hath said, It profiteth a man nothing that he should delight himself with God.

Job xl. 5.—Once have I spoken, but I will not answer; yea twice, but I will proceed no further.

Ps. lxxviii. 45.—He sent frogs which destroyed them.

Ps. cxxix. 4.—The Lord is righteous, he hath cut asunder the cords of the wicked.

Ps. cxlvii. 1.—For it is pleasant, and praise is comely.

Prov. xx. 23.—Divers weights are an abomination to the Lord.

Prov. xxii. 29.—Seest thou a man diligent in his business? he shall stand before kings.

Isaiah xix. 14. — The Lord hath mingled a perverse spirit in the midst thereof.

Mat. x. 16.—Be ye therefore wise as serpents.

Mat. xii. 44.—Findeth it empty, swept and garnished.

Mark ix. 47.—It is better for thee to enter into the kingdom of God with one eye, than having two eyes, to be cast into hellfire.

John iv. 49.—The nobleman saith unto him, Sir, come down ere my child die.

Acts xiv. 8.—A certain man at Lystra, impotent in his feet.

Rom. ix. 10.—When Rebecca als o had conceived by one, even by our father Isaac.

2 Cor. xIi. 3.—Whether in the body I cannot tell, or whether out of the body I cannot tell, God knoweth.

Rev. xii. 5.—She brought forth a man child, who was to rule all nations with a rod of iron.

In trying to make the record of Apostolic life as near a counterpart as possible to what prevailed in England in his own day, Wyclif occasionally introduced into his Bible words that had not been adopted by the Church, at the date of the incidents to which they are made to refer. At the present day, the words *baptize* and *christen* are used synonymously: but we cannot think it other than an anachronism, as well as an unliteral translation, to make St. Luke say (as Wyclif does), Acts xviii. 8, that " many of the corinthies herden, and bileueden and werun *cristened."* In Wyclif's Bible, again, the designation generally given to idols is "mawmets." "Ze ben conuerted to God fro *mawmetes*," 1 Thess. i. 9. "Mi litil sones kepe ze zou fro *mawmetes*," 1 John v. 21. The word *mawmet* is a corruption of Mahomet; and as Mahomet was not born for five hundred years after Paul had written his epistles, it is a violation of the principles of dramatic unity to represent the Apostle cautioning his readers against "mawmets." And it may be here remarked, that there never was more injustice done to a man's name than was by Christians done to Mahomet's, in making it a synonym for idol; for there never was a religion that denounced and condemned idolatry more vehemently than does Mahometanism. Another anachronism in Wyclif's Bible (also in Tyndale's Testament) is the introduction into Paul's writings of the word *whitsuntide*. This is a word of ecclesiastical and post-pauline origin. It could not possibly, therefore, have been used by St. Paul himself: and although it came to be considered only as another name for Pentecost, it expressed certain facts or associations which could not have been before the mind of the Apostle when he spoke of the Pentecostal solemnity. Wyclif, nevertheless, introduces the word into St. Paul's writings. He makes the Apostle say, 1 Cor. xvi. 8, "I schal dwelle at effecie til to *witsuntide*." There is at least one anachronism in our authorised version, however, which does not appear in Wyclif's translation. It is said of Herod, who killed James the brother of John, that he put Peter into prison, "intending after *Easter* to bring him forth to the people," Acts xii. 4. Before the days of Christianity the word Easter seems to have been applied to the April festival in honour of the goddess of light and spring. But in that application, it had no place in the calendar of either Jews or Christians: and it was not till it came to be applied by the Church to the festival of the resurrection that any Christian writer could have referred to it as a date. St. Paul does not use the word in any of his Epistles: and the word should not be given as the translation or equivalent of any of St. Paul's terms. The revisers of 1881 have properly excluded it from their version of the testament; and have substituted for it, in the passage quoted, the word *pass-*

over, which is the literal translation and the true equivalent of the Greek original. Wyclif also adheres to the Apostle's own term, and does not even translate it *passover*, but "paske," which is the English form of the Greek and Latin *pascha*. Another anachronism of Wyclif's occurs in the Gospels. In the parable of the lost coin, a woman is represented in our authorised version of the Bible as having ten pieces of silver. In some old English translations, Tyndale's, Coverdale's, &c., these ten coins are called "grotes;" bnt in Wyclif's Bible they are termed *besauntis*, a word that had no place in numismatology till the Byzantine empire was founded, four hundred years after Christ had left the world.

That Wyclif's Bible is at all to be compared to either the authorised or the revised version of the Scriptures, as an accurate translation or as a work of literature, cannot be pretended; but it is a notable production notwithstanding, and worthy of an honoured place in England's remembrance. It cannot be supposed that even Wyclif himself considered it a final translation of the Bible, perfect, entire, and needing no amendment. It was not a translation from the original Scriptures, but only from a Latin version of these. It was written at a time when the English language was only taking shape, and it was thus doomed to become prematurely archaic. But it answered the immediate end for which it was published. It gave to the English people of Wyclif's own generation a substantially fair and faithful English version of the holy Scriptures; and it thus enabled Englishmen of that day to refer the doctrines and usages of the Church to the fundamental and authentic test of Christian truth.

Besides issuing copies of his Bible in different sizes, and at different prices, to suit the taste and means of different classes of readers, Wyclif endeavoured to make his Bible practically beneficial to the very poorest and most ignorant of the public by instituting an order of readers and preachers, who "gede aboute" all England, reading the gospels and epistles, and giving simple expositions of what they read. The result was that there grew up in the land a body of religionists, who held a purer faith, walked in a clearer light, and led a holier life, than their neighbours. These Puritans, as they may be termed, were at first called Wycliffites, because it was from Wyclif's preaching, Wyclif's preachers, Wyclif's writings, and Wyclif's Bible that their inspiration was drawn. Afterwards, and down till the Reformation, they went by the reproachful designation of Lollards, or idle babblers. They were not confined to English territory, either, but they had habitations in Scotland also. In the central district of Ayrshire, in what are now the parishes of Mauchline, Tarbolton, Stair, Loudoun, and Galston, they had an important settlement. Finally they were absorbed in the ranks of Protestantism; but they have this honourable testimony and memorial, that they were a shining light in the land, till the day dawned and the day star of Reformation rose. Their peculiar heritage and dearest possession was Wyclif's Bible, which may thus be termed the light of the Lollards.

The Reformers' Bibles.

TYNDALE'S TESTAMENT, 1526; REVISED, 1534.

Editions consulted and quoted from—
    Original version, 1526. Fry's facsimile.
    Revised version, 1534. Reprint in Bagster's Hexapla.

THE place that the Bible should hold in men's estimation is the fundamental question on which the Protestant Church and the Catholic Church are at issue. Both Churches honour the Bible, and acknowledge the Bible as a divine revelation. Both Churches also found on the Bible for their doctrines. But the Protestant Church founds on the *Bible alone* for her teaching; whereas the Catholic Church founds partly on the Bible, and partly on special communications, or increased enlightenment, given to the Church from age to age by the Holy Spirit. The promised guide of the Church, Catholics assert, is the Holy Ghost; and that guidance is an ever-living inspiration, which has neither yet ceased nor been exhausted. According to Catholics, therefore, the Church receives accessions of truth from time to time; and the new revelations made to the Church to-day are quite as authoritative as the old revelations made in the days of the Apostles. The Church's own constitutions, the decrees of her councils, and the official utterances of her Popes, being all divinely inspired, have thus, with Catholics, a degree of authority equal to that of the sacred Book itself. Hence the Church's warrant for the worship of the Virgin, for worship by images, for priestly absolutions, for sale of indulgences, for the dogma of the immaculate conception. On the other hand, the fundamental doctrine of Protestantism is that the Bible is the only divine revelation given for our spiritual direction; that nothing contrary to, or at variance with what is written in the Bible can be allowed in the Church; that the teaching of the Bible is never to be annulled or superseded;

and that nothing which does not appear in the Bible can be imposed by the Church on her members as an essential obligation of Christian life or Christian ritual. As the Reformers came to recognise and realise their true doctrinal position, they saw more and more clearly, and they felt more and more strongly, that the Bible must be given to the people of all nations and kindreds in their own tongues, so that every Christian man might be able to judge for himself what doctrines are to be received, what ordinances are to be observed, and what duties are to be practised, by those that name the name of Christ.

When the great revolt against Papal power and Popish doctrine which ended in the Reformation arose in England, there were, and for a hundred and forty years there had been, in this country not a few manuscript copies of the Bible in English. Wyclif's translation had been published in 1380, and Purvey's amendment of it in 1388; and although both of these publications had been condemned, and their perusal prohibited under pains and penalties, copies of them were still in existence, and access to them could easily be obtained. It may seem, therefore, that nothing more was requisite to satisfy the demands of the Reformers than to have Wyclif's Bible republished by means of the recently invented printing press. But such a re-publication would not have sufficed to meet either the views of the leading Reformers or the wants of the age. The language in which Wyclif's Bible was written had, in the sixteenth century, become antiquated. It had ceased to be the daily spoken language of the English people. Many of its words had become obsolete, and others had assumed new meanings. The structure and orthography of the language had been radically changed; and Wyclif's Bible, even if it could have been accepted as a satisfactory translation, would have required to be modernised in its diction, in order to be made intelligible to ordinary readers. But Wyclif's Bible was only a translation of a translation. It was only a rendering in English of the Latin Vulgate; and by the time we speak of (say 1520), copies of the Old Testament in Hebrew, and of the New Testament in Greek, were to be had in England, and they could be read by some English scholars. Those that desired to give the English people a version of the Bible in English could not content themselves, therefore, with any translation that was not made from the tongues in which the Bible was originally written. The living water must be drawn from the fountain-head. Wyclif's Bible was, accordingly, left to lie on the secret shelves of the Lollard and the antiquary; and a new version of the Bible, as accurate and as clearly expressed as care and scholarship could make it, was felt to be a necessity of the times.

The first of the English Reformers to set about the task of translating the Bible anew, and the most notable of all who gave themselves to that great and good work, was William Tyndale. History says, "he was born about the borders of Wales;" tradition adds, in Gloucestershire; and the latest phase of accepted opinion is that his birth took place in 1484. At an early age he was sent to the University of Oxford, where "by long continuance, he grew and increased in the knowledge of tongues and other liberal arts, and specially in the knowledge of the Scriptures, whereunto his mind was singularly addicted." After "proceeding in degrees of the schools," he removed from Oxford to Cambridge, where he "likewise made his abode a certain space, and ripened further in the knowledge of God's word."

About 1521, Tyndale left Cambridge, to act as tutor or chaplain in the family of Sir John Walsh, of Little Sodbury. Here his religious views and character were markedly developed. In those days there was much in the Catholic Church to provoke and grieve, if not alienate, the worthiest of her members. Many of the most important bishoprics in England were held by foreigners, who lived abroad, and who never entered appearance within the bounds of their dioceses. The greed and extortion, too, of the clergy had no limits; so that when Tyndale took pen in hand, he wrote in one of his books :—"The parson sheareth, the vicar shaveth, the parish priest polleth, the friar scrapeth, and the pardoner pareth : we lack but a butcher to pull off the skin." What was exhibited in the Church as the Christian religion was a senseless mummery, which had no root in the intellect, and no moral influence on the lives of those that affected to find salvation in it. On these scandals and corruptions Tyndale looked with scorn and indignation, and out of the abundance of his heart his mouth began to speak with greater plainness than prudence. "Being in good favour with his master, he sat most commonly at his (master's) own table, which kept a good ordinary, having resort to him many times divers great-beneficed men, as abbots, deans, and arch-deacons. . . . Amongst whom commonly was talk of learning . . . and the said Master Tyndale being learned . . . did many times therein shew his learning . . . until in the continuance thereof those great-beneficed doctors waxed weary, and bore a secret grudge in their hearts against Master Tyndale."[1] And, considering the vehemence of language that Tyndale displays in his writings, we may be quite sure that in his post-prandial discussions he would not be very careful to express himself in measured terms. We can easily understand, too, that the great-beneficed dignitaries bore a grudge at him, and that murmurs arose about his holding opinions at variance with the faith of the Church. Tyndale, in fact, at this early period, and while occupying a position that was not independent, had made himself a marked man. He was promptly taken to task, therefore, by his superiors. In the absence of the non-resident bishop, the chancellor of the diocese took occasion to summon before him all the priests in the district where Tyndale resided. Tyndale had his own suspicions of what was meant by this act of authority; and he prayed heartily that God would "strengthen him to stand fast in the truth." What took place at the meeting can only be gathered somewhat dubiously from the partial accounts on the one hand by Tyndale himself, and on the other by the adversary of his later years, Sir Thomas More. "When I came before the Chancellor," Tyndale writes, "he threatened me grievously, and reviled me, and rated me as though I had been a dog: and laid to my charge (things) whereof there could be none accuser brought forth, as their

---

[1] Foxe.

manner is not to bring forth the accuser: and yet all the priests of the country[1] were the same day there." Sir Thomas More, on the other hand, avers that as Tyndale "glosed his words with a better sense, and said and swore that he meant no harm, folk were glad to take all to the best."

It was during his tutorship, or chaplaincy, at Little Sodbury, about the year 1522, when he was thirty-eight years of age, that Tyndale seems first to have announced his purpose of translating the Scriptures into English.[2] Falling into argument with an ecclesiastical brother, about God's laws and the Pope's laws, Tyndale said in the heat of his temper:—"I defy the Pope and all his laws: and if God spare my life, ere many years I will cause a boy that driveth the plough shall know more of the Scriptures than thou doest." And the motives that led Tyndale to cherish this high and grand design, he detailed many years afterwards, in the preface to his translation of the Pentateuch. The rulers of the Church, he there said, " be all agreed . . . to keep the world in darkness: to the intent they may sit in the consciences of the people, through vain superstition and false doctrine to satisfy their filthy lusts, their proud ambition and unsatiable covetousness, and to exalt their own honour above King and compeer, yea, and above God himself. . . . Which thing only moved me to translate the New Testament. . . . I perceived by experience how that it was impossible to establish the lay people in any truth, except the Scripture were plainly laid before their eyes in their mother-tongue, that they might see the process, order, and meaning of the text: for else, whatsoever truth is taught them, these enemies of all truth quench it again, partly with the smoke of their bottomless pit . . . that is, with

---

[1] Pref. to Pentateuch. Demaus, p. 57.
[2] In Scrivener's Introduction to Notes on the New Testament (1845), the following statement occurs, p. 78-9: "In his 'Memoirs of Tyndale' Mr. Offer has recently brought to light a few manuscript translations of various parts of the New Testament, bearing the signature of W. T., and the date of 1502, just twenty years before the publication of any portion of Luther's Bible. From these most curious fragments it appears that Tyndale's version of Scripture was no hasty compilation to serve an emergency, but the matured fruit of careful practice and patient study, continued through the course of four and twenty years."

apparent reasons of sophistry, and traditions of their own making, founded without ground of Scripture, and partly in juggling with the text, expounding it in such a sense as is impossible to gather of the text, if thou see the process, order, and meaning thereof."

It is evident that the stand which Tyndale was taking against ecclesiastical authority was not altogether in keeping with the dependent position he occupied in Sir John Walsh's family, and that it might possibly bring Sir John Walsh himself into trouble. Tyndale was not slow to realise these facts; and he accordingly intimated his desire to be released from his tutorship. "I perceive," he said to the worthy knight, in whose hospitable house he had received much kindness, "that I shall not be suffered to tarry long here, nor will you be able to keep me out of their (the clergy's) hands; and what displeasure you might have thereby is hard to know, for the which I should be right sorry."

Tyndale, therefore, "with his master's good will," took leave of Little Sodbury and Gloucestershire, and made his way to the metropolis, where he hoped to be able to accomplish in peace the great undertaking on which he was bent. He obtained, and took with him, a note of introduction from Sir John Walsh to Sir Harry Guildford, controller of the royal household, who was thought likely to be able to further the views of the poor tutor. Shortly before this time, a new bishop had been installed in London; and this new bishop, Cuthbert Tunstall, was not only of high repute as a scholar, but was supposed to have some sympathy with the liberal views that were spreading at the seats of learning. On reaching London, Tyndale repaired without delay to Sir Harry Guildford, who received him with all the courtesy anticipated, and promised to recommend him to the bishop's favourable notice. It was then arranged that Tyndale should, at a fitting time, wait upon the bishop personally; and, after submitting credentials of his scholarship, endeavour to ascertain if the bishop could find for him any service that would enable him to reside in London, and prosecute the work to which he meant to devote his energies. The desired interview was obtained, but the result was disappointing. Men that are besieged with applications for sympathy and help, as bishops are apt to be, are often compelled to be reserved and coldly polite to suitors. It may very well be supposed, also, that considering the disfavour with which translations of the Bible into different tongues had come to be regarded by many churchmen, Tunstall would be chary about committing himself to the project of an adventurer, whose ardour might possibly have outrun his discretion. After hearing what Tyndale had to say, therefore, the Bishop replied that "his house was full, and that he had more (chaplains) than he could well find."[1] And he politely added, that he did not doubt, if Master Tyndale would look about him in London he would not long lack service.

While residing in London, Tyndale preached occasionally in the Church of St. Dunstan's in the West. One that heard him preach there was Humphrey Monmouth, a wealthy cloth merchant in the east end of the city, who had begun "to be a Scripture man, and to smell the Gospel." Tyndale made the acquaintance of this well-to-do hearer, and was installed for half a year as chaplain in his house, at a salary of ten pounds sterling, to pray for all Christian souls, and especially for the souls of Monmouth's father and mother. During the half-year he was so employed, "he lived," said Monmouth, "like a good priest as methought. He studied most part of the day and of the night at his book ; and he would eat but sodden meat by his good will, and drink but small single beer."

In England, the Bible was, at this time, to all intents and purposes, an interdicted book. No scholar was allowed to publish, and no person was allowed to peruse, under pains and penalties, a translation of the Holy Scriptures, "until the said translation had been approved by the ordinary of the place, or, if the case so required, by the council provincial." It accordingly became more and more clear to Tyndale, that not only was there "no room in my lord of London's palace to translate the New Testament, but also, that there was no

---

[1] "Find" here means "provide for."

place to do it in all England." He resolved, therefore, to embark for the continent, and achieve abroad what he was unable to accomplish at home. Early in 1524, he left England, never to revisit her shores; and he made his way in the first instance to Hamburg. He took with him the ten pounds he received from Monmouth as payment for prayers; and in about a twelvemonth afterwards, when his translation was ready for the press, there was transmitted to him from England a second sum of ten pounds, from friends whose names are unknown.

It may be assumed as probable that Tyndale's original intention was to translate the whole Bible into English. It was more practicable, however, to do the work by instalments than to do it all at once. And, as the object he had in view was to indoctrinate the people of England in the true principles of the Christian religion, he wisely determined that the first instalment of his work should be a translation of the New Testament.

Although Tyndale landed at Hamburg in 1524, and was at Hamburg again in 1525, when the ten pounds were sent him from England, it is commonly supposed that he did not reside at Hamburg during the interval. Where he went to is matter of conjecture, and more than one hypothetical account of his movements has been put into print. His latest biographer, Mr. Demaus, is of opinion that from Hamburg Tyndale went direct to Wittemberg, where Luther lived, and that he remained at Wittemberg till the translation of the New Testament was finished.

But it was not at Wittemberg that Tyndale's Testament was printed. Cologne was the place chosen by Tyndale for putting his work in type. Instead, however, of going direct to Cologne from Wittemberg, he came round by Hamburg in order to lift the friendly contribution that was sent him from England to meet his printer's bill. At Cologne a mischance occurred, which somewhat retarded the publication of his book. There happened at that time to be residing at Cologne a noted ecclesiastic, named John Cochlaeus, who was one of the fiercest and bitterest enemies of the Reformation. For the vehemence and virulence with which he assailed the Protestant doctrines, he was styled in some quarters "the scourge of Luther." In his opinion, the root of all evil was the dissemination of the Scriptures among the people in their own mother tongues. He declared that translations of the New Testament, such as Luther's, were the food of death, the destruction of discipline, a wellspring of vice, a nourishment of contempt, and high treason against the truth.[1] Unluckily, it reached the ears of Cochlaeus that a translation of the New Testament into English was being rapidly pushed through the press at Cologne; that the printers had already "advanced as far as the letter K in the order of the sheets; that the expenses were abundantly supplied by English merchants, who when the work was printed, were to convey it secretly, and disperse it widely through all England, before the King or the cardinal could discover or prohibit it." This was startling intelligence to a man of Cochlaeus' temperament. He lost no time in communicating his information to a civilian of high rank, who "went to the senate of Cologne, and procured an order interdicting the printers from proceeding further with their work." Tyndale deemed it expedient to hurry off from Cologne with all his papers and prints, and make his way to Worms, where he could be sure of protection against the Church's persecution. At Worms, the work, commenced and interrupted at Cologne, was continued and finished. This was the quarto edition of Tyndale's Testament, with glosses or marginal notes, published in 1526. Along with this edition in quarto, another in octavo, without notes, was simultaneously issued at Worms; and large consignments of both editions were without delay smuggled over to England.

The name of Tyndale did not appear on the title-page of

---

[1] Cochlaeus' own words are so choice that they are worthy of preservation in the records of bigotry :—"Novum Testamentum, a Luthero in patriam linguam traductum, vere pabulum est mortis, fomes peccati, velamen malitiae, praetextus falsae libertatis, inobedientiae praesidium, disciplinae corruptio, morum depravatio, concordiae dissipatio, honestatis interitus, vitiorum scaturigo, virtutum lues, rebellionis incendium, superbiae lac, esca contemptus, pacis mors, charitatis peremptio, unitatis hostis, veritatis perduellio." Tyndale by Demaus, p. 387.

either of these prints; and for some time it was not known who was the person that had dared, in the face of a penal prohibition, to publish a translation of the New Testament into English, without the prescribed ecclesiastical licence.

It was at a most opportune juncture that Tyndale's translation appeared. The people of England were thirsting to know what the word of God really contained; whether it sanctioned the doctrines and practices of the Church or confirmed the allegations of the Reformers. The two editions of Tyndale's Testament, therefore, although they each comprised three thousand copies, were soon bought up by the reading public, small as it was in those days. Before the close of 1526, another edition, printed at Antwerp, apparently as a private speculation by an enterprising publisher, was sent over to England, to meet the unsated demand. And it was not only in that part of Great Britain which is specially termed England, and which was then under the sway of a separate King, that this grand hunger for the Bible existed; but in the northern part of the island there was evinced a similar eagerness to have the word of God presented to the people, in a language they could understand. In January 1527, one of Cardinal Wolsey's emissaries in the low countries wrote to his patron, that divers merchants of Scotland had been buying Testaments, and had taken them home, "a part to Edinburgh, and most part to the town of St. Andrew."

All the more eagerly that Tyndale's Testament was purchased by the people of England the more fiercely was it denounced by the chief authorities in the Church. In the course of the summer of 1526, a copy of the book came into the hands of one of the English bishops, and with the zeal of his order, this bishop submitted the book to his ecclesiastical superior. A meeting of prelates was forthwith summoned; and, after deliberation, it was resolved that the book should be called in and suppressed. To awaken the public mind to an adequate sense of the danger attending the circulation of such a pestilent volume, it was also agreed that a great gathering

---

[1] Tyndale by Demaus, p. 173.

should be convened at Paul's Cross, London, to hear a true and an unvarnished account of the mistranslations and heresies with which the book was filled, and then to witness its consignment, as a thing accursed, to the flames. The bishop on whom devolved the task of preaching this inflammatory sermon was the accomplished Tunstall, the friend of Erasmus, and the patron of learning, who was expected by Tyndale to aid him in his project of translating the Bible. Tunstall, as the supposed gravity of the occasion required, discharged his duty vigorously, and denounced the obnoxious book lustily. He declared that in the book he had found of mistranslations the good round number of three thousand. What could be said of a book so replete with errors? It was, we may imagine Tunstall saying, like the ground which instead of bringing forth herbs meet for them by whom it is dressed, beareth only thorns and briars, and is therefore to be rejected, as nigh unto cursing, whose end is to be burned.[1]

The action of the prelates in reference to Tyndale's Testament did not end with this scene at Paul's Cross. An injunction was issued by the Bishop of London to his arch-deacons, to require all persons, within the bounds of his diocese, that had in their possession a copy of the denounced book, to surrender the same under pain of excommunication.[2] In this injunction,

---

[1] In May 1530, Tyndale's Testament was publicly burned a second time, at Paul's Cross, under the superintendence of Tunstall. (Demaus, p. 224.) It is difficult to make out from the confused and contradictory accounts given of the burning of Tyndale's Testament, whether there was not a third conflagration. It is said by all the biographers of Tyndale that his brother John and Thomas Patmore, a London draper, were taken before the Star Chamber, and accused of importing and selling the forbidden Testament; and having been found guilty, they were condemned to do penance in ridiculous guise. Loaded with as many of the obnoxious books as could be tacked to their gowns, they were marched through the city on horseback, with their faces towards the tails of their nags, and on reaching the place where the fire was kindled, were compelled to cast into the flames, with their own hands, the Testaments with which they were derisively adorned. Mr. Demaus says that this procession (he makes no mention of the subsequent burning) took place in 1531. For different accounts of these scenes, *vide* Dr. Mombert's English versions, Mr. Paterson Smith's "How we got our Bible," etc., etc.

[2] At a later date, 1531, May 25, an edict was published by the King, with advice of his council and prelates, "that the translation of Scripture corrupted by

the book was not described as the work either of Tyndale singly, or of Tyndale and some associate, but of "many children of iniquity, maintainers of Luther's sect." And the special charges brought against these translators were, that they had intermingled with the text "heretical articles and erroneous opinions," and had attempted, "by their wicked and perverse interpretations, to profane the Majesty of Scripture . . . and craftily to abuse the most holy word of God." Offensive, however, as Tyndale's glosses in his quarto edition may have been to the Catholic clergy, it would be a mistake to suppose that the stir that was made about the English Testament was all or mainly on that account. There was a widespread horror of Scripture translations, whether accompanied with notes or not, and however faultlessly executed. Towards the close of 1525, a churchman who came afterwards to be Archbishop of York, wrote from the continent to his Majesty, about a translation of the New Testament into English, "by an Englishman . . . at the solicitation and instance of Luther," which was within a few days to be sent over to England. In that letter, which has been preserved and printed in more than one book, the writer takes on himself to tell the King's grace, that "this is the next way to fulfil your realm with Lutherans. For all Luther's opinions be grounded upon *bare words* of Scripture, not well taken nor understood." What the Catholics in 1526, therefore, were afraid to trust to the people, were "the bare words of Scripture;" for as Tyndale in one of his books remarks, the way in which churchmen sought to establish their superstitions and dumb ceremonies was by "destroying the literal sense, (of Scripture) and setting up a false feigned sense of allegories, when there is none such."[1]

William Tyndale . . . should be utterly expelled, rejected, and put away out of the hands of his people, and not be suffered to get abroad among his subjects. To give this tyrannical edict an appearance of clemency, there was added a promissory note, "that the King would see to it that the New Testament should be faithfully and purely translated."

[1] Answer to Sir T. More's Dialogue, (Parker Society Edition) p. 44.

Despite the stringent measures adopted by the Church to prevent the circulation of Tyndale's Testament in England, and notwithstanding the oratorical artifices employed to create in the minds of the public a prejudice against its accuracy as a translation, it continued to be purchased and read in secret, with the greatest avidity. In a postscript subjoined to his octavo edition of the Testament, 1526, Tyndale entreated that his work should be regarded "as a thing not having his full shape,[1] but as it were born afore his time, even as a thing begun rather than finished." And he added, "in time to come, if God have appointed us thereunto, we will give it his full shape; and put out, if aught be added superfluously; and add to, if aught be overseen through negligence; . . . and seek in certain places more proper English; . . . and will endeavour ourselves to seethe it better, and to make it more apt for the weak stomachs; desiring them that are learned and able, to remember their duty and to help thereunto." It was not till 1534, that Tyndale redeemed this pledge, by the publication of a revised edition of his Testament; but, in the meanwhile, several reprints, more or less accurate, or rather inaccurate, of his first edition came into England from the continent. To suppress the work, it was seen that something more than denunciation and combustion was needed. And so other devices were resorted to. It happened that, in 1529, Tunstall was in Antwerp, where he forgathered with one Augustine Packington, a London mercer, "of great honesty." In the course of conversation with Packington, who was secretly a friend of Tyndale's, although to the bishop he "shewed himself the contrary," Tunstall intimated that in order to destroy the interdicted Testaments, he would gladly pay for all that could be brought to him. "If it be your pleasure to do so," said Packington, "I will assure you to have every copy of them that is imprinted and is unsold in Antwerp." "The bishop," so runs the story, "thinking he had God by the toe, when indeed he had . . . the Devil by the fist, said, 'Gentle Mr. Packington, do your diligence and

---

[1] *His* was, in Tyndale's day, used as *its* is now.

get them; and with all my heart I will pay for them, whatsoever they cost you, for the books are erroneous and nought, and I intend surely to destroy them all, and to burn them at Paul's cross.' Packington thereupon hurried to Tyndale, and said, 'William, I know thou art a poor man, and hast a heap of New Testaments by thee, . . . and I have now gotten thee a merchant, which with ready money shall despatch thee of all that thou hast.' 'Who is the merchant?' asked Tyndale. 'The Bishop of London,' said Packington. 'Oh, that is because he will burn them,' said Tyndale. 'Yea, marry,' quoth Packington. 'I am the gladder,' said Tyndale, for 'these two benefits shall come thereof: I shall get money to bring myself out of debt, and the whole world will cry out against the burning of God's word; and the overplus of the money that shall remain to me shall make me more studious to correct the said New Testament, and so newly to imprint the same once again.' . . . And so forward went the bargain. The bishop had the books; Packington had the thanks; and Tyndale had the money."

Another, and a better, device of Tunstall's for undoing the mischief caused by Tyndale's Testament, was to expose the errors of its text and confute the heresies in its annotations. And this he had set himself to do, or rather to get done, even before his interview with Packington at Antwerp. On the 7th March 1528, he wrote to Sir Thomas More, one of the most accomplished and most esteemed men in England: "You will never be able to make a better use of your spare hours . . . than by publishing in our native tongue something that will expose even to rude and simple people the crafty malice of the heretics, and make them better prepared against those impious enemies of the Church." More took in hand the task suggested, and, in June 1529, published a book bearing the title: " A Dialogue of Sir Thomas More, Knight, one of the Council of our Sovereign Lord the King, and Chancellor of the Duchy of Lancaster, wherein be treated divers matters, as of the veneration and worship of images and relics, praying to saints and going on pilgrimage: with many other things touching the pestilent sect of Luther and Tyndale, by the tone begun in Saxony, and by the tother laboured to be brought into England." The scope of this treatise included, but extended further than, a criticism of Tyndale's Testament; and it called for an answer from Tyndale, in respect of the pointed manner in which his name was associated with certain alleged heresies. More's dialogue has the credit of being " written in a witty, pleasant, and popular style." This is more than can be said of Tyndale's reply, which was published in 1531. The verdict of Sir Thomas Cromwell, that it was " unclerkly done," must be the finding of every one that attempts to read through its dreary pages. It nevertheless contains a few interesting remarks, which will bear quotation, regarding objections to some of his renderings in the English Testament.

Eight years intervened between the publication of the first and the revised edition of Tyndale's Testament. During these eight years, however, from 1526 to 1533, Tyndale was by no means idle. On the contrary, he was busily employed in literary work. Besides a translation of the Pentateuch, with a general preface, a separate preface to each book and marginal notes, and a translation of the prophecies of Jonah, with a prologue, Tyndale during these years published several works of a polemical character. These publications of Tyndale's are all more or less interesting to the student of the English Bible, as shewing what theories Tyndale held in regard to Biblical interpretation and the true foundation of the Christian religion, what charges he made against the Catholic Church in connection with these matters, and of what a keen, combative, and vehement spirit he was possessed. The fundamental doctrine of Protestantism is that Christianity is founded solely and entirely on the Scriptures. This was what Tyndale maintained; and he said further, that " Scripture hath but one sense, which is the literal sense." And in eloquent words he added: "That literal sense is the root and ground of all, and the anchor that never faileth, whereunto if thou cleave, thou canst never err or go out of the way."[1] In another of his writings, he tells how the Catholics, in opposition to this sound doctrine, had by false

---

[1] Obedience of a Christian man.

glosses and fantastical interpretations, perverted Scripture from its true meaning in order to bolster up their own pretensions. "When they come to the law," he says, "they put gloses to, and make no more of it than of a worldly lawe which is satisfied with the outward work. When they come to the gospel, there they mingle their leuen, and say, God now receiveth us no more to mercy, but of mercy receiveth us to penaunce, that is to witte, holy deedes that make *them* fat bellies, and *us* their captives both in soule and body."[1] And, as may be seen from this last extract, it was not in minced words nor with bated breath that Tyndale spoke and wrote. His biographer apologises as far as truth will allow for this vehemence; but he is constrained to admit that Tyndale hated the system of Popery "with his whole heart, and condemned it with his whole strength. In his eyes the Pope was Anti-Christ, and the whore of Babylon . . . the monks and friars were caterpillars, horse-leeches, drone-bees, and draff. In short, Tyndale's indignation, sharpened by years of exile and home-sick longing, knew no bounds, and his words knew no moderation."[2] In his controversies with individual persons, too, Tyndale was very little restrained by delicate consideration of an honourable opponent's feelings.[3] But sometimes he was pithy without being abusive. At other times he railed and reviled, and brought himself down to the level of his Popish assailants. It is admitted by his biographer, that through misinformation, he made odious charges against Sir Thomas More,[4] which had no foundation in fact; and, in addition to

---

[1] Prologue to Book of Jonah.

[2] *Tyndale*, Demaus, p. 254.

[3] For instance, in reply to Sir Thomas More's averment, that Apostles and Saints were prayed to when alive and God was not dishonoured thereby, Tyndale says: "What helpeth that your carnal purpose? I have answer:d you unto that, and many things more . . . against which ye reply not, but keep your tune, and unto all things sing, Cuckoo, Cuckoo." *Reply to More* (Parker Society Edition) p. 119. In similar style, he says again in the same book, p. 15: "As the wise people, when they dance naked in nets, believe that no man seeth them; even so, Master More thinketh that his errors be so subtilly couched that no man can espy them."

[4] Demaus' *Tyntale*, p. 272.

that, he applied to his learned opponent terms of the coarsest opprobrium. For such indecencies in Tyndale's writings the only valid apology that can be offered is that they corresponded with the culture and courtesies of the times in which the author lived.[1]

Towards the end of 1530, an effort was made to induce Tyndale to return to his native country. This effort originated with Thomas Cromwell, who possibly thought that, in the liberation policy on which he had entered, Tyndale would be both inclined and able to afford him material support. Cromwell's overtures seem to have had the King's sanction and nominal approval. One of the English envoys in the low countries was accordingly instructed to discover, if possible, the residence of Tyndale; and to hint that if he were content, as was rumoured, to repair and come to England on promise of a safe conduct from the King, influence would be used to procure for him "whatsoever surety he would reasonably desire, for his coming in and going out of the realm." Tyndale, however, could not be prevailed upon to venture home, albeit the King should "promise him never so much surety;" for he feared that such a promise would "shortly be broken, by persuasion of the clergy, who would affirm that promises made with heretics ought not to be kept." In this determination, Tyndale displayed a prudence that was fully vindicated by subsequent events. The King was too variable to be much depended on; and there were many statements in Tyndale's writings with which crafty courtiers could easily poison the mind of Henry against the Reformer. It happened that just about this time, when inducements were held out to Tyndale by the English envoy, Stephen Vaughan, to return to England, the bitterest of all Tyndale's polemical works made its appearance, and attracted notice in high quar-

---

[1] Among other things Tyndale says of More, "His mighty arguments prove not the value of a poding prick." . . . "He rageth, and fareth exceeding foul with himself. There he biteth, sucketh, gnaweth, towseth and mowseth Tynedale." . . . "Master More was their special orator, to feign lies for their purpose." . . . "Controversies blinded the eyes of that gleering fox more and more, and hardened his heart against the truth." *Answer to More*, p. 141, 151, 168. *Exposition of Sermon on Mount*, p. 100.

F

ters. In this book, the prosecution of the suit for Henry's divorce was denounced as a scandalous attempt on the part of the clergy to set aside the obligations of divine law. Early in 1531, it reached the ears of Tyndale that the King had been much displeased at the publication of this book; whereof, said Tyndale in a conversation with Vaughan, "I have no little marvel, considering that in it I did but warn his grace of the subtle demeanour of the clergy of his realm towards his person, and of the shameful abuses by them practised, not a little threatening the displeasure of his grace and weal of his realm." In the course of further conversation, Tyndale added that he had finished a reply to Sir Thomas More's dialogue, but would not put it in print till the King had had the opportunity of perusing it. Part of this unprinted work, "sewed and inclosed in leather," was thereupon forwarded by Vaughan for the King's private perusal. This intended mark of dutiful respect to the King was only a further contribution of fuel to the fire that was burning in Henry's bosom. The King's rage became unbounded, and Cromwell was instructed to direct his envoy to be less officious, and to desist from his efforts to induce Tyndale to return to England.[1]

Soon after this incident, Henry had the meanness to issue orders for the apprehension of his loyal but outspoken subject.

---

[1] The letter that Cromwell despatched to Vaughan is so characteristic, and so clearly explains the situation, that a few sentences of it may be here quoted. "Stephen Vaughan, I commend me unto you, and have received your letters, dated at Antwerp the 18th day of April, with also that part of Tyndale's book . . . which ye, with your letters, directed to the King's Highness. . . . And albeit I might well perceive that his Majesty was right well pleased, and right acceptably considered your diligence and pains taken in the writing and sending of the said book, as also in the persuading and exhorting of Tyndale to repair into this realm; yet his Highness nothing liked the said book, being filled with seditions, slanderous lies, and fantastical opinions, shewing therein neither learning nor truth. . . . The King's Highness, therefore, hath commanded me to advertise you that ye should desist and leave any further to persuade or attempt the said Tyndale to come into this realm; alleging that he . . . is very joyous to have his realm destitute of such a person. . . . For his Highness right prudently considereth that if he were present, by all likelihood he would shortly do as much as in him were to infect and corrupt the whole realm, to the great inquietation and hurt of the commonwealth of the same."—*Demaus.*

The person employed in this ignoble task was Sir Thomas Elyot, a friend of Sir Thomas More's; and, sad to say, Elyot devoted himself to his unhallowed work with a zeal that was worthy of a better cause. Tyndale was not only in exile but in hiding. Elyot accordingly wrote (1532), "Albeit the King willeth me . . . to remain at Brussels some space of time for the apprehension of Tyndale, which somewhat minisheth my hope of soon return, considering that like as he is in wit movable, semblably so is his person uncertain to come by: and so far as I can perceive, hearing of the King's diligence in the apprehension of him, he withdraweth him into such places where he thinketh to be farthest out of danger. In me there shall lack none endeavour."

Sir Thomas Elyot's endeavours, whatever they were, to apprehend Tyndale were not successful. The Reformer was in wit too moveable to be caught by such a garrulous detective; and although Sir Thomas, according to his own account, "gave many rewards" to the Emperor's servants and others to reveal or discover for him Tyndale's place of concealment, the service so handsomely paid for beforehand was never rendered. But the enemies of Tyndale were not content to rest satisfied with the abortive efforts of Sir Thomas Elyot to secure the Reformer's person. They resolved that another effort, conducted with more skill and vigour, should be made. Towards the end of 1534, or early in 1535, a new plan of campaign was secretly concocted in England. It has not been ascertained who were the authors of that plan, but it is supposed that neither the King nor any of his ministers was cognisant of it. The execution of the plan was entrusted to a Londoner, named Henry Philips, and a friar, named Gabriel Donne. Tyndale was then residing in Antwerp, and he did not require to make any secret of his residence there, for at the date referred to it was one of the privileges enjoyed by residents in that city that they could not be "arrested in their houses except for some great crime." Strange to say, however, a man could be seized on the streets of Antwerp and whipped off to another place, where the Church's laws regarding heresy could be enforced against him. Philips and Donne, therefore, were to make their way to Antwerp. Philips, who was "a comely fellow," was to act the part of gentleman, and cultivate acquaintance with the leading Englishmen in the city. Donne was to act the humbler part of valet, and by surrounding his master with a semblance of dignity make his society the more coveted. The two together were to find ways and means of abducting Tyndale, and how they did so may be best told in the words of the martyrologist Foxe. "Master Tyndale divers times was desired forth to dinner and supper among merchants, by the means whereof this Henry Philips became acquainted with him, so that within short space Master Tyndale had a great confidence in him, and brought him to his lodging, . . . and had him also once or twice with him to dinner and supper. . . . . One day Philip called at Tyndale's lodging and requested to be allowed to entertain Tyndale in his own house with such good meat as the market could give. 'No,' said Master Tyndale, 'I go forth this day to dinner, and you shall go with me and be my guest, where you shall be welcome.' So when it was dinner-time, Master Tyndale went forth with Philips, and at the going out of the house was a long narrow entry, so that two could not go in a front. Master Tyndale would have put Philips before him, but Philips would in no wise, but put Master Tyndale afore, for that he pretended to show great humanity. So Master Tyndale, being a man of no great stature, went before, and Philips, a tall comely person, followed behind him, who had set officers on either side of the door upon two seats, and coming through the same entry Philips pointed with his finger over Master Tyndale's head down to him, that the officers which sat at the door might see that it was he whom they should take." The officers, as directed, seized Tyndale and carried him off with so little show of resistance "that they pitied to see his simplicity." He was marched in the first instance to the residence of the Emperor's attorney, where he dined, and "from thence he was had to the Castle of Vilford (or Vilvorde) eighteen English miles from Antwerp."

Tyndale was now formally charged with venting heretical doctrines, and, according to the common practice in cases of heresy, special commissioners were nominated for conducting his trial. The trial was a tedious process, but the issue was never doubtful. Tyndale had certainly vented opinions that the Church considered heretical. Whether they should have been called heretical is another question. Tyndale maintained that all his alleged heresies were the very doctrines of Christ and his Apostles. But the Commissioners who tried Tyndale had only to say whether or not Tyndale's opinions fell under the designation of heretical, as that term was defined by the Church.

The friends of Tyndale did what they could to procure his release but, although the influence of Cromwell was obtained on behalf of the prisoner, the law was allowed to take its course. For sixteen weary months Tyndale lay in the jail that was dignified by the name of castle. What rigours he had to submit to in that lordly place of confinement may be seen from the tenor of a letter he penned in his chamber, and addressed to the governor of the castle, the Marquis of Bergen-op-Zoom. "If I am to remain here during the winter," he wrote, "you will request the procureur to be kind enough to send me from my goods, which he has in his possession, a warmer cap, for I suffer extremely from cold in the head . . . . .: a warmer coat also, for that which I have is very thin." And then he adds pathetically, "I wish his permission to have a candle in the evening, for it is wearisome to sit alone in the dark."[1] From that cold and lonely prison Tyndale never was removed till, on the morning of the 6th October, 1536, he was led forth to be burned at the stake. And all for saying that he believed certain doctrines, which seemed to him to be plainly stated in the Scriptures on which Christianity is founded, were the truth of God! His last prayer, like that of his Divine Master, was for his enemies; and especially that the Lord would "open the King of England's eyes."

There were three advantages that Tyndale had over Wyclif in translating the New Testament into English. First of all,

---

[1] The letter was written in Latin, and is printed verbatim in Demaus' *Life of Tyndale*, p. 475-6

Tyndale was a Greek scholar, and had access to a copy of the New Testament in its original Greek language. In the next place, he had Luther's translation of the New Testament into German to refer to. And in the third place, he had the opportunity of comparing a new translation of the Testament into Latin with the old translation known as the Vulgate. It was a matter of great consequence for Tyndale to be able to say that his translation was made from the original, even although subsequent research has shown that the text from which he translated contains many readings that are not authentic. The purest text in Greek was not then known to Biblical critics. And it was no slight benefit to Tyndale that, living at Wittemberg, the city of Luther's residence, he had both Luther's German translation and Luther himself at hand to consult on the right rendering of many Greek words and Greek phrases. It is admitted that in his notes and prologues Tyndale was largely indebted to the labours of the German Reformer; and it is generally conceded that the inspiration of Luther can be detected in some of Tyndale's renderings.[2] It can scarcely be doubted, too, that Tyndale both learned and unlearned something from the Latin translation of the New Testament by Erasmus. The Vulgate had so long held possession of the public mind that many of its words and phrases had come to be regarded as the divine original. Both usages and doctrines were founded by the Church on these expressions in the Vulgate. But, in the several Latin translations of the New Testament issued by the Reformers a new phraseology was introduced; time-honoured words were discarded, and the sacred page was made to exhibit a new meaning. It was in Beza's Latin version of the Testament, published in 1556, that these departures from the readings of the Vulgate became most marked, but they were visible also in the earlier translation by Erasmus. For instance, the word *sacramentum* (sacra-

---

[1] Mr. Demaus says, "Of the whole number of *ninety* marginal glosses which occur in the fragment of Tyndale's quarto (1526) that has come down to us, *fifty-two* have been more or less literally taken from Luther," p. 129.

[2] See Eadie's *Hist. of English Bible*, and Mombert's *English Versions*.

ment), Eph. v. 32, was by Erasmus changed into *mysterium* (mystery); the Catholic term *calix* (chalice), Mat. xxvi. 27, was secularised into *poculum* (cup); the sacerdotal word *ecclesia* was in some places, Rom. xvi. 5, 1 Cor. xiv. 4, etc., transformed into *congregatio*, and in other places, Acts xix. 32, and Heb. xii. 23, substituted by *concio*; and that great rock of offence to Calvinistic heretics, "*promeretur Deus* (God is conciliated, or satisfied by the merits of men's good works) was replaced by the colourless phrase *placetur Deo* (we please God)."[1] These and other verbal alterations affected questions of high doctrine, on which Catholics and Protestants were at issue; and they doubtless strengthened the hands of Tyndale, and made him very independent of the Vulgate, in translating the Testament from the Greek.

That Tyndale had eminent qualifications for the great work to which he devoted his mind is universally conceded. He had good knowledge of Greek, and, what is of as much importance, his style of English was singularly clear, terse, unaffected and simple. His Testament, says one critic, "is a noble translation, the basis of every subsequent English version, and on several accounts better than all subsequent versions; it has an individuality as pronounced as Luther's; its Saxon is racy and strong, sometimes majestic, and above all things, it is hearty and true; the reader feels that the translator felt what he wrote, that his heart was in his work, and that he strove in prayer to reproduce in his own mother-tongue, to the very best of his ability, what he believed to be the true sense of the word of God, as he understood it." "To Tyndale belongs," says Prof. Plumptre, "the honour of having given the first example of a translation based on true principles, and the excellence of later versions has been almost in exact proportion as they followed his. . . . Throughout there is the pervading stamp, so often wanting in other like works, of the most thorough truthfulness. No word has been altered to court a King's favour, or please bishops, or

---

[1] Although on Calvinistic grounds the phrase *mereri supplicia* (deserve punishments), is allowable, the expression, Heb. x. 29, is by Erasmus changed into *afficietur suppliciis*, and by Beza into *supplicio dignus censebitur*.

make out a case for or against a particular opinion." The merits of what is called *his* Testament, too, are all his own. He had no collaborateur. The name of Father Roye was sometimes associated with Tyndale's, as if the English Testament of 1526 had been their joint production. In reality, Father Roye was only an amanuensis, who helped Tyndale to compare texts, but had nothing to do with the translation. Roye, moreover, was a source of much trouble and annoyance to Tyndale. He "professed wonderful faculties and made boast of no small things." He was both reckless and unscrupulous, wrote squibs about people in high places, and although his rhymes were as destitute of poetical merit as they were of Christian decency, they were very provocative, and not only brought himself into deserved odium but put his friends to inconvenience. "When that was ended which I could not do alone without one," says Tyndale, " I took my leave, and bade him farewell for our two lives, and as men say, a day longer."

The first edition of Tyndale's Testament was published in 1526. A revised edition appeared in 1534. This edition of 1534 is the one that is printed in Bagster's Hexapla, and is the one therefore that is best known to English readers at the present day. It is acknowledged to be a very considerable improvement on the earlier version. Besides these two, there were at least six other editions of Tyndale's Testament published during the translator's life time. Some of these editions were issued without Tyndale's supervision. One was edited by a man named George Joye, who took the liberty of amending the translation in several places. This liberty was keenly resented by Tyndale, and as it was never graciously apologised for, it was never altogether forgiven. An edition published in 1536 was characterised by a very peculiar style of spelling. At one time, it was supposed that this peculiar spelling was intended to represent the provincial pronunciation of the peasants of Gloucestershire; and a romantic interest was created in the book, as if it had been the promised volume that was to make the plough-boys of South England wiser than their priests. What was imagined to be Gloucestershire phonetics has turned out to be Dutch ignorance. The book was printed after Tyndale's arrest, and the proof sheets were left to the correction of a Dutch compositor, who "naturally introduced, in many cases, Flemish equivalents for the English vowel sounds."

Except for book collectors, the only editions of Tyndale's Testament that are of much interest are the original edition of 1526 and the amended edition of 1534. Of the first issue in 1526, only three copies are now in existence. One of these is a quarto copy, with glosses; and the other two are octavo copies without glosses. Of the words and phrases in this edition that were changed in the edition of 1534, the following may be noted: Mat. v. 28, eyeth a wyfe (1), looketh on a wyfe (2); Acts xiii. 15, after the lecture (1), after the lawe and the prophets were redde (2); Gal. iv. 15, digged out your awne eyes (1), plucked out your awne eyes (2); 1 Cor. iv. 9, the hynmost off all (1), the lowest of all (2); 1 Cor. iv. 16, counterfayte me (1), follow me (2); 1 Cor. xvi. 2, in some Sabothe day (1), upon some Sondaye (2); 2 Cor. i. 12, without doublenes (1), in syngleness (2); 2 Cor. xii. 20, lest there be founde among yon lawynge (1), debate (2); 1 Tim. ii. 8, lifting up pure handes without wrath or arguing (1), without wrath or doubtinge (2); 1 Tim. ii. 9, that they araye themselves in manerly aparell (1), in comlye aparell (2); 2 Tim. i. 7, honest behaviour (1), sobrietie of mynde (2); James vi. 17, Helias was a man in danger to tribulacioun as we are (1), mortal even as we are (2).

A better comparison of the two versions will be afforded by the following complete sentences taken respectively from Fry's reprint of the 1526, and Bagster's reprint of the 1534 edition:

EDITION 1526.	EDITION 1534.
Acts xviii. 5.—When Silas and Timotheus wer come from Macedonia, Paul was payned in the sprete as he testified to the Jewes that Jesus was Christ.	Acts xviii. 5.—When Sylas and Timotheus were come from Macedonia, Paul was constrayned by the sprete to testifie to the Jewes that Jesus was very Christ.
Rom. xv. 28.—When I have performed this, and have shewed them this frute, I will come back agayne by you into Spayne.	Rom. xv. 28.—When I have performed this, and have brought them this frute sealed, I will come back agayne by you into Spayne.
Rom. xvi. 19.—Youre obedience is spoken of among all men.	Rom. xvi. 19.—Youre obedience extendeth to all men.
1 Cor. i. 25.—For godly folyshnes is wyser than men, and godly weaknes is stronger than are men.	1 Cor. i. 25.—For the folishnes of God is wyser than men, and the weakness of God is stronger than men.

2 Cor. vi. 11. — O ye Corinthyans, oure mougth is open unto you, oure herte is made large, ye aie nott brought into combraunce by us, though that ye were youre selves off a true meanynge. I speake unto you as unto chyldren whych have lyke rewarde wyth us, stretche youre selves therefore out, beare nott the yooke wyth the unbelevers.

2 Thess. ii. 7. — For already the mistery off iniquytie worketh. Only he that holdeth let him nowe holde untill hit be taken out of the waye, and then shall that wicked be uttered.

1 Tim. i. 11. — Accordynge to the glorious gospell off the holy God, which gospell is committed unto me.

Heb. xi. 3. — Thorowe fayth we understonde that the worlde was ordeyned by the worde off God. That by the menes of thynges whych apeare thynges whych are invisyble myght be knowen.

2 Cor. vi. 11. — O ye Corinthyans, our mouth is open unto you. Oure herte is made large, ye are in no strayte in us, but are in a strayte in youre awne bowelles. I promyse you lyke rewarde with me as to m.y children. Set youre selves therefore at large, and beare not a straungers yoke wyth the unbelevers.

2 Thess. ii. 7. — For the mistery of that iniquitie doeth he all readie worke which onlie loketh untill it be taken out of the waye, and then shall that wicked be uttered.

1 Tim. i. 11. — According to the gospell of the glory of the blessed God, which gospell is committed unto me.

Heb. xi. 3. — Thorow fayth we understonde that the worlde was ordeyned by the worde of God: and that thynges which are sene were made of thynges which are not sene.

It is the amended version of 1534 that we must consider to be Tyndale's Testament. It was in that edition that his translation took its permanent form. It is of that edition, therefore, that we have here more particularly to speak.

In respect of the language in which they are written, there is a wide difference between Tyndale's Testament and Wyclif's Bible. The one was written a hundred and fifty years before the other, and during these hundred and fifty years the English language underwent great changes.

Tyndale, for instance, never uses such words as "weren" for were, "schulen" for shall, "crieden" for cried, "kittiden" for cut, "ijen" for eyes, "schon" for shoes. He never uses such phrases either as "mai not be undo" for may not be undone, "hadde not be born" for had not been born, "kepe ze as ze kunnen" for keep ye as ye can, "gauen me to eten" for gave me to eat.[1] The language in which he writes is not much different from that in which the authorised version of the Bible is written. But for the spelling one might read many verses,

---

[1] An exception to what is here said will be found in Acts xi. 17, where St. Peter is made by Tyndale to say: "What was I that I should *have with stonde* God?" An obsolete inflexion used by Tyndale is *lewch* for "laughed": "They lewghe him to scorne" (Luke viii. 53).

perhaps a whole chapter, without knowing that one was reading anything else than what is called Queen's English, and yet, when gathered together, the archaisms in Tyndale's Testament form a goodly collection.

In Wyclif's Bible, pronouns, as we have seen, are not used with very uniform regard to modern rules of gender. *He* and *it* are applied indiscriminately to the same nouns. In one passage about the offending eye, it is said "pull *hym* out," and in another, "pull *it* out." In both of these passages, Tyndale uses *him*—"Yf thy right eye offende thee, pluck *hym* out and cast *hym* fro thee." And so also, in John xv. 18—"Yf the worlde hate you, ye know that *he* hated me before *he* hated you." There is no instance, in Tyndale's Testament, of "them" and "their" being spelt *hem* and *her;* but of "other" and "others" there are very peculiar spellings, as in Mark vi. 15, "*wother* said, it is Helyas," and in Gal. i. 19, "*no nother* of the Apostles sawe I, save James the Lorde's brother."[1]

Of obsolete words, and obsolete forms of words, there neither are in Tyndale's Testament so many, nor are there to be found such antiquated specimens, as occur on the pages of Wyclif's Bible. Few of the obsolete terms quoted in last chapter from Wyclif's version of the Testament are to be met with in Tyndale's. But some are : such as "gobbetes," in the sense of fragments—"They gadered up of the gobbetes that remayned twelve baskets full," Mat. xiv. 20.[2] And there are many words which are now out of use, although not included in that list of obsoletisms from Wyclif. One such word, of frequent occurrence, is "yer." "He that cometh after me was before me, because he was *yer* than I,"[3] John i. 15 ; and, "We which live, and are remayninge in the comminge of the Lorde, shall not

---

[1] The word *other* is sometimes used as a conjunction by Tyndale, for "or," as in Rom. x. 7 ; "*other* who shall descend into the depe?" and Rom. xiv. 10, "*other* why doest thou despyse thy brother?"

[2] Wyclif seems to use the word "gobet" in a slightly different sense. In Mat. xiv. 20, he says, "thei token the relifis of *brokun* gobeites twelve cofyns full ;" and in 1 Cor. v. 6, "a litil sourdough apeirith *al* the gobet."

[3] Yer is an old form of ere, and it appeared in the first edition, 1611, of the authorised version—"Syr, come downe *yer* my child die," John iv. 49.

come *yerre* they which slepe," 1 Thess. iv. 15. We meet with the word *fet*, also, an old form of *fetch*; as in John xx. 15— " Yf thou have borne him hence, tell me where thou hast layde him, that I may fet him." We find *lyvelod*, too, an old form of *livelihood*, used for land or field; as in Acts v. 3—" How is it that Satan hath filled thyne hert that thou shuldest lye unto the holy goost, and kepe away parte of the pryce of the lyvelod." For "continued," we find *bidden*; as in Luke xxii. 28—" Ye are they which have bidden with me in my temptacions." In one passage, *peased* is used for "quieted" or "silenced;" "All the multitude was peased, and gave evidence to Barnabas and Paul," Acts xv. 12. In more than one passage, *arede* occurs where "prophesy" is now the word employed; as in Mark xiv. 65—" Some beganne to spit at him, and to cover his face, and to bete him with fistes, and to say unto him, *arede* unto us." In the sense of *rob*, the term *pill* appears in 2 Cor. xii. 17; and a question that seems very un-apostolic is thereby put into the mouth of St. Paul—" Did I *pill* you by any of them which I sent unto you." This unapostolic phrase of Tyndale's, however, is more than compensated for by another very interesting expression of his, shewing the derivation of the theological terms "atone" and "atonement," which occurs in 2 Cor. v. 20—" So praye we you in Christe's stede that ye be *atone* (at one) with God."[1]

Much larger than the number of obsolete words in Tyndale's Testament is the number of common current words that are used in an archaic sense. The question, "Why *troublest* thou the master," Mark v. 35, appears in Tyndale's version, "Why *diseasest* thou the master; the phrase "uncomely parts," 1 Cor.

---

[1] Among other obsolete words, and forms of words, in Tyndale's Testament may be mentioned: *afyre*, for "on fire," Jas. iii. 6; *comened*, for "talked," Acts xx. 11; *conspiracion*, for "conspiracy," Acts xxiii. 13; *despicious*, for "reasoning," Acts xxviii. 29; *hagge on me*, for "weary me," Luke xviii. 5; *harberous*, for "hospitable," 1 Tim. iii. 2; *lever*, for "rather," 1 Cor. xiv. 19; *loweth*, for "depth," Rom. viii. 39; *pistle*, for "epistle," 1 Cor. v. 9; *perceavaunce*, for "prudence," Eph. i. 8; *ungostly*, for "profane," 1 Tim. iv. 7. The "profane and vain babblings," which Timothy was exhorted to avoid, are designated by Tyndale, "ungostly vanities of voyces."

xii. 23, is rendered *ungodly parties ; busynes* is used, Mark xiv. 2, in the sense of tumult; *submitted*, 2 Cor. xi. 7, in the sense of abased; *avoid*, Mat. iv. 10, in the sense of "get thee hence;" *inordinatly*, 2 Thes. iii. 7, in the sense of "disorderly;" and *enfoarce*, 2 Peter i. 15, in the sense of "endeavour," or "give diligence." As it may still be heard in provincial speech, the word "*learn*" is sometimes used by Tyndale for "teach;"— "They verely for a feaue dayes nurtred us after their awne pleasure, but he *learneth* us unto that which is proffitable," Heb. xii. 10. The term *soft*, which in its reference to a man's character conveys now the imputation of feebleness, is by Tyndale employed in the sense of "gentle." In his epistle to Titus, St. Paul is made to say :— " Warne them . . . that they speake evyll of no man, that they be no fyghters, but *softe*, showing all meknes unto all men." And so, also, in Phil. iv. 5 :—" Let your softenes be knowen unto all men." A remonstrance that, at the present day, might be very ridiculously misconstrued, appears in Tyndale's version of Gal. vi. 17 :— " From henceforth let no man put me to *busyness*." The word " business," however, signified, in Tyndale's time, carefulness or anxiety: and the phrase " put me to busynes" meant, accordingly, " put me to trouble," or " trouble me."

It was remarked that, in Wyclif's Bible, the word *minister* stands for " officer," in the verse where men are counselled to agree with their adversaries, rather than go to law over their quarrels. In that verse, the word *minister* is used by Tyndale also. It is used for "servant," too, by both Wyclif and Tyndale, in John ii. 9 :—" When the ruler of the feast had tasted the water that was turned unto wyne, and knewe not whence it was, the *ministres* which drue the water knew." And still more strange is Tyndale's use of the word " minister," in Rom. xvi. 1 :—" I commende unto you Phebe, oure sister, which is a *minister* of the congregacion at Chenchrea." But if these references to ministers have mirth-provoking associations for Scotsmen, what will Englishmen say of Tyndale's rendering of 1 Cor. v. 13, " Put awaye from you that evyll *parson?*"[1]

---

[1] In Coverdale's Bible we read, Is. v. 27, " There is not one faynt nor feble

And besides ministers and parsons, the *laity* are introduced to us by Tyndale in a rather uncomplimentary way. The Greek word *idiotai*, from which comes the English *idiot*, is, in Acts iv. 13, translated by Tyndale *laye people*; and unfortunately for laymen this translation is not very wide of the mark.[1] The term *idiot*, too, suggests another expression of Tyndale's that cannot but sound strange to modern readers. The heading of the first epistle to Timothy is by Tyndale translated: "Paul, an apostle of Jesus Christ, . . . unto Timothe, his *naturall sonne* in the faith;" and what is still more remarkable, the expression here italicised has been retained in the Great Bible, in the Geneva Bible, and in the Bishops' Bible.

Other instances of words used in Tyndale's Testament in an obsolete or archaic sense will be seen in the following quotations:—Mat. xvi. 3, "O ye ypocrites, ye can discern the *fassion* of the sky;" Mat. xxi. 24, "I also will axe of you a certayne question, which if ye *assoyle* me I in lyke wyse wyll tell you by what auctorite I do these things;"[2] Mark vii. 2, "When they sawe certayne of his disciples eate breed with *commen* hondes (that is to say, with unweshen hondes) they complayned;" Luke iii. 11, "He that hath two coottes, let him *parte with* him that hath none;" Luke vii. 14, "He went and touched the *coffyn*" (*i.e.* the bier, or common coffin for carriage but not for burial); John xix. 2, "And they *dyd* on him a purple garment;"[3] Acts xi. 26, "It chaunced that a whole yere they had their *conversacioun* (residence) with the congregacion there;" Acts xviii. 18, "He shore his heed;" Acts xix. 35, "When the town-clarcke had *ceased* the people;" Rom. iii. 23, "All have synned, and laeke the prayse that *is of valoure* before God;" Rom. xiii. 7, "Geve to every man, therfore, his *duetie*," *i.e.*, what is due to him; 1 Cor. ix. 13, "They which minister in the temple have their *fyndynge* of the temple," *i.e.*, their *living* from the temple; 2 Cor. ii. 11, "Lest Satan shuld *prevent* us," *i.e.*, circumvent us, or over-reach us;" Gal. v. 7, 'Ye did runne well, who was a *let*, unto you," *i.e.*, a hindrance to you.

---

amonge them, no not a slogish nor slepery *parsone*." Of course *parson* is an old form of "person."

[1] "By the expression *idiotai* are meant private persons, as opposed to those who hold any office, ecclesiastical or civil." (Bloomfield's *Greek Test.*) Matthew Henry's comments on the verse are amusing but scarcely warrantable. "They were *private men*, men that had not any public character or employment. . . . They were *idiots*, so the word signifies; they were looked upon with as much contempt as if they had been mere naturals." On the other hand the Catholic, Gregory Martin, holds the translation of *idiotai* by the English term "laymen" to be altogether indefensible.

[2] Assoyle, from *absolvo*. We still retain the phrase, "solve the question."

[3] This form of expression was noticed in Wyclif's Bible—"do on thy hoosis."

One of the special charges brought against Tyndale by his adversaries was, that in his English Testament he inserted novel expressions, in lieu of ancient ecclesiastical terms on which the Catholic Church had founded some of her dogmas and practices. It was complained, in particular, that for *priests*, *church*, and *charity*, he had substituted respectively, *seniors*, *congregation*, and *love*. And there were other objectionable words that he had introduced. What should have been rendered "grace," he had in some places translated *favour ;* what should have been designated "confession," he had termed *knowledging ;* and to what was known as "penance" he had given the new name of *repentance*. It was alleged that by these and other innovations he designed to "make the people believe that such articles of the faith as he laboured to destroy, and which were well proved by Scripture, were in holy Scripture nothing spoken of, but that the preachers had all this fifteen hundred years misrepresented the gospel, and Englished the Scripture wrong, to lead the people purposely out of the way."[1] While denying that he handled the word of God deceitfully, Tyndale practically confessed that some of his renderings objected to by the spokesmen of the Church were unhappy. In his revised translation of the New Testament, 1534, he introduced the word *grace* into almost every passage where we find it now in the authorised version. In a few passages, however, he still retained the obnoxious term *favour*, as in Rom. iv. 4, "To him that worketh is the rewarde not reckened of *favour* but of duty ; and in Rom. iv. 16, "By fayth is the inheritance geven that it myght come of *favour*." In regard to *senior*, Tyndale, in his reply to More, 1531, wrote that "of a truth it is no very good English, . . . but there came no better in my mind at that time. Howbeit, I spied my fault since, long ere Master More told it me, and have mended it in all the works which I (have) since made, and call it an *elder*." Then, apprehending that the word *elder* might be as objectionable to churchmen as *senior*, Tyndale proceeds to say that if it be heresy to translate

---

[1] More, quoted by Mombert, 103-4.

the Greek word *presbyteros* by the English word *elder*, the Vulgate itself, which is daily read in the Catholic Church, will be convicted of heresy; "For thus standeth it in the Latin text, 1 Peter v. 1, '*Seniores ergo qui in vobis sunt obsecro consenior.*'"[1] To his other novations in ecclesiastical nomenclature, Tyndale tenaciously adhered. He continued to flaunt the word *congregation* in the face of the Church, and he defended his conduct therein by declaring that the clergy had of old beguiled the people in "making them to understand by this word *Church* nothing but the shaven flock of them that shore the whole world;" whereas the term *ecclesia*, which churchmen insist on translating *church*, is, "of right, common unto the whole congregation of them that believe in Christ." He cited high scholastic authority, also, for rendering *ecclesia* "congregation." "How happith it," he asked, "that Master More hath not contended against his darling Erasmus all this long while? Doth he not change this word *ecclesia* into *congregatio*, and that not seldom?"[2] In Tyndale's revised translation, 1534, we accordingly read, Mat. xvi. 18, "Thou arte Peter, and upon this rocke I wyll bylde my *congregacion*." We also read, Gal. i. 2, "All the brethren which are with me, unto the *congregacions* of Galacia."[3] And this is not all ; but, as if by way of assuming the *role* of the prophet of ecclesiastical democracy, Tyndale in one place introduces the term *congregation* in such a connection as to give, by an ambiguous expression, apparent warrant of Scripture for the popular election of Church office-bearers. He translates Acts xiv. 23, "And when they had ordened them elders by *eleccion* in every con-

---

[1] Tyndale was no stickler for the three separate orders of Bishops, Priests and Deacons. He says, "all that were called elders (or priests, if they so will) were called bishops also, though they have divided the names now : which thing thou mayest evidently see by the first chapter of Titus, and Acts xx., and other places more."—*Reply to More*, p. 17.

[2] Reply to More, p. 13.

[3] Notwithstanding his objection to use the word *church*, where Catholics averred it should have been used, Tyndale has not scrupled to introduce the word where it was not appropriate. Instead of translating Acts xiv. 13, "Then the priest of Jupiter . . . brought oxen and garlands unto the *gates*," he renders the last part of the sentence, "oxen and garlondes unto the *Churche porche*."

gregacion, after they had prayde and fasted, they comended them to God on whom they beleved." Tyndale, in like manner, defended his use of the word *love* in all those places where it was alleged that the "known and holy term" *charity* would have been a preferable translation.[1] And in this matter Tyndale's judgment has been confirmed by the New Testament revisers of 1881.

The Church of Rome has always laid great stress on the efficacy of her sacraments. The very word *sacrament*, in its ecclesiastical sense at least, is a word of her own creation. It occurs over and over in the Vulgate; and she esteems it so precious a word, that on no account should it be allowed to drop out of the book of life. But in Tyndale's translation, the word is conspicuous by its absence from those passages where it was supposed to give special countenance to certain Catholic doctrines. What appears in the Vulgate as *dispensatio sacramenti*, Eph. iii. 9, is rendered by Tyndale, *the felyshippe of the mistery;* and the famous statement, *sacramentum hoc magnum est*, Eph. v. 32, on which the sacramentarian theory of marriage is built, is minimised by Tyndale into *this is a great secrete*. All appearance of Scripture authority for penance and auricular confession is likewise excluded by Tyndale from the English Testament. Instead of rendering Mat. iii. 11, "I baptize you in water *unto penance*," which is the literal translation of the text in the Vulgate, Tyndale makes the Baptist say—"I baptize you in water *in token of repentaunce*." Equally careful was Tyndale to abstain from using the word *confess* in any connection where it could be construed as giving authority for the kind of confession enjoined and practised in the Catholic Church. Confession, he said, is a term with which priests have long "juggled, and so made the people, as oft as they spake of it, understand shrift in the ear." He accordingly avoided the use of a word that was so liable to misconstruction; and, both in Rom. x. 10, and James v. 16, he substituted for *confess* the

---

[1] For instance he translated 2 Peter i. 5-7:—"In youre fayth minister vertue . . . in brotherly kyndnes *love*." Coverdale renders the passage more explicitly—"in brotherly love general love."

antiquated verb *knowledge;* "To *knowledge* with the mouth maketh a man safe," Rom. x. 10.

Catholics have always maintained that images may be set up in Churches, not only for ornament but for instruction. And in saying so, they have constantly disavowed idolatry as strongly as Protestants. An image they say is one thing, and an idol is another. The veneration shewn to an image and the worship offered to an idol are therefore, they aver, quite different. In all their versions of the New Testament, whether in Latin or in English, they are careful to make the distinction between an idol and an image appear. But they complain of Protestant translators for not observing this distinction. "It is a known treachery of heretics," they allege, "to translate *idola* 'images' . . and they do it of purpose, to seduce the poor ignorant people, and to make them think that whatsoever is spoken in Scripture against the idols of the Gentiles is meant of pictures, sacred images, and holy memories of Christ and his saints."[1] To this stricture, Tyndale laid himself specially open. In many places, he translated *idola* "images," instead of *idols*. His rendering of 2 Cor. vi. 16, is—"how agreeth the temple of God with *ymages;*" and his translation of 1 Thess. i. 9, is—"how ye tourned to God from *ymages*, for to serve the livynge and true God."

In last chapter some remarks were made on the introduction of the word *easter* into the English Testament. For this anachronistic sin it is Tyndale that must be held chiefly responsible. And it is not in one place only, but in many places, that Tyndale introduces the unseasonable expression. He makes it be said, John, vi. 4, that "*ester*, a feast of the Jewes, was nye;" Mark, xiv. 16, that "the disciples came to the cyte, and made ready the *ester* lambe;" Acts, xx. 6, that "we sayled awaye from Philippos after the *ester holydayes;*" and, 1 Cor. v. 7, that "Christ oure ester lambe is offered up for us." And that there might be no incongruity in his free rendering of Jewish terms, Tyndale not only calls the passover *easter*, but he designates the preparation *good friday:*—"The

---

[1] Rhemes Testament. Annotation on 1 John v. 21.

nexte daye that foloweth *good frydaye* the hye prestes and pharises got themselves to Pilate."—Mat. xxvii. 62.[1]

From ecclesiastical terms to proper names the transition is easy; and a word may be here said on Tyndale's treatment of the names of persons and places. In many cases it may be an open question whether, in translating the New Testament, proper names should be Englished or given in their original Greek form. Tyndale has not in this matter gone upon the same lines as the translators of the authorised version have done. Several proper names and technical terms he has transformed into what he considered their nearest English equivalents. For "Decapolis," he substitutes *the ten cities;* for "Areopagus," *Mars-street;* for "the Areopagite," *a senator;* for "Pentecost," *the fiftieth day;* for "the Christ," *anointed*. Some words and phrases, on the other hand, that are Englished in the authorised version he leaves untranslated. Instead of "Mary the mother of James," we find in Tyndale's Testament, *Mary Jacobi;* and instead of "the quick-sands," Acts xxvii. 17, *Syrtes*. In the latter of these two cases, Tyndale's judgment has been confirmed, and his example followed, by nearly all subsequent translators.

More interesting than the individual words, dissociated from their context, which occur in the writings of old authors are the combinations of words. Next to scholastic accuracy, it is adroitness in the art of phrasing, that stamps a translation with merit. And to show how skilful Tyndale was in this noble art, the right course would be to cite some of the many happy turns of expression that have been transferred from his to the authorised version of the Testament in English. So far as subsequent translators have adopted Tyndale's renderings, they have borne testimony to the excellence of these renderings; and how much of Tyndale's diction appears in the version of

---

[1] In Coverdale's Bible, 1535, we read, '2 Kings, xxiii. 21.—"And the kyng commanded the people, and sayde: Kepe *easter* unto the Lord your God, as it is wrytten in the boke of this covenant." Both in Tyndale's Testament and in Coverdale's Bible, 1 Cor. xvi. 8, is rendered—"I will tary at Ephesus untyll whitsontyde."

the Testament in use at the present day, will be seen by comparing the following columns :—

TYNDALE, 1534.	AUTHORISED VERSION, 1611.
Mat. xii. 43-45.—When the unclene sprite is gone out of a man, he walketh through*out* dry places, seking reest and syndeth none. Then he sayeth: I will retourne *ageyne* into my housse, from whence I came oute. And when he is come, he fyndeth *the housse* empty *and* swepte and garnisshed. Then he goeth *his waye,* and taketh unto him seven other spretes *worsse* then him silfe, and *so* entre they in and dwell there. And the *ende* of that man is worsse then the *beginning.* Even so shall it be *with* this *evell nacion.*	Mat. xii. 43-45.—When the unclean spirit is gone out of a man, he walketh through dry places seeking rest and findeth none. Then he saith, I will return into my house from whence I came out. And when he is come, he findeth *it* empty, swept and garnished. Then goeth he, and taketh with himself seven other spirits *more wicked* than himself, and they enter in and dwell there. And the *last state* of that man is worse than the *first.* Even so shall it be also *unto* this *wicked generation.*
Luke xv. 17-24.—*Then* he came to him selfe *and* sayde: how many hyred servauntes *at* my fathers have breed ynough, and I *dye for* honger. I will aryse and goo to my father, and will saye unto him: father, I have synned agaynst heven and before the, and am no moare worthy to be called thy sonne, make me as one of thy hyred servauntes. And he arose and *went* to his father. *And* when he was yet a greate waye of, his father sawe him and had compassion, and ran and fell on his necke and kyssed him. And the sonne sayd unto him, Father, I have synned agaynst heven, and in thy sight, and am no moare worthy to be called thy sonne. But *his* father sayde to his servauntes, Bringe forth *that* best *garment* and put it on him, and put a rynge on his hoode and showes on his fete. And bringe hidder *that* fatted caulfe and kyll *him,* and let us eate and be mery: for this my sonne was deed and is alyve agayne, he was loste, and is *now* founde. And they began to be merye.	Luke xv. 17-24.—*And when* he came to himself, *he* said, How many hired servants *of* my father's have bread enough and to spare, and I *perish with* hunger! I will arise and go to my father, and will say unto him, Father, I have sinned against heaven and before thee, and am no more worthy to be called thy son, make me as one of thy hired servants. And he arose and *came* to his father. *But* when he was yet a great way off, his father saw him, and had compassion, and ran, and fell on his neck, and kissed him. And the son said unto him, Father, I have sinned against heaven and in thy sight, and am no more worthy to be called thy son. But *the* father said to his servants, Bring forth *the* best *robe* and put it on him, and put a ring on his hand and shoes on his feet. And bring hither *the* fatted calf, and kill *it,* and let us eat and be merry: For this my son was dead, and is alive again; he was lost, and is found. And they began to be merry.
1 Cor. xv. 50-53.—This saye I, brethren, that flesshe and bloud cannot inheret the kyngdome of God, nether corrupcion inhereteth uncorrupcion. Beholde I shewe you a mystery. We shall not all slepe, but we shall all be chaunged, *and that* in a moment, *and* in the twinclinge of an eye, at the sounde of the last trompe. For the trompe shall *blowe,* and the deed shall *ryse* incorruptible, and we shalbe chaunged. For this corruptible must put on *incorruptibilite* and this mortall must put on immortalite.	1 Cor. xv. 50-53.—*Now,* this I say, brethren, that flesh and blood cannot inherit the kingdom of God, neither *doth* corruption inherit incorruption. Behold I shew you a mystery: we shall not all sleep, but we shall all be changed: in a moment, in the twinkling of an eye, at the last trump. For the *trumpet* shall *sound,* and the dead shall *be raised* incorruptible, and we shall be changed. For this corruptible must put on *incorruption,* and this mortal must put on immortality.

It is obviously to the disadvantage of Tyndale to compare his translation with the authorised version, in respect of the points wherein they differ. The changes made on Tyndale's version may be presumed to indicate the places where Tyndale's translation was most imperfect, and yet it will be found that in many passages where Tyndale's translation has not been adopted, his renderings are marvellously good. Laying aside for a moment the question of scholastic accuracy, and judging of phrases merely in respect of their inherent clearness, vigour, and beauty, it may be matter of opinion whether Tyndale's renderings are not, in some places, preferable to those substituted for them in the authorised version. Instead of "it came to pass," we read in Tyndale's Testament, "it chaunced" that he went through the corn fields; and some people may think that of these two renderings the older is the simpler and better. The word *stambered*, again, used by Tyndale, Mark vii. 32, in reference to one that was deaf and could not articulate distinctly, is, whether strictly accurate or not as a translation, at least better English than the long, lumbering phrase, "had an impediment in his speech." In reminding the Galatians of his first visit to them, and how they had then received him "as an angel of God, or even as Christ himself," St. Paul is made, in the authorised version, to say: "where is then the blessedness you speak of?" In Tyndale's translation, the apostolic appeal is much more terse and tender: "How happy were ye then."[1] There is not only freedom but felicity, too, in Tyndale's rendering of Luke xx. 21: "Master, we knowe that thou sayest and teachest ryght, *nother considerest thou eny mannes degre* but teachest the waye of God truly."

Some of Tyndale's phrases are very forcible and emphatic. In the authorised version Peter is represented, John xiii. 8, as saying to Jesus, "Thou shalt never wash my feet." This declaration is not so strongly worded as it is in the original Greek; and the spirit of the original is much better brought out in Tyndale's version: "Thou shalt not wesshe my fete *while the worlde stondeth*." In respect of its literal accuracy, no fault

---

[1] A similar rendering is given by Dr. Doddridge, and approved by Dr. Bloomfield in his notes on the Greek Testament.

can be found with the translation of Titus ii. 14, "A peculiar people, zealous of good works," (if the meaning of *peculiar* be not mis-apprehended), but, without sacrificing accuracy in the least degree, Tyndale animates the passage with spirit and life by rendering it : " A peculiar people, *fervently geven* unto good workes." This tendency to accentuate and emphasise is shown by Tyndale in many other expressions. The phrases, "God forbid," "would to God," "bid him God speed," which we find so often in the English Bible, are mostly of Tyndale's manufacture, [1] and in emphasis they even go beyond the words of the original. The Greek for which they stand would be literally rendered by "be it not so," (Rom. iii. 4), " I wish," (1 Cor. iv. 8), and " say to him, hail," (2 John 10).[2] But such is the fascination of a strong phrase that these emphasised renderings of Tyndale's have been retained by Coverdale in the Great Bible, by the Puritan divines in the Geneva Bible, by the Bishops in their Church Bible, by the Catholic priests in the Douay Bible, and by the King's translators in the national authorised Bible. In the account of the woman " which had an issue of blood twelve years, and had suffered many things of many physicians, and had spent all she had," it is mildly said in the authorised version, Mark v. 26, that she " was nothing bettered but *rather* grew worse." Tyndale brings against the physicians a heavier indictment, by making the evangelist aver that after they had drugged and tortured the woman all they could, she "felte none amendment at all, but *wexed worsse and worsse.*" One verse that cannot be said to be happily, although literally, rendered in the authorised version, is Phil. i. 8 : " God is my record, how greatly I long after you all *in the bowels* of Jesus Christ." The Apostle's meaning is, I appeal to God, that I yearn after you all with the greatest Christian affection ; and

---

[1] In several passages—e.g., Rom. iii. 4, Gal. ii. 17, Gal. iii. 21, where Tyndale uses the phrase " God forbid "—the same expression is found in Wyclif's Bible. But, in 1 Cor. iv. 8, Wyclif is content to say "I wold," instead of *I would to God*, and in 2 John 10, Wyclif translates literally " nether seie ze to him heil " instead of "nether bid him God spede."

[2] The Geneva divines coined one or two other phrases of a similar strain. They make Judas Iscariot say to Jesus, Mat. xxvi. 49—" God save thee, Master," instead of—" Hail, master."

this meaning is brought out with strong accentuation in the rendering of Tyndale: "I longe after you all from the *very herte rote* in Jesus Christ." This clear and forcible, if somewhat free and paraphrastic, translation was adopted both by Coverdale in the Great Bible, and by the exiles at Geneva in the Breeches Bible. The phrase, *in the bowels of Christ*, appeared first in the Bishops' Bible, and is one of the unhappy legacies we have inherited from that prelatic source.[1]

It may seem a Hibernian statement, that many of Tyndale's translations would be admirable, if they were only accurate. Such a statement, however, is not far from the truth. How well, for instance, does the following translation of John xv. 24, 25, read: "But now have they sene, *and yet* have hated bothe me and my father: *even that* the sayinge myght be fulfilled that is written in theyr lawe, they hated me without a cause." This is a clear, sequent, and conclusive statement; but, apparently with the view of making it clear, sequent, and conclusive, Tyndale has introduced connecting and illative particles, "*yet*" and "*even that*," which are not represented in the original. A similar remark may be made on this other sentence in Tyndale's version, "they have beaten us openly, uncondemned, *for all that* we are Romans." So also on the following, 1 Thess. ii. 15, "*as* they kylled the lorde Jesus and their awne prophetes, *even so* have they persecuted us." The objection to each of these three renderings is that, for the sake of force and perspicuity, the translator has interpolated emphatic and convenient little words of his own. Sometimes Tyndale takes even greater liberties with the text than the interpolation of a single word. In the fourth chapter of the Epistle to the Galatians, we read in the authorised version: "But when the fulness of the time was come, God sent forth His Son made of a woman, made under the law, to redeem them that were under the law, that we might receive the adoption of sons." The last clause in this passage—descriptive of God's purpose towards men—is, in Tyndale's testament, ampli-

---

[1] The word "bowels" is used in the sense of *heart* by Tyndale in 2 Cor. vi. 12, Philem. xii. 20.

fied into—" that we, *thorow eleccion*, myght receave the inheritance that *belongeth unto the naturall sonnes.*" As a marginal note of explanation nothing could have been better than these words of Tyndale's; but, as a translation, they are faulty, in containing more than can be found in St. Paul's own writings. The same may be said of Tyndale's translation of James ii. 15, 16. It is explanatory instead of literal; and it looks like an attempt to improve the Apostle's mode of statement: " If a brother or a sister be naked or destitute of dayly fode, and one of you saye unto them, Departe in peace. *God sende you* warmnes and fode, . . . what helpeth it them."

One of the alleged peculiarities of diction in Tyndale's Testament is the inversion of the natural sequence of verbs to their nominatives. Tyndale does not always place the verb before its nominative; but he frequently does, and so frequently that the frequency has occasioned remark. And because this mode of expression is common in German literature it has been called a Germanism. Be it a German importation or not, it is a form of expression that in many cases is very effective, and every reader of the Bible must be thankful that it has not been banished from the pages of even the most recent version of the English Scriptures. No one would wish to see any alteration on the phraseology of the statement, 1st John, i. 3— " That which we have seen and heard *declare we* unto you." Still less would any one wish to see an attempted improvement on the words attributed to Peter in Acts iii. 6—" Silver and gold *have I* none, but such as I have, *give I* thee." These italicised phrases are all Tyndale's coining; and there are similar phrases of his that were received into the authorised version which we regret to see excluded from the revised; such as, " Though he were Goddes sonne, yet *learned he* obedience by tho thynges which he suffered," Heb. v. 8; and, " We are comforted because ye are comforted: yee, and excedyngly the moare *joyed we* for the joye that Titus had," 2 Cor. vii. 13. Some other of Tyndale's Germanisms were not so happy, and we are well rid of them. Of these may be mentioned: " *Met* him the *people*," John xii. 18; " entred they " into Caesarea, Acts x. 24; " so *lefte he* them and departed," Mat. xvi. 4.

It might be expected that in Tyndale's Testament we should find many expressions, besides a few Germanisms, that have been changed for the better in subsequent translations. That was inevitable. And it must be admitted that in Tyndale's version there are both words and phrases that, to modern ears, sound very inapt and infelicitous. In one place we read that Jesus charged his disciples, "that they should not *utter* Him." For "get thee behind me, Satan," we find in Tyndale's translation—*go after me, Satan;* for "deny himself," *forsake him silfe;* for "good to be here," *here is good being for us;* for "began to be much displeased with James and John," *began to disdayne at James and John;* for "the assembly was confused," *the congregation was all out of quiet;* for, "be it far from thee Lord," *Master faver thyself;* for, "Israel after the flesh," *Israel which walketh carnally;* for, "a linnen cloth cast about his naked body," *cloothed in lynnen upon the bare;* for, "the Jews have no dealings with the Samaritans," *the Jews medle not with the Samaritans*; for, "the Pharisees began to urge him vehemently," *the Pharisees began to wexe busye aboute him.* Instead of the sonorous interdict, "whom God hath joined together let not man put asunder," Tyndale gives for the wedding charge the crabbed order: "whom God hath cuppled let not man separate." And it may shock some people to hear that in Tyndale's Bible it is written, "all men at the beginnynge set forth good wyne, and *when man be dronke,* then that which is worsse." It is a very unphilosophic account of St. Paul's preaching, too, that Tyndale attributes to the philosophers of Athens, "They sayd he semeth to be a tydnges bringer of *newe devyls.*"

In Tyndale's Testament, as in Wyclif's, there are homely phrases without number. Some of these are very happy and pathetic, others are not worthy of such praise. Very simple and graphic, for instance, are the words "*comers and goers,*" in the narrative, "he said unto them, come ye apart into the wylderness and rest a whyle. For there were many *comers and goers,* that they had no leisure so moche as to eat." Equally simple and graphic is the account of the conveyance of the paralytic into the room at Capernaum, where Jesus was teaching: "They went up on the toppe of the housse, and let him doune thorowe the tylinge, *beed and all.*" Very graphic, if not very classic, again, is the statement, "all the city was on a roore," which is Tyndale's way of saying that "the city was filled with confusion." In the expression, "*that lost child,*" applied by our Lord to Judas, there is a sad tenderness which does not appear in its modern substitute, "that son of perdition." There is an honest warmth in the simple asseveration, 2 Cor. ii. 17, "we are not as many which *choppe and chaunge* with the worde of God." There is a touching cogency in the argument, also, Rom xiv. 20, "destroye not the worke of God for a *lytel meates* sake." In the quaint words, "there arose agaynste their purpose a *flawe of wynde out of the north-easte,*" there is a fine picturesqueness, which is not preserved in the statelier translation, "there arose a tempestuous wind called Euroclydon." And there is a similar picturesqueness in Tyndale's account of the discovery of Jesus in the temple, when he was found, "sittinge in the middes of the doctours, both hearynge them and *posinge* them." The hit, too, in Luke xxii. 25, at the folly of titular usages, which is somewhat obscure in the authorised translation, is well brought out by Tyndale: "They that beare rule over them are called *gracious lords!*" Other homely expressions of Tyndale's will be admired by some people and not relished by others. There is a pleasant pic-nic aspect, for instance, given to the grand scene in the wilderness, where it is said, in Tyndale's Testament, that the people "sate down *here a rowe and there a rowe* by hundreds and fifties." A curious homely phrase, also, occurs in St. Matthew's account of the Lord's supper: "When they had sayde *grace*, they went out into mounte Olyvete." There is a colloquial aptness, again, in the following rendering: "Whosoever shall saye unto this mountayne, *take away* thy silfe and cast thy silfe into the sea, and shall not waver in his herte . . . whatsoever he sayeth shall be done to him." Very graphic and true, also, is the account given by St. Paul to Timothy, of the preacher that sets himself against Church authority, and will not content himself with the wholesome words of Christ: "He is pufte up and knoweth nothinge, but wasteth his braynes aboute questions and stryfe of wordes.' And an exhortation that would not be out of place at the present day is Eph. iv. 31, as rendered by Tyndale: " Let all bitterness, fearsnes, and wrath, *rorynge* and *cursyd speakynge* be put awaye from you." Some of Tyndale's colloquialisms, however, are of questionable taste ; and we cannot wonder that subsequent translators "excommunicated" them from the English Bible. The tenth verse of the second chapter of the First Epistle to the Corinthians, for instance, is translated by Tyndale: " The sprete searcheth all thinges, ye the bottome of Goddes secretes." The fifth verse of the first chapter of the Epistle of James, again, is rendered : " Yf eny of you lacke wysdom, let him axe of God, which geveth to all men indifferentlie, and *casteth no man in the teth*." In a similarly blunt way it is said, Mat. iv. 24, that there were brought unto Jesus "all sicke people that were taken with divers diseases and gripinges ;" Mark. vi. 27, that Herod "sent the hangman" to bring into his banqueting hall the head of John the Baptist; Luke xi. 46, that lawyers lade men with burdens grievous to be borne, but will not themselves touch "the packes with one of (their) fyngers ;" and Titus ii. 10, that Christians who occupy the position of servants, should not be "pickers, but shewe all good faythfulnes."

It is evident that the meaning of a passage may be greatly modified by either the omission or the insertion of an article. Tyndale's Testament reads, from this cause, very differently in many places from the authorised version. In most of these instances, Tyndale's renderings make good enough sense, and sometimes they seem more in accordance with the idiom of the English tongue than the literal translations substituted for them in later versions. One sentence in the prayer at Gethsemane is rendered by Tyndale : " I desire not that thou shouldst take them out of the world, but that thou keep them from evil ;" instead of from "*the evil*," as in the authorised version, or " *the evil one*," as in the revised version. In the narrative of our Lord's temptation, Tyndale says, "he was then in the wilderness forty days, and was with wilde beestis," instead of " with *the* wild beasts." The only objection to these renderings of Tyndale's is that they take no account of the article in the original Greek. There are cases, however, in which Tyndale's misuse of the article takes away the point of particular statements or allusions. The question put to our Saviour, John i. 21, was not as given by Tyndale: "Art thou a prophet?" but, "Art thou *the* prophet?"—the prophet that is expected in Israel. And so, also, the statement, John i. 9, which appears in Tyndale's version: "That was *a* true light, which lighteth all men that come into the world," is far short of the evangelist's meaning. Another misapplication of the article in Tyndale's Testament is so ludicrous and absurd that we may wonder how it ever was made by a man so careful as Tyndale was to express himself unambiguously and sensibly: "Have not I chosen you twelve and one of you is *the* Devil?" Sometimes Tyndale's accentuation of passages, by means of the article, not only gives good sense, but is more accurate as a translation than its counterpart in the authorised version. His rendering of 1 Tim. ii. 8: "I wyll therfore that *the* men praye everywhere, liftynge up pure hondes without wrath or dowtinge," has been confirmed by the revisers of 1881; and although Tyndale's rendering of the following verse, "Lykwyse also *the* wemen that they araye themselves in comlye aparell," does not appear in the revised version, it is because the revisers have translated from a slightly different text in the Greek.

It is interesting to note that some of Tyndale's renderings that were changed by the King's translators in 1611 have been restored by the revisers in 1881. It is said, for instance, in the authorised version, Mark vi. 19, that "Herodias had a *quarrel* against" John the Baptist. In Tyndale's Testament the statement is, that "Herodias layd wayte for" John; and in the revised version the words attributed to the evangelist are, "Herodias *set herself against* John." A verse in Tyndale's Testament that reads more smoothly, and flows more naturally out of the context, than its counterpart in the authorised translation, is John xii. 13. In the latter-named translation the crowds that accompanied Jesus on his triumphal entry into Jerusalem are represented as crying, "Hosanna, blessed is the king of Israel that cometh in the name of the Lord." Tyndale's rendering of the passage is, " Hosanna, blessed is he that in the name of the Lorde commeth kynge of Israel ;" and this is substantially what appears in the revised version. In the letter of "Claudius Lysias unto the most excellent governor Felix," there is an expression which must have led many of its readers to suspect that the "chief captain," although a Roman, was rather given to the trick of exaggerating. "This man, Paul," he writes, "was taken of the Jews and should have been killed of them ; then came I with an *army* and rescued him." In Tyndale's translation of the letter this apparent exaggeration does not occur. Instead of " I came with an army," it is said, "I cam with *soudiers;*" and that old rendering, slightly modified into *the soldiers*, to signify the force under the charge of Lysias, appears in the version of 1881. It is not unworthy of note, too, that some of Tyndale's homely phrases have been restored by the revisers. In the account of the mishap that befell the young man who went asleep during the sermon of St. Paul at Troas, the Apostle is represented in the authorised version as saying, " *Trouble not yourselves*, for his life is in him." The words of Paul, as given by Tyndale, are, " make nothing ado ;" and as given by the recent revisers, " make ye no ado." A statement in the authorised version that is open to misconstruction, by persons unlearned in the mysteries of etymology, is the often-quoted passage in 2 Thess. i. 10—"When He shall come to be glorified in His saints, and to be *admired* in them that believe." In Tyndale's Testament the sentence reads, "When He shall come . . to be made marvellous ;" and in the revised version of 1881, "When He shall come to be *marvelled at*." It is well known, also, that in the revision, 1881, there is a very important change on a verse that bears on the doctrine of the Bible's inspiration. The familiar words, " All Scripture is given by inspiration of God, and is profitable for doctrine, for reproof, for correction, and for instruction in righteousness," have been altered by the revisers into " Every Scripture inspired of God is also profitable for teaching," etc. This rendering gives a very different meaning to the passage. It is not a new reading or rendering, however, but a restoration of the old reading and rendering of Tyndale's.

As might be expected, there are many cases in which Scripture is made to present in Tyndale's Testament a different meaning from what it bears in the authorised translation. But it is mostly in regard to small matters which have little or no bearing on questions of faith or life that these differences appear. An interesting version of one of our Lord's sayings that we find in Tyndale's Testament is: "Yf salt have loste hyr saltness what shall be seasoned therewith." A very odd reading, also, that we find in Tyndale's translation is: "He which hath prepared the housse hath *most honoure in* the housse," Heb. iii. 3. By the substitution of *was* for *is*, Tyndale clothes one of the charges that Jesus gave to his seventy emissaries with a sadder significance than it is commonly supposed to have had: "Yf they receave you not, goo youre wayes out into the stretes . . . and saye, even the very dust which cleaveth on us of your citie we wipe of agaynst you; notwithstondinge marke this that the kyngdome of God *was* come nie upon you," Luke x. 11. A reading again in Tyndale's Testament that gives a different doctrinal and practical aspect to a passage in Scripture is Acts iii. 26: "Fyrst unto you hath God raysed up his sonne Jesus, and him he hath sent to blysse you that every one of you shuld turne (instead of, in turning every one of you) from youre wickednes."[1]

Some of Tyndale's peculiar readings and renderings are, if the expression may be pardoned, amusing. One instance in point is, Mat. ix. 18, 24: "Whyls he thus spake unto them, beholde ther came a certayne ruler, and worshipped him, sayinge, My doghter is euen now deceased, but come and lay thy honde on her and she shall live. And when Jesus came into the ruler's housse and sawe the minstrels and the people *raginge*, he said unto them, get you hence, for the mayde is not deed but slepeth." At the close of the second Epistle to the Thessalonians, again, it is said, both in the authorised and the revised version, "if any man obey not our word by this epistle, note that man, and have no company with him that he may be ashamed." But according to Tyndale, a different course was

---

[1] An odd rendering of Tyndale's is, 2 Cor. v. 7, "We walke in fayth and so not."

to be adopted with the refractory convert: "Yf eny man obey not oure sayinges, *sende us worde of him by a letter, and have no companie with him.*" Among the things, also, required of a bishop, (which, according to Presbyterians, means a parish minister), the clergy of Scotland will be glad to hear, and their congregations should take note of the fact, that one specified in Tyndale's version of 1 Timothy iii. 2, is that he be "honestly aparelled."[1] And a strange sight that St. John is said by Tyndale to have seen at Patmos was "a *grene* horsse, and his name that sat on him was deeth," Rev. vi. 8.[2]

There are clauses and sentences in Tyndale's translation, too, that diverge much farther from the authorised than any of those that have yet been cited. In Acts xiii. 33, for example, there are certain words given by Tyndale as a quotation from the *first* instead of from the second psalm. In another part of the Acts of the Apostles, xvii. 11, where we are accustomed to read that the Jews in Berea "were more noble than those in Thessalonica, in that they received the word with all readiness of mind and searched the Scriptures daily," it is stated in Tyndale's version, "these were the *noblest of byrthe among them of* Thessalonica, which receved the worde," etc. A passage that cannot be said to be clearly rendered in plain language, in either the authorised or revised version of the Scriptures, is 2 Cor. vi. 11, 13.[3] The closing words of that passage are, "be ye also enlarged:" and then there follows a new verse (and in the revised version a new paragraph) which begins: "Be ye not unequally

---

[1] The word so translated is *kosmios*, which in the Vulgate is rendered *ornatus*, and in the Rhemes Testament *comely*. In the authorised version it is translated *of good behaviour*, and in the revised version *orderly*.

[2] Some of Tyndale's expressions read very like puns. One that has been often taken notice of, occurs in 2 Cor. v. 11, "Seynge then that we knowe how the lorde is to be *feared*, we *fare fayre* with men." Another that is not so elaborate occurs in James ii. 20—"Wilt thou understonde, O thou vayne man, that fayth without *dedes* is *deed*." A stiff piece of alliteration occurs in Acts iii. 11, "the *halt* which was *healed helde* Peter."

[3] The meaning of the passage is well brought out in Mr. Conybeare's translation, "Corinthians, my mouth has spoken to you freely, my heart has opened itself fully towards you. You find no narrowness in my love, but the narrowness is in your own. I pray you, therefore, in return for my affection (I speak as to my children), let your hearts be opened in like manner."

yoked together with unbelievers." In Tyndale's Testament these two clauses, the last of one paragraph and the first of another, are connected and made to read as one sentence: "Set yourselves therfore at large, and beare not a straunger's yoke wyth the unbelevers." In the ordination of ministers in Presbyterian churches, again, there is a ceremony gone through which is called "giving the right hand of fellowship." The phrase by which this ceremony is designated is to be found in almost all English Bibles, in Gal. ii. 9; and many people, who do not consider themselves ritualists, may possibly imagine that the ceremony is required by Scripture as an essential part of an ordination service. But Tyndale, who was an ecclesiastical democrat, bitterly opposed to everything that wore a priestly aspect, does not in his translation of Gal. ii. 9, use the expression *right hand of fellowship* at all. He makes the Apostle say, "when they perceaved the grace that was geven unto me, then James, Cephas, and John, which semed to be pilers, gave to me and Barnabas the ryght hondes, and *agreed with us* that we should preache amonge the Hethen and they amonge the Jewes."

The variations from the authorised version that appear in Tyndale's Testament arose, in some cases, from his having a different Greek text to translate from, and in other cases, from his giving to the text an English rendering, which subsequent translators have not seen fit to accept. How many of his variations arose from the former, and how many from the latter, of these causes, might be approximately determined by a comparison of them with the old texts, from which he is supposed to have translated. It will suffice for us to shew how some of his variations can be accounted for, by what in modern editions of the Greek Testament are noted as alternative readings. In the Greek Testament, as commonly printed, the last word in 1 Thess. v. 12, is *heautois*, but in some old manuscripts the word is *autois*. The consequence is that while in some English versions the passage is translated: "We beseech you, brethren, to know them which labour among you, and are over you in the Lord . . . and to esteem them very highly in love for their workes sake, and be at peace among *yourselves*;" in other versions, Tyndale's, Coverdale's, and the Rhemes Testament, the last clause is rendered "be at peace with *them*," that is, with your spiritual guides and governors. There are also two Greek readings in Rom. xii. 11. One of these is *kurio* and the other is *kairo*. In some English versions, therefore (such as the authorised, the Geneva, and the Bishops), we read : "Fervent in spirit, serving the Lord ;" but in others (to wit, Tyndale's, Coverdale's, and the Great Bible), "Be fervent in the sprete. Apply yourselves to the *time*." In the Greek text of James ii. 18, there are two alternative readings, which do not bear much resemblance to each other. The one is *choris*, and the other is *ek*. Some English translators have adopted the one reading, and some have adopted the other. In the authorised version we read, "Show me thy faith without *(choris)* thy works, and I will show thee my faith by my works." And this statement, every one will see, is pertinent to the subject under the Apostle's discussion. The fact, nevertheless, remains that in many of the earlier English versions of the Testament (Tyndale's, Coverdale's, the Geneva, and the Bishops'), the passage was rendered, "Shewe me *thy* fayth *by (ek)* thy dedes, and I will shewe the *my* fayth by my dedes." In another part of St. James' Epistle, Tyndale's version presents a different reading from what is found in the authorised. For "ye kill," we read in Tyndale's Testament, James iv. 2, *ye envy ;* and although the reason for that difference of reading in the two English versions does not appear on the margin of the Greek Testament, as usually printed, the reason nevertheless is obvious. The Greek word for *ye kill* is *phoneuete*, and the Greek for *ye envy* is *phthoneite*.[1] The latter word had evidently found its way into some copies of the Greek text; and not only Tyndale, but the exiles in Geneva, 1570, and the Bishops, 1572, had accepted it as the true reading. Strange to say, the following chapter in St. James' Epistle furnishes another instance of Tyndale's variation from the authorised version, through the adoption of a different

---

[1] Bloomfield says, "For *phoneuete* some would conjecture *phthoneite* . . . but for an alteration so unauthorised no real necessity exists."

reading in the Greek text. What is usually printed, v. 12, *hypo crísin*, appears in some copies of the Greek Testament *hypócrisin;* and it happens that, while the King's translators, 1611, have accepted the former of these readings, Tyndale has accepted the latter. In Tyndale's version, therefore, we read : " Let youre ye be ye, and youre naye naye, [not, as is commonly said, lest ye fall into *condemnation*, but] lest ye faule into *ypocrecy.*"

Many other cases of divergence between Tyndale's and the authorised version of the Testament could easily be adduced. In the authorised version, it is said, Acts xiii. 42, that "when the Jews were gone out of the Synagogue the Gentiles besought that these words might be preached to them *the next Sabbath* ;" but the statement in Tyndale's version is that the Gentiles besought the Apostles to " preache the worde to them *bitwene the Saboth dayes.*" Of the Philippian jailor it is said, in the authorised version, Acts xvi. 34, that when he had brought Paul and Silas " into his house, he set meat before them and rejoiced, believing in God with all his house." According to Tyndale, the jailor "joyed *that* he with all his housholde beleved on God." In the account of St. Paul's voyage to Rome it is said, in the authorised version, Acts xxvii. 9, that " sailing was now dangerous, *because* the *Fast was now already past*," and it was consequently far on in the autumn. A very different statement is made in Tyndale's translation. The whole verse reads there, " When moche tyme was spent, and saylinge was now jeoperdeous, *because also that we had ouerlonge fasted*, Paul put them in remembraunce." For " weak and beggarly elements," Gal. iv. 9., Tyndale, like a zealous Puritan, has " weake and bedgarly cerimonies "; for " being found in fashion as a man," Phil. ii. 8., Tyndale has, " founde in his *aparell* as a man " ; for " beware of the concision," Phil. iii. 2., Tyndale has, " beware of *dissencion* ; " for "Devil," Tyndale has in one place, Eph. iv. 27, " *backbyter*," and in other places, 1 Tim. iii. 6-7, *evyll-speaker* ; for " hast borne," Rev. ii. 3., Tyndale has "*dydest wasshe* thy self " ; and for " religious proselytes " Acts xiii. 43, that is, proselytes to the Jewish religion, Tyndale has " verteous *convertes*," which, whatever it was intended to mean, would be construed to signify converts to Christianity.

Besides a translation of the New Testament, Tyndale published a translation of the five books of Moses, and a translation of the prophecies of Jonah. Both of these books were printed abroad, the former in 1530 and the latter in 1531. He is believed, also, to have left behind him, in manuscript, a translation of the historical books in the Old Testament from Joshua to 2 Chronicles inclusive. It seems now to be acknowledged that all these translations were made direct from the original Hebrew, although use was made by Tyndale of both Latin and German versions for instruction and correction.

The enduring glory of Tyndale, however, is that he laid the foundation of the English version of the New Testament. That work of his has never been set aside or superseded, but only revised and amended. It is to a very large extent in the words of Tyndale that English-speaking Christians at the present day express their dearest hopes and richest consolations.

The Reformers' Bibles.

Coverdale's Bible, 1535.
Matthew's Bible, 1537.
Taverner's Bible, 1539.
The Great Bible, or Coverdale's second Bible, 1539. Revised Edition, with prologue by Cranmer, 1540.

Editions consulted and quoted from :—
Coverdale's Bible.—Bagster's Reprint, 1838.
Matthew's Bible.—Edition, 1537, (Glasgow University Library).
Taverner's Bible.—Edition, 1539, (Glasgow University Library).
Great Bible.—Grafton's Edition, 1541, (printed Nov. 1540).—New Testament, Reprint in Bagster's Hexapla of edition 1539.

THE demand for a Bible in English was every day becoming louder and more urgent in England, as the Reformation advanced. The questions at issue between Churchmen and Protestants must, it was felt, be decided by an appeal to the Bible. The whole system of ecclesiastical teaching, ecclesiastical worship, ecclesiastical mediation, and ecclesiastical government must, said the Reformers, be tried and judged by the Scriptures on which it is alleged to be founded. Besides Tyndale, therefore, other men were engaged in the work of translating the Bible into English. One of the most notable of these was Miles Coverdale.

Some authors have represented Coverdale as a *collaborateur* of Tyndale's at Hamburg ; but according to recent writers, there is no evidence to support that statement. He is said to have been born in 1488, and at an early age to have espoused the principles of the Reformation. For so doing he " found himself in danger, and fled beyond sea, where he chiefly applied himself to the study and translation of the Holy Scriptures." [1]

---

[1] Lewis' *History of the several Translations of the Bible into English*, p. 92.

Where he resided while engaged in this work is not known; nor is it definitely ascertained where he found his first printers. He did not, like Tyndale, issue his translation by instalments, but published the whole Bible in English at once. This was in 1535, while Tyndale was still living.[1] The book bore no publisher's name; and it presented itself to national notice, says Dr. Eadie, "unheralded and unanticipated."

This version of the Bible, by Coverdale, was not a translation from the original tongues in which the Scriptures were written. On its title page there was an honest confession that the translation was made out of "Douche and Latyn." It was, therefore, only a secondary version of the Scriptures in English: the translation of a translation. It consequently had not the scholastic and theological value it should have had, if it had been drawn direct from the fountain head. And not only so, but while Coverdale's Bible may be acknowledged to be in part an independent translation from the "Douche and Latyn," it is in part not even that. Coverdale was preceded by Tyndale in the translation of the New Testament, the Pentateuch, and the Book of Jonah. And as far as these portions of Scripture are concerned Coverdale's translation was only a revision of Tyndale's labours. Two parts of Coverdale's Bible have thus to be considered separately: the part that was an original translation, and the part that was not.

It is in the former of these parts that Coverdale's most notable renderings occur. His Bible is sometimes spoken of as the "treacle" Bible, and sometimes as the "bug" Bible, from these words being used in his Bible in an odd sense and an odd connection.[2] The passages containing these readings are

---

[1] Some have surmised that it was printed at Frankfort by Egenolph; others that it was printed at Cologne; but, Dr. Eadie says, "there is a very strong presumption that Frosehover of Zurich, who printed the edition of 1550, also printed that of 1535." In an old French biography there is a statement, which till recently was overlooked, that Jacob van Meteren "was at pains and very zealous at Antwerp, towards the translation of the English Bible, and employed for that purpose a certain learned scholar, called Miles Coverdale." This statement, Dr. Mombert remarks, "renders it *probable* that the first edition of Coverdale was printed at Antwerp."

[2] It might, also, for a similar reason be termed the "beer" Bible. One of the

found in the part translated at first hand. Where in the authorised version of the Bible we read: "Is there no balm in Gilead," Jer. viii. 22, it is said in Coverdale's Bible: "There is no more triacle at Galaad:" and where again in the authorised version we read: "Thou shalt not be afraid of the terror by night," Ps. xci. 5, it is said in Coverdale's translation, "thou shalt not nede to be afrayed for any *bugges* by night."[1] Other odd renderings in this part of Coverdale's Bible might be instanced. The invocation, "put them in fear, O lord,"[2] Ps. ix. 20, is with unconscious humour rendered by Coverdale, "set a schoolmaster over them:" Solomon's note on the inconvertibility of fools, Prov. xxvii. 22, is translated, "though thou shuldest bray a foole with a pestell in a morter *like otemeel*, yet will not his foolishness go from him": Shebna, the shame of his Lord's house (Revised version, 1885) is denounced, Is. xxii. 18, as "thou *vyllene* of the house of thy Lorde": in comparison of the Almighty, the isles of the earth are declared, Is. xl. 15, to be "as the *shadowe of the sonnebeame*": "the word that

---

judgments it pronounces on the people of Israel for their sins is, "The beer shall be bytter to them that drinke it," Is. xxiv. 9.

[1] The designation "treacle" Bible is sometimes given to Matthew's Bible also. In the verse referred to, the word treacle occurs in all the Reformers' Bibles, (Coverdale's, Matthew's, Taverner's and the Great Bible) and also in the Bishops' Bible; but as Coverdale's was the first published of these versions, it should have the credit or discredit of the phrase. By bibliographers the term "bug Bible" is applied specially to a particular edition of Matthew's Bible, printed in 1551; although the word "bugges" appeared long before that date, not only in Matthew's but in Taverner's and Coverdale's translation of Ps. xci. 5. In the sense of terror, or scare-crow, "bug" appears in Shakespeare also:—"Warwick was a *bug* that feared us all."—*Henry VI. Part iii. Act 5, Scene 2.*

[2] "Constitue, Domine, *legislatorem* super eos."—*Vulgate.* In some other Latin versions this rendering is changed into: "Pone, Jehovah, timorem eis."—*Zurich*, 1564.

To Coverdale's mind teaching and flogging were nearly synonymous terms. His rendering of 1 Kings, xii. 11, was "My father correcte you with scourges, but I will *nurtoure* you with scorpions;" and of Ps. xciv. 10, "He that nurtureth the heithen and teacheth a man knowledge shal not be *punysh*." A phrase quite worthy of Coverdale, however, (and it is not a phrase of his) stands in both the authorised and revised versions of the Bible: "He took the elders of the city, and thorns of the wilderness and briers, and with them he *taught* the men of Succoth," Judges, viii. 16.

came to Jeremiah from the Lord" is paraphrased, "this is another *sermon* which the Lord commanded Jeremy for to preach": and the two staves of Zechariah, which are known to us by the names of Beauty and Bands, are strangely designated *Louynge Mekenesse* and *Wo*.

The diction of Coverdale's Bible, it will thus be seen, is characterised by the same quaintness and homeliness as that of Wyclif's and Tyndale's translations. And this remark applies not to one portion of Coverdale's Bible only, but to the whole of it. A word of very frequent occurrence in his version is *tush*: "The foolish bodyes saye in their hertes, *Tush*, there is no God," Ps. xiv. 1; "*Tush*, God will not destroy us utterly," Jer. xii. 5; "He [the war horse] feareth not the noyse of the trompettes, but as soone as he heareth the shawmes blowe, *Tush*, sayeth he," Job xxxix. 25. A passage whose sublimity is made well nigh ridiculous by Coverdale's Arcadian phraseology, is Ps. xlii. 7: "One depe calleth another with the voyce of thy *whystles*." In its simplicity and homeliness, however, Coverdale's style is sometimes very racy: "There be thre thinges that are neuer satisfied, and the fourth saieth neuer *hoo*," Prov. xxx. 15; "He that is geven to much slepe shal go with a *ragged cote*," Prov. xxiii. 21; "Death and we are *at a poynte*; and as for hell, we haue made a *condicion* with it," Is. xxviii. 15. At other times, Coverdale's renderings are, in their homely phraseology, extremely picturesque: "There be thre thinges that *go stiffly*, but the goinge of the fourth is the *goodliest of all*. A lyon which is kynge of beestes, and geueth place to no man; a cock ready to fight; a ramme; and a kynge that goeth forth with his people."[1] Now and again, however, the realism in

---

[1] Of homely diction, specimens without number could be gathered from Coverdale's Bible. The following will serve as additional examples here:—"When Jacob sawe that there was moch corne in Egypte, he sayde unto his sonnes, *Why gape ye?*" Gen. xlii. 1; "The kyne . . . wente on *blearynge*," 1 Sam. vi. 12; "We trust in the Lorde oure God: *A goodly god*, indede! whose hie places and aulteres Ezechias toke downe," Is. xxxvi. 7; "There went a *rygge* wall rounde aboute them. . . . Then sayde he unto me, This is the *kechin*, where the ministers of the house shall dight the slayne offerynges of the people," Ezek. xlvi. 23-24; "They call not upon me with their hartes, but lye *youlinge* upon their beddes," Hos. vii. 14; "*Laye to* youre sythes, for the haruest is rype," Joel. iii. 13.

Coverdale's renderings verges on coarseness of expression, as in Isaiah xix. 14: "The Lorde hath made Egypte droncken with the sprete of erroure, and they shal use it in all matters; euen as a dronken man *goeth spewinge aboute.*" But, on the other hand, his wording is occasionally so delicate that we wonder why it was not retained in subsequent versions. Many a jocund peal of irreverent laughter at David's denuded warriors might have been left unstirred in the tents of the Philistines if Coverdale's translation of 2 Sam. x. 4 had been quietly adopted by the king's translators in 1611 : "Then toke Hanun the seruantes of Dauid and shore of the one halue of their beerdes, and cut of the halfe of their garments euen by the *girdell*, and so let them go." Not infrequently the narrative is clearer and more pathetic in Coverdale's Bible than in either the authorised or revised versions, as in Lam. ii. 11-12: "The children and babes dyd swowne in the stretes of the cite, euen when they spake to their mothers, where is meate and drynke? for, whyle they so sayde, they fell downe in the stretes of the cite, like as they had bene wounded, and some dyed in their mothers bosome." It has been complained by critics that the freeness of Coverdale's renderings makes his Bible in some places a paraphrase rather than a strict translation; but although this is a fault, it now and then proves helpful to the reader.[1] Statements are accentuated, and arguments put in more cogent form, so that the narrative is followed with greater ease. A good example of this paraphrastic freedom occurs in Is. xxviii. 7: "They go wronge by the reason of wyne, they fall and stacker because of stronge drynke. Yee, euen the prestes and prophetes themselues go amisse, they are dronken with wyne, and weake braned thorow stronge drynke. They erre in seinge, and in judgment they fayle."[2] Still, it must be said that, taken as a whole, the part of Coverdale's

---

[1] A quaint paraphrastic rendering occurs in Is. viii. 4: "Or euer the childe shal haue knowledge to saye, Abi and Im, that is, Father and Mother."

[2] Another graphic account of the drunkard is given by Coverdale in his translation of Prov. xxiii. 35 :—"They wounded me, but it hath not hurte me, they smote me, but I felt it not. When I am wel wakened I wil go to the drynke agayne."

Bible that was a first translation from "the Douche and Latyn" is, in point of rhythm and dignity, much inferior to some later English versions of the Scriptures. Many of the fine Biblical expressions that are now familiar to us as household words are not to be found in Coverdale's Bible. One or two selected passages will show how much Coverdale's diction has been improved on by the King's translators:

COVERDALE, 1535.	AUTHORISED VERSION, 1611.
Ps. xciii. 4.—The wawes of the see are mightie and rage horribly: but yet the Lorde that dwelleth on hye is mightier.	Ps. xciii. 4.—The Lord on high is mightier than the noise of many waters, yea, than the mighty waves of the sea.
Prov. iv. 18.—The path of the righteous shyneth as the light, and is euer brighter and brighter unto the parfecte daye.	Prov. iv. 18.—The path of the just is as the shining light, which shineth more and more unto the perfect day.
Is. xliv. 22.—As for thyne offences I dryue them awaye like the cloudes and thy synnes as the myst.	Is. xliv. 22.—I have blotted out as a thick cloud thy transgressions, and as a cloud, thy sins.
Is. liii. 2.—He shal haue nether bewty ner fauore. When we loke upon him there shalbe no fayrnesse: we shal haue no lust unto him.	Is. liii. 2.—He hath no form nor comeliness, and when we shall see him there is no beauty that we should desire him.
Is. lxiii. 1.—What is he this that cometh from Edom, with stayned reade clothes of Bosra (which is so costly cloth) and cometh in so neembly with all his strength?	Is. lxiii. 1.—Who is this that cometh from Edom, with dyed garments from Bozrah, this that is glorious in his apparel, travelling in the greatness of his strength?
Jer. iv. 19.—How longe shall I se the tokens of warre, and heare the noyse of the trompettes?	Jer. iv. 19.—O, my soul, the sound of the trumpet, the alarm of war!
Jer. viii. 20.—The haruest is gone, the somer hath an ende, and we are not helped.	Jer. viii. 20.—The harvest is past, the summer is ended, and we are not saved.
Jer. ix. 1.—O, who will geue my heade water ynough, and a well of teares for myne eyes,	Jer. ix. 1.—Oh, that my head were waters, and mine eyes a fountain of tears.
Jer. xxii. 10.—Mourne not ouer the deed, and be not wo for them: but be sory for him that departeth awaye for he commeth not agayne, and seeth his natyve countre no more.	Jer. xxii. 10.—Weep ye not for the dead, neither bemoan him: but weep sore for him that goeth away for he shall return no more, nor see his native country.

It goes without saying that in Coverdale's Bible, as in Tyndale's Testament, there are to be found many obsolete words, and many words that although not obsolete are used in an obsolete sense. One curious word that we find is *perquellies*: "Who so euer smyteth the Jebusites, and optayneth the *perquellies*,"[1] . . . shall be made chief and captain, 2 Sam. v. 8.

---

[1] In the edition, 1537, perquellies is spelt perquylles, and is doubtless equivalent

Another word repeatedly used in a connection that makes it open to very flagrant misconception is *damn*: " The Lorde sente ye in to the waye, and sayde: Go thy waie and *damne the synners*, the Amalechites, and fighte against them tyll thou haue utterly destroyed them," 1 Sam. xv. 18. Every one has heard of the Roundheads in the reign of Charles the Second, but some people may possibly be ignorant of the derivation of the term. For such persons the following sentence from Coverdale's Bible will be instructive: " In all Israel there was not so fayre and so marvuelous goodly a man as Absalom. From the sole of his fote unto the toppe of his heade there was not one blemysh in him, and whan his *head was rounded* (that was comonly euery yeare, for it was too heuy for him, so that it must nedes have bene *rounded*) the heer of his heade weyed two hundreth sicles after the kynges weight," 2 Sam. xiv. 25, 26. Of the many other antiquated words, or antiquated inflexions found in Coverdale's Bible, the following may be mentioned: *shope*, " The Lorde God shope man euen of the moulde of the earth," Gen. ii. 7; *turne grese*, " That they might go up to the myddest stacion by a turne grese," 1 Kings vi. 8; *reconcile*, " Reconcile me with Isope, and I shal be clene," Psal. li. 7; *wrutt*, " The wilde bore out of the wod hath wrutt it up," Psal. lxxx. 13; *chaft bones*, " With their chaft bones they consume and deuoure the symple," Prov. xxx. 14; *redebush*, " A fyre in a wod or a redebush," Is. ix. 18; *hilchapel*, " The hye hilchapels off Isaac must be layed waist," Amos vii. 9; *handreachinge*, " The disciples concluded to sende . . . an handreachinge unto the brethren that were in Jewry," Acts xi. 29; *goodmeaninge*, " I saye my goodmeanynge" (mind or opinion), 1 Cor. vii. 25; *childshippe*, " Unto whom pertayneth the childshippe," Rom. ix. 4; *Jewshippe*, " I . . . preuayled in the Jeweshippe, above many of my companyons in my nacion," Gal. i. 13.

In respect of the New Testament and Pentateuch, and especially the New Testament, the indebtedness of Coverdale

---

to *percullis*, which (although stated in some modern Dictionaries to be a corrupt form of *portcullis*) should from its etymology mean gutter or watercourse.

to Tyndale is very apparent. A large number of Tyndale's most notable expressions—both those that are specially apt and those that are specially inapt—are, in these parts of Scripture, adopted verbatim by Coverdale. In both Coverdale's and Tyndale's version of the New Testament it is said, Mat. vi. 7, " When ye praye, *bable not moche* as the heathen do, for they thincke that they shal be herde, for their *moche bablynges sake*." In both versions it is said, also, Mat. ix. 23, " When Jesus came into the ruler's housse, and sawe the minstrels and the people *raginge*, he sayde unto them, *get you hence*." In the passage, Mat. xxiv. 40, 41, about two that shall be working in the fields and two that shall be grinding at the mill, it is said in both versions: "One shall be *receaved* and the other shall be *refused*." The strange expression, " The *Jewes ester* was nye at hand," occurs, John xi. 55, in both versions; so does the statement, Acts viii. 1, " Saul had *pleasure* in his death ;" and so does the exhortation, Heb. xii. 1, " *Laye awaye* all that *presseth downe*, and the synne that *hangeth on*, and let us run with pacience *unto the batayl* that is set before us."

Coverdale's version of the New Testament is, nevertheless, by no means a reprint of Tyndale's. The changes that Coverdale made on Tyndale's renderings are numerous, and, in not a few cases, of some importance. One principle in translation laid down by Coverdale was in direct antagonism to Tyndale's practice. In the use of ecclesiastical terms Tyndale thought it necessary to be very particular. He always translated *presbyteroi*, *elders* and not *priests ; metanoia*, *repentance* and not *penance ; ecclesia*, *congregation* and not *church*. But Coverdale was not so rigid. In his prologue to the reader, he says : " Be not thou offended, though one call a *scribe* that another calleth a *lawyer;* or *elders*, that another calleth *father and mother ;* or *repentance*, that another calleth *penaunce* or *amendment*. For, yf thou be not deceaved by men's traditions, thou shalt fynde no more dyversitie betwene these terms than betwene foure pens and a grote. And this maner have I used in my translacyon, callying it in some place *penaunce* that in another place I call *repentance* ; and that not only because the interpreters have done so before me, but that the adversaries of the truth may see how that we abhorre not this word *penaunce*, (as they untruly report of us), no more than the interpreters of latyn abhorre *penitere* whan they reade *resipiscere*."[1] What Tyndale almost uniformly translates *repentance*, Coverdale, therefore, translates with indifference, *repentance*, *penance*, and *amendment of life*. In his version of the third chapter of St. Matthew's Gospel, we find all the three renderings: "*Amende youre selves, the kyngdom of heuen is at honde*," verse 2; "*Brynge forth due frutes of penaunce*," verse 8; "*I baptise you with water to repentaunce*," verse 11. Following out the principles advocated in his prologue, Coverdale has also, in one or two instances, used the word *elders*, where strict regard for the original should have required a translator to write *parents*. The phrase, "disobedient to parents," 2 Tim. iii. 2, is paraphrastically rendered by Tyndale, "disobedient to father and mother;" and both loosely and erroneously rendered by Coverdale, "dishobedient to their *elders*."[2] Where the word Cæsar occurs in the Testament, Coverdale translates it *the emperor*, as in Luke, xx. 25 : "Geue then unto the *Emperoure* that which is the *Emperoures*," and in Phil. iv. 22 : "All the sayntes salute you, but especially they that are of the *Emperours* house." He makes free with the title *centurio* also, and instead of being content to put it into the English form of *centurion*, he translates it *captain*.[3]

Among other verbal changes that Coverdale made on Tyndale's translation, some for the better and some for the worse, the following may be mentioned :—the substitution of *married* for *betrothed*, Mat. i. 18 ; of *Lord, Lord*, for *Master, Master*,

---

[1] A very curious use of the word *grace* occurs in Coverdale's Bible:—"The ungodly (though he haue receaued *grace*) yet lerneth he not rightuousnesse," Is. xxvi. 10.

[2] The word *fore-elders* in the sense of ancestors, occurs in Coverdale's Bible : as in Prov. xxii. 28, "Thou shalt not remoue the lande marcke, which thy fore-elders haue sett "; and Ecclasiasticus, (Apocrypha) xliv. 1, "Let us commende the noble famous men, and the generation of our fore-elders and fathers." See *Bishops' Bible* also.

[3] In his translation of *Centurio*, Coverdale is more consistent than Tyndale. The latter sometimes renders the word *centurion*, sometimes *captain*, and sometimes *under captain*. Tyndale, also, uses the word *Cæsar* in one place, Luke xx, and *emperor* in another, Phil. iv.

Mat. vii. 21; of *shew breds* for *halowed loves*, Mat. xii. 4; of *the enemy* for *the envious man*, Mat. xiii. 28; of *avoyde* for *take thy self away*, Mat. xxi. 21; of *two murderers* for *two theves*, Mat. xxvii. 38; of *helped* for *saved*, Mat. xxvii. 42; of *ungrekes* for *no Greeks*, Rom. i. 13; of *no respecte of personnes* for *partialy'c*, Rom. ii. 11; of we *holde*, for we *suppose* that a man is justified by faith, Rom. iii. 28; of *letteth us not come to confusion*, for *maketh not ashamed*, Rom. v. 5; of *ministers* for *deacons*, Phil. i. 1; of *the more haistely*, for *diligentliar*, Phil. ii. 28: of *maketh you the surer*, for *to you it is a sure thynge*, Phil. iii. 1; of *manerly*, for *honestly aparelled*, 1 Tim. iii. 2.

It is only by means of parallel columns that larger variations of rendering can be shown; and with the view of exhibiting to the eye some of the changes of more than one word that Coverdale made on Tyndale's translation, a few entire sentences, from one of the four Gospels in each version, shall here be set opposite one another, with differentiations italicised :—

TYNDALE, 1534.	COVERDALE, 1535.
Mat. xiii. 57.—And they were offended by him. Then Jesus said to them, A Prophet is not without honour, save in his awne countre and among his awne *kynne*.	Mat. xiii. 57.—And they were offended *at* him. *But* Jesus sayde unto them, A Prophet is *nowhere lesse sett by than at home* and amonge his owne.
Mat. xxii. 10.—The weddinge was furnysshed with guestes.	Mat. xxii. 10.—The *tables were all full*.
Mat. xxvi. 8.—When his disciples saw that, they had indignacion, sayinge, what neded this wast?	Mat. xxvi. 8.—When his disciples saw that, they *diszdayned, and sayde, Where to serveth* this waist?
Mat. xxvii. 6.—And the chefe prestes toke the sylver plattes, and sayd, It is not lawfull *for* to put them in to the treasury, because it is the pryce of bloud.	Mat. xxvii. 6.—*So the hye* prestes toke the sylver *pens*, and sayde, It is not lawfull to put them in to the *Gods chest, for* it is *bloudmoney*.
Mat. xxvii. 24.—When Pilate sawe that he prevayled nothinge, but that more busines was made, he toke water and wasshed his hondes before the people, sayinge, I am innocent of the bloud of this juste person, *and that* ye shall se.	Mat. xxvii. 24.—*So* whan Pilate sawe, that he *could not helpe*, but that *there* was *a greater uproure*, he toke water, and waszhed his handes before the people, *and sayde*, I am *ungiltie* of the bloud of this *righteous man*. *Se ye thereto*.
Mat. xxviii. 1.—The Sabboth daye at even which dauneth the morowe after the Sabboth, Mary Magdalene and the other Mary came to se the sepulchre.	Mat. xxviii. 1.—*Upon the euenynge of* the Sabbath *holydaye*, which dawneth the morow *of the first daye of the Sabbathes*, came Mary Magdalene, etc., etc.
Mat. xxviii. 9.—And as they went to tell his disciples, beholde, Jesus met them, sayinge, All hayle.	Mat. xxviii. 9.—And as they *were going* to tell his disciples, beholde, Jesus met them, *and sayde, God spede you*.
Mat. xxviii. 14.—And if this come to the rulers eares, we wyll pease him, and save you harmles.	Mat. xxviii. 14.—And yf this come to the *debytes* eares, we wyll *styll* him, and bringe it so to passe that ye shall be safe.

A reference to the authorised and revised versions of the English Testament will show that more of Tyndale's original renderings than of Coverdale's variations, in the above table, have been retained in subsequent translations of the Bible. It may be admitted that many of Coverdale's changes on Tyndale's text are improvements; but it will probably be found that over the whole Testament, as well as in the above quoted verses, more of the renderings of Tyndale which Coverdale attempted to improve have, by subsequent revisers, been retained than have been displaced.[1]

Considering that Coverdale confessedly translated the Scriptures "out of Douche and Latyn in to English," it may be presumed that the changes he made on Tyndale's version of the New Testament were inspired by Dutch and Latin readings. It may interest us to ascertain what particular translations in Latin and Dutch gave most inspiration to Coverdale's renderings. The versions we should think he was most likely to have consulted and followed were the Vulgate, the translation in Latin by Erasmus, and the translation in Dutch (German) by Luther. Taking for examination a chapter at random, Luke xxiii., and comparing Tyndale's and Coverdale's renderings of it, it will be found that, exclusive of minor variations of particles, such as *and, but, then,* etc., there are about thirty-three places in which Coverdale departs, more or less, from the text of Tyndale. In several of these places the translation by Coverdale harmonises with the Latin of both Erasmus and the Vulgate; as in v. 2, where *give tribute* is substituted for *pay tribute;* in v. 23, where *lay still upon him* is put for *cried;* and in v. 25, where *do with him what they would* is changed into *their will.* But the most distinctive of the changes that Coverdale made on the text of Tyndale—such as, the *emperor* for *Cæsar,* v. 2; *none of the causes* for *no fault,* v. 14; *after the custom of the feast* for *at that feast,* v. 17; *the time will come* for *the days will come,* v. 29; *rent in two* for *rent even through,* v. 45; *stode by and beheld* for *came together at that sight,* v. 48—could not have been inspired by either of the two Latin versions, and it is remarkable that these specially distinctive

---

[2] A very unhappy rendering of Coverdale's is, Rom. xi. 16: "Yf the begynnynge be holy, then is all the dowe holy."

renderings of Coverdale's are all literal translations of Luther's version in German. And it is no less noteworthy that of all the thirty-three instances in which Coverdale has made amendments on the translation by Tyndale there is only one in which his rendering does not accord with Luther's. That one rendering, of which no account is given in any of the three named Latin and Dutch versions, is "here and there in all the londe of Jewry," v. 5, for "throughout all Jewry." It seems clear, therefore, that Luther's Dutch version contains the text from which Coverdale made his translation of the New Testament;[1] and that all the use he could have made of either the Vulgate or the Latin version by Erasmus was merely in the way of reference.

This conclusion is confirmed by an examination of the more notable changes that Coverdale made on Tyndale's renderings. Of the twenty-one mentioned in the paragraphs beginning on page 107, there are only two, *married* for *betrothed*, Mat. i. 8, and *amende yourselves* for *repent*, Mat. iii. 2, that do not correspond with the Dutch text in Luther's Bible. And not only are the other nineteen renderings of Coverdale's consistent with Luther's version, but many of them, such as *two murderers* for *two theves*, Mat. xxvii. 38; *ungrekes* for *no Grekes*, Rom. i. 13; *maketh you the surer* for *to you it is a sure thing*, Phil. iii. 1; *mannerly* for *honestly apparelled*, 1 Tim. iii. 2, were obviously inspired by the German Reformer. Of Coverdale's variations from Tyndale, again, that appear in the eight verses in the parallel columns on page 109, the most striking are literal renderings of their counterparts in Luther's Testament, and they bear no affinity to the words in either the Vulgate or the Latin version by Erasmus. The passages to which this remark specially applies are: "A prophet is nowhere lesse set by than at home," Mat. xiii. 57; "The tables were all full," Mat. xxii. 10; "It is not lawful to put them into the God's chest, for it is blood-money," Mat. xxviii. 6; "Bring it to pass that ye shall be safe," Mat. xxviii. 14.

---

[1] "*Seems* clear." As the Zurich version followed Luther's very closely in the New Testament, Coverdale may have, for anything shown above, translated direct from that version.

Of Dutch and Latin translations of the Bible, from which Coverdale might have drawn his English version of the Old Testament, there were several. Those that, from the frequency with which they are spoken of by historians of the Bible, may occur to us most readily are the German translation by Luther, the Vulgate, and the Latin translation by Pagninus. Between Coverdale's English and Luther's German version of the Old Testament there are many instances of more than accidental correspondence, but the correspondence between these two versions is by no means so all-pervading in the Old Testament as in the New. Among the notable readings and renderings in Coverdale's Old Testament which have been, or will in succeeding pages be, referred to in this chapter, the following may be specified as according literally with the German translation by Luther: "It goeth all over me," (all these things are against me), Gen. xlii. 36; "Reuben stode hye in his awne consayte," (for the divisions of Reuben there were great thoughts of heart), Judges v. 15; "He knewe how shamefully his children behaued themselues and hath not once loked sowerly therto," (he restrained them not), 1 Sam. iii. 13; "O, who will geve my heade water ynough, (oh, that my head were waters), Jer. ix. 1; "After the King had clipte his shepe," (after the king's mowings), Amos vii. 1. The following, again, have no correspondence with the words in Luther's translation, but harmonise with the readings in the Vulgate: "David stackered towards the dores of the gate" (scrabbled on the doors of the gate), 1 Sam. xxi. 13; "A styll softe hissing" (a still small voice), 1 Kings xix. 12; "between the mawe and the lungs" (between the joints of the harness), 1 Kings xxii. 34; "hath comprehended all the earth of the world in thre fyngers" (hath comprehended the dust of the earth in a measure), Is. xl. 12; "A cake of bread and else no dight meate" (a piece of bread out of the baker's street), Jer. xxxvii. 21. There are other distinctive readings and renderings in Coverdale's Bible, however, for which no warrant can be found in either Luther's translation or the Vulgate. In some of these there is an echo of the Latin version by Pagninus, as in Jer. viii. 22, "There is no more triacle at Galaad," *theriaca non est in Gilead*; and in

Psal. xlii. 7, "One depe calleth another with the voyse of thy whystles," *vorago voraginem vocat ad sonitum fistularum tuarum.*[1] But in Coverdale's Old Testament there are other peculiar readings and renderings still, which do not harmonise with their counterparts in either Luther's Bible, the Vulgate, or the Latin translation by Pagninus. Of these may be mentioned: "His cheeks were not fallen" (his natural force was not abated), Deut. xxxiv. 7; "A cock ready to fight" (a grey hound), Prov. xxx. 31; "A vineyard of Muscatel" (a vineyard of red wine), Is. xxvii. 2; "He shall be the most symple and despised of all" (he is despised and rejected of men), Is. liii. 3; "Come, let us cut out his tongue" (come, let us smite him with the tongue), Jer. xviii. 18; "The boyes are hanged up upon trees" (the children fell under the wood), Lam. v. 13. There must have been some other Dutch or Latin version, therefore, from which Coverdale drew largely in his translation of the Old Testament. One Dutch version, besides Luther's, that was in high repute in the days of Coverdale, was known by the name of the Zurich Bible. It was a translation into German by the preachers of Zurich, and was published at Zurich in 1530. And that this German-Swiss translation was the version that Coverdale chiefly followed in his rendering of the Old Testament, appears from the following remarks of Dr. Moulton's:—

"In the Pentateuch and in the New Testament the Swiss translators, to a very large extent, followed Luther, merely adapting his work to the dialect of their country. In the prophets and some other books of the Old Testament, the Zurich Bible differs widely from Luther's; and here Coverdale's preference for the Swiss version is strongly marked. . . Dr. Ginsburg, in his *Commentary on Ecclesiastes*, gives a number of passages in which Coverdale has literally followed the Zurich Bible, and remarks that in this book of Scripture the instances in which Coverdale follows the Vulgate and Luther are comparatively few. Professor Westcott goes carefully into this subject. He examined fifty-five passages in which Coverdale has shown some doubt as to the meaning, and has therefore given one interpretation in the text and an alternative in the margin. Here then, reckoning text and margin, we have more than one hundred renderings to trace. Dr. Westcott discovers almost all in one or more of the following five versions, the Vulgate, Pagninus's Latin version, Luther, the Zurich Bible, and Tyndale. In seven instances only does he not identify the rendering. A more recent examination of early editions of the two German versions has brought to light this small remainder, so that we have now presumptive evidence that the sources of Coverdale's work are completely before us."

---

[1] *Fistula*, a shepherd's pipe.

Coverdale's translation was dedicated to Henry VIII., as "defendour of the fayth, and under God the chefe and suppreme heade of the Church of Englonde." This was both right and politic. To the dedication was prefixed a profuse invocation of divine blessings on the King, in the following Scriptural terms: "The ryght and just administracyon of the lawes that God gave unto Moses and unto Josua; the testimonye of faythfulnes that God gaue of Dauid: the plenteous abundaunce of wysdome that God gaue unto Salomon: the lucky and prosperous age, with the multiplicacyon of sede, which God gave unto Abraham and Sara his wyfe: be geven unto you most gracyous Prynce, with your dearest just wyfe, and most vertuous Pryncesse, Queen Anne. Amen." In the dedication itself, Coverdale refers in grateful language to a most blessed change that had recently been witnessed in England. The word of God, he said, is no longer "clene shut up, depressed, cast asyde, and put out of remembraunce." The King has commanded, like Josias of old, that the Scriptures "shulde be redde and taught unto all the people." And so, Coverdale adds: "I thought it my dutye, and to belong unto my allegiaunce, when I had translated this Bible, not only to dedicate this translacyon unto your highnesse, but wholy to comytte it unto the same: to the intent that yf any thynge therin be translated amysse (for in many things we fayle, euen when we thinke to be sure) it may stonde in your graces hondes, to correcte it, to amende it, to improve it, yee and clene to rejecte it, yf your godly wysdome shall thynke it necessary." A good deal of diplomacy was, nevertheless, required to procure, through the King, free course for the new translation. Without entering into the details of that diplomacy, it will suffice to say here that not only was Coverdale's Bible not seized and burned, but it was allowed to be openly circulated. An edition, published in 1537, was declared on the title page to be "sett forth with the Kynges most gracious license."

In 1537, there appeared another notable version of the Bible in English. The name of the translator was given on the title page as Thomas Matthew. That, however, was a pseudonym, and the real name of the person responsible for the work was

John Rogers. This John Rogers was Tyndale's literary executor: and the Bible he published was not a new and an original translation, but only a well edited version of other men's translations. It comprised, or substantially comprised, a reprint of Tyndale's Testament and Pentateuch; a first print of the translations Tyndale left behind him in manuscript: and a reprint from Coverdale's Bible, of the remanent portion of Scripture, from Ezra to Malachi. Like Coverdale's translation, this of Matthew's was protected by Royal License.[1] The protection was obtained at the suit of Cranmer, who, in 1534, had tried but failed to induce the bishops to undertake a translation of the Bible. Having failed in that endeavour, Cranmer, in 1537, wrote to Cromwell, that it would be well if Matthew's book were shown to the King, and permission craved for its free circulation, "until such time that we bishops shall set forth a better translation, which I think will not be till a day after doomsday." As a translation, Matthew's Bible was in some respects, of higher merit than Coverdale's; but it was accompanied by prologues and notes of Matthew's own, which were too fierce and free to be palatable to all sorts of people. Like his master Tyndale, Matthew (or Rogers) was a zealous and an extreme Reformer; and as Tyndale, in 1536, was strangled and burnt by Churchmen on the continent, so had Rogers the uncoveted honour of being burned at Smithfield, in 1555, during the persecution of Protestants by Mary of England.

A few specimens of his annotations will show what kind of bread it was that Rogers gave the people of England to eat with the pure milk of the word. Commenting on Isaiah lviii. 3, "wherefore have we fasted and thou seest not," Rogers remarks: "The fast remayneth yet amonge ye Christen, for true chastenynge of the body and abstenynge from vice will we yet nether understande nor heare of: but still thinke with the Jews both that we do God a great pleasure when we fast, and

---

[1] The licensing of Matthew's Bible was enough to have waked the ashes of Tyndale into laughter. Matthew's Bible was just a revised edition of Tyndale's translations, (which had been so fiercely denounced), with a new part, from Ezra to Malachi, added! How little do some people know what they condemn and what they commend!

also that we then fast when we absteyne from one thynge, and fill our belyes with another." Good Catholics who thought they did God service by subjecting themselves to an alterative diet on Fridays could not but bristle at such reflections as these on their religious customs. In some other notes, Rogers made observations on the office and the modern practices of bishops, which must have been very annoying to the mitred occupants of episcopal sees. Comparing Titus i. 5, "I left the in Crete that thou shuldest . . . ordeyne *elders* in every citie," with Titus i. 7, "a bisshoppe must be fautelesse," he took occasion to lay downe the Presbyterian doctrine that, "Bisshopes and elders is all one, an officer chosen to governe the congregation in doctryne and lyuyng."[1] On 1 Tim. iii. 1, "Yf a man covet the office of a bysshope he desyreth a good worke," Rogers remarks that, "Bysshoppe is as moche to say, as a sear to, a taker heade to, or an ouer sear; which when he desyreth to feade Christes flocke with the fode of healeth, that is, with his holy worde, as the bysshopes dyd in Paul's tyme, desyreth a good worcke, and the very office of a bysshope. But he that desyreth honoure; gapeth for lucre; thirsteth greate rentes; seketh preeminence, pompe, dominion; coveteth abundance of all thinges without want, rest and hertes ease, castelles, parckes, lordshyppes, yerldomes, etc., desyre not a worcke, moch lesse a good worcke." On the subjects of faith, holy life, and repentance, Rogers shewed, by his notes, that he was in full touch with the most advanced protestantism. He describes faith, Mat. ix. 2, as "the rightwesnes of a christen man, which setteth at peace the conscience, and receaveth the herytage euerlastynge." He declares that reward, Mat. v. 12, "is geven to men for their worcke, but is not due to the worcke." And he says that to repent, Mat. iv. 17, "is to forthynck, and to leve and chaunge the euell lyfe for the loue of virtue and hate of synne." His scholastic annotations are sometimes instructive, and when not instructive they are sometimes entertaining, which is almost better. The locusts that furnished fare for John the Baptist

---

[1] Coverdale and the Bishops had their episcopal revenge for this outrage on sacerdotal traditions. In 1 Tim. iii. 8, and elsewhere, they give to *deacons* the designation of *ministers*.

were, he tells his readers, "certen beastes which the people of Parthia and of Ethiopia did comenly use to eate, . . . yet do some holde opinion that they be the toppes or, as we call them, the buddes of treas or frutes."[1] The vipers again, to whom Jesus compared the men of the evil generation in which he lived on earth, were, "certen serpentes that breake their mothers belyes at their byrth, and so kil them."

Neither Coverdale's nor Matthew's Bible was altogether satisfactory. Both seemed capable of improvement. "The boldness of the pseudo-Matthew," says Dr. Plumptre, "had frightened the ecclesiastical world from its propriety, and Coverdale's version was too inaccurate to keep its ground." It was necessary, therefore, that an effort should be made to meet a widely felt want, by a revision of all existing translations. One person induced to enter on this undertaking was Richard Taverner: and notwithstanding certain stories told of him to his literary discredit, he had some considerable qualifications for the work. He was an excellent Greek scholar, and was quite competent, therefore, to correct the translation of the New Testament wherever it required amendment. His competency to revise the translation of the Old Testament has not been so freely acknowledged. Some of his *corrections* there have been cited by critics as proofs that " he knew no Hebrew."[2] One virtue, however, he is well entitled to be credited with. He had a clear and just sense of the arduousness of his task. "The prynters," he says in his dedication, "were very desirous to have the Byble come forth as faultlesse and emendatly as the shortness of tyme for the recognysing of the same would require, and they desyred me, for default of a better learned, diligently to overloke and peruse the hole copy, and in case I shold fynd any notable default that neded correction, to amende the same according to the true exemplars." The re-

---

[1] Wyclif's translation of Mat. iii. 4, is "his mete was hony soukis (honey-suckles) and hony of the wode."

[2] Mombert, p. 198. In Coverdale's Bible we read, Gen. xlix. 6, "they houghed an oxe." Taverner changed this into "they threw down the walls of the city." Our authorised version retains Taverner's reading, with a marginal note, "or houghed oxen." The revised version has restored Coverdale's reading, and in the margin makes no reference to a wall.

vision he undertook was not intended to be exhaustive and final. It was only "notable defaults" he was desired to amend. And it was absurd, he said, for any one to suppose that a faultless translation of the Bible could be made in a year's time by any single man. "It is a worke," were his words, "of so great difficultie so absolutely to translate the holie Bible that it be faultlesse that I feared it could scarce be done of one or two persons, but rather requyred both a deeper conferryng of many learned wittes together, and also a juster tyme and longer leysure." [1]

On subsequent versions of the Bible in English Taverner's labours had very little influence. His revision was, nevertheless, a work of some merit. "The reviser's scholarship," says Dr. Eadie, "appears on every page in many minute touches." Some other reviewers of his Bible are less eulogistic. "His recognition (that is revision) in the Old Testament consisted mainly," says Dr. Mombert, "in suppressing many of Rogers' notes, in correcting Rogers' English by the Vulgate, and in endeavouring to give a clear sense to the text. His *improvements* in the Old Testament are, therefore, with few exceptions, of a very doubtful character. In the New Testament, where his knowledge of Greek stood him in good stead, the changes introduced are at once more numerous, and often also felicitous . . . although through haste he has left uncorrected errors, which could not have escaped him, if he had paid greater attention to his work." [2]

As specimens of the changes that Taverner made on Tyndale's renderings, the

---

[1] A story told of Taverner is that, on one occasion, when over three score years old, he went with a gold chain about his neck and a sword by his side, to preach to a company of young scholars, and commenced his discourse in the following terms :—"Arriving at the Mount of St. Mary's, in the stony cage where I now stand, I have brought you some fine biscuits, baked in the oven of charity, and carefully conserved for the chickens of the church, the sparrows of the spirit, and the sweet swallows of salvation." Such a story would need to be well authenticated before it is believed ; and with the literary structure of the above quoted sentence, there is nothing to correspond in either Taverner's "recognition" of the Bible or in his dedication of that work.

[2] Dr. Westcott remarks that Taverner probably undertook a revision of the New Testament, "for which his scholarship fitted him, first : and only afterwards extended his labours to the Old Testament, for which he had no special aptitude."

following may be quoted :—" He had never a word to say," Mat. xxii. 12, for "he was even speechless"; "Stopped the Sadducees mouths," Mat. xxii. 34, for "put the Sadducees to silence"; "Move," Mat. xxiii. 4, for "Heave" at them with one of their fyngers; "Shall hew him," Mat. xxiv. 51, for "will divide him"; "When they had given praises," Mat. xxvi. 30, for "said grace"; "Which was deare to him," Luke vii. 2, for "whom he made moche of"; "bier," Luke vii. 14, for "coffin"; "Be not carried in the clouds," Luke xii. 29, for "neither climb ye up on high," (be not of doubtful mind—*A. V.*); "Hath enfraunchised," Rom. viii. 2, for "hath delivered" me from the law of sin; "Fordelles unto me," Phil. iii. 7, for "vauntage unto me"; and "He is our mercy-stock," 1 John, ii. 2, for "he it is that obtaineth grace." Taverner's adherence to the English text of Tyndale, however, is much more noticeable and strange than his occasional departures from it. In 1 Tim. vi. 17, the rendering of both Tyndale and Taverner is— "Charge them that are ryche in this world that they be not *exceedynge wyse*."

As the contents and history of Matthew's Bible came to be more fully known, the advisers of the King realised the unpleasant fact that, in procuring for it a royal license, they had befooled his majesty. Matthew's Bible contained a reprint, very little altered, of Tyndale's Testament and Tyndale's Pentateuch; and Matthew's own annotations were more offensive than anything Tyndale had ever penned. In regard both to Tyndale and Tyndale's Testament, the King had put his royal judgment on public record. "With the deliberate advice" of the reverend fathers of the spiritualty, he had ordered Tyndale's Testament to be burned as "an untrue translation." Several years later, he had employed an agent on the Continent to search for Tyndale, and apprehend him as a broacher of heresies and seditions. It was extremely awkward for Henry's advisers, therefore, that they had persuaded him to grant licence, unawares, for the circulation of what were practically Tyndale's Testament and Tyndale's other translations of Scripture. The license had been procured by Cromwell, the Chief Secretary of State, at the suit of Cranmer, Archbishop of Canterbury. On discovering the real import of this act, Cromwell must have felt it necessary to minimise the effects of the license as quickly and quietly as possible. He resolved, therefore, to supersede Matthew's Bible by a new version, of which Matthew's Bible should be in part the basis, but from which all Matthew's polemical annotations should be excluded, and in which all Matthew's mistranslations should be corrected. The person to whom he committed the execution of this project was Coverdale, who had already given proof of his skill and taste in translating and of his moderation and courtesy in the treatment of ecclesiastical questions.

For some reason or other, it was determined that the printing of the new version should be executed in Paris. Good paper and good types, it was alleged, could easily be had there; and possibly it was thought that the work would be less subject to interference there than in England. The sanction of the French King was accordingly solicited and obtained, and the work proceeded. Signs of ill-affected espionage, however, were soon descried; and, eventually, an order was issued by the inquisitor-general to stop the work and seize whatever papers were already printed. On hearing of this edict, Coverdale and his printer, Grafton, took flight and left behind them all of their property that was confiscated. The printed sheets, which were to have been "burned in the place Maubert," were saved by a smart haberdasher, who bought them for paper "to lay caps in," and then consigned them to England in four large vats. People in those days of adventure and hazard were not much disconcerted by small mishaps. Coverdale and Grafton were, therefore, soon at their work again in London; and in April 1539, a few weeks or months before the issue of Taverner's Bible, the new version was in the hands of the public.

On account of its large dimensions and massy appearance, this new version of the Scriptures in English, which was designed and expected so to supersede all previous versions, whether licensed or unlicensed, as virtually to put them out of the market, obtained the honourable name of "The Great Bible." By that name it is still known; and by that name it will be convenient for us to designate not only the first edition, but all subsequent editions of the same version. In one of these subsequent editions, published in 1540, there is a long and valuable prologue by Cranmer. For this reason, it has been called Cranmer's Bible, and so have all later editions that contain the Archbishop's prologue. But the title is not a just one. If any person's name is to be associated with the Great Bible, it should be Coverdale's. He alone is responsible for the English text. But it cannot be called Coverdale's Bible, in the same sense as the Bible formerly published by him was called his. That former version was Coverdale's own translation of the Bible, from the Latin and Dutch. The Great Bible was only a revised version, by Coverdale, of his own and other people's translations. The revision, nevertheless, was no mean work. The Hebrew and Greek texts were examined; the readings and renderings of the best translations in Latin and German were considered; the true meaning of the original was thereafter determined according to the light of the times; and the diction of former versions in English was smoothed and perfected. To what extent the corrections and amendments thus made, by Coverdale, on the earlier versions of the English Bible were real improvements, is a matter on which opinion may be divided.[1]

In order that the Great Bible might achieve the object for which its publication was designed—of superseding and driving out of the market all former licensed versions of the Scriptures—a royal order was issued (at Cromwell's instance we may be sure), while the printing was going on at Paris, that every clergyman in England should " provide on this side the feast of—next commyng, one boke of the whole Bible of the *largest* volume in Englysche, and have the same sett up in summe convenient place within the churche that he has the cure of, whereat his parishners may most commodiously resort to the same and rede yt." This injunction was not universally honoured by the clergy. But it was partially obeyed, and in a large number of churches, Bibles were set up for free and public reading. In some churches, St. Paul's in London for example, there were as many as six copies of the Bible located; and his-

---

[1] The under-noted amendments introduced by Coverdale into the Great Bible, may strike the English reader as somewhat odd and lame versions of Scripture :— " Made us sytte together with him amonge them of heaven in Christ Jesus," Eph. ii. 6 ; " Having shoes on your feet, that ye may be prepared for the gospell of peace," Eph. vi. 15 ; " As new borne babes, desyre ye the mylke (not of the body but of the soule) which is without disceate," 1 Pet. ii. 2 ; " Seyng that we have soch an offyce, even as God hath hed mercy on us, we go not out of kynde," 2 Cor. iv. 1.

torians relate, that "it was wonderful to see with what joy this book of God was received, not only among the learneder sort and those that were noted for lovers of the Reformation, but generally all England over, among the vulgar and common people. Everybody, that could, bought the book, or busily read it, or got others to read it to them, if they could not themselves, and divers elderly people learned to read on purpose."[1]

This was not all that Cromwell did to ensure for the Great Bible a preference and pre-eminence over other Bibles in English. He contrived, in Nov. 1539, to obtain for himself a Royal patent, "to take special care and charge that no manner of persone or persones within this our realme shall enterprise, attempt, or sett in hand, to print any Bible in the English tonge of any manner of volume, during the space of fyve yeres next ensuying after the date hereof, but only such as shall (by him) be deputied, assignid, and admitted." This patent put it in Cromwell's power to prevent for five years the publication in England of any English version of the Scriptures except the Great Bible.

In the five years between 1535 and 1539 there were thus put into the hands of the English people no fewer than four translations of the Bible into English, viz., Coverdale's, Matthew's or Rogers', Taverner's, and the Great Bible.[2] There was a

---

[1] The privilege procured for the people was, in some instances, abused. Complaints were heard that "people read mostly during service and sermon," shewing, thereby, in their zeal for the word, contempt for the worship of God. How ignorant of the Bible the very clergy were, may be gathered from the fact, that in May 1542, Bonner thought it necessary to issue the following order:—"By the authority givin to me of God . . . I exhort, require, and command that every parson, vicar and curat shall read over and diligently study every day one chapter of the Bible . . . proceeding from . . . the beginning of the gospel of Matthew to the end of the New Testament : : . . and to come to the rehearsal and recital thereof, at all such times, as they or any of them shall be commanded by me, or any of my officers or deputies."—*Eadie*, Vol. I. p. 400-1.

[2] In some books, such as Adam Clarke's Commentary, reference is made to Becke's Bible and Carmarden's Bible, as if they were translations of Becke's and Carmarden's own. Becke's Bible was simply a reprint of Taverner's in 1549, with dedication to the King by Becke, and "supputation of the yeares and time from Adam unto Christe," by the same person. Carmarden's Bible, again, was a reprint, at Rouen in 1566, of the Great Bible, "at the cost and charges of Richard Carmarden." *Lewis*, p. 178 and 214.

In the Ewing Collection of Bibles in the Glasgow University Library, there is

plethora of Bibles in those days, and there was some advantage in that. People became curious to see wherein translations differed, and by comparing different versions they made themselves well acquainted with the contents of Scripture. Each of the four versions has still for us a special interest. Each was the outcome of an effort to give to the English people a true account of the word of God, on which so many current dogmas and practices in those days were said by Churchmen to be founded. Each was the work of a Reformer. Each was a material contribution to the Reformation; and between them they made the Reformation in England complete. But while each of these Bibles has for us a special interest, the Great Bible has most. It was the culmination of all the work in English Bible-making that had been going on from the day that Tyndale set about his translation of the New Testament. And not only does it represent the final shape that the Bible of the English Reformers assumed; but, down to 1662, it supplied the Church of England, in her Prayer-book, with the lessons to be read in all her acts of divine service. And to this day, part of the Great Bible lives in the Prayer-book of the Church of England. The Psalter there is just the version of the Psalms given in the Great Bible; and from the Great Bible also are taken words of Scripture to be repeated in the office of communion.

To determine the merits and demerits of the Great Bible, as a translation of Scripture, it will be necessary to divide it into three parts, and to examine each part separately. The three parts into which, for this end, the Great Bible must be divided, are the New Testament, the Old Testament from Genesis to Chronicles inclusive, and the Old Testament from Ezra to Malachi. And the questions we have to consider are, whether Coverdale in the Great Bible mainly follows his own or Tyndale's version of the New Testament, whether he mainly

---

another edition of the English Bible that bears Becke's name. This is a revision of "Taverner's Recognition . . . (called Matthew's translation on the title page), printed by John Daye in 1551." (Notice of Ewing Collection, etc., by James Lymburn, Librarian, 1888).

follows his own or Matthew's translation of the first part of the Old Testament, and how far in the second part of the Old Testament he deviates from his own former version printed in 1535. And as the Great Bible passed through several editions which embodied considerable variations,[1] it must be stated here that while in the New Testament our references shall be to the 1539 edition as reprinted in Bagster's Hexapla, our quotations of the Old Testament shall be taken from the edition issued by Grafton in 1541.[2]

---

[1] To speak only of the two editions, 1539 and April 1540, the following, among scores of other, instances of differentiation will be found in the volumes of Westcott, Eadie, Mombert, etc. :—

Eccles. xi. 1. Sende thy vitayles ouer the waters, and so shalt thou fynde them after many days. 1539.
,, ,, Lay thy bread upon weate faces, and so shalt thou fynde after many days. 1540.
Is. liii. 5. The pain of our punishment. 1539.
,, ,, The chastisement of our peace. 1540.
Joel i. 18. O what a syghynge make the cuell! 1539.
,, ,, O what a syghynge make the kyne! 1540.
Nahum ii. 3. His archers are not well deckte and trimmed. 1539.
,, ,, His spere shafts are soked in venom. 1540.
2 Cor. ix. 6. Soweth plenteously shall reap. 1539.
,, ,, Soweth in giving largely and freely shall reap. 1540.
Gal. i. 10. Speak unto men. 1539. Persuade men. 1540.
Jas. i. 13. For God cannot tempt unto evil, because he tempteth no man. 1539. For as God cannot be tempted with evil, so neither he himself tempteth any man. 1540.
Jas. v. 17. A man mortal. 1539. A man under infirmities. 1540.
Jude 12. Feeding themselves. 1539. Living lawless and after their own pleasures. 1540.

To these may be added :—

1 Cor. iv. 9. Us (whych are Apostles) for the lowest of all. 1539
,, ,, Us (whych are the last Apostles). 1541 (Nov. 1540).

[2] Grafton's reprint, 1541, from which quotations in this chapter are taken, is not, although it was "oversene and perused" by Tunstall and Heath, free from errata. In the heading of Gen. xxxix., Joseph is said to have been tempted by *Pharaoh's wife*. The following readings I found on reference to other editions in the Library of Glasgow University are misprints :—"He that hath *no* respecte unto the cloudes shall not reape," Eccles. xi. 4; "Heare me, O ye that are of an hye stomacke but *are* (instead of *farre*) from righteousness," Is. xlvi. 12; "A thre-fold *gable* (cable) is not easily broken," Eccles. iv. 12; "All nations shall *preach* (press) unto him," Is. ii. 2; "Yea, and thou Juda kepest an *harlotte* (harvest) for thyself," Hos. vi. 11; "*Who* (woe) shall come to them when I departe from them," Hos. ix. 12.

One would naturally expect that the Great Bible should, in that portion which comprises the New Testament, bear the impress of Coverdale's translation, 1535, more than of Tyndale's, 1534. But it does not. The Great Bible follows Tyndale's version much more closely than Coverdale's. In the paragraphs that begin on page 107 in this chapter, there are specified twenty-one cases of verbal difference between Coverdale's and Tyndale's renderings. In twelve of these cases, the renderings in the Great Bible agree with Tyndale's, and in only six with Coverdale's. In the parallel columns on page 109, there are indicated by italics thirty-three points of difference between the translations of Coverdale and Tyndale; and on twenty-three of these points the Great Bible agrees with Tyndale's Testament, and on four only with Coverdale's first translation. It is stated, also, on page 110 that an examination of Coverdale's and Tyndale's version of the twenty-third chapter of St. Luke's Gospel reveals thirty-three places in which the two translations diverge more or less.[1] In twenty-eight of these places Tyndale's renderings (with, in one or two instances, slight modifications) have been retained in the Great Bible.

The strange fact comes out, therefore, that in the great Bible Coverdale exalts the New Testament renderings of Tyndale above the emendations that he himself made of them in 1535. Some of these emendations, however, are still happily preserved. One verse that in Tyndale's Testament reads very awkwardly is Rom. xiv. 7—"None of us lyveth his awne servant: nether doeth eny of us dye his awne servant." Coverdale, in 1535, changed this crudely worded statement into—"None of us lyueth to himselfe, and no man dieth to himselfe;" and he transferred this amendment,[2] into the Great

---

Also "bleate" for *bleare*, Is. xv. 4; "harvest" for *her nest*, Is. xvi. 2; "theyr measures" for *thre* measures, Is. xl. 12, etc.

[1] In Tyndale's Testament there are several cases of odd spelling, and some of the strangest of these are to be found also in Coverdale's Bible, 1535, and in the Great Bible, 1539. In all the three translations we read, Heb. iv. 12—"The worde of God is quicke . . . and entreth through even unto the divyding of . . . the joyntes and the *mary*."

[2] Almost, but not quite, verbatim. Other amendments of Tyndale's renderings that Coverdale did well to transfer from his own Bible, 1535, to the Great Bible

Bible. What again will strike the English reader as a very odd rendering of Tyndale's is, 1 Cor. ii. 14,—"The naturall man perceaveth not the thinges of the sprete of God. For they are but folyshnes unto him. Nether can he perceave them, because *he* is spretually examined." The last clause of this verse is made by Coverdale, in the Great Bible, to read, "*they* are spiritually examined," which is a proper correction. It is worthy of note, however, that a phrase which appears in Coverdale's own translation, 1535, and was by Coverdale allowed to be superseded in the Great Bible by the expression used in Tyndale's Testament, was restored in the authorised version, 1611, viz., "spiritually *discerned.*" But while Coverdale, as we see, excluded from the Great Bible some renderings in his own translation that were good, he had the bad taste to insert others that were not good. In Acts xx. 7, the Greek Testament contains a conventional phrase, which means "on the first day of the week." The words themselves might be literally translated "upon one of the Sabbath days." Both in his own translation, 1535, and in the Great Bible, 1540, Coverdale has erroneously given the literal, instead of the conventional, rendering of the phrase: so that the early Christians are represented as meeting together for communion on occasional Saturdays, instead of every Sunday.

Of New Testament renderings in the Great Bible, 1539, that exhibit improvement on what preceded them in either Tyn-

---

were :—" Give us this day our daily bread," for *oure dayly breed geve us evermore,* Luke xi. 3; " O ye of lytle faith," for *O ye endued with litell faith,* Luke xii. 28 ; ' It is your father's pleasure to geve you the kingdome," instead of *a kingdom,* Luke xii. 32 ; " Verely this was a righteous man," for *of a surtie this man was perfecte,* Luke xxiii. 47 ; " Bewitched them with sorceries " for "*with sorcery he had mocked them,*" Acts viii. 11 ; " Have they therefore stombled that they shuld utterly fall awaye together," for *shuld but faule only,* Rom. xi. 11; "Stewardes of the secretes of God," for *disposers of the secretes of God,* 1 Cor. iv. 1 ; " Deeth is swallowed up in victory," for *deeth is consumed in to victory,* 1 Cor. xv. 54 ; " Before them all," for *before all men,* Gal. ii. 14 ; " The slaunder of the crosse," for *the offence which the crosse geveth,* Gal. v. 11 ; " Crucified unto me, and I unto the worlde," for *crucified as touching me, and I as concerninge the worlde,*" Gal. vi. 14 ; " Hye mynded," for *exceedinge wyse,* 1 Tim. vi. 17 ; " Watch unto prayer," for *be apte to prayers,*" 1 Peter iv. 7 ; " Ye shall never fall," for *ye shall never erre,* 2 Peter i. 10 ; etc., etc.

dale's Testament or Coverdale's Bible, 1535, the following will serve as instances:—

"Let her alone," for *let her be in reest*, Mark xiv. 6; "Yf they do this in a grene tree," for *if they do this to a grene tree*, Luke xxiii. 31; "He saved other men, let him save himselfe," for *he holpe other men let him helpe himselfe*, Luke xxxii. 35; "There stondeth one amonge you," for *one is come amonge you*, John i. 26; "Taried with them," for *haunted with them* (Tyndale), and *hed his beyinge there with them* (Coverdale), John iii. 22; "At the poynt of death," for *readie to dye* (Tyndale), and *lay deed sicke* (Coverdale), John iv. 47; "Rather geve place unto wrath," for *geve roume unto the wrath of God*, Rom. xii. 19; "man's judgement," for *man's daye*, 1 Cor. iv. 3; "the singlenes that ye had toward Christ," for *the singlenes that is in Christ*, 2 Cor. xi. 3; "Fayth which worketh by loue," for *faith which by love is mighty in operacion*, Gal. v. 6; "By nature," for *naturally*, the children of wrath, Eph. ii. 3; "The thynges which happened unto me," for *my busyness*, chaunced unto the greater furtherance of the gospel, Phil i. 12; "Be lyke mynded," for *drawe one waye*, Phil. ii. 2; "Fathers, provoke not," for fathers, *rate not* your children, Col. iii. 21; "Naked and open," for *naked and bare* unto the eyes of him of whom we speak, Heb. iv. 13; "Obtained a good reporte," for *well reported of*, Heb. xi. 2; "One messe of meate," for *one breakfast*, Heb. xii. 16; "Maruayll not that ye are proued by fyre," for *be not troubled in this heate*, 1 Pet. iv. 12.

As in the New Testament, so in the Old Testament from Genesis to Chronicles inclusive, the Great Bible follows the renderings of Tyndale (or Matthew) much more closely than it follows the renderings given by Coverdale in 1535. Opening the Bible at random, in three places, we light on the following chapters, Exodus xvi., 2 Sam. xxiv., and 2 Kings xi. In the first named of these chapters there are thirty-six verses, in the second twenty-five verses, and in the third twenty-one verses. Out of all these eighty-two verses there is only one in which the words of the Great Bible correspond exactly with those in Coverdale's translation. And in this verse, Ex. xvi. 36, it would have been difficult to devise more renderings than one— "A gomer is the tenthe part of an epha." In every other of the eighty-two verses, there is a divergence more or less great. Sometimes in one verse there are two or three points of difference, and sometimes a verse is different all through. In the greater number of these eighty-two verses, there is more or less difference, also, between the renderings in the Great Bible, and those in Matthew's translation. But there are, in the two last named Bibles, nearly a score of these eighty-two verses that are absolutely identical, and many more verses that differ in only one unimportant word.[1]

To give the reader some definite notion of what is the real amount of agreement and disagreement, sameness and difference, in the texts of the three English Bibles (Coverdale's 1535, Matthew's 1537, and the Great Bible 1540), in that part of the Old Testament which is comprised between Genesis and Chronicles, a short passage from each of the three Bibles shall here be presented in parallel columns.

COVERDALE, 1535.	MATTHEW, 1537.	GREAT BIBLE, 1541.
1 Sam. ii. 30 - 33. — Therefore sayeth the Lorde God of Israel : I have spoken that thy house and thy father's houses houlde walke before me for ever. But now sayeth the Lorde, That be farre fro me. But who so ever honoureth me, him will I honoure also, as for those that despyse me they shall not be regarded. Behold the tyme shal come, that I wyll break thyne arm in two, and the arm of thy father's house, so that there shal no oldeman be in thy house. And thou shalt see thine adversaries in the habitacion, in all the good of Israel, and there shal neuer be olde man in thy father's house. Yet wyll I not rote out euery man of the fro myne altare but that thyne eyes may be consumed, and that thy soul may be sory : and a great multitude of thy house shal dye, when they are come to be men.	1 Sam. ii. 30·33. — Wherefore *the Lorde God of Israel sayth* : I *sayde* that thyne house and *the house of thy* father shulde haue walked before me for ever. But now *the Lorde sayeth*, That be farre from me : for *them that worshippe me I will worshippe, and they* that despyse me shalbe despysed. Beholde the *dayes* will come that I will *cut of* thine arme, and the arme of thy father's house, that there shall *not be an* elder in thine house. And thou shalt see thine *enemy* in the *tabernacle*, in all that shall please Israel, and there shall *not be an elder* in thine house while the world standeth. *Nevertheless I will not destroye all* thy males from my aultare to dase thy sight withal and to *make thyne hert melte*. And *all* the multitude of thyne house shall dye younge.	1 Sam. ii. 30 - 33. — Wherefore the Lord God of Israel sayeth, I *sayde*, that thy house and *the house of thy* father shoulde walke before me for ever. But now *the Lord sayth* That be farre from me : for *them that worship me I wyl worship and they* that despyse me *shall come to shame*. Behold the *dayes* come that I wyll *cutte of* thine arm, and the arm of thy father's house that there shall *not be an* olde man in *thine* house : and thou shalt se thyne *enemy* in the *tabernacle (of the Lord)* and in all the *wealth which (God) shall give* Israel, and there shall *not be an elder* in thyne house *for ever*. *Neverthelesse I wyll not destroy all the males that come of the* fro myne altar. But *to make thyne eyes base*, and *to make thyne herte melte*. And *all they that be multyplyed in* thyne house shall dye, *yf they be* men.

In the passage above cited, it will be observed that there is not, in any of the three Bibles quoted from, either any notable expression, or any great variation of expression. But it would be a mistake to infer that there are no notable expressions to

---

[1] Westcott says that the Great Bible is simply a revision of "the text of Matthew, which was laid down as the basis, by the help of Munster," that is, of Munster's Latin translation.

be found in any of these three English versions of the first part of the Old Testament. In each of these translations the curious reader will find many obsolete words, and obsolete forms of words, with many quaint and antiquated phrases. In Coverdale's Bible, it is said, Ex. xvi. 21, that "as soon as (the manna) was *whote* of the sonne it melted away"; and 31, that the manna "was like Coriander sede and whyte, and had a taist like *symnels* with hony." In the Great Bible, the antiquated term *whote* is not retained; but, in lieu of the modern phrase "melted away," the obsolete inflexion *moulte* is substituted. In the subjoined parallel columns will be found a few of the many peculiar readings and archaic renderings that may be culled from the historical books of the Old Testament in the Reformers' Bibles. And it will be seen that these extracts confirm the conclusion stated in a previous paragraph that the readings and renderings in the Great Bible correspond far more closely with those in Matthew's than with those in Coverdale's version. Taverner's Bible is so nearly a verbatim copy of Matthew's, that its deviations from Matthew's are all that need be noted in the columns below.

COVERDALE, 1535.	MATTHEW, 1537.	GREAT BIBLE, 1540.
Gen. viii. 11.—And she returned unto him aboute the euen tyde: and beholde she had broken of a leafe of an olyve tre and bare it in her *nebb*.	Gen. viii. 11.—And *the doue came* to hym agayne about euentyde: and beholde there was *in hyr mouth* a lefe of an olyve tree, *whyche she had plucked*.	Gen. viii. 11.—And *the doue came* to hym in the euen tyde, and lo *in her mouthe* was an olyue leafe *that she had plucte*.
Gen. xxxix. 2.—And the Lord was with Joseph, in so moch that he became a *luckye* man.	Gen. xxxix. 2.—And the Lorde was with Joseph, and he was a *luckie* felowe, (and he prospered. —*Taverner*.)	Gen. xxxix. 2.—And God was with Joseph and he became a *luckye* man.
Gen. xlii. 36.—*It goeth all ouer me.*	Gen. xlii. 36.—*All these things* fall upon me.	Gen. xlii. 36.—*All these thynges* are agaynst me.[1]
Gen. xlix. 4.— *Thou passeth forth swiftly as the water.* Thou shalt not be the chefest.	Gen. xlix. 4.—As unstable as *water* wast thou, thou shalt therefore not be the chefest.	Gen. xlix. 4.—*Unstable as water* thou shalt not be the chefest.

---

[1] A strange account of Joseph and his brethren is given in the Great Bible, Gen. xliii. 34.—"And they drinking, *were droncke* with him." In Coverdale's own Bible the passage reads—"And they droncke and were mery with him."

Lev. xix. 27.—Ye shal *shave no crowns* upon your heade, nether shalt thou *clyppe thy beerde cleane off.*	Lev. xix. 27.—Ye shall not *rounde the lockes* of your heades, nether shalt thou *marre the tuftes* of thy bearde.	Lev. xix. 27.—Ye shall not *rounde the lockes* of your heades, neyther shalte thou *marre the tuftes* of thy bearde.
Deut. xxxii. 10.—He founde him in the wildernesse, euen in the drye deserte, *where he roared.*	Deut. xxxii. 10.—He founde hym in a *deserte land,* in a *voyde ground,* and a *rorynge wilderness.* (A wild wilderness.—*Taverner*).	Deut. xxxii. 10.—He founde hym in a *deserte lande,* in a *voyde grounde,* and in a *roarynge wildernesse.*
Deut. xxxiv. 7.—His eyes were not dymme, and his *chekes were not fallen.*	Deut. xxxiv. 7.—His eyes were not dym nor hys chekes *abated.*	Deut. xxxiv. 7.—Hys eye was not dymme, nor hys naturall coloure *abated.*
Judges v. 12.—Arise, Barak and *catch him that catched thee,* thou sonne of Abinoam.	Judges v. 12.—U p Barak, and *take thy praye* thou sonne of Abinoam.	Judges v. 12.—Aryse Barak, and *leade the captiuitie captiue,* thou sonne of Abinoam.
Judges v. 15.—Because Ruben stode hye in his awne consayte, and separated him selfe from us.	Judges v. 15.—But in the *devysions* of Rueben were great ymaginations of herte.	Judges v. 15.—When in the *departyng awaye* of Ruben there were great men and wyse of hert.
Judges xv. 5.—And thus he brent the *stoukes* and the standynge corne.	Judges xv. 5.—And burnt up bothe the *reped corne,* and also the standynge.	Judges xv. 5.—And burnt up bothe the *reped corne* and also the standyng.
Judges xv. 8.—He smote them sore both upon the *shulders and loynes.*	Judges xv. 8.—He smote them *legge and thighe* with a mighty plage.	Judges xv. 8.—He smote them *legge and thygh* with a mightye plage.
1 Sam. iii. 13.—He knewe how shamefully his children behaued themselues and hath not once *loked sowerly thereto.*	1 Sam. iii. 13.—For the wickednesse whyche he knoweth, how his sonnes are ungraciouse and he was not wroth therewith (and he chastised them not.—*Taverner*.)	1 Sam. iii. 13.—When the people cursed hys sonnes, for the same wyckednes, he hath not corrected them.
1 Sam. xvii. 4.—Then stepte there forth from amonge the Philistynes a *stoute bolde* man, named Goliath.	1 Sam. xvii. 4.—And then *came* a man, and stode in the myddes *out of the tents* of the Philistines, named Goliath.	1 Sam. xvii. 4.—And there *came* a man betwene them both *out of the tentes* of the Philistines named Goliah.
1 Sam. xviii. 6.—The wemen wente out of all the cities of Israel with songes and daunses to mete kynge Saul with tymbrels, with myrth and with *fyddels.*	1 Sam. xviii. 6.—Women came out of all cyties of Israel *syngyng and daunsynge agaynst* Saul, with tymbrelles, with *ioye* and with *fydilles.*	1 Sam. xviii. 6.—Women came oute of all cyties of Israel *syngynge and daunsynge agaynste* Kynge Saul, and with tymbrels, with *ioye* and with *instruments* of musyke.
1 Sam. xxi. 13.—And Dauid . . . shewed himselfe as he had bene madd in their handes, and *stackered* towarde the dores of the gate, and his *slauerynges ranne* downe his beard.	1 Sam. xxi. 13.—And he . . . raved in their handes, and *scrabbled* on the doores of the gate, and *let his spittel falle* downe upon his bearde.	1 Sam. xxi. 13.—And Dauid . . . fayned hym selfe mad in theyr handes and *scrabbled* on the dores of the gate, and let his *spettle fall* downe upon his beerde.
1 Kings iv. 26.—And Salomon had fortye thousande *cart* horses.	1 Kings iv. 26.—And Salomon had fourtie thousand *stalles* of horses for *charettes.*	1 Kings iv. 26.—And Salomon had XLM *stalles* of horses for *charettes.*

1 Kings xviii. 28.—And they cried loude and *prouoked* themselues with knyues and *botkens*, as their maner was, tyll the bloude folowed.

1 Kings xix. 12.—And after the fyre came there a styll softe *hyssinge*.

1 Kings xxii. 34.—A certayne man bended his bowe harde, and shott the kynge of Israel betwene the *mawe and the longes*.

2 Kings xii. 12.—Namely, to the *dawbers* and masons, and to them that boughte tymber and fre stone.

1 Kings xviii. 28.—And they cryed lowde and *cut* themselves, as their manner was with knyues and *launcers* tyll the bloude folowed *on them*.

1 Kings xix. 12.—And after the fyre came a styll *small voyce*.

1 Kings xxii. 34.—And a certen man drew a boowe *ignorantly*, and smote the kinge of Israel betwene the *ribbes* of his *harnesse*.

2 Kings xii. 12.—To masons and hewers of stone to bye tymbre and fre stone.

1 Kings xviii. 28.—And they cryed loude, and *cutte* themselues as theyr maner was with knyues and *launcers* tyll the bloode folowed *on them*.

1 Kings xix. 12.—And after ye fyre came a *small* styll *voyce*.

1 Kings xxii. 34.—A certaine man drue a bowe *ignorantly*, and (*by chaunce*) smote the kynge of Israel betwene the *rybbes* and *hys harnesse*.

2 Kings xii. 12.—To masons and hewers of stone. And they brought tymbre and fre stone.

In the other part of the Old Testament, from Ezra to Malachi, Coverdale had simply in the Great Bible to revise his own former version. The Great Bible, therefore, does not present the same amount of divergence from Coverdale's own in this part of the Old Testament as in the preceding part. Out of every hundred consecutive verses here, there will (probably) be found about fifty that, in the two Bibles, are identical in their terms; and out of the other fifty, a considerable number in which the difference of phraseology is very slight. Take at random four chapters, one here and another there. The four we light on are Job xix., Prov. xx., Isaiah xxxii., and Hosea xiii. In these chapters the number of verses that are word for word the same in the two Bibles are:—in Job xix., fifteen out of twenty-nine: in Prov. xx., sixteen out of thirty: in Isaiah xxxii., seven out of twenty: in Hosea xiii., eight out of sixteen: in all, forty-six out of ninety-five. Many of the variations counted in this enumeration, too, are the closest possible approaches on imperceptible distinctions. In one case the whole change on a verse is the substitution of *a* for *the*: in another case, it is *that man* for *he*: in a third case, it is the alteration of *would be* into *are*: and in a fourth, it is the suppression of the adverb *too*.

And this statement fails to shew the amount of identity there is in the two versions. Many peculiar words and phrases, and not a few defective renderings, which appear in Coverdale's translation, 1535, and which we should have expected a reviser to change, are retained in the Great Bible. In both translations, it is said, Is. xxxix., 2, that Hezekiah shewed to the couriers of Merodach-baladin "all that was in his *cubburdes*." In both translations, the famous prophecy regarding Zerubbabel, Zech. iv., 7, is rendered: "He shall brynge up the fyrst stone, so that men shal crye unto hym, *good lucke, good lucke*:" a very different exclamation it will be observed from "grace, grace."[1] And in both translations, there is an expression that will probably sound strange, if not meaningless, in the ears of Scotsmen, but may nevertheless be dear to the students and lovers of ancient ritual:[2] "*byd* nether prayse nor prayer for them," Jer. xi., 14. Of the renderings, moreover, that have been transferred without change from Coverdale's Bible to the Great Bible, there are many that may be called peculiar, although they contain no words that are antiquated. One that, whatever may be said of its accuracy as a translation, has much intrinsic reasonableness to recommend it as a directory of conduct occurs in Prov. xxvi., 4-5: "Geve not the foole an answer *after* his foolishnesse,[3] lest thou become like unto him: but make the foole an answer *to* his foolishnesse lest he be wise in his own conceate." A rendering that not only differs considerably from what appears in the authorised version, but is expressed in a quaint antithetical form occurs in the last clause of Jer. xxx., 19: "I shall *endue* them with honoure, and no man shall *subdue* them." The account that Nebuchadnezzar, accord-

---

[1] Matthew Henry's remark on this verse is:—"The acclamations are not huzzas, but grace, grace: that is the burthen of the triumphant songs the Church sings." What would the Commentator have said of Coverdale's rendering of the verse?

[2] Of other words, little less notable than those mentioned above, that appear in both Bibles may be mentioned:—*querne* for "millstone," Is. xlvii. 2; *gelded chamberlains* for "eunuchs," Is. xxxix. 7; *rammes* of the flock for "principal of the flock," Jer. xxv. 34; *worthies* for "young lions," Ezek. xxxviii. 13; and the adjective *bayrded* (Coverdale) or *barbed* (Great Bible) prefixed paraphrastically to "horses," Joel ii. 4.

[3] In the Latin version of the Bible published at Zurich 1564, it is said:—"Ne respondeas stulto *juxta* stultitiam ejus, ne adaequeris ei etiam tu, Responda stulto *secundum* stultitiam suam, ne forte sit sapiens in oculis suis."

ing to Coverdale, gives of his dream, Danl. ii. 3, is well worthy of remark also as a curious study in royal psychology: "I have dreamed a dreame, and my sprete was so troubled therewith that I have clene forgotten what I dreamed."

It is necessary, however, to have before us the corresponding passages in the authorised version in order to see the striking peculiarity of some of the readings and renderings that were transferred without change from Coverdale's Bible, 1535, into the Great Bible, 1540. A few passages shall, therefore, be submitted for comparison in parallel columns.

COVERDALE'S BIBLE & GREAT BIBLE.

Job. xxxix. 19.—Hast thou geuen the horse his strength or *lerned him to bowe downe his neck with feare: that he letteth himself be dryuen forthelike* a greshopper, whereas *the stoute neyenge that he maketh* is fearfull.

Ps. lxviii. 6.—He is the God that *maketh men to be of one mynde in a house*, and bryngeth the presoners out of captiuitie in due season, but letteth the *rennagates continue in scarcenesse*.

Prov. xxvii. 19.—Like as in *one water there apeare dyuerse faces*, euen so *dyuerse men haue dyuerse herts*.

Jer. xv. 12.—Doth *one yron hurte another*, or *one metall that cometh from the north, another*.

Lam. v. 13.—They haue taken yonge *men's lynes from them*, and the boyes are *hanged up upon trees*.

Hosea x. 11.—Ephraim was unto me as a cow that is *used to go to plowe, therefore I loued him, and fell* upon his fayre neck. I *droue* Ephraim, Juda plowed, and Jacob *played the huszbonde man*.

Joel i. 18.—O what a *sighinge make the catell?* the *bullocks are in very euell likynge*, because they have no pasture and the sheep are fameszshed away.

Amos vii. 1.—The Lorde God shewed me soch a vision: beholde, there stode *one that made greszshoppers*, euen when the corne was shutynge forth, after the kynge *had clipte his shepe*.

Micah ii. 11.—Yff *I were a fleshly felowe*, and a preacher of lyes, and told them *that they might sit bebbinge and bollynge and be droncken*: O that were a prophet for this people.

Hab. ii. 2.—Wryte the vision planely

AUTHORISED VERSION.

Job. xxxix. 19.—Hast thou given the horse strength! Hast thou clothed his neck with thunder! Canst thou make him afraid as a grasshopper? The glory of his nostrils is terrible.

Ps. lxviii. 6.—God setteth the solitary in families: he bringeth out those which are bound with chains but the rebellious dwell in a dry land.

Prov. xxvii. 19.—As in water face answereth to face, so the heart of man to man.

Jer. xv. 12.—Shall iron break the northern iron and the steel.

Lam. v. 13.—They took the young men to grind, and the children fell under the wood.

Hosea x. 11.—And Ephraim is as an heifer that is taught, and loveth to tread out the corn; but I passed over upon her fair neck. I will make Ephraim to ride, Judah shall plow, and Jacob shall break his clods.

Joel i. 18.—How do the beasts groan the herds of cattle are perplexed, because they have no pasture, yea the flocks of sheep are made desolate.

Amos vii. 1.—Thus hath the Lord God shewed unto me: and beholde he formed grasshoppers in the beginning of the shooting of the latter growth: and lo it was the latter growth after the king's mowings.

Micah ii. 11.—If a man walking in the spirit and falsehood do lie, saying, I will prophesy unto thee of wine and of strong drink: he shall even be the prophet of this people.

Hab. ii. 2.—Write the vision and

upon thy tables, that *whoso commeth by may rede it.* Mal. ii. 15.—Therefore loke well to youre sprete, and let no man despyse the wife of his youth. *Yf thou hatest her put her awaye,* sayeth the Lord God of Israel, and *geue her a clothinge for the scorne,* sayeth the Lorde of hoostes.	make it plain upon tables that he may run that readeth it. Mal. ii. 15.—Therefore take heed to your spirit, and let none deal treacherously with the wife of his youth. For the Lord, the God of Israel saith that he hateth putting away: for one covereth violence with his garment, saith the Lord of hosts.

Although, in the second part of the Old Testament, the Great Bible reads in many places as if it were little else than a transcript of Coverdale's Bible, 1535, there are between the two versions many notable points of difference notwithstanding. About fifty *per cent.* of the verses in this part of the Great Bible diverge more or less from the corresponding verses in Coverdale's earlier translation. And although many of these variations are unimportant, some are not. Words are altered, phrases are refined, renderings are corrected. Of antiquated and peculiar words in Coverdale's Bible, which have not been retained in the Great Bible, there will be found in the prophecies of Isaiah alone: *rowneth* (whispereth)—" The Lorde of hosts rowneth me thus," v. 9; *flakred*—" From above flakred the seraphims," vi., 2; *colled*—" All their heads were colled, and all their beardes shauen," xv., 2; *myslinge*—" There fel a myslinge shower like a dew," xviii., 4; *muscatel* (red wine)— " Shall men synge of the vynyarde of muscatel," xxvii., 2; *neeres* (kidneys)—" The fatnesse of neeres of the wethers," xxxiv., 6. A word that in Coverdale's first translation is used in a very objectionable manner is *fellow.* In Job xxi., 15, the man of patience, who in all his afflictions sinned not with his lips, is represented as making the astounding exclamation: " What maner of *felowe* is the Almightie that we should serve him." This coarse and irreverent utterance is in the Great Bible toned down to the short and simple form it assumes in the authorised version. A sentence that underwent a very curious change in Coverdale's hands is Ps. lxviii., 10. In his first translation that verse reads sensibly enough: "Thou sendest gracious rayne upon thine inheritaunce, and refreshest it when it is drye, that thy *beastes* may dwell therein." In the Great Bible the word "congregation" is substituted, and rightly substituted, for *beastes*. A more notable correction, however, was made by Coverdale on his first rendering of Jer. xviii., 18. In that verse mention is made of a proposal by some of Jeremiah's enemies to take ways and means of stopping the mouth of the prophet. According to Coverdale's first translation, the method suggested was to excise the prophet's tongue. In the Great Bible, a less malignant aspect is given to the plot; and the prophet's enemies are represented as forming only a constitutional project to " smite him *with* the tongue." All these, and many other changes that Coverdale, in the Great Bible, made on his former translation may be counted improvements. But Coverdale sometimes miscorrected himself, as most people do in the course of their lives. His original rendering of Ps. lxxvii., 2, was: "In the tyme of my trouble I sought the Lorde, *I helde up my hands unto him in the night season*, for my soul refused all other comfort." The words here italicised are, in the Great Bible, changed into " my sore ran and ceased not in the night season:" and this revised rendering was adopted both by the Geneva translators, in 1560, and by the King's translators, in 1611. But, in such a popular commentary as Dr. Adam Clarke's this is declared to be " a most unaccountable translation: the literal meaning of the Hebrew words which we translate, ' my sore ran ' is *my hand was stretched out*, that is, in prayer." And so, Coverdale's original rendering of the passage, after having been discarded by himself, and shelved by authority for 345 years, has at length been vindicated and restored to the Church in the latest English version of the Bible, 1885.

Other corrections and amendments that Coverdale, in the Great Bible, made on his former renderings, will be seen in the following extracts.

COVERDALE'S BIBLE, 1535.

Job iv. 16.—" The wether was still so that I herde this voyce.

Job vii. 15. — My soule wyssheth rather to be hanged, and my bones to be deed.

Ps. cxviii. 27.—O garnish the solempne feast with grene braunches.

Ps. cxxx. 6.—My soule doth pacient-

GREAT BIBLE, 1540.

Job iv. 16.—In the stilnesse herde I a voyce.

Job vii. 15.—My soule wyssheth rather to peryshe and dye, then my bones to remayne.

Ps. cxviii. 27.—Bynde the sacrifice with cordes.

Ps. cxxx. 6.—My soul flyeth unto the

ly abyde the Lorde, from the one mornynge to the other. Prov. x. 8.—A wyse man wil receave warnynge, but a foole will sooner be smytten in the face. Eccles. xii. 12.—Therefore, bewarre (my sonne) that aboue these thou make the not many and innumerable bokes, nor take dyverse doctrynes in hande, to weery thy body withal. Is. xxviii. 10.—Byd that may be bydden; forbyd that may be forbydden; kepe backe that may be kept backe; here a litle, there a litle. Jer. xxxvii. 21.—Dayly to be geuen him a cake of bred, and els no dighte meate, untill all the bred in the cite was eaten up. Jer. xlviii. 12.—I shall sende hir trussers to trusse her up, to prepare and season hir vessels, yee hir tankerdes rattell and shake to and fro.	Lorde, before the mornyng watche (I saye) before the mornyng watche. Prov. x. 8.—A wyse man wyll receyue warnynge, but a pratynge foole shal be punyshed. Eccles. xii. 12.—Therefore, beware (my sonne) of that doctryne that is besyde thys: for, to make many bokes it is an endlesse worke; and too loude criynge weryeth the bodye. Is. xxviii. 10.—After one commaundement another commaundement, after one rule another rule, after one instruccion another instruccion, there a lytle and there a lytle. Jer. xxxvii. 21.—Dayly to be geuen hym a kake of breade out of the baker's streate untyll all the breade in the cytie war eaten up. Jer. xlviii. 12.—I shall sende her trussers to trusse her up, which shal remoue her from her dwellyng, and empty her vesselles, and breake her wyne pottes.

To the people of England, and of Scotland also, the English versions of the Bible that were published during the struggle for Reformation, in the reign of Henry the Eighth, were boons of no common magnitude. They thoroughly served the special and immediate purpose for which they were issued. They acquainted men with the true doctrine of Scripture; they exposed the corruptions of the Roman Catholic Church; and they laid the foundations of a great spiritual and social revolution in the country. But, as translations, they were not perfect. Each successive version was meant to be an improvement on its predecessor; and with the production of the Great Bible the translator's labours in that age were practically exhausted. The translation had been amended and polished, several times over, till it admitted of no further refinement from the same hands. But, with all its merits, the Great Bible is neither as an accurate translation nor as a readable book equal to the version that for more than two hundred and seventy years has been read in our Churches. By dint of superior literary skill, there has been given in our authorised version a new sublimity to many of the most impressive passages in Scripture. Racy enough are some of Coverdale's renderings, as the verses already quoted, both from his own translation, 1535, and from the Great Bible, must have shown. Very graphic, for instance, is the statement of Job as rendered by Coverdale—" My bone hangeth to my skin, and the flesh is away : only there is left me the skynne about my teth." In its own way, too, as according with civilised notions of the fitness of things, nothing can be more admirable than the wise man's precept as rendered by Coverdale, Prov. xxiii. 1—" When thou syttest at the table to eat with a lord, order thyself manerly wyth the thynges that are set before thee. Measure thine appetite, and yf thou wylt rule thine owne self, be not *ouer gredye of his meate.*"[1] But, notwitstanding the "uncommonly good ear" with which Coverdale has been credited by some of his admirers, his rendering of many of the grander passages of Scripture comes, in respect of melody and majesty, immeasurably short of the literary standard that has been reached in the authorised version. One or two extracts will speak for themselves :

Great Bible. 1540.	Authorised Version, 1611.
Job xxix. 25.—When I agreed unto theyr waye, I was the chefe, and sat as a Kyng wyth his armye about hym. And when they were in heuynes I was theyr comfortour.	Job. xxix. 25.—I chose out their way, and sat chief, and dwelt as a king in the army, as one that comforteth the mourners.
Ps. lxxii. 6.—He shall come downe like the rain into a flese of woll, euen as the droppes that water the earth.	Ps. lxxii. 6.—He shall come down like rain upon the mown grass : as showers that water the earth.
Isaiah xl. 31.—But unto them that haue the Lord before their eies shal strength be increased. Aegles winges shall grow upon them ; when they runne they shall not fall ; and when they go they shall not be werye.	Isaiah xl. 31.—But they that wait upon the Lord shall renew their strength : they shall mount up with wings as eagles ; they shall run and not be weary ; and they shall walk and not faint.
Jer. ii. 13.—My people have done two euyles. They have forsaken me the *well of the water of lyfe*, and *dygged them pyttes*, yea vyle *and broken pyttes* that can hold no water.	Jer. ii. 13.—My people have committed two evils : They have forsaken me the fountain of living waters, and hewed them out cisterns, broken cisterns, that can hold no water.
Lam. v. 16.—The garland of our heed is fallen : alas, that we ever synned so sore.	Lam. v. 16.—The crown has fallen from our head, woe unto us that we have sinned.
Micah iii. 7.—They shal be fayne, all the packe of them, to stop theyr mouthes, for they haue not Goddes word.	Micah iii. 7.—They shall all cover their lips, for there is no answer of God.

---

[1] A free rendering in the Great Bible that makes an obscure passage of prophecy very intelligible is Isaiah, xxvii. 4 :—There is no displeasure in me, els when the vineyarde bryngeth me forth breers and thornes I wolde go thorowe it by warre and burne it up together."

A matter to which in recent years public attention has been pointedly called is the variety of readings alleged to be found in old manuscript copies of the Hebrew and Greek Scriptures. The number of these duplicate readings is set down at thousands. And it is a very difficult question for Biblical critics to determine, which of two, or even three, readings in a particular passage is the true original. On the margin of the revised Bible will be found such remarks as, "another reading," or "according to some ancient authorities." In the days of the Reformers, many of these alternative readings were unknown; but in books to which a certain amount of deference was paid by the scholastic public of those days, different readings of verses, here and there, were found. Words, and clauses, and sentences that appeared in one version of the Scriptures were awanting in another. Coverdale thought proper, in the Great Bible, to present to the English public some of the controverted passages which he personally was not disposed to accept as part of the sacred text. These dubious passages are, in the Great Bible, inserted in their alleged proper places, but are inclosed within brackets, and are printed in different characters from the surrounding text. They might be entitled supplementary readings from the Vulgate. In many, or in most, instances their presence or absence is of little consequence. Some of them read like interpolated explanations, as, " Benoni [*the son of my sorrow*], Gen. xxxv; and " Mara [*that is to say bitternesse*]," Ex. xv. Others look like an editor's insertions, to complete unfinished sentences, and make the author's meaning more clear; as, " The waters that came down from above, dyd ryse up upon an heape [*and appeared as great as a mountayne*], Josh. iii.; and " The man that fulfylleth the thinges [*contayned in the lawe*] shall lyve in them," Gal. iii. In other cases they introduce new matter into the record, as in the following sentence appended to 1st Sam. v. 6—" The villages also and the feldes in the myddes of the countre were ful, and there came up myce, and there was a confusyon of greate death in the cytie." One of the largest of these interpolations appears in Ps. xiv., after the third verse, so as to make the Psalm harmonise with the words quoted, apparently from different sources, by St. Paul, in Romans iv. 10-18.

It only remains to be added that Coverdale, to whose labours the people of England were indebted, in 1535, for a useful and most readable translation of the Bible, and, in 1539, for the version called the Great Bible, which was the Bible *par excellence* of the Reformers, was not only a fellow-worker, but a fellow-sufferer with Tyndale and Rogers in the service of God. He was not, like them, crowned with the crown of martyrdom; but he was sorely persecuted. Having been promoted, during the reign of Edward the Sixth, to the bishopric of Exeter, he was, after the death of Edward, removed, on a frivolous pretext, and sent to a felon's prison. For two years he lingered in his place of confinement; and but for the intercession of the King of Denmark, to whom a brother-in-law of Coverdale was chaplain, he might have been left to end his days in a dungeon. And when set free, Coverdale had to flee from England to preserve his freedom. As was natural, he made his way, in the first place, to the country of his benefactor. He afterwards proceeded to Geneva, where many of the English Reformers were at that time enjoying a peaceful and literary retreat. On the death of Mary, the Catholic Queen of England, he returned home; but not to be reinstalled in his former see, or to be appointed to another episcopal benefice. His Geneva connections prejudiced his interests; and till 1564 he had, notwithstanding all his public services, to be satisfied with what in Scotland is contemptuously termed a *vagum ministerium*. In the course of that year, however, he was settled in a humble charge at London Bridge; but even this small piece of prosperity he was not privileged for any length of time to enjoy. Bent down by age and hardships, he was compelled, in 1566, to resign his living. To the shame of his church and country, he was then allowed to close his life in neglect and penury.

The Puritans' and People's Bible, otherwise termed the Geneva or Breeches Bible.

Editions consulted and quoted from :—
> First Geneva version of New Testament, 1557.—Reprint in Bagster's Hexapla.
> Second Geneva version of New Testament, 1560.—Barker's Print, 1580.
> Third Geneva version of New Testament, (Tomson's revision) 1576.—Print by Barker's deputies, London, 1599.
> Geneva Bible, 1560.—London, Barker, 1580.

FOR nearly twenty years after the publication of Taverner's Bible and the Great Bible with Cranmer's prologue, very little was done in the way of perfecting or improving the English version of the Scriptures. A small fragment of the New Testament was, by Sir John Cheke, translated into a sort of Doric, or un-latinised English; with the view, apparently, of giving the common people of England a Bible, in a language more truly native than that of either Tyndale or Coverdale. This project of Cheke's, if it could be seriously termed a project, was never completed. A very small portion of the New Testament —the gospel according to St. Matthew (with two or three passages awanting) and the first chapter of St. Mark's Gospel— is all that has come down to us. In reality, Cheke's translation, although generally referred to in histories of the English Bible, is not worthy of mention, except as Cheke's own biographer candidly avows "for the reader's diversion." It never, till 1843, was put into print or obtained circulation: and it has not exercised any influence on subsequent versions of the Bible in English. While some churchmen thought that the English translators of the Bible had gone too far in the substitution of common English words, which were in daily secular use, for Latin terms of vaguer meaning and holier association, Cheke considered they had not gone far enough in that direction. As substitutes for some of the uncouth words of foreign extraction which he found in the English Bible, he, therefore, manufactured new terms out of purely Saxon elements. And in this process of verbal fabrication he shewed not a little adroitness. He called apostles *frosents;* publicans *tollers;* centurions *hunderders;* proselytes *freschmen;* and parables *biwords.* The phrase, "possessed with devils," he shortened into *develd;* and such Latin derivatives as "crucified" and "lunatic," he transmuted into *crossed* and *mooned.* He was not altogether consistent, however, in his proclivity to Saxonise. For "locusts" he substituted *acrids,* which is just the Greek word *akrides* in an English form; and for the simple, common word "spirit" he substituted, in Mat. xiv., 26, the much more scholastic term *phantasm,* which is just, again, the Greek original *phantasma,* with its Greek ending cut off. More unaccountably still, he, in one place at least, uses the Latin *vel* for the English *or:* "Whosoever sweareth bi the gold of the temple he is bound to perform it, *vel* he fauteth."

Some of the archaisms that abound in Wyclif's and Tyndale's Testaments appear in Cheke's fragment also. The Greek words that, in Mat. xvi., 23, are by Tyndale rendered, "Come after me Satan" (instead of get thee behind me Satan) are so translated by Cheke, too, in Mat. iv., 10. The phrase "chimnei of fiir," which occurs in Wyclif's version, Mat. xiii., 42, is used by Cheke in the same connection. The word *nigheth,* likewise, which we often meet with in Wyclif's Bible, is introduced by Cheke into Mat. xv., 8: "This pepil *nigheth* me with their mouth." A very unecclesiastical rendering of Cheke's is his translation of Mark i., 8: "I have *wasched* you with water, but he schal *wasch* you with the holi ghoost." Of other renderings, quaint and curious, by Cheke, the following may be given as examples:—"Happi be the beggars in spirit, for the kingdom of heeven is theers," Mat. v. 3; "The eie is the candel of the body, if theerfoor thyn eie be cleen al thy hool bodi wil be lightsom, but if thyn eie be not wel thi hool bodi wil be darksome," Mat. vi. 22-23; "Wisdoom is cleen rid from her own children," Mat. xi. 19; "Thei have winked hard with theer own eies least thei schold se with theer eies," Mat. xiii. 15; "He wrong him bi the neck saeing, Pai me that thou ouest me," Mat. xviii. 28;

"I sai to you again that it is easier for a cable to passe through a nedel's eie, than for a rich man to enter into the kingdom of heeven," Mat. xix. 24 ; " Then roos all thees virgins and furnisched theer lampes," Mat. xxv. 7.

Like other early translations of Scripture, Cheke's version of St. Matthew's gospel is garnished with marginal notes. Some of these are more entertaining than comments on Scripture usually are. On Mat. x. 18, for instance, it is said :—

"The Jues called all men besid themselves sumtime grecians but comunli hethen ; euen as the aegyptian and the grecian called everi contree, in despite, beside theer own barbarous ; the romans called other externos, and our old Saxons called the liik *welsch men*. We now call them strangers and outborns and outlandish."

In the note on Mat. xvi. 18, there is a remark that should be grateful to the ears of Scotsmen. twitted for their ecclesiastical provincialisms :—

"This word *church*, into the which we torn (turn) *ecclesia*, is the hous wheer the outcalled do meet, and heer goddes word, and use common praier and thankesgeving to God. For it cometh of the greek *kuriakon*, which word served in the primitiv church for the commons house of praier and sacramentes, as appeareth in Eusebius. . . We folowing the greek calle this house, as the north doth yet moor truli sound it, the *kurk*, and we moor corruptli and frenchlike, the *church* !"

So much, then, for Sir John Cheke's translation of St. Matthew's Gospel. Although it was the first instalment of a work by one of the best scholars of his age, and was supposed to have been designed to supplement, if not supersede, the Testaments of Tyndale and Coverdale, it seems to us of the present day more like the freak of a young patriotic schoolman, who, in zeal for his mother tongue, had purposed to interdict the growth of a national language by the importation of foreign words, than an earnest effort to make the Scriptures plainer or more intelligible to the common people.

From 1553 to 1558, England was under the rule of a Catholic Queen—Mary, daughter of Henry the Eighth by his first wife, Catharine of Arragon. During the reign of that "most vertuous, most wittie, and most studious ladie," as a Catholic admirer has described her, the circulation of the Scriptures in the English tongue was not encouraged. The public reading of the Bible was positively prohibited by a proclamation, dated 18th August 1553; the importation of certain books, including the works of Tyndale, Coverdale, and Cranmer, was prohibited by another proclamation in June 1555; and in 1558, the delivery of wicked and seditious writings, by which were meant the writings of such authors as we call Reformers, was required under pain of death. A relentless persecution, too, was directed against all who endeavoured to promote the Reformers' opinions, or, in other words, called in question the doctrines of the mother Church. Nearly three hundred persons in England were, for this ecclesiastical offence, burned at the stake; and far more were imprisoned, or otherwise evil entreated. The first to perish in the flames during this persecution was John Rogers, *alias* Thomas Matthew, the friend and literary executor of Tyndale. Coverdale was honoured with apartments in a prison; whether, as commonly alleged, for his zeal in the work of Reformation, or, as averred by the Queen, for debts due to the Crown, may be left for historians to determine. Whatever the offence may have been that was laid to his charge, his position was reckoned so perilous that even after his liberation was obtained through the royal influence of the King of Denmark, he saw reason to provide for his safety by voluntary exile. Sir John Cheke, too, was disendowed of all his possessions, and would have been sent the way of Rogers if he had not made his peace with the Church, by a professed repentance of his Protestant follies. But he purchased liberation from the stake at a greater price than he counted on. In trying to save his life, he lost his life. The insincerity of his conduct preyed so much on his mind that within a year after his recantation he died of a broken heart. So it is said.

Besides Coverdale, many Reformers were fain, at this time, to seek shelter abroad. It is commonly stated that no fewer than eight hundred Englishmen were, from fear of persecution at home, scattered over the Continent. A favourite place of resort for them was Geneva. In that city, Protestantism was supreme. The form of government there was a kind of theocracy, in which civil and ecclesiastical authority were blended according to the Judaistic-Presbyterial notions of John Calvin. The ruling spirit of the city was Calvin himself, and the man of his right hand was Theodore Beza.[1] To Geneva, accordingly, so many Englishmen were attracted that they formed by themselves a considerable congregation; and they had for their minister, or pastor, in 1556-57, no less a personage than John Knox. Another distinguished exile at Geneva was William Whittingham, who married a sister of Calvin's wife, and, in 1557, succeeded Knox in the pastorate of the English Congregation. Whittingham was a scholarly man; and, both before and after his admission to the pastorate at Geneva, he devoted himself to the high and useful work of endeavouring to perfect the English version of the Scriptures. The first instalment of his Biblical labours was a revised translation of the New Testament, with "most profitable annotations of all harde places," which was published at Geneva in 1557. To this translation of Whittingham's was prefixed an epistle by his brother-in-law, Calvin, which, doubtless, helped to introduce the book to the favourable notice of the Protestant and Bible-reading section of the English people.

One or two outward peculiarities characterised this new version of the Testament in English. Not only were the several books of the Testament broken up into chapters and sections, but the chapters were divided into verses, and to each verse was prefixed its number. This had never been done before in an English Testament; but it had been done "in the best editions (of the Scriptures) in other languages," ever since 1551, when Robert Stephen's edition of the Greek Testament was given to the world.[2] And, as affording facilities for refer-

---

[1] At the date here referred to, Beza was not actually resident in Geneva, but was in constant communication with Calvin. "In October, 1548, he retired to Geneva, and joined the Reformed Church. In the following year, he was made Professor of Greek at the Academy of Lausanne, where he remained for ten years, communicating frequently with Calvin at Geneva. . . . In 1558, he removed to Geneva, and succeeded Calvin as Professor in 1564."—*Encyc. Brit.*

[2] "In the Old Testament the division into short verses was ready to hand in the

ence, it was a matter of considerable consequence. Besides dividing chapters into verses, Whittingham also indicated, in characters different from those of the surrounding text, the supplemental words that were inserted in order to express the full sense of the original. This, also, was a benefit to the reader.

"As touching the perusing of the text," the translator, in his prefatory address says, "it was diligently revised by the most approved Greek examples, and conference of translations in other tongues, as the learned may easily judge both by the faithful rendering of the sentence and also by the propriety of the words and perspicuity of the phrase." As the translation was made in the city where Beza was held in special honour, we should naturally expect that it would be, strictly speaking, a revision, "by the most approved Greek examples," of the New Testament contained in the Great Bible, 1540, with "conference" of Tyndale's Testament in English, 1534, and Beza's Testament in Latin, 1556.

To see whether this is so, let us examine the renderings of Whittingham in some particular chapter, taken at random. The chapter we light on is the second in the Epistle to the Philippians. It contains thirty verses; and in these thirty verses there are only forty-two changes, of word or phrase, worthy of notice that Whittingham has made on either Tyndale's renderings, 1534, or on those in the Great Bible, 1539. In other words, the rendering of this chapter is, except in forty-two cases, verbatim the same in Tyndale's Testament, in the Great Bible, and in the Geneva Testament of 1557. This amount of concord is remarkable, and cannot be accidental. The words, "Let the same mynde be in you that was in Christ Jesus," v. 5, which we find in all the three English versions, is not such a literal translation of the original Greek that it would inevitably occur to three independent translators, who had no communication with each other. The same may be said of the

---

Hebrew Bible. Through Pagninus, 1528, this division became familiar to readers of Latin. In the New Testament there was no precedent of this kind till 1551."—*Moulton.*

statements in *v.* 6 and 7, "thought it no robbery to be equal with God: but he made himself of no reputation :" and also of the quaint expression " make moche of soche," *v.* 29. Beyond all question, therefore, Whittingham's version, 1557, is based either on the Great Bible or on Tyndale's Testament, or on both jointly. It is evidently, however, a free and careful revision of the translation or translations on which it is based. In a chapter of thirty verses there are eight instances in which the rendering agrees with Tyndale's, and differs from that in the Great Bible; thirteen in which it agrees with that in the Great Bible, and differs from Tyndale's; and twenty-one in which it differs both from Tyndale's and from what is given in the Great Bible.[1] In fifteen of these twenty-one cases, Whittingham's renderings are literal translations of Beza's version in Latin, and in the other six they might pass for translations of Beza. As specimens of unmistakeable Bezaisms in Whittingham's translation of this chapter, the following phrases may be quoted :—" At the name," *v.* 10, for " in the name," *ad nomen;* " make an end of your own salvation," *v.* 12, for " work out your salvation," *salutem conficite* (operamini, Vulgate); " his free benevolence," *v.* 13, for " his good will," *gratuita sua benevolentia* (bona voluntate, Vulgate); " putting forth," *v.* 16, for " holding fast," *praetendentes* (continentes, Vulgate); " your messenger," *v.* 25, for " your apostle," *vestrum legatum* (apostolum, Vulgate); " such things as I wanted," *v.*

---

[1] It has to be remarked, however, that although these figures indicate in Whittingham's translation rather more concordance with the Great Bible than with Tyndale's Testament, an examination of other chapters will indicate differently. In some chapters there are two, or even three, variations from the Great Bible for every one from Tyndale's Testament. And not only so, but the renderings of Tyndale are in some cases adopted, where those in the Great Bible are preferable. In Tyndale's translation of Acts xv. 39, there is a very irrelevant statement :— "The dissencion was so sharp between them that they departed asunder one from the other: *so that Barnabas took Mark and sayled unto Cyprus.*" In the Great Bible this irrelevancy is made to disappear, by the substitution of "and so" for "so that "; and yet, notwithstanding this improvement, Tyndale's rendering is retained by Whittingham. In Tyndale's Testament again, Gal. ii. 14 is very crudely translated :—" I said unto Peter *before all men,*" and this crude rendering is also adopted by Whittingham, although in the Great Bible it had been corrected into " before *them all.*"

25, for "at my nedes," *quibus mihi opus erat* (necessitatis meae, Vulgate); "when ye should see him again ye might rejoice," *v.* 28, for "when ye see him ye may rejoice again," *eo rursus viso, gaudeatis* (viso eo *iterum gaudeatis*, Vulgate). The Geneva version of the New Testament, 1557, was so soon superseded by another Geneva version that it is not necessary for us to scan here its merits and demerits minutely. To show, however, that some not inconsiderable alterations (not always, although generally, for the better) were in 1557 made by Whittingham on the text of previous English versions of the Testament, a few specimens of his translation may be submitted to the reader's inspection, alongside of the corresponding passages in Tyndale's Testament, in the Great Bible, and in Beza's Latin version of the Testament :[1]

TYNDALE, 1534.	GREAT BIBLE, 1539.	WHITTINGHAM, 1557.	BEZA'S LATIN, 1556.
Luke xiii. 7.—Cut it doune, why *combreth* it the ground.	Luke xiii. 7.—Cut it downe, why *combereth* it the ground.	Luke xiii. 7.—Cut it downe, why *kepeth it the ground barren*.	Luke xiii. 7.— Exscinde eam : quorsum etiam *terram inutilem reddit?*
John ii. 10. — When men *be droncke*.	John ii. 10. — When men *be droncke*.	John ii. 10. — When men *have well drunk*.	John ii. 10. — *Affatim biberunt*.
Acts xxvii. 13.— They . . . lowsed *unto Asson*, and sayled paste all Candy.	Acts xxvii. 13.— Same as in Tyndale's Testament.	Acts xxvii. 13.— They . . . lowsed *nearer*, and sailed by Candia.	Acts xvvii. 13.— Solvissent *propius* praeteriegebant Cretam.
Rom. iii. 2.— Unto them was committed the *word* of God.	Rom. iii. 2. — Unto them were commytted the *wordes* of God.	Rom. iii. 2. — Unto them was committed the *oracles* of God.	Rom. iii. 2. — Quod eis credita sunt *eloquia* Dei (oracula Dei.—Zurich, 1564).
Rom. vi. 19.— I will speake *grossly* because of the infirmitie of your flesshe.	Rom. vi. 19.— I speak *grosly* because of the infirmitie of your fleshe.	Rom. vi. 19.— I speake *as men commonly use* because of the infirmitie of your flesh.	Rom. vi. 19.— *Hominum more* loquor, propter infirmitatem carnis vestrae.
Rom. xiv. 1.— Him that is weak in the fayth *receave* unto you, *not in disputynge and troublynge his conscience*.	Rom. xiv. 1.— Same as in Tyndale's Testament.	Rom. xiv. 1.— Him that is weak in the fayth, *take* unto you, *but not to enter into doutful disputations of controversies*.	Rom. xiv. 1.— Eum vero qui fide est infirmus, assumite : non tamen ad certamina disceptationum.

---

[1] The copy of Beza quoted from is of modern date.

148 *Bibles of England.*

1 Cor. xi. 2.—That ye remember me in all things.	1 Cor. xi. 2.—Same as in Tyndale's Testament.	1 Cor. xi. 2.—That ye remembre all my things.	1 Cor. xi. 2.—Quod *omnia mea* meministis.
2 Cor. v. 8.—To *be absent from* the body and to *be present* with the Lord.	2 Cor. v. 8.—To be absent from the body and to be present with God.	2 Cor. v. 8.—To *remove out of* the body, and *to go to dwel with* the Lord.	2 Cor. v. 8.—*Migrare* e corpore et ad dominum *ire habitatum*.
2 Cor. xi. 9.—And when I was present with you and had need I was *grevous to no man*.	2 Cor. xi. 9.—And when I was present with you and had nede I was *chargeable to no man*.	2 Cor. xi. 9.—And when I was present with you and had nede I was *not slothful to the hinderance of any man*.	2 Cor. xi. 9.—Et quum apud vos essem et egerem *non obtorpui* cum cujusquam *incommodo*.
Gal. ii. 21.—I *despise* not the grace of God.	Gal. ii. 21.—Same as in Tyndale's Testament.	Gal. ii. 21.—I do not *abrogate* the grace of God.	Gal. ii. 21.—*Irritam* non *facio* gratiam Dei.
Gal. v. 5.—We *loke for and hope in the spirite to be justified thorow fayth*.	,, ,,	Gal. v. 5.—We *wayte for (by the spirit through faith) the hope of the righteousness*.	Gal. v. 5.—Nos enim, *spiritu ex fide, spem justitiae exspectamus*.
Ephes. vi. 24.—Grace be with all them which love our Lorde Jesus Christ in *puerness*.	Ephes. vi. 24.—Grace be with all them which love our Lord Jesus Christ *unfaynedly*, (syncerely, 1541).	Ephes. vi. 24.—Grace be with all them which love our Lord Jesus Christ *to their immortalitie*.	Ephes. vi. 24.—Gratia sit cum omnibus diligentibus Dominum nostrum Jesus Christum *ad immortalitatem*.
Phil. i. 21.—For Christ is to me lyfe, and deeth is to me a vauntage.	Phil. i. 21.—Same as in Tyndale's Testament.	Phil. i. 21.—For Christ is to me *both in life and in death* advantage.	Phil. i. 21.—Mihi enim est Christus *et in vita et in morte* lucrum.
Col. ii. 16.—Let no man, therefore, *trouble your conscience* aboute meate and drink.	,, ,,	Col. ii. 16.—Let no man, therefore, *condemn you* about meat and drink.	Col. ii. 16.—Nequis igitur *vos damnet* ob cibum vel potum.
Heb. xi. 21.—*Bowed himself towarde the toppe of his cepter*.	,, ,,	Heb. xi. 21.—*Leaning on the end of his staffe, worshipped* (God).	Heb. xi. 21.—*Adoravit, baculo innixus*.
1 Peter ii. 2.—And as new-born babes, desire that *reasonable* mylke which is *without corruption* that ye may growe therein.	1 Peter ii. 2.—And as new-borne babes, desyre ye the mylke (not of the body but of the soul) which is without disceate: that ye may grow thereby (unto salvation).	1 Peter ii. 2.—And as new-born babes, desire the *syncere* milke of the word, that ye may grow thereby.	1 Peter ii. 2.—Ut modo nati infantes, lac illud sermonis *sincerum* expetite, ut per illud adolescetis.

Immediately after the publication of Whittingham's Testament, the Geneva exiles entered on a much larger work. This was a revision of the whole of the English Bible. How many of the refugees had a hand in this undertaking it is hard to say. Coverdale was residing at Geneva at the time, and some writers have claimed for him a share of the honour. Scotsmen have, of course, put in a similar claim on behalf of John Knox. The biographer of Knox uses language that might lead his readers to infer that the Scottish Reformer was the chief person on the staff of the Geneva revisers. "Knox," he says, "returned to Geneva in the beginning of the year 1558. During that year he was engaged, along with several learned men of his congregation, in making a new translation of the Bible into English, which, from the place where it was composed and first printed, has obtained the name of *The Geneva Bible*."[1] Whatever help, if any, was given to this noble work at Geneva by Coverdale and Knox, it seems now to be admitted that the chief credit of the work is due to Whittingham, and that his principal assistants were two Englishmen, named Thomas Sampson and Anthony Gilby. "For the space of two years and more, day and night," these three worthy men toiled at their task; and in 1560 they gave to the world the fruit of their labours in the book that is now known as the Geneva Bible. The New Testament, in this book, is by no means a reprint merely of the translation published by Whittingham three years previously. It is a new translation. There were thus, in 1560, two Geneva Testaments in the market; and in 1576, there was published a revised edition of the second of these, with so many amendments, by Laurence Tomson, secretary to Sir Francis Walsingham, that it may be said there were then three Geneva Testaments in circulation.

In a prefatory epistle, it was avowed by the Geneva divines that they were moved to undertake the translation, 1560, by a conviction that, in their exile, they could bestow their "labours and study in nothing more acceptable to God and comfortable to his Church." And the reason they gave for this conviction was, that although there were already several translations of the Bible into English these translations "required greatly to

---

[1] That Knox could not have had much to do with this work may be inferred from certain dates which Dr. M'Crie himself supplies. Knox went to Geneva in the autumn of 1556. He demitted his charge there in 1557, and left Geneva in October of that year. He returned to Geneva in the beginning of 1558, and in January 1559, he "took his leave of Geneva for the last time."

be perused and reformed." But, besides *reforming* previous translations, the Geneva exiles set themselves to provide the English people with both a cheaper and a better annotated Bible than they had ever had. The authorised Bible, called the Great Bible, and which from 1540 to 1560 was the Bible in most request in England, was both costly and unwieldy. It was well adapted for public reading, either in churches or in the halls of gentlemen's mansions. But it was inconvenient for private use; and its cost was a hindrance to its circulation. The Geneva exiles, accordingly, resolved that their version of the English Bible should be issued in a handier and cheaper form than the one in common use. They resolved, also, to furnish the reader with such marginal notes as it was supposed the average man in those days required for the elucidation of Scripture. And in this there was nothing new, but only a reversion to an old practice. It was, nevertheless, a very questionable practice; and something could be said against it as well as for it. It was the offensiveness of the notes in Matthew's Bible that led Cromwell to order the publication of another version, in which there should be either no notes at all, or none of a controversial character. And most people, now, will heartily concur with the old writer who expressed a desire that "the Scripture were so puerly and plyantly translated, that it needed nether note, glosse, nor scholia; so that the reder might once swymme without a corke." But in 1560 annotations were popular; and the Geneva translators took a correct estimate of the popular taste and popular demand, when they resolved to accompany their translation of the Bible with prologues, headings of chapters, and notes on the margin.

For a multitude of reasons, the Geneva version of the Bible, 1560, became a great favourite. It was reckoned a better translation than any that had ever been printed before. It embodied the latest results of Biblical criticism. It was portable, and moderate in price. For convenience in quotation, it was cut up, like Whittingham's Testament, 1557, into chapters and verses. Its origin was associated with romance. Its authors, like the evangelist in Patmos, had suffered exile "for the Word of God and the testimony of Jesus Christ." It was the sweet fruit of suffering ; and it contained notes unmistakeably evangelical, sublimely predestinarian, conspicuously anti-papal, and slyly democratic.

To Scotsmen, the Geneva Bible has an especial interest. It was the Bible of their Reformed Church ; the Bible of Knox and Melville ; the Bible that was read in all places of worship in Scotland from 1560 to 1611, and in not a few places of worship for many years longer. In some of the earlier public documents of the Church of Scotland, such as the Confession of Faith, 1560, and the Order of the Ecclesiastical Discipline, 1561 (revised, 1567), it is from the first edition of the Geneva Testament, 1557, that quotations are made.[1] In later writings, quotations from the Geneva Testament are mostly taken from the second (1560) or third (1576) version. And not only Presbyterian, but Episcopalian ministers in Scotland continued to use the Geneva Bible, after the King's translation, 1611, was issued and "appointed to be read in churches." It is from the Geneva Bible that Bishop Cowper of Galloway draws his citations of Scripture, both in " Good news from Canaan," 1613, and in " Pathmos," 1619. In the writings and sermons of the heroes of the Second Reformation (1638), Henderson, Dickson, and Rutherford, Geneva renderings are quoted occasionally, but only occasionally.[2] Traces of the Geneva version are even to be found in the Epistle to the Reader, prefixed to the Westminster Confession of Faith, 1647 : *e. g.*, " *Above* all getting, get understanding," Prov. iv. 7 ; " Without knowledge, the mind cannot be good," Prov. xix. 2.

The first version of the Bible in English that issued from the Scottish press was the Geneva version, and the publication of it was gone about with characteristic national caution.

---

[1] Calderwood, vol. ii., pp. 15 and 63. Quotations in these and other old records are not always verbatim.

[2] In the printed copy of the sermon preached by Henderson at the opening of the Assembly, 1639, the text is given in the words of the Geneva version, and at least one verse is quoted from that translation, viz. : " The word of God is *lively* and *mightie in operation,*" Heb. iv. 12. In No 27 of Rutherford's Letters (Bonar's edition), it is said of Dives, in the words of the Geneva version,—"he fared *well* and *delicately* every day."

In the early days of the Reformed Church of Scotland, the General Assembly required all writings bearing on religious questions to be revised by the Kirk, previous to their publication. When Thomas Bassandyne, the printer, therefore, along with Alexander Arbuthnot, merchant burgess, projected the publication at Edinburgh of a version of the Bible in English, they had at the outset to obtain for their project the sanction of the Church. With that view they drew up a set of articles in 1575, and submitted them to the judgment of the General Assembly. One of these "godly propositions," as they were courteously termed by the ecclesiastical authority, astricted the printers faithfully to "follow" a copy of the Bible delivered to them by the Kirk as "authentick." Another stipulated that certain visitors, named by the Assembly, should supervise the printing, and receive "a reasonable gratitude therefor, at the cost of the said Alexander and Thomas." On the other hand, the "Bishops, Superintendents, and Commissioners," in that General Assembly, 1575, bound and obliged themselves, to "do their utter and exact diligence, for purchasing of such advancement as might be had and obtained within every one of their respective jurisdictions,"[1] and to "try how many of (the lords, barons, and gentlemen of every parish), would be content to buy one of the saids volumes." It was also agreed by the Assembly that "every person that is provided of old as well as of new be compelled to buy a Bible for their parish kirk, and to advance therefor the price foresaid, £4 13s. 4d., Scottis." Terms having thus been made with the Church, the printers next procured from the Privy Council an exclusive license for ten years to print and sell "within this realme or outwith the samin, Bibillis in the vulgare Inglis toung, in haill or in partis, with ane callindaire to be insert therein." The work of printing was thereafter commenced, and before the end of 1576 the whole of the New Testament was in type. In the execution of the remaining part of the work some delay occurred, and it was not till 1579 that the whole Bible was given to the public.

---

[1] This recommendation became afterwards a statutory obligation. See Balfour's *Practicks*, p. 33.

Meanwhile, Bassandyne had died; and Arbuthnot, who had previously quarrelled with Bassandyne, and had obtained sole possession of the printing house, was left to bring the work to completion. On the title-page of the book, therefore, the printer's name was Arbuthnot, and the year of publication 1579, while within the book there was a separate title-page for the New Testament, on which the printer's name appeared as Thomas Bassandyne, and the year of publication 1576.[1]

Down to 1610 this edition of the Bible was the one that was commonly read in Scottish churches. It was printed from what the General Assembly represented to be an "authentic copy" of the Geneva version. But the copy selected to be "followed" was not so faultless as was supposed. It belonged to an edition published at Geneva in 1562, and contained two astounding misprints. The benediction, "blessed are the *peace-makers*," Mat. v. 9, was converted into "blessed are the *place-makers*"[2]; and the heading of Luke xxi. was changed from "Christ *commendeth*" into "Christ *condemneth* the poor widow." These errata, however, were too glaring to escape the notice of the lynx-eyed visitors appointed by the Kirk, and they were accordingly corrected in the Scottish issue. As was fit and proper in a country where Church and State were associated, this first edition of the Bible printed in Scotland was, by the General Assembly, dedicated to His Majesty King James. And in this dedication there is an interesting allusion by the Assembly to the great and grateful change "between thir days of light, when almaist in every private house the buike of God's law is red and understand in oure vulgarie language, and that age of darkness . . . . when the false namit clergie of this realme, abusing the gentle nature of your hienes maist noble gudshir of worthie memorie, made it an capital crime to be punished with the fyre to have or read the New Testament in the vulgar language: and when to make them to all men more odious (as if it had been the detestable name of a pernicious sect) they were called New Testamenters."[3]

---

[1] See *History of the Bassandyne Bible*, by W. T. Dobson, 1887.

[2] For this reason called the Whig Bible. Date on title page, 1562; New Testament, 1561.

[3] The heading of this dedication runs:—"To the richt excellent, richt heich and

In 1610 another edition of the Bible in English was published at Edinburgh. The printer's name was Andro Hart, and the version printed was the Geneva, with Tomson's amendments in the New Testament. And it is worthy of note that although in 1611 the present authorised version of the English Bible, (on which it was known that for several years a large company of learned divines had at the King's instance been labouring), was published, the Synod of Fife, at their April meeting that year, not only ordained "that their be in every Kirk ane commoune Byble," but directed that "evrie brother should urge his parochinares to buy ane of the Bybles laitlie printed be Andro Hart." There is reason to believe that in some churches in Scotland Hart's Bible continued to be used for more than half a century after that date. At a Presbyterial visitation held at Kintore in 1674, the minister reported that there "is a byble for publick reading in the Church, but of the *old translation*, yrfore its recommended to cause provyde one of the new translation."[1]

To this day, the Geneva Bible is well known in Scotland, not only to biblical scholars, but to a large number of people in almost all ranks of the lay community. Copies of it, more or less perfect or imperfect, are to be had almost daily in the shops of antiquarian booksellers. The name by which it is commonly known is *The Breeches Bible*, from the rendering given in it of the last clause of Gen. iii. 7 : " They sewed figge tree leaves together, and made themselves breeches." The

---

michtie prince James the sext, King of Scottis ; " and in the body of the dedication it is stated, that by James' "autoritie it was of a certane time bypast ordanit that this holy buke of God sulde be set forth and imprentit of newe, within zour awne realme, to the end, that in every Paroch kirk there sulde be at leist ane thereof kepit, to be callit the common buke of the kirke, as a maist mete ornament for sik a place, and a perpetuall register of the worde of God." The Vulgate is referred to in this dedication rather contemptuously, as being written in "ane strange tongue of latine, not gud but mixed with barbaritie, used and red be fewe, and almaist understand or exponit be nane."

[1] This fact was communicated to me by the Rev. Dr. Gammack, Aberdeen. In his memorial for the Bible Society, 1824, Principal Lee states that, "till within the last forty years, a Bible of Geneva translation was used in the Church of Crail."

popular cognomen, however, is in this instance scarcely warranted. It is not in the Geneva Bible only, that the first human garment is, contrary to all the principles of evolution, described as a divided skirt. That tegumentary heresy is as old as the days of Wyclif, or older;[1] and it is to be found in both Hereford's and Purvey's translations of the Bible, and in other pre-Reformation writings. Another notable word in the Geneva Bible is *cratch*, instead of "manger," in Luke ii. 7 : " She brought forth her first begotten sonne, and wrapped him in swadling clothes, and layed him in a *cratch*." This rendering is often quoted as a peculiarity in the Geneva version, and as one of the distinctive marks by which a copy of the Geneva Testament may be identified. But it is not peculiar to the Geneva version. It will be found in Wyclif's Bible, both in Luke ii. 7, and in Luke ii. 12.

Of the New Testament there are, as has already been remarked, no fewer than three Geneva versions; namely:—the translation by Whittingham, published at Geneva in 1557; the translation by Whittingham and his co-exiles, published at Geneva in 1560; and the revision by Lawrence Tomson, published at London in 1576. It will be convenient to designate

---

[1] In the one version of Wyclif's Bible the passage reads :—"Thei soweden to gidre leeues of a fige tree and maden hem brechis"; and in the other version, "maden brechis to hem silf." In 1582, there was published by Gregorie Martin, whom his literary antagonist, Dr. W. Fulke, designates "one of the readers of Popish Divinitie in the traitorous seminarie of Rhemes," a polemical work, entituled, " A discoverie of the Manifold Corruptions of the Holy Scriptures by the Heretikes of our days, specially the English sectaries, since the time of the schisme." In the preface to this book, it is alleged that it has been customary in all ages for heretics "to make false translations of the Scriptures for the maintenance of errors"; and, curious to say, one of the cases of mistranslation adduced is that of Gen. iii. 7 *by a Pelagian*, who rendered the last clause, "fecerunt sibi *vestimenta*, for *perizomata* or *campestria*, that is, *they made themselves garments*, whereas the word of the Scripture is *breeches* or *aprons*." In some books it is stated that "it was really only one edition (of the Geneva Bible) published by Barker that contained the reading '*made themselves breeches*.'" This is not correct. The expression occurs not only in editions printed at London, but in the editions printed at Geneva, both in 1560 and in 1562. In one edition of the Geneva Bible, however, published at London by M. Lewis in 1775, the word breeches is changed into "aprons."

these respectively, the first, second, and third Geneva versions of the New Testament.

Of the Old Testament, there is only one Geneva version: that published by the exiles in 1560.

We have seen that in the first Geneva version of the New Testament there is a considerable amount of departure both from Tyndale's translation, and from the translation in the Great Bible; and that that departure is largely due to the influence of Beza's Latin renderings. Let us now enquire how far the second Geneva version departs from the first, and try to discover how that departure originated.

If we turn, at random, to any chapter in the Testament, we shall find a great difference between the first Geneva version of that chapter and the second Geneva version of it: a greater difference, possibly, than between Tyndale's version of the chapter and the version given in the Geneva translation 1557. Take the second chapter of the Epistle to the Colossians. In that chapter there are twenty-three verses. In fourteen of these, the first Geneva translation deviates more or less from Tyndale's; and in twenty, the second Geneva translation varies less or more from the first. In most of these changes that in 1560 were made by the Geneva divines on the earlier renderings of Whittingham's, increased conformity to the Latin of Beza may be traced; and in some, the inspiration of Beza is decidedly manifest. In verse eight, for instance, "deceitful vanity" is changed into *vain deceit*, which is the literal English of Beza's *inanem deceptionem*; in verse sixteen, "for a peece of an holy-day," becomes *in respect of an holyday*,[1] which is the literal English again of Beza's *respectu festi*; and in verse eighteen, the strange rendering "wilfully rule over you by humbleness," is amplified into, *at his pleasure bear rule over you in humbleness of mind*, which is practically no change at all except that it shews a more slavish adherence to the words of Beza, *ultro sumat in submissione animi*. On the other hand, it must be acknowledged, that in the last clause of the twenty-third verse,

---

[1] The Greek words of the original might be literally rendered "in parte," and in the Vulgate they are translated *in parte diei festi*.

it is the first and not the second Geneva translation that bears the impress of Beza's Latin.[1]

The changes made on the first Geneva version of the New Testament, by the authors of the second, were, as might have been expected, of two kinds. There were variations of a larger, and variations of a lesser degree—variations that involved considerable difference of meaning, or considerable change on the structure of a sentence—and variations that were merely artistic touches or scholastic refinements, which gave to particular passages either greater faithfulness to the original or more literary grace.

Of the former class of amendments there are not so many as of the latter. Still, there are not a few cases in which the structure or meaning of an entire sentence is, in the second Geneva version, broadly altered from what it was in the first. What, without any irreverence, may be called an amusing instance of this kind of change occurs in a verse referred to in last paragraph, Col. ii. 23. The statement made in the first Geneva translation of that verse is: The traditions, touch not, taste not, handle not, on which some people set much store, are really matters of little consequence, not pertaining directly to spiritual life, but only to the things with which the body is fed and pampered. The statement that seems to be made in the second Geneva version of the passage is: These traditions, so much made of by some persons, are fundamentally erroneous representations of religious doctrine, in as much as they are founded on the false principle that it is not a matter of "estimation" to satisfy the wants of the body. In other words, the old Rechabite rules—touch not, taste not, handle not—

---

[1] VERSION, 1557.

Which things have indeed a shew of wisdom in voluntary worshipping and humbleness, and in not sparing the body: *yet are of no value but apperteine to those things wherewith the flesh is crammed.*

VERSION, 1560.

Which things have indeed a shewe of wisdom in voluntary religion and humbleness of mind, and in not sparing the body: *neither have they it in any estimation to satisfie the flesh.* (Non in honore aliquo ad expletionum carnis. —*Calvin.*)

BEZA'S LATIN.

Quae rationem quidem habent sapientiae in cultu voluntario, et submissione animi, et in eo quod corpori non parcant: *nec tamen ullius sunt pretii, quum ad ea spectent quibus farcitur caro.*

were stoutly declared by the Geneva divines of 1560 to be contrary to the principles of Christian faith; and in a marginal note on the verse, they remarked, for the reader's warning, that the advocates of these unauthorised traditions only "pinch and *defraude* their body to shew themselves greater hypocrites"! In the first Geneva version, again, Rom. xii. 3 reads the same as in Tyndale's Testament, and nearly the same as it does in the authorised translation: "For I say through the grace that is geven unto me, to every man among you, that no man esteme of himselfe more than it becometh him to esteeme, but that he discretly judge of himself." In 1560, however, the Geneva divines, slavishly following the Latin translation of Beza, rendered the passage: "For I say . . . to every man that is among you, that no man presume to understand above that which is meete to understand, but that he understand according to sobriety."[1] By the change of one very small word, there is a considerable difference of meaning, also, between the first and second translations of Mark x. 21. In the former, Jesus is represented as saying to the man who had kept all the commandments of God from his youth up, and desired to know what more he should do to inherit eternal life: "Go and sel all that thou hast and geue to the poore, and thou shalt have treasure in heaven; and come, folowe me and take up *thy* crosse." In other words, deny yourself, to the extent of crossing your own inclinations and temporal interests in every way, for my sake and for the good of your fellow-men. In the second Geneva version, the italicised word *thy* is changed into *the;* as if Jesus, contrary to all probability, spake beforehand, in a manner that could not have been understood by his hearers, of the popular name by which his doctrine was destined to become known in the world, *the cross*, and simply enjoined the man to become a disciple, and make a public profession of the gospel. There is a difference of meaning, too,

---

[1] It may be mentioned in passing that this rendering has the approval of Calvin, who remarks upon it: "Sic enim intelligere malo, quam secundum quod Erasmus vertit. 'Nequis superbe de se sentiat': quia et hic sensus est aliquanto a verbis remotior, et ille melius quadrat orationis contextui."

between the first and second Geneva readings of 2 Cor. ii. 17. In the former St. Paul is represented as saying: "We do not, as many, disguise and counterfait the worde of God; but as of syncere affection, but as of God, in the sight of God, so speake we in Christe." This means, we do not distort the word of God to suit our own convenience, or to advance any selfish end we have in view, but we deliver to you the word of God as it was spoken to us. But in the second Geneva version the Apostle's statement is rendered: "We are not as many, which make merchandise of the word of God;" that is, who preach it, soundly or unsoundly, purely or corruptly, in its integrity or in a mutilated form, for the sake of filthy lucre. And in regard to this passage, it may be remarked that, while the translation in the second Geneva version is a literal rendering of the original Greek, the translators were probably led to the phrase they used by the Latin expression of Beza, *cauponamur*, instead of *adulterantes*, as in the Vulgate.

The refinements made by the Geneva revisers, 1560, on the first Geneva version of the Testament, are very numerous, and in many cases not unimportant. There is nothing specially striking or beautiful, perhaps, in the simple narrative given in the second Geneva version of Acts ix. 26: "When Saul was come to Jerusalem, he assayed to joyne himself with the disciples, but they were all afraid of him, and believed not that he was a disciple." If we consider, however, that in the first Geneva version Saul was said to have "assayed to *couple* himself with the disciples," we shall see that we are indebted to the revisers of 1560 for some improvement on the diction of the verse. And none will refuse to admit that the simple words, "among whom ye be also, the called of Jesus Christ," which form the second Geneva version of Rom. i. 6, are much preferable to the more inflated rendering in the first version, "of whose numbers ye be also, which are Jesus Christ's by vocation." And there might be adduced ever so many instances to the same effect: as "the kingdom of heaven suffereth violence, and the violent *take it by force*," Mat. xi. 12, for "the violent plucke it unto them": "the place *was shaken* where they were assembled," Acts iv. 31, for "the place *moved*": "the days of *un-*

leavened bread," Acts xii. 3,[1] for "the days of *swete* bread":
"the *ruines thereof* will I build again," Acts xv. 16, for "that
which is fallen in decay of it will I build again": "when they
fell into a place where *two seas met*," Acts xxvii. 41, for "they
chanced on a place, *which had the sea on both the sydes*":
"bringeth *forth*," for "bringeth" patience, Rom. v. 3 : . "the
Israel of God," Gal. vi. 16, for "Israel that pertayneth to God."[2]
Occasionally the little touches or refinements given by the revisors in 1560 to the first Geneva renderings are not only literary improvements, but scholastic amendments, which bring out more forcibly and clearly the meaning of the passages in which they appear. It cannot be said that the translation of John xi. 16, in the first Geneva version, is positively incorrect; but it requires the supplementary words introduced into the second version to make it perfect: "Then saith Thomas, which is called Didymus, unto *his fellow* disciples, let us also go that we may die with him."

The following quotations, without comments, will still further illustrate the little changes, for, good, that were made on the first Geneva version, by the revisers in 1560.

SECOND GENEVA VERSION, 1560.

Mark v. 38.—Saw the *tumult*, and them that wept and wayled greatly.

Luke ix. 33.—It is good for us to be here.

Luke x. 30. — Jesus answered and said, A certain man went down from Jerusalem to Jericho.

Luke xii. 56.—Hypocrites, ye can discern the face of the earth and of the sky.

John vii. 20.—Be ye angry at me because I have made a man every whit whole on the Sabbath day.

Acts xvii. 23.—Beheld your devotions.

Romans ii. 20.—An instructor of them which lack discretion, a teacher of the unlearned, which hast the form of knowledge.

FIRST GENEVA VERSION, 1557.

Mark v. 38.—Saw the *wonderyng* and them that wept and wayled greatly.

Luke ix. 33.—It is good *being* here for us.

Luke x. 30.—Jesus *taking his word* said, A certain man *descended* from Jerusalem to Jericho.

Luke xii. 56.—Hypocrites, ye can *skyl of the fasshyon* of the earth and of the sky.

John vii. 20.—*Disdayne* ye at me because I have made a man every whit whole on the Sabbath day.

Acts xvii. 23.—Behelde *the maner how ve worship* your goddes.

Romans ii. 20.—An *informer* of them which lack discretion, a teacher of unlearned, which hast the *information* of knowledge.

---

[1] Leaven was termed by Wyclif "sourdough," and *unleavened* bread was consequently *unsoured* or sweet bread.

[2] "The Israel of God" is one of the phrases that were first introduced into the English Testament by Taverner.

| Romans ii. 29. — But he is a Jew which is one within, and the circumcision is of the heart, not in the letter, whose praise is not of men, but of God. | Romans ii. 29.—But he is a Jew which is *hyd* within, and the circumcision *of the heart is the true circumcision, which consisteth* in the spirit, *and* not in the letter, *the which Jewes* praise is not of men but of God. |

Romans vii. 6.—Now we are delivered from the law, being dead unto it, wherein we were holden, that we should serve in newness of spirit.

Romans vii. 6.—But now we are delivered from the law, being dead unto it, wherein we were *in bondage* (hat we should serve in *a new conversation of the spirit*.

1 Cor. ii. 10.—The spirit searcheth all things, yea, the deepe things of God.

1 Cor. ii. 10.—The spirit searcheth all things, yea the *bottome of Goddes secretes*.

1 Cor. xi. 29.—Discerneth not the Lord's body.

1 Cor. xi. 29.—*Maketh no difference of* the Lordes body.

1 Cor. xvi. 9.—A great door and effectual is opened unto me.

1 Cor. xvi. 9.—A great dore and a *fruteful* is opened unto me.

2 Cor. viii. 2.—Their most extreme poverty abounded unto their riche liberalitie.

2 Cor. viii. 2.—The povertie *which had consumed them, even to the very botome*, abunded unto their most riche liberalitie.

Phil. iv. 8.—If there be any virtue, or if there be any praise, think on these things.

Phil. iv. 8.—If there be any vertuous thing, if there be any laudable thing, *those same haue ye in your minde.*

2 Tim. ii. 19.—The foundation of God remaineth sure.

2 Tim. ii. 19.—The *sure ground* of God remaineth.

2 Tim. iii. 5.—A show of godliness.

2 Tim. iii. 5.—A *similitude of godly living.*

2 Tim. iii. 10. — Thou hast fully known my doctrine.

2 Tim. iii. 10.—Thou hast *sene the experience* of my doctrine.

It can scarcely be maintained that all the new renderings in the second Geneva version are improvements on those they displaced. In the first Geneva version we read, Acts xx. 21, "none of these things move me." This, it may be admitted, is not a literal, but a free, translation of the passage, as it stands in all modern Greek texts. It is a very happy translation, however, and it has been received into the authorised version. But it was discarded by the Geneva revisers of 1560. And had they substituted for it a more literal, and an equally intelligible translation, there wonld have been no cause of complaint. But, for plain words, they substituted words of very hazy import; and for a rendering that was correct in meaning, they gave a rendering that is neither correct in meaning, nor literal in form of expression: *I passe not at all.* Another faultless phrase in the first Geneva version, which we find also in the King's translation, is, "their eyes have they closed," Acts xxviii. 27. This, in the second Geneva version, is changed into, *with their eyes they have winked.* And here the influence of Beza is evident. While in the Vulgate we read, *oculos suos compresserunt*; we find in Beza's Latin translation, *oculis suis conniverunt*. A verse that is crudely rendered in the first Geneva translation is, 1 Cor. xiv. 10: "Ther are so many kyndes of voyces, as it commeth to passe, in the world, and none of them are so that they cannot be discerned." Only one alteration, however, is made on this verse by the revisers of 1560, and that alteration is for the worse. A single but ill chosen word, *dumb*, is substituted for the last member of the second clause, so that the whole verse reads: "There are so many kyndes of voyces (as it commeth to passe) in the world, and none of them is *domme*."

Notwithstanding these instances, and others which might be cited, of change for the worse, the Geneva version of 1560 is, all things considered, a very great improvement on that of 1557. It was a distinct step in the line of progress, and it brought the New Testament a long way nearer the shape it was made to assume, fifty years later, in the authorised version which is still in use.

The third Geneva version of the New Testament—that is, the revision, by Tomson, of the 1560 edition—was by no means so great an improvement on the second version as the second was on the first. The changes introduced into the third version were neither so numerous nor so important as those introduced into the second. The variations between the third and second versions, too, are far more numerous in some books of the New Testament than in others. They abound much more in the writings of St. John, for instance, than in the writings of St. Paul, as the following summary will shew :—

Chapter examined.	Number of verses in chapter.	Verses in which 1st and 2nd Geneva differ.	Verses in which 3rd and 2nd Geneva differ.
Luke xvi.	31	22	5
John i.	51	26	24
Romans ix.	33	23	2
Philippians iii.	21	13	0
James v.	20	12	1
1 Peter v.	14	8	2
1 John ii.	29	18	16
Total	199	122	50

It will be seen, from the above table, that out of the eighty verses in St. John's writings that happened to be examined, there are no fewer than forty in which the third version differs from the second; while of the 119 verses taken from the writings of St. Luke, St. Paul, St. James, and St. Peter, there are only ten in which the third version presents any difference from the second. Many of the variations enumerated, too, are very insignificant. Most, but not all, are simply accentuations of the article. This, indeed, is the most outstanding feature of Tomson's revision. The first chapter of St. John's gospel in that revision opens as follows:—" In the beginning was *that* word, and *that* word was with God, and *that* word was God. *This same* was in the beginning with God. All things were made by it: and without it, was made nothing that was made. In it was life, and *that* life was the light of men. And *that* light shineth in *the* darkness, and the darkness comprehended it not."[1]

Although Tomson was considered one of the best linguists of his day, his renderings of the Greek article have not been uniformly approved by modern scholarship. While the revisers, 1881, have, like Tomson, emphasised many passages by the introduction of definite articles where in the authorised version there are no articles; they have never gone, as Tomson did, beyond the letter of the Greek text by converting articles into demonstrative pronouns. In some cases, again, the revisers have inserted articles where Tomson did not. A passage that, under the light of the revised version of the Testament, 1881, will show the misaccentuations of Tomson in both excess and deficiency, is Rom. v. 17 :—

REVISED VERSION, 1881.	TOMSON'S REVISION, 1576.
For if, by the trespass of *the* one, death reigned through *the* one: much more shall they that receive the abundance of grace, and of the gift of righteousness, reign in life, through *the* one, even Jesus Christ.	For if, by the offence of one, death reigned through one, much more shall they which receive *that* abundance of grace, and of *that* gift of *that* righteousness, reign in life through one, that is, Jesus Christ.

---

[1] A passage oddly accentuated in Tomson's revision of the Geneva Testament is Rev. xviii. 18, where, for the phrase "the smoke of her burning," we find "*that* smoke of *that* her burning."

Not a few of Tomson's *thats*, however, have found their way into the authorised version, and become familiar to us, in oft quoted phrases, as dear household words. In the second Geneva version, 1560, we read, John vi. 48, "I am *the* bread of life." This is the translation given in the revised version, 1881, and it is the translation in the Bishops' Bible, 1572. But it was changed by Tomson in the third Geneva version, 1576, into "I am *that* bread of life." And although the authorised version is professedly based on the Bishops' Bible, the Bishops' rendering was, in this verse, rejected by the King's translators, and Tomson's was adopted. The same has to be said of 1 John iii. 12—"Not as Cain, who was of *that* wicked one, and slew his brother." We see the inspiration of Tomson, also, in the following expressions which occur in the authorised version: John i. 21, "art thou *that* prophet"; 1 John i. 2, "shew unto you *that* eternal life"; Rev. i. 3, "blessed . . . are they that hear the words of *this* prophecy." Indeed, it may be said, with good shew of reason, that Tomson's theory has been carried out by the King's translators, in some places where it was not by Tomson himself. In the authorised version, we find the phrases "*that* saying," John iv. 37, and "*that* spirit," 2 Cor. iii. 17, where in Tomson's Testament the words are "*the* saying," and "*the* spirit."[1]

While it was mainly, it was not exclusively in accentuations of the article that Tomson's Testament varied from the Geneva version of 1560. Sometimes Tomson changed important words, and sometimes he altered whole clauses. In John i. 12, he changed *power* into *prerogative*:—"To them he gave prerogative to be the sonnes of God." In Rom. xiii. 3, he transformed *princes* into *magistrates*:—"Magistrates are not to be feared for good workes, but for euill." In 1 Cor. vi. 7, he substituted

---

[1] In most of the above quoted cases Tomson has followed Beza's Latin version in rendering the Greek article by a demonstrative pronoun, as in John i. 1, *ille sermo*; John i. 5, *lux ista*; John vi. 48, *panis ille*; 1 John i. 2, *vitam illam aeternam*; 1 John iii. 12, *ex illo malo*, etc. In other cases Tomson has emphasised the Greek article where Beza has not, as in Rom. v. 17, "of that gift of that righteousness," *doni justitiae*; and Rev. xviii. 18, "that smoke of that her burning," *fumum incendii ejus*.

infirmity for *fault* :—" Now, therefore, there is altogether infirmity in you, in that ye go to law one with another." One statement in the Geneva translation, 1560, he literally reversed : —" He that cometh after me is preferred before me, for he was before me," John i. 15. This announcement he changed into " He that cometh after me was before me, for he was better than I."[1] Another passage that he altered largely was Rom. ii. 18, where he substituted " Triest the things that differ from it," for "allowest the things that are excellent." And a verse that he translated with more pith than propriety is Gal. ii. 13 :—"The other Jews *played the hypocrites* likewise with him."

Of the Old Testament, there is only one Geneva version, that, namely, which was first published at Geneva in 1560. The authors of this translation, Whittingham, Sampson, and Gilby, were Hebrew scholars ; and they translated, as Tyndale did, direct from the Hebrew original. They were guided in their translation, however, by the labours of other translators. They had the Great Bible before them ; and their object was not so much to make an absolutely new translation as to correct the version in use, wherever its renderings were faulty, and to improve its diction wherever that was defective. They, accordingly, read and studied all that could help or guide them in their work : Latin translations of the Bible, German translations, French translations, Italian translations. Of Latin translations, they had quite a store: the Vulgate, the translation by Pagninus, 1528, that by S. Munster, 1534, and that by Leo Jude, 1542. Of German translations, they had Luther's, and the one that went by the name of the Zurich version. It also happened that while they were at work in Geneva on the English Bible, others were at work, in the same city, on a revision of versions in the French and Italian languages. International conferences, therefore, we may well suppose, would be held by those who were labouring in the same cause for different peoples. The city wherein they resided, moreover, was the city of Calvin and Beza ;[2] and the translators were

---

[1] Qui post me venit, prelatus est mihi, quia praestantioi me est, Zurich, 1564.
[2] Beza came back to Geneva before 1560.

neither ignorant of the privilege they thereby had, nor were they slow to take advantage of it. In a book, whose authorship is attributed to Whittingham, on the troubles of those distracted times, it is stated that, in order to have "the texte off the Scriptures faithfully and truly translated," the exiles at Geneva, in preparing their version of the Bible in English, were moved "with one assent to requeste two off their brethern, to witt, Caluin and Beza, efsonnes to peruse the same, notwithstandynge their former trauells." While they were themselves competent scholars, the Geneva translators had thus the benefit of a no inconsiderable amount of help and counsel, in the prosecution of their work.

Learned critics have analysed passages in different parts of the Geneva version of the Old Testament, and have pointed out the probable inspiration of many of its differential expressions. In one place, the inspiration seems to have come from Pagninus; in another, from Munster; in another, from Leo Jude; and in another still, from Luther. A phrase we are very familiar with, in the authorised version of the Bible, is "the tabernacle of the congregation." This phrase was introduced into the English Bible by the Geneva translators. Both in the Great Bible and in Coverdale's Bible, the corresponding phrase is in ever so many places "the tabernacle of witness." In changing the designation of the tabernacle, the Geneva translators followed the Latin version of Pagninus. While in the Vulgate we meet with the words, "tabernaculum testimonii," the tabernacle of witness (Exodus xxix. 44, and elsewhere), and "tabernaculum foederis," the tabernacle of the covenant (Exodus xxxiii. 7, and elsewhere), Pagninus in all these places uses the terms "tabernaculum ecclesiae." And so with other words and phrases in the Geneva Bible; one seems to have come from this source, and another from that, second hand so to speak.

The question of main interest to us, in connection with the Geneva version of the Old Testament, is, to what extent it differs from, and is an improvement on, the version in the Great Bible. It was the Great Bible that, from 1539 to 1560, was practically the Bible of England. It had the privilege of being read in all English churches. It had virtually superseded, as it was meant to supersede, all other versions of the Bible in English. It must have been of the Great Bible, therefore, that the Geneva translators more particularly spoke, when, in their epistle to the brethren of England, Scotland, and Ireland, they said, " We thought we could bestow our labours and study in nothing which could be more acceptable to God, and comfortable to his church, than in the translating of the Scriptures into our native tongue: the which thing albeit that others have endeavoured to achieve, yet, considering the infancy of those times and imperfect knowledge of the tongues in respect of this ripe age and clear light which God hath now revealed, the translations required greatly to be perused and reformed." To what extent, then, was the Great Bible corrected and amended by the Geneva exiles?

To a very great extent indeed. Many verses are quite remodelled—changed all over—and made to express a different meaning from what they did before. A still larger number of verses are improved in their diction, so that they are made to read more clearly and smoothly, and to come home to the heart more impressively. A few verses, however, that are altered, are not altered for the better ; and several changes are made, by way of correction, which we are almost sorry were necessitated.

One passage in the Great Bible that we should have been thankful to see retained, so well does it give expression to a noble religious hope, which, but for the anachronism involved, might be called Christian, is Job xix. 25, 26 : " For I am sure that my redemer lyueth, and that *I shal ryse out of the earth in the latter daye ; that I shal be clothed agayne with this skynne, and se God in my fleshe.*" The Geneva translators had, of course, to render the words of Scripture as they found them in the original text, and they accordingly made the passage read : ' For I am sure that my redeemer liveth, and he shall stand the last[1] on the earth. And though, after my skinne,

---

[1] This strange reading is countenanced by the Latin version Zurich, 1564. Noui redemptorem meum esse viuentem et nouissimum qui super terram surget.

wormes destroy this body, yet shall I se God in my flesh." Another verse in the book of Job that found a new rendering in the Geneva version is chap. xxxiv. 29. In the Great Bible, that verse reads : " If he graunt pardone, who wyll condemne ? and if he hyde awaye his countenance who shall be able to se it. Whether it be to the people, or to any man, thus wyll he do." The Geneva translators changed this rendering into substantially the form it now assumes in the authorised version : " When he *giveth quietnesse*, who can *make trouble* ? and when he hideth his face, who can behold him, whether it be *upon nations or upon a man only* ? " A very odd reading that we find in the Great Bible is : " Geve part seuen dayes and also upon the eighth ; for thou knowest not what misery shall come upon the earth."[1] Eccles. xi. 2. The appearance of this reading in the Great Bible is all the more strange, too, that Coverdale, in his own translation, 1535, had previously given the right reading. The Geneva divines restored Coverdale's first rendering ; and put the verse in the form it still retains in the authorised Bible. A message from the Lord, in very homely terms, appears in the Great Bible, Is. xl. 2 : " Comfort Jerusalem at the herte, and tell her, that her trauayle is at an end, that her offence is pardoned, that she hath receyued of the Lordes hande sufficient correccion for all her synnes." The terms of this message have at least the merit of perfect clearness, if nothing else ; and some commentators are of opinion that they express the true mind of the spirit. But this opinion is open to question. The words of the original admit of another interpretation ; and the Geneva translators have accordingly given a literal rendering of the passage, which neither adds to nor takes anything from the original text : " She hath received of the Lord's hand *double* for all her sins." The alternative meaning of this rendering they have also set before the reader, in a marginal note, which says : " sufficient and full correction " (as stated in the Great Bible) " *or double grace*, whereas she deserved double punishment."

---

[1] In the Vulgate the words are so incomplete and ambiguous that they will bear either translation, " Da partem septem, necnon et octo." In other Latin versions, such as Zurich, 1564, the words are, Da partem *panis* septem *indigentibus.*

The following extracts will further illustrate the different meanings that verses of Scripture were represented to bear in the Great Bible and the Geneva Bible respectively :—

GREAT BIBLE, 1540.

Lev. viii. 33-34.—For seven days shall he *fyll your hande*, as he dyd this day.

1 Sam. ix. 20.—Moreover whose shall the *beautifull thynges* of Israel be ? Belonge they not to the, and to all thy father's house ?

Job ix. 3, 4.—Yf he (man) will argue with hym, there is not *one among a thousand that can answere hym*. Concernynge soch as be *wyse of herte* or myghtie in strength who euer prospered, that tooke parte agaynste hym.

Prov. xvii. 8.—A rewarde is a precious stone unto hym that hath it ; but unto whomsoever it turneth, *it maketh hym unwyse*.

Prov. xix. 18.—Chasten thy sonne whyle there is hope ; but let not thy soule be *moued to slaye hym*.

Prov. xxvii. 19.—Lyke as in one water there appere dyuerse faces, euen so dyuers men have dyuerse hartes.

Eccles. v. 1.—When thou comest into the house of God, kepe thy foot *and draw nigh, that God which is at hande maye heare that* thou geve not the offrings of fooles : for they knowe *nought but* to do euell.

Eccles. v. 8.—If thou seest the poore to be oppressed and wrongfully delt withal, so that equitie and ryghte of the lawe is wrested in the lande, maruayle not thou at soche a thynge, *for one great man kepeth touch with another and the myghtie men are in auctorytie ouer the poore*.

Is. xlii. 3, 4.—But faythfully and truely shall he geue judgement, *not be pensive nor carefull*, that he may restore righteousnes unto the erth.

Is. liii. 8.—Whose *generacion* yet who may *nombre?*

Is. liii. 10.—Yet hath it pleased the Lorde thus to burste him with plages, and to smyte him with infirmyties, *that* when he had made his soul an offering for synne he myght se longe lasting seed. And *this devyce* of the Lorde shall prospere in his hande.

Hab. iii. 2.—The worke that thou hast taken in hande, *shalt thou perfourme*

GENEVA BIBLE, 1560.

Lev. viii. 33-34.—For seven days, said the Lord, shall he *consecrate you*, as he hath done this day.

1 Sam. ix. 20.—On whom *is set all the desire of* Israel, is it not upon thee, and all thy father's house ?

Job ix. 3, 4.—If he (man) would dispute with him, he coulde not answere him *one thing* of a thousand. *He is wise in heart* and mighty in strength ; who hath been fierce against him and hath prospered ?

Prov. xvii. 8.—A reward is a stone pleasant in the eyes of them that have it ; *it prospereth* whithersoever it turneth.

Prov. xix. 18.—Chasten thy sonne whyle there is hope, and let not thy soul *spare for his murmuring*.

Prov. xxvii. 19.—As in water, face answereth to face, so the heart of man to man.

Eccles. v. 1.—Take heede to thy foote when thou entrest into the house of God, and *bee more neare to heare than to give* the sacrifice of fooles : for they know not that they do euill.

Eccles. v. 8 (v. 7 in Geneva Bible).—If in a countrey thou seest the oppression of the poore, and the defrauding of judgement and justice, be not astonyed at the matter : for he *that is higher than the highest regardeth, and there be higher than they*.

Is. xlii. 3, 4.—He shall bring forth judgment in trueth. *He shall not fayle nor be discouraged* till he have set judgment in the earth.

Is. liii. 8.—Who shall *declare his age ?*

Is. liii. 10.—Yet the Lord would breake him, and make him subject to infirmities ; when he shall make his soul an offering for sin, he shall see his seede and shall prolong his daies, and *the wil* of the Lord shall prosper in his hand.

Hab. iii. 2.—O Lord, *revive thy* work in the middes of the people ; *in the*

in his tyme, O Lord ; and *when thy tyme cometh thou shalt declare it.* In thy very wrathe *thou thynkest upon mercy.*

Zech. iv. 10.—For *he that hath ben despised* a lytle season shall rejoice, *when he seeth the tynne weight in Zorababel's hand.*

Zech. vi. 3.—In the fourth charet were horses of dyuerse colours and *stronge.*

middes of the yeres make it knowne ; in wrath *remember mercy.*

Zech. iv. 10.—For who hath *despised the day of the small things :* but they shall rejoice and shall see the stone of tinne in the hand of Zerubabel.

Zech. vi. 3.—In the fourth charet horses of dyuerse colours and *reddish.*

Even more than by the accuracy of its translation, the Geneva version asserted superiority over the Great Bible by the refinement of its diction. A large number of words and phrases and entire sentences, which have ever since been retained in the English Bibles of the Protestant Churches, were first introduced into these Bibles by the Geneva translators. A large number, also, of other phrases and sentences that we find in the authorised version made their first appearance, in a crude and unfinished form, in the Geneva Bible.

Not to speak of such archaisms as *ouerthwarte*, in the phrase, "an ouerthwarte tonge," Prov. xvii. 20 ; and *perbrake*, in the statement, "the morsels that thou hast eaten shalt thou perbrake," Prov. xxiii. 8 ; or of such malapropisms as *abundance*, in the oft-recurring expression "the abundance of the liver," (the caul above the liver): there are in the Great Bible not a few terms that are not as meet as they should be for the place they occupy. One of these, which has already been commented on, is *luck*. Whether from a sense of literary propriety, or because the term seemed to countenance a certain metaphysical theory at variance with Calvinistic views, this word is in the Geneva Bible left out of more than one passage where it is found in the Great Bible. The statement, "we have wished you good lucke," Ps. cxviii. 26, is converted into "we have blessed you" ; and the ecphonesis "good lucke, good lucke," which is represented by Coverdale to have greeted the ears of Zerubabel, when the head stone of the second temple was set in its place, is transformed into the more reverent acclamation of "grace, grace." A phrase in the Great Bible that very imperfectly expresses the meaning it is intended to convey is *the noblenesse of my dignity* :—" Reuben, myne eldest sonne, thou art my might and the beginning of my strength, the noblenesse of my dignity and the noblenesse of my power." By the substitution of *excellency* for "noblenesse," the Geneva divines gave to this utterance all the majesty that was wanted, and nearly all the clearness that was possible. Another amendment that was made by the Geneva divines on an old rendering in the Pentateuch, is one that must be remitted to the faculty of physicians to express their opinion upon. Both in Coverdale's Bible and in the Great Bible the wives of the Israelites are said, Ex. i. 19, to have been "sturdy wemen," and to have been delivered of their children in Goshen, "yer" the midwives came at them. The word *sturdy*, suggestive of plebeian vigour, was by the Geneva divines courteously changed into another adjective more consonant with cultured notions of physical grace.[1] A not overly delicate phrase, again, that was in high repute and much vogue during the later struggles of Puritanism in England was "hip and thigh." The phrase, as every one knows, occurs in the authorised version of the Bible, Judges xv. 8. But it must have been gratifying to the muscular Christians of the Puritan party in the days of "stout, religious" Cromwell to think that that church-militant expression, which rose so oft to their lips and sounded so sweet in their ears, was coined by their Puritan fathers in Geneva. The castigation that Samson gave the Philistines is said in the Great Bible to have been administered on "the legge and thigh"; but that, it will be observed, was a much milder "instruction" than the sainted legions of the Lord Protector thought it their duty to bestow on Cavaliers and Churchmen. And, to pass from the scourge of the rod to the scourge of the tongue, it may be remarked that never was lofty taunt expressed in choicer terms than in Lam. ii. 5, where strangers are described as pointing to the humbled daughter of Jerusalem, and saying, "Is this the city that men call the perfection of beauty, the joy of the whole earth"! This rendering, which we find in the authorised Bible, is just a transcript of what is

---

[1] The reading in the Vulgate is curious, "Ipsæ enim obstetricandi habent scientiam." The literal meaning of the Hebrew word translated *lively* in the Geneva and Authorised Bibles is, according to Dr. A. Clark, "strong, hale, and vigorous."

given, and was first given, in the Geneva version. In the Great Bible the verse reads, " Is this the cytie that men call so fayre, wherein the whole land rejoyseth " : a pathetic utterance, too, but a very rudimentary exclamation compared with what it was matured into by the Geneva divines. It is only by means of parallel columns, however, that we can fully perceive the amount of improvement effected by the exiles at Geneva on the diction of the English Bible. The following extracts are accordingly, with this view, submitted, without comment, for comparison.

GREAT BIBLE, 1540.

Gen. xxv. 8.—And then fell sycke, and dyed in a lusty age, when he had lived ynough, and was put to his people.

Deut. xxxii. 7.—Remember the days of the world that is past, consyder the years from tyme to tyme.

1 Sam. iv. 13.—Eli sat upon a stole, and looked toward the waye.

Job xxx. 23.—Sure I am, that thou wilt delyver me unto death, even to the lodging that is due unto all men lyuing.

Job xxxvii. 4.—His glorious magesty geveth soche a thondre clappe that (though a man heare it) yet may he not perceave it afterwarde.

Eccles. i. 2.—All is but moost vayne vanytie, sayeth the Preacher, and all is moost vayne.

Eccles. xii. 1.—Remembre thy maker the sooner in thy youth, or ever the days of adversitie come.

Is. i. 4.—Alas for this synful nation, a people of great iniquitie.

Is. i. 16.—Washe you, make you cleane, put away your euell thoughtes out of my syght, cease from doynge of euell, learne to do ryght, applie yourselves to equitie, deliuer the oppressed, helpe the fatherlesse to his ryght, let the wydowes complaint come before you.

Is. xi. 3.—He shall not give sentence after the thing that shall be brought before his eyes.

Is. xxxii. 2.—The shadow of a great rock in a dry land.

Is. l. 11.—But take hede, ye al kyndle a fyre of the wrath of God, and steare up the cooles, walk on in the glisteryng of your owne fyre and in the cooles that ye have kyndled.

Is. lxi. 3.—That I might geve, I saye,

GENEVA BIBLE, 1560.

Gen. xxv. 8.—Then Abraham yeelded the spirit, and died in a good age, an olde man and of great yeeres, and was gathered to his people.

Deut. xxxii. 7.—Remember the dayes of olde, consider the yeeres of so many generations.

1 Sam. iv. 13.—Eli sate upon a seate by the wayside, waiting.

Job xxx. 23.—Surely, I know that thou wilt bring me to death, and to the house appointed for all the living.

Job xxxvii. 4.—He thundereth with the voice of his majestie, and he wil not staie them when his voyce is heard.

Eccles. i. 2.—Vanitie of vanities, sayeth the Preacher, vanity of vanities, all is vanity.

Eccles. xii. 1.—Remember now thy Creator in the dayes of thy youth, whiles the euill dayes come not.

Is. i. 4.—Ah, sinnefull nation, a people laden with iniquitie.

Is. i. 16.—Wash you, make you clean, take away the euil of your workes from before mine eyes, cease to do euil, lerne to do well, seeke judgment, relieve the oppressed, judge the fatherlesse, and defend the widow.

Is. xi. 3.—He shall not judge after the sight of his eyes.

Is. xxxii. 2.—The shadow of a great rock in a weary land.

Is. l. 11.—Beholde, all you kindle a fire, and are compassed about with sparkes : walke in the light of your fire, and in the sparkes that ye have kindled.

Is. lxi. 3.—To give unto them beautie

Geneva	Authorised
beauty instead of ashes, joyful oyntment for syghing, pleasant raiment for an hevy mynde.	for ashes, the oyle of joy for mourning, the garment of gladness for the spirit of heaviness.
Jer. ix. 1.—Who wyll geve my heade water ynough, and a well of teares for myne eyes that I maye wepe nyghte and daye for the slaughter of my people.	Jer. ix. 1.—Oh that mine head were ful of waters and mine eyes a fountain of teares that I might weepe day and night for the slain of the daughter of my people.
Jer. x. 4.—It standeth as styffe as the palme tree, it can neyther speake nor go one fote, but must be borne.	Jer. x. 4.—The idols stand up as the palme tree, but speake not; they are borne because they cannot go.
Jer. xxiii. 11.—The prophets and the priests themselves are polluted hypocrites.	Jer. xxiii. 11.—Both the prophet and the priest do wickedly.
Hag. ii. 7.—I wyll move all heathen, and the comforte of all heathen shall come, and so wyll I fyll this house with honoure, sayeth the Lord of hoostes.	Hag. ii. 7.—And I will move all nations, and the desire of all nations shall come, and I will fill this house with glory, saith the Lord of hosts.
Zech. i. 5.—What is nowe become of your forefathers, and the prophetes, are they yet styll alyue?	Zech. i. 5.—Your fathers, where are they, and do the prophets live for ever?
Zech. ii. 5.—Yee, I myself (sayeth the Lorde) wyll be unto her a wall of fyre round aboute, and wyll be honoured in her.	Zech. ii. 5.—For I, sayth the Lorde, wil be unto her a wall of fire rounde aboute, and will be the glory in the middes of her.

It will be seen that, in a considerable number of the foregoing extracts from the Geneva version, the amendments made on the renderings in the Great Bible have been retained in the authorised translation. This is the best certificate that, at the end of fifty years, could have been given to their intrinsic excellence. In many cases, however, the amendments made by the Geneva divines have not been retained in the authorised version, but have been themselves amended. Still, although they failed to receive the honour of being adopted into the national Bible of 1611, they furnished, in not a few instances, the lines on which the King's translators worked. They were, in other words, not only improvements on the renderings in the Great Bible, but they suggested and contributed materials for still further improved renderings, which appear now in the authorised version. They were scrolls or drafts of revision, which were finally adjusted, by a national committee, fifty years afterwards.

In some instances, it must be admitted, the changes of diction made by the Geneva revisers on the English Bible were not improvements. This was to be expected. Wherever many changes are made, they can scarcely be all for the better. It is satisfactory if a large majority are.

The Geneva translators were neither invariably fortunate in their choice of words, invariably successful in their composition of phrases, nor invariably happy in their renderings. It is a sound maxim in revision, to let well alone; and so, when the Geneva divines found it said in the Great Bible, Prov. vi. 6, "Go to the *emmet*, thou sluggard, and consider her wayes," it may be asked, in the name of wonder, why they could not have allowed that rendering to stand, but should have substituted for the word italicised an unsavoury term of nauseous and obvious etymology.[1] With the title *dame* no fault need be found. It is a simple, good, old-fashioned term, perhaps a little out of date now, but current enough at one time. And quite a proper application is made of it in the Geneva version, Gen. xvi. 8, where Hagar is represented as saying to the angel of the Lord: "I flee from my *dame* Sarai." Still, it was unnecessary to introduce the word into that verse, when there was in the Great Bible another word quite as good, and as well understood, "mastresse." One rendering in the authorised Bible that has been disallowed in the revised is Hos. x. 1—"Israel is an *empty* vine." This rendering is, in more ways than one, objectionable. It is not a happy phrase, and even readers who know nothing of Hebrew will see that it does not harmonise with the context. On the Geneva divines must rest the discredit of having introduced it into the English Bible. In the Great Bible there was a different rendering, not very far removed in meaning from what is given in the revised version, 1885; and, apart from its accuracy or inaccuracy as a translation, it contained a very cogently worded declaration for the people of Israel to reflect on :—"Israel was a *goodly* vine, but he hath brought forth unprofytable frute : yea, the more frute he had, the more aultares he made : the more good I dyd to their lande the more frendshypp shewed they to theyr ymages." [2] A verse admitted to be obscure and of doubtful meaning in the Hebrew Scriptures is Gen. iv. 23.

---

[1] Pismire.

[2] In the Vulgate the words are "vitis frondosa Israel"; in the translation by Pagninus, "vitis vacua Israel."

By some people the words of Lamech, recorded in that verse, have been regarded as an expression of contrition and sorrow, as if their purport were, " I slew a man, and I thereby brought on myself a sore misfortune." By other people they have been regarded as an exultation, " A young man wounded me, and I gave him his quietus. So shall perish all the enemies of Lamech." In the Great Bible it is the former of these interpretations that is put on the passage, " I have slayne a man to the woundynge of myselfe, and a young man to mine own punyshment." The Geneva divines adopted, as their marginal note shews, the other interpretation; and that interpretation is the one that at the present day finds most favour. But the Geneva rendering is ill-worded and obscure, and is thus, from the English reader's point of view, the reverse of an improvement on what it superseded. Its tenor is, " I would slay a man in my wound, and a yong man in mine hurte."[1] Another verse in the Hebrew Scriptures that has presented itself in different lights to different minds is Song vii. 5. In the authorised Bible this verse reads, " Thine head upon thee is like Carmel, and the hair of thine head like purple: the King is held in the galleries." What the meaning of the last clause of this sentence can be, and what connection its words have with those in the clause preceding, must be left to men of more than common discernment to explain. In the revised version, 1885, a rendering is given which admits of easier comprehension :—" The King is held captive in the tresses thereof." A still different, and a very picturesque, rendering of the verse appears in the Great Bible :—" That heade that standeth upon thee is lyke Carmell : and the heare of thy heade is lyke purple, lyke a King going forth with his gard about him." This imagery, also, we can understand, and its aptness strikes us forcibly. Yet another rendering of the verse, and, whether accurate or not, "the goodliest of all" is given in Coverdale's Bible :—" The hayre of thy heade is like

---

[1] The marginal note on the verse is, " His wives, seeing that all men hated him for his cruelty, were afraid ; therefore he braggeth that there is none so lusty that were able to resist, although he were already wounded."

the kynges purple, folden up in plates." It may well be asked, how did the authorised translators ever stumble on the rendering they have given in their version? They found it in the Geneva Bible, not exactly in the words in which they have presented it to us, but in these words :—" Thine heade upon thee is as scarlet, and the bushe of thine heade like purple : *the king is tyed in the rafters.*"[1] Another notable phrase that we find in the authorised version, Is. li. 20, is "a wild bull in a net." This, also, is an importation from the Geneva version. To many readers, it conveys the idea of bridled fury. But this is not the idea that the prophet meant to express, as will appear from the context :—" Thy sons have fainted, they lie at the head of all the streets, as ——" something very helpless. And this helpless object to which the sons of Zion are compared is, in the Great Bible, pathetically called "a taken venyson."

Between the issue of the last of what we have termed the Reformers' Bibles and the first of the Geneva versions of the Testament, there intervened a period of nearly twenty years. This is not a long period, even in the history of a human life, and it bulks much less in the history of a language. It is seldom that, in so short a time, a language undergoes much change. But wherever there is literary activity, language is always changing ; and in the days between the reigns of the last Henry and Elizabeth, the English language was at that particular stage of growth when appreciable changes could, at very brief intervals, be discerned in its aspect. It thus happens, that between the diction of the Geneva versions and that of the Reformers' Bibles there is a perceptible difference. Many of the quaint antiquated words that abound in the

---

[1] The words in the Geneva Bible are a literal rendering of what appears in the Latin version printed at Zurich in 1564 :—Caput tuum super te veluti coccinum et coma capitis tui sicut purpura, Rex ligatus in *tignis.*" For *tignis* we find *canalibus* in the version by Pagninus. The reading in the Vulgate is :—" Comae capitis tui sicut purpura regis vincta canalibus," which in the Douay Bible, 1610, is rendered :
—" The hairs of thy head as a King's purple tyed to *cundite pipes.*" The rendering in the Bishops' Bible, 1572, is :—" The heare of thy head is like purple, and like a King dwelling among many water conduites."

writings of Tyndale and Coverdale are replaced in the Geneva versions by terms of more modern and familiar usage. And yet in the Geneva versions, also, there is not a little interesting archaism to be found.

There are, for instance, a few cases of antiquated inflexions and of antiquated compoundings to be met with. It is perhaps scarcely justifiable to call participles prefixed or preceded by *a* antiquated forms of verbal construction, seeing that not only in the authorised but also in the recently revised version of the Bible, it is said in Luke ix. 42, " as he was yet *a* coming " ; and in Heb. xi. 21, " Jacob when he was *a* dying blessed the sons of Joseph." This form of speech, however, is at least less common in modern writings than in writings three hundred years old ; and we find instances of it in the Geneva version which are not retained in the authorised, such as, " Fourty and six yeres was this temple *a* building," John ii. 20. Some prefixes of *be*, also, which are seldom or never heard in modern speech, may be found in one or other of the Geneva versions. In the Testament, 1557, it is said, Rev. xviii. 9:—"The kynges of the earth shal *bewepe* her and wayle ouer her." In the same version, 1557, we find " holpe " for *helped* :—" He *holpe* other men, let him help himself " ; in both the first and second versions, " gnew " for *gnawed* :—" They *gnew* their tongues for sorowe " ; in all the three versions, " pight " for pitched :—" The true tabernacle which the Lord *pight* and not man " ; and " werest " for *wert* :—" I woulde thou *werest* cold or hotte." And not only do we, in the first of these versions, meet with " other " for *either*, but in that version we repeatedly meet with " no nother " for *none other* :—Now preach I man's doctrine or God's ? *other* go I about to please men ? " Gal. i. 10 ; " *No nother* of the Apostles sawe I, save James the Lord's brother," Gal. i. 19. An expression in the first Geneva version of the Testament that has an antique appearance is, " geve *accountes* of thy stewardship," Luke xvi. 2 ; and in the subsequent versions, this expression is changed into one still further removed from modern phraseology, " give *an accounts* of thy stewardship."

The obsolete words to be found in the Geneva versions are

N

few in number, compared with those in earlier versions. Several words that appear in Tyndale's are retained in the first Geneva version of the Testament, but not in the two subsequent ones. Of these may be mentioned, "arede" for *prophesy*, "bide" for *abide*, "let" for *hindrance*, "yer while" for *already*, "eareth" for *ploweth*. Other words in Tyndale's Testament that seem equally antiquated are introduced into all the three Geneva Testaments, such as "griece" or "grece" for *stair*, "mete" for *measure*, "polle money" for *tribute*. There are antiquated words, too, in the Geneva Testaments, which do not appear in the corresponding passages in Tyndale's version. For instance, in all the three Geneva versions, we read in the Acts of the Apostles, chap. v. 33., "They *brast* for anger," (were cut to the heart); chap. xxi. 15, "We *trussed* up our *fardels*," (took up our carriages);[1] chap. xxiv. 22, "I will *decise* your matter," (I will know the uttermost of your matter).

A most unregrettably-obsolete word that appears in the first Geneva version of the new Testament is "giltieship": "The giltieship came of one offence unto condemnation, but the gyft is geven to justifie from many sinnes."[2] A less objectionable word that appears in the same version is "refection," in the sense of a luncheon or refreshment: "He entred into the house . . . to take his refection," Luke xiv. 2.

Of common words used in a peculiar and archaic sense, a very considerable number will be found in the different Geneva translations. In the first Geneva version of the Testament, the

---

[1] By using the word *carriage* in this peculiar sense, the shepherd David is made, in the authorised version, to conduct himself like a modern dandy in the field of battle : "Israel and the Philistines had put the battle in array, army against army. And David left his *carriage* in the hand of the keeper of the *carriage*, and ran into the army." 1 Sam. xvii. 21, 22. See revised version. See also Is. x. 28.

[2] In the second Geneva version of the New Testament, St. Paul is made to say, Acts xxii. 28: "With a great sum obtained I this *burgess-ship*." A very homely word used in the Geneva Bible (and in the Great Bible) is "nippers": "I gave my back unto the smiters, and my cheekes to the *nippers*," Is. l. 6. Another homely rendering that occurs in all the Geneva versions of the Testament is 1 Pet. iii. 6: "Sarah obeyed Abraham, and called him, *Syr*." And what will probably be considered another homely phrase in the Geneva versions is James ii. 16—"Warme yourselves, and fill your bellies."

word *depart* is used, as it is by Wyclif, in the sense of divide: "They solde their possessions and goodes, and *departed* them to all men, as every man had need," Acts ii. 45: "Nether height, nether depth, nether any other creature shal be able to *departe* us from the love of God," Rom. viii. 39. The word *separate* is also in that version used in a peculiar sense. In the authorised translation, 1611, we read, Luke xii. 46: "The Lord of that servant will come in a day when he looketh not for him, and at an hour when he is not aware, and *will cut him in sunder.*" The last clause of this verse is rendered by Wyclif, "will departe him;" by Tyndale, "will devyde him;" by Coverdale, in the Great Bible, "will hew him in pieces;" by the Geneva divines, 1560, "will cut him off;" and by Whittingham, in the first Geneva Testament, 1557, "will separate him."[1] A word, again, that from time immemorial has had a place in the ritual of the Church of England, and has lately been heard in some Presbyterian churches in Scotland, is *lesson*, in the sense of a portion of Scripture to be read publicly. And in this sense of the term, "lesson" occurs in at least one English version of the New Testament, the Rhemes or authorised Catholic translation: "After the *lesson* of the law and the prophets, the princes of the synagogue sent to (Paul and Barnabas), saying, Men, brethren, if there be among you any sermon of exhortation to the people, speak," Acts xiii. 15. But, what may seem strange to Scotsmen, the word *lecture*, which in their country has for more than two hundred years been synonymous with expository discourse, is, in all the Geneva versions, the term used in this passage for *lesson* or *reading*. This curious fact indicates that the original Church *lecture*, in Scotland as well as elsewhere, was not an extempore exposition or running commentary, but a bare reading of Scripture. And this conclusion is corroborated by the name *lectern*, which in olden times was given to the *reader's* desk in Scottish churches. Of other words used in an obsolete or almost obsolete sense in one or other of the

---

[1] Whittingham's rendering, 1557, is a literal translation of Beza's Latin version of the passage, "separabit eum." In the Vulgate the words are "dividet eum," and in the version of Erasmus, "dissecabit eum."

Geneva versions of the Testament may be mentioned :— *improve*, in the sense of reprove, 2 Tim. iv. 2, "improve, rebuke ;" *slander*, in the sense of an evil report, whether false or true, Titus i. 6, "faithful children, not slandered of ryot;" *honest*, in the sense of respectable or of good social position, Acts xvii. 12, " honest women, which were Grekes ";[1] *wealth*, in the sense of welfare, Rom. xiii. 4, " He (the civil magistrate) is the minister of God for thy wealth"; *harness*, in the sense of armour, Luke xi. 22, "When a stronger than he commeth upon hym at unawares, and overcometh hym, he taketh from him all his harnes wherein he trusted"; and *commodity*, in the sense of privilege or blessing, Rom. xiv. 16, "Cause not your commodity to be evil spoken of: for the kingdom of God is not meat and drinke, but righteousness, peace, and joy in the holy ghost." One word used in a very peculiar sense in the first Geneva version of the Testament is *patron*—" The under captayne beleued the gouernor and the *patron of the ship* better than those things which were spoken of Paul," Acts xxvii. 11.

We have seen how wakeful the watchmen of the Catholic Church were lest any of their approved ecclesiastical terms should not receive in the English Bible their proper place and honour. Wyclif was faulted for using the word *repentance* instead of *penance*, and Tyndale was exclaimed against for using the plain and well understood word *favour*, instead of juggling with the more mystical term *grace*. The refugees at Geneva were mostly ultra-Protestants, Reformers of the radical type represented by Calvin and Beza ; and it might have been expected, therefore, that their version of the Bible would bristle all over with the most consummately barbed ecclesiastical spikes. They had the discretion, however, to make their ecclesiastical proclivities known by their annotations rather than by their text of Scripture. Their translation exhibits nothing that is ecclesiastically startling, but there is some extremely

---

[1] Both in Tyndale's Testament and the Great Bible they are designated "worshypful wemen," and in the revised version, 1881, "women of honourable estate." An odd application of the word "honest" occurs in the Great Bible, "Up, Zion, up, take thy strength unto thee : Put on thy *honeste* rayment, O Jerusalem, thou holye cittie," Is. lii. 1.

plain speaking in their marginal notes. A few of their renderings, nevertheless, must have been offensive to conservative Catholics. Following the Latin Vulgate, both Wyclif and the Popish exiles at Rhemes have translated Acts ii. 38, "*Do penance*, and be every one of you baptized . . . and you shall receive the gift of the holy ghost." For the phrase "do penance" Tyndale and the framers of the authorised version, translating directly from the original Greek, substituted *repent*. The Geneva translators went a step further in the rationalistic and anti-ceremonial direction, by rendering the first article of St. Peter's instruction, " amend your lives." There is at least one instance, too, in which the Geneva translators have followed Tyndale in the use of *favour* for *grace* : "To him that worketh, wages is not counted by *favour* but by debt." The terms *bishop* and *bishopric* had long before the Reformation come to have such specific meanings, and to signify in common acceptation so much more than they originally did, that a presbyterian may be excused for saying they should never have been introduced into the English Bible at all, any more than the word *priests* in passages where *presbyteroi* occurs in the Greek. And the Geneva translators have shewn how this might have been done. " His bishopric let another take," they render, " *his charge let another take.*" The democratic theory of church government, too, which recognises the right of every congregation to elect its own office-bearers, is shown pretty clearly to have been the theory in vogue among the Reformers at Geneva. In the postscripts attached to several of the Epistles, the Geneva divines make use of the word *elected* instead of *ordained*, in reference to bishops; as if to indicate that episcopal appointments were originally conferred by popular vote, and not by ecclesiastical ceremonial. In one case we read, " Unto Timotheus, the first Bishop *elected* of the Church of Ephesus;" and in another, "Unto Titus, *elect* the first Bishop of the Church of the Cretians."

It may be supposed, that in a version of the Bible so popular as the Geneva version was in this country for nearly a hundred years, there will be not only many well chosen expressions, which have been adopted by subsequent translators ; but also, that of those not so adopted and continued, there will be many of considerable merit notwithstanding. And such is the case. But there is, likewise, in the Geneva versions a large number of readings that are much inferior to those in the authorised translation. Proofs of this statement could, with little difficulty, be adduced in scores. The following, however, will suffice to establish the assertion. In all the Geneva versions we read, Luke xix. 8, "If I have taken anything from any man by *forged cavillation* I restore him fourfold." In the account of St. Peter's denial of his Master, it is stated in all the Geneva versions, Luke xxii. 58, that after the Apostle had been challenged by one of the *maids* in the palace,[1] "another *man* saw him, and sayd, Thou art also of them." The immortal description that Jesus gave of John the Baptist, "a burning and a shining light," is with more than pre-raphaelite realism converted by the Geneva divines into "a burning and a shining *candle*." Of Peter and John it is said in the Geneva versions, Acts iii. 1, that they "went up together into the temple, at the *ninth hour of prayer.*" The clear direction, "what God hath cleansed call not thou common," is ambiguously represented in all the Geneva versions, "what God hath purified pollute thou not." The generous rule of Christian courtesy, so finely and delicately given by the way as it were, Rom. xii. 10, "In honour preferring one another," is in the Geneva and earlier versions statuted into what looks more like an order of ceremonial than a law of loving kindness, "In giving honour, *go one before another.*" The Apostle's entreaty to the Galatians, "Let no man trouble me," is in all the Geneva versions, as well as in Tyndale's and Cranmer's, rendered, "Let no man *put me to business.*" By the employment of the word *preach* for *proclaim*, a ludicrous effect is produced by the Geneva translators on one of the grandest passages in the book of Revelation : " I saw a strong angel, which *preached with a loud voice.*" And in another passage of the Apocalypse, a similar unhappy effect results from their use of the culinary word "boiled" where

---

[1] In the corresponding passage, Mat. xxvi, the word "maid" is correctly given in all the three Geneva versions.

in the authorised version we find the term "scorched." The fourth angel, it is said, poured out his vial on the sun, "and power was geven unto him to vex men with heat of fyre, and men *boyled* in great heate, and blasphemed the name of God." [1] A very coarse word, again, which need not be emphasised, occurs in all the Geneva versions of 1 Cor. vi. 9-10: "Be not deceived, neither fornicators, nor idolaters, nor adulterers, nor wantons, nor buggerers, nor thieves, nor covetous, nor drunkards, nor extortioners shall inherite the kingdome of God." [2]

In the Old Testament, too, we meet in the Geneva version with many phrases that have been set aside by choicer ones in the authorised translation. A wonderfully feeble ending, for instance, is given to the twenty-third Psalm: "Doubtless kindness and mercy shall follow me all the days of my life, and I shall remain a long season in the house of the Lord." An odd and infelicitous phrase, again, is introduced into Gen. xxix. 1: "Iaakob lift up his feete, and came into the east country." Sweet, simple, and melodious are the words in which, in the authorised translation of the Bible, the consolations of death are sadly sung by the afflicted patriarch: "There the wicked cease from troubling, and there the weary are at rest." In comparison with these artless strains, the rendering of the Geneva divines is painfully halt: "The wicked have there ceased from their tyrannie, and there they that laboured valiantly are at rest." In respect of majesty and melody, again, there is a wide difference between the Geneva rendering of Jer. ii. 21, "How then art thou turned unto me into the plantes of a strange vine," and the authorised, "How art thou turned into

---

[1] The same rendering is given in the Rhemes Testament, 1582; while in Tyndale's Testament the passage reads, "The men *raged* in gret heate." The word both in the Vulgate and in Beza's Latin translation, which has been rendered *boyled* is *aestuaverunt (aestuaverunt aestu magno)*.

[2] As specimens of odd rendering in the Geneva versions of the New Testament the following may be instanced: Acts xix. 27. "Not only this thing is dangerous unto us that the *state should be reproved* but also that the temple of the great goddess Diana should be nothing esteemed," (second version); 2 Cor. vii. 2, "We have done wrong to no man, we have *consumed* no man," (second version), "We have *wasted no man's goods*," (first version).

the degenerate plant of a strange vine unto me." Between the two phrases, "rejoice and blossom," and "be glad and flourish," it may seem to some people that there is little to choose, and yet the choice may seriously affect the rhythm of a noble sentence. In the Geneva rendering of Is. xxxv. 1, " The waste ground shall be glad and flourish as the rose," there is neither the swell nor the jubilancy that there is in the more recent translation, " The desert shall rejoice and blossom as the rose." Worse than unmelodious, too, is the strange and unhappy expression ascribed to the Lord by the Geneva translators in Is. xliii. 24 : " Thou broughtest me no sweete sauour with money, neither hast thou *made me drunke* with the fat of thy sacrifices." [1]

More than to aught else, the popularity of the Geneva Bible was due to its prologues and marginal notes. These annotations, however, are so numerous and miscellaneous that it is not easy to give, in a brief statement, a fair representation of their general tenor.[2] Many of them are strongly anti-papal, and for that reason they were idolised by immoderate Reformers. The abuse bestowed on the Pope is quite unparliamentary. In one note, on Rev. ix. 11, he is bluntly designated, "Anti-Christ, King of hypocrites, and Satan's ambassador." The odious number 666 is unhesitatingly assigned him ; for, "these characters χξϛ signify 666, and the number is gathered of the small number λατεινος which . . . signifieth Latin,

---

[1] An odd rendering in the Geneva version of the Old Testament is Zeph. i. 12 : "The men that are *frosen* in their dregs."

[2] The marginal notes are not the same in all editions of the Geneva Testament. In the two editions referred to in the heading of this chapter, viz., London, 1580 (*second* version), and London, 1599 (*third* version), the notes are quite different. For instance, on Acts xxiii. 5—"I knew not, brethren, that he was the high priest, for it is written, thou shalt not speak evil of the ruler of thy people,"—the note in edition 1580 (and 1560) is, "He made this excuse as it were in mockerie, as if he would say, I know nothing in this man worthy the office of the hie priest." In edition 1599 (Tomson's revision) the note is, " We must willingly and from the heart give honour to magistrates, although they bee tyrants." A curious ethical note on the following verse is given in this edition, 1599, "We may lawfully sometimes set the wicked together by the eares, that they may leave off to assault us " ! The notes quoted in this chapter are taken from the edition 1580, and are, strictly speaking, the *Geneva* notes. The notes in editions that contain Tomson's revisions are of more modern date.

and noteth the Pope or Anti-Christ who useth in all things the Latin tongue, and in respect thereof he contemneth the Hebrew and Greek wherein the word of God was first and best written." The phrase, "worship the image of the beast," Rev. xiii. 15, is paraphrased on the margin, "Receive the ordinances and decrees of the seat of Rome, and kisse the villain's foot, if he were put thereto." Equally polite things are said of the other dignitaries of the Catholic Church. The locusts that issued, during the apocalyptic vision, from the smoke of the pit are declared to be "worldly subtle Prelates, with Monks, Friars, Cardinals, Patriarchs, Archbishops, Bishops, Doctors, Bachelors, and Masters, which forsake Christ to maintain false doctrine." The statement of St. Peter, that "through covetousness shall they with feigned words make merchandise of you," is applied to "the Pope and his Priests, which by lies and flatterie sell men's souls, so that it is certain he is not the successor of Simon Peter but of Simon Magus." And, worse than all, the "noisome and grievous sores, which fell upon the men that had the mark of the beast," are identified with the "boyles or pocks, which reigneth commonly among Canons, Monks, Friars, Nunnes, Priests, and such filthy vermin."[1]

As might be expected, the Geneva notes are also Calvinistic. At the time the Geneva Bible was first published, Calvin was the ruling spirit in Geneva. All the features of his theological, ecclesiastical, political, and social system are accordingly reflected in the marginal annotations of the English Bible that issued from the city of his residence. The doctrine of predestination is proclaimed to be the head corner stone of the gospel. In one note, on Luke x. 21, it is remarked that, "Jesus attributed it to the free election of God that the wise and worldlings know not the gospel, and yet the poor base people

---

[1] In the edition 1599 (Tomson's revision) the annotations on the book of Revelation are by Franc. Junius, and are of a very different strain from those quoted above. For instance, the note by Junius on Rev. xvi. 2 is: The sore here referred to "doth signifie a spirituall ulcer, and that torture or butchery of conscience seared with an hote yron, which accuseth the ungodly within, and both by truth of the word (the light whereof God hath now so long shewed forth) and by bitterness stirreth up and forceth out the sword of God's wrath."

understand it." In another note, on Rom. xi. 29, it is said that "those to whom God giveth his spirit of adoption, and whom he effectually calleth, cannot perish, for God's eternal purpose never changeth." The anti-episcopal, pari-presbyterial form of Church government, advocated by Calvin and instituted in the Church of Scotland by Melville, is also indoctrinated in the Geneva Bible. One page is headed, "S. Luke, Chap. xxii. 26, God's ministers equal."[1] The pertinent comment on Phil. i. 1 is, "By Bishops, the Apostle meaneth them that had charge of the word, and governing, as pastors, doctors, elders." Following the text of Tyndale, the Geneva exiles translated Acts xiv. 23, "Ordeined them elders by *election* in euery Church," and noted on the margin opposite that "the word signifieth to elect, by putting *up* the hands,[2] which declareth that ministers were not made without the consent of the people." This was the democratic theory of ordination held by the first Reformers in Scotland, as may be seen from their Book of Discipline, 1560. And another point of coincidence between the Geneva annotations and the ecclesiastical government set up in Scotland at the Reformation was the recognition of *superintendents* in the ministry, who were, in matters ecclesiastical, very much like what inspectors of schools are now in matters educational. On the statement, Acts xxi. 18, that "Paul went in with us to *James,*" the note is, "who was the chiefe or superintendant of the Church of Jerusalem."

One of the most outstanding features of Calvinism was its Puritanism, both in respect of worship and in respect of social conduct. The Geneva notes accordingly teem with denunciations of idle and beggarly ceremonies, and of Church usages not divinely appointed. The apostolic statement, "bodily exercise profeteth nothing," is fancifully interpreted to mean that no good can be got from "ceremonies and such things as

---

[1] This heading, taken from the edition 1580, does not appear in the edition 1560.
[2] The Scottish Reformers objected to the "laying *on* of hands" in ordination. "Other ceremonie than the public approbation of the people, and declaration (thereof by) the chief minister . . . we cannot approve: for albeit the Apostles used imposition of hands, yet seeing the miracle is ceased, the using of the ceremonie we judge not necessarie." First Book of Discipline, Cap. iv., sec. 10.

delite the fantasie of man." The phrase, "risen with Christ," is said to describe a spiritual condition that men attain to "after they have become dead to beggarly ceremonies." Equally unsparing are the Geneva annotations in their denunciation of all worldly vanities however amiable, and of all gaieties supposed to be inconsistent with the gravity of Christian deportment. One page is headed, "the inconveniency of dancing," and half-way down the page there is a note in almost identical terms in reference to the calisthenics of Herod's step-daughter.[1] Opposite the injunction that women array themselves in comely apparell and go with their hair unbraided, there is a note explaining that the word "broyd" means "to plat, to crispe, to folde, to busk, to curle, or to lay curiously: whereby all pompe and wantonness is condemned, which women use in trimming their heades."[2]

In respect of things civil, also, as well as of things ecclesiastical, the Geneva annotations display a decided spirit of Calvinistic radicalism. The civil government in Geneva was theocratic, as distinguished from human and monarchical. The city and state were governed by God's ministers and according to God's laws. The political notes in the Geneva Bible were, consequently, as much disliked by Kings of the absolute order, as were the ecclesiastical notes by infallible Popes, and by cardinals of expectant infallibility. One of the reasons that led King James, in 1604, to express his desire for a new translation of the Scriptures, was his dislike of the politics preached on the margins of the Geneva Bible. In one note, the conduct of King Asa was condemned in sparing the life of his mother, the Queen Regent, after she had outraged the national conscience by her public idolatry. "He gave

---

[1] Some editions of the Geneva Testament, *e.g.*, London, 1599, 12mo., have no heading, and do not contain the note here referred to on Mark vi. 22.

[2] The word "broid" is an old form of "braid." In most early versions of the English Testament the expression "broided hair" occurs. In the Bishops' version, as printed in Fulke's Texts, 1633, *broided* is changed into *braided*, as it also is in the revised Testament, 1881. Strange to say, however, while the phrase "broided hair" appears in the authorised version, 1611, it is in many modern editions of that version transformed into "*broidered* hair."

place to foolish pity," said the merciless annotators, "and he betrayed lack of zeal : for, both by the covenant and by the law of God, his mother should have been put to death." The statement in Exodus i. 17, that the Hebrew midwives in Goshen "feared God and did not as the King of Egypt commanded them," was backed with an annotation that " their disobedience was lawful but their dissembling evil." The freedom of these remarks, applicable as they were to events in Scottish history, made the Geneva version very distasteful to the Scottish monarch, although in other parts of the margin considerable concessions were made to royal prerogative.[1] Very unacceptable to the bearers of hereditary titles must, also, have been the Geneva comment on the words of Festus, Acts xxv. 26 : " I have no certain thing to write unto *my Lord*." This was a designation, said the Geneva politicians, that " flatterers first advised to call Tyrants by, ... and after, it so growed into use that virtuous Princes refused it not."[2]

Of quaint and curious notes, illustrative of customs and social life, not a few will be found on the margin of the Geneva Bible. The leprosy that Jesus healed, Mat. viii. 2, is said to have been " not like that leprosy that *is now*, but was a kind thereof which is incurable."[3] Of the man referred to in Mark ix. 18, it is remarked, with more detail than was either needful or edifying, that " when the spirit cometh upon him he teareth him with inwarde sorrowe and pangs, as in a colike a man feeleth such griefe as if his bowels were rent asunder." Very plain, sensible, and matter of fact, however, is the note on marriage in heaven : " Since marriage is ordained to maintain and increase mankind, when we shall be immortal it shall not be in any use." On the other hand, we cannot but think that in the note on Heb. vi. 2, there is a futile attempt to explain apostolic precepts anachronistically by modern customs. The principles of the doctrine of Christ, specified

---

[1] The note on Titus iii. 1, is : Although rulers be infidels we are bound to obey them in civil policies, when they command nothing against the word of God.

[2] Hence perhaps the Geneva translation, "Sarah called Abraham, *Sir*," (not Lord).

[3] In Wyclif's Bible leprosy is called " mysels," that is, measles.

there by the Apostle, are said by the Geneva divines to have been the "five points of the Catechism *which was then in use.*" On the word "novice," 1 Tim. iii. 6, the pert remark is made: "proud of his degree." On the term, "Lord's day," Rev. i. 10, it is said with an obvious hit at certain people: "Which some call sunday." To the expression, "pinnacle of the temple," Mat. iv. 5, is appended the not very well worded explanation: "Vane, which shewed where the wind *stood*." And quite in keeping with this last annotation is the heading of a page on which some results of human learning are exposed: "*Isaiah xlvii., vaine sciences.*"

Amid a mass of annotations that are more entertaining than instructive, a few may nevertheless be cited as really good specimens of sound exposition. As good a commentary on faith and works as might be desired at the present day will be found in the note on James ii. 14: "Paul sheweth the causes of our justification and James the effects: there it is declared how we are justified, here how we are known to be justified: there, works are excluded, as not the cause of our justification: here, they are approved, as effects proceeding thereof: there, they are denied to go before them that shall be justified: and here, they are said to follow them that shall be justified." Very sound, also, if honestly read and interpreted, is the note on Mark ii. 27: "Seeing the Sabbath was made for man's use, it is not meet that it should be used to his hindrance and incommodity." Worthy of all acceptation, too, is the remark on Mat. xvi. 19: "The preachers of the gospel open the gates of heaven with the word of God, which is the right key." A fine specimen of allegorical interpretation, again, is the disquisition on Rom. vii. 2: "The husband and wife must be considered within ourselves. The first husband was sinne, and our flesh was the wife. Their children were the fruits of the flesh. In the second marriage, the spirit is the husband, the new creature is the wife, and their children are the fruits of the spirit." A verse in the Old Testament that may puzzle plain folks, who have nothing but mother-wit to guide them in the interpretation of Scripture, is Hos. vii. 8: "Ephraim hath mixt himself among the people: Ephraim is as a cake on the hearth not turned." The marginal note on this verse in the Geneva Bible is, whether original or not, at least ingenious and racy, and continues to hold its place as the orthodox explanation of the passage. Ephraim hath mixed himself among the people, "he counterfaiteth the religion of the Gentiles, yet is but as a cake baked on the one side, and raw on the other; that is, neither through hot nor through colde, but partly a Jew and partly a Gentile."

THE BIBLES OF THE CHURCHES.

No. I.

Bible of the Church of England, commonly called the Bishops' Bible.

Editions consulted and quoted from :—
   First version, 1568.
      Jugge's folio, 1568.
   Second Version, 1572.
      Barker's quarto, 1584 ; Barker's Folio, 1585 (for Psalms).
      New Testament in Fulke's Texts, 1633.

THE popularity of the Geneva Bible was somewhat disquieting to the two churches of England and Rome. The Church of England had from the day of her institution, as a national, reformed, and anti-papal Church, been zealous for the dissemination of the Scriptures in the English tongue. The reading of the Scriptures in English was part of her canonical service. The Great Bible was mainly the work of one of her own bishops ; and it was prefaced, in some editions, by another of her prelates, of still higher eminence. But, notwithstanding the civil and ecclesiastical patronage and protection it enjoyed, the Great Bible did not hold its ground, in public estimation, against the Geneva version. The churchmen of England had the mortification, therefore, of seeing an unauthorised version of the Scriptures preferred to one that was read, and ordered to be read, in their own places of worship. And not only did churchmen see the Geneva version purchased, possessed, and prized by private persons ; but they heard it extolled by scholars and divines, as a better translation than the large and costly volume associated with the names of Cranmer and Cromwell.

Nor was this all. While the Geneva version was preferred to the Great Bible for its better English and its superior accuracy as a translation, its margins bristled with annotations which were about as galling to the chiefs of the Church of England as they were to the faithful members of the old Church of Rome. Not only was the papacy denounced in these annotations, but prelacy was held up to scorn. The locusts of the apocalypse were declared to be "worldly subtil Prelates with . . . Archbishops, Bishops," etc.; and the "crowns like unto gold," on the heads of the locusts, were interpreted to mean titles of honour which certain of the priests affected to wear, but "which in deede belongeth nothing unto them." The *jus divinum*, or divine foundation, of Episcopacy was also assailed. By the word "bishops," the Apostle was said to mean "pastors, doctors and elders;" and by the word "deacons," such as had charge of the distribution to the poor and sick. The proprieties of ritual, too, were scoffed at in a way that was well-nigh profane. What St. Paul termed "beggarly elements" were stoutly asserted to be nothing else than ceremonies in worship. The religious observance of days, such as Easter, Whitsuntide and the Feast of Tabernacles, was called a "superstitious slavery," and a hankering after "beggarly ceremonies, most pernicious to them which have received the sweet liberty of the Gospel." Such remarks could not fail to give offence to many Anglican Protestants. They were virtually attacks on the constitution of the Church of England. For, it was patent to every one that the Church of England, after renouncing the Pope's supremacy and rejecting such Popish doctrines as she held to be unwarranted by Scripture, purposely retained in her ritual many ceremonies. Her priests were clothed in sacerdotal vestments that were much more ornate than Geneva gowns. Postures in worship were matters of ecclesiastical regulation, confirmed by acts of Parliament. In the administration of the sacraments, certain formalities, such as crossing in Baptism, which rigid Puritans held to be neither necessary nor beneficial, were ordered to be observed. The theological strain of the Geneva annotations on matters of Christian doctrine was, we may suppose, less objectionable to the then guardians of the national faith. The Arminianism commonly attributed to the Church of England was of a date subsequent to that which we are now considering ; and in the first days of the Reformation, when the thirty-nine articles were drawn up, the Church of England as well as the Church of Scotland, was both ostensibly and really Calvinistic in her creed. Apart from matters of doctrinal theology, however, the Geneva notes were so irritating to Anglican divines, that the dignitaries of the Church of England had to consider whether it was not expedient, or even necessary, to provide the English people with a new version of the Bible, which, from its intrinsic excellence, might supplant in their affections the popular, but obnoxious, version that hailed from Geneva.

There were other considerations that might have led the ministers of any Church to desire a new translation of the Bible into English. The Geneva version, although the best in the field, was far from being perfect. It admitted of improvement, like all its precursors. And the ministers or members of any Church may not only be excused but commended for saying : We will never rest satisfied till we have the Bible translated into our mother tongue as accurately and aptly, as by human scholarship and skill it can be translated.

A resolution was accordingly formed by some of the leading lights of the Church of England, that a revised version of the Bible, which should be *de facto* the Church's own version, should with all convenient speed be issued to the people. As early as 1564, that resolution was come to. The project is generally attributed to Parker, the archbishop of Canterbury, who saw, or imagined he saw, in the Puritanism around him a mutinous spirit of individualism and dissension, incompatible with ecclesiastical order, and which, if unrepressed, might undo in England the whole work of the Reformation. If the scheme did not originate with Parker, he at least put himself at the head of the movement. He is represented in Hudibras as having broached the matter to the Queen, and persuaded Her Majesty to call a convocation to hear and discuss the proposal. This statement of the Popish satirist, with his caricature of the archbishop, has been keenly resented by a worthy historian of the English Bible, as "a falsehood of that buffoon's own inventing, in order to make the English Reformation as ridiculous as his little wit and ill manners could."[1] The same historian states that the archbishop's project was never submitted to convocation at all ; but was carried out privately, by such bishops and members of the Universities as his grace considered best qualified for the work.

That the project, too, was not wholly an ecclesiastical manœuvre to defeat the anti-prelatic designs of the Puritans, appears from the tenor of a letter written by Parker, after it had been announced that a new translation was contemplated. The exclusive privilege of printing the Geneva Bible in England for a period of seven years, had been conferred on John Bodleigh, father of the more famous man who founded in Oxford the Bodleian library. Before the expiry of this patent, it was proposed to publish a revised edition of the Geneva version ; and, in March 1565, Bodleigh wrote to Cecil, the Secretary of State, on the subject, knowing that Parker and some of the bishops were "intending themselves speedily to publish an English translation of their own providing." Cecil was unwilling to give any encouragement to the new Geneva edition, without the advice of these prelates, and he therefore submitted to them the communication he had received from Bodleigh.[2] Parker replied to the Secretary, in a spirit of much greater generosity than was common in those days, or is even yet, that "he and the Bishop of London thought so well of the first impression of this Bible (the Geneva), and the review of those who had since travelled therein, that they wished it would please him (Cecil) to be a means that twelve years longer term might be, by special privilege, granted to Bodleigh, in consideration of the charges sustained by him and his associates in the first impression and the review since ; that though another special Bible, for the churches, was intended by them to be set forth, as convenient time and leisure should hereafter permit, yet it should nothing hinder, but rather do much good, to have diversitie of translations and readings."

---

[1] Lewis' *History of the Translations of the Bible.*   [2] Lewis, p. 234-5.

In the prosecution of his scheme, Parker adopted the principle of divided and distributed labour. He "sorted out the whole Bible into parcels," and distributed these for examination and revision among qualified divines. The task of reviewing the corrections and amendments of the several revisers he reserved to himself. To each of the revisers he sent a copy of instructions regarding the spirit and method in which their task was to be conducted. These instructions were of a most praiseworthy conservative character. The labours of previous translators were to be respected. Alterations were not to be made in a spirit of wantonness. The first of the instructions, or "observations," as they were courteously termed, gave direction that the revisers should " follow the common translation used in the Churches, and not recede from it, but where it varieth manifestly from the Hebrew or Greek original," in other words, that the new version should be based on the Great Bible. Another instruction was that the editors should " make no bitter notes upon any text, nor yet set down any determination in places of controversy." And a third recommendation was that "all such words as sound in the old translation to any offence of lightness or obscenity be expressed with more convenient terms and phrases."

Four years were spent on this commendable undertaking of Parker's, and in 1568 the new translation was published. Most of the persons to whom the work of translation and revision was entrusted were occupants of the episcopal bench. The book accordingly obtained the soubriquet, by which it is still known, of the Bishops' Bible. "Every thing was done to make it attractive." It was issued in magnificent style; profusely ornamented with wood engravings; embellished in questionable taste with copper-plate portraits of the Queen, Leicester, and Burleigh; furnished with a map of Palestine; and supplemented by an elaborate series of genealogical tables. When all had been done that could be done by mechanical means to make the book perfect, Parker wrote to the Queen, "beseeching her highness that it might have her gracious favour, license, and protection, to be communicated abroad; as well for that in many Churches they want their books and have long time looked for this, as for that in certain places be publicly used some translations which have not been laboured in (this) realm, having inspersed diverse prejudicial notes, which might have been also well spared."

For some reason or another the favour thus besought was not granted, and the Bishops' Bible never was, in the regal or parliamentary sense of the term, authorised. In some editions it is stated on the title-page to be " set forth by authoritie," but this authority was only ecclesiastical. In 1571, an order was issued by convocation that "every arch-bishop and bishop should have at his house a copy of the holy Bible of the largest volume, as lately published at London, and that it should be placed in the hall or large dining room, that it might be useful to their servants or to strangers. The order was likewise extended to Cathedrals ; and to all Churches, as far as it could be conveniently done."[1] But this order met with the general fate of ecclesiastical edicts. It received only partial attention from ecclesiastical persons. In 1587, the primate wrote to one of the bishops : " I am credibly informed that divers, as well parish churches as chapels of ease, are not sufficiently furnished with Bibles, but some have either none at all, or such as be torn and defaced, and yet not of the translation authorised by the synod of bishops. These are, therefore, to require you strictly in your visitations, or otherwise, to see that all and every the said churches and chapels in your diocese be provided of one Bible or more, at your discretion, of the translation allowed as aforesaid."

In 1659, a second edition of the Bishops' Bible was published; and in 1572, a third. In the last named of these editions, a considerable number of amendments or changes were introduced into the New Testament. In the ninth chapter of St. John's gospel, for instance, which contains forty-one verses, there are about a dozen of such variations, of which the most notable are *parents*, for " father and mother," *v.* 2 ; *made manifest*, for " shewed," *v.* 3 ; *anointed the clay upon the eyes*, for " anointed with the clay the eyes," *v.* 6 ; *of age*, for " old enough,"

---

[1] Mombert, p. 270, 271.

v. 21; *had agreed*, for "had decreed," *v.* 22; *doeth his will*, for "obedient unto his will," *v.* 31. Of six variations in Acts xiv. the only one worth noting is *speaking boldly*, for "quit themselves boldly," *v.* 3. About twelve variations may be counted in 1 Cor. ix., such as, *by all means*, for "at the least wey," *v.* 22; *be partaker*, for "have my part," *v.* 23: *know ye*, for "perceive ye," *v.* 24; and *a corruptible crown*, for "a crown that shall perish," *v.* 25. But a more important amendment than any of the foregoing was made on the sixth verse of that chapter. In the first edition, 1568, that verse reads, as in the Great Bible: "Either only I and Barnabas have not power this to do." In the edition 1572, this rendering was changed into, "Is the liberty of not labouring taken from me and Barnabas only?"[1] One of the oddest readings in the first edition is, Col. ii. 13, "Ye being dead *to* sin, and *to* the uncircumcision of your flesh, hath he quickened." The version that in this chapter shall be treated, and quoted from, as the Bishops' Bible is that of 1572.[2]

Practically, the Bishops' Bible was a failure. It was issued from laudable motives, and it was framed under excellent instructions, but it lacked the qualities that procure popularity. It was too timid a version. It got a footing in the Church of England by the force of ecclesiastical precept, but it never succeeded in ingratiating itself into the favour of either laity or clergy. "Of all the English versions," says a living dignitary of the English Church, "the Bishops' Bible had probably the

---

[1] In the Epistle to the Ephesians, the 1572 version of the Bishops' Bible differs from the 1568 version in about fifty places; and among the new readings in the later of these editions are the now familiar phrases "*less than the least of all saints*," "*middle wall* of partition," and "*fellow-citizens* with the saints." Moulton's *History of the English Bible*, 178. See also Westcott.

[2] The edition of the 1572 version quoted from in this chapter, viz., Barker's quarto, 1584, is not free from misprints. In Prov. ix. 17, it is said that "stolen wares," instead of *stolen waters* are sweet. and in Amos ii. 14, "the flight shall *not* perish," instead of "*shall perish* from the swift." The other edition of the 1572 version of the New Testament quoted from in this chapter, viz., that printed along with the Rhemes Testament in Dr. Fulke's folio, 1633, is erroneously stated in several books of high authority, such as Cotton's *Editions of the Bible* (p. 68), and Eadie's *History of the English Bible* (vol. ii. p. 294), to be not the Bishops' translation at all, but the authorised translation of 1611.

least success. It did not command the respect of scholars, and its size and cost were far from meeting the wants of the people. Its circulation appears to have been practically limited to the Churches that were ordered to be supplied with it."[1] The following remarks on the Bishops' Bible by an American divine are not only just in the verdict they convey, but probably sound also in the theory they present: "It is a work of unequal merit from first to last; there being in the edition of 1568 a very marked difference qualitatively between the different books, and a very great improvement in the edition of 1572 over that of 1568. Perhaps, the peculiar plan adopted in the preparation, the want of concert and discussion of the different parts of the work by all the collaborators, and the impossibility of the archbishop, with such aid as he could command, to stamp upon the whole a consistent and harmonious unity of spirit, style, and expression, are sufficient to account for all its faults."

Parker himself was a scholarly, judicious man; but his team were not all that could have been desired. Not to speak of their learning or literary taste, some of them had special crotchets, theories, and prejudices, which, if allowed indulgence, might have led the bishops to play havoc with what they were only very cautiously to amend. It is, in these circumstances, rather strange that the Bishops' Bible is so colourless a revision. The archbishop was sorely put to it by some of his employés. They afflicted him with tiresome letters, in which they postulated untenable principles of translation, and submitted to him impracticable suggestions. But Parker managed them with tact. He did not enter into fruitless controversy with them, but quietly took note of their folly, and contrived to set them to a piece of work in which they would have little scope to air their whims. Grave, stolid doctors of divinity, in recounting this adroitness of Parker's, grow radiant with smiles, and

---

[1] Professor Plumptre, in Dictionary of the Bible, article "Versions." "It seems to have fared somewhat the worse through the intemperate zeal of the sticklers for the Geneva translation, and Broughton's ambition of being employed in making a new one."—Lewis.

lighten their listless pages with sparks of sacerdotal humour. One bishop, to whom the Book of Psalms had been sent for revision, innocently wrote to his superior:—"I have not altered the translation but where it gave an occasion to an error: as, at the first Psalm, at the beginning, I turn the praeter-perfect tense into the present tense, because the sense is too harsh in the praeter-perfect tense. Where, in the New Testament, one piece of a Psalm is reported, I translate it in the Psalms according to the translation thereof in the New Testament,[1] for the avoiding of the offence that may arise to the people upon divers translations." In regard to this episcopal confession, one historian of the English versions mildly remarks, that if the principle of distorting truth for the sake of edification, by means of a pious fraud, has sometimes been acted on by ecclesiastics, it has seldom at least been "so explicitly avowed." On the subject of the Psalms, another bishop suggested to Parker that "the translation of the verbs be used uniformly in one tense." Apropos of this suggestion, another historian of the English versions naively remarks, "The archbishop *accordingly* gave to this prelate Acts and Romans"!

The Bishops' Bible does not occupy an important place in history. As stated in Parker's letter to Cecil, already quoted, it was designed for use in churches principally. And from 1568 to 1611, when the version now called the authorised was issued, it was in common use in the churches of England. It does not appear ever to have obtained a footing in Scotland.

The Bishops' Bible was avowedly nothing more than a revision of the Great Bible; and its correspondence with the Great Bible, over a large part of both Testaments, is very marked. That correspondence, however, is not by any means so close as is commonly represented. Keeping in mind that "the version was entrusted to many hands, and that each reviser seems to have acted independently," Dr. Moulton

---

[1] This Bishop was not the first to adopt that principle. In the Vulgate, Ps. viii. 3 is rendered : " Ex ore infantium et lactentium *perfecisti laudem*," (hast perfected praise).

remarks justly, that "the version must be examined in various parts, and that no one book must be taken as representing others." Dr. Moulton has, himself, in a way that looks fair and satisfactory, made the kind of examination he suggests. He has collated seven passages (each from a separate book in the Old Testament) as they appear in the Great Bible, the Geneva Bible, and the Bishops' Bible, and the result of his collation is as follows:—

"In Num. xxiv. 15-24, the Bishops' Bible agrees in almost every point with Cranmer's (*i.e.*, Great Bible). In 2 Sam. xxiii. 1-7, the Bishops' and the Great Bible differ about eighteen times. Fifteen of the new renderings in the former version are taken from the Geneva Bible. In 1 Kings xix., which is a fair specimen of a chapter of the historical books, the Bishops' Bible can hardly be distinguished from Cranmer's. In Prov. viii. 22-35, not more than six words of the Bishops' Bible differ from Cranmer's, and in Eccles. xii. not more than twelve, though in each chapter the Genevan Bible contains some useful corrections. In two difficult verses (12 and 13) of Is. xliv., in which the Genevan Bible departs from Cranmer's at least twenty times (and usually for the better) the Bishops' Bible agrees with Cranmer's as far as the last word. On the other hand, in Job xix. there are few verses of the Great Bible which have not been altered in the revision."

The fact is pointed out, therefore, by Dr. Moulton that while in some chapters of the Old Testament the text of the Bishops' Bible departs very little from that of the Great Bible, there are other chapters, presumably not so many as those of the former class, in which a considerable number of the Geneva renderings are adopted. Even this definite statement fails to convey a clear and correct idea of the extent to which the Bishops' Bible in some places agrees with, and in other places deviates from, the Great Bible, especially in the Old Testament. There are some books in which the bishops adhered almost slavishly to the Great Bible, and appropriated very few of the amendments presented to them in the Geneva version. There are other books, again, in which the bishops departed very conspicuously from the text of the Great Bible, and borrowed very freely from the Bible of Geneva.

The following table shews (approximately) the result of an examination of several chapters, taken at random, from different parts of the Old Testament, in the Bishops' Bible. It will be seen that, in the chapter taken from the prophecies of Hosea, the bishops have departed far more frequently from the text of the Great Bible, and have borrowed far more from the Geneva Bible, than they have done in the other chapters mentioned in the table. And to this statement it should be added, that so widely different are some of the renderings of Hosea's words, in the Great Bible and the Bishops' Bible, that it is difficult to say how the variations should be counted.

Chapter.	No. of verses.	No. of variations from Great Bible.	No. of these variations found in Geneva Bible.	No. not found in Geneva Bible.	No. of new renderings adopted in Authorised Version.
Gen. xlix.,	33	36	18	18	8
Judges v.,	31	26	20	6	2
Eccles. xii.,	14	9	4	5	1
Isaiah xl.,	31	37	16	21	2
Jeremiah v.,	31	16	8	8	2
Hosea viii.,	14	56	48	8	0

It is by extracts, however, that the extent to which the bishops, in different parts of the Old Testament, have deviated from or adhered to the text of the Great Bible, and appropriated from or disregarded the Geneva version, will be best exhibited. Two passages of several continuous verses shall therefore be selected which will show that, in some places, the bishops have adhered to the text of the Great Bible very closely, and that, in other places, they have borrowed from the Geneva version very largely.

First passage: in which the bishops slavishly adhered to the text of the Great Bible and disregarded the Geneva amendments:

GREAT BIBLE.	GENEVA BIBLE.	BISHOPS' BIBLE.
Jer. xvii. 1.—Your synne, O ye of the trybe of Juda, is wrytten in the table of youre hertes, and grauen so upon the hedges (sic) of youre aulters with a penne of yron, and with an adamante clawe.	Jer. xvii. 1.—The sin of Judah is written with a penne of yron, and with the point of a diamond, and graven upon the table of their heart, and upon the hornes of your altars.	Jer. xvii. 1.—Your sinne, O ye of the tribe of Juda, is written in the table of your hearts, and graven so upon the edges of your altars with a penne of yron, and with an adamant clawe.

That as the fathers thyncke upon theyr chyldren, so thyncke you also upon youre aulters, woddes, thycke trees, hye hilles, mountaines and feldes.	2. They remember their altars as their children, with their groves by the greene trees upon the hie hills.	2. That as the fathers thinke upon their children, so thinke you also upon your altars, woods, thicke trees, high hilles, mountaines, and fieldes.
Wherefore I will make my mounte that standeth in the felde, al your substaunce and treasure to be spoyled, for the greate synne that ye have doone upon youre hye places thorowe oute all the coastes of your land.	3. O my mountain in the field. I will give thy substance, and all thy treasures to be spoyled, for the sinne of thy high places throughout all thy borders.	3. Wherefore, O my mount that standeth in the fields. I will make all thy substance and treasure to be spoyled, for the great sinne that thou hast done upon thy high places, thorowout all the coasts of thy land.
Ye shall be cast out also from the heritage that I gave you. And I wyl subdue you under the heauye bondage of youre enemies, in a land that ye knowe not: For ye have ministered fyre to myne indignacion, which shall burn euermoare.	4. And thou shalt rest, and in thee shall be a rest from thine heritage that I gave thee, and I will cause thee to serve thine enemies in the lande, which thou knowest not: for ye have kindled a fire in mine anger, which shall burn for ever.	4. Thou shalt be cast out also from the heritage that I gave thee: and I will subdue thee under the heavie bondage of thine enemies, in a lande that yee know not: for ye have ministered fire to mine indignation, which shall burn evermore.
Thus sayth the Lorde: Cursed be the man that putteth his truste in man, and that taketh fleshe for his arme, and he whose herte departeth from the Lorde.	5. Thus sayeth the Lord, Cursed be the man that trusteth in man, and maketh flesh his arme and withdraweth his heart from the Lord.	5. Thus sayeth the Lord, Cursed be the man that putteth his trust in man, and that taketh flesh for his arm, and he whose heart departeth from the Lord.
He shall be like the heath, that groweth in the wyldernesse. As for the good thyng that is for to come, he shall not see it, but dwell in a drye place of the wildernes, in a salte and unoccupied land.	6. For he shalbe like the heath in the wilderness, and shall not see when any good cometh, but shall inhabit the parched places in the wilderness, in a fair land and not inhabited.	6. He shall be like the heath that groweth in wildernesse: As for the good thing that is for to come, he shall not see it, but dwell in a dry place of the wildernesse, in a salt and unoccupied land.

And to show that the above quoted passage from the prophecies of Jeremiah[1] is not one in which the bishops have, in their translation of that book, adhered with more than usual closeness to the text of the Great Bible, and disregarded with more than usual heedlessness unquestionable improvements, in diction at least, that were set before them in the Geneva Bible, a few other verses from different chapters of the same book shall now be submitted.

---

[1] The bishop that revised the translation of the prophecies of Isaiah and Jeremiah was Horne of Winchester.

GREAT BIBLE AND BISHOPS' BIBLE.

Jer. iii. 1.—Commonly when a man putteth away his wife, and she goeth from him, and marrieth with another, then the question is, Should he resort unto her any more after that?

Jer. iv. 25.—I looked about me and there was no body, and all the birdes of the ayre were away.

Jer. vi. 13.—For from the least to the most they hang all upon covetousness.

Jer. ix. 2.—Would God that I had a cottage some where far from folk, that I might leave my people and go from them, for they be all adulterers and a shrinking sort.

Jer. x. 19.—Alas, how am I hurt, alas, how painful are my scourges unto me, for I consider this sorrow by myself, and I must suffer it.

Jer. xi. 9, 10.—It is found out that whole Israel, and all the cities of Jerusalem are gone back. They have turned themselves to the blasphemies of their forefathers which had no lust to hear my worde.

Jer. xvii. 9.—Amonge all thynges man hath the most disceatful and stubburne hert. Who shall then knowe it?

GENEVA BIBLE.

Jer. iii. 1.—They say, If a man put away his wife, and she go from him, and become another man's, shall he return again unto her?

Jer. iv. 25.—I beheld, and lo, there was no man, and all the birdes of the heaven were departed.

Jer. vi. 13.—For, from the least of them even unto the greatest of them, every one is given unto covetousness.

Jer. ix. 2.—Oh that I had in the wilderness a cottage of wayfaring men, that I might leave my people and go from them: for they be all adulterers and an assembly of rebels.

Jer. x. 19.—Wo is me for my destruction, and my grievous plague: but I thought, Yet it is my sorrow, and I will bear it.

Jer. xi. 9, 10.—A conspiracy is found among the men of Judah and among the inhabitants of Jerusalem. They are turned back to the iniquities of their forefathers, which refused to hear my words.

Jer. xvii. 9.—The heart is deceitful and wicked above all things: who can know it?

Second passage: in which the bishops depart widely from the text of the Great Bible, and draw largely from the amendments in the Geneva version.

GREAT BIBLE.	GENEVA BIBLE.	BISHOPS' BIBLE.
Hosea xi. 3.—I learned Ephraim to goe, and bare them in myne armes, but they regarded not me that wolde have helped them. I led them wyth cordes of frendschyp and with bandes of loue. I was euen he that layd the yoke upon theyr neckes. I gave them fodder myself. That they shuld not go agayne into Egypt. And now is Assur theyr kyng. For they wolde not turne unto me. Therefore shall the swerde begyn in theyr cityes, the store that they have layde up shalbe de-	Hosea xi. 3.—I led Ephraim also, as one should beare them in his armes, but they knew not that I healed them. I led them with cordes of a man, euen with bandes of loue: and I was to them as he that taketh off the yoke from their jawes, and I laid the meate unto them. He shall no more returne into the land of Egypt: but Asshur shall be his king, because they refused to conuert. And the sworde shall fall on his cities, and shall consume his barres and devoure them, because of	Hosea xi. 3.—I gave to Ephraim one to leade him, who should beare him in his armes, but they knew not that I healed them. I led them with cordes of a man, euen with bandes of loue: and I was to them as hee that taketh off the yoke from their jawes, and I layde meate to them. He shall no more returne into Egypt: but Asshur shall be his king, because he refused to convert. Therefore shall the sworde fall on his cities and shall consume his branches, and devoure

Great Bible	Geneva	Bishops'
stroyed and eaten and that bycause of theyre owne ymaginacyons.	their owne counsels.	them, because of their owne counsels.
And my people shall stand in a doubt whyther to turne them, for when the prophetes called them to the most hiest, not one yet wolde gyve hym hys glorye.	And my people are bent to rebellion against me: though they called them to the most hie, yet none at all would exalt him.	And my people shall be in a doubt for their rebellion against me: for when the prophets called them to the most high not one yet woulde give him his glory.
What great thynges haue I gyven the, O Ephraim: howe faythfully haue I defended the O Israel: haue I dealt with the as with Adama, or haue I entreated the lyke Seboim. No my hert is otherwyse mynded. Yea, my mercye is to fervent.	How shall I give thee up, Ephraim: how shall I deliver thee, Israel: howe shall I make thee as Admah: how shall I set thee as Zeboim: mine heart is turned within me, my repentings are rouled together.	Howe shall I give thee up, Ephraim: how shall I deliver thee, Israel: howe shall I make thee as Adama: how shall I set thee as Zeboim: mine heart is turned within me, my repentings are kindled within me.
Therefore haue I not turned me to destroye Ephraim in my wrathful dyspleasure.	I will not execute the fiercenesse of my wrath, I will not return to destroye Ephraim.	I will not execute the fiercenesse of my wrath, I will not return to destroy Ephraim.

It is clear that in the above quoted passage the bishops have borrowed freely and frequently from the Geneva version. And that they have done so all through the book of Hosea [1] will be seen from the following renderings, in which they not only adopt the Geneva translation but deviate widely from the text of the Great Bible:

Great Bible.	Geneva Bible and Bishops' Bible.
Hos. iv. 19.—A wynde shal take hold of theyr fethers: and they shalbe confounded in theyr offrynges.	Hos. iv. 19.—The wind hath bound them up in her wings, and they shall be ashamed of their sacrifices.
Hos. v. 8.—Crye out at Bethauen upon the yonde-side of Ben Jamin.	Hos. v. 8.—Cry out at Bethaven, after thee, O Benjamin. [1]
Hos. vii. 5.—Euen so goeth this daye with oure kynges and princes, for they	Hos. vii. 5.—This is the day of our king: the princes have made him sick

---

[1] The bishop that was entrusted with the version of the minor prophets, from Hosea to Malachi, was Grindal of London, who was a Protestant of the Geneva type. Quoting Strype, Dr. M'Crie in his Life of Knox (fourth edition, vol. i., p. 388), says that when Grindall was appointed to the Bishopric of London, "he remained under some scruples of conscience about some things, especially the habits and certain ceremonies required to be used of bishops." Quoting from Burnet, Dr. M'Crie says further (vol. i., p. 389), that "Grindal and Horne (of Winchester) wrote to Zurich that they did not approve of, but merely suffered, kneeling at the eucharist, and signing with the cross in baptism, etc., hoping that they would speedily obtain their abrogation."

begyn to be wood dronken thorowe wyne, they use familyarityte with suche as deceyue them.

Hos. vii. 6.—Their slepe is all the nyght lyke the slepe of a baker. [2]

Hos. ix. 11.—Ephraim flyeth lyke a byrde, so shal theyr glorye also. Insomuch that they shal neyther beget, conceyue, nor beare chylde.

Hos. x. 10.—I wyll chasten them, euen after myne owne desyre: the people shalbe gathered togyther ouer them, when I punysh them for theyr great wyckednesse.

Hos. x. 11.—Ephraim was unto me as a cow that is used to go to plowe, therefore I loued hym, and fell upon hys fayre necke: I droue Ephraim, Juda plowed, and Jacob played the husbandeman.

Hos. xii. 7.—But thou art lyke the marchant, that hath a false wayght in his hand, he hath a pleasure to occupye extorcion.

with flagons of wine. He stretcheth out his hand to scorners.

Hos. vii. 6.—Their baker sleepeth all the night.

Hos. ix 11.—Ephraim, their glory shall flee away like a bird: from the birth, from the womb, and from the conception.

Hos. x. 10.—It is my desire that I should chastise them, and the people shall be gathered against them, when they shall gather themselves in their two furrows.

Hos. x. 11.—And Ephraim is as an heifer used to delight in threshing: [3] but I will pass by her fair neck, I will make Ephraim to ride, Judah shall plow, and Jacob shall break his clods.

Hos. xii. 7.—He is Canaan, the balances of deceit are in his hand, he loveth to oppress.

But while in some parts of the Old Testament the Bishops' Bible presents both very many and very notable deviations from the text of the Great Bible, it must admitted that, over the Old Testament generally, the points of correspondence between these two Bibles are far more striking than the points of difference. And it is not only where the translation in the Great Bible would, at the present day, be considered preferable to that in the Geneva version that the bishops retained the old renderings, but in many instances where the translation in the Great Bible had been improved by the Geneva exiles, the bishops clung, with a half commendable conservative partiality, to the rendering which they found in the version they were instructed mainly to follow.

In some cases where, judging by the revised version of the Old Testament, 1885, we must consider the readings in the Great Bible incorrect, and the Geneva readings right, the

---

[1] In these verses the Bishops' renderings sometimes differ by a word from the Geneva translation.

[2] A marginal note in the revised version says that according to some ancient authorities the verse should read "their anger" instead of "their baker" sleepeth all night.

[3] "Treading out the corne," Bishops'.

bishops had the unwisdom to retain the evil and reject the good. The following curious version of Prov. xvi. 10, appears in the Great Bible: "When the prophecye is in the lyppes of the kynge, his mouth shall not go wronge in judgment." This is as much as to say that at certain times and on certain occasions, but not always nor perhaps generally, we may expect sound judgment to come from the throne. This may be true in fact, but it can scarcely be supposed to be what Solomon meant to say. It does not inspire reverence for the institution of monarchy, and we find in both the authorised and revised versions a very different reading of the passage. The authorised translation is: "A divine sentence is in the lips of the king, he transgresseth not in judgment." And this is substantially the statement that appears in the Geneva version. But the bishops, notwithstanding their reverence for the throne, disregarded what, not only on scholastic but on common-sense grounds, must be held as the true reading of the verse, and adopted without a word of change the old rendering they found in the Great Bible. Another peculiar reading in the Great Bible, which has been retained by the bishops, is Eccles. x. 3: "A foole wyl shewe himself when he goeth by the waye, yet thynketh he that euerye man doth as foolyshly as hym self." So far as its intrinsic truthfulness is concerned this is a statement that might quite well appear in the book of Ecclesiastes. But it is not what we are told by approved English interpreters of the Scriptures is the right translation of the real words of the preacher. By the revisers, 1885, the verse is made to read: "Yea also, when the fool walketh by the way, his understanding faileth him, and he saith to every one that he is a fool." And this reading, in a very slightly different form of expression, was set before the bishops in the Bible of Geneva. Many other instances to the like effect, probably better instances, could easily be culled from the Bishops' version of the Old Testament, but the following will suffice to confirm the averment made in this paragraph:

GREAT BIBLE AND BISHOPS' BIBLE.	GENEVA BIBLE.
Prov. x. 6.—The mouth of the ungodly keepeth mischief in secret.	Prov. x. 6.—Iniquity shall cover the mouth of the wicked.

Eccles. x. 4.—If a principall spirite be given thee to beare rule, be not negligent then in thine office: for he that can take care of himself avoydeth great offences.

Is. xvi. 2.—For, as for the daughters of Moab, they shall be as a trembling bird that is put out of her nest: for they shall carry them unto Arnon.

Is. xxiv. 16.—I know a thing in secret, I know a thing in secret.

Is. xxv. 6.—Most pleasant and dainty dishes.

Micah v. 1.—Now shalt thou be robbed thyself, O thou robber's daughter.

Nah. ii. 3 (Bishops').—The charet is compassed with flaming torches in the day of his expedition and the fyrre staues are drenched in poyson.

(Great Bible).—Hys charettes are as fyre, when he maketh him forwarde, and his spere shaftes are soked in venom.[1]

Eccles. x. 4.—If the spirite of him that ruleth ryse up against thee, leave not thy place: for gentleness pacifieth great sins.

Is. xvi. 2.—For it shall be as a bird that flieth, and a nest forsaken: the daughters of Moab shall be at the fords of Arnon.

Is. xxiv. 16.—My leanness, my leanness, woe is me.

Is. xxv. 6.—Wines fined and purified.

Micah v. 1.—Now assemble thy garrisons, O daughter of garrisons.

Nah. ii. 3 (Geneva).—The charets shall be as in the fire and flames in the day of his preparation, and the firre trees shall tremble.

(Revised 1885).—The chariots flash with steel in the day of his preparation, and the spears are shaken terribly.

The bishops were in like manner content, in many cases, to accept crude and careless expressions from the Great Bible, when more correct forms of speech were submitted to them in the Bible of Geneva. It is not worth while to dwell at length on this point, but the following instances may be adduced to speak for themselves.

GREAT BIBLE AND BISHOPS'.

Gen. xlix. 5.—Simeon and Levi brethren, are cruell instruments in their habitations. (Bish.)

Judges xviii. 7.—They dwelt carelesse, after the maner of the Sidons, still and without casting of perils.

Eccles. xi. 1.—Lay thy bread upon wet faces.[2]

GENEVA BIBLE.

Gen. xlix. 5.—Simeon and Levi, brethren in euill, the instruments of crueltie are in their habitations.

Judges xviii. 7.—Which dwelt carelesse, after the maner of the Zidonians, quiet and sure.

Eccles. xi. 1.—Cast thy bread upon the waters.

---

[1] Some readings adopted by the Geneva divines, but rejected by the King's translators, 1611, and by the revisers, 1885, were also disallowed by the bishops. Of these may be mentioned:

GENEVA VERSION.

Job xxxvi. 5.—Beholde, the mighty God casteth away none that is mightie and valiant of courage.

Is. xliii. 8.—I will bring forth the blinde people, and they shall have eyes: and the deaf, and they shall have ears.

BISHOPS' VERSION.

Job. xxxvi. 5.—Behold the great God casteth away no man, for he himself is mightie in power and wisedome.

Is. xliii. 8.—Bring forth that people which is blind and yet hath eyes: which are deafe, although they have eares.

[2] The word *faces* is here equivalent to *surfaces*, as in the familiar expression "face of the earth."

Is. xlv. 15.—O, howe profounde art thou, O God, thou God and Saviour of Israel.

Is. xlv. 15.—Verily thou, O God, hidest thyself, O God, the Saviour of Israel.

Is. xlvi. 11.—As soon as I think to devise a thing, I do it.

Is. xlvi. 11.—I have purposed it, and I will do it.

While the bishops failed, in so many instances, to take advantage of amendments on the Great Bible which were presented to them in the Geneva version, they also not infrequently adopted Geneva readings and renderings when these were not improvements on the older English text, or were, at least, far from being satisfactory. One or two examples from the prophecies of Micah will make this apparent. In both the authorised and revised versions we read, ch. ii. 8, "Ye pull off the robe with the garment (strip the robe from off the garment, Revised) from them that pass by securely *as men averse from war.*" Very different from this, in expression at least, is the statement given in the Great Bible: "They take away both cote and cloke from the symple, *ye have turned yourselves to fyght.*" In the Geneva version another reading appears, "They spoyle the beautifull garment from them that passe by peaceably, *as though they returned from the warre*;"[1] and this reading was adopted without any amendment by the bishops. A verse that is at least elliptical, if not also open to serious misapprehension, in the authorised and revised Bibles is Micah iii. 5, "Thus sayeth the Lord concerning the prophets that make my people err, that bite with their teeth, and cry, Peace: and he that putteth not into their mouths, they even prepare war against him." Of this verse a somewhat free but most racy rendering, in which the true meaning of the prophet is picturesquely exhibited, is given in the Great Bible: "As concernyng the prophetes that deceave my people, thus the Lord sayeth agaynst them, When they have any thing to byte upon, then

---

[1] In the Latin version printed at Zurich in 1564, the passage reads (in accordance with the Geneva translation): "Pallium expoliatis a transeuntibus confidenter *qui* reuertuntur e praelio." In the Vulgate (Clementine version) there is still another reading of the passage:—"Desuper tunica pallium sustulistis: et eos qui transibant simpliciter convertistis in bellum": which in the Douay Bible is literally englished:—"You have taken away the cloak off from the coat, and them that passed harmless you have turned to war."

they preach that al shalbe wel, but yf a man put not some thing into their mouths, they preach of warre agaynst hym." In substituting for this free translation a more literal one, the Geneva divines have, by the interposition of one word (*them*), given to the verse a most peculiar rendering, suggestive of a meaning very different from what they intended to convey; and the bishops adopted both the Geneva rendering and the Geneva marginal note of explanation.[1] This faulty and misleading rendering made first by the Geneva divines, and then adopted by the bishops, is: "Thus saith the Lord concerning the prophets that deceive my people, and bite *them* with their teeth, and cry, Peace etc." Another very racy description of the evil doers in Israel, in the degenerate days in which Micah lived, is given in the Great Bible, in the second and third verses of the seventh chapter of that prophet's testimony, "They labour all to shede bloud, and euery man hunteth his brother to death; yet they say they do wel, when they do euyl. As the prynce wyl, so sayth the judge, that he may do hym a pleasure agayne. The great man speaketh what his hert desyreth, and the hearers alowe hym."[2] Be this reading a correct or an incorrect rendering of the true original—the Hebrew verity—it is at least plain English; and it has been superseded in the Geneva and Bishops' Bibles by a translation that is much less explicit: "They all lye in wayte for blood, euery man hunteth his brother with a net. To make good for the euil of their handes, the prince asked, and the judge judgeth for a reward; therefore the great man hee speaketh out of the corruption of his soule; so they wrap it up."[3]

---

[1] The marginal note on this verse in the Geneva Bible is, "They (the prophets) devour all their (the people's) substance, and then flatter them, promising that all shall go well: but if one restraine from their bellies, then they invent all ways to mischief."

[2] "Alowe," used here in the old sense of approve or praise. See Skeat's Dict. The words in the Latin version (Zurich, 1564) are "corroborant illam." In old or middle English there are words *loue, lowe,* and *louen* (laudo, Latin), signifying to *praise*; so that in Gau's "Richt vey to the kingdome of Heuen" we find Is. xxvi. 19 rendered "vaik up and *lowff* God," and Ps. cxxxvii. 4 "nay man cane sing my *lowine* in ane fremmit land."

[3] The Bishops' rendering is slightly different from this. The Authorised and Revised versions follow the track of the Geneva, but introduce some changes.

The bishops did not obtrude into their version of the Old Testament either many original translations or many original expressions. They have left, however, here and there on the pages of the English Bible traces of their literary taste, if not also of their scholastic insight. One verse in the authorised translation that may be said to have been moulded by the bishops is the opening verse in the ninth chapter of the prophecies of Isaiah: "Nevertheless the dimness (darkness, Bish.) shall not be such as was in her vexation, when at the first he lightly afflicted the land of Zebulon, and the land of Naphtali, and afterward did more grievously afflict her by the way of the sea, beyond Jordan, in Galilee of the nations," (heathen, Bish.) Another beautiful verse that was perfected and brought into its present shape by the bishops is Job iii. 22 : "Which rejoice exceedingly and are glad when they can find the grave." Other alterations on the Geneva text that were made by the bishops, and have left their mark on later versions of the Bible, are Gen. xlix. 6, "O my soule, come not thou into their secretes, neither unto their congregation let *mine honour be united*"; Prov. xi. 15, "He that is suretie for a stranger shall *smart for it*"; Prov. xxii. 9, "He that hath a *bountiful* eye shall be blessed"; "Joel ii. 13, "Rend your hearts and not your *garments*"; Joel ii. 23, "Moderate rain"; for *the teacher of righteousness*, G. B., and the *rain of righteousness*, Gen. ; Amos i. 2, "The dwelling places of the shepherds shall *mourn*," (*perish*, Gen.); Nah. iii. 2, "The *rattling* of wheels, the *pransing* of horses, and the *jumping* of chariots"; "Hab. iii. 2, "Revive thy work in the midst of the *years*," (people, Gen.); and Mal. iii. 15, "Now we call the proud *happy*." Certain words, too, that in our authorised version are treated as proper names, or technical terms, have, by the bishops, been translated into plain English, and one may be excused for thinking that, in some cases, a certain picturesqueness and a little light have by that means been thrown by the bishops on the pages of Scripture. In both the authorised and revised versions it is said, Num. xxiii. 14 : "And he took him into the field of Zophim, to the top of Pisgah, and built seven altars." The statement in the Bishops' Bible is : "And he brought him into a field, *where men might see farre off*, to the top of an hill, and built seven altars." In like manner we read in the authorised version, Deut. xxxiii. 8: "And of Levi, he said, Let thy Thummim and thy Urim be with thy holy one." But the blessing here pronounced on Levi is rendered by the bishops: "*Right and light* shall be with thee, and with every one that is godly in thee."

It must be said, however, that the larger half of the original emendations, whether as new readings or new renderings, made by the bishops on the English text of the Old Testament, have failed to find a permanent place in the English Bible. They stand neglected on the disused pages of the Bishops' version, and on the pages of that version only. In the burden of Nineveh, as translated by the divines of Geneva, the following pitiable story is told, Nahum ii. 10: "She is emptie and voide, and waste, and the heart melteth, and the knees smite together, and sorrowe is in all loines, and the faces of them all gather blackness." With only two verbal alterations for the better, the substitution of "anguish" for "sorrow," and "are waxed pale" for "gather blackness," this rendering has been retained by the recent revisers, 1885. It did not satisfy the bishops, however, and they set it aside for the following translation, which in the italicised words is original, and in the last four words is taken from the Great Bible: "*Sacking, resacking, rasing, a dissolved heart*, and *collision* of knees, sorowe in all loynes also, and the faces of them all as blacke as a potte." In a previous paragraph in this chapter, several verses were quoted from Hosea to show that the bishops in some cases deviated considerably from the text of the Great Bible and drew largely from the Geneva translation. In one of these verses the bishops have made a faint show of originality. They have departed from the Geneva text in one word, by changing *bars* into *branches*, and making the sixth verse read: "Therefore shall the sword fall on his cities, and shall consume his *branches*.[1] This rendering of the bishops has been retained

---

[1] Matthew Henry's note on this verse is worth quoting, as a sample of ingenious interpretation, which covers and explains all readings. "This judgement shall spread far: the sword shall fasten upon *his cities*, those nests of people and store-

in the authorised version, but in the revised version the Geneva rendering has been restored. Other instances of unappreciated originality or research, on the part of the bishops, will be seen in the following quotations from the Old Testament:

GREAT BIBLE.	GENEVA BIBLE.	BISHOPS' BIBLE.
Gen. xlix. 20. — Of Asser: his bread shalbe fat, and he shall give pleasures for a kynge.	Gen. xlix. 20.—Concerning Asshur: his bread shalbe fat, and he shall give pleasures for a kynge.	Gen. xlix. 20.—Out of *the fat land of Aser* shall be his bread, and he shall give pleasures for a king.
Job iii. 23. — That should be joye to that man whose joye is hydde, and God kepeth it backe from hym.	Job. iii. 23.—Why is the light given to the man whose waye is hid, and whome God hath hedged in?	Job. iii. 23.—From whom *their endes are hid* and concealed by God.
Job. iv. 12.—And to me came the worde secretly, and myne eare hath receyued a lytel thereof.	Job. iv. 12. — But a thing was brought to mee secretly, and myne eare hath receiued a little thereof.	Job. iv. 12.—But where as *a thing was hid from me*, yet mine eare hath receiued a little thereof.
Hos. ix. 9.—They be gone to far, and haue destroyed themselves, lyke as they did aforetyme at Gabaa.	Hos. ix. 9.—They are deeply set: they are corrupt as in the days of Gibeah.	Hos. ix. 9.—They have *gone to the bottome*, they are corrupt as in the days of Gibea.
Nahum i. 3. — The Lorde goeth forth in tempest and stormye wether.	Nahum i. 3.—The Lord hath his way in the whirlwinde, and in the storm.	Nahum i. 3. — The Lordes *dealing is with blustering tempest* and whirlewinde.
Nahum ii. 7. — The quene her selfe shalbe led away captyue, and her gentylwemen shall mourn as the doues, and grone with theyr hartes.	Nahum ii. 7. — And Huzzah, the Queene shall be led away captive, and her maidens shall leade her as with the voyce of doues, smiting upon their brests.	Nahum ii. 7.—Huzah is brought forth captive, made to ascende into the charets, her handmaydens also *leading one another as in the voyce of doues*, knocking upon their breastes.

The Bishops' version of the New Testament, especially their revised version, 1572, has received much more favourable criticism than has been accorded to their translation of the Old Testament. Their version of the New Testament, however, like that of the Old, is not of uniform merit throughout. Some

---

houses of wealth: it shall likewise reach to *his branches*, the country villages, so some (the Bishops' in marginal note): the citizens themselves, so others: or the *bars* (so the word signifies) and gates of their cities: or, all the *branches* of their revenue and wealth: or, their children, the *branches* of their families." In the Latin version, Zurich, 1564, the words are "consumetque villas ejus"; and in the Vulgate "consumet electos ejus."

of the bishops did their work better than others. "The verdict of the student will," therefore, says Professor Moulton, "vary according to the portion which he is examining." But the judgment pronounced on some parts of the Bishops' translation by such a competent scholar as Dr. Westcott, must be held to imply very high praise. In a passage of ten verses, Eph. iv. 7-16, the bishops have made twenty-six departures from the text of the Great Bible. "Of these twenty-six variations, no less than sixteen," says Dr. Westcott, "are new, while only ten are due to the Genevan version; and the character of the original corrections marks a very close and thoughtful revision, based faithfully upon the Greek. The anxiously literal rendering of the particles and prepositions is specially worthy of notice; so, too, the observance of the order and of the original form of the sentences, even where some obscurity follows from it."[1]

Similar remarks to what have, in this chapter, been made on the Bishops' version of the Old Testament may, nevertheless, be made on their version of the New. While their principle of adhering as closely as possible to the text of the Great Bible is laudable, they sometimes carry that principle too far, and retain renderings given in the Great Bible, when better renderings were set before them in the Geneva version. In adopting Geneva amendments, again, they sometimes shew good discretion, and sometimes not. Their original renderings, also, are sometimes happy and sometimes unhappy. We cannot do better than illustrate and establish these points in the order in which they are here stated.

Some readings and renderings in the New Testament of the Great Bible that, at the present day, cannot but be held as incorrect have been retained by the bishops. One verse in the Great Bible that presents a studied appearance of literal translation, is Mat. viii. 7. A centurion had come unto Jesus and said:—"Master, my seruant lyeth at home sicke of the palsye, and is grevously payned." To this statement Jesus is

---

[1] It may be doubted whether the "observance" here commended is entitled to commendation.

represented in the Great Bible as having replied in the following terms :—"*Whan* I come unto hym I wyll heale hym." This is scarcely what we should have expected Jesus to say; and it is not what modern scholars declare to be the true rendering of the evangelist's peculiar phraseology. But the bishops adopted that strange rendering into their Bible, although common sense might have made them distrustful of the correctness of the translation, and the Geneva Bible held up to their view another rendering of the passage, which was much more consonant with our Lord's courtesy and charity :—" I will come and heal him." Following the Great Bible, again, and disregarding the corrected rendering in the Geneva version, the bishops, in Acts xxvii. 13, translate the Greek word *asson* as a proper noun, instead of an adverb meaning *nearer*, and make the passage read : "loosed unto *Asson*, and sayled paste all Candye." The odd rendering of James ii. 18 that appears in the Great Bible is also adopted by the bishops :—" Thou hast a fayth and I have deedes. Shew me thy fayth by thy dedes, and I wyll shew the my fayth by my dedes." This rendering, in its natural interpretation, harmonises so ill with the context, and is so irrelevant to what goes before, that one might be excused for wondering if the word *by* were not used here in two different senses :—in the sense of *beside* or *without* in the second clause, and in the sense of *through* or *by means of* in the third. As shewn in a previous chapter, however, there are two readings of the verse in Greek manuscripts, and the bishops' rendering is simply a literal translation of what must be considered an incorrect Greek text. A very peculiar rendering, or reading, which the bishops took from the Great Bible, is Heb. xi. 9 : " By faith Abraham *removed* into the land of promise, as into a strange country, *when he had dwelt in tabernacles* with Isaac and Jacob." Another odd rendering, for which Tyndale was originally responsible, that the bishops appropriated from the Great Bible, is 2 Cor. iii. 18 : "We all beholding as in a myrror the glorie of the Lorde with *his* face open are changed unto the same image."

Besides incorrect translations, the bishops took from the New Testament in the Great Bible many renderings whose diction was very far from being apt or felicitous; and in not a few of these cases, alterations for the better might have been found in the Geneva version. For instance, Mat. vi. 7, is in the Bishops' Bible translated: "When ye pray, *babble* not much, as the heathen do; for they think that they shall be heard for their much babbling's sake." This is the translation given in the Great Bible also. But it is not choice diction, and it does not correspond in dignity with either the speaker or the subject of discourse. It was so far improved by the Geneva divines that " babble " in the first clause of the verse was changed into "use no vain repetitions," and to that extent it might have been amended by the bishops without strain on their literary resources.[1] There are cases, again, in which the bishops adopted in part the Geneva amendments on the Great Bible, but would have done better to accept these amendments without abatement. One verse that the Geneva divines put into a form of expression well-nigh perfect is 1 Cor. x. 16: "The cup of blessing which we bless, is it not the communion of the blood of Christ? The bread which we break, is it not the communion of the body of Christ?" This rendering was a great improvement on the unrhythmical translation that appears in Tyndale's Testament and the Great Bible; and the bishops did well to accept the new order of words submitted to them in the Geneva version. They declined, however, to retain the most distinctive word in the whole verse, the word *communion*, but restored the word that had been used by Tyndale and Coverdale, *partaking*. This fact is the more strange, too, that the term used by the puritans is a churchly one, while that adopted by the prelatists is non-churchly.[2]

---

[1] Beza's rendering of this passage is—"Precantes autem ne eadem *blaterate*." In the Vulgate the translation is—"Orantes autem nolite multum loqui ;" and in the Zurich version, 1564—"Ne sitis loquaces." The Rhemes translators, in their marginal note, say that what is here condemned by Jesus is not "long prayer," but "long rhetorical prayers" such as those by which heretics "thinke to persuade God : whereas the Collects of the Church are most briefe and most effectuall."

[2] The following statement appears in the eleventh of the fourscore questions of Ninian Winzet :—" Quhy vse ze this terme communioun for the Lordis Supper nocht contenit in Scriptuir in that significatioun, and samekle abhorris fra the terme Missa expresslie contenit in the original Hebrew text for an oblatioun, Deut. xvi."

Wonderful to tell, also, the bishops, in their rendering of James i. 5, preferred to retain the slang phrase, "Casteth no man in the teeth," which they found in the Great Bible, rather than adopt the staider words, "reproacheth no man," which appear in the second Geneva version. A very obscure translation, to non-classical readers at least, which the bishops were content to take from the Great Bible, is Heb. iii. 14: "For we are made partakers of Christ, if we keep sure unto the end the *beginning of the substance.*" But in this case the substitute offered in the Geneva version was little more satisfactory: "We are made partakers of Christ, if we keep sure unto the end the beginning, wherewith *we ure upholden.*" And so of Heb. ix. 25. The rendering of that verse, in the Great Bible and the Bishops' Bible, is very inexplicit; but all the improvement on it in the Geneva Bible is the substitution of *other* for *strange*: "Not that he should offer himself often, as the High Priest entereth into the holy places every year *in strange blood.*" But it will scarcely be disputed that in the following passages the Bishops' version might have been improved, either in propriety or in dignity of expression, by the adoption of the Geneva renderings:

GREAT BIBLE AND BISHOPS' BIBLE.	GENEVA BIBLE.
Acts iv. 31.—As soon as they had prayed the place *moved* where they were assembled.[1]	Acts iv. 31. — When as they had prayed the place *was shaken* where they were assembled.
Acts xix. 32.—The Assembly was *all out of quiet*.	Acts xix. 32.—The Assembly was *out of order*.
Acts xxv. 21.—But when Paul had appealed to be *kept unto the knowledge* of Augustus.	Acts xxv. 21.—But because he appealed to be *reserved to the examination* of Augustus.
Rome vi. 10.—For *as touching* that he died, he died *concerning* sin once.	Rom. vi. 10.—And *in* that he died he died once *to* sin.
Rom. vii. 9.—I *once lived without law*.	Rom. vii 9.—I *once was alive*, without the law.
Rom. x. 21.—A people that believeth not, but speaketh against me.	Rom. x. 21.—A disobedient and *gainsaying* people.
Rom. xiv. 5. — This man putteth *difference between day and day*.	Rom. xiv. 5.—This man esteemeth one day above another.
1 Cor. xi. 29.—Eateth and drinketh	1 Cor. xi. 29.—Eateth and drinketh

---

The words *Missa* and *mass* are not Hebrew words at all. They are derived from the Latin formula in dismissing a congregation, *ite, missa est*: as much as to say, "hearers go, and communicants remain." The word referred to by Winzet was probably *matstsah*, unleavened bread.

[1] In the passages here cited the Bishops' Bible and Great Bible do not in all instances agree verbatim.

damnation to himself, *making no difference* of the Lord's body.	his own damnation, because he *discerneth not* the Lord's body.
Col. i. 16.—Whether they be *majesties* or *lordshippes*, either *rulers* or *powers*.	Col. i. 16.—Whether they be *thrones* or *dominions*, or *principalities*, or *powers*.
2 Thess. iii. 8.—Wrought with labour and *sweat* night and day.	2 Thess. iii. 8.—Wrought with labour and *travail* night and day.
Heb. xi. 24.—Moses, when he was *great*, refused to be called.	Heb. xi. 24.—Moses, when he was *come to age*, refused to be called.
James iv. 11.—*Backbite* not one another, brethren. He that *backbiteth* his brother *backbiteth* the law.	Jas. iv. 11.—Speak not evil one of another, brethren. He that speaketh evil of his brother . . . speaketh evil of the law.
3 John 14.—Thy *lovers* salute thee.[1]	3 John 14.—Thy *friends* salute thee.
Rev. xvi. 2.—There fell a noisome and a sore *botch* upon the man which had the mark of the beast.	Rev. xvi. 2.—There fell a noisome and a grievous *sore* upon the man which had the mark of the beast.

It is not to be supposed, however, that there are no cases in which the judgment of the bishops is to be approved in adhering to the text of the New Testament in the Great Bible, and rejecting the changes made thereon by the Geneva divines. In the Geneva Bible there is a very peculiar rendering of Acts xxiv. 22: "When Felix heard these things, he deferred them and said: When I shall more perfectly know the things which concern this way, by the coming of Lysias, the chief captain, I will decise your matter."[2] This is so like what Felix should have said that we are tempted to think it must be the correct rendering of the verse. But it is a strained rendering of the words as they stand in the Greek text. The bishops did right, therefore, to adhere to the reading in the Great Bible, and translate the original Greek, not as they might have it to be, but as they actually found it. In the following further cases, the bishops showed a wise discretion in rejecting the changes made on the Great Bible by the Geneva exiles:

GREAT BIBLE AND BISHOPS' BIBLE.	GENEVA VERSION.
Mat. xviii. 26.—The servant fell down, and besought him, saying, Lord, *have*	Mat. xviii. 26.—The servant fell down, and besought him, saying, Master, *ap-*

---

[1] In the Great Bible the words are, "*The* lovers salute thee": a fine synonym for, "The believers," or "The Christians." In the revised version, 1881, the words are, "*The friends* salute thee."

[2] The Geneva translators here followed Beza's Latin:—"Felix distulit eos, Postquam exquisitius pernovero quae ad viam istam pertinent, inquiens, quum tribunus Lysias descenderit, pernoscam vestrum negotium."

patience with me, and I will pay thee all.
  Luke xxii. 11.—Where is the *guest-chamber*, where I shall eat the Passover with my disciples.
  Acts xvi. 12.—And a *free city*.

  Acts xxvii. 14-15.—But not long after their arose against their purpose a *flaw of wind* out of the North-east (which is called Euroclydon, Bishops'). And when the ship was caught, and could not resist the wind, we let her go, and were *driven with the weather*.[2]
  Rom. viii. 6.—*To be carnally minded* is death; but *to be spiritually minded* is life and peace.
  2 Tim. ii. 6.—The husbandman that laboureth must *first receive* of the fruits. (The labouring husbandman must first be partaker of the fruites, Bishops'.)

pease thine anger towards me, and I will pay thee all.[1]
  Luke xxii. 11.—Where is the *lodging*, where I shall eat my Passover with my disciples.
  Acts xvi. 12.—And *whose inhabitants came from Rome to dwell there*.

  Acts xxvii. 14-15.—But anon after there arose by it a *stormy winde* called Euroclydon. And when the ship was caught, and could not resist the wind, we let her go and were *carried away*.

  Rom. viii. 6.—*The wisdom of the flesh* is death, but *the wisdom of the spirit* is life and peace.
  2 Tim. ii. 6.—The husbandman must *first labour before* he receive the fruits.

While the bishops, in their translation of the New, as well as of the Old Testament, followed in the main the text of the Great Bible, they also in the New, as in the Old Testament, adopted a very large number of the Geneva renderings. The extent to which they deviated from the Great Bible,[3] and appropriated from the Geneva Bible, may be gathered from the following tabulated figures:—

Chapter.	No. of Verses.	No. of variations from Great Bible.	No. of these variations found in Geneva Bible.	No. of these variations not found in Geneva Bible.	No. of new renderings received into Authorised Version.
Luke xvi.,	31	30	13	17	4
Acts xi.,	30	21	11	10	7
1 Corinthians xi.,	34	51	33	18	14
Hebrews ix.,	29	67	29	38	23
Revelation xxi.,	27	22	12	10	9
Total,	151	191	98	93	57

The amount of deviation in the Bishops' Bible from the text of the Great Bible, is shewn here to have been very considerable. For every three verses there are, on an average, four cases of

---

[1] Cohibe iram adversus me, Beza; Patientiam habe in me, Vulgate.

[2] The translation here commended is both free and paraphrastic, which by some people are reckoned grievous faults, but it has the rare merits of being *really* true, and singularly graphic.

[3] The edition of the Great Bible consulted in the formation of this table is that of 1539, as reprinted in Bagster's Hexapla.

deviation. As nearly as possible, too, one half of these deviations consist of Geneva renderings. Of the other half, again, which are presumed to be original amendments by the bishops, more than sixty per cent. have been retained in the authorised version. All this indicates a fair measure of revisional care and skill. Speaking at present, however, of the renderings appropriated by the bishops from the Geneva Bible, it may be said that they were sometimes renderings which modern taste and judgment would approve, and sometimes not. The cases that shall now be undernoted, are cases in which it will hardly be disputed that the bishops did well to accept the amendments made by the Geneva divines on the Great Bible.

GREAT BIBLE.	GENEVA AND BISHOPS' BIBLE.
Mat. xxiii. 4.—They bynde together hevy burthens and grevous to be borne, and laye them on mennes shoulders: but they themselves wyll not *heave at* them wyth one of theyr fyngers.	Mat. xxiii. 4.—They bind together hevy burthens and grevous to be borne, and laye them on mennes shoulders: but they themselves will not *move* them with one of their fingers.
Mat. xxvi. 18.—My tyme is at hande, I wyll kepe *myne Easter* by the, wyth my disciples.	Mat. xxvi. 18.—My time is at hand, I make (will kepe, Geneva) *the Passover* at thy house with my disciples.
Acts viii. 23.—For I perceive that thou arte *full of bytter gall* and *wrapped in* iniquitie.	Acts viii. 23.—For I perceive that thou art *in the gall of bitterness*, and *in the bond of* iniquity.
Acts xxvii. 9.—When sailynge was nowe jeopardous, because also that *they had ouerlonge fasted*.	Acts xxvii. 9.—When sailing was now jeopardous, because also that *the fast was now already past*.
Rom. vii. 1.—Knowe ye not brethren . . how that the lawe hath power over a man as longe as *it endureth*.	Rom. vii. 1.—Know ye not, brethren . . how that the law hath power (dominion, Geneva) over a man as long as *he liveth*.
Rom. vii. 6.—That we shuld serve in *a new conversacyon* of the sprete and not in *the olde conversacyon* of the letter.	Rom. vii. 6.—That we should serve in *newness* of spirit, and not in *the oldness* of the letter.
Gal. iv. 5.—That we thorow eleccion might receyue the inherytaunce that belongeth unto the naturall sonnes.	Gal. iv. 5.—That we might receive the adoption of children (of the sons, Geneva).
Heb. x. 33.—Partly whyle *all men wondred and gazed at you for the shame and tribulacyon that was done unto you:* partly while ye became companyons of them which *so passed their tyme*.	Heb. x. 33.—Partly while ye were made *a gazing stocke, both by reproaches and afflictions*, and partly while ye became companions of them which *were so tossed to and fro*.

In other cases, the bishops did not exercise a wise discretion in adopting the Geneva renderings. In the Great Bible, Acts viii. 33 is translated: "Because of his humbleness he was not esteemed." This is a statement that accords with fact, and it is in meaning not very remote from the rendering given in both the authorised and the revised versions. But the bishops, following the Geneva divines, translate the verse—"in his humility his judgment is *exalted;*" which is fancifully explained in the margin of the Geneva version—"the punishment he suffered was the beginning of his glory." One verse in which it might have been thought, a few years ago, that the bishops did well to follow the Geneva translators is Heb. v. 7, in which the Apostle is made to say that our Lord "was heard in that which he feared." This is one of the renderings that Catholic divines specially impugn, as a pernicious and presumptuous corruption of the sacred text, in order to give apparent sanction to the Protestant heresy, that Christ was in terror of damnation! In their English version of the Scriptures, the Catholics accordingly give a different rendering of the passage. They make it read: he was "heard for his reverence." This, too, is how the verse reads in the Great Bible; and now at length, with a slight variation of words, in the revised version, 1881.

As shown in the table on page 218, the bishops introduced into the Testament a considerable number of new renderings of their own; at all events, renderings that are not found in either the Great Bible or the Geneva Bible. A goodly proportion, too, of the bishops' original renderings have been retained in later versions. Two, of which more has been said than their importance warrants, will be found in Mat. xvii. In the Great Bible, the 25th verse of that chapter reads: "Of whom do the kynges of the earth take trybute or tolle, of their chyldren or of straungers?" And so, also, in the first edition of the Bishops' Bible, 1568; but in the second version, 1572, the words "their children" were changed into "their *own* children," and this alteration was hailed by scholastic critics as a very important amendment. Alas, for the fickleness of scholastic judgment! This amendment, which in 1572 was deemed a matter of high consequence, and in 1611 was retained in the King's translation, has by the revisers of 1881 been discarded in favour of the earlier and less emphatic rendering. Two verses further on in the chapter, Jesus is represented in the Great Bible to have said to Peter: "Go thou to the see, and cast an *angle,* and take the fish that first cometh up." In

1572, the italicised word *angle* was by the bishops changed into *hook;* and this change also was proclaimed as a notable correction, although it was really an ostensible distinction without a shade of difference.

While few of the changes made by the Bishops on previous renderings of Scripture are of great importance, some are improvements. In the Great Bible it is said, Mat. xxiv. 12: "Because iniquitie shall *have the upper hand*, the love of many shall *abate*." The expressions here italicised were, in the Geneva Bible, changed into *be increased*, and *be cold;* but a finishing touch was given to the sentence by the bishops, who made it read, as it still does in the authorised version, "because iniquity shall *abound*, the love of many shall *wax* cold." In some cases, archaisms of obscure and doubtful meaning which are found in the Great Bible and Geneva Bible are in the Bishops' Bible replaced by simple and definite terms; as in Acts i. 21, where the words *had all his conversacyon* (Great Bible) and *was conversant* (Geneva Bible) are changed into "went out and in;" and in Acts xiii. 15, where the term *lecture* is changed into "reading." Here and there a cumbrous phrase is replaced by a happier expression; as in Rom. viii. 17, where *joint-heirs* is substituted for "heirs annexed" with Christ. Some verbal inaccuracies are likewise corrected; as in 1 Cor. iii. 2, which in the Great Bible and the Geneva Bible reads, "I gave you milk to *drink*, and not *meate*," but in the Bishops' Bible is rendered, "I have nourished you with milk, and not with meate."

As further specimens of amendments made by the bishops on the diction of previous versions, the following passages may be cited:—

GREAT BIBLE.	GENEVA BIBLE.	BISHOPS' BIBLE.
Rom. ix. 33.—A rocke that men shall be offended at.	Rom. ix. 33.—A rocke to make men fall.	Rom. ix. 33.—A rock of offence.
Rom. x. 10.—To beleue wyth the hert justifyeth: and to knowledge wyth the mouth maketh a man safe.	Rom. x. 10.—With the heart, man believeth unto righteousness, and with the mouth man confesseth to salvation.	Rom. x. 10.—With the heart man believeth unto righteousness, and with the mouth confession is made unto salvation.
Rom. xii. 18.—As muche as is in you, lyve peaceably wyth all men.	Rom. xii. 18.—As much as in you is, have peace with all men.	Rom. xii. 18.—As much as lyeth in you, live peaceably with all men.

2 Cor. iv. 2.—Reporte ourselves to every mannes conscience.	2 Cor. iv. 2.—Approve ourselves to every man's conscience.	2 Cor. iv. 2.—Commending ourselves to every man's conscience.
2 Cor. ix. 5.—To prepare youre good blessynge promysed afore, that it might be ready, so that it be a blessyng and not a defraudynge.	2 Cor. ix. 5.—To finish your benevolence appointed afore, that it might be ready, and come as of benevolence and not as of sparing.	2 Cor. ix. 5.—And prepare your fore-appointed beneficence, that it might be ready as a beneficence and not as an extortion.
Eph. i. 5.—Ordeyned us before thorow Jesus Christ, to be heyres unto hymself.	Eph. i. 5.—Predestinated us to be adopted through Jesus Christ unto himself.	Eph. i. 5.—Predestinated us unto the adoption of children by Jesus Christ unto himself.
Phil. iv. 17.—Not that I desyre gyftes : but I desyre aboundaunt frute on your parte.	Phil. iv. 17.—Not that I desire a gift, but I desire the fruit that may further your reckoning.	Phil. iv. 17.—Not that I desire a gift; but I desire fruit abounding to your account.
1 Thess. iv. 11.—That ye studye to be quyet and to medle with youre awne busynes.	1 Thess. iv. 11.--That ye studie to be quiet and to medle with youre awne busines.	1 Thess. iv. 11.—That ye study to be quiet and to doe your awne businesse.
2 Peter iii. 10. — The heauens shall passe awaye in maner as a tempest, and the elementes shall melt wyth heat.	2 Peter iii. 10. — The heavens shall passe away with a noyse, and the element shall melt with heat.	2 Peter iii. 10. — The heavens shall passe away with a great noyse, and the elements shall melt with fervent heate.

All the changes, however, that the bishops made on previous translations, are not entitled to praise. Some of them are positively mistranslations; as "*Hearts grief* and misery are in their ways," Rom. iii. 16; " All have sinned, and *have need* of the glory of God," Rom. iii. 23; " Let us fear, therefore, lest at any time, by forsaking the promise of entering into his rest, any of you should seem to *be defrauded*," Heb. iv. 1; " The first covenant then had verily *justifying* ordinances," Heb. ix. 1; " Justifyings of the flesh, which were *laid up* until the time of reformation," Heb. ix. 10.[1] Infelicitous words, too, were sometimes substituted by the bishops for better words that were to be found either in the Great or in the Geneva Bible ; as, " Then will I *confess* unto them, That I never knew you," Mat. vii. 23 ; " Pray ye, therefore, the Lord of the harvest,

---

[1] The bishops may have been influenced in these renderings by words in Latin versions :—*Contritio*, Rom. iii. 16, Vulgate ; *Egent* gloria Dei, Rom. iii. 23, Vulgate ; Aliquis ex vobis fuisse *frustratus*, Heb. iv. 1, Beza ; " Any of you should seem to be deprived," Geneva Version. The following verse either exhibits a very peculiar reading in some Greek text, or is a misprint :—" Let the peace of God have the victorie in your hearts, to the which also *we* (ye) are called in one body," Col. iii. 15.

that he will *thrust forth* labourers into his harvest," Mat. ix. 38; "While they *were conversant* (abode, Gen.) in Galilee," Mat. xvii. 22; "Repent ye, therefore, and *revert* that your sins may be blotted out," Acts iii. 19; "That every mouth may be stopped, and that all the world may be *endangered* to God," Rom. iii. 19; "Not *lither* (slothful, G.B.) in business," Rom. xii. 11; "Praying night and day exceedingly to see you personally, and *repaire the wantings* of your faith," 1 Thess. iii. 10; "For there hath appeared the grace of God, which *is healthfull* to all men," Titus ii. 11; "When he would have inherited the blessing, he was *reprobated*," Heb. xii. 17. An oft-quoted, beautiful verse in the authorised translation, is Mat. vi. 28:— "Consider the lilies of the field; how they grow: They toil not, neither do they spin." This rendering is taken all but one word, *toil* instead of *labour*, from the Great Bible; and yet the bishops, with such a model before them, cumbered the passage as follows:—"*Learne of* the lilies of the field, how they grow: They *weary not themselves with labour*, neither do they spinne." The phrase, "land of Sodom and Gomorrha," which appears both in the Great and Geneva Bible is, in like manner, inflated by the bishops, Mat. x. 15, into "land of the Sodomites and Gomorrhœans." A verse that reads well enough in both the Great Bible and Geneva Bible, is Heb. xiii. 7. The bishops, however, were not satisfied with that verse as it stood in these Bibles, and they remodelled it in a way which, it will be enough to say, no subsequent revisers have ever copied:— "Whose end of conversation ye considering, follow their faith."

A goodly proportion of the original emendations made by the bishops on the text of the Great Bible, in both the Old and New Testaments, have, as will be seen by reference to pages 210 and 221-2, been retained in the present authorised version of the Scriptures. This retention is a valuable testimony to their scholastic and literary merits. Some of these accepted emendations, too, being improvements in expression, may be said to have permanently enriched the English Bible. We owe the bishops something for their labours, therefore; and that obligation should be cordially acknowledged. Of Bible phrases coined by the bishops, instances may be found in almost every other chapter of the New Testament. Out of a very few chapters read specially for that purpose, the following have been culled: "*Children of the bridechamber*," Mat. ix. 15; "*faithless and perverse nation*," Mat. xvii. 17; "*with* (hearty) *desire I have desired* to eat this Passover, Luke xxii. 15; "they that have authority upon them are called *benefactors*," Luke xxii. 25; "where prayer was *wont to be made*," Acts xvi. 13; "*set at nought* thy brother," Rom. xiv. 10; "*rightly* dividing the word of truth" 2 Tim. ii. 15; "sought it *carefully* with tears," Heb. xii. 17; serve God *acceptably* with reverence and godly fear, Heb. xii. 28; "*superfluity of naughtiness*," and "*engrafted word*," Jas. i. 21; "an inheritance *incorruptible* and undefiled, and that fadeth not away," 1 Pet. i. 4; "not of *corruptible* seed, but of *incorruptible*," 1 Pet. i. 23; "since the fathers *fell asleep*," 2 Pet. iii. 4; "*led away* with the error of the wicked," 2 Pet. iii. 17.

Of ill-chosen words again in the Great Bible or Geneva Bible that were displaced by the bishops for other and happier terms may be mentioned: "*avoid* Satan," Mat. iv. 10; "for fear of him the keepers *were astonied*," Mat. xxviii. 4; "counted worthy to suffer *rebuke* for his name," Acts v. 41. One verse, in the rendering of which a very marked progressive improvement may be traced, is Rom. xiv. 4. In the Great Bible, the first part of this verse is clumsily translated: "What art thou, that judgest another mannes seruaunt whether he stande or fall? That pertayneth unto his owne master." A much simpler rendering is given in the Geneva version: "Who art thou that condemnest another man's servant? he standeth or falleth to his own master." But with very little change of words there is an epigrammatic finish given by the bishops to this rendering: "What art thou that judgest another man's servant? *To his own master he standeth or falleth.*"

It is commonly alleged that the bishops shewed a tendency to introduce into the Bible inflated and latinised diction. Their translation, says Dr. Eadie, is "more stately than precise," and it abounds in "mouth-filling words" and "rounded periods." And in confirmation of this statement, their rendering of 2 Cor. ix. 5, which has been quoted in this chapter as a

favourable specimen of their emendations, has been adduced:—
"I thought it necessary to exhort the brethren, that they should come before unto you, and prepare your fore-promised beneficence, that it might be ready as a beneficence, and not as an extortion." Other verses, besides, might doubtless be quoted, and quoted with more force,. in justification of the above-mentioned criticism. The bishops, for instance, following the text of the Great Bible,[1] make Heb. vii. 12 read:—"If the priesthood be *translated*, of necessity also there is made a *translation* of the law." And, in James i. 14, they introduce a phrase of their own coinage for no apparent purpose, unless to fill the mouth of the reader and give rotundity to the sentence:—"Every man is tempted, when he is drawn away, and enticed *with the baite* of his owne concupiscence." Turning to the Old Testament, we find an instance of similar padding in the first verse of the twenty-third Psalm:—"God is my shephearde, therefor I can lacke nothyng: he wyll cause me to repose myself in pasture full of grasse, and he wyll leade me unto calme waters." And a still more emasculated piece of English will be found in the opening verse of the last chapter of Nahum's prophecies. In the Great Bible that verse reads:—"Wo to the bloudthursty citye, which is all full of lyes and robberye, and wyll not leaue of from rauyshynge." Without any assistance from the Geneva divines, the bishops have transformed this strong and heart-penetrating cry of the prophet into the following flabby malediction:—"O bloody citie, stuffed throughout with falshoode, with extreme dealing, nor will be broughte from spoyling. . . . . lo, I against thee, saith the Lorde of hostes." Another pompous rendering of the bishops is Prov. xxv. 26:—"Curiously to search the glory of heavenly things is not commendable." But the bishops' diction is not generally characterised by "great

---

[1] A large number of the stilted renderings in the Bishops' Bible are taken from the Great Bible: such as, "Provoke the presence of his majestie to anger," Is. iii. 8; "In the day see that ye sing of the congregation, which is the vineyard that bringeth forth the best wine," Is. xxvii. 2; "No man shall invade thee, to hurt thee," Acts xviii. 10; "Abhorring fighting, abhorring covetousness," 1 Tim. iii. 3.

swelling words." As a rule, the bishops adhered to the homely and vernacular style of the Great Bible, when in the Geneva version there was presented to them a more inflated form of expression; and, taken all over, the Bishops' Bible is less sonorous and stately in its style than the Geneva, as the following extracts will tend to shew:—

BISHOPS' BIBLE.	GENEVA BIBLE.
John v. 27.—Power also to *judge*.	John v. 27.—Power also to *execute judgment*.
Acts i. 13.—And when they were come in they went up into a *parlour* where abode both Peter and James.	Acts i. 13.—And when they were come in they went up into an *upper chamber* where abode, etc.
Acts xviii. 28.—He *overcame* the Jews *mightily*, and *that openly*.	Acts xviii. 28.—Mightily he *confuted publicly* the Jews with *great vehemencie*.
Acts xix. 23.—And the same time there arose no *little ado* about that way.	Acts xix. 23.—And the same time there arose no *small trouble* about that way.
Acts xix. 29.—And all the city was *on a rore*.	Acts xix. 29.—And the whole city was *full of confusion*.
Acts xix. 31.—Desiring him that he would not *preasse into* the common hall.	Acts xix. 31.—Desiring him that he would not *present himself* in the common place.
Acts xxi. 14.—And when we could not *turn his mind* we ceased.	Acts xxi. 14.—And when he would not *be persuaded* we ceased.
Acts xxi. 24.—*Do cost on* them that they may shave their heads.	Acts xxi. 24.—*Contribute* with them that they may shave their heads.
Acts xxvii. 27.—As we were *sailing in Adria* about midnight.	Acts xxvii. 27.—As we were *carried to and fro in the Adriatical sea* about midnight.
Deut. xxxiii. 7.—His hands shall be *good ynough* for him, if thou helpe him against his enemies.	Deut. xxxiii. 7.—His hands shall be *sufficient* for him, if thou helpe him against his enemies.
Deut. xxxiii. 10.—They shall put incense *to thy nose*.	Deut. xxxiii. 10.—They shall put incense before thy face.
Job. vii. 3.—Many a careful night have I told.	Job vii. 3.—Painful nights have been appointed unto me.
Job. ix. 32.—He that I must give answer unto and *with whom I go to the law*, is not a man as I am.	Job ix. 32.—He is not a man as I am that I should answer him if we *come together to judgment*.
Job xvii. 1.—I am *hard at deaths doore*.	Job xvii. 1.—The grave is ready for me.
Ps. xxvii. 13.—·If I had not believed verily to see the goodness of God in the land of the living, (*their spite had killed me*.)	Ps. xxvii 13.—*I should have fainted* except I had believed to see the goodness of the Lord in the land of the living.
Ps. xxviii. 1.—*Make not* as though thou wert deafe *at* me.	Ps. xxviii. 1.—Be not deaf toward me.
Ps. xxviii. 4.—*Pay them home* that they have deserved.	Ps. xxviii. 4.—*Render* them their *reward*.
Ps. xxxviii. 6.—I am become crooked and am exceedingly *pulled down*.	Ps. xxxviii. 6.—I am bowed and crooked very sore.
Prov. xvi. 28. — A frowarde *bodie* acuseth strife, and he that is a *blabbe of his tongue* maketh division among princes.	Prov. xvi. 28. — A froward *person* soweth strife, and a *tale teller* maketh division among princes.

Prov. xvii. 17. – In adversitie a man shall know who is his brother.
Prov. xvii. 22.—A merie heart maketh a *lusty age.*
Eccles. x. 18.—Through slothfulnesse the *balkes fall down.*
Is. xxx. 27.—His presence is *so hot that* no man is able to abide.
Is. xxxii. 18.—Dwell in the *innes* of peace.
Is. lxii. 6.—Ye that remember the Lord, ye shall not *keep him close.*
Is. lxvi. 3.—He that killeth a sheep for me (*is as one that*) *knetcheth* a dogge. (Choketh a dog, Coverdale.)
Jer. xxiii. 9.—My heart breaketh *in my body.*
Jer. xxvi. 20.—There was a prophet that *preached stiffly* in the name of the Lord, called Urias.

Prov. xvii. 17.—A brother is *born for* adversity.
Prov. xvii. 22.—A joyful heart causeth good health.
Eccles. x. 18.—By slouthfulnesse the *roof of the house goeth to decay.*
Is. xxx. 27.—His face is burning and the burden thereof is heavy.
Is. xxxii. 18.—Dwell in the tabernacles of peace.
Is. lxii. 6.—Ye that are mindful of the Lord, *keep not silence.*
Is. lxvi. 3.—He that sacrificeth a sheep (*is*) as if he cut off a dogges necke.
Jer. xxiii. 9.—Mine heart breaketh within me.
Jer. xxvi. 20.—There was also a man that prophesied in the name of the Lord, one Uriah.

Considering that even in the authorised version there are many antiquated words and phrases, we cannot be surprised to find that in the Bishops' Bible there have been retained, from the older translations, a goodly number of archaic terms and forms of expression. Some of these, however, are more antique than we might be prepared for. The following phrases among others were adopted by the bishops from the Great Bible : "the owne accord," Acts xii. 10 ; "other many," Acts xv. 35 ; "a good many of days," Acts xxi. 10 ; although in each of these instances there had been introduced into the Geneva version a phraseology of more modern aspect. Where we are accustomed to read, Mat. xxi. 44, "it shall grind him to powder," we find it said in the Bishops' Bible, "it shall *all to* grinde him;" that is, it shall grind him utterly and completely.[1] Other archaic words in the Bishops' Bible are: "depart from," in the sense of *part* with, or *give away;* "The nigarde having inough will depart from nothing, and yet is euer in povertie," Prov. xi. 24; "sprong," in the sense of

---

[1] This expression "all to," which was common in the early translations of the Bible, and less common in subsequent ones, still lives in the authorised version :— "A certain woman cast a piece of a millstone upon Abimelech's head, and *all to* brake his skull," Judges ix. 53. In the Geneva Version we read, Matthew vii. 6. "Neither cast ye your pearles before swine, lest they tread them under their feet, and turning again *all to* rent you."

sprinkled, "Their blood shall be sprong upon my clothes," Is. lxiii. 3; "safe," in the sense of *whole*, "Thy faith hath made thee *safe*," Mat. ix. 22; "occupying," in the sense of trading, "Howe much every one had gayned in occupying," Luke xix. 15; "tarried," in the form of a verb transitive; "These going before, *tarried us* at Troas," Acts xx. 5; "fet," for *fetched*, "From them we *fet* a compass," Acts xxviii. 13;[1] "pight," for *pitched*, "The true tabernacle which the Lord *pyght*, and not man," Heb. viii. 2; "herberous," for hospitable, "Be ye *herberous* one to another, without grudging," 1 Pet. iv. 9; and "raines," for *fine linen*; "To her was granted that she should be arayed with pure and goodly *raynes:* for the *raynes* is the righteousness of Christ," Rev. xix. 8. An odd expression taken by the bishops from the Great Bible occurs in James i. 24, "For hee hath considered himselfe, and is gone his wayes, and hath forgotten immediately what his *fashion* was." Another odd and antique phrase, which the bishops themselves introduced into the English Testament, is, "make you careless," in the old sense of secure. "If this come to the Deputy's ears we will persuade him and make you *careless*." A quaint, antique, and expressive word that the bishops found in the Great Bible, and retained in their own version, is "huswifely," "A huswifely woman is a crowne unto her husband," Prov. xii. 4.

The marginal notes in the Bishops' Bible are not very numerous, not nearly so numerous as in the Geneva Bible, and they are generally not interesting. They are mostly designed for the instruction of readers of weak capacity. A few of them, however, are racy and entertaining. Some of them, too, are of a theological and ecclesiastical strain that we should scarcely have expected in a Bible issued by a body of prelates. To use a phrase of Cardinal Wiseman's, applied to another matter, "they remind us of Geneva caps, and smack of predestination." And, in truth, the raciest and best of the bishops' notes are

---

[1] Although the word *fet* does not occur in modern editions of the authorised Version, it appears in the first edition of that version, 1611. See *English Hexapla*, Acts xxviii. 13.

taken verbatim, and without grace of either acknowledgment or thanks, from the Geneva Bible. On the statement, Gen. xxxvi. 24, "this was that Ana that found mules in the wilderness as she fed her father Gibeon's asses," there is appended, in the margin, a note that, "Man's vanitie cannot be content with God's distinction of beastes, but inventeth the prodigious generation of mules, between the asse and the mare." This is very spicy criticism, but it lacks the virtue of originality; for, if we turn to the Geneva Bible, we shall find there the same ethical reflection expressed in the same words.[1] From the Geneva Bible, also, is taken the sour and unjust remark on Gal. vi. 14: "*By the world* he meaneth all outwarde pompes, ceremonies, and thinges which please mens fantasies." The quaint exposition of Heb. ii. 1, which we find in the Geneva Bible, that "we must diligently keep in memorie the doctrine which we have learned, lest like vessels full of chops, we leake and run out on every part," is likewise appropriated by the bishops. The Geneva note on 1 Peter v. 1, that, "By *elders* he understandeth all them which preach, teach, or minister in the Church," appears in the Bishops' Bible also; but not the note on Phil. i. 1, that, "By *Bishops*, the Apostle meaneth them that had charge of the word and governing, as pastours, doctours, elders;"[2] nor the note on Acts xiv. 23, "That ministers were not made without the consent of the people." The sweeping inference, deduced by the Geneva divines, from 2 Pet. ii. 3, that the Pope "is not the successor of Simon Peter, but of Simon Magus," is, also, unscrupulously inserted by the bishops in their marginal annotations. Episcopal prudence restrained the bishops, however, from adopting the Geneva note on Rev. ix. 3, that the locusts, which came out of the smoke of the bottomless

---

[1] The reflection is out of place, for the passage was mistranslated of old, and now reads in the revised version, "found the *hot springs* in the wilderness."

[2] Many dignitaries in the Church of England in the first days of the Reformation would have acquiesced in this statement. "Cranmer expressed his opinion formally in writing that bishops and priests were not two things, but both one office in the beginning of Christ's religion. Thirteen bishops, with a great number of other ecclesiastics, subscribed this proposition, that in the New Testament there is no mention made of any degrees or distinctions in orders, but only deacons or ministers, and priests or bishops." M'Crie's "Life of Knox," Note R, Vol. I.

pit, were "worldly, subtil Prelates . . . with Archbishops, &c., &c." Of sturdy doctrinal notes, taken by the bishops from the margin of the Geneva Bible, many might be cited, but one will be sufficiently illustrative: 1 Peter i. 2, "The free election of God is the efficient cause of our salvation; the material cause is Christes obedience; our effectual calling is the formal cause; and the final cause is our sanctification."

An interesting, although not very numerous, class of notes in the Bishops' Bible, is that in which the Geneva annotations are either modified or controverted. The conduct of Jacob in passing himself off for Esau, in order to obtain his father's blessing, is a matter that is differently regarded according as the facts of the case are apprehended. The marginal note on the subject in the Geneva Bible is: "Although Jaakob was assured of his blessing by faith, yet he did euill to seeke it by lyes, and the more because he abused God's name thereunto." The bishops were not prepared to endorse this condemnation, in an unqualified way; and, for the Geneva note, they substituted the following: "The subtill dealing of Rebecca and Jacob with Isaac, considered by itself, is altogether blameworthy; but if it be referred to the will of God, and setting forth of his decree, it is commendable." In his speech to the men of Shechem, about a treaty of intermarriage with the Israelites, Hamor is reported, Gen. xxxiv. 23, to have said: "Shall not their goods and their substance, and all their cattel be ours; let us only consent unto them, and they will dwell with us." In the Geneva Bible, the note on this statement is: "They lacke no kind of perswasion, whiche preferre their own commodities before the common welth." By the bishops, the more apposite remark is made: "Euile magistrates *pretend a common welth*, and yet all is but for their owne cause."

Of original notes (or at least notes uninspired from Geneva), that appear on the margin of the Bishops' Bible, the following may be quoted as favourable specimens of those that are other than common-place: Gen. xxiv. 49, "He treateth with the mother and brother concerning the maiden, whereby it may appeare that priuie contractes, without the knowledge and consent of their parents, are not good"; Gen. xxv. 25 ("hee was all ouer as it were a hearie garment, and they called his name Esau"), "The crueltie of his minde answered to the roughness of his body"! Phil. ii. 12 ("work out your own salvation, &c."), "Our health hangeth not on our workes, and yet are they sayd to worke out their health, who doe runne in the race of justice. For although we be saved freely in Christ by faith, yet must we walke by the way of justice unto our health"; Rom. xvi. 1 ("Phoebe, our sister, which is a minister of the Church of Cenchraea") "In the primitive Church, ancient widowes and other vertuous women were chosen and appointed to minister unto the needy, and therefore called ministers ; and not because they had any publique authoritie to teach in the congregation."

The distribution of notes over the margin of the Bishops' Bible is very irregular and unequal. In some books hard to understand, such as the prophecies of Isaiah and Jeremiah, the notes are very sparse, so sparse that five or six consecutive pages may be found, here and there, ungarnished by a single annotation; while in other books, such as Genesis, Exodus, Job, and the Epistles of St. Paul, the notes are "thick as autumn rains." It is not a little remarkable that while the bishops have incorporated some of the Geneva observations on the ritual, doctrines, and ecclesiastical assumptions of the Catholic Church, they have scarcely a note on the margin of the book of Revelation, where the most obnoxious of their anti-Papal reflections were inserted by the Geneva divines.

One of the features of the Great Bible was the number of interpolations it contained. These were enclosed in brackets, and were printed in a different type from the surrounding text. Few of these interpolations were transferred to the Bishops' Bible, but a few were, such as: "*They did flye in the aire* as it were two cubits high," Num. xi. 31 ; "desiring to be refreshed with the crumbes which fell from the rich man's boord, *and no man gave unto him*," Luke xvi. 21 ; "providing aforehande things honest, *not only before God, but also* in the sight of all men," Rom. xii. 17 ; "that ye may grow thereby *unto salvation*," 1 Pet. ii. 2 ; "*he that knowledgeth the sonne hath the father also*," 1 John ii. 23. But into the Bishops' Bible (at least into some editions of it), there were introduced a number of interpolations that are not found in the Great Bible. To the question, "where is he, or who is he?" Job. ix. 24, is appended, by the bishops, the supplementary clause, "*that can shewe the contrarie.*" In the eighteenth chapter of St. John's Gospel, two interpolations have been inserted by the bishops, viz., v. 13, "*And Annas sent Christ bound unto Caiaphas the high priest;*" and v. 22, "one of the officers which stood by smote Jesus *with a rodde.*" With the text of Acts ix. 22, the bishops incorporated a note (which appears on the margin of the Geneva Bible), so as to make the verse read : " Saul increased the more in strength, and confounded the Jews which dwelt at Damascus, proving by conferring *one Scripture with another* that this is very Christ."[1] On the other hand, there are in the Bishops' Bible many instances in which words and phrases, printed as part of the text in the Great Bible, appear in different type as interpolations. In most of these cases, the interpolations are simply supplementary words, supposed to be necessary to convey the meaning of the original Scripture, by completing the sentences in which they appear. Of these may be mentioned, " have I therefore seen an angel of the Lord face to face, *that I should die*," Judges vi. 22 ; " to go dwell where he could find

---

[1] In Fulke's edition of the bishops' version of the New Testament (published along with the text of the Rhemes Testament, 1633), the passage interpolated in John xviii. 13 is given on the margin, as a reading advocated by some authorities ; and the words interpolated in Acts ix. 22 are given on the margin, as a comment or explanation. In Fulke's Defence of the English translations of the Bible, chap. xx., sec. 2, there is a curious statement regarding the latter interpolation. Gregory Martin had alleged that this interpolation appears in a version bearing date 1577, and that it was added by the Protestant translators "in favour of their presumptuous opinion, that conference of Scripture is enough for any man to understand them." To this averment, Fulke replies :—" Either you make a loud ly or else some one print which you have of the Bishops' Bible, which you call Bib. 1577, hath put that in the line which should be the note in the margent. For, of foure translations that I have, never a one hath that addition." To Fulke's statement Dr. Mombert adds :—" The only edition of the Bishops' Bible known to have the obnoxious clause is that of 1584, which Martin could not have used, because he wrote in 1583," p. 292. The interpolation here referred to may be seen, exactly as printed by Martin (that is, in brackets), in a handsome folio bearing date 1577, and said on the last page to be printed by Henrie Denham and Richard Watkins. It will also be found in Barker's folio, 1588. Both of these volumes are in the library of the University of Glasgow.

a convenient place," Judges xvii. 8 ; " and he made two pommels of moulten brass, *after the fashion of a crown,* to set on the toppes of the pillars," 1 Kings vii. 16 ; "*last of all,* when we *women* did sacrifice," Jer. xliv. 19 ; " as he sat *at the boord,*" Mat. xxvi. 7 ; " that we should *be apostles* unto the heathen," Gal. ii. 9 ; " Apollyon, *that is to say, a destroyer.*"[1] Some of these italicised expressions, or equivalents to them, will be found in the authorised version also ; and what may seem more remarkable, as a reversion to the form of the Great Bible, two of them will be found unitalicised, as a part of the legitimate text, in the revised version of the New Testament, 1881.

---

[1] In Fulke's edition, 1633, this interpolation is given as a marginal note.

THE BIBLES OF THE CHURCHES.

No. II.

Bible of the Catholic Church, commonly called the Douay Bible.

Editions consulted and quoted from :—
    Original version. 1609.
        Old Testament, vol. I., Genesis to Job. Douay, 1609.
        Old Testament, vol. II., Psalms to Malachi. Rouen, 1635.
        New Testament. Bagster's Hexapla.
    Challoner's Revision.
        Coyne, five volumes. Dublin, 1811.

WHATEVER may be said of the scholastic merits of the bishops' translation of the Scriptures, the watchmen of the Church of England, in 1564, are at least to be commended for taking measures to prevent prejudice to the doctrines and constitution of their church, by the circulation of annotated Bibles in which contumelious remarks were made on prelates and ceremonies. There was urgent need for similar action on the part of the Church of Rome, if she desired to retain any hold on the English people.

The popish clergy, and popish statesmen, had hitherto more than discountenanced the circulation of Bibles in English. Not to speak of earlier edicts on the subject, the Council of Trent, which sat from 1545 to 1563, ordained that "The Holy Scriptures, though truly and catholikely translated into vulgar tongues, may not be indifferently read of all men, nor of any other than such as have express license thereunto of their lawful ordinaries, with good testimony from their curates and confessors that they be humble discreet, and devout persons, and like to take much good and no harm thereby."[1] Instead

---

[1] Preface to Rhemes Testament. Some Catholic prelates at that date opposed even these concessions. In 1553, three bishops wrote a joint letter to the Pope in

of proclaiming *freedom*, the Catholic Church, it will thus be seen, insisted on the necessity of *license* to read the Scriptures even when truly and catholikely translated ;[1] and in defence of that principle it was said by their apologists :—" We must not imagine that in the primitive church either every one that understood the learned tongues wherein the Scriptures were written, or other languages into which they were translated, might without reprehension read, reason, dispute, turn and toss the Scriptures; or that our forefathers suffered every schoolmaster, scholar, or grammarian, that had a little Greek or Latin, straight to take in hand the holy Testament; or that the translated Bibles into the vulgar tongues were in the hands of every husbandman, artificer, prentice, boy, girl, mistress, maid, man; that they were sung, played, alleaged, of every tinker, taverner, rhymer, minstrel; that they were for table talk, for ale-benches, for boats and barges, and for every profane person or company."[2]

---

which they represented "that as little as possible of the Gospel (especially in the mother tongue) be read in all countries subject to your jurisdiction. That little which is usually read at Mass is sufficient, and beyond that no one whatever must be permitted to read." (Brown's edition of Ortuinus Gratius' *Fasciculus Rerum*, London, 1690, vol. ii., p. 648.) The words in the original Latin are :—" Denique (quod inter omnia consilia, quae nos dare hoc tempore beatitudini tuae possumus, omnium gravissimum, ad extremum reservavimus) oculi hic aperiendi sunt, omnibus nervis adnitendum erit, ut quam minimum evangelii poterit (praeserim *(sic)* vulgari lingua) in iis legatur civitatibus, quae sub tua ditione ac potestate sunt. Sufficiatque tantillum illud quod in Missa legi solet, nec eo amplius cuiquam mortalium legere permittatur. Quamdiu enim pauculo illo homines contenti fuerunt, tamdiu res tuae ex sententia successere; eadem-que in contrarium labi coeperunt, ex quo ulterius legi vulgo usurpatum est. Hic ille (in summa) est liber qui praeter caeteros hasce nobis tempestates et turbines concitavit quibus prope abrepti sumus. . . . Quare occultandae pauculae illae chartae erunt, sed adhibitae quadam cautione ac diligentia, ne ea res majores nobis turbas ac tumultus excitet."

[1] On this point the attitude of the Catholic Church is still practically unchanged: " Less than ten years ago it was forbidden to buy in Ireland a Douai version (the authorised Roman Catholic version) of the Bible without being furnished with a license from the priest. And to-day if a Roman Catholic ventures to open a Bible —even the carefully annotated Douai version which is supposed to be permitted— he is bound to confess such act to his priest." (*The Pope and the Bible*, Christian Life Publishing Co., London, 1888.)

[2] Preface to Rhemes Testament.

It was ostensibly, however, on the grounds that all English versions of the Scriptures, hitherto published, were incorrect and untruthful translations of God's word, and that they tended to pervert and corrupt the minds of those who read them, that the circulation of the Bible *in English* was denounced and opposed by Catholic prelates. But it was soon discovered that the prohibition and denunciation of English versions of the Bible could not prevent the spread of heresy. In spite of prohibition and denunciation, the Bible in English continued to be read by more and more of the English people. The attempt, by the Catholic clergy, to suppress English versions of the Bible created, in fact, a prejudice against the Catholic Church. It seemed an admission of the Protestant doctrine, that the Scriptures are the sole standard of Christian faith ; and it created a suspicion, that the Catholics were so conscious of their defection from the truth that they were afraid to appeal to the divine word. As time wore on, many Catholics felt that something more must be done than merely exclaim against the foul dealing of the English sectaries with the holy Scriptures, by means of " partial and false translations, to the advantage of their heresies, in their English Bibles used and authorised since the time of their schism." If the Catholic Church considered these English Bibles corrupt and heretical, it was clearly her wisest policy as well as her bounden duty, both to her own children and to those that had declined from her communion, to issue a new version of the Bible in English, which she could warrant to be authentic and genuine.

During the reign of Elizabeth, the Church of Rome could scarcely do in England what we have seen was done by the Reformed Church. The mass was prohibited, and the English liturgy was established in its stead. All beneficed ecclesiastics were compelled to take the oath of supremacy, and " renounce the spiritual as well as temporal jurisdiction of every foreign prince or prelate, on pain of forfeiting their office or benefice." From that date, there ceased to be a popish hierarchy, or face of a Catholic Church, in all England. Popish bishops could not unite together as Protestant bishops did, in 1564, to revise the English Bible, and issue a new version of the Scriptures under high ecclesiastical patronage. The faithful Catholics of England were scattered abroad. But, to their praise be it said, some of these poor persecuted Papists, true to their principles and professions, did in their exile what the Protestant refugees had done before at Geneva. They set themselves to the task of translating the Bible. And, in 1582, they brought out, from the press at Rhemes, an English translation of the New Testament. "Lack of good means," in their poor estate of banishment, prevented them from publishing, at the same time, their translation of the Old Testament; but in 1609-1610, they were enabled to give the public the full benefit of their labours, in an English version of that part of the Bible also, which was printed at Douay, and has hence come to be designated the Douay Bible.

The credit of this version of Scripture, translated on Catholic principles, devolves mainly on three men, *tres diversi eruditissimi theologi*, whose names were Gregory Martin, William Allen, and Richard Bristow. Of these, Martin was the most eminent;[1] and he seems to have been the one that made the translation. He was a man of considerable learning, "reputed the best Hebrew and Greek scholar of his college," when he took his degree at Oxford; and he was distinguished also as a polemical writer of both vigour and asperity.

The title on the Rhemes Testament, 1582, indicated both the source from which that translation was derived, and the special objects the translators had in view by its publication. The source from which the Rhemes Testament came was "the authentical Latin, diligently conferred with the Greek and other editions in diverse languages." The objects, again, for which the Rhemes Testament, with its "annotations and other necessary helps," was published, were "the discovery of the corruptions of diverse late translations, and of the clearing of controversies in religion."

The title-page of the Douay Bible, 1609-1610, bore a similar declaration.

The first thing, therefore, to be noted in regard to the

---

[1] Allen attained the rank of cardinal.

Rhemes Testament and the Douay Bible, is that, like Wyclif's Bible, they were translated from the Latin Vulgate. In other words they are translations of a translation. They were not drawn from the fountain head, like the translations by Tyndale, and the Geneva exiles. It was not, however, because Martin and his colleagues wanted the necessary scholarship. They were, from all accounts, quite competent to have translated from the Greek and Hebrew originals; and, indeed, they were careful to state, on the title pages of both the Rhemes and the Douay publications, that the original Scriptures had not been overlooked or disregarded.[1] The Vulgate was compared "with the Hebrew, Greek, and other editions in diverse languages." But the apparently strange theory was held, that the Vulgate Latin is of more authority, and more to be relied on for accuracy, than any copy we have of the Scriptures in Hebrew and Greek. In a prologue prefixed to the Rhemes Testament, the translators say, that, besides its antiquity and the commendation it receives from the Fathers, the Latin Vulgate is declared by the Holy Council of Trent to be "not only better than all other Latin translations, but than the Greek text itself in those places where they disagree." In an epistle to the English reader, prefixed to the Douay Bible, 1609-1610, it is said to the same effect:—" Another question may be proposed why we translated the Latin text, rather than the Hebrew or Greek which Protestants prefer as the fountain tongue, wherein holy Scriptures were first written. To this we answer, that if indeed those first pure Editions were now extant, or if such as

---

[1] That the Rhemes translators of the New Testament had a Greek text before them, is held to be conclusively proved by the way in which *articles*, unexpressed in the Vulgate, are introduced into the English version. "It might well be supposed," says Dr. Moulton, "that of all English versions the Rhemish would be least accurate in this point of translation. The very reverse is actually the case. There are many instances in which, of all versions, from Tyndale's to the authorised inclusive, this alone is correct in regard to the article." While the Greek article, however, is in many instances correctly rendered in the Rhemes Testament, it is in many other cases left untranslated, and an English article is sometimes introduced where there is no article in the original: as—" Five loaves among five thousand," (instead of " *The* five loaves among *the* five thousand ") Mark viii. 19; "The way of truth," (instead of " The way of *the* truth "), 2 Pet. ii. 2; and, " You are not under *the* law," (instead of " under law "), Rom. vi. 14.

be extant were more pure than the Latin, we would also prefer such fountains before the rivers, in whatsoever they should be found to disagree. But the ancient best learned Fathers and Doctors of the Church do much complain and testify to us that both the Hebrew and Greek editions are foully corrupted by Jews and Heretics, since the Latin was truly translated out of them, while they were more pure; and that the same Latin hath been far better conserved from corruptions."

The text from which the Rhemes Testament and Douay Bible are translated is termed, on the title pages of both of these publications, "the *authentical* Latin." And an explanation of the term *authentical* is given in the prologue to the Rhemes Testament, where it is stated that the Vulgate was the only one of all the Latin translations of the Scriptures declared by the Council of Trent to be "authentical." This account of the Council of Trent's declaration is a slight over-statement. All that the Council of Trent affirmed was that in public readings, disputations, sermons, and lectures, the Vulgate edition should be held as authentic.[1] The Council of Trent gave orders, also, that the Vulgate should, henceforth, be printed with all the accuracy attainable. But, for years after the Council of Trent had brought its sessions to a close, there was no copy of the Vulgate that was pronounced authoritatively to contain the standard text of Scripture. It was reserved to Pope Sixtus V. to supply this want for the Church. In 1590, that pontiff published a carefully collated copy of the Vulgate, with the following proclamation attached to it:—"By the fulness of Apostolical power, we decree and declare that this edition . . . approved by the authority delivered to us by the Lord, is to be received and held as true, lawful, authentic and unquestioned, in all public and private discussion, reading, preaching and explanation." Even the decree of a Pope, however, will not make any text or version of Scripture "authentical," in the sense of being absolutely without error. And the

---

[1] The terms of the Council's declaration were:—"Statuit et declarat, ut haec ipsa vetus et vulgata editio, quae longo tot seculorum usu in ipsa ecclesia probata est, in publicis lectionibus, disputationibus, praedicationibus et expositionibus *pro authentica habeatur.*"

character of this true, lawful and authentic edition of the Vulgate is thus described by Canon Westcott:[1] "He (Sixtus) had changed the readings of those whom he had employed to report upon the text with the most arbitrary and unskilful hand, and it is scarcely an exaggeration to say that his precipitate self-reliance had brought the Church into the most serious peril." Sixtus died soon after the publication of this authentic Vulgate; and so great was the scandal created in learned circles by his arbitrary and unskilful editing, that within little more than a year after his death, Bellarmin, with consummate casuistry, proposed that a new and corrected edition of the Vulgate should with all convenient speed be printed, "under the name of Sixtus, with a prefatory note, that several errors had crept into the former edition through the carelessness of the printers." The result was that in 1592 a new authentic edition of the Vulgate was published under the authority of another Pope, Clement VIII. This second authentic Vulgate differed widely from the first; more widely, it is said, than did the first from almost any unauthenticated copy in circulation.

It is quite clear, therefore, that in 1582, when the Rhemes Testament was published, there was no "authentical" Vulgate to found upon, for an absolutely correct version of the Scriptures in Latin. One critic says, "it is impossible to tell what edition of the Vulgate was used by the Rhemish translators, but it must have been one of the very worst."[2] To do them justice, however, it should be mentioned that in the preface to their translation of the New Testament they have the candour to say: "We bind not ourselves to the points of any one copy, print, or edition of the vulgar Latin, in places of no controversy, but follow the pointing most agreeable to the Greek and to the fathers' commentaries." The translation of the Old Testament was, like that of the New, completed before the publication of either the Sixtine (1590) or the Clementine (1592) authorised edition of the Vulgate; but having been left unpublished till 1609, it was revised and "conformed to the most perfect Latin text" before it was issued to the English public.

---

[1] Article, Vulgate, in Smith's "Dictionary of Christian Antiquities."
[2] Mombert.

The principle on which the Rhemes and Douay translators proceeded is indicated in the preface to the first edition of the Rhemes Testament. " We wish it," they say, " to be most sincerely, as becometh, *a Catholic translation,* and have endeavoured so to make it ; we are very precise and religious in following our copy, the old vulgar approved Latin ; not only in sense, which we hope we always do, but sometimes in the very words also and phrases, which may seem to the vulgar reader and to common English ears not yet acquainted therewith rudeness or ignorance. . . . . Moreover, we presume not, in hard places, to mollify the speeches and phrases, but religiously keep them word for word, and point for point, for fear of missing or restraining the sense of the Holy Ghost to our phantasie." This procedure was in strict accordance with the principles of Scripture translation that had long previously been propounded by Catholic Churchmen. In 1542, when the Church in England was in a transition state between Popery and Protestantism, with some of its benefices held by reforming and some by reactionary divines, a proposal was made in Convocation that the Great Bible should be revised according to the Vulgate. To this proposal was added a rider by Gardiner, the Popish bishop of Winchester, that something like a hundred Latin words in the Vulgate, which he enumerated, should in the new translation be either retained in their original form " for their genuine meaning and the mystery of the matter in them contained," or be " fitly Englished with the least alteration." Gardiner's list of words comprised, as might be expected, *poenitentia* (penitence or penance) ; *caritas* (love or charity) ; *gratia* (favour or grace) ; *ecclesia* (congregation or church) ; *sacramentum* (mystery or sacrament) ; and such other ecclesiastical terms as have in previous chapters of this volume been referred to. Besides these controverted words, too, Gardiner's list included *simulacrum* (image) ; *idolum* (idol) ; *spiritus sanctus* (holy ghost) ; *benedictio* (blessing) ; *adorare* (to worship) ; *elementa* (rudiments) ; *hostia* (an animal offered in sacrifice), etc., etc. In the preface to the Douay Bible, 1609-1610, the translators accordingly say :—" Now for the strictness observed in translating some words, or rather the not translating of

R

some, which is in more danger to be disliked, we doubt not but the discreet learned reader, deeply weighing and considering the importance of sacred words, and how easily the translator may miss the sense of the Holy Ghost, will hold that which is here done for reasonable and necessary. We have also the example of the Latin and Greek, where some words are not translated, but left in Hebrew, as they were first spoken and written; which seeing they could not, or were not convenient to be translated into Latin or Greek, how much less could they or was it reason to turn them into English. . . . Briefly, our apology is easy against English Protestants; because they also reserve some words in the original tongue, not translated into English, as *Sabbath, Ephod, Pentecost, Proselyte*, and some others."

Adherence to this principle has exposed the Douay[1] version of the Bible to much unfavourable criticism. There are so many Latin words printed in it unchanged, or only changed in termination, that one English divine has called it a translation which needs to be translated. Another critic says, it is probably to the general reader the least intelligible of all the English versions of Scripture. Another author remarks that the style has few admirers. Even a Catholic scholar, who himself tried his hand at translation, has not scrupled to pronounce the Douay Bible a barbarous translation. It would be correct to say it is just what the translators themselves professed it was their aim to make it—a semi-translation—or a translation to the extent they felt they could safely go, without compromising some Catholic doctrine or some Catholic sentiment. The argument of the editors was, it would be easy to give a more smoothly-flowing translation, a simpler narrative, and a finer specimen of English literature, but it would be at the risk of taking from, or adding to, the meaning of God's own revelation. They were of opinion, therefore, that duty both to God and man, required the translators to be accurate rather than entertaining, and to quote the *ipsissima verba* of inspira-

---

[1] The phrase Douay Bible is here, and in some other places, applied to the Rhemes Testament also—in other words, to the Catholic version in English of the whole Bible.

tion rather than bring themselves under the condemnation of handling the word of God deceitfully.

Let us now turn to the Douay Bible itself, and see how the translators have done their work ; and first in the New Testament. One thing that specially strikes the reader of the Rhemes Testament is the number of long words, obviously of Latin extraction, that appear on almost every page. If we refer to the Latin Vulgate we shall find that a very large proportion of these long words are just the words of the Vulgate slightly anglified. Some of them are words we seldom, or never, meet with anywhere else ; others are words that, although not uncommon, are used in a sense quite different from what they bear in modern speech ; and others are words that, although intelligible enough, might with much advantage be displaced by shorter and simpler terms of Saxon origin.

As furnishing examples of the first of these three classes of words—those, namely, that are rare, antiquated, or obsolete—the following passages may be quoted : " He shall be great before our Lord, and wine and *sicer* (*vinum et siceram*) he shall not drink," Luke i. 15 : " And Joseph buying *sindon* (*sindonem*) and taking him down, wrapped him in the sindon and laid him in a monument" (*in monumento*), Mark xv. 46 ; " *Captiving* me in the law of sin," Rom. vii. 23 ; " Purge the old leaven, that you may be a new paste, as you are *azymes* (*azymi*), 1 Cor. v. 7 ; " *Contristrate* not (*nolite contristrare*) the holy spirit of God," Eph. iv. 30 ;[1] " Fathers, provoke not your children to anger, but bring them up in the discipline and *correption* (*correptione*) of our Lord," Eph. vi. 4 ; " *Acception* of persons (*personarum acceptio*) is not with him," Eph. vi. 9 ; " I pursue to the marke, to the price of the *supernal vocation* (*supernal vocationis*) of God," Phil. iii. 14 ; " Elias was a man like unto us *passible*" (*passibilis*), James v. 17 ; " As we went to prayer, a certain wench, having a *pythonical* spirit (*spiritum pythonem*) met us," Acts xvi. 16 ; " Give us to-day our *supersubstantial* bread" (*panem supersubstantialem*), Mat. vi. 11.[2]

---

[1] More simply expressed by Wyclif, "nyle ye make the holi goost of God sorie."
[2] In the parallel passage, Luke xi. 3, the phrase in the Rhemes Testament is

Of the second class of Latin-English terms found in the Rhemes Testament—those, namely, which are used in an etymological and archaic sense different from the meaning they now bear in common speech—examples to any number might be cited. The "shew-bread," for instance, is called "the loaves of *proposition*," that is, the loaves placed or set before the Lord on the altar. In accordance with a special meaning of *prevaricor* in Latin, the words *prevaricate* and *prevarication* are used by the Rhemes translators, not in the sense of dissembling or shuffling, but in the sense of sinning or transgressing. It is said of Judas Iscariot, that "he *prevaricated*, that he might go to his own place," and St. Paul is made to say, what to the ears of modern litigants and legal counsel must be curiously suggestive, "Where is no law, neither is there *prevarication*." Another word that appears in the Rhemes Testament in an odd connection is *mortification*: "We bear about in our body the *mortification (mortificationem)* of Jesus," 2 Cor. iv. 10. And as a synonym to mortification, in this sense, the word *resolution* occurs also: "The time of my *resolution (tempus resolutionis)* is at hand," 2 Tim. iv. 6. In like manner, for "fruit of the vine," we find "*generation* of the vine"; for "deceive himself," "*seduce* himself"; for "power of God," "*virtue* of God"; for "fatherless," *pupils;* and for "disbelief," *diffidence*. In two verses, almost contiguous to each other, we meet with *form* and *reform* in the sense of their Latin counterparts in the Vulgate: "Be followers of me, and observe them that walk so as you have our *form*" (*formam nostram*). . . For our conversation is in heaven, whence also we expect the Saviour, who will *reform (qui reformabit)* the body of our humility, *configured (configuratum)* to the body of his glory," Phil. iii. 17-21.

Of the third class of Latinistic words imported into the Rhemes Testament from the Vulgate—those, namely, which although used in a current and popular sense might with ad-

---

daily bread, and in the Vulgate, *panem quotidianum*. In the Greek Testament the word used to designate the bread prayed for is in both passages *epiousion*. But this Greek word has been differently interpreted. By some scholars it is rendered in Latin *quoditianus*, and by others, who trace it to a different source, *substantificus*, *supersubstantialis*, or *superessentialis*. See Scapulae Lexicon.

vantage be replaced by simpler terms of Saxon origin—there is no end to the examples that might be quoted. On almost every page we encounter foreign terms, which to our "profane and delicate ears sound hard and barbarous." Where, for instance, the word *filled* might have been used the word *replenished* is introduced. People are spoken of as being *replenished* with fear, *replenished* with madness, *replenished* with zeal, *replenished* with the Holy Ghost. Another word that is used where a simpler might have been found is *assumpted*. The day on which Jesus ascended into heaven is called, Acts i. 2, the day on which He was *assumpted*; and when the hour for His assumption came, it is said, Acts i. 9, that "in their sight he was *elevated*." In like manner, "the Lord's day" is designated, Rev. i. 10, the *dominical* day; "the household of faith," Gal. vi. 10, the *domesticals* of faith; "The redemption of the purchased possession," Eph. i. 14, the redemption of *acquisition*. For "harden not your hearts," Heb. iii. 15, we read, do not *obdurate* your hearts; for "drawn away of his own lust and enticed," Jas. i. 14, of his own *concupiscence abstracted and allured*; for "beholding his natural face," Jas. i. 23, beholding the *countenance* of his *nativity*; and for "pass the time of your sojourning," 1 Pet. i. 17, *converse* ye the time of your *peregrination*. As if with the view of bewildering plain people, and suggesting to them supersubstantial significance in the most realistic things, "drunkenness and revellings" are Gal. v. 21, termed *ebrieties* and *commesations*; "vile affections," Rom. i. 26, *passions* of *ignominy*; "filthiness" and "spots," 2 Cor. vii. 1, and 2 Pet. ii. 13, *inquinations* and *coinquinations*.

Not only, too, are the words of the Latin Vulgate translated in the Rhemes Testament, as far as practicable, by their English *derivatives*, rather than by their best understood *equivalents*, but in some cases, Latin words are transferred bodily, without any change whatever, into the English version. In one place, 1 Tim. vi. 20, we read:—"Oh Timothee, keep the *depositum*"; in another, Heb. ix. 3—"The tabernacle, which is called *sancta sanctorum*"; in a third, John v. 2—"There is at Jerusalem upon *Probatica* a pond." The retention of the Latin word in its native form, in the last cited passage, may possibly be considered practically justified by the fact, that the word Probatica (which appears in the Greek text as well as in the Vulgate) has been differently Englished by different translators. Wyclif renders it "a waischynge place;" Tyndale, "the slaughter-house"; the Geneva exiles "the place of the sheep"; the bishops, "the sheep-market"; and now the international revisers, 1881, have adopted, what in the Bishops' Bible and the authorised version appears as the alternative rendering on the margin, "the sheep gate." Other untranslated words in the Rhemes Testament are:—*Parasceue*, Mat. xxvii. 62, for "day of preparation"; *archysynagogue*, Mark v. 35, for "ruler of the synagogue"; *scenopegia*, John vii. 2, for "feast of tabernacles"; and *Euro-aquilo*, Acts xxvii. 14, for, what in familiar nautical language is called "Nor-easter."

In the Rhemes Testament, again, we find not only a slavish adherence to the very words of the Vulgate, but an adherence almost equally slavish to the idiom of the Vulgate. In some cases, the structure of a sentence, down to its minutest details, is carefully reproduced not only word for word but "point for point." This at times is done with good enough effect, but at other times not so happily. At Luke vii. 44, we read:—" And turning to the woman, Jesus said unto Simon. Dost thou see this woman? I entered into thy house. Water to my feet thou didst not give, but she with tears hath watered my feet, and with her hairs hath wiped them." The order of words here may not, perhaps, be considered the best possible, but it at least occasions no ambiguity nor difficulty of interpretation. That, however, is more than can be said of the following rendering of 1 Thess. iv. 14 :—" For if we believe that Jesus died and rose again, so also God them that have slept by Jesus will bring with him." But the Rhemes divines were never at a loss for a reason with which to vindicate their procedure. When ambiguity resulted from the excessive literalness of their renderings, they justified the ambiguity, on the ground that what in the original admits of more meanings than one should in the translation be as open to several constructions. They pronounced it "a common fault and intolerable" in Protestant versions of the Scriptures, that the sense of the Holy Ghost was abridged "to one particular understanding." They, therefore, translated 1 Pet. ii. 2: "As infants even new-born, reasonable, milk without guile desire ye, that in it you may grow unto salvation." The grammatical chaos of this sentence was intentional. "Here," they said, "we do so place *reasonable* of purpose, that it may be indifferent both to infants going before, as in our Latin text, or to milk that followeth after, as in other Latin copies, and in the Greek." One thing that, from (we suppose) regard to the verbal inspiration of the Scriptures, they were very chary of doing was the insertion, in their English text, of supplementary words that had no counterparts in the original. Some sentences in their translation have, for this reason, a look of incompleteness; others are obscure; and others still are out of harmony with the context. One sentence that, from this cause, is both elliptical and obscure is Rev. xxi. 17 : "He measured the wall thereof of an hundred fourtie foure cubites, the measure of a man which is of an angel."[1] One sentence, again, that is obviously at variance with what follows is 1 Tim. iv. 3: "Forbidding to marie, to abstaine (*i.e., forbidding*, instead of *commanding* to abstain) from meates which God created to receave with thankes-giving for the faithful." And it may here be remarked that not only is it often necessary for translators to supply a word in order to set forth the meaning of the original, but it is sometimes necessary to do so in order to make their translation literal as well as intelligible. In the Rhemes Testament, for instance, we read, 2 Cor. iii. 7: "If the ministration of death, with letters figured in stones, was in glory, so that the children of Israel could not behold the face

---

[1] A sentence that by this means is shorn of its Apostolic dignity is 2 Cor. xi. 24, "Of the Jewes five times, did I receive *fourtie*, saving one."

One verse that has its theological import affected by the punctuation is 2 Cor. v. 17. According to the punctuation in the Greek text as commonly printed, the verse is correctly rendered—"If any man (be) in Christ, (he is) a new creature : old things are past away." If otherwise pointed, the verse might be rendered, as in the Vulgate—"Si qua ergo in Christo nova creatura, vetera transierunt." The Rhemes translation, like good money, "answereth all things." "If then any be in Christ a new creature : the old are passed, behold all things are made new."

of Moses, for the glory of his countenance, *that* is made void." But the question arises, what is it that is here said to be made void? The relative pronoun *that* might apply to any one of several nouns. In the Latin and Greek Texts, however, the gender of the word translated *that* removes the ambiguity. In order, therefore, to be strictly literal, the Rhemes translators should have done as Tyndale did before them, and rendered the last clause of the verse, "*which glory* is made void."

A feature in the Rhemes and Douay version of the Scriptures that has been much commended by scholastic critics is the uniformity of its renderings. It may be remarked, however, that the renderings in the Rhemes Testament are not absolutely uniform. In Mark i. 30, 31, two Latin words derived from the same root, are englished not only by dissimilar words, but by words that although originally of identical meaning have come now to signify respectively the *hot* and the *cold* stages of an intermittent malady: "Simon's wife's mother lay in a fit of a *fever* . . . and comminge neere, he lifted her up, taking her by the hand; and incontinent the *ague (febris)* left her." The Rhemes translators are nevertheless consistent, as a rule, in their rendering of words; and they are sometimes careful to make distinctions overlooked in both the authorised and revised versions, as in Mark viii. 19, 20, "When I brake five loaves, among five thousand, how many *baskets* ful of fragments tooke ye up? When also, seven loaves among four thousand, how many *maundes* of fragments took you up?"

It need scarcely be said that the Rhemes translators are extremely careful to use no English word in reference to things ecclesiastical that would in the remotest degree discountenance any dogma or custom cherished in the Catholic Church. One of their charges against Protestants was, that, by false translation of Scripture, "they had, instead of God's law and testament, and for Christ's written will and word, given people their own wicked writing and phantasies, most shamefully in all their versions . . . corrupting both the letter and sense . . . and altering all the authentical and ecclesiastical words used sithence our Christianity into new profane novelties of speeches agreeable to their doctrine." Among other things, Protestants were charged with using "in ill part, where they are not in the original text," the words, procession, images, excommunicate; and with avoiding the following other words, when they do occur in the original, church, altar, sacrament, priests, Catholic, traditions, etc. There is marvellous acuteness shewn, too, by the Rhemes translators in detecting Protestant heresies. In the early Protestant versions of the Bible in English, Rom. viii. 18 is translated:—"I am certainly persuaded that the afflictions of this time are not *worthy of the glory* which shall be shewed upon us." The words here italicised, said Martin, are meant to indicate "that the tribulations of this life, be they never so great, and though suffered for Christ, do not merit or deserve heavenly glory"—in other words, that justification is to be obtained through faith only, and in no manner or measure by good works. But, he added, the word *worthy* is a mis-translation; and in this contention, he has been supported by the framers of the authorised version, who have changed the words *worthy of* into "worthy to be compared with." In the Vulgate the verse reads:—"Existimo enim quod non sunt *condignae passiones* hujus temporis ad futuram gloriam," which in the Rhemes Testament is literally rendered, "I think that the *passions* of this time are not *condign* to the glory to come." Another Protestant rendering faulted by Catholics is, Luke xxii. 20:—"This cup is the New Testament in my blood which is shed for you." Translated directly and literally from the Vulgate this clause reads in the Rhemes Testament:— 'This is the chalice, the New Testament in my blood, which shall be shed for you." By this rendering, two points were supposed to be scored for catholicism. The use of the word "chalice" was meant, as Dr. Fulke says, "to make fools believe that Christ used not a common cup, usual to be drunken in at meat, but a consecrated vessel such as is occupied at masse." It was alleged, also, by the translators, that the word "which" being made to refer to *chalice* and not to *blood*, "taketh away all cavillations and shifts from the Protestants, both against the reall presence and the true sacrificing; for it sheweth evidently, that the blood as the contents of the chalice, or as in

the chalice, is shed for us, and not only as upon the cross." [1]
Another of the points of abstruse doctrine in regard to which
Catholics and Protestants, in the sixteenth century, were at
variance, was the freedom of man's will. The Scottish Reformers in their Confession of Faith, 1560, declared " that the
cause of good works (is) not our free-will, but the spirit of the
Lord Jesus, who, dwelling in our hearts by true faith, bringeth
forth such works as God hath prepared for us to walk in."
This was not Catholic doctrine ; and we find, accordingly, that
certain verses of Scripture, which three hundred years ago
were supposed to bear very directly on the question of
free-will, are differently rendered in the Catholic and
Protestant translations of the New Testament. One of
these verses is 1 Cor. xv. 10, which in the Great Bible, the
Geneva Bible, and the Bishops' Bible, is translated—" By the
grace of God I am that I am, and his grace which is in me,
was not in vain ; but I laboured more abundantly than they
all ; yet not I, but the grace of God *which is* with me." The
words italicised are omitted in the Rhemes Testament, so that
the last clause reads simply—" yet not I, but the grace of God
with me." This rendering, which is a literal translation of the
Vulgate (non ego autem sed gratia Dei mecum) " may," says
Gregory Martin, " have this sense, ' not I, but the grace of God
which is with me,' as St. Hierome sometime expoundeth it ; or
this, ' not I, but the grace of God *which laboured* with me.'
And by this latter is most evidently signified, that the grace of
God and the Apostle both laboured together ; and not only
grace, as though the Apostle had done nothing, like unto a

---

[1] On this annotation, Dr. Fulke remarks, with the ecclesiastical etiquette of his times :—"All your trifling of the reall presence and true sacrificing is nothing but vaine and unlearned insultation. For no ancient writer, for a thousand years after Christ, or more, ever observed any such matter out of this text. And whereas you say that Beza turneth himselfe roundly upon the holy Evangelist, charging him with Soloecisme or false Greeke . . . except you would be taken for such ignorant asses that you know not the difference of Soloecismus and Soloecophanes your malicious slander can have no excuse. . . . So miserable be your slights and shifts of falsehood, forged upon impudent lies, and malicious slanders and unlearned collections, God be praised who daily maketh your folly and madness more and more manifest to all men."

block forced only; but that the grace of God did so concurre, as the principal agent, with all his labour, that his free-will wrought withall. Against which trueth and most approved interpretation of this place, you translate according to the former sense only, making it the *very* text, as your masters Calvin and Beza taught."

From what has been said in previous chapters, it may be surmised that in several places where the word "mystery" occurs in our authorised version of the Scriptures, the word "sacrament" will be found in the Rhemes Testament. And so it is. In that translation, Eph. i. 9 is rendered: "That he might make known unto us the sacrament of his will;" Eph. iii. 3, "According to revelation the sacrament was made known to me;" 1 Tim. iii. 16, "It is a great sacrament of piety which was manifested in flesh;" Rev. i. 20, "The sacrament of the seven starres . . . the seven starres are the angels of the seven churches," &c.[1] The word "penance" is, also, of frequent occurrence in the Rhemes Testament. It is said of John the Baptist, Luke iii. 3, that he came into all the country of Jordan, preaching the baptism of penance; and of St. Peter, that he exhorted the strangers in Jerusalem, on the day of Pentecost, to "do penance, and be baptized in the name of Jesus Christ." And it may be said generally, that by an apt use of particular words, an appearance of Scriptural authority is, in the Rhemes Testament, given to almost all the pecular dogmas and customs, institutions and nomenclature of the Catholic Church. Instead of "ordain elders," we read, Titus i. 5, "ordain *priests*"; instead of "remember them which have the rule over you," Heb. xiii. 7, "remember your *Prelates*";[2] instead of "to the end ye may be established," Rom. i. 11, "*to confirm you*"; instead of "saved us by the washing of regeneration," Titus iii. 5, "saved us by the *laver* of regeneration"; instead of "the laying on of the hands of the presbytery," 1 Tim. iv. 14, "*imposition* of the

---

[1] In some modern versions of the Rhemes Testament the word *sacrament* is in all these passages changed into *mystery*.

[2] Better still, as an inculcation of good manners, "Salute all your prelates," Heb. xiii. 24!

hands of *priesthood*; and instead of "messengers" and "ambassadors" for Christ, 2 Cor. v. 20 and Eph. vi. 20, "*legates*" for Christ.[1]

Three words that Catholics consider particularly ecclesiastical and sacred are grace, charity, and justice; and one of the gravest faults imputed by Catholics to Protestant translations of the Bible is the suppression of these words, or the substitution of others for them, in places where they should have been found. In the Bishops' Bible we read 2 Cor. i. 15: "In this confidence was I minded first to have come unto you, that ye might have had one *pleasure* more." The Greek word here translated pleasure is *charis*, and the usual rendering of *charis* in Latin is *gratia*, and in English *grace*. The Rhemes divines accordingly translate 2 Cor. i. 15 more ecclesiastically: "In this confidence I would first have come to you, that you might have a second *grace*." But their Catholic rule of translating *charis* in Greek, and *gratia* in Latin, by the English word *grace*, was not invariable. In Acts xxv. 3, they translate *postulantes gratiam* "requesting favour." And as with grace so with charity. Wherever the word *caritas* occurs in the Vulgate, it is by the Rhemes divines translated *charity*; but although *caritas* stands, in the Vulgate, for *agape* in the Greek original, it does not follow that wherever *agape* is found in the Greek Testament *charity* appears as its counterpart in the Rhemes translation. In the Vulgate, *agape* is sometimes rendered *caritas*, and sometimes *dilectio*. In the former case it is, by the Rhemes divines, Englished *charity*, and in the latter *love*. Thus, in one place, we read:—"God is charitie, and he that abideth in charitie abideth in God"; and in another passage of the same Apostle's writings—"Greater love than this no man hath, that a man yeld his life for his frendes." In regard to the meaning and application of the last of the three specially sacred terms, *justice*, the Rhemes theologians had a

---

[1] An argument for Purgatory is founded on Acts ii. 27, "thou wilt not leave my soul *in hell*" (in inferno, Vulgate); and on Gen. xxxvii. 35, "I will go down into the *grave* unto my son" (in infernum, Vulgate). It was not "grave," says Martin, "for Joseph was not *buried*"!

very curious theory. They found that in some places where the word *justus* occurs in the Vulgate, the corresponding word in English translations is *just*, while in other places it is *righteous*. In this diversity of rendering, they imagined that Protestants had a deep design. "They put the word *just* when faith is joined withal, as 'the just shall live by faith.' But if works be joined withal, and keeping the commandments, there they say *righteous* to suppresse justification by works." A glance at a common concordance will shew that there is no ground for this charge against Protestants; and Dr. Fulke was warranted in saying, "there is no professor of justification by faith only that esteemeth it the worth of one haire whether you say in any place of Scripture *just* or *righteous*." The Rhemes translators, however, with this fanciful distinction in their minds, were very particular in using the word *just*, and its English derivatives, whenever in the Vulgate they found *justus* or any of its Latin derivatives. And in this way they were often led to use expressions that to English ears are obscure as well as uncouth, as, Luke i. 6, "They walked in all the commandments and *justifications* of our Lord"; and Rom. iv. 11, Abraham "received the sign of circumcision, a seal of the *justice* of faith that is in prepuce, that he might be the father of all that believe by the prepuce, that unto them also it may be reputed to *justice*."

It could easily be shewn that the Vulgate, from which the Rhemes version of the Testament is derived, is with all its merits, not perfect as a Latin translation. In its rendering of particular words there is a want of uniformity. The word *agape*, as we have seen, is sometimes rendered *caritas* and sometimes *dilectio*. In some places *mysterion* is translated *mysterium*; and in others, *sacramentum*. In some instances *metanoesate* and *metanoeite* are rendered *poenitemini*; and in others, *poenitentiam agite*. There are many cases, again, of antitheses presented to us in the Greek original which are not preserved in the Latin Vulgate; such as *apeithousi* and *peithomenois*, Rom. ii. 8, equivalent to *obedient* and *disobedient*, but rendered by Jerome, *non acquiescunt* and *credunt*; *ekdusasthai* and *ependusasthai*, 2 Cor. v. 4, equivalent to *unclothed* and *clothed upon*, but rendered *exspoliari* and *supervestiri*; *endemountes* and *ekdemoumen*, 2 Cor. v. 6, equivalent to *at home* and *from home*, but loosely rendered *dum sumus in corpore* and *peregrinamur*. The consequence is that the Rhemes renderings, being literal translations of the Vulgate, are, in all these cases, exceedingly feeble and pointless, as a repetition of them will shew : Rom. ii. 8, " To them that obey not the truth, but give credit to iniquity, wrath and indignation "; 2 Cor. v. 4, " We would not be spoiled but overclothed "[1]; and 2 Cor. v. 6, " While we are in the body we are pilgrims from God."

It will thus be seen that from close and literal adherence to the words and phrases of the Vulgate the Rhemes divines gave to their English version of the Testament several uncommendable peculiarities. The translators were afraid to translate. They had no lack of scholarship or command of good English. They could discuss the meaning of words learnedly, and when untrammelled they could write trenchant English. But in translating the Scriptures they were hampered by their own maxim—" not in hard places to mollifie the speeches or phrases, but religiously keep them word for word, and point for point, for fear of missing or restraining the sense of the Holy Ghost to our fantasie." Apart, however, from any reference to the Vulgate, we have to consider what kind of book, from a literary point of view, the Douay Bible is. It was not intended for those that could read the Vulgate, but for those that could not. Besides being accurate, therefore, it was requisite that it should be readable ; a book that plain people could understand, and a book that both educated and uneducated could peruse with pleasure.

In previous chapters we have criticised, separately, the words and phrases that occur in different English versions of the Bible. In this chapter we shall follow the same method. One feature of some of the older versions is the number of archaic

---

[1] The translation of this verse in the Bishops' Bible is singularly prosaic, which is the more to be wondered at that the passage is well rendered in the Great Bible. The bishops' rendering is, "we would not put off our clothing, but upon the same put on more."

and obsolete words they contain. Of such words there are not so many specimens to be found in the Rhemes testament. The outstanding literary characteristic of that version, as has already been remarked, is the latinity of its expressions. For the simple precept "study to be quiet," we read in the Rhemes Testament, *employ your endeavour to be quiet ;* for "the sky is red," *the element is red ;* for "lose his soul," *sustain the damage of his soul ;* for "trance," *excess of mind ;* and for "vexed with the filthy conversation of the wicked," *oppressed by the injury and luxurious conversation of the abominable men.* For "workfellow," we find *coadjutor ;* for "preach the gospel," *evangelise ;* for "a gluttonous man," *a gurmander ;* for "songs," *canticles ;* for "built up," *superedified ;* and for "novice," *neophyte.* Some interesting archaisms may nevertheless be found in the Rhemes Testament. It is said, 1 Cor. xi. 4, "Every man praying or prophesying with his head covered *dishonesteth* his head"; Gal. i. 7, "There be some that trouble you and will *inuert* the gospel of Christ"; Gal. vi. 6, "Let him that is *catechized* in the word communicate to him that *catechizeth* him, in all his goods."[1] Sometimes simpler and homelier words will be found in the Rhemes than in the authorised Testament; as "the manor," for *the parcel of ground* that Jacob gave to Joseph," John iv. 5 ; "judge not according to the face," for *judge not according to the appearance,* John vii. 24 ; "my dearest," for *beloved,* 3 John v. 2 ; and "ouergoe," for *go beyond* or *over-reach,* 1 Thess. iv. 6.

Passing now from single words and brief expressions to whole clauses and sentences, we shall again find much to note with disfavour in the Rhemes Testament. Statements are often indistinct, and sentences ill constructed. One verse in the first Epistle of Peter has already been referred to, as having been purposely and professedly left obscure by the translators,

---

[1] The words translated, "that is catechized," are in the Vulgate, *qui catechizatur,* and in the original Greek *ho catechoumenos.* The meaning of the Greek verb *catecheo* is, not to put questions, but to din in people's ears, or teach by word of mouth. Some of the old Catechisms were not in the form of question and answer, but were simple expositions of faith and duty. See Prof. Mitchell's Introduction to Gau's *Richt Vay to the Kingdom of Heuine,* p. xxviii.

"for fear of missing or restraining the sense of the holy ghost." Another verse avowedly left obscure for the same reason is Eph. vi. 12 : "Our wrestling is not against flesh and blood, but against Princes and Potestats, against the rectors of the world of this darkenes, against the *spirituals* of *wickednes in the celestials*." For the following sentences, some of which are crude and incomplete, some hazy and well nigh meaningless, and some grammatically open to misconstruction, no apology is offered by the translators; and some readers will be inclined to think it would be difficult to frame a satisfactory apology: "This think in yourselues, which also in Christ Jesus," Phil. ii. 5; "See the dogges, see the euil workers, see the concision," Phil. iii. 2; "To illuminate al men what is the dispensation of the the sacrament hidden from worldes in God," Eph. iii. 9; "He that is in secrete is a Jew," Rom. ii. 29; "I will doe my diligence, you to haue often after my deccase also, that you may keepe a memorie of these things," 2 Pet. i. 15.

It would be strange, however, if there were not some quaint and happy phrases in the Rhemes Testament along with the clumsy and incoherent ones that have been cited. We have seen that in some of the early versions of the English Bible there is occasionally what looks like an intended and a pleasant play on words. And, notwithstanding their avowed aversion to a "meretricious manner of writing" the Rhemes translators sometimes, in the Testament, treat their readers to a little of this pleasantry. Their rendering of Rom. iii. 24, is "justified *gratis* by his *grace*," a neat expression, but not so neat in English as in the Latin from which it is derived, "justificati *gratis per gratiam* ipsius.[1] An unconscious idyllic simplicity, as well as a pointed antithesis, appears also in the account of the Sodomites, 2 Pet. ii. 8, "who from day to day vexed *the just soule* (Lot) with unjust workes." A quaint colloquialism, too, which few will find fault with, is : "See (*quod he*) that thou make al things according to the exempler," Heb. viii. 5.

---

[1] Another phrase of the same kind may be found in modern editions of the Douay Bible (e.g., Dublin, 1811), in Eph. i. 6, "Unto the praise of the glory of his *grace*, in which he hath *graced* us in his beloved son."

Another not unpleasant colloquialism, which it may be remarked in passing is a literal rendering of the Vulgate[1] (temporaneum et serotinum), appears in James v. 7 : "The husbandman expecteth the pretious fruite of the earth ; patiently bearing till he receive the *timely* and the *lateward.*" Free and racy again are such renderings as : " Who euer *plaieth the souldiar* at his owne charges," I Cor. ix. 7 ; and "Fallen into a place betwene two seas, they *graueled* the ship," Acts xxvii. 41. More forcible still are the following : " *Thratled* him, saying, Repay that thou owest," Mat. xviii. 28 ; " Euery one that falleth upon this stone shal be *quashed,*" Luke xx. 18 ; and "*Damned* them with subuersion," 2 Pet. ii. 6. There is a fine ecclesiastical ring, which may well come home to the hearts of Churchmen, in the words, "the *stipends* of sin is death ;" and there is all the appositeness of every day speech in the exhortation, " be not *easily moued from your sense,* nor be terrified . . . as though the day of our Lord were at hand." A very clumsy phrase, introduced by Tyndale, and retained in both the authorised and revised versions, occurs in Mark ii. 12, "They were all amazed and glorified God, saying, we never saw it *on this fashion.*" The Rhemes divines rendered the last clause more simply : " We neuer saw the like."

That there should be in the Rhemes Testament some different readings, and different renderings of the same readings, from what we find in the authorised version of the Testament in English, will occasion no surprise. A large proportion of these differences are of a very minute kind. Some of them have, nevertheless, been founded on for verification of important dogmas. We have already seen how much was made of the Rhemes rendering of Luke xxii. 20 : " This is the chalice, the New Testament in my blood, which shall be shed for you." Authority for another sacramentarian doctrine of the Catholic Church was drawn by the Rhemes divines from their rendering of Acts ii. 42 : " And they were perseuering in the doctrine of the Apostles, and in the *communication of the breaking of bread.*" This, they say, was the blessed sacrament, " which the Apostles

---

[1] Erasmus has "*pluviam* tempestivam et serotinam."

daily administered to the Christians, at least *in one kind.*"[1] Another verse that has both a Catholic and a Protestant reading is 1 John iv. 3. The Protestant reading is: "Every spirit that confesseth not that Jesus Christ is come in the flesh is not of God." The Catholic reading, as given in the Rhemes Testament, is: "Euery spirit that *dissolueth* Jesus (*qui solvit Jesum*, Vulgate) is not of God;" and the annotation on this obscure reading is, that "to dissolve, loose, or separate Jesus asunder was proper to all those old heretics that taught either against his Divinity or Humanity, or the unity of his person." Sometimes it is difficult to determine to which of two nouns in the original a certain adjective, participle, or relative pronoun should be referred, and in such circumstances it is not to be wondered at that different renderings are given by different translators. In the Greek text of 2 Cor. vii. 10, there is a word *ametameleeton*. It is not agreed, says Dr. Bloomfield, whether that word should be applied to *salvation* or *repentance*. In our authorised translation of the Bible, the latter interpretation is adopted, and the verse reads: "Godly sorrow worketh repentance to salvation not to be repented of." In the Rhemes Testament the other interpretation is adopted, and the verse reads there: "The sorow that is according to God worketh penance unto saluation that is stable," (*salutem stabilem*, Vulgate).

Some of the peculiar readings and renderings in the Rhemes Testament might fitly be included in the chapter of Biblical curiosities; such as, "He departed, and went and hanged himself *with an halter*," Mat. xxvii. 5; "Where is my *refectorie*, where I may eate the pasche with my disciples," Mark xiv. 14;

---

[1] A reading in the Rhemes Testament on which Catholics set much store is the italicised clause in 2 Pet. i. 10, "Wherefore, brethren, labour the more that *by good works* you may make sure your vocation and election." In the annotation on this version of St. Peter's admonition, it is said that "Protestants not much liking these words *by good works* . . . leave them out of their translations by their wonted policy." There is really, however, no force in this insinuation; for, as Dr. Fulke remarks, "if in any translation, *by good works* be left out, it is because they were left out of the text which we translated, yet we always confess that the circumstance of the place doth of necessity require that good works be understood though they be not expressed."

"Forthwith his feete and *soles* were made strong," Acts iii. 7; "If . . . al speake with tongues, and there enter in *vulgar persons* or infidels, will they not say that you be madde," 1 Cor. xiv. 23; "We shall *al* in deede *rise againe*, but we *shall not al be changed*," 1 Cor. xv. 51; "It was tedious unto us euen to liue," 2 Cor. i. 8; "The Holy Ghost being sent from heauen, on *whom* the angels desire to looke," 1 Peter i. 12.

Considering the strain of the foregoing remarks, and the vehemence with which the Rhemes Testament has been decried by Protestants as a corruption of the word of God, the reader will perhaps be scarcely prepared to hear now that a large number of its peculiar readings and renderings have been confirmed and adopted by the framers of the Revised New Testament, 1881. This fact, which may easily be verified, is a remarkable testimony to the intrinsic value of the Latin Vulgate, as a faithful representation of the most ancient and approved manuscript copies of the original Greek Testament. One passage in the authorised version that the revisers, 1881, have altered, is Mat. xix. 17: "Why callest thou me good?" For these words they have substituted, "Why askest thou me concerning that which is good?" and this reading is just what had been given as the true Scripture in the Rhemes Testament three hundred years before. Another passage that the revisers have altered is Rom. v. 1. In the authorised translation that verse reads: "Being justified by faith, *we have* peace with God." The statement "we have peace," is by the revisers changed into an exhortation, "Let us have peace with God"; and this change is also a reversion to the Rhemes reading. What appears in the authorised version, Gal. iv. 14, as "*my* temptation," is in the Rhemes Testament called "*your* temptation"; and it is the latter reading that the revisers have accepted. In the Rhemes Testament we read, 1 Tim. vi. 17-19, "Commaund the riche of this world . . . to doe wel, to become riche in good workes, to giue easily . . that they may apprehend *the true life*." Instead of "the true life," we find in the authorised version, and in all the early English Protestant versions, *eternal life;* but now in the revised translation "the life that is life indeed." And so, also, in Rev. xxii. 14, the revisers have, for the authorised reading, "Blessed are they that do his commandments," inserted the Rhemes, "Blessed are they that wash their robes."[1]

It is well known that many words, clauses, and sentences, which are found in the authorised version of the New Testament, are omitted in the revised. And it is a very instructive fact that not a few of the passages so excluded from the revised Testament are awanting in the Rhemes also. Of these it will suffice to mention: "For thine is the kingdom, and the power, and the glory, for ever, Amen," Mat. vi. 13; "And to be baptized with the baptism that I am baptized with," Mat. xx. 22; "Verily, I say unto you, it shall be more tolerable for Sodom and Gomorrha in the day of judgment than for that city,"[2] Mark vi. 11; "But if it be of works then is it no more grace, otherwise work is no more work," Rom. xi. 6.

To the student of ecclesiastical history, not the least interesting reading in the Rhemes Testament are the annotations. The notes in the Geneva Bible are well "powdered with salt," but they are not much more saline and savoury than those of the Rhemes translators. Every thing in the Church of Rome that the Geneva divines allege to be inventions of the man of sin, are by the Rhemes translators vindicated with confident shew of Scripture authority; while, on the other hand, the monstrous blasphemies of Protestants are triumphantly exposed and lustily denounced.

The following will serve as samples both of the notes that are polemical, and of those that are doctrinal:—

Mat. vi. 24.—*Two masters.* Two religions, God and Baal, Christ and Calvin, Masse and Communion, the Catholic Church and Heretical Conventicles. Let

---

[1] The revised rendering of 1 Cor. iv. 4, "I know nothing *against* (instead of *by*) myself, yet am I not hereby justified," may be said to have been anticipated in the Rhemes translation, "I am not guilty in conscience of anything, but I am not justified herein." Wyclif's rendering was, "I am nothing ouertrowinge to my silf, but not in this thing I am justified."

[2] The passage omitted in the Rhemes and revised versions of Mat. xx. 22, is given in Mark x. 38, and the words omitted in these versions of Mark vi. 11 are given in Mat. x. 15.

them mark this lesson of our Saviour, that think they may serve all masters, all times, all religions.

Acts xx. 29.—The governors of the Church are foretold of the great danger that should fall to the people by wolves, that is to say by heretics, whose cruelty towards the Catholics is noted by this term. . . . Such wolves came afterwards indeed in diverse ages, Arius, Macedonius, Nestorius, Eutyches, Luther, Calvin, great blood-sucking wolves and wasters of the flock of Christ.

2 Pet. ii. 19.—Who ever promised more liberty to their followers than Luther, Calvin, and the like, taking away penance, fasting, continency or chastity, keeping of vows, necessity of good works (because faith doth all), obedience.

1 Tim. ii. 12.—In times of licentiousness, liberty, and heresy, women are much given to reading, disputing, chatting, and jangling of the holy Scriptures ; yea, and to teach also, if they might be permitted. But St. Paul utterly forbiddeth it ; and the Greek doctors upon this place note that the woman taught but once, that was when after her reasoning with Satan, she persuaded her husband to transgression, and so she undid all mankind. And in the ecclesiastical writers we find that women have been great promoters of every sort of heresy, which they would not have done, if they had, according to the apostle's rule, followed piety and good works, and lived in silence and subjection to their husbands."

2 Cor. ii. 17. "The Greek word signifieth to make commodity of the word of God, as vulgar vintners do of their wine. Whereby is expressed the peculiar trade of all heretics, and exceeding proper to the Protestants, that so corrupt Scriptures by mixture of their own fantasies, by false translations, glosses, colourable and pleasant commentaries, to deceive the taste of the simple, as taverners and tapsters do, to make their wines saleable by manifold artificial decoctions. The Apostles contrarywise, as all Catholics, deliver the Scriptures and utter the word of God sincerely and entirely."

2 Tim. iv. 8. *A crown of justice.* This place convinceth for the Catholics, that all good works done by God's grace, after the first justification, be truly and properly meritorious, and fully worthy of everlasting life ; and that thereupon heaven is the due and just stipend, crown, or recompense, which God by his justice oweth to the persons so working by his grace, for he rendereth or repayeth heaven as a just prize, and not only as a merciful giver ; and the crown which he payeth is not only of mercie, or favour, or grace, but also of justice ; it is his justice for these merits to give us a crown correspondent in heaven. . . . The parable also of the men sent into the vineyard proveth that heaven is our own right, bargained for and wrought for, and accordingly paid unto us as our due at the day of judgment.

John iii. 5. "Born again of water." We see, first, this sacrament to be called our regeneration. . . . and that no man can enter the kingdom of God. . . . without it. Whereby the Pelagians and Calvinists be condemned that promise everlasting life to young children that die without baptism. . . . Lastly, it is proved that this sacrament giveth grace *ex opere operato*, that is of the work itself, which all Protestants deny, because it so breedeth our spiritual life in God, as our carnal birth giveth the life of the world.

In the Douay version of the Old Testament we find, if not to the same extent, still to a considerable extent, all the literary peculiarities that so markedly characterise the diction of the Rhemes version of the New Testament. Peculiar ecclesiastical words and phrases are there, reading in some cases like strange anachronisms in the old records of the pre-Christian dispensation. We meet with such terms as penance, chalice, and bishopric. In Lev. v. 5-6, we read: "Let him *do penance* for his sinne, and offer of the flocks an ewe lamb, or a she-goat, and the priest shall pray for him." In Ps. xxiii. 5, it is said: "Thou hast fatted my head with oil; and my *chalice* inebriating, how goodlie is it!" And an explanatory note on the verse states that by *chalice* we are here to understand "the blessed sacrament and sacrifice of Christ's bodie and bloud." Among the curses imprecated in Ps. cix. is "Let another take his *bishopric*." This was a strange malediction for the Psalmist to utter, if it was meant for the traitor Ahithophel. But to show how completely the words of the Old Testament were, by the Douay divines, interpreted in a secondary and mystical sense, it is stated in the marginal notes that the Psalm is a prophecy, written with reference to Judas Iscariot, and that by "bishopric" was meant the apostleship of him "who fell and went to his own place." The word "Christ," also, frequently occurs in the Douay version of the Old Testament, and not as a general term signifying *anointed*, but as a proper name, and in reference to our Lord and Saviour. The latter part of 1 Sam. ii. 10, is rendered: "Our Lord shall judge the endes of the earth, and shall give empire to his king, and shall exalt the horne of his *Christ*." And *apropos* of this statement it is remarked on the margin: "Neither David nor Solomon, much less any other king, possessed or judged the endes of the earth: but Christ's inheritance reacheth to the world's end."

Like the Rhemes New Testament the Douay version of the Old Testament abounds in long and unfamiliar words, which are taken from the Latin Vulgate, either *literatim* or in a very slightly altered form. Of these may be mentioned[1]: "apos-

---

[1] Besides *long* there are also *short* unfamiliar words in the Douay Bible, as "gith" for *fitches*, Is. xxviii. 27; "mamzer" for *bastard*, Deut. xxiii. 2;

tate" for worthless person, Prov. vi. 12; "calends" for *new moons*, Is. i. 14: "conculcation" for *treading down*, Is. xxii. 5; "dominator" for *sovereign*, Is. iii. 1: "ecclesiastes" for *preacher*, Eccles. i. 12; "excelse" for *high place*, 1 Sam. ix. 25; "exprobating" for *reproaching*, Job xvi. 11; "holocaust" for *burnt-offering*, Is. i. 11; "hyacinth" for *blue*, Ex. xxviii. 5; "immolated" for *offered*, 1 Sam. ii. 13; "libaments" for *drink-offerings*, Num. vi. 17; "peregrination" for *sojourn*, Ruth i. 22; "rationale" for *breast-plate*, Ex. xxv. 7; and "recordation" for *memorial*, Num. v. 18. A very strange expression in the Douay Bible is "the plague of the bed": "Thus sayth our Lord: As if a pastour should get out of the lion's mouth two legges, or the tippe of the eare: so shall the children of Israel, that dwell in Samaria, be delivered in the plague of the bed, and in the couche of Damascus," Amos iii. 12. The word *plague* was evidently introduced into this passage from a misapprehension of the Vulgate text, and disregard of the Hebrew original. The words in the Vulgate translated "plague of the bed" are *plaga lectuli*, but in the Latin language there are two words spelt *plaga*; one of which, *plāga*, means a blow or a plague, and the other, *plăga*, means a region or district, and also a net, and so when used with *lectus* or *lectulus* may signify the curtain or corner of a bed.¹

"musach" for *canopy*, 2 Kings xvi. 18; "nables" for *psalteries*, 1 Chron. xv. 16; "pomes" for *fruits*, Deut. xxxiii. 14; "ptisane" for *bruised corn*, Prov. xxvii. 22; "sciniphes" for *lice*, Ex. viii. 16 "sculptils" for *graven images*, Is. xxi. 9; and "title" for *pillar*, 2 Sam. xviii. 18. Some of the above quoted words, such as mamzer and musach, are Hebrew words Latinised in the Vulgate. Sciniph, on the other hand, is a Greek word imported into the Vulgate from the Septuagint.

1 The word *plăga* is of frequent occurrence in the Vulgate as the counterpart of *peah* in the Hebrew, especially when *peah* is in our authorised version translated *side* or *quarter*. In many places, however, where *peah* is in the authorised version rendered *corner*, its counterpart in the Vulgate is not *plaga* but *angulus*. And in some Latin translations of the Bible, (*e.g.*, Zurich, 1564), *angulus* is the substitute for *peah* in Amos iii. 12. In Gen. iv. 16, the words "*ad orientalem plagam Eden*" occur in the Vulgate, and are rendered in the Douay Bible, "at the East side of Eden." But we have seen that in Wyclif's translation of that verse the word *plaga* is Englished by its derivative *plage* or *plaag*, a word now obsolete, which meant a district, region or country. It may occur to the reader, therefore, that the word *plague* in the Douay version of Amos iii. 12, is a misprint for *plage* in the sense of

In the Douay Bible, again, there are not only words of inordinate length and barbarous aspect, but there are cumbrous combinations of Latinisms, which, if they do not positively bewilder unscholastic readers, might at least with much advantage be displaced by simpler phrases. In the prophecy pronounced on Gad by Moses, Deut. xxxiii. 21, it is said in the revised English version, 1885 : " He provided the first part for himself, for there was the lawgiver's portion reserved." This is a clear, intelligible statement, which no reader is likely to misunderstand. But the Douay rendering of the passage might be propounded as a riddle for philosophers: " He saw his principalitie, that in his part the *doctor was reposed*."[1] It was the extreme fidelity with which the Douay Divines adhered to the text of the Vulgate that mainly led to the introduction of such sentences into their version of the Bible. And some of the dark renderings in the Douay translation are, when cleared, not without form and beauty of a kind. " The doctor is reposed " in them. The soul-destroying woman, for instance, is described, Prov. vii. 11, as " babling and wandering, *impatient of rest, nor able to consist in the house on her feet*." (Quietis impatiens, nec valens in domo consistere pedibus suis). In most cases, however, the Latinisms in the Douay Bible have little to commend them, as the majority of the following examples will shew.

Douay Bible.	Authorised Version.
Gen. l. 10.—They celebrated the exsequies (celebrantes exequias).	Gen. l. 10.—They mourned.
Lev. xix. 5.—If ye immolate an hoste of pacifiques to the Lord, (si immolaveritis hostiam pacificorum Domino).	Lev. xix. 5.—If ye offer a sacrifice of peace-offerings to the Lord.

---

district, side, or corner. This will appear the more probable, too, from the fact that in modern editions (or revisions) of the Douay Bible the passage in question is rendered "in a piece of a bed." This theory, however, is scarcely tenable. The word is spelled *plague* both in the Douay print, 1610, and in the Rouen reprint, 1635. In Wyclif's Bible the passage reads, "that dwellen in Samaria, in plage, or *wound*, of the litil bed."

[1] " Vidit principatum suum, quod in parte sua doctor esset repositus," Vulgate. In the Latin translation, Zurich, 1564, the same passage is rendered:—" Vidit principium sibi, quod illic esset portio legislatoris tecta."

Deut. xv. 9.—An impious cogitation, (impia cogitatio).
1 Sam. ii. 6.—Our Lord mortifieth and quickeneth, (Dominus mortificat et vivificat).
2 Sam. xiii. 8.—Taking meal, tempered it, and resolving it in his sight, she made suppinges.
2 Kings xix. 25.—Fenced cities shall be into ruin of little hills bickering together, (in ruinam collium pugnantium).
2 Chron. xxi. 19.—When day succeeded day, and the spaces of time passed about, the circuite of two years was complete, (Cumque diei succederet dies, et temporum spatia volverentur, duorum annorum expletus est circulus.)
Job xxxii. 4.—Elihu expected Job speaking, (expectavit Job loquentem).
Ps. xlix. 4.—I will open my proposition on a psalter, (Aperiam in psalterio propositionem meam).
Ps. cix. 24.—My flesh is changed by reason of oil, (immutata, propter oleum).
Prov. xi. 25.—He that inebriateth, himself shall also be inebriated, (Qui inebriat ipse quoque inebriabitur).
Is. xxiv. 3.—With dissipation shall the earth be dissipated, (Dissipatione dissipabitur terra).
Is. lxi. 3.—They shall be called in it the strong of justice, planting of the Lord to glorify, (vocabuntur in ea fortes justitiae, plantatio domini ad glorificandum).
Jer. ii. 22.—If thou shalt wash thyself with nitre, and multiply to thyself the herb borith, (multiplicaveris tibi herbam borith).
Jer. xxx. 3.—I will convert the conversion of my people Israel.
Amos i. 13.—Dilate their limit.
Zech. iv. 14.—These are the two sons of oil which assist the dominator of the whole earth, (Duo filii olei, qui assistunt dominatori universae terrae).

Deut. xv. 9.—A thought in thy wicked heart, (a base thought.—*Revised*).
1 Sam. ii. 6.—The Lord killeth and maketh alive.
2 Sam. xiii. 8.—She took flour and kneaded it, and made cakes in his sight, and did bake the cakes.
2 Kings xix. 25.—Lay waste fenced cities into ruinous heaps.
2 Chron. xxi. 19.—It came to pass in process of time, after the end of two years.
Job. xxxii. 4.—Elihu had waited till Job had spoken,
Ps. xlix. 4.—I will open my dark saying upon the harp.
Ps. cix. 24.—My flesh faileth of fatness.
Prov. xi. 25.—He that watereth shall be watered also himself.
Is. xxiv. 3.—The land shall be utterly emptied.
Is. lxi. 3.—That they might be called Trees of righteousness, The planting of the Lord, that he might be glorified.
Jer. ii. 22.—Though thou wash thee with nitre, and take thee much soap.
Jer. xxx. 3.—I will bring again the captivity of my people Israel.
Amos i. 13.—Enlarge their border.
Zech. iv. 14.—These are the two anointed ones that stand by the Lord of the whole earth.

In the predilection of the Douay divines for long words of ecclesiastical association, and in their Balaamitish resolution not to go beyond the text of the authentical scriptures, less or more, although sentences should thereby be left ever so incomplete and obscure, there is a certain air of austere and dignified High Churchism, which, it might have been supposed, would have led to the exclusion of all colloquialisms or literary whims from the Catholic version of the old Testament. But such has not been the case. The Douay version of the Old Testament is full of quaint and odd phrases, archaic and obsolete words, free, naive, and vigorous renderings. These curiosities of diction are, indeed, a very outstanding feature of the Douay translation.

Of the words referred to as obsolete or archaic, in our notice of earlier versions, a few are to be found in the Douay Bible. The word "chimney," for instance, is used in the sense of furnace or fire-place, as in Ex. ix. 8, "Take your handes full of ashes out of the chimney." The antiquated term "fardels," also, has a place in the Douay Bible. One of the gracious speeches made to Ruth by Booz was, "If thou shalt thirst, go to the *fardels*, and drink the waters whereof the servants drink," Ruth ii. 9. And in the painful story of the Levite, to whom the churls, of Gibeah refused a night's lodging, it is said, that the man was found "sitting with his fardels in the streete of the city."

But besides these and similar obsolete words, which have already been commented on in former chapters, there are other antique terms in the Douay translation worthy of note. One common word that occurs in an old and unfamiliar sense is "esquire," as in 1 Sam. xvi. 21, "David came to Saul and stood before him . . . and was made his *esquier*." In 2 Sam. xviii. 15, the word is abbreviated into *squire*; and we read there, that "when as yet Absolom panted for life, sticking on the oke, there ran ten young men, the *squyers* of Joab, and striking they killed him." A less familiar word in the Douay Bible is *manchet*. "When thou shalt come to the oak Thabor," said the prophet to Saul, 1 Sam. x. 3, "three men going up to God into Bethel shall finde thee there, one carrying three kiddes, and another three *manchettes* of bread, and another a flegon of wine." A phrase, also, that to many people will probably seem inscrutable occurs in the Douay version of Isaiah i. 31, "Your strength shall be as the *isles of towe*, and your work as a spark." The word here spelt *isles* may possibly, however, be recognised by Scotsmen as an old Scottish word,[1] usually printed *issilis*, which means ashes or embers. And this surmise will be confirmed by the amended reading which

---

[1] It is what is termed a middle-English word.

appears in modern editions of the Douay translation: "Your strength shall be as the ashes of tow." Another word in the Douay Bible that must be pronounced an archaism, in so far as it stands for the name of an ornamental article of female attire, is "sloppes;"[1] "In that day shall our Lord take away . . . the sheading combes, and *sloppes*, and tablets, and sweet balles and earlets," Is. iii. 20.

Besides what are strictly speaking antiquated *words*, there are, also, in the Douay Bible not a few antiquated *forms* of words.[2] Specimens of these will be seen in the following sentences: "Thou shalt make a silken mitre, and a *bawdrike* (baldric) of embroidered worke," Ex. xxviii. 39: "The first among thirtie, but yet the three he *raught* not" (reached not), 1 Chron. xi. 25: "The mouth of fooles *bolyeth* forth follie," Prov. xv. 2: "Behold I will *screake* under you, as a wayne *screaketh* loden with hay," Amos ii. 13: "Can horses run upon rocks, or can there be ploughing with *buffles*?"[3] Amos vi. 12.

Of notable, simple English phrases, sometimes quaint and sometimes queer, sometimes tender and sometimes tart, a

---

[1] Periscelidas, Vulgate, literally what goes round the legs, breeches or garters.

[2] Some words in the Douay Bible are strangely spelt. In several places "champaign" is spelt *champion*, as in Num. xxxvi. 13, where we read :—"These are the commandments, etc., which the Lord commanded . . . in the *champion* countrie of Moab": and in Deut. xi. 11, where it is said :—"The land which thou goest to possess . . . is hilly and *champion*, expecting raine from heaven." In 1 Kings x. 12, "vials" is printed for *viols* or *violins*. But it has to be admitted that neither the 1609 nor the 1635 edition, which are the two editions quoted from in this chapter, is free from obvious misprints. In Vol. I. of the edition 1609, I have happened to note "carcasse of *cartaine*," for "carcass of *caraine*," or *carrion*, (morticini, Vulgate), Lev. vii. 24; "a stranger, or a natural *sinne*," for "a stranger, or a natural *sonne*," (peregrinus, sivi civis, Vulgate), Lev. xxiv. 22; and "coler of a *wate*," for "collar of a *coate*," (capitio tunicae, Vulgate), Job. xxx. 18. In Vol II. of edition 1635, which is very carelessly printed, a strange reading is, by the omission of "not," given to Is. xi. 9 :—"They shall *(not)* hurt, and they shall not kill in all my holie mountayne."

[3] One word in the Douay Bible that, we should say, must have been very *modern* when inserted there, especially if it was inserted when the translation was first made out in manuscript, (before 1582) is *coaches* :—"In chariots, and in horse litters, and on mules, and in coaches," Is. lxvi. 20. It is commonly said that it was in 1580 that a coach was first seen in England. The word *cochere*, also, is used in the Douay Bible, for chariot driver, 1 Kings xxii. 34.

goodly store could without much difficulty be gathered out of the Douay translation of the Old Testament. A very dainty expression is "penury of wit:" and no maxim is more worthy of perpetual remembrance than the Douay version of the second clause of Pro. x. 21 : "They that are untaught shall die in the penury of their wite." A curious anthropopathic picture, again, of the delightful life that was led in chaos, before creation, is given in the words of Wisdom, as rendered by the Douay divines, in Prov. viii. 27-30 : "When he prepared the heavens I was present. . . . when he hanged the foundations of the earth I was with him framing all things; and was delighted every day, *playing before him at all time, playing in the world*; and my delights to be with the children of men." Sweetly picturesque, too, in their primitive metaphors and pastoral simplicity are the opening verses of the fifth chapter of Isaiah: "I will sing to my beloved the *canticle of my cosin* concerning his vineyeard. A vineyeard was made to my beloved in *horne, the sonne of oile*, and he hedged it, and chose stones out of it, and *planted it elect*, and built a towre in the middes, thereof, and set up a presse therein: and looked that it should yeald grapes, and it yealded wild grapes." Of the other homely and semi-colloquial phrases in the Douay Bible, some are more forcible than refined. The impotent rage of Saul, in his jealousy of David, is thus depicted: "The evil spirit of God invaded Saul, and he prophesied. . . . And David played with his hand as every day. And Saul held a speare, and threw it, thinking that he could *nail David to the wall*," 1 Sam. xviii. 10-11. Very blunt, again, are the terms in which the prophet is said to have denounced the feckless watchmen of Israel, Is. lvi. 11: "Dumb dogs and not able to bark. . . . and most *impudent dogs.*" But, not to dwell on individual cases, the following passages may be cited in slump, as further specimens of the quaint, homely, and realistic renderings of the Douay divines in their version of the Old Testament.

"Ranne to the heard, and tooke from thence a calfe verie tender and verie good, and gave it to a young man, who made hast and *boiled it*," Gen. xviii. 7; "Lia was *bleare-eyed*," Gen. xxix. 17; "Knowe ye not that there is not *the like to me* in the science of divining," Gen. xliv. 15; "Samson, who brake the bands, as if a man should breake a thread of *toe twyned with spittle*," Judges xvi. 9 ; "Tast first a little bread, and *strengthen thy stomach*," Judges xix. 5 ; "Heli sate upon a stoole¹ over against the way looking . . . and all the city howled," 1 Sam. iv. 13 ; " Being gathered *in a plumpe* into one troupe they stood in the toppe of one hil," 2 Sam. ii. 25 ; "If he shal *slippe away*, thy life shal be for his life, or thou shalt pay a talent of siluer," 1 Kings xx. 39 ; " Be not caught with her *becks*," Prov. vi. 25 ; "Taking the young man she kisseth him, and with *malepert countenance speaketh fayre*," Prov. vii. 13 ; " Be not with them that *stick down their hands* and that offer themselves sureties for debts," Prov. xxii. 26 ; " (The Lord) shall *whistle* to him of the ends of the earth," Is. v. 26 ; " Sobna, the *provost* of the temple," Is. xxii. 15 ; " He that killeth a sheep in sacrifice, as he that should *braine* a dog," Is. lxvi. 3 ; " I am become as a drunken man, and as a man *wet with wine*," Jer. xxiii. 9 ; " Be ruler in the house of our Lord, upon everie man *raving and prophesying*, to put him into the stocks," Jer. xxix. 26 ; " All faces are turned into *the jaundice*," Jer. xxx. 6 ; "The sunne beate upon the head of Jonas, and he *broyled for heat*," Jon. iv. 8.

As distinguished from the foregoing, there are many renderings in the Douay Bible that may be entered in the category of oddities. Much has been said of Coverdale's version of Jer. viii. 22, " There is no more triacle at Galaad." Quite as remote from spiritual associations is the Douay rendering of the same verse : " Is there noe *rosen* in Galaad ? "² Much has been heard, also, of Coverdale's version of Ps. xci. 5, " Thou shalt not nede to be afrayed for any *bugges* by night." The Douay rendering of the verses that follow suggests ideas quite as ludicrous : " Thou shalt not be afrayed . . . of business walking in darkness . . . and the *midday divel*." What every one, again, will consider a very odd reading in the Douay Bible is Is. xxii. 17 :—" Behold our Lord will cause thee to be carried away *as a cock is carried*." And a glance at the Vulgate will remove all doubt about the kind of cock that is here referred to. It is neither a cock of hay nor a weather-cock ; but a *gallus gallinaceus*, which lexicographers say is the full and

---

¹ *Stool* is one of the words whose meaning has been degraded. In Anglo-Saxon it meant a seat or throne.

² Numquid resina non est in Galaad ? Vulgate. Some resins are still used for medicinal purposes. The *theriaca* of Pagninus, or *treacle* of Coverdale, originally meant an antidote against the bite of poisonous animals.—Facciolati Lexicon. So far from being a product of the sugar-cane, it is said to have been a decoction of viper's flesh, and its efficacy as a medicine was accounted for on the homœopathic and tippler's principle of " eating a hair of the dog that bit you."

proper appellation of the domesticated chanticleer, in distinction from *gallus simpliciter*, which might mean a Frenchman! Another verse in the Douay Bible that to some people may seem odd is 1 Sam. ii. 8 :—" The *poles* of the earth are our Lord's, and upon them he hath sette the world." In both the authorised and revised versions the same rendering appears, except that for "poles" the word *pillars* is substituted. It might be concluded, therefore, but erroneously, that by *poles* the Douay divines meant pillars; and it might be supposed that in this Douay expression the origin of the terms North and South Pole, with the underlying theory of them, may be discovered. In this passage, however, the word "poles" is used by the Douay divines in the sense of hinges and not of pillars, *cardines terrae;* in the sense, in fact, in which the terms North and South Pole are really used, as the pivots on which the earth revolves.

Among other odd readings in the Douay version of the Old Testament the following are worthy of notice :—

"The land of Heuilath, where gold *groweth*," Gen. ii. 11; "He (Samson) stroke them with a great plague, so that astonied they *laid the calfe of the leg upon the thigh*," Judges xv. 8; "Thou shalt not bring his hoare head *peaceably unto hel*," 1 Kings, ii. 6; "With a shell scraped the corruption, sitting on a *dunghill*," Job ii. 8; "The *spirit of my bellie* streyneth me," Job xxxii. 18; "There Benjamin, a young man, *in excesse of mind*," Ps. lxviii. 27; "The price of an harlot is *scarce worth one loaf*," Prov. vi. 26; "Behold not wine when it waxeth *yellow*, when the colour thereof shall shine in the glass," Prov. xxiii. 31; "As a lame man *hath fayre legs in vain:* so a parable is undecent in the mouth of fools," Prov. xxvi. 7; "The bed is streitned, so that one must fall out, and a short mantel cannot cover both," Is. xxviii. 20; "He shall humble his glory with *dashing of his hands*," Is. xxv. 11; "Attend to the rocke whence you are hewen out, and to the *cave of the lake* from the which you are cut out," Is. li. 1; "Ruddier than the *old yvorie*," Lam. iv. 7; "Cut your ploughs into swords, and your *spades* into spears," Joel iii. 10; "I have given you *dulness of the teeth* in all your cities," Amos iv. 6; "Our Lord God prepared an *yvie tree*, and it came up over the head of Jonas," Jonah iv. 6.

A great many words that in the authorised version of the Scriptures are given as proper names, are, in the Douay Bible, translated as if they were common nouns. Sometimes this gives realism and picturesqueness to the narrative, as in Gen. xiv. 3, "All these came together into the *woodland vale* (vale of Siddim), which now is the Salt Sea"; and Gen. xxiii. 9, "That he give me *the double cave* (cave of Macpelah) which he hath in the uttermost part of his field." At other times the effect produced is not good. The narrative is obscured, and the reader is set on a wrong track of interpretation, if he is not left in absolute bewilderment. Proof of this statement will be found in the following passages: Gen. xxii. 2, "Take thy only begotten sonne, whom thou lovest, Isaac, and goe into the land of *vision*"; Gen. xxiv. 62, "Isaac walked along the way, that leadeth to the well *of the living and the seeing*"; Judges ii. 1, "The angel of our Lord went up from Gilgal to *the place of weepers*"; Is. xvi. 11, "For this my bellie shall sound as an harpe to Moab, and my bowels to *the wal of baked bricke*." The Douay divines, moreover, were not strictly uniform and consistent in their way of dealing with proper names. In the seventh chapter of 1 Chronicles, there is what might be termed a garden of genealogical trees. The stems and scions are for the most part designated by their Hebrew names, Manasses, Ezriel, Machir, Galaad, etc. But in the eighteenth verse, this rule is departed from; and instead of reading there, as in the authorised version, "his sister *Hammoleketh* bare *Ishod*," etc., we read that "his sister *Queen* bare *Goodlieman*, and Abiezer and Mohola." And the reason for this procedure is stated on the margin in the following note: "We leave the Hebrew names in this place, because St. Jerome and the whole Church doth so in the Latin text, which we translate."

What, however, to the English Protestant reader, will probably appear the chief peculiarity of the Douay Bible is the large number of readings it contains that vary considerably in meaning from their corresponding passages in the authorised and revised versions. The number of such distinctive readings is legion. Some of them should, perhaps, be called renderings rather than readings. They give one translation of a text while their counterparts in the authorised version give another. Turning, for instance, to Is. xxvi. 18, we read in the Douay Bible: "We have conceived, and as it were travailed, and *brought forth the spirit*"; and in the authorised Bible, "We have been with child, we have been in pain, we have as it were *brought forth wind*." Between these two statements there is apparently a very wide difference, but the difference is one of translation only. The Latin word in the Vulgate (spiritus) which the Douay divines have translated *spirit* means *wind* also, and in Challoner's revision of the Douay, as well as in the authorised Protestant, version *spiritus* receives this latter rendering. Turning, again, to 1 Sam. xiii. 19-21, we find it said in the Douay Bible, "There was not found an yron smith in all the land of Israel. . . . All Israel therefore went down to the Philisthijms, that euerie man might whette his plough culter, and spade, and axe, and rake. *Therefore the edges of the shares, and spades, and forkes with three teeth, and axes, were blunt, even to the goad prick, which was to be mended.*" Instead of the sentence here italicised, we read in the authorised version: "Yet they had a file for the mattocks, and for the coulters, and for the forks, and for the axes, and to sharpen the goads." Between the Douay and the authorised version of this passage there is thus not only variation but positive variance, not only difference on points of detail but disagreement all through. How it may be asked can so much divergence be accounted for? On the margin of the revised version there is a note, which says that the Hebrew text of this passage is obscure, and that instead of being translated, "they had a file for the mattocks," it might be rendered, "When the edges of the mattocks . . . and of the axes were blunt." The peculiarity of the Douay reading in this passage is, therefore, due to translation also, not to the Douay translation of the Vulgate text, but to the translation in the Vulgate of the original Hebrew text. But although some, or even many, of the peculiar readings in the Douay Bible may be made out to be only peculiar renderings either *of* the Vulgate or *in* the Vulgate, a large number of them must be attributed to differences in the texts from which the Vulgate and the authorised English version have been respectively taken. Both in the Vulgate, and in the Douay translation of the Vulgate, there are to be found whole clauses, and even whole sentences, that have no place in the authorised English version. In the book of Proverbs, particularly, these Catholic interpolations are numerous. There is one attached to the fifth verse of the sixteenth chapter, and it gives expression to a most important doctrine of biblical religion: "The beginning of a good way is to doe justice; and it is more acceptable with God than to immolate hosts." Another is appended to the last verse of the twenty ninth chapter, and is to the effect, that "the sonne who keepeth the word shall be out of perdition."[1] In addition to these interpolations, there are in the Douay Bible many readings so widely different from those in the corresponding parts of the authorised version that, without referring to the Hebrew original, we might say at once that they can only be accounted for by a difference in the text from which the Catholic and the Protestant English versions have been at first derived. But without pursuing this question, or attempting to shew how this and that peculiar reading in the Douay Bible originated—whether by a mistranslation *of* the Vulgate—or from a mistranslation *in* the Vulgate—or from a translation in the Vulgate of a different text from that which underlies the authorised English version—we shall consider the peculiar readings in the Douay Bible as *readings* simply, and indicate a few of these to shew how widely, in some places, the Douay and authorised versions differ.[2]

One verse that reads with a curious, although unimportant, difference of meaning in the Douay and authorised transla-

---

[1] A somewhat grotesque reading, occasioned no doubt by a small interpolation, is given by the Douay divines to 1 Chron. xiii. 9 :—"When they were come to the floore of Chidon, Oza stretched forth his hand, to holde up the Arke; for the oxe *being wantone* had made it leane a little a side." The words of the Vulgate are, "bos quippe lasciviens paululum inclinaverat eam." In the Latin version, Zurich, 1564, the words are simply, "quoniam declinaverant boves."

[2] Although the Douay version of the Old Testament is said to have been conformed to the Clementine text of the Vulgate, the statement can scarcely be accepted as quite accurate. There are several interpolations added to the Douay Bible by modern revisers, and these are found in the Clementine text (as usually printed). One of these occurs in Prov. xviii. 22 :—"He that driveth away a good wife, driveth away a good thing." There are renderings, also, in the original Douay version which do not correspond with the Clementine text, such as Job. iii. 23 :—"To a man whose *life* is hid." The reading in the Clementine Vulgate is : "Viro cujus abscondita est *via,*" and Catholic revisers have accordingly changed the word *life* into *way*. Instead of *via* the Douay divines had doubtless found *vita* in the copy from which they translated; and *vita* is the word given also in the Protestant version, Zurich, 1564.

T

tions, is Joshua xv. 18. In the latter named version it is said that " it came to pass, as she (Achsah) came unto him, that *she moved him* to ask of her father a field : and *she lighted off her ass* : and Caleb said unto her, What wouldest thou ?" The reading in the Douay Bible is : " *She was moved by her husband* to ask a field of her father, and *she sighed as she sate on her asse.* To whom Caleb said, What aileth thee ?" A sentence in the prophecies of Isaiah that conveys, in the Douay Bible, a meaning very remote from what it does in the authorised version of the Scriptures, is chap. xvi. 1. In the latter named version the prophet is represented calling on the children of Moab to pay, as of old, their tribute to the King of Israel[1] : " Send ye the lamb to the ruler of the land, from Sela to the wilderness, unto the mount of the daughter of Zion." The Douay divines, on the other hand, represent the prophet praying for the advent of Messiah : " Send forth, O Lord, the lambe, the dominatour of the earth, from the rocke of the desert, to the mount of the daughter of Zion." In the writings of Amos, again, there is a judgment proclaimed, chap. iv. 2, against the rulers of Israel, which, as rendered in the authorised version, was fearful enough to contemplate : " The Lord God hath sworn by his holiness, that the days shall come upon you, that he will take you away *with hooks* and your posterity *with fish hooks.*" As given in the Douay Bible, however, the prediction sounds much more dreadful : " They shall lift you *upon poles*, and your remnant *in pots boyling hot.*" Other passages that read differently in the two versions will be seen in the subjoined parallel columns :

Douay Version.	Authorised Version.
Gen. xlix. 3.—My strength, and the beginning of my *sorrow*.	Gen. xlix. 3.—My might, and the beginning of my strength.
Gen. xlix. 22.—Joseph, a *child encreasing, encreasing and comelie to behold :* the *daughters coursed* to and for (fro ?) upon the wall.	Gen. xlix. 22.—Joseph is a fruitful bough, even a fruitful bough by a well, whose branches run over the wall.

---

[1] It is recorded in 2 Kings iii. 4-5, that "Mesha, King of Moab, was a sheepmaster, and rendered unto the King of Israel an hundred thousand lambs, and an hundred thousand rams, with the wool. But it came to pass when Ahab was dead, that the King of Moab rebelled against the King of Israel."

Lev. xxi. 18.—Neither shall he approach to his ministerie . . . if he have a *litle or a great, or a crooked nose*.

Ruth. ii. 14.—She therefore sate at the side of the reapers, and she heaped to herselfe polent, and did eat and was filled and *tooke the leavinges*, (Tulit reliquias, Vulgate).

I Sam. xvii. 4.—And there came forth a man that was a *bastard* (vir spurius, Vulg.) from the camp of the Philistians, named Goliath.

I Sam. xix. 24.—And he stripped himselfe of his garments, and prophecied with the rest before Samuel, and *sang* naked all that day and night.[1]

Ps. iv. 4.—Be ye *angrie* and sinne not: *the things that you say in your harts, in your chambers be ye sorrie for*.

Ps. xix. 12-13.—From my secret sins cleanse me, and from *other men's spare thy servant*.

Ps. lxxvii. 3.—I was mindful of God, and was *delighted*.

Prov. xxvi. 8.—As he that casteth a stone *into the heap of mercurie;* so he that giveth honour to the unwise.

Jer. xxxvii. 21.—There should be given him a piece of bread every day, *beside broth*.

Lam. iv. 14.—They were polluted with bloud; and *when they could not, they held their skirts*.

Hos. xiii. 2.—To these they say, *Immolate men* adoring calves, (sacrifice men, ye that adore calves, Challoner; Immolate, homines vitulos adorentes, Vulg.).

Joel i. 17.—The beasts are rotted *in their dung*.

Amos viii. 2.—What seest thou Amos? And I said, *an apple-hook*.

Amos viii. 3.—And the *hinges* of the temple shall *creak* in that day.

Zech. iv. 7.—He will bring forth the principal stone, and will make *grace equal to the grace thereof*.

Lev. xxi. 18.—He shall not approach : . . . he that hath a flat nose or any thing superfluous.

Ruth ii. 14.—She sat beside the reapers; and he reached her parched corn, and she did eat and was sufficed, and *left*, (Reliquum fecit, Zurich 1564).

I Sam. xvii. 4.—And there went out a champion out of the camp of the Philistines, named Goliath.

I Sam. xix. 24.—He stripped off his clothes also, and prophesied before Samuel in like manner, and lay down naked all that day and all that night.

Ps. iv. 4.—Stand in awe, and sin not : commune with your own heart upon your bed and be still.

Ps. xix. 12-13.—Cleanse thou me from secret faults; keep back thy servant also from presumptuous sins.

Ps. lxxvii. 3.—I remembered God, and was troubled.

Prov. xxvi. 8.—As he that bindeth a stone in a sling; so is he that giveth honour to a fool.

Jer. xxxvii. 21.—They should give him daily a piece of bread, *out of the bakers' strect*.

Lam. iv. 14.—They have polluted themselves with blood, *so that men could not touch their garments*.

Hos. xiii. 2.—They say of them, Let the men that sacrifice kiss the calves.

Joel i. 17.—The seed is rotten under their clods.

Amos viii. 2.—Amos what seest thou? And I said, a basket of summer fruit.

Amos viii. 3.—And the songs of the temple shall be howlings in that day.

Zech. vii. 7.—He shall bring forth the head stone thereof, with shoutings, crying, grace, grace unto it.

As setting forth not only the special doctrines of the Catholic Church, but the spirit of Catholic churchmen in the age succeeding the Reformation, there is no part of the Douay

---

[1] The word in the Vulgate corresponding to *sang* is *cecidit* which means *fell* or *lay down*, and is so rendered by Challoner. One is tempted to express a conjecture that in the copy of the Vulgate from which the Douay divines made their translation *cecidit* had been printed *cecinit*, and was thus rendered *sang*.

Bible more interesting than the marginal notes, and the annotations on whole books and chapters. It is impossible, however, in a single paragraph to convey an adequate notion of their contents. They all proceed upon the theory that Catholic doctrines, and Catholic institutions, are mystically taught and enjoined in every part of the Old Testament. There is a marginal note, for instance, on Gen. xlviii. 14, that when Jacob placed his right hand on the head of Ephraim, and his left on the head of Manasseh, "he made a cross, prefiguring the cross of Christ." In another note, on Gen. xlix. 11, countenance is given to a fanciful opinion of one of the fathers, that by the wine in which it was prophesied that Judah should "wash his stole," was meant "the wine of the chalice of our Lord's blood." Almost every doctrine, rite, custom, practice, and institution of the Catholic Church is, in this way, grounded or sought to be grounded upon some statement or other in the Old Testament. And while instant in season and out of season in expounding, establishing, maintaining, and defending the tenets of their own church, the Douay annotators were no less assiduous in exposing and denouncing the heresies and mal-practices of other churches. "Sons of God and sons of men," they remark, in reference to Gen. vi. 2, was in the days before the flood "such a distinction as now is Catholiques and Hereticks." In their annotations on Ex. xx., they accuse Protestants of "egregious lies against the whole church militant, and blasphemous reproaches against the glorious sainctes." Touches of a gentler spirit are, nevertheless, discernable in some other of the Douay notes. In reference to the incident that occurred when Jacob and Rachel made their first acquaintance at the well in the east, Gen. xxix. 11, it is noted on the margin, that "St. Augustine commendeth familiar kissing of kinsfolke and friends as a laudable custom in some countries." And to this statement, it is courteously added by the doctors of Douay, for the gratification of their "right well beloved English readers," that this familiar kissing "is nowhere more civil and modest than in England."

That the Douay and Rhemes version of the Old and New Testament have merits of a kind, will not be disputed. They were framed on principles that able and learned men thought were the true principles of biblical translation. The translators, too, were scholars of no mean repute, and theologians of no mean ability. " They were well known to the world, to have been excellent in the tongs, sincere men, and great divines." [1] And to this day, there are scholastic persons that see in the Douay Bible and Rhemes Testament, much to admire. In these versions they meet with Catholic and ecclesiastical expressions, which delight their minds. Some of the words and phrases referred to in this chapter as dark, crude and uncouth, are the very ones in which these people discern mysterious, if not mystic, charms. The Latinisms awake both classic and spiritual associations. They are pleasant echoes of 'the dear old Vulgate; and, to change the metaphor, they recall to memory the rock from which they were hewn. Such in particular are the phrases, "supersubstantial bread"—" the time of my resolution "—" every spirit that dissolveth Christ "—" keep the good depositum "—" with such hosts God is promerited." And there are in all parts of the Douay Bible both evidences and fruits of advanced scholarship; so that, as a good Protestant divine says, "there is no other English version of the Scriptures that will prove more instructive to the student, who will take the pains to separate what is good and useful from what is ill-advised and wrong." [2]

But the Douay Bible was not a people's book. It was not even intended to be. It was given to the laity with some reluctance. It was "a benefit bestowed as of necessity"; on account of the wide circulation of "false and impious translations," through which many good souls were endangered, both ecclesiastically and spiritually. And it was not a free and frank translation into current English. The translators both shewed and avowed far more fear to commit mistakes, by the substitution of plain Saxon words for words of ecclesiastical Latin, than honest desire to satisfy the yearnings of common people after the knowledge of biblical truth. Instead of

---

[1] Preface to Douay Bible, 1609.
[2] Moulton.

opening up the holy of holies unreservedly, they only drew the veil a few inches aside. To make the Douay Bible a popular book, therefore, some revision of it was necessary. One good Catholic on whom this conviction lay heavily was Cornelius Nary, "Consultissimae Facultatis Parisiensis Doctor." He accordingly, in 1719, published a Catholic version of the New Testament, "translated out of the Latin Vulgate, and with the original Greek and divers translations in vulgar languages diligently compared and revised": and, in a preface to this translation, he indicated the reasons that had mainly induced him to undertake the work. "We had no Catholic translation of the Scriptures in the English tongue," he said, "but the Douay Bible and the Rhemish Testament, which have been done now more than an hundred years since, the language whereof is so old, the words in many places so obsolete, the orthography so bad, and the translation so very literal, that in a number of places it is unintelligible, and all over so grating to the ears of such as are accustomed to speak, in a manner, another language, that most people will not be at the pains of reading them."[1] It was reserved for Dr. Challoner, however, thoroughly to accomplish what Nary aimed at, the superseding of the Rhemes and Douay versions of the Scripture by a Catholic version written in a simpler and more popular style. In 1749, he published what may be termed a revised version of the Rhemes New Testament, and in 1750 a revised version of the Douay Old Testament, both "corrected according to the Clementine edition of the Scriptures."[2] A second edition of Challoner's New Testament, with some amendments, was published in 1750, and a third edition with more amendments in 1752. In 1783 a revision of Challoner's versions, both of the Old and New Testament, was made by the Rev. Bernard M'Mahon, with the approbation of Dr. Troy, the Catholic Archbishop of Dublin, whence it is commonly known as Troy's Bible. At the present day the Catholic version of

---

[1] Lewis' *History of English Translations of Bibles*, p. 357.

[2] The Old Testament published at Douay, in 1609, was itself said to be corrected in the manuscript, according to the Clementine edition of the Vulgate.

the Scriptures commonly used in this country is Challoner's version of the Old Testament, and either one of Challoner's versions or Troy's of the New.[1] In America, Challoner's version is strictly adhered to, except where Kenrick's Testament, 1849-51, is adopted.

Some Catholic dignitaries have declared themselves not very much taken with Challoner's revisions. The old wine they allege is better than the new; and with all its imperfections and faults they prefer the Douay-Rhemes version to its modern substitutes. That version, says Cardinal Wiseman, " has been altered and modified till scarcely any verse remains as it was originally published; and so far as simplicity and energy of style are concerned, the changes are in general for the worse. For though Dr. Challoner did well to alter many too decided Latinisms, which the old translators had retained, he weakened the language considerably, by destroying inversion where it was congenial, . . . and by the insertion of particles where they were by no means necessary.[2] And it had been well,"[3] the Cardinal adds, "if Dr. Challoner's alterations had given stability to the text. . . . But, far from this being the case, new and often important modifications have been made in every edition which has followed, till at length many may appear rather new versions than revisions of the old. . . . And these systematic variations are not the only vicissitudes to which the text has been subject. The mass of typographical errors to be found in some editions is quite frightful,[4] and not so much disfiguring them . . . as transforming them into others that give a correct grammatical but unsound theological sense."

---

[1] "Ever since 1800, Challoner's versions of the New Testament have been constantly intermixed, and with them Troy's text, till it is nearly impossible to dissociate them. It is only in the New Testament that Troy's reading is retained: Challoner's now remaining almost verbatim in the Old. . . . . The edition of Coyne" (quoted from in this chapter) "is as near an approach to Challoner's original as any other." (Private letter from a Catholic Prelate.)

[2] Wiseman's Essays.   [3] Ibid.

[4] One misprint in the Dublin edition, 1815, is "the *wickedness* (weakness) of God is stronger than man," 1 Cor. i. 25.

In a popular and generally excellent handbook on English versions of the Scriptures, it is stated "that Challoner's text is substantially that of the original Catholic version, the changes relating chiefly to syntax and spelling, and only rarely to the meaning . . . ": and "that the grand difference between the current edition of the Rhemes-Douay versions and the original editions is the suppression of many of the savage, fanatical notes, although quite a number of these remain." This is not a correct statement of facts. It is true that Challoner's version rarely differs in meaning from the Douay-Rhemes version, except where the Clementine edition of the Vulgate differs from the old edition used by the Rhemes translators of the New Testament. But Challoner's version differs very widely in diction, as well as in syntax proper and spelling, from the Douay-Rhemes; and its new diction has, in some parts, been to a very large extent imported from the Protestants' authorised version of 1611.

One of the most outstanding features in the Rhemes Testament and Douay Bible is, as we have seen, the large number of "inkhorn" terms they contain. For many of these scholastic terms, common words are substituted in Challoner's revision, especially of the New Testament. Instead of "celestials, terrestrials, and infernals," Phil. ii. 10, we read, "those that are in heaven, on earth, and under the earth." So also, in the fourth chapter of the Epistle to the Ephesians, we find the phrase "*consummation* of the saints," verse 12, displaced by "perfecting of the saints"; the clause "*impudicity* to the *operation* of all uncleanness," verse 19, altered into "lasciviousness, to the working of all uncleanness"; and "*contristrate* not the holy spirit of God, by which you are *signed* unto the day of redemption, verse 30, changed into "grieve not the holy spirit of God, whereby you are sealed." And it is not in a verse here and there that this simplification of diction appears, but on almost every page. "Repairing their nets," Mat. iv 21, is transformed into "mending their nets"; "ministers," John ii. 9, into "waiters"; "dissolve this temple," John ii. 19, into "destroy this temple"; "exalted the serpent," John iii. 14, into "lifted up the serpent"; "docible of God," John vi 45, into "taught of God"; "execration," Acts xxiii. 14, into "a great oath"; "hostes," 1 Cor. x. 18, into "sacrifices"; "diffidence," Eph. ii. 2, into "disobedience"; "evacuating," Eph. ii. 15, into "making void"; "prefinition of worlds," Eph. iii. 11, into "eternal purpose"; "affiance," Eph. iii. 12, into "boldness"; "subministration," Phil. i. 19, into "supply"; "exinanited," Phil. ii. 7, into "debased"; "odible," Titus iii. 3, into "hateful"; "agnition," Philemon 6, into "acknowledgment"; "exasperate," Heb. iii. 16, into "provoke"; "sabbatism," Heb. iv. 9, into "rest"; "proposition of loaves," Heb. ix. 2, into "setting forth of loaves"; "magnifical glory," 2 Peter i. 17, into "excellent glory"; "dominical day," Rev. i. 10, into "the Lord's day."

Besides these and scores of similar scholastic terms, there are many odd and archaic, super-homely and inapt words in the Douay Bible, that have in Challoner's version been displaced by less *outre* expressions. Of such amendments the following may serve as examples :

RHEMES TESTAMENT, 1582.

Mat. viii. 16.—Al that were *ill at ease* he cured.

Acts xxiii. 5.—The prince of thy people thou shalt not *misspeake*.

Acts xxvii. 39.—Into the which they minded, if they could, to *cast a land* the ship.

1 Cor. xv. 53.—This corruptible must *doe on* in corruption.

Phil. ii. 22.—And know ye an *experiment* of him.

Philemon 7.—The bowels of the sainctes have *rested* by thee, brother.

Heb. xi. 16.—God is not *confounded* to be callèd their God.

3 John 10.—With malicious wordes *chatting* against us.

Rev. i. 7.—Euery eie shall see him, and they that *pricked* him.

CHALLONER'S REVISION, (Coyne, 1811).

Mat. viii. 16.—All that were sick he healed.

Acts xxiii. 5.—Thou shalt not speak evil of the prince of thy people.

Acts xxvii. 39.—Into which they minded, if they could, to *thrust in* the ship.

1 Cor. xv. 53.—This corruptible must put on incorruption.

Phil. ii. 22.—Now know ye the proof of him.

Philemon 7.—The bowels of the saints have been refreshed by thee, brother.

Heb. xi. 16.—God is not ashamed to be called their God.

3 John 10.—Prating against us with malicious words.

Rev. i. 7.—Every eye shall see him, and they also that pierced him.

It will be seen that in a very large number of the above cited cases in which Challoner has amended the phraseology of the Rhemes Testament, he has adopted the words of what we call the authorised version. The extent, however, to which he has plumed the Catholic version, especially in the New Testament, with Protestant feathers, will be more fully realised when we have examined passages that have not only been altered in respect of a significant word or a significant phrase, but have been recast all over. Some of these reconstructed verses will be found to correspond word for word with the translation in the authorised Bible, and others to come very near that measure of identity.

RHEMES TESTAMENT, 1582.	CHALLONER'S REVISION (Coyne, 1811).
Rom. iii. 3.—Hath their incredulitie made the faith of God frustrate?	Rom. iii. 3.—Shall their unbelief make the faith of God without effect?
Rom. viii. 18.—For I think that the passions of this time are not condigne to the glory to come.	Rom. viii. 18.—For I reckon, that the sufferings of this present time are not worthy to be compared with the glory to come.
1 Cor. xv. 19.—If in this life only we be hoping in Christ, we are more miserable than al men.	1 Cor. xv. 19.—If in this life only we have hope in Christ, we are of all men most miserable.
Phil. iii. 7.—But the things that were gaines to me, those haue I esteemed for Christ, detriments.	Phil. iii. 7.—But what things were gain to me, those I have counted loss for Christ.
Phil. iii. 10.—To know him, and the vertue of his resurrection, and the societie of his passions, configured to his death.	Phil. iii. 10.—That I may know him, and the power of his resurrection, and the fellowship of his sufferings, being made conformable to his death.
Heb. iii. 13.—But exhort yourselues euery day, whiles to-day is named, that none of you be obdurate with the fallacie of sinne.	Heb. iii. 13.—But exhort one another every day, whiles it is called to-day, lest any one of you be hardened through the deceitfulness of sin.
Heb. ix. 17.—For a testament is confirmed in the dead; otherwise it is yet of no value, whiles he that tested liveth.	Heb. ix. 17.—For a testament is of force after men are dead: otherwise it is as yet of no strength, whilst the testator liveth.
Heb. xi. 34.—Extinguished the force of fire, repelled the edge of the sword, recouered of their infirmitie, were made strong in battel, turned away the camp of forainers.	Heb. xi. 34.—Quenched the violence of fire, escaped the edge of the sword, recovered strength from weakness, became valiant in war, put to flight the armies of the aliens.
Heb. xii. 10.—And they indeede for a time of few daies, according to their will, instructed us; but he, to that which is profitable in receiuing of his sanctification.	Heb. xii. 10.—And they indeed for a few days chastised us according to their own pleasure; but he, for our profit, that we might be partakers of his holiness.
Heb. xiii. 16.—And beneficence and communication do not forget.	Heb. xiii. 16.—And do not forget to do good and to impart.

While Challoner made such great changes on the diction of the Catholic Bible, there was also a large number of notable words and phrases in the old version that he left unaltered. In the ninth chapter of the Epistles to the Hebrews, the following phrases of the Rhemes translators have been retained by Challoner:—"*justifications* (ordinances, A.V.) of divine service, verse 1; cherubims of glory overshadowing the *propitiatory* (mercy-seat, A.V.), verse 5 ; divers washings and *justices of the flesh* (carnal ordinances, A.V.), verse 10 ; offered once to *exhaust* (bear, A.V.) the sins of many," verse 28.[1] Of other Latinisms in the Douay Bible that Challoner thought proper to retain may be mentioned :—" The redemption of *acquisition*," Eph. i. 14 ; " All *paternity* in heaven and earth is named," Eph. iii. 15 ; " Aliens from the *conversation* of Israel," Eph. ii. 12 ; " Every spirit that *dissolveth* Jesus," 1 John iv. 3 ; " Elias was a man *passible* like unto us," James v. 17. Some quaint and homely expressions in the Rhemes Testament have also been preserved by Challoner, as :—" Every *soul* got safe to land," Acts xxvii. 44 ; " By faith, he abode in the land of promise, dwelling in *cottages*,"[2] Heb. xi. 9; " Both now, and unto the day of eternity," 2 Pet. iii. 18 ; " Two pound of wheat for a penny and *thrice two pounds* of barley for a penny," Rev. vi. 6.

It is evident that Challoner did not set so much store, as the Rhemes translators did, on words that were held to be ecclesiastical and Catholic terms. The phrase "our Lord," which constantly occurs in the Rhemes Testament, and which Cardinal Wiseman specially lauds as Catholic and affectionate (although not invariably scriptural), is, in all cases where in the Vulgate it is represented by the unadjectived noun *Dominus*, changed by Challoner into "*the* Lord." In one verse at least, Rom. viii. 39, the word " love " is substituted by Challoner for *charity*; in several passages, Eph. i. 9, 1 Tim. iii. 16, and Rev. i. 20, " sacrament " is displaced by *mystery*; and in one part of his writings, Eph. vi. 20, St. Paul is made to doff the Roman title of *legate*, and assume the British *rôle* of ambassador.

In modern editions of the Catholic version of the New Testament, annotations of all kinds, good and indifferent, liberal and illiberal, may possibly be found. They are certainly not in every case fanatical or offensive. Those in the edition of Challoner's revision from which the foregoing extracts have been taken are neither lengthy nor virulent, and of neither much literary nor much scholastic merit. But, in so far as they

---

[1] Ad *exhaurienda* peccata, Vulgate. Ut pecata *tolleret*, Erasmus.
[2] "In *casulis*, Vulgate. In *tabernaculis*, Erasmus.

set forth the distinctive points of the Catholic doctrine, they are instructive, and any Protestant may read them without the slightest detriment to his nervous system. Among those that contain statements of, or apologies for, Catholic tenets, the following may be quoted for entertainment:

Mat. i. 25.—These words "assure us that our Blessed Lady was a virgin when she brought forth her Son," which is the great point the Evangelist has here in view; without meddling with the question what was done afterwards. But, by Apostolical tradition we are assured that she always remained a virgin.

Luke i. 48.—*All generations shall call me blessed.* These words are a prediction of that honour which the Church of all ages should pay to the Blessed Virgin. Let Protestants examine whether they are any way concerned in this prophecy.

Mat. vi. 11.—*Give us this day our supersubstantial bread.* In St. Luke the words "supersubstantial bread" are rendered *daily bread*. They are understood of the bread of life, which we receive in the blessed sacrament.

1 Cor. xi. 27-29.—*Guilty of the body and of the blood of the Lord . . . not discerning the body of the Lord.* This demonstrates the real presence of the body and blood of Christ, even to the unworthy communicant, who otherwise could not be guilty of the body and blood of Christ, or justly condemned for not discerning the Lord's body.

Mat. xii. 32.—*Not be forgiven him, neither in this world, nor in the world to come.* From these words St. Austin and St. Gregory gather that some sins may be remitted in the world to come; and consequently that there is a Purgatory, or a middle place.

1 Peter iii. 19.—*Spirits in prison.* See here a proof of a third place, or middle state of souls; for, these spirits in prison, to whom Christ went to preach, after his death, were not in heaven, nor yet in the hell of the damned; because heaven is no prison, and Christ did not go to preach to the damned.

Rom. iii. 28.—*Justified by faith, without the works of the law.* The faith to which the Apostle here attributes man's justification, is not a presumptuous *assurance* of our being justified; but a firm and lively belief of all that God has revealed or promised; in short, a faith which takes in hope, love, repentance and the use of the sacraments. And the works which he here excludes are only *the works of the law*: that is, such as are done by the law of nature, or that of Moses, antecedent to the faith of Christ; but, by no means such as follow faith and proceed from it.

1 Cor. ix. 5.—*A woman a sister.* Protestants have corrupted this text, by rendering it *a sister a wife*; whereas, it is certain St. Paul had no wife (Chap. vii. 7, 8), and that he only speaks of such devout women, as, according to the custom of the Jewish nation, waited upon the preachers of the gospel, and supplied them with necessaries.

Rev. ix. 3.—*Locusts.* It is commonly understood of heretics, They are not able to hurt the green tree, that is, such as have a lively faith, working by charity—but only the reprobate. They are represented as prepared to battel, as being ever ready to contend. They wear counterfeit gold on their heads, for all is but pretence and fiction. In shape they are as *men*; in smoothness of speech as *women*; in fury and rage against all that oppose them as *lions;* their breasts and hearts are as hard as iron; they are full of noise and shuffling; the sting of their pestiferous doctrine is worse than that of a scorpion; but their reign is generally for a short time only.

THE NATIONAL BIBLE,

*Sometimes called, The King's Translation,
Commonly termed, The Authorised Version.*

Editions consulted and quoted from :—
    For text as commonly printed, modern copies.
    For original text as printed in 1611—Old Testament, Parallel Bible, Oxford, 1885 ; New Testament, Bagster's Hexapla ; Parallel New Testament, 1882, Oxford.
For Preface :—
    Pulpit Bible, Cambridge (modern).

AT the close of the sixteenth century, there were in England three very notable Protestant versions of the Bible, in the vernacular tongue. The Great Bible, which bore on its title page the imprimatur of civil authority, still retained some of its pristine celebrity ; and from its pages the Service Book of the Church of England was furnished with its gospels, epistles, and psalter.[1] The Geneva Bible, on the other hand, had lost none of its prestige with the people. The Bishops' Bible, again, presented all the improvement on the Great Bible and the Geneva Bible that, in 1572, could be effected by the learning and piety of the Church of England.

But there was still a cry for another and better translation of the Bible than any that had yet been printed. Possibly the cry was neither very loud nor very general, but it happened to be raised at a juncture so opportune that action followed.

In 1603, James the Sixth of Scotland succeeded to the throne of England. At that date, there were in the Church of England two parties that may be described respectively as

---

[1] At this date, the Psalter was not printed with the Book of Common Prayer, but was read out of the Bible. Lewis, p. 258.

Ritualists and Puritans. The latter complained of certain grievances to which they were subjected. Ceremonies that they disliked were made part of the Church's ritual; and from the compulsory observance of these obnoxious formalities they desired to be relieved. They accordingly put themselves in the way of the King on his journey to London, and submitted to him a petition for redress of their grievances. This petition purported to represent the views of a thousand ministers in the National Church; and was, therefore, called the millenary petition. In response to this petition, the King appointed a conference to be held at Hampton Court the following January, 1604; at which representatives of both parties in the Church should have an opportunity of stating their views to His Majesty, on the matters of complaint. The result of this conference was not what the Puritans anticipated. The King avowed himself to be, in the main, favourable to the courses of the High Church party; and he intimated his resolution, while amending some abuses, to maintain in the kingdom "one doctrine, one discipline, and one religion in substance and ceremony."

But there was one point in which James met the wishes of the Puritans. A request was made by their representatives that there should be "a new translation of the Bible, because those which were allowed in the Reign of King Henry VIII. and Edward VI. were corrupt and not answerable to the truth of the original." In the Psalter appointed to be read in church, one verse, Ps. cv. 28, was rendered, "They were not *obedient*" (instead of *disobedient*) "unto his word"; and another verse, Ps. cvi. 30, was translated, "Then stood up Phinehas *and prayed*," instead of *and executed judgment*. The Epistle, again, set down in the Prayer-book for the fourth Sunday in Lent, contained the extraordinary geographical mis-statement, Gal. iv. 25, "Mount Sinai is Agar in Arabia, and bordereth upon the city which is now called Jerusalem." The version from which these citations were made was the Great Bible; but the Bishops' Bible was, in part, open to the same criticism. It con-contained the false rendering of Gal iv. 25; and although the Bishops themselves corrected the rendering of Ps. cvi. 30, their version of the Psalms, not being appointed to be read or sung in Churches, was not printed in some editions of their Bible.[1]

To the surprise and chagrin of some of the bishops, the Puritans' motion for a new translation of the Bible happened to fall in with the King's humour. "I have never yet," said the royal theologian, "seen a Bible well translated into English; and the worst of all the translations I have seen is the Geneva." The unexpected outcome of this episode in the Hampton Court discussions was the expressed desire of His Majesty that "some special pains should be taken . . . for one uniform translation, . . !. to be done by the best learned in both Universities; after them, to be reviewed by the bishops and the chief learned of the Church; from them to be presented to the Privy Council; and lastly, to be ratified by his royal authority." With his characteristic imperial notions of one doctrine, one discipline, and one form of worship, he said further, that to this new translation, and none other, the whole Church in the kingdom should be bound.

The people of England have cause to be thankful to the King for the action he took on this occasion. For whatever were the merits of the Great Bible, the Geneva Bible, or the Bishops' Bible, the new translation desired by the King, and through him procured a few years later, for the English people, was better than all its precursors. It is a curious fact, however, that the issue of the new translation, in 1611, did not remove the complaint of the Puritans, that in church they were obliged to read and listen to mis-renderings of Scripture. Although the King had said that the whole Church in the realm should be bound to the new version of the Bible and to none other, the old translation of the Psalter and the Epistles continued long afterwards to be used in public worship as before. It was not till the reign of Charles II. that the Gospels and Epistles according to the translation 1611, were

---

[1] In the quarto edition of the Bishops' Bible, 1584, quoted from in chapter v. of this volume, the Psalms are printed according to the translation in the Great Bible. In the edition, 1572, there are two versions of the Psalms, the Bishops' own, and the one in the Great Bible, which was the authorised version.

admitted into the Prayer-book; and the Psalter according to that translation has not been admitted yet. In the Church of England, people to this day hear it read on Sundays that Phinehas stood up "*and prayed.*"

Some Churchmen, as was remarked, did not go in very heartily with the King's wishes. They thought that enough had been done in the way of changing the words of Scripture. The bishop of London is alleged to have said cynically at the conference, that "if every man's humour should be followed there would be no end of translating." The King took the matter in hand, nevertheless, and the work went on. In the summer of 1604, a list of men well qualified to be employed in the work of translation was submitted to, and approved by, his Majesty. The bishops were thereupon directed to invite learned men within their several dioceses to send in to the Hebrew reader at Oxford, or to the dean of Westminster, any notes they had made of errors or obscurities in former translations. But three years passed before the work of translation was actually begun.

The list of translators comprised originally fifty-four names; but only forty-seven persons came forward to take part in the labours of revision. The translators, or revisers, as we choose to term them, were divided into six companies; and to each company was assigned a separate portion of Scripture. Three companies were set to the Old Testament; two companies to the New Testament; and the sixth company to the Apocrypha. Each of the translators was required to make his own translation, chapter by chapter, of the portion of Scripture assigned to his company. Each company held meetings from time to time, to hear and compare translations, and to draw out a scroll of what was eventually agreed on as the company's renderings. After an entire book had been gone over in this way, the scroll was sent the round of the other companies, to be "considered of seriously and judiciously"; and it was then, with remarks, remitted to the company from whom it came. By that company these remarks or criticisms were, in turn, reviewed; and if not approved, they were referred to a select committee of final revisers. The execution of the work occupied about three years; and both the length of time employed in the work, and the elaborate mode of procedure adopted, indicate the pains that were taken to make the translation worthy of its high design. In 1611 the new version was given forth to the public; and before the year was out a second edition was issued.

Considering the interest that the King had taken in the matter, it was fitting that his name should be permanently associated with the new translation. Practically, he was the originator of the undertaking; it was he, also, that apparently laid down the lines of procedure; and when means were awanting to remunerate the translators for their labours, he did all he could to procure for them such promotion in the Church as was meet "for men of their deserts." Patrons of prebends and parsonages were requested not to fill up vacant appointments in their gift till the King had an opportunity of "commending for the same some such of the learned men" on the translation staff, "as he should think fit to be preferred thereto." Through the good offices of James, seven of the forty-seven translators were raised to episcopal dignity, and more than twice seven were settled in other comfortable livings.

The new version was accordingly dedicated to the King, "as the principal mover and author of the work"; and, in the epistle dedicatory, His Majesty's gifts and graces were extolled in the adulatory language peculiar to such writings at that period. He was described as the "sanctified person, who under God is the immediate author of (his loyal and religious people's) true happiness." His zeal for the house of God was said to be manifested "every day at home, by religious and learned discourse, . . . by hearing the word preached, by cherishing the teachers thereof, and by caring for the Church, as a most tender and loving nursing-father." The renown of his literary achievements was declared to have reached "the farthest parts of Christendom"; and his writings in defence of the truth were averred to have "given such a blow unto the man of sin, as will not be healed." The approbation and patronage of so learned and judicious a Prince shall, therefore, said the dedicators, "more honour and encourage us than all the calumniations and hard interpretations of other men shall dismay us. So that if, on the one side, we shall be traduced by Popish persons . . . because we are poor instruments to make God's holy truth to be yet more and more known, . . . or if, on the other side, we shall be maligned by self-conceited brethren, who run their own ways, and give liking unto nothing but what is framed by themselves and hammered on their anvil, we may rest secure, supported within by the truth and innocency of a good conscience, . . . and sustained without by the powerful protection of your Majesty's grace and favour." The writer of this courtly document was Dr. Miles Smith, whose compliments to the King and labours in the work of revision were deservedly rewarded by his preferment from the canonry of Hereford to the bishopric of Gloucester.

Along with this dedication, there was prefixed to the new version a lengthy preface, explaining the design of the translators, and vindicating the spirit in which their work had been executed. This prefatory epistle was also the composition of Dr. Smith, and it set forth the important fact that the translators " never thought from the beginning that they should need to make a new translation, nor yet to make of a bad one a good one, . . . but to make a good one better, or out of many good ones one principal good one." This statement of Dr. Smith's is fully confirmed by the tenor of the King's instructions. The first of these directed that in the revision the Bible ordinarily read in church, and commonly called the Bishops' Bible, should be followed, and as little altered as the truth of the original would permit. Another of the instructions specified the particular translations that should be adopted, when they agreed better with the text than the Bishops' Bible did. These were Tyndale's Testament, Coverdale's Bible, Matthew's Bible, the Great Bible, and the Geneva Bible. The Rhemes Testament, it will thus be seen, was excluded from reference; but this exclusion may be sufficiently accounted for, irrespective of ecclesiastical prejudice, by the fact that that translation was made from the Vulgate and not from "the original tongues." Among the other instructions to the translators were the following:—The names of prophets and holy writers to be retained, as near as may be, according to former usage; old ecclesiastical words to be used, such as, church instead of congregation; the rendering of words that have different meanings to be that which has most authority from eminent fathers, being agreeable to the propriety of the place and the analogy of faith; the divisions of chapters to be altered either not at all, or as little as possible; no notes to be printed on the margin except for the explanation of such Greek or Hebrew words as cannot without circumlocution be fully translated in the text.[1]

The scholastic attainments of the translators, and the reverent spirit in which they entered on their work, are referred to in the preface with honest pride. "Many," says Dr. Smith, "were chosen that were greater in other men's eyes than in their own, and that sought the truth rather than their own praise. They came, or were thought to come, not *exercendi causa*, but *exercitati*, that is *learned*, not *to learn*: for the chief overseer under His Majesty, to whom not only we, but also our whole Church was much bound, knew by his wisdom . . . that it is a preposterous order to teach first and to learn after. And in what sort did these assemble? In the trust of their own knowledge, or of their sharpness of wit, or deepness of judgment, as it were an arm of flesh? At no hand. They trusted in Him that hath the key of David, opening and no man shutting: they prayed to the Lord, the father of our Lord, to the effect that St. Augustine did—*Oh, let thy Scriptures be my pure delight, let me not be deceived in them, neither let me deceive by them.* In this confidence, and with this devotion, did they assemble together; not too many, lest one should trouble another; and yet many, lest many things haply might escape them."

As stated on the title page, the translation 1611 was made

---

[1] The Geneva notes were incorporated in several editions of the authorised version published at Amsterdam between 1642 and 1715, for the use of "the exiled English Church abiding for the present" in Holland. *Athenæum*, 1st December, 1888.

from the original languages of holy Scripture; and every available help in the translation of obscure and difficult passages was freely used. All the English versions specified in the instructions were carefully studied. And not only so, but "neither did we think much," says Dr. Smith, "to consult the translators or commentators, Chaldee, Hebrew, Syrian, Greek, or Latin; no, nor the Spanish, French, Italian, or Dutch: neither did we disdain to revise that which we had done, and to bring back to the anvil that which we had hammered: but having and using as great helps as were needful, and fearing no reproach for slowness, nor coveting praise for expedition, we have at the length, through the good hand of the Lord upon us, brought the work to that pass that you see."

It need scarcely be said that the chief aim of the translators, in preparing the national version of the Bible, now commonly called the authorised version, was to express without addition or diminution the exact meaning of the original Scriptures. They adhered with great strictness to the diction of the Bishops' Bible; but wherever the truth of the original, or what they held to be so, required any change of expression, they made alterations according to their instruction. And this scrupulous regard to "the truth of the original" exposed their work, when first published, to not a few unfavourable comments. "The English translation of the Bible," said Selden, "is the best translation in the world, and renders the sense of the original best. But the Bible is rather translated into English words than into English phrases. . . This is well enough so long as scholars have to do with it, but when it comes among the common people, Lord, what gear do they make of it."[1] Notwithstanding what was said by Selden, however, the framers of the authorised version were not unmindful of literary grace in their translation. They changed many expressions and phrases in the Bishops' Bible, from regard to sound as well as to sense. Indeed, according to the revision committee of 1881, they went too far in this direction. They gave to Greek and Hebrew words a diversity of render-

---

[1] Gear. In some editions of Table Talk printed *jeer*.

ings, in order to please the ear, and prevent a too frequent recurrence of the same sound. And they were sensible that in so doing their procedure was open to cavil and criticism: for they took occasion in their preface to vindicate their conduct in that particular. "Another thing," said their apologist, Dr. Smith, "we think good to admonish thee of, gentle Reader, that we have not tied ourselves to an uniformity of phrasing, or to an identity of words, as some peradventure would wish we had done. Truly, that we might not vary from the sense of that which we had translated before . . . we were especially careful, and made a conscience, according to our duty. But that we should express the same notion in the same particular word, as, for example, if we translate the Hebrew or Greek word once by *purpose*, never to call it *intent*; if one where *journeying*, never *travelling*; if one where *think*, never *suppose*:
. . . thus to mince the matter, we thought to savour more of curiosity than wisdom."

One thing for which the framers of the authorised version claimed to themselves special credit was their steering a middle course between Puritanism and Papistry. "We have on the one side," they said, "avoided the scrupulosity of the Puritans, who leave the old ecclesiastical words, and betake them to other, as where they put *washing* for *baptism*, and *congregation* instead of *church*; as also, on the other hand, we have shunned the obscurity of the Papists, in their *azymes, tunike, rational holocausts, pasche*, and a number of such like, whereof their late translation is full, and that of purpose to darken the sense, that since they must needs translate the Bible, yet by the language thereof it may be kept from being understood." Notwithstanding this disclaimer, critics have taken on themselves to say that the theological and ecclesiastical bias of the translators betrays itself in the authorised version. The Church of England was from the first prelatic in its constitution, and was in 1611 far more Calvinistic in its actual creed than it is supposed to be now; and it has accordingly been observed that Prelacy and Calvinism obtain in several passages of the authorised version a show of countenance which is scarcely warranted. The Calvinistic phrase, "such as should be saved," introduced by Tyndale and retained in the Geneva, Douay, and Bishops' Bible, appears in the authorised version at Acts ii. 47, where modern scholarship has substituted the expression, "those that were being saved." The prelatic word "bishopric," also, appears in Acts i. 20, where modern scholarship has substituted the more general term "office."

It was not all at once that the new national version of the Bible displaced previous translations. Although its title-page bore the statement that it was appointed to be read in Churches, it is not known where that appointment came from. "No evidence," says Dr. Westcott, "has yet been produced to show that the version was ever publicly sanctioned by Convocation, or by Parliament, or by the Privy Council, or by the King." It is believed that in many Churches the Bishops' Bible continued to be read for years after the publication of the King's version. Indeed, we can understand that, in those impecunious times of dear books, if a Church were supplied with a good copy of one version, neither the preacher nor the parish would care to be at the expense of providing a copy of any other translation. But "the printing of the Bishops' Bible was at once stayed when the new version was undertaken." It may be presumed, therefore, that churches unsupplied with Bibles were, after 1611, supplied with the new version. By the visitation articles of Laud, 1622, a copy of the "whole Bible of the largest volume and latest edition" was required to be placed in each of the Churches within the diocese (St. David's) of that prelate. On the promotion of Laud to the see of London, in 1628, a similar order was issued to the clergy under his new episcopacy. And in 1636, when he unwisely and unfortunately took in hand to direct the ecclesiastical affairs of Scotland, it was inserted in the obnoxious book of canons, that the Bible used in Church "shall be of the translation of King James." In the homes of the people, the Geneva version held its ground long after 1611. It is said that no fewer than thirteen editions of the Geneva version were issued from the press between 1611 and 1617. The conspicuous merits of the new version, however, gradually gained recognition. It was not only pronounced a more scholarly, but it was found to be a more readable, book than any other English translation of the Scriptures.

Surprise has often been expressed at the number of different readings found in ancient manuscripts of the Bible. That surprise will be lessened when we hear how many variations are to be found in the several editions of the authorised version of the Scriptures in English. In a printed book, of which proof sheets are read, examined, and corrected previous to publication, we should not expect one-tenth part of the errata that may appear in a manuscript copy of the same work. But so difficult is it to ensure absolute accuracy that there scarcely are, or at least till recently there scarcely were, any two editions of the authorised version of the Bible in English exactly alike. The two editions published in 1611 differed from each other considerably. A subsequent edition, 1613, is accredited with more than four hundred variations from the original; and in later issues the number of variations increased. "Some of these were very important, and others extremely ludicrous; so that, after a lapse of time, a careful correction of the current editions became indispensably necessary. This important task was first executed by Dr. Scattergood in the year 1683; but the latest and most complete revision was performed by Dr. Blayney, Oxford, in the year 1769. He collated the original edition of 1611; that of Bishop Lloyd, 1701; and two Cambridge editions; thoroughly revised the punctuation, examined and corrected the italics, added a translation of proper names, altered the summaries of the chapters and the running titles, corrected some errors in the chronology, and greatly increased the number of the marginal references."[1] To the Cambridge paragraph Bible, 1873, there is appended a catalogue of the variations from the text of the original authorised version, 1611, which are found in different modern editions, and so long is this catalogue that it occupies sixteen closely printed quarto pages.

The strange misprints that have been made in successive editions of the authorised version of the Bible form one of the

---

[1] Preface to Bagster's Hexapla.

most interesting chapters in the curiosities of literature. It is well known that in one of these editions, 1631, the seventh commandment was, by the omission of the word *not*, transformed from a prohibition into an injunction. For this oversight the printers were mulcted in a penalty of £300. But the 1631 edition of the Bible was not the only one in which a prank was played with *not*. In one of the early editions, 1613, St. Paul is made to say, 1 Cor. ii. 17, "In this that I declare unto you *I praise you* [instead of, I praise you *not*] that you come together, not for the better, but for the worse"; and in another edition, 1653, the same Apostle is made to say, 1 Cor. vi. 9, "Know ye not that the unrighteous *shall* (instead of *shall not*) inherit the kingdom of God." An Edinburgh edition, 1760, contains a new reading of Luke vi. 29, which may, at least, claim the credit of accordance with modern notions of self-protection, "Him that taketh away thy cloke *forbid* [instead of *forbid not*] to take thy coat also"; while another Scottish edition, published the following year, represents the Psalmist as praying, Ps. cxix. 35, "Make me *not* to go in the path of thy commandments." Among other misprints that have been noted in different editions are: "vinegar," for *vineyard;* "loves," for *loaves;* "ate her," for *hate her;* "oul," for *soul;* "eyes," for *ears;* "he killed," for *he is killed;* "deliver up their children to the *swine*," instead of *to the famine;* "covereth," for *converteth* a sinner; "liked," for *licked* his blood; "seventy" [instead of *seven*] years from her virginity; "let all tongues [instead of *all things*] be done decently."[1]

---

[1] Mombert, p. 363-4. Other instances will be found in the pages of Dr. Eadie; such as, in one of the editions, 1611, Lev. xvii. 14, "Ye shall *not* eat the blood of no manner of flesh"; and in the edition of 1613, Lev. xix. 10, "Thou shalt (not) glean thy vineyard." It is commonly alleged that the expression "strain *at* a gnat," Mat. xxiii. 24, was a misprint in the first edition for "strain *out* a gnat"; and that the misprint has been continued ever since, except in one edition published in 1754. The words "strain *out*" occur in Tyndale's Testament, the Great Bible, the two Geneva versions, 1557 and 1560, and the Bishops' Bible. In the edition, 1599, of the third Geneva version (Tomson's revision) quoted from in chapter iv. of this volume, the phrase is changed into "strain at." In other editions of Tomson's revision that I have examined, one of them being a copy of the

One misprint, over which a considerable commotion arose, was the substitution of "ye" for "we," in Acts vi. 3. This misprint found its way into many editions of the Bible that were issued from the press between 1638 and 1682. That was a period in which a strong democratic spirit displayed itself among Presbyterians in Scotland; and the misprint was supposed to be cherished by some of these Presbyterians as a declaration of the people's scriptural right not only to elect, but to ordain, their own ministers. One English parson, named Gipps, with more zeal than discretion, preached and published a sermon, in which Presbyterians, and particularly those of Scotland, were charged with being corrupters of the word of God, in countenancing this misprint, for the bearing it had on the question of Church government. The charge was both groundless and ridiculous; but it was reckoned at the time so grave, that the General Assembly, in 1698, thought proper to give it formal denial in a public and solemn declaration, which still stands in the printed Acts of the Church of Scotland. In this declaration, the Assembly "unanimously declare that as they allow no power in the people, but only in the pastors of the Church, to appoint or ordain Church officers, so they disclaim the above-named error of the press, if any such be found in any Bibles printed in this nation; and do declare that they do not own any other reading of that text to be according to the original but "look ye out among you seven men of honest report, full of the holy ghost and wisdom, whom *we* may appoint over this business."[1]

Geneva Bible printed the same year, 1599, by the same publishers, "strain out" is the rendering given. The most notoriously careless printer of Bibles that ever disgraced her craft was a Mrs. Anderson, who, from 1676 to 1711, enjoyed the exclusive right of printing Bibles in Scotland. "Nothing came from her press," writes her adversary, James Watson, "but the most illegible and incorrect Bibles and books that ever were printed in any one place in the world." As a specimen of her typography the following sentence may be quoted from one of her prints, 1705: "Whyshoulditbethoug tathingincredible w^{t}you, y^t God should raise the dead?" See *History of Bassandyne Bible*, by W. T. Dobson, p. 187-190.

[1] One early misprint that has to the present day continued to hold its place in the authorised version is *shamedfacedness* instead of "shamefastnesse," 1 Tim. ii. 9, as it was spelt in the first edition. See Bagster's Hexapla.

The authorised version of the Bible in English, as commonly printed at the present day, deviates in many places from the text of the original edition, 1611. The most notable of these deviations, whether "due to corrections of the edition of 1611, or to errors which have subsequently crept in," are indicated on the left hand margin of a well-known modern book, the Oxford Parallel Bible, 1885. They are mostly very trivial, but there are some that affect the meaning of Scripture considerably. Of what appear to be errata in the first edition, the following may be mentioned :—"Behold thou art taken *to*" (instead of *in*) "thy mischief," 2 Sam. xvi. 8 ; "They shall bury them in Tophet till there be no place *else* to bury," Jer. xix. 11 ; "She poured it" (instead of *poured it not*) "upon the ground," Ezek. xxiv. 7 ; "A *new* building" (instead of *a row of building*), Ezek. xlvi. 23 ; "Approved" (instead of *appointed*) "to death," 1 Cor. iv. 9 ; and "Helps *in* governments" (instead of *helps, governments*), 1 Cor. xii. 28.[1] In more than one place there is a whole clause awanting in the edition 1611, and these omissions, we cannot but think, must have been due also to the negligence of the printer. In the inventory of St. Paul's personal requirements, 2 Tim. iv. 13, the words *and the books* are omitted ; so that the only articles said to be solicited by the Apostle for his bodily and mental comfort were his cloak and parchments. A stranger and a more serious omission was made in Lev. xxvi. 40. That verse, as usually printed now, contains a promise of pardon and grace to the unfaithful children of Israel, if they would "confess *their iniquity, and* the

---

[1] The words "helps *in* governments" were regarded by George Gillespie as something worse than a misprint. He recognised in these words a covert attack on the constitution of the Church of Scotland. In his Assertion of the Government of that Church, 1641, he says : "We cannot enough admire how the authors of the new English translation were bold to turn it *helps in governments*, so to make one of two, and to elude our argument (for the office of ruling elder). The original hath them clearly distinguished. And I find some late editions of the English translation to have it as it is in the Greek, *helps, governments*. How this change hath been made in the English Bible, I know not," p. 40. Although Gillespie here speaks of the authorised version as "the new English translation," it is from that translation, and not from the Geneva Bible, that all quotations in his "Assertion" are taken.

iniquity of their fathers." In the edition of 1611, the words here italicised were left out; and the Lord was thus represented as making overtures of reconciliation to men if they would only acknowledge *their fathers'* transgressions!

Some curious amendments, too, have been made on the original punctuation of the authorised version. In Ps. xlii. 9, we are accustomed to read, "I will say unto God my rock, Why hast thou forgotten me." As originally punctuated, the Psalmist was made in this passage to assume rather more familiarity with his Maker, "I will say unto God, *My rock*, why hast thou," etc. As now printed, there is no comma after the word *pray*, in Luke xxii. 40, "Pray that ye enter not into temptation." According to this punctuation, our Lord sets before us in this precept what should be one of the subjects of our petitions at the throne of grace. But in the edition of 1611, there was a comma after the word *pray*, which made the exhortation mean, Have recourse to prayer as an exercise that will defend you against the wiles of your adversary.

Passing from these curiosities of printing to a consideration of the work by the King's translators in 1611, we remark that the National Bible and the Bishops' Bible were framed on similar lines. Both of these English versions of the Scriptures were conservative in their character. Neither of them was a radically new and original translation; but each of them was a revision and an amendment of the version in use in the Church of England at the date of their publication. The first of the instructions given to the translators in King James' reign was that "the ordinary Bible read in the Church, commonly called the Bishops' Bible, be followed, and as little altered as the truth of the original will permit." We have seen how observation No. 1 was attended to by the Bishops, let us see now how instruction No. 1 was carried out by the King's translators. And in pursuing this inquiry, we may take note, at the same time, of the way in which instruction No. 14 was obtempered, especially in regard to the Geneva version.[1] As the Rhemes

---

[1] Instruction 14. "These translations to be used when they agree better with the text than the Bishops' Bible:—Tyndale's, Coverdale's, Matthew's, Whitchurch's, Geneva."

Testament was not included in the list of translations to be perused, we may, likewise, examine whether there is any evidence of its having been unauthorisedly consulted and utilised.

For this purpose, we shall take, at random, two portions of Scripture, one from the New Testament and one from the Old, and see in how many places the King's translators have deviated from the text of the Bishops' Bible, and in how many of these deviations they have accepted the rendering given in the Geneva and Douay Bibles respectively.[1]

Let the passage for examination in the New Testament be the sermon on the mount, as recorded by St. Matthew. In this portion of Scripture, extending over three chapters and comprising more than a hundred verses, it will be found that there are not quite sixty cases of variation between the authorised and the bishops' renderings. In about a third of these cases, the Geneva translation has been adopted; in fully a fourth of them, the Rhemes version has been followed; and in the others, original amendments have been introduced. The most notable importations from the Geneva version are the following: v. 11, "falsely," after, "all manner of evil"; v. 13, "lost his savour," for, *become unsavoury;* v. 39, "smite thee on thy right cheek," for, *give thee a blow on thy right cheek;* vi. 7, "use not vain repetitions," for, *babble not much;* vi. 19, "lay not up for yourselves treasures, for, *hoard not up treasures;* vi. 29, "Solomon in all his glory," for, *Solomon in all his royalty.* Of distinctive renderings taken from the Rhemes Testament the following may be noted: v. 18, "one jot or one tittle shall in no wise pass from the law," for, *one jot or one tittle of the law shall not scape;* v. 25, "deliver thee to the officer," for, *deliver thee to the minister;* v. 47, "what do ye more than others," for, *what singular thing do ye;* vi. 2, "do not sound," for, *do not blow* a trumpet before you; vi. 26, "nor gather," for, *nor carry* into barns; vi. 30, "the grass of the field, which to-day is," for, *the grass of the field which though it stand to-day;*

---

[1] Very few, if any, renderings in the Old Testament were taken from the Douay Bible. The first volume of that Bible was published in 1609, and the second in 1610, while the King's translation was issued from the press in 1611.

vii. 25, "founded," for, *grounded* on a rock. Of the new renderings, by the King's translators, in the sermon on the mount, the most characteristic are: v. 21, "ye have heard that it was said *by* (instead of, *to*) them of old time"; v. 22, "angry with his brother without a cause," for, *angry unadvisedly;* v. 44, "despitefully use you," for, *hurt you;* vi. 2, "have glory of men," for, *be esteemed of men* (Bishops), *praised of men* (Geneva), *honoured of men* (Rhemes); vi. 24, "hold to the one," for, *lean to the one;* vi. 25, "take no thought," for, *be not careful;* vii. 4, "let me pull out the mote," for, *suffer me, I will cast out a mote;* v. 6, "trample them under their feet, and turn again and rend you," for, *tread them under their feet, and turn again, all to rent you.*[1]

The passage from the Old Testament that we shall name, in a similar hap-hazard way, for examination is the book of the prophecies of Micah, which contains seven chapters, and, like the sermon on the mount, comprises fully a hundred verses. In this portion of the Old Testament Scripture, there is a much

---

[1] The above remarks may leave on the reader's mind an impression that the authorised version of the New Testament contains very few, and only insignificant, amendments, on the Bishop's renderings. This is not the case, as the subjoined quotations, not laboriously selected, will help to show:

AUTHORISED VERSION.	BISHOPS' VERSION.	GENEVA VERSION.	RHEMES VERSION.
2 Cor. v. 13.—Whether we be besides ourselves it is to God: or whether we be sober it is for your cause.	2 Cor. v. 13.—If we be too fervent, to God are we too fervent: or if we keep measure, for your cause keep we measure.	2 Cor. v. 13.—Whether we be out of our wit, we are to God: or whether we be in our right mind we are unto you.	2 Cor. v. 13.—Whether we exceed in mind, to God: or whether we be sober, to you.
Gal. v. 4.—Christ is become of no effect unto you.	Gal. v. 4.—Christ is become but vain to you.	Gal. v. 4.—Ye are abolished from Christ.	Gal. v. 4.—You are evacuated from Christ.
Gal. vi. 1.—If a man be overtaken in a fault.	Gal. vi. 1.—If a man be prevented in any fault.	Gal. vi. 1.—If a man be fallen by occasion into any fault.	Gal. vi. 1.—If a man be pre-occupated in any fault.
Eph. vi. 4.—The nurture and admonition of the Lord.	Eph. vi. 4.—Instruction and information of the Lord.	Eph. vi. 4.—The instruction and information of the Lord.	Eph. vi. 4.—The discipline and correption of our Lord.
1 Tim. vi. 6.—Godliness with contentment is great gain.	1 Tim. vi. 6.—Godliness is great lucre if a man be content with what he hath.	1 Tim. vi. 6.—Godliness is great gain, if a man be content. with what he hath.	1 Tim. vi. 6.—Piety with sufficiency is great gain.
1 Tim. vi. 15.—The blessed and only Potentate.	1 Tim. vi. 15.—Blessed and Prince only.	1. Tim. vi. 15.—Blessed and Prince only.	1 Tim. vi. 15.—The blessed and only Mighty.
Heb. iv. 11.—Let us labour, therefore, to enter into that rest.	Heb. iv. 11.—Let us study, therefore, to enter into that rest.	Heb. iv. 11. Let us studie, therefore, to enter into that rest.	Heb. iv. 11.—Let us hasten, therefore, to enter into that rest.
Heb. vi. 6.—Put him to an open shame.	Heb. vi. 6.—Making a mocke of him.	Heb. vi. 6.—Make a mock of him.	Heb. vi. 6.—Making him a mockery.
2 Peter iii. 1.—I stir up your pure minds by way of remembrance.	2 Peter iii. 1.—I stir up and warn your pure minds.	2 Peter iii. 1.—I stir up and warn your pure minds.	2 Peter iii. 1.—I stir up by admonition your sincere mind.

greater amount of variation between the King's and the Bishops' renderings than there is in the portion of the New Testament that was examined. In the first five verses of the fourth chapter, which are in no way exceptional verses, the King's translators have made no fewer than thirty-six departures from the text they were directed to adhere to as closely as possible. And it is noteworthy that thirty out of these thirty-six variations are retrogressive, and conduct us back to the Geneva text. Of these the most important are the substitution of "exalted," *v.* 1, for "set up higher"; "flow," *v.* 1, for "press"; "nations," *v.* 2, for "people"; and "vine," *v.* 4, for "vineyard." The remaining six departures from the text of the Bishops' Bible we may assume to be original amendments; and that they were either corrections or improvements may be inferred from the fact that they have all been retained in the revised version of 1885. The most notable of these are "established," *v.* 1, instead of "prepared"; "pruning hooks," *v.* 3, instead of "scythes"; and the noun "war," *v.* 3, instead of the verbal expression "to fight." It would be tedious to enumerate all the changes made by the King's translators on the Bishops' version of the whole book of Micah. There is only one verse in the book that is absolutely identical in the two translations. That verse is the tenth of the third chapter—"They build up Zion with blood, and Jerusalem with iniquity." And although in the case of some verses, the difference between the King's and the Bishops' renderings is extremely slight, there are other cases in which the difference is very considerable; as the following examples will show:

AUTHORISED VERSION.	BISHOPS' VERSION.
Chap. iii. 6.—Night shall be unto you, that ye shall not have a vision, and it shall be dark unto you that ye shall not divine.	Chap. iii. 6.—Night shall be unto you for a vision, and darknesse shall be unto you for a divination.
Chap. v. 1.—Now gather thyself in troops, O daughter of troops.	Chap. v. 1.—Now shalt thou be robbed thyself, O thou robber's daughter.
Chap. v. 4.—They shall abide: for now shall he be great unto the ends of the earth.	Chap. v. 4.—When they be converted, he shall be magnified unto the farthest partes of the world.

On the other hand, while the King's translators, in departing from the text of the Bishops' Bible, did in many instances adopt and revive the Geneva renderings, they betrayed no conspicuous deference to the scholastic authority of the Puritan fathers. They made frequent and notable departures from the Geneva text as well as from the Bishops'. Indeed, while there are many passages in the prophecies of Micah that read almost the same in the Geneva and the King's translations, there are only nine verses that are exactly alike.

The outcome of our investigation, therefore, is that the King's translators, although in some parts adhering very closely to the text of the Bishops' Bible, have everywhere deviated from it more or less, and in some places widely; that a large number of these deviations, both in the Old and New Testament, are reversions to the text of the Geneva Bible; that, in the New Testament, a goodly number of them accord with the Rhemes renderings; and that a further goodly number of them in both the Old and New Testament are entitled to the credit of being original emendations.

In the instructions issued to the King's translators, it was not only declared that the Bishops' Bible was in a general way to be made the basis of the new version, but that its diction was to be " as little altered *as the truth of the original would permit.*". It was further intimated, that when any of the other English Protestant versions were used or followed, it should be "when they agreed better with the text than the Bishops' Bible."

It would appear, therefore, that the King's translators were required to adhere literally to the bishops' version, except when the translation in that version was not merely infelicitous or feeble but positively inaccurate or imperfect. And renderings were not to be borrowed or appropriated from other versions, unless these renderings were not only terser or happier, more sonorous or more rhythmical, but more accordant with the letter and spirit of the original Scripture than were the corresponding translations in the Bishops' Bible. Let us see, whether, in this matter, the King's translators adhered strictly to their instructions, or assumed a little more latitude than they were ostensibly allowed.

This question might be determined by considering instances

of change on the bishops' text that have already been adduced from the sermon on the mount, and from the prophecies of Micah. Many of these changes are obviously alterations for the sake of literary improvement. They give no new meaning to the Scriptures, but simply express the old meaning in another way. Let us investigate this matter afresh, however, and with that view let us turn to the 8th chapter of the Epistle to the Romans. In the last fourteen verses of that chapter, it will be found that the reading in the authorised version departs in forty-four instances from the words of the Bishops' Bible; and some of these departures are evidently made with a view to greater accuracy of translation. It really agrees "better" with the truth of the original (whether completely or not is another question) to say, in verse 26, "we know not what we should *pray for* as we ought," than, as in the Bishops' Bible, to say, "we know not what to *desire* as we ought." The phrases, "work together," *v.* 28; "freely give," *v.* 32; and, "are more than conquerors," *v.* 37, are plainly also more correct translations of the Greek Scripture (*sunergei, charisetai*, and *hypernikōmen*) than are the unsupplemented verbs *work, give*, and *overcome*, which are used in the Bishops' Bible. It is not only a more easily accepted doctrine, again, but a more faithful rendering of the word, that we find in the King's translation, *v.* 28, "all things work together for *good*," than appears in the Bishops' Bible, "all things work for the *best*, to them that love God."

But in other, and far more cases, the changes that were made by the King's translators on the bishops' rendering of Romans viii. 26-39, were introduced for the sake of good plain English, and pleasant cadence in reading. There was no difference of meaning occasioned by the substitution of "uttered" for *expressed*, *v.* 26; of "whom he did foreknow," for *those which he knew before, v.* 29; of "conformed to the image of his son," for "*like fashioned unto the shape of his son*, *v.* 29; of "he also," for "also he," *v.* 30; of "elect," for *chosen, v.* 33; or of "persuaded," for *sure*, *v.* 38. But it will be found that in these and other instances where verbal changes, not affecting the meaning of the passage, have been made on the Bishops' Bible by the King's translators, a sweeter, smoother, or statelier diction has been introduced into our English version of the "dearworth" book. And this has been no small gain. The English Bible is designed for public reading, and whatever makes it read more smoothly, and in a style of pathos or majesty more accordant with its subject matter, is a help to the reader, and a benefit to the hearer. The statements of the Bible, again, that bear on our conduct and comfort, on our sanctification and salvation, are meant to be remembered, so as to be present in our minds whenever temptations or afflictions come our way; and whatever choice or arrangement of words makes these statements of the Bible more striking or impressive, more pleasant to the ear or more fascinating to the imagination, makes them also more easily remembered, and more potent for good. It is not enough that our English Bible be a mathematically correct translation of the original Scriptures, word for word, and point for point; but it should, both in its literary charms and its divine revelations, be a wellspring of spiritual life in the broadest, as well as the highest, sense of the terms. We cannot be too grateful, therefore, that the framers of our authorised version were not only skilled in the "discernment of tongues," but were gifted with an ear for melody. "Who will not say," writes a famous Catholic dignitary, in words that have been often quoted, "that the uncommon beauty and marvellous English of the Protestant Bible is not one of the great strongholds of heresy in this country? It lives on the ear like a music that can never be forgotten, like the sound of church bells. Its felicities often seem to be things rather than words. It is part of the national mind, and the anchor of national seriousness."

It is scarcely worth while to enquire whether all the Geneva renderings that have been imported into the authorised version were adopted on the ground of their stricter fidelity to the original than were their counterparts in the Bishops' Bible, or whether some of them were appropriated on the ground of choicer diction. From what we have already seen, we may be quite confident that the King's translators would not scruple to borrow a phrase either from the Geneva Bible or from the

Great Bible, if, for any reason whatever, they found it advantageous to do so. In the 2nd chapter of St. John's first Epistle there are about fifty-two changes made by the King's translators on the Bishops' Bible. Assuming that every distinctive expression in the authorised version which we find in the Geneva and not in the Bishops' Bible was imported from the Geneva translation, there could not have been, out of these fifty-two changes, more than ten that were drawn from the people's favourite. And of these ten changes that may have been derived from that source, at least one-half are simply improved phrases, which present no difference of signification from those they displaced. For "sins of all the world," which appears in the Bishops' Bible, *v.* 2, we find in the Geneva, as well as in the authorised, version, "*sins of the whole world*"; for "verity," in the Bishops' Bible, *v.* 4, *truth;* for "cannot tell," *v.* 11, *knoweth not;* and for "babes," *v.* 12, *little children.* It will thus be seen, that wherever the King's translators found in the Geneva version a happier word or phrase than they found at the same place in the Bishops' Bible, they appropriated that word or phrase, to adorn and enrich their own translation.

Among Geneva renderings not found in the Bishops' Bible, but imported direct (with almost no change) from their original source into the authorised version, the following, in addition to others mentioned in former chapters, may be specified:

"Canst thou by searching find out God, canst thou find out the Almighty unto perfection," Job xi. 7; "Not judge after the sight of his eyes," Is. xi. 3; "The land shadowing with wings," Is. xviii. 1; "To whom is the arm of the Lord revealed," Is. liii. 1; "The Lord hath laid on him the iniquity of us all," Is. liii. 6; "He shall see of the travail of his soul," Is. liii. 11; "O, thou afflicted, tossed with tempest," Is. liv. 11; "The angel of his presence," Is. lxiii. 9; "The fountain of living waters," Jer. ii. 13; "Is there no balm in Gilead," Jer. viii. 22; "The joy and rejoicing of mine heart," Jer. xv. 16; "Because his compassions fail not," Lam. iii. 22; "It is good for us to be here," Luke ix. 33; "Men of like passions with you," Acts xiv. 15; "A disobedient and gainsaying people," Rom. x. 21; "We see through a glass darkly," 1 Cor. xiii. 12; "Our light affliction, which is but for a moment," 2 Cor. iv. 17; "We walk by faith, not by sight," 2 Cor. v. 7; "Ambassadors for Christ," 2 Cor. v. 20; "The love of Christ, which passeth knowledge," Eph. iii. 19; "The glorious gospel of the blessed God," 1 Tim. i. 11; "The eyes of him with whom we have to do," Heb. iv. 13; "A man subject to like passions as we are," Jas. v. 17.

Little esteemed as the Rhemes Testament is, either on scholastic or literary grounds, it has nevertheless helped, and in no small degree, to enrich the national Bible with living words. A familiar phrase in the authorised translation is "subverting your souls." It occurs in Acts xv. 24, "Forasmuch as we have heard that certain, which went out from us, have troubled you with words, *subverting your souls*, saying, Ye must be circumcised and keep the law." That phrase is an importation from the Rhemes Testament, and although it has no special power or beauty or aptness, it has the merit of being a great improvement on what it superseded. In the New Testament of Tyndale, in the Great Bible, in the Geneva Bible, and in the Bishops' Bible the verse reads: "We have heard that certain, which departed from us, have troubled you with words, and *cumbered your minds*."[1] Another oft-quoted expression in the authorised version, which appears also in the Rhemes Testament, is, "Thanked God and took courage," Acts xxviii. 15. In most of the earlier versions the rendering is *thanked God and waxed bold:* which describes a state of feeling somewhat different from *took courage*, and a state of feeling not so natural to the situation. A still more familiar and oftener quoted phrase, which has come to us from the Rhemes version is "the goodness and severity of God," Rom. xi. 22. Tyndale's words, in this version, are, "the kyndnes and rigourousnesse of God"; and that rendering is, strange to say, retained in all its hirsute barbarity by Coverdale in the Great Bible, and by the bishops in theirs. In the second Geneva version the phrase was recast and changed into *the bountifulness and severity of God*, which was an improvement certainly, but left room for further improvement in the way of smoothness and simplicity. Other phrases appropriated from the Rhemes Testament will be found in the following quotations: "a faithful saying and worthy of all acceptation," 1 Tim. i. 15; "to me to live is Christ, and to die is gain," Phil. i. 21; "the form of sound words," 2 Tim i. 13; "evil communications corrupt good manners," 1 Cor

---

[1] In Wyclif's version, the rendering is *turneden upsodoun your soulis*.

xv. 33; "speech contemptible," 2 Cor. x. 10; "giveth to all men liberally (*abundantly*, Rhemes), and upbraideth not," Jas. i. 5; "unction from the holy one," 1 John ii. 20; "perfected praise," Mat. xxi. 16; "one shall be taken, and the other left," Mat. xxiv. 40; "commendeth his love" (*charity*, Rhemes), Rom. v. 8; "as ye see the day approaching," Heb. x. 25; "the spirits of just men (*the just*, Rhemes) made perfect," Heb. xii. 23.[1] It will thus be seen that not a few of our household Bible words and phrases have come to us from a source that is not usually considered a well of English undefiled. All the more honour to the King's translators, that, in their search for the right word for the right place, they left no corner unexplored.

It may be said roughly that each successive version of the English Bible (barring the Rhemes-Douay version, which has characteristic merits and demerits of its own) was an improvement on the one of which it professed to be a revision. In version after version there are increased accuracy and increased felicity of expression to be found; and there are many clauses and sentences that, in their transition from one version to another, indicate growth and development at almost every stage.

In successive translations, the meaning of Scripture is in some verses presented to us in a series of different lights. For instance, in Prov. xi. 17, we are accustomed to read: "The merciful man doeth good to his own soul, but he that is cruel troubleth his own flesh." The proverb, however, does not bear this meaning in all the English versions of the Bible. By changing subject into predicate, and predicate into subject, in one or other or both clauses of the verse; and by transforming *kinsmen* into *own flesh*, the proverb comes before us in the Bibles of England, in no fewer than five forms, as will be seen from the following quotations:

---

[1] Another of the Rhemes renderings that the King's translators would have done well to adopt is Acts v. 30: "Jesus whom you did kill, hanging him upon a tree." Instead of that, the translation of Tyndale, continued in the Great Bible, the Geneva Bible, and the Bishops' Bible, was retained: "Whom ye *slew and hanged* on a tree."

"A merciful man doith wel to his soule : but he that is cruel casteth awei, zhe kynsmen."—*Wyclif.*

"He that hath a gentle liberall stomacke is mercifull : but whoso hurteth his negboure is a tyraunt."—*Coverdale.*

"He that is mercifull doeth himselfe a benefite : but whoso hurteth his neighbour is a tyrant."—*Great Bible and Bishops' Bible.*

"Hee that is mercifull rewardeth his owne soule : but he that troubleth his own flesh is cruel."—*Geneva Version.*

Turning to the New Testament, we find verses there, also, interpreted in four, five, or six different ways in the principal translations of the Bible. Reference has already been made to 1 Cor. xv. 34, which in the authorised version is rendered, "Awake to righteousness." And so is it in the first Geneva version 1557, and in the Bishops' Bible; but in Wyclif's Bible and the Douay Bible the verse reads, "Awake, ye just"; in Tyndale's Testament and the Great Bible, "Awake truely oute of slepe"; in Coverdale's Bible, "Awake righte up"; and in the Geneva Bible, 1560, "Awake to live righteously." It is by means of extracts, however, without comment that the diversity of meaning given to particular passages of Scripture in different translations will be best exhibited. The following are specimens of instances to this effect that might be adduced in considerable numbers :

JOB VI. 18.

"For the paths that they (my brethren) go in are crokid, they haist after vaine things and shall perish."—*Coverdale's Bible, Great Bible,* and similarly in *Douay Bible.*

"They (the rivers) depart from their way and course, yea they vanish and perish."—*Geneva Bible.*

"They (the rivers) depart from the course of their wonted channel to other places, they run in vain and perish."—*Bishops' Bible.*

"The paths of their (the rivers') way are turned aside, they go to nothing and perish."[1]—*Authorised Version.*

JOB XXXI. 35.

"Who zyueth an helpere to me, that Almyzti God here my desire? that he that demeth write a book."—*Wyclif.*

"Lo this is my cause. Let the Almightie geue me answere : and let him that is my contrary party sue me with a lybell."—*Coverdale.*

---

[1] "The caravans that travel by the way of them turn aside: They go up into the waste and perish."—*Revised Version.*

"Lo, this is my cause. In the which the Almyghty shall answere for me, though he that is my contrary party hath wrytten a boke agaynst me."—*Great Bible.*

"Beholde my signe that the Almightie will witnesse for me: though mine adversarie should write a booke against me."—*Geneva Bible* and *Bishops' Bible.*

"Behold my desire is that the Almighty would answer me, and that mine adversary had written a book."[1]—*Authorised Version.*

JOB XXXVI. 33.

"He shal heren heringe in gastnesse of his vois, and the soun goende out of the mouth of hym."—*Wyclif* (Hereford).

"He tellith of it to his freend, that it is his possessioun: and that he may stie to it."—*Wyclif* (Purvey), *Douay Bible.*

"The rysinge up thereof sheweth he to his frendes, and to the catell."—*Coverdale* and *Great Bible.*

"His companion sheweth him thereof, and there is anger in rising up."—*Geneva Bible.*

"Which dashing upon the next cloudes, shewe tokens of wrath."—*Bishops' Bible.*

"The noise thereof sheweth concerning it, the cattle also concerning the vapour."[2]—*Authorised Version.*

ISAIAH XXVII. 8.

"In measure azens measure, whanne it schal be cast awei, he schal deme it : he bithouzte in his hard spirit, bi the day of hecte."—*Wyclif* (Purvey). Modernised in Douay Bible.

"Every man recompenseth with the measure that he receaveth : He museth upon his sore wynde, as upon the days of extreme heate."—*Coverdale.*

"In measure doth he smyte hym whyle he sendeth to him soch thingis whereby he commeth to his mynde agayne, for in the day that the East wind bloweth sore, it taketh away the fruits."—*Great Bible.*

"In measure in the branches thereof wilt thou contend with it, when he bloweth with his rough winde in the day of the Eastwynde."—*Geneva Bible.*

"Thou wilt punish it in the branches, yet not beyond measure : for in the day that the East wind bloweth sore it taketh away the fruits."—*Bishops' Bible.*

"In measure, when it shooteth forth, thou wilt debate with it : he stayeth his rough wind in the day of the east wind."[3]—*Authorised Version.*

---

[1] In the revised version, 1885, the passage, including prefatory exclamation, reads: "Oh that I had one to hear me! (Lo, here is my signature, let the Almighty answer me) ; And that I had the indictment which mine adversary hath written."

[2] "The noise thereof telleth concerning him,
The cattle also concerning (the storm) that cometh up."
—*Revised Version*, 1885.

[3] "In measure, when thou sendest her away, thou dost contend with her : he hath removed her with his rough blast in the day of the east wind."—*Revised Version.*

Acts ix. 31.

"And the chirch by alle judee and galilee and samarie hadde pees, and was edified, and walkid in the drede of the Lord, and was filled with comfort of the holi goost."—*Wyclif.* (Same rendering modernised in Coverdale's Bible and Rhemes Testament).

"Then had the congregacyons rest throwout all Jewry and Galilee and Samary, and were edified and walked in the fear of the Lord, and multiplied by the comfort of the holy ghost."—*Tyndale.* (Geneva and Bishops' Bible, except *churches* for *congregations*).

"Then had the Churches rest throughout all Judaea and Galilee, and Samaria, and were edified: and walking in the fear of the Lord, and in the comfort of the Holy Ghost were multiplied."—*Authorised Version.*

2 Peter ii. 13.

"Thei gessen delicis of defoulinge and of wemmen to be likynges of day."—*Wyclif.*

"Count it pleasure to live deliciously for a season."—*Tyndale, Coverdale, Great Bible, Geneva Bible, Bishops' Bible.*

"Esteeming for a pleasure the delights of a day."—*Rhemes Testament.*

"Count it pleasure to riot in the day time."—*Authorised Version.*

The foregoing extracts exhibit such amendments, by the King's translators, on previous versions of the English Bible, as affect the meaning and interpretation of Scripture. But we have seen that on the Bishops' Bible there were made, by these translators or revisers, many changes that were only literary improvements. Some of these literary improvements were the culmination of a long process of development. It may not occur to people that in the statement, Luke xxi. 14, "*Settle it,* therefore, in your hearts, not to meditate before what ye shall answer," there is anything that from a literary point of view is strikingly felicitous. It is merely a plain statement of a plain instruction. But in its simplicity and directness, it presents a great improvement on the diction of the earlier translations. Tyndale's rendering of the passage was, "*Let it stick, therefore, fast* in your hearts, not once to study before what ye shall answer." In the Great Bible, and also in the Bishops' Bible, the verse was made to read, "*Be at a sure point* in your hearts not to study before"; while, in 1560, the Geneva divines gave the precept a third form of expression,[1] "*Lay it by,* therefore, in your hearts, that ye premeditate not." In the impeachment of St. Paul, again, by the orator Tertullus, as recorded in the authorised version of Acts xxiv. 5, there is a very concise and graphic account of the alleged misdemeanour of the Apostle: "We have found this man a pestilent fellow, and a mover of sedition among all the Jews throughout the world, and a *ringleader* of the sect of the Nazarenes." The term *ringleader* is so forcible and expressive, and likewise so natural for any one to use in the circumstances, that we might suppose there never could have been any other word put for it in this part of the English Bible. But what is natural in expression seldom comes naturally to people. As a rule, it is the slow result of long whittling. And so, in one English version of the Bible after another, from Tyndale's to the Bishops', we find, instead of *ringleader*, "maintainer" or "chief maintainer" of the sect of the "Nazarites."[1] A very beautiful exclamation of our Lord's, which has served as a text for many a sermon, is, "Behold an Israelite indeed, in whom is no guile." Short and simple as that exclamation is in English, it passed through a great deal of rounding before it assumed the final and perfect form it now has in the authorised and revised versions. Tyndale's rendering of it was very prosaic: "Behold a right Israelite." Both the Geneva and the Rhemes divines had well nigh won for themselves the honour of perfecting the sentence; but the one, by an inharmonious order of words, "indeed an Israelite" for *an Israelite indeed*, and the other, by an overly emphasised statement, "an Israelite in *very* deed," precluded the rhythm they had almost attained. A most grateful relief, again, not unworthy of mention, that the King's translators have in many instances brought to the ears and minds of readers, is the alteration of verbs from the subjunctive to the indicative mood, or from the past-perfect to the past-imperfect tense. Both in the Bishops' and the Geneva Bible, for instance, we find it said, John xii. 12: "On the morrow, a great multitude that were come to the feast, when they heard that Jesus *should come* to Jerusalem,

---

[1] The distinguished Catholic scholar, Dr. Alexander Geddes, who died about the beginning of the present century, says of the authorised version of the Bible in English: "Every sentence, every word, every syllable, every letter and point, seem to have been weighed with the nicest exactitude, and expressed either in the text or margin with the greatest precision."

took branches of palm trees," etc. The reading of these, and such like forms of expression, strains the mind. But the strain is removed, and the verse is made clear and simple, when the words *should come* are changed, as they are in the national Bible, into *was coming*.

The following quotations will, without comment, illustrate further the progressive improvement in phraseology that characterises the successive versions of the Bible in English :

PROVERBS III. 17.

"The weies therof ben feire weis, and alle the paths therof ben pesible."—*Wyclif* (Purvey).

"Her wayes are pleasant wayes and all her paths are peaceable."—*Coverdale, Great Bible, Bishops' Bible.*

"Her wayes are wayes of pleasure, and all her paths prosperity."—*Geneva Bible.*

"Her ways are ways of pleasantness, and all her paths are peace."—*Authorised Version.*

PROVERBS XXVI. 7.

"Like as it is an unseemly thing to have legges and yet to halte, even so is a parable in the foole's mouth."—*Coverdale's Bible.*

"Like as in a lame man his legges are not equal, so is a parable in a fool's mouth."—*Great Bible, Bishops' Bible.*

"As they that lift up the legs of the lame, so is a parable in a foole's mouth."—*Geneva.*

"As a lame man hath fair legs in vain, so a parable is unseemly in the mouth of a fool."—*Douay Bible* (modern).

"The legs of the lame are not equal, so is a parable in the mouth of fools." [1]—*Authorised Version.*

ISAIAH IX. 5.

"A cloth meddlid with blood."—*Wyclif.*

"But a cote fyled with blood." [2]—*Coverdale.*

"Defying their garments with blood."—*Great Bible* and *Bishops' Bible.*

"With tumbling of garments in blood."—*Geneva Bible.*

"With . . . garments mingled with blood."—*Douay Bible* (modern version).

"With . . . garments rolled in blood."—*Authorised Version.*

---

[1] "The legs of the lame hang loose :
So is a parable in the mouth of fools."—*Revised Version.*

[2] The whole sentence in Coverdale's Bible differs widely from modern renderings : "Moreover all temerarious and sedicious power (yee where there is but a cote fyled with bloude) shalbe burnt and fede the fyre."

LUKE XIX. 42.

"If thou haddist knowen, thou schuldist wepe also, for in this day the thingis ben in pees to thee."—*Wyclif.*

"If thou haddest knowen those thinges which belonge unto thy peace, even at this thy tyme."—*Tyndale.*

"Yf thou knewest what were for thy peace. thou shuldest remember it euen in this present daye of thine."—*Coverdale.*

"If thou haddest knowen those thynges whyche belong unto thy peace, euen in this thy daie, thou woudeste take hede."—*Great Bible.*

"If thou haddest euen knowen, at the least in this thy day, those things which belong unto thy peace."—*Geneva Bible.*

"If thou haddest knowen those things which belong unto thy peace, euen in this thy day."—*Bishop's Bible.*

"If thou also hadst known, and that in this thy day, the things that pertain to thy peace."—*Rhemes Testament.*

"If thou hadst known, even thou, at least in this thy day, the things which belong unto thy peace."—*Authorised Version.*

ROMANS XIII. 12.

"The nyzt went bifor, but the dai hath nyzed."—*Wyclif.*

"The night is passed, the day is come nigh."—*Tyndale, Coverdale, Great Bible, Bishops' Bible.*

"The night hath come unto us, and the day is at hand."—*Geneva Testament,* 1557.

"The night is passed, and the day is at hand."—*Geneva Bible,* 1560, *Rhemes Testament.*

"The night is far spent, the day is at hand."—*Authorised Version.*

I PETER I. 8.

"Schuln haue joie and gladnesse that mai not be teeld out, and ze schuln be glorified."—*Wyclif.*

"Ye . . . rejoice with joy unspeakable and glorious."—*Tyndale, Great Bible, Geneva Bible, Bishops' Bible.*

"Ye rejoice also with unoutspeakable and glorious joye."—*Coverdale.*

"You rejoice with joy unspeakable and glorified."—*Rhemes Testament.*

"Ye rejoice with joy unspeakable and full of glory."—*Authorised Version:*

HEBREWS XIII. 8.

"Jhesus crist zistirdai, and to dai, he is also in to worldis."—*Wyclif.*

"Jesus Christ yesterdaye, and to daye, and the same continueth for ever."—*Tyndale, Coverdale, Great Bible.*

"Jesus Christ yesterday, and to day, the same also is for ever."—*Geneva Bible.*

"Jesus Christ yesterday, and to day, and the same for ever."—*Bishops' Bible.*

"Jesus Christ, the same yesterday, and to-day, and for ever."—*Authorised Version.*

These examples of successively amended renderings, so far as they go, make it plain that the authorised version of the

English Bible is, in respect of those particulars which specially make a translation of the Scriptures precious to the common reader, a very great improvement on all preceding versions. The language is clearer and choicer, more impressive and more capable of making itself remembered; and it may be assumed that the translation is at least quite as faithful and accurate as in any former version, if not more so. But the examples given fail to exhibit the full extent of the improvement made by the King's translators on the versions they were set to amend. The improvement is not here and there only, nor is it only very markedly in a few special points; but it is all over, and although for the most part faint it is still perceptible both to the judgment and the ear. And both from a literary and a spiritual point of view, there are few things more to be desired by a Christian community than a translation, as good as care and skill can make, of those holy Scriptures which are the guide and the solace of life and which make their readers wise unto salvation.

Not content with expressing, in general terms, their admiration of the authorised version of the Scriptures in English, some critics have set themselves to form a catalogue of its peculiar and particular excellences. In a sentence that probably cost him a great deal of study, Dr. Eadie says of the authorised version that :—" It has the fulness of the Bishops', without its frequent literalisms or its repeated supplements; it has the graceful vigour of the Geneva, the quiet grandeur of the Great Bible, the clearness of Tyndale's, the harmonies of Coverdale's, and the stately theological vocabulary of the Rhemes." There is too much judgment crowded here into one sentence; and the characterisation of the different versions is not very accurate. The basis of the authorised version, so far as the New Testament and the greater part of the historical portion of the Old Testament are concerned, is Tyndale's translation; and, so far as the rest of the Old Testament is concerned, the basis of the authorised version may be held to be the Great Bible. The phraseology of these old translations is accordingly, in a large degree, retained in the authorised version. In every chapter, we have distinctive expressions that were shaped by Tyndale and Coverdale. But the diction, as well as the renderings of these ancient worthies, has been much altered ; and in these alterations, the inspiration of Geneva and Rhemes as well as of the English Bishops of 1572 is clearly traceable. Rhythm and majesty, terseness and vigour, pathos and tenderness are extracted from all previous versions ; so that nearly every special feature of excellence in each of these versions is appropriated and utilised. Dr. Moulton says, that on the authorised version of the New Testament the Geneva and Rhemes translations have exercised far more influence than the Great Bible and the Bishops' Bible. This must mean that, in cases of different and distinctive renderings, the Geneva and the Rhemes versions were more followed than the home ones. But the fact remains that the Bishops' Bible, of which the authorised version is simply a revision, supplied verbatim four fifths, if not nine tenths, of the whole text in the King's translation ; and the Great Bible, of which the Bishops' Bible is a revision, supplied verbatim four-fifths, if not nine-tenths, of all the bishops' text.[1]

A considerable number of archaic words and forms of expression are to be found in the authorised version.[2] For the word *its*, the modern possessive case of the neuter personal pronoun, we find *his* used times without number ; as in Ex.

---

[1] Examining the chapter, Rom. x., that accidentally turns up on opening the testament, I find that that chapter in the authorised version contains 461 words, and of these only 50 are different from the text in the Bishops' Bible. In the Bishops' Bible the chapter contains 468 words, and only 51 of these are different from what are given in the Great Bible, 1539.

[2] In the original edition of the Authorised Bible, 1611, the word *its* did not occur once. In modern editions, it will be found in Lev. xxv. 5 :—"That which groweth of *its* own accord, etc." This originally read—" That which groweth of *it* own accord "; and the verse, as thus printed, is referred to by some grammarians as affording an instance in which " *hit* or *it* was sometimes used (as a possessive) in place of *his* (neuter) or *its*."—*Bain's Higher English Grammar*, p. 139. An example of *it* for *its* will be found in Gau's *Richt way*, p. 75, " of *it* aune natur."

At one time it was customary to use *his* as the sign of the possessive case, and in the first edition (and many subsequent editions) of the authorised version *Asa's heart*, 1 Kings xv. 14, and *Mordecai's matters*, Est. iii. 4, were printed "Asa his heart" and "Mordecai his matters." In the Geneva Bible (ed. 1580) we read, *Asas heart* and *Mordecais matters*.

xxxv. 11, " The tabernacle, *his* tent and *his* covering, *his* taches, *his* boards, *his* bars, *his* pillars, and *his* sockets"; Ps. i. 3, " Like a tree that bringeth forth *his* fruit in *his* season"; and 2 Sam. vi. 17, " They brought in the ark of the Lord, and set *it* in *his* place." The pronoun *either*, also, is used in some connections where *each* would now be reckoned the proper word; as in Lev. x. 1, where it is said that " Nadab and Abihu, the sons of Aaron, took *either* of them his censer"; and in 2 Chron. xviii. 9, where it is said that " the king of Israel and Jehosaphat king of Judah, sat *either* of them on his throne." The verb *be* is, in like manner, often used archaically in an indicative sense for "are"; and, from failing to apprehend this fact, people sometimes misinterpret the language of Scripture. The sentence, " Thy sins be forgiven thee," Mat. ix. 2, does not mean, as some readers of the Bible suppose, " let thy sins be forgiven," as if forgiveness were to follow the words of Jesus, but "thy sins are forgiven" even now. The curious word "all to," meaning completely or thoroughly, which occurs frequently in the earlier versions of the English Bible, has in one place been allowed to remain in the authorised version, " A certain woman cast a piece of millstone upon Abimelech's head, and *all to* brake his scull," Judges ix. 53. A few colloquialisms, too, which belong to a past age, still survive in our church Bibles; as, " They said, *Go to*, let us make brick," Gen. xi. 3; " With weeping shall they *go it up*," Is. xv. 5; " The calling of Assemblies, I *cannot away with*," Is. i. 13; " The thieves also *cast the same in his teeth*," Mat. xxvii. 44. Of words entirely, or nearly obsolete now, a considerable number may be found in the authorised version. For *chest* or *box* the word *ark* is frequently used, as it still is in the rural districts of Scotland; *ear* (verb) and *earing* (noun) occur more than once in the sense of *plough* and *ploughing;* *charger* is the stately term employed in some cases for *bowl* or *dish;* *withs* is, in one or two instances, made to do duty for *wands;* and the phrase *worse liking* stands in one place for *worse like* or *worse looking*.[1] Besides obsolete

---

[1] To these examples of obsoletisms may be added :—"parcel," for *a little part*, Gen. xxxiii. 19; "taches" for *buttons*, Ex. xxvi. 11; "neesing" for *sneezing*,

words," there are also in the authorised version of the Bible many familiar words used in an archaic sense. The word *carriage*, for instance, is again and again used not in the modern sense of *vehicles*, by which travellers are conveyed from place to place, but in the sense of *luggage*, or that which people carry with them in their journeys, 1 Sam. xvii. 22, Acts xxi. 15. The high-sounding term *artillery*, again, by which now-a-days is designated the heavy ordnance of an army, is, 1 Sam. xx. 40, applied to a sportman's or a soldier's personal equipment of bow and arrows. In one passage the word *road* is used for *raid* or *foray*: "David and his men went up and invaded the Geshurites, . . . and Achish said, Whither have ye made a *road* to-day," 1 Sam. xxvii. 8-10; in another passage *title* is used for *monument*: "What *title* is that that I see? . . . It is the sepulchre of the man of God," 2 Kings xxiii. 17;[1] and in more passages than one *prevent* is very oddly used in the sense

---

Job xli. 18; "ouches" for *sockets*, Ex. xxviii. 11; "sith" for *since*, Ezek. xxxv. 6; "taber" for *beat*, Nah. ii. 7; "fray" for *frighten*, Zech. i. 21; "ought" (o whit) for *aught* (a whit), Mat. v. 23; etc., etc.

Of obsolete forms of words, the following, quoted by Archbishop Trench (*English Past and Present*), may be mentioned:—"sod" for *seethed*, Gen. xxv. 29; "chode" for *chid*, Gen. xxxi. 36; "slang" for *slung*, 1 Sam. xvii. 49; "strake" for *struck*, Acts xxvii. 17; "ought" (in edition 1611) for *owed*, Luke vii. 41; "lift" for *lifted*, Luke xvi. 23.

An antiquated phrase in the authorised version of the New Testament is "on sleep" for *asleep*, Acts xiii. 36. This is a phrase of Coverdale's, which occurs frequently in his translation of the Old Testament; and in his translation of the New Testament, 2 Pet. iii. 4. It was introduced into Acts xiii. 36, by Coverdale, in the Great Bible, then passed on to the Bishops' Bible, after being set aside by the Geneva divines, and was subsequently adopted by the King's translators, 1611.

In the original edition, 1611, of the authorised version, there were many other archaisms, which have since been removed: e.g., "It came to pass in the six hundredth and *one* (first) year," Gen. viii. 13; "all manner (of) plague of leprosy," Lev. xiv. 54; "the child *neesed* (sneezed) seven times," 2 Kings iv. 35; "had *dedicate*," 2 Kings, xii. 18; "hast thou not poured me out as milk, and *cruddled* (curdled) me like cheese," Job. x. 10; "oh that thou wouldest *rent* (rend) the heavens," Is. lxiv. 1; "they *returned* (turned) not when they went," Ezek. i. 17.

[1] The Hebrew word here rendered *title* is in Jer. xxxi. 21 rendered *waymark*. In the Douay Bible the word *title* is used for *pillar* or *memorial*; Gen. xxviii. 18, 22, "This stone which I have set up for a *title*." (Lapis iste, quem erexi in titulum, Vulgate.)

of *precede*: "I *prevented* the dawning of the morning," Ps. cxix. 147. A strange use of *several*, in the sense of *separate*, occurs in 2 Kings xv. 5, "The Lord smote the king, so that he was a leper unto the day of his death, and dwelt in a *several* house." And so of Jehoram the wicked son of Jehoshaphat, who "died of sore diseases, and for whom his people made no burning like the burning of his fathers," the quaint and curious statement is made, 2 Chron. xxi. 20, "He reigned in Jerusalem eight years, and departed without being *desired*," that is, without being *regretted*.

Of other current words used in the authorised version of the Bible in an archaic sense,[1] the following may be mentioned:—"strakes" for *streaks*, "pilled white strakes in them," Gen. xxx. 37; "challenge," for *claim*, "which another challengeth to be his," Ex. xxii. 9; "tablet," for *a personal ornament*, Ex. xxxv. 22; "profane," for *polluted*, "a divorced woman or profane . . . shall he not take," Lev. xxi. 14; "nephews," for *grandsons*, Judges xii. 14, 1 Tim. v. 4; "eyed," for *envied*, "Saul eyed David," 1 Sam. xviii. 9 (Non rectis oculis Saul aspiciebat David, Vulgate); "avoided" for *withdrew*, "avoided out of his presence twice," 1 Sam. xviii. 11; "discovered" for *laid bare*, "the foundations of the world were discovered," 2 Sam. xxii. 16; for *disclosed*, "discover not a secret to another, Prov. xxv. 9; "oracle," for *holy place*, "to set there the ark of the covenant," 1 Kings vi. 19"; "ranges" for *enclosures*, "have her forth without the ranges" (extra septa templi, Vulgate), 2 Kings xi. 15; "castles" for *encampments*, "these are their dwelling places throughout their castles," 1 Chron. vi. 54 (vicos, Vulgate : palatia, Zurich 1564; towns, Geneva); "perfected," for *finished*, "the house of the Lord was perfected," 2 Chron. viii. 16 (was all prepared, Coverdale; was perfite, Geneva); "wealth" for *weal* or *welfare*, "seeking the wealth of his people," Esth. x. 3; "Let no man seek his own, but every man another's wealth," 1 Cor. x. 24; "vile," for *lightly esteemed*, "Behold, I am vile,' Job xl. 4 (contemptibilis, Zurich, 1564); for *foul*, "a poor man in vile raiment," James ii. 2 (sordida, Zurich, 1564); "room," for *place*, "Thou hast set my feet in a large room," Ps. xxxi. 8; "vagabond," for *homeless wanderer*, "Let his children be continually vagabonds," Ps. cix. 10; "quick," for *alive*, "they had swallowed us up quick," Ps. cxxiv. 3; "in continuance," for *after many days*, "which in continuance were fashioned," Ps. cxxxix. 16 (diebus multis, Zurich, 1564); "organs," for *pipes*, Ps. cl. 4, etc.; "prudent," for *supernaturally wise*, "the prophet, and the prudent, and the ancient," Is. iii. 2; "bravery," for *beauty*, "the bravery of their tinkling ornaments," Is. iii. 18; "renowned," for *have a name*, "the seed of evil doers shall never be renowned," Is. xiv. 20; "reckon," for

---

[1] There are several books in print that treat of this subject. They have not been consulted by me, but the reader who desires to investigate this subject further will probably find in them a more interesting as well as a much longer list of Bible archaisms than is here given.

reason with one's self, "I reckoned till morning," Is. xxxviii. 13; "confirm" for *strengthen,* "confirm the feeble knees," Is. xxxv. 3; "converted for *turned,* "the abundance of the sea shall be converted unto thee," Is. lx. 5; "Zion shall be redeemed with judgment, and her converts with righteousness," Is. i. 27; "equal" for *just* (well weighed), "Is not my way equal? are not your ways unequal," Ezek. xviii. 25; for *of the same age,* "profited . . . above many mine equals," Gal. i. 14; "worthies"¹ for *braves,* Nah. ii. 5; "secure" for *free from care,* "we will persuade him, and secure² you," Mat. xxviii. 14; "by and by" for *immediately,* "give me by and by in a charger the head of John the Baptist," Mark vi. 25; "cousin" for *kinsman,* "thy cousin Elizabeth," Luke i. 36; "allow" for *praise,* "ye allow³ the deeds of your fathers," Luke xi. 48; "worship" for *honour,* "then shalt thou have worship in the presence of them," Luke xiv. 16; "occupy" for *trade* or *traffic,* "occupy till I come," Luke xix. 13; "passion" for *suffering,* "after his passion," Acts i. 3; "proper" for *one's own,* "called in their proper tongue, Aceldama," Acts i. 19; "lively" for *living,* "lively oracles," Acts vii. 38; "lewdness" for *villainy,* "a matter of wrong or wicked lewdness," Acts xviii. 14; "entreat" for *treat,* "Julius courteously entreated Paul," Acts xxvii. 3; "let" for *hindered,* "was let hitherto," Rom. i. 13; "convenient" for *becoming,* "things which are not convenient," Rom. i. 28; "revenger" for *avenger,* "a revenger to execute wrath," Rom. xiii. 4; "secondarily" for *secondly,* "first Apostles, secondarily Prophets," 1 Cor. xii. 28; "offend" for *stumble,* "if meat make my brother to offend," 1 Cor. viii. 13; "tables" for *tablets to write on,* "not in tables of stone but in fleshy tables of the heart, 2 Cor. iii. 3;" "experiment" for *proof,* "the experiment of this ministration," 2 Cor. ix. 13; "sometime" and "sometimes" for *formerly,* "ye who sometimes were far off are made nigh," Eph. ii. 13; "record" for *witness,* "God is my record," Phil. i. 8; "broided" for *braided,* "not with broided hair," 1 Tim. ii. 9;⁴ "profit" for *progress,* "that thy profiting may appear," 1 Tim. iv. 15; "heady for *headstrong,* 2 Tim. iii. 4; "dressed" for *cultivated,* "bringeth forth herbs meet for those by whom it is dressed," Heb. vi. 7; "conversation" for *conduct,* "Let your conversation be without covetousness," Heb. xiii. 5; "admiration" for *wonder,* "I saw the woman drunken with the blood of the saints, . . . and when I saw her I wondered with great admiration," Rev. xvii. 6; "delicacies" for *wantonness,* Rev. xviii. 3.

It is not necessary to say much about the headings of chapters, and the marginal references, that appeared in the

---

¹ A better example of "worthies" in the sense of *braves* occurs in Coverdale's translation of the Bible:—"Of the Gaddites resorted there unto Dauid to the castell in the wyldernesse mightie Worthies and men of armes, which handled spears and swerdes, and had faces like lions, and were as swifte as the Roes upon the mountaynes," 1 Chron. xiii. (xii.) 8.

² Secure literally means free from care. An old author writes, "We care not to be safe, but to be secure."—*Dictionary.*

³ See note on p. 209.

⁴ Often printed "broidered," and not only in modern editions of the authorised translations, but in modern revisions of the Rhemes Testament, *e.g.,* Dublin, 1811.

King's translation, 1611. The headings were new. In the Bishops' Bible, the Geneva Bible, and the Great Bible, all the chapters were headed with a short table of contents; but the King's translators made out tables of their own. And these tables, which were drawn up in 1611, appear in many editions at the present day unaltered, save in some twelve instances.[1] The most notable of these few alterations is in the heading of Psalm cxlix. That heading in modern editions reads as follows: "The prophet exhorteth to praise God for his love to the Church, and for that power which he hath given to the Church." To this was added, in the original edition, 1611, "*to rule the consciences of men.*" How much the headings in the authorised version differ from those in the Bishops' and Geneva Bibles, may be seen by a comparison of two, taken at random, from the Old and New Testaments respectively:

AUTHORISED VERSION. Cambridge. Large issue. 1854.	BISHOPS' BIBLE. Barker. 1584.	GENEVA BIBLE. Barker. 1580.
Jer. x.—1. The unequal comparison of God and idols. 17. The prophet exhorteth to flee from the calamity to come. 19. He lamenteth the spoil of the tabernacle by foolish pastors. 23. He maketh an humble supplication.	Jer. x.—1. The constellation of the starres are not to be feared. 5. Of the weakness of idols, and of the power of God. 21. Of euell Curates.	Jer. x.—1. The constellations of the starres are not to be feared. 5. The weaknesse of idols, and of the power of God. 21. Their pastours are become bruite beastes.
John xii.—1. Jesus excuseth Mary anointing his feet. 9. The people flock to see Lazarus. 10. The high priests consult to kill him. 12. Christ rideth into Jerusalem. 20. Greeks desire to see Jesus. 23. He foretelleth his death. 37. The Jews are generally blinded: 42. yet many chief rulers believe, but do not confess him: 44. therefore Jesus calleth earnestly for confession of faith.	John xii.—3. Marie anointeth Jesus feete. 37. Wherefore the Jewes beleeue not.	John xii.—7. Christ excuseth Maries fact. 13. The affection of some towards him, and the rage of others against him and Lazarus. 25. The commoditie of the crosse. 27. His prayer. 28. The answer of the Father. 32. His death and the fruits thereof. 36. He exhorteth to faith. 40. The blindness of some and the infirmities of others.

---

[1] The statement commonly made, even in works of high authority, that there are only twelve variations between our present headings of chapters and those of 1611, is misleading. The headings of chapters are not the same in all modern issues of the Bible. Those, for instance, in the edition that lies on my study table, published

In the original edition, 1611, of the authorised version, the number of marginal references to corresponding passages was, including those in the Apocrypha, about 9,000. Large as that number seems, it is but a small fraction of what the references now amount to, in some well edited Bibles. To some people, these references are doubtless helpful, but to thoughtful students of Scripture they are not of much expository value. Many of them obscure the meaning of the statements to which they are attached. It is different, however, with what are called the marginal notes. In the original edition, 1611, these notes were nearly as numerous as the marginal references. In the Old Testament there were 6,588 references and 6,637 notes; in the New Testament 1,517 references and 765 notes; in the Apocrypha 885 references and 1,017 notes. These notes are both brief and non-polemical; and, in these respects, they differ very markedly from the annotations in both Matthew's and the Geneva Bible. They indicate, for the most part, either alternative or more literal renderings. In some cases they specify different readings in the original text; and, in other cases, they give brief explanations of words or expressions. Not a few of the alternative renderings they present have been adopted, either verbatim or substantially, in the revised version of 1881-1885; as for instance, in the Old Testament: "They houghed an ox," instead of "digged down a wall," Gen. xlix. 6; "The way of the righteous is raised up as a causey" (made an high way, Rev. version), instead of "made plain," Prov. xv. 19; "The north wind bringeth forth rain," instead of "driveth away rain," Prov. xxv. 23; "He that hath an evil eye hasteth to be rich," instead of the converse, "He that hasteth to be rich hath an evil eye," Prov. xxviii. 22; "Wisdom is as good as an inheritance, yea better," instead of "Wisdom is good with an inheritance, and by it there is profit," Eccles. vii. 11; "Hast thou not heard how I have made it long ago, and formed it of ancient times," instead of "Hast thou not heard long ago, how

---

by Cowan & Co., Edinburgh, 1858, are much mutilated. It was published by royal authority, "*but so far as regards the text only.*" Hence the liberty taken with the ancient headings.

I have done it; and of ancient times, that I have formed it," Is. xxxvii. 26; "Saying of the soder, It is good," instead of "Saying, It is ready for the sodering," Is. xli. 7; and in the New Testament, "I praise you brethren, that you keep the traditions," instead of "keep the ordinances," 1 Cor. xi. 2; "Eateth and drinketh judgment," instead of "damnation" to himself, 1 Co. xi. 29; "Under the rudiments," instead of under the elements "of the world," Gal. iv. 3; "I am perplexed for you," instead of "I stand in doubt of you," Gal. iv. 20; "Fulfil," instead of, make full proof of, "thy ministry," 2 Tim. iv. 5; "The grace of God, that bringeth salvation to all men, hath appeared," instead of "The grace of God, that bringeth salvation, hath appeared to all men," Titus ii. 11; "The word preached did not profit them, because they were not united by faith to them that heard it," instead of "did not profit them, not being mixed with faith in them that heard it," Heb. iv. 2. Even in cases where they have not been adopted by the revisers of 1881-1885, the alternative renderings on the margin of the authorised version are worth noting. For "wring off his head," Lev. i. 15, the alternative rendering submitted on the margin is, "pinch off the head with the nail"; for "mincing as they go," Is. iii. 16, "tripping nicely"; for "bushes," Is. vii. 19, "commendable trees"; for "unicorns," Is. xxxiv. 7, "rhinocerots"; for "cast him out," John ix. 34, "excommunicated him"; for "false accusers," Titus ii. 3, "make-bates"; for "no place of repentance," Heb. xii. 17, "no way to change his mind." Delightfully quaint and amusingly odd, too, are some of the explanatory notes as well as the alternative renderings. The reader is told, for instance, that the Hebrew words translated, "the man whose hair is fallen off his head," Lev. xiii. 40, literally mean, "the man whose head is *pilled*"; that "idols," Deut. xxix. 17, would be more correctly designated "*dungy gods*"; that the phrase "a word fitly spoken," Prov. xxv. 11, is in the original, "a word *spoken upon his wheels*"; that what is rendered "tablets" in the authorised version, and "perfume boxes" in the revised version, literally signifies "*houses of the soul*." Simple and informatory, however, are the terms that most correctly describe the notes in general. In some cases they give the meaning of the names applied to persons or places: as, "Allonbachuth, the oak of weeping"; "Benoni, the son of my sorrow," Gen. xxxv. 8 and 18. In other cases, they explain expressions that are supposed to need explanation, as "the caul above the liver," Ex. xxix. 13 :—"It seemeth by anatomy and the Hebrew doctors to be the midriff." In other cases, still, they show the way in which the translators endeavoured, in idiomatic English, to convey the force and spirit of peculiar Greek and Hebrew phrases. Some of this last mentioned class of notes are particularly interesting in showing that consideration, judgment, taste, and literary art are all required for the effective translation of a book from an ancient language of primeval structure into a modern tongue. As samples of this class of notes, the following may be cited: "Thou mayest freely eat," Gen. ii. 16, "Hebrew, *Eating thou shalt eat*"; "thou shalt surely die," Gen. ii. 17, "Hebrew, *Dying thou shalt die*"; "the humble person," Job xxii. 29, "Hebrew, *Him that hath low eyes*"; "a very fruitful hill," Is. v. 1, "Hebrew, *The horn of the son of oil*"; "He feedeth on ashes," Is. xliv. 20, "Hebrew, *That which comes of a tree*"; "It is a very small thing that I should be judged of you, or of man's *judgment*," 1 Cor. iv. 3, "Greek, *Day*"; "in a voluntary humility," Col. ii. 18, "Greek, *Being a voluntary in humility*"!

THE INTER-NATIONAL BIBLE,

Commonly called the Revised Version.

New Testament, 1881.   Old Testament, 1885.

As was stated in last chapter, the National Bible did not on its appearance in 1611 supersede at once all earlier English versions of the Scriptures. Long after 1611 the Geneva version continued to be the household Bible of a large portion of the English people, and in some parts of England the Bishops' Bible retained its place in church. As recently as 1703 the bishop of Carlisle found that in several churches within his diocese the Bible used was "of the old translation." [1]

This tardiness on the part of the public to appreciate the new version, of 1611, was only what the translators expected or professed to expect. The tone of their preface was apologetic, as if the publication of such a book as theirs required defence, and as if a somewhat cold reception of their work were a foregone conclusion. It was, they said, the uniform fate of all novations, however well intended, to meet with opposition. "Zeal to promote the common good, whether it be by devising anything ourselves, or revising that which hath been laboured by others, deserveth certainly much respect and esteem, but findeth cold entertainment in the world. It is welcomed with suspicion instead of love, and with emulation instead of thanks; and if there be any hole left for cavil to enter (and cavil, if it do not find a hole, will make one), it is sure to be misconstrued,

---

[1] The phrase "of the old translation" would in Scotland have meant the Geneva version, but notwithstanding what has recently been said on the subject (Athenæum, December, 1888), it must in England have meant the bishops' revision of the Great Bible.

and in danger to be condemned. . . . Whosoever attempteth anything for the public (especially if it pertain to religion and clearing of the word of God), the same setteth himself upon a stage to be gloated upon by every evil eye ; yea, he casteth himself headlong upon spikes, to be gored by every sharp tongue. For he that meddleth with men's religion in any part meddleth with their custom, nay, with their freehold ; and though they find no content in that which they have, yet they cannot abide to hear of altering." The augury implied in these remarks was not unverified. Hostile criticism of the new translation was soon heard ; and, along with a daily increasing measure of appreciation, there has down to the present time been a constantly swelling murmur of dissatisfaction.

The first person of note to raise his voice against the new version was Hugh Broughton, one of the most learned Hebraists of his age, but a man of overweening spirit, whose conceit made him intolerable and impracticable. No translation of the Bible pleased him, and his own translations pleased nobody but himself.[1] " Our Bishops' Bible," he said, " might well give place to the Alcoran, pestered with lyes." And so, when the King's translation was issued, he wrote : " Tell his Majesty that I had rather be rent in pieces with wild horses than any such translation, by my consent, should be urged on poor churches." For obvious reasons, Mr. Broughton was not included in the list of translators submitted to, and approved by, James ; and the question may fairly be raised, whether his dissatisfaction with the new version was not partly due to mortification at

---

[1] He published translations of the prophecies of Daniel (1597) and Jeremiah (1608) ; also, of the books of Ecclesiastes (1609) and Job (1610). Specimens of his translation are given by Lewis : of which the following is one.

Job i. 4-6, " An age passeth, and an age cometh, though the truth abideth still. Both the sun ariseth and the sun goeth down, and to his place doth he breath, there he ariseth. He walketh unto the south, and compasseth unto the north : The wind whirleth, whirleth, walketh, and unto his circuits returneth the wind."

Broughton's rendering of Daniel iii. 5, bears such a resemblance to the authorised rendering that Lewis is led to make the remark (which, strange to say, is repeated by Dr. Westcott without correction) that the King's translators cannot have wholly neglected the vain-glorious man's labours. The King's translators, however, did not need to go to Broughton's Daniel for their rendering. It stood before their eyes in the Geneva Bible.

that exclusion. Even Selden, however, accorded to the King's translation only modified praise. He admitted it to be the best translation in the world, as rendering "the sense of the original best," but he complained of its un-English phrases which were much ridiculed by the common people.

In little more than thirty years after its first issue, a serious proposal was made for a revision of the national Bible. It was urged on Parliament in 1645. A distinguished member of the Westminster Assembly, in the course of a sermon preached that year before the House of Commons, entreated his hearers "to think of a review and survey of the translation of the Bible"; so that, by a revised translation, "exact, vigorous, and lively," the people of the three kingdoms might come to know the proper and genuine sense of the Scriptures. It is clear, therefore, that some of the Westminster divines did not suppose that the King's translation would continue for ever to be the only Bible appointed to be read in Churches. And so, in their directory for public worship, which was adopted by the General Assembly of the Church of Scotland in 1645, it is said, under the heading of public reading of the Scriptures :— " All the canonical books of the Old and New Testament shall be publicly read in the vulgar tongue, *out of the best allowed translation.*"

A bill was actually brought into the long Parliament, shortly before its dissolution in 1653, to appoint a committee to review and revise the "new translation," as the King's or authorised version was then termed. It was alleged that that translation had been "wronged by the prelates, or printers, or others"; and it was proposed that all the injuries so done to that translation, in malice or in ignorance, should be repaired by this committee, "before there be any further printing of the Bible." It was further alleged to be a common stumbling-block to the weak, and a subject of cavil for scoffers, that, in sermons preached and printed, people heard or found it said, " the original bears it better thus and thus." It was accordingly proposed that the committee appointed by Parliament should carefully consider all translations, annotations, and marginal readings that they knew of; and give their approbation to what, "after seriously looking up to the Lord for his gracious assistance in so weighty a work, and advising together amongst themselves, they should judge to be nearest to the text, and to the mind of the Lord." And that there might be security against the hasty adoption, and unadvised insertion, of fanciful and unfaithful renderings in the English Bible, it was proposed that another committee of three divines should be "appointed and authorised to be supervisors of what is so approved, and that what those (supervisors) should so approve, should be printed and published for the general edification and benefit of the whole nation, to be read both privately and in the public congregations."

The sudden dissolution of the long Parliament put an end to this scheme. It is evident, however, that the scheme was something more than a pedantic project of some whimsical layman's, which had no countenance either in the Church or country. It was fostered, if not devised, by some of the leading divines of the age. On the proposed committee of review and revision stood the names of Dr. John Owen and Dr. Ralph Cudworth; and on the proposed committee of supervision, the names of Dr. Thomas Goodwin and Mr. Joseph Caryl. On the committee of review there was the name of a Scotsman also, Mr. John Row, Professor of Hebrew at Aberdeen. This Mr. John was son of the more famous John of Carnock, but was one of the unstable zealots who in those days of ecclesiastical revolt deserted the Presbyterian Church of their fathers and adopted the principles of congregational independence. So ready was he to undertake the duties proposed for him in the bill brought into Parliament, that he had a programme of his committee's procedure, cut and dry upon paper. "For ye bettering of ye Inglish translation of ye Bible (first printed A.D. 1612) . . . five things are to be endeavoured," said Mr. John. These five things are, "a more proper, rational, and dexterous" division of chapters, verses and sentences; an amendment of " needless transposition of words or stories, pretending to Hypall or Synchyses"; the excision of all useless additions "that debase the wisdom of the spirit "; the reparation of "all sinful and needless detractions"; and the introduction of certain specified "mutations and changes." Under several of these heads, detailed explanations and instructions were given. The useless additions to be removed from the Bible were, all the apocryphal writings; all popish prints, plates, and pictures; all prefixes of *saint* to evangelists and apostles; and all spurious subscriptions of particular epistles. Among the mutations and changes recommended, were, the printing of God's names and titles in capital letters; magisterial correction of all misprints; an "idiomatization" of English words not understood in Scotland; a substitution of English for Hebrew, Greek and Latin terms; and "something equivocal to Keri and Kethib!"

From 1653 to 1871, demands more or less loud continued to be made from time to time by divines and biblical scholars for a revision of the King's, or what we are more accustomed to call the authorised, version of the Scriptures. In 1659, "An essay toward the amendment of the last English translation of the Bible," was published by Dr. Robert Gell; and in 1702 a similar essay was published by "H. R., a minister of the Church of England." In the middle of the eighteenth century, revision was advocated by several men of note, including Lowth and Secker. Towards the end of the century the agitation was renewed. In 1788, a book was printed at Cambridge under the title of "Reasons for revising by authority our present version of the Bible." From the same University town were issued, in 1789, "Observations on the expediency of revising the present English version of the four Gospels and the Acts of the Apostles," by Professor John Symonds; and five years later there was published, by the same author, another set of observations on the expediency of retranslating the Epistles. In 1792, Archbishop Newcome gave the weight of his name and influence to the movement for revision, and cited high authorities of unquestioned orthodoxy, who were all in favour of the project. Among those that, in the present century advocated the desirability of a new translation of the Bible into English, it will suffice to name Dr. Marsh, Bishop of Peterborough (1828), Professor Scholefield (1832), Professor Selwyn (1856), Dr. Trench, Archbishop of Dublin (1858), Dr.

Ellicott, Bishop of Gloucester (1870), Dr. Lightfoot, Bishop of Durham, (1871). It must be admitted however, that men of equal or almost equal eminence, both in the first and second half of the present century, set themselves sternly against the project of revising the King's version. In 1819, an able vindication of the authorised translation of the Bible was published by the Rev. Henry John Todd. In 1820, Archbishop Lawrence took up his episcopal pen, and, on the grounds that it was impossible to restore the original text of the Hebrew Testament, and to clearly establish the text of the Greek Testament, contended that no revision of the English Bible could be satisfactory or beneficial. During the first decade of the present half century, when Selwyn and Trench were advocating revision, and holding forth the benefits that would result therefrom, Mr. Malan, Mr. Scrivener,[1] Dr. Cumming, and Dr. M'Caul were as vigorously enforcing the duty of "holding fast what we have."

And not only has there, from 1645, been a demand, more or less loud and widespread, for a revision of the King's version of the Bible, but not a few attempts have been made to furnish such a revision in whole or in part. As far back as 1639, a translation of the Pentateuch, Psalms, and Canticles was published by Dr. Henry Ainsworth, a member of the Brownist persuasion. So well thought of, too, in the time of the commonwealth was this work of Dr. Ainsworth's, that, in the bill before Parliament in 1653, his translation was specially commended to the favourable consideration of the proposed committee of review. But it does not appear to have been a really meritorious work. The translation was literal beyond all propriety, and the diction was even more archaic than that of the version it was meant to supersede. In the ninety-fifth

---

[1] In his "Supplement to the Authorised English Version of the New Testament," 1845, Mr. Scrivener writes :—"I hope it is no presumptuous belief, that the Providence of God took such care of His Church in the vital matter of maintaining His Word pure and uncorrupted, that He guided the minds of the first editors, in their selection of the authorities on which they rested." An argument of that kind, if accepted, would prove too much. It would prove that the Vulgate is the authentic Bible, which Catholics assert and Protestants deny.

Psalm the following renderings occur: "Let us *prevent* his face with confession." . . . "Whose the sea is, for he made it; and the dry land his hands have formed." . . . "Come let us bow down ourselves and *bend*." . . . "Forty years I was *irked* with that generation; and said, they are a people erring in heart."[1]

The catalogue of private translations of parts of the Scriptures that, since 1639, have been issued from the English press is very large. But, to ordinary readers, it is very uninteresting. Few of these translations have any literary or scholastic value. They are rarely found even on the shelf of the antiquary. They lie buried in the recesses of great libraries, where human eye seldom sees them, and where human hands more seldom open them. But to this rule, as to most others, there are exceptions. A book that is very deservedly held in high repute at the present day is Dr. Philip Doddridge's Family Expositor. No book in the English language more truly bears out its designation. It is about the briefest, clearest, and most complete commentary on the New Testament that the common English reader can find. On the margin is printed the text of the authorised version; and alongside of each verse, in the body of the page, there is a copious paraphrase, bringing out by circumlocution the full scope and meaning of the verse, as apprehended by Dr. Doddridge. Within this paraphrase are to be seen, here and there,—*rari nantes in gurgite vasto*—words printed in italics. These words, if not carefully noted, might be supposed to be the same as the words on the margin. But they are a little different, and they are Dr. Doddridge's own translation of the Testament, as appears from the following statement, in the preface to the first volume of the original edition: "I thought it might be some additional improvement of this work, and some entertainment to the more accurate reader, to give the text in a *new version:* which I have accordingly done from the *original*, with all the care I could. There are so few places

---

[1] Lewis: who remarks, apropos of this specimen of translation, "would any one now imagine that Ainsworth was an Englishman, and that he understood his own language?"

in which the general sense will appear different from our received translation, that some will perhaps think this an unnecessary trouble ; but I can by no means repent it, as it has given me an opportunity of searching more accurately into several beauties of expression which had before escaped me, and of making some alterations, which, though they may not be very material to the edification of men's souls, may yet in some degree do a further honour to Scripture ; raising some of these ornaments which were before depressed ; and sufficiently proving that several objections urged against it were entirely of an English growth." Dr. Doddridge, like many another person, has in this passage rather misjudged the work of his own hands. His translation has done very little literary honour to Scripture, and has revealed very few beauties that were formerly concealed. His renderings, as a rule, are clear and vigorous, but they want the smoothness and simplicity that give charm to the King's translation. He had a great gift, and by means of it he did great service to the church. But his gift was exposition, rather than translation : not tongues, but interpretation of tongues. In some cases he has anticipated, substantially, the revised renderings of 1881 ; as in Rom. i. 17, " the righteousness of God by faith is revealed to faith"; Rom. i. 18, "who restrain the truth in unrighteousness"; Phil. ii. 7, "emptied himself, taking the form of a servant"; Heb. ii. 16, " for truly he took not hold of the angels, but he took hold of the seed of Abraham"; 1 Pet. v. 3, " not assuming dominion over those who fall to your lot." In his translation, too, of the line from Menander, quoted by St. Paul, 1 Cor. xv. 33, he gives not only a good and forcible, but a rhythmically happy rendering of the original :

"Good manners are debauched by talk profane."

His translation, however, is very faulty. It abounds in Johnsonian words and inflated phrases. For the simple expression, "did eat their meat," Acts ii. 46, it has the long, connotative statement, *partook of their refreshment;* for "higher powers," Rom. xiii. 1, *superior authorities;* for "fitly framed together," Eph. ii. 21, *harmoniously cemented;* for "ambassador in bonds," Eph. vi. 20, *discharge my embassy in a chain;* for "sincere milk of the word," 1 Pet. ii. 2, *rational and unmingled milk*, etc., etc.

On the north as well as on the south side of the Tweed, attempts were made, from time to time, by ministers of scholastic proclivities, to provide the reading public with translations of the Bible, or parts of the Bible; in the hope of thereby representing the mind and meaning of the Spirit more faithfully and clearly than is done in the authorised version. The best as well as the best known of these, it will probably be admitted, is the literal translation of the "Apostolic Epistles" by Dr. James M'Knight of Edinburgh. Although first published in 1795, this work still finds appreciative readers; more, however, like Doddridge's "Expositor," on account of the accompanying commentary, than on account of the translation itself. As specimens of Dr. M'Knight's translation, the following may be submitted :

AUTHORISED VERSION.	M'KNIGHT'S TRANSLATION.	REVISED VERSION.
Gal. iii. 1.—O foolish Galatians, who hath bewitched you, that you should not obey the truth, before whose eyes Jesus Christ hath been evidently set forth crucified among you ?	Gal. iii. 1.—O *senseless* Galatians, who hath *deceived* you, *not to* obey the truth *to whom visibly* Jesus Christ *was* set forth crucified *for* you ?	Gal. iii. 1.—O foolish Galatians, who did bewitch you . . . before whose eyes Jesus Christ was openly set forth, crucified?
2 Cor. ii. 5.—But if any have caused grief, he hath not grieved me, but in part : that I may not overcharge you all.	2 Cor. ii. 5.—*Now, if a certain person hath grieved me,* he hath not grieved me, *except by a part of you,* that I may not *lay a load on* you all.	2 Cor. ii. 5.—But if any hath caused sorrow, he hath caused sorrow, not to me, but in part (that I press not too heavily) to you all.
Gal. iv. 18.—But it is good to be zealously affected always in a good thing, and not only when I am present with you.	Gal. iv. 18.—But it is *honourable* to be *ardently in love with* a good *man, at all times,* and not *merely* when I am present with you.	Gal. iv. 18.—But it is good to be zealously sought in a good matter at all times, and not only when I am present with you.
Eph. iv. 29.—Let no corrupt communication proceed out of your mouth, but that which is good to the use of edifying that it may minister grace unto the hearers.	Eph. iv. 29. — Let no *rotten speech come* out of your mouth : but *if any speech be* good *for* the use of *edification, speak it,* that it may minister *pleasure* to the hearers.	Eph. iv. 29.—Let no corrupt speech proceed out of your mouth, but such as is good for edifying as the need may be, that it may give grace to them that hear.
Eph. v. 4. — Neither filthiness, nor foolish talking, nor jesting, *which* are	Eph. v. 4.—*Also obscenity, and* foolish talking, *and double meanings* are	Eph. v. 4.—Nor filthiness, nor foolish talking or jesting, which are not be-

not convenient : but rather giving of thanks.	*things* not *proper*, but *thanksgiving* rather *is proper.*	fitting : but rather giving of thanks.
Eph. v. 31.—For this cause shall a man leave his father and mother, and shall be joined unto his wife, and they two shall be one flesh.	Eph. v. 31.—For this *reason* shall a man leave his father and mother, and shall be *glued to* his wife, and *the* two shall *become* one flesh.	Eph. v. 31.—For this cause shall a man leave his father and mother, and shall cleave to his wife : and the twain shall become one flesh.

From these specimens of Dr. M'Knight's translation, it is clear that its diction was northern and rugged, and had no beauty to make it desired for household reading. It claims, however, to be a *literal* translation ; and consequently, if it satisfies the demands of faithfulness and accuracy, it should not be complained of for want of smoothness and grace. In some of its distinctive renderings it has been followed by the revisers of 1881, but in others it has not.

Another private translation of the New Testament which, on account of local associations, may be here mentioned is that of the Rev. William Thomson of Ochiltree. It was published at Kilmarnock in 1816. Mr. Thomson was a vigorous evangelical preacher, an indefatigable pastor, and a man of great parochial renown. He was also a scholarly and studious man, who, in his quiet rural parish, gave "attendance to reading (as well as) to exhortation and to doctrine." For nearly twenty years he "employed his leisure time principally in studying, writing, and repeatedly transcribing his translation and notes." But his labours on the revision of the New Testament, although considerable, have not been highly lauded. One of the subscribers for his book was Thomas Carlyle, who was then sojourning at Annan, the town of Mr. Thomson's birth, and had become a vagrant from the paths of orthodoxy. Carlyle bitterly grudged his subscription, which was "one pound four," and wrote to a fellow-student that whatever might be the merit of Mr. Thomson's new renderings, his "style both of writing and thinking was dull and sluggish as the clay itself." And from other quarters a similar strain of criticism has been heard. In his *Bibliotheca Sacra*, Mr. Orme pronounces a very unfavourable judgment on the Ochiltree version. "The English idiom," he says, "is continually sacrificed to the Greek, and grammatical propriety is often violated, and the desire to render the translation very faithful and very clear has often made it obscure and incorrect. The author never departs from the received text in a single instance, so that for him Mill, and Wetstein, and Griesbach, have all laboured in vain." Notwithstanding these strictures, however, Mr. Thomson's volumes may be consulted with both entertainment and profit. His translation being "studiously made as literal as possible," is in some places dull and sluggish enough, but in other places it is terse and vigorous, and in many passages it shows the courage of peculiar convictions on questions of scholarship. It contains above two hundred "renderings that exhibit a meaning somewhat different from that which is expressed in the common version." Of these distinctive renderings, "a few," says the author, "have been adopted from the works of former translators: but the greater number are entirely new," and the propriety of them being vindicated in the notes, "they will," he adds, "be found so literal, so simple, and so consistent with the context that they will be readily understood and admitted." As samples of Mr. Thomson's sluggish literalism the following renderings may be cited : "The disciples having taken him by night, let him down over the wall, *having suspended him* in a basket," Acts ix. 25 ; "Ye who are wives be obedient to your *appropriate* husbands," Col. iii. 18 ; "Speak thou the things which become sound doctrine, that aged men may be vigilant . . . . *healthy by the faith*, by the love, by the patience : that aged women in like manner be *sacredly decent in deportment*," Titus ii. 1-3 ; "Reject younger widows : for when they have waxed wanton to a disregard of Christ, they desire to marry : . . . . and at the same time they learn also to be idle, ... and not only idle, but also tatlers . . . . speaking things that are *not proper*," 1 Timothy, v. 11-13 ; "The overseer (bishop) ought to be blameless, the husband of one wife . . . . *decent*, hospitable . . . . not a *tippler* . . . . not a pursuer of dishonourable gain," 1 Tim. iii. 2-3 ; "Deacons in the same way ought to be *respectable*, not double-tongued." As happier specimens of Mr. Thomson's translation, showing how clearly and vigorously, if not tersely, he sometimes rendered the original, the following passages may also be quoted : " If any one wrestle, he is not crowned, unless he wrestle *according to the rules,*" 2 Tim. ii. 5 ; "If he hath wronged thee in any thing or oweth any thing, *charge that to me,*" Philemon 18 ; " Faith is a *realising* of things hoped for, a *conviction* of things not seen," Heb. xi. 1 ; " Who have received the law *as ordinances* of angels, and have not kept it," Acts vii. 53. In not a few passages Mr. Thomson has anticipated the renderings of the revised version, 1881 ; as for instance, in Gal. vi. 11, " ye see with *how large letters* I have written to you"; in 1 Tim. i. 16, " that in me a *chief sinner* Jesus Christ might shew forth all long-suffering"; in 1 Tim. vi. 10, " *a* root of all the evils is the love of money "; in Tit. ii. 11, " the grace of God, which *bringeth salvation to all men* "; and in Heb. vi. 5, " the powers of *the future age.*" One rendering of Mr. Thomson's that seems to deviate very far from the received translation will be found in Heb. ix. 1, where for " worldly sanctuary" *holy ornature* is substituted. This rendering, or one similar to it, *sacred furniture*, has had the countenance of several scholars of repute,[1] and it certainly, to an ordinary English reader, makes the passage have a clearer meaning. Another interesting rendering of Mr. Thomson's is Rom. viii. 33-34, " Who will bring a charge against the elect of God ? *will* God who justifieth ? Who is he that condemneth ? *Is it* Christ who died, yea rather who was raised again, who also intercedeth for us ?"

But although ever since 1645 there has been a clamour raised from time to time to have the received version of the Bible in English revised and corrected, and although many scholars 'have, in part, responded to that demand by issuing translations of special portions of Scripture, it was not till the year 1870 that steps were taken in earnest to have a thorough revision of the whole Bible instituted. The honour of being the first to take action in this matter is due to the convocation of the province of Canterbury. And the action taken by that convocation, in 1870, was not taken a day too soon. So many statements had been scattered abroad, on high authority, that

---

[1] See Bloomfield's Testament.

the received version of the Scriptures contains a large number of errors, both in text and translation ; and so customary had it become for preachers to tell their hearers that the true text or the true translation, in this and the other passage, is something altogether different from what common people found in their Bibles, that it became necessary for the Church to show her members plainly what the true Bible really is, and what is the total amount of change that modern scholarship alleges should be made on King James's translation. And now that a revised version of the whole Bible has been issued to the English speaking peoples a distinct gain has been secured. The public have before them what they are told is as faithful and correct a translation as present scholarship can give of what is held, on the authority of ancient manuscripts, to be the best authenticated texts in the original of both the Old and the New Testaments.

Not only did the proposal for a revision of the authorised translation of the Bible emanate from the Convocation of Canterbury, in 1870, but the work of revision was undertaken by that Convocation itself. A committee of its own members was nominated, "to undertake the work of revision, (with) . . . liberty to invite the co-operation of any eminent for scholarship, to whatever nation or religious body they might belong." This committee separated itself into two companies ; one for revision of the Old and the other for revision of the New Testament. To each company were added, by invitation, distinguished scholars from different churches in the United Kingdom.[1] In both companies Scotland was well represented, not only by ministers of the established Church, but by ministers of the non-established Churches. The Churches of America, also, were invited to form a committee of co-operation. And it was agreed that to this American committee, the English

---

[1] " It was in my account a serious breach of Church order that . . . a body of divines, professing to act under the authority of the Southern Convocation, should spontaneously associate with themselves ministers of various denominations, Baptists, Congregationalists, Wesleyan Methodists, Independents, and the like ; and especially that a successor of the Apostles should have presided over the deliberations of this assemblage of Separatists " ! Burgon, p. 505.

revisers should send confidentially their revision in its successive stages; that all suggestions from the American committee should be specially considered by the companies at home; that before publication of the revision the American committee should be furnished with copies of the translation in its final shape, and should be allowed to present, in an appendix, all the unadopted readings and renderings they had submitted to the English companies. On the other hand, the American revisers pledged themselves "to give their moral support to the authorised editions of the University presses, with a view to their freest circulation within the United States,[1] and not to issue a rival edition for a term of fourteen years."

Long as was the time expended on the production of the authorised version, that expended on the recent revision was still longer. In the month of June, 1870, the revisers commenced their labours. Their translation of the New Testament was completed in November, 1880,[2] and their translation of the Old Testament on the 20th June, 1884. The time devoted to the revision of the New Testament was thus ten years and a half; while that devoted to the revision of the Old Testament was about fourteen years. A session of four days each month, except August and September, was held by the New Testament company every year from the commencement till the close of their work. "The revision of the Old Testament was completed in 85 sessions, and it occupied 792 days. The greater part of the sessions were for ten days each, and each day the company usually sat for six hours."[3] And this statement does not indicate anything like the total amount of time and toil expended on the revision. Each member of each company was expected to have the subject set down for discussion at each session carefully studied beforehand in private.

There perhaps never was such a demand for any book as there was for the revised version of the New Testament, in

---

[1] Mombert's English Versions, p. 454.
[2] Published on 17th May, 1881.
[3] Preface to revised version of Old Testament.

1881. Early in the spring of that year it was announced that the long expected volume would be issued on the 17th May. It was near the 17th June before some of the earliest applicants, in Scotland at least, could be supplied with a copy of the edition that was most coveted.[1] The demand for the revised version of the Old Testament, in 1885, was not so urgent; partly, it may be presumed, because the Old Testament has not so many readers as the New; and partly, because the revised version of the New Testament, after satiating curiosity, failed to kindle popular enthusiasm.

The revised version of the Bible is, in the strictest sense of the terms, *only a revision.* It is based on the authorised version, 1611; as that was based on the Bishops' Bible, 1572; and as the Bishops' Bible, in its turn, was based on the Great Bible, 1540; and the Great Bible on Tyndale's and Coverdale's translations. In what are termed the "fundamental resolutions," adopted by the convocation of Canterbury, in May, 1870, it was declared that a new translation of the Bible was not contemplated, and that no alteration was proposed to be made on the language of the authorised version, "except where, in the judgment of the most competent scholars, such change is necessary."

The revision embraced both a revision of the text in the original languages and a revision of the translation, besides a revision of " the headings of chapters, pages, paragraphs, italics, and punctuation."

It cannot be said that the revisers were rash in making changes on the text that was presumed to underlie the authorised version. They resolved " to introduce as few alterations (of that kind) as possible, consistently with faithfulness"; and, although changes on the text might, on the first review, be carried by a majority of votes, they were not, in the final

---

[1] Of the many impatient and disappointed applicants for the best edition the writer of this volume had the misfortune to be one, and in reply to what may possibly have been a somewhat petulant letter he was, on the 31st May, informed by the publishers that the edition he was in quest of had been issued as advertised, but the demand for it was so great "that all the morocco binders in London could not have succeeded in keeping up the supply."

revision, to be retained, unless "two thirds of those present approved the same." And in determining questions of reading, they proceeded on the principle "That the text to be adopted be that for which the evidence is decidedly preponderating; and that when the text so adopted differs from that from which the authorised version was made, the alteration be indicated in the margin." The revisers of the New Testament found it impracticable to carry out the second part of this resolution. The English reader is, therefore, not shewn on the margin the extent of textual change made on the New Testament by the revisers. He sees, here and there, "some authorities" or "many authorities," read so and so; but these marginal notes do not represent the tenth part of the changes made on the text. It is stated, however, in the revisers' preface, that a better mode of giving publicity to these changes has been found. Instead of indicating them on the margin of the English Testament, it has been thought preferable to "introduce them into a continuous Greek text, and to set at the foot of each page the readings which they displace." This continuous Greek text of the revised version of the English Testament, with displaced readings, has now been published in several forms, so that we can with very little trouble ascertain the extent to which the revisers have really departed from the presumed text of the authorised version. The author of this volume has had the curiosity to count the number of displaced readings so indicated,[1] and the following table exhibits the result of his investigation. Each displacement is counted *one*, whether it comprises one word or several words.

Textual variations in revised and authorised versions of New Testament :

In Gospel by St. Matthew, - 425	In Epistle to the Galatians, -	49
,, ,, ,, Mark, - - 614	,, Epistle to the Ephesians, -	80
,, ,, ,, Luke, - - 799	,, ,, ,, Philippians, -	49
,, ,, ,, John, - - 503	,, ,, ,, Colossians, -	60
,, Acts of the Apostles, - 725	,, 1st Epistle to the Thessalonians	47
,, Epistle to the Romans, - 160.	,, 2nd ,, ,, ,,	25
,, 1st Epistle to the Corinthians, 246	,, 1st Epistle to Timothy, -	47
,, 2nd ,, ,, ,, 137	,, 2nd Epistle to Timothy, -	31

[1] In the Parallel New Testament, Greek and English. Oxford, 1882.

In Epistle to Titus,	· ·	20
,, ,, ,, Philemon, ·	·	13
,, Epistle to the Hebrews,	·	131
,, the Epistle of James, ·	·	59
,, 1st Epistle of Peter, ·	·	73
,, 2nd ,, ,, ,,	· ·	34
,, 1st Epistle of John,	· ·	51
In the 2nd Epistle of John,	·	11
,, the 3rd ,, ,,	·	10
,, the Epistle of Jude, ·	·	21
,, the Revelation of St. John,		582
Total in New Testament,[1]	·	5002

From this table, it will be seen that there are no fewer than 5000 readings in the Greek Text, "presumed to underlie the authorised version" of the New Testament that have been set aside and changed by the revisers of 1881. The amount of divergence caused by these changes is not so great, however, as might be supposed. A very large number of the readings noted as displacements scarcely deserve to be counted changes. Some of them do not affect the English version, either in sense or in sound, either in meaning or in form of expression. For instance, we read in the authorised version, Luke xiv. 15, "Blessed is he that shall eat bread in the kingdom of God"; and, in the revised version we find the same words. But there is a different reading in the Greek texts from which the two English versions have been derived. In the one Greek text there is *hos*, where in the other there is *hostis*. In other cases, the new reading is a particle equivalent to *and*, or *but*, or *now*. Sometimes it is the substitution of a personal pronoun for the noun to which it refers, as, Mark vii. 27, " *He*," instead of *Jesus*, "said unto her; let the children first be filled." Sometimes it is the substitution of a personal name for a title, or of one title for another, as Acts x. 48, " He commanded them to be baptized in the name of *Jesus Christ*," instead of, *in the name of the Lord*. Sometimes it is a trifling verbal change, which involves no difference of meaning, as in Luke xx. 28, "He be," for *he die*, "childless," or in Mark i. 27, "What is this? a new teaching?" for *what new teaching is this*. Sometimes it is only the transposition of two words or two clauses, as in Mark xi. 18, "The chief priests and the scribes," for *the scribes and the chief*

---

[1] "The traditional text has been departed from by them (the Revisers) nearly six thousand times—almost invariably for the worse." Burgon, Revision Revised, p. 107.

priests. Sometimes it is a transposition which can scarcely be indicated by the inelastic forms of English speech, as John i. 37, *hoi duo matheetai autou,* for *autou hoi duo matheetai;* or Mark xii. 17, "The things of Cæsar render to Cæsar," instead of *render the things of Cæsar to Cæsar.*

There are cases, however, in which a very slight change on the words, or even the letters, of the Greek text has made a great alteration on the meaning of a verse. In 2 Cor. vii. 12, there occur in the Greek text two words, which differ from each other in only one letter, *hēmou* and *humou*. But by the transposition of these words, the verse has been completely transformed —and transformed from plain sense to what is not so clear—by the revisers. Instead of reading, "that *our* care for *you* in the sight of God might appear to you," we are now bidden read, "that *your* earnest care for *us* might be made manifest unto *you* in the sight of God." It is quite possible, therefore, that although a large number of the new readings adopted in the revision of the New Testament are only insignificant variations of expression, there might still remain many that make serious changes on the text of Scripture. To ascertain roughly whether such is the case or not, let us take at random some particular Epistle, and examine the most notable of the new readings introduced there. The Epistle to the Galatians should, in respect of length, be suitable for this purpose. The revised version of it contains forty-nine new readings, and of these there are only five that by plain English readers would be considered of any importance. In these five cases certain words that appear in the authorised version are omitted in the revised ; and how little these omissions affect the teaching of Scripture will be seen by comparing the old and new readings in the subjoined parallel columns.

Authorised Version, 1611.	Revised Version, 1881.
Gal. iii. 1.—O foolish Galatians, who hath bewitched you, *that you should not obey the truth.*	Gal. iii. 1.—O foolish Galatians, who did bewitch you.
Gal. iii. 17.—The covenant that was confirmed before of God *in Christ* the law . . . cannot disannul.	Gal. iii. 17.—A covenant confirmed beforehand by God the law . . . doth not disannul.
Gal. v. 19.—The works of the flesh are manifest, which are these, *adultery,* fornication, uncleanness, lasciviousness.	Gal. v. 19.—The works of the flesh are manifest, which are these, fornication, uncleanness, lasciviousness.

Gal. v. 21.—Envyings, *murders*, drunkenness, revellings, and such like.

Gal. vi. 15.—For *in Christ Jesus* neither circumcision availeth any thing nor uncircumcision, but a new creature.

Gal. v. 21.—Envyings, drunkenness, revellings, and such like.

Gal. vi. 15.—For neither is circumcision anything, nor uncircumcision, but a new creature.

The ground on which changes were made by the revisers on the received text of the Greek Testament, was the weight of evidence from ancient manuscripts that these changes were reversions to the true original.[1] In the sixteenth century it was alleged by Catholics that the Vulgate was of higher authority than any Greek text of the New Testament that was then known to be in existence. The question may be asked, therefore, if in the textual changes adopted by the revisers, in 1881, there is any considerable return to the readings in the Vulgate. There certainly are not a few cases of such reversion. In the

---

[1] Some biblical scholars deny that the new readings adopted by the revisers are supported by the authority of the most trustworthy manuscripts. The following extracts from Dean Burgon's work on *The Revision Revised*, 1883, will shew what these objectors have to say on the subject :—

"The most learned of our living prelates (Wordsworth of Lincoln), says it is well known that there are two opposite schools of biblical criticism among us, with very different opinions as to the comparative value of our manuscripts of the New Testament." P. 502.

"Singular to relate, the first, second, fourth, and fifth of these codices, but especially the codex Vaticanus and the codex Sinaiticus, have within the last twenty years established a tyrannical ascendancy over the imagination of the critics, which can only be fitly spoken of as a blind superstition." P. 11.

"How it came about that . . . the revisers of 1881 should have deliberately gone back to those vile fabrications, from which the good providence of God preserved Erasmus and Stunica, Stephens and Beza, and the Elzevirs, three centuries ago, it is useless to enquire." P. 238.

"Just five days before [the appearance of the revised version], under the editorship of Drs. Westcott and Hort, revisionists themselves, had appeared the most extravagant text which has seen the light since the invention of printing. No secret was made of the fact that, under pledges of the strictest secrecy, a copy of this wild performance, marked 'confidential,' had been entrusted to every member of the revising body ; and it has since transpired that Dr. Hort advocated his own peculiar views in the Jerusalem Chamber with so much volubility, eagerness, pertinacity, and plausibility, that in the end, notwithstanding the warnings, remonstrances, and entreaties of Dr. Scrivener, his counsel prevailed ; and the utter shipwreck of the revised version has been, as might have been confidently predicted, the disastrous consequence. Dr. Hort is calculated to have *talked for three years* out of the ten." P. 365.

Strong language like the above refutes itself, and shews on what side sound judgment may be looked for.

gospel by St. Matthew the revisers have made 425 changes on the received Greek text. Only twenty-six of these, however, are likely to strike the cursory reader as of much consequence. And even these are not of consequence, in the sense of altering the Evangelist's meaning; but of consequence only in having caused changes of notable words or whole clauses, and not merely of particles, in the English Testament. In nineteen of these twenty-six departures from the old *textus receptus* the reading in the Vulgate is revived. The doxology for instance is omitted in vi. 13; entire clauses are left out in xv. 8, xx. 7, xx. 22-23, xxiii. 19, and xxviii. 9; and in xix. 17 the question, "Why callest thou me good?" is transformed into, "Why askest thou me concerning that which is good?"

In St. John's gospel, again, the revisers have made 487 changes on the Greek text that is believed to have formed the basis of the King's translation. Only thirteen of these are in any way notable, and seven of the thirteen are reversions to the Vulgate. Both in the Rhemes and the International versions the clauses italicised in the following quotations are omitted: v. 16, "And therefore did the Jews persecute Jesus, *and sought to slay him*"; viii. 9, "And they which heard it, *being convicted by their own conscience*, went out one by one"; viii. 59, "Jesus hid himself, and went out of the temple, *going through the midst of them, and so passed by*.

To indicate a little more fully, however, the amount and nature of the changes introduced into the English Testament by the revisers, through the adoption of a different Greek text from what was received in 1611, a few verses may here be quoted from other parts of the book. Those quoted in the first table give readings in the revised version that do not accord with the Vulgate, and those in the second table readings that appear in the Vulgate also.

TABLE I.

Readings in the revised version that do not accord with Vulgate.

Revised Version, 1881.	Authorised Version, 1611.
Mat. xi. 19.—Wisdom is justified by her works.	Mat. xi. 19.—Wisdom is justified of her children.

Luke xxii. 64.—And they blindfolded him, and asked him saying, Prophesy: who is he that struck thee?

Luke xxiii. 15.—Nor yet Herod: for *he sent him back unto us*: and behold nothing worthy of death hath been done *by* him.

Luke xxiii. 38.—And there was also a superscription over him, This is the king of the Jews.

Luke xxiv. 17.—What communications are these that ye have one with another, as ye walk? *And they stood still*, looking sad.

Acts iii. 26.—Unto you first God, having raised up his *Servant*, sent him, etc.

Acts xv. 18.—Saith the Lord *who maketh these things known* from the beginning of the world.

1 Cor. ii. 1.—Proclaiming to you the *mystery* of God.

2 Cor. xii. 1.—I must needs glory, though it is not expedient.

Eph. v. 15.—*Look therefore carefully*, how ye walk, not as unwise but as wise.

Col. iv. 8.—Whom I have sent unto you for this very purpose, that *ye* may know *our* estate.

1 Tim. i. 4.—Questionings, rather than *a dispensation of God* which is in faith.

Luke xxii. 64.—And when they had blindfolded him, *they struck him on the face*, and asked him, saying, etc.

Luke xxiii. 15.—Nor yet Herod: for *I sent you to him*, and lo, nothing worthy of death is done *unto* him.

Luke xxiii. 38.—And a superscription also was written over him, *in letters of Greek and Latin and Hebrew*, This, etc.

Luke xxiv. 17.—What manner of communications are these that ye have one to another as ye walk, and are sad?

Acts iii. 26.—Unto you first, God, having raised up his *Son Jesus*, sent, etc.

Acts xv. 18.—*Known unto God are all his works* from the beginning of the world.

1 Cor. ii. 1.—Declaring unto you the *testimony* of God.

2 Cor. xii. 1.—It is not expedient for me, doubtless, to glory.

Eph. v. 15.—See that ye *walk circumspectly*, not as fools but as wise.

Col. iv. 8.—Whom I have sent unto you for the same purpose, that *he* might know *your* estate.

1 Tim. i. 4.—Questions, rather than *godly edifying*, which is in faith.

TABLE II.

Readings in revised version that accord with Vulgate.

REVISED VERSION, 1881.

Luke ii. 43.—His *parents* knew it not.

Luke xxi. 19.—In your patience ye shall *win* your souls.

Acts xiii. 42.—And as *they* went out *they* besought that these words might be spoken to them the next Sabbath.

Rom. v. 1.—Being therefore justified by faith, *let us have* peace with God through our Lord Jesus Christ.

2 Cor. ix. 10.—And he that supplieth seed to the sower and *bread for food shall supply* and multiply your seed for sowing, etc.

Eph. iii. 9.—To make all men see what is the *dispensation* of the mystery which from all ages hath been hid in God who created all things.

Eph. v. 9.—The fruit of the *light* is in all goodness, and righteousness, and truth.

AUTHORISED VERSION, 1611.

Luke ii. 43.—Joseph and his mother knew not of it.

Luke xxi. 19.—In your patience *possess ye* your souls.

Acts xiii. 42.—And when *the Jews* were gone out of the *synagogue*, *the Gentiles* besought that these words might be preached to them the next Sabbath.

Rom. v. 1.—Therefore, being justified by faith, *we have* peace with God through our Lord Jesus Christ.

2 Cor. ix. 10.—Now he that ministereth seed to the sower, *both minister* bread for your food and multiply your seed sown.

Eph. iii. 9.—To make all men see what is the *fellowship* of the mystery, which from the beginning of the world hath been hid in God, who created all things *by Jesus Christ*.

Eph. v. 9.—The fruit of the *spirit* is in all goodness and righteousness and truth.

1 Thess. iv. 1.—Ye received of us how ye ought to walk and to please God, even as ye do walk.
1 Tim. iii. 16.—Without controversy great is the mystery of godliness : *He who* was manifested in the flesh, etc.
Jas. iii. 12.—Neither can *salt water yield* sweet.
Rev. xv. 3.—Righteous and true are thy ways, thou King of the *ages*.
Rev. xv. 6.—The seven angels . . . arrayed with precious *stone*, pure and bright.

1 Thess. iv. 1.—Ye have received of us, how ye ought to walk and to please God.
1 Tim. iii. 16.—Without controversy great is the mystery of godliness : *God* was manifest in the flesh, etc.
Jas. iii. 12.—So can no *fountain both yield salt water and* fresh.
Rev. xv. 3.—Just and true are thy ways, thou king of *saints*.
Rev. xv. 6.—The seven angels . . . clothed in pure and white *linen*.

It is certainly a remarkable circumstance that so many of the Catholic readings in the New Testament, which in reformation and early post-reformation times were denounced by Protestants as corruptions of the pure text of God's word, should now, in the last quarter of the nineteenth century, be adopted by the revisers of our time-honoured English Bibles. Some of the watchmen of Zion may possibly see in this circumstance an indication of the re-ascendency of Popery in England, or possibly an evidence of concealed Jesuitism in the Protestant churches. There is no cause for alarm on the subject. The revisers have simply accepted the readings which they found best supported by the testimony of ancient manuscripts. If other manuscripts, of ancient date and well-established authenticity, should come to light, the divines who fixed the text of the revised version of the Bible will most cordially, in a spirit of truthfulness, adopt such new readings as shall then have the greatest weight of authority in their favour. The concordance, in some or in many points, of the Revised version of the New Testament with the Rhemes version simply proves, what no one should be sorry nor need be surprised to find proved, that St. Jerome, when he wrote the Latin Vulgate, had before him Greek manuscripts of the New Testament very much akin to those that have since the Reformation been discovered ; that the Vulgate, in short, is a purer and better version of the Scriptures than Protestants at one time were willing to believe. We need not be surprised either to find that when Stephen and Beza astonished and confounded the world of their day by the unearthing of old and lost Greek manuscripts of the New Testament which presented many points of difference from the Vulgate, they had not lighted on either the oldest or the most incorrupt versions that had been stowed away in times of ignorance. The manuscripts first found were not the most valuable. Other finds have brought to light more precious treasures, and by a careful collation of these a text supposed to be nearer the original has been gradually obtained. And so far from being a matter of mortification, it should be to us a matter of thankfulness to learn that recent discoveries have raised rather than lowered the authority of the Vulgate, and that the only version of the Bible which the Western Church for centuries possessed was not so corrupt as was by some people supposed and represented.[1]

Besides rectifying the text from which to translate, the revisers have given new renderings to many verses of the New Testament in which the old text was not altered.

Notwithstanding all the pains taken by King James's translators to make their work perfect before the Lord, and notwithstanding all the praise they have received for their faithful rendering of the original, there are many passages where they have failed to exhibit to their English readers the true and full meaning of the inspired writers. This is not disputed; and in adducing instances of their mis-translation, only such shall be here quoted as have been faulted by acknowledged authorities. In the authorised version we read, Acts iii. 19-20: "Repent ye therefore, and be converted, that your sins may be blotted out, when the times of refreshing shall come from the presence of

---

[1] In an article written by Cardinal Wiseman, in 1849, the following remarks will be found:—

"The oldest and best manuscripts, and the most ancient versions, almost invariably agree with the Vulgate; and their concurrent testimony establishes the fact, that the Vulgate represents manuscripts more accurate than have been used to form the received Greek text."

"When we consider the scorn cast by the Reformers upon the Vulgate, and their recurrence in consequence to the Greek as the only accurate standard, we cannot but rejoice at the silent triumph which truth has at length gained over clamorous error. For, in fact, the principal writers who have avenged the Vulgate, and obtained for it its critical pre-eminence, are Protestants." *Essays*, Vol. I. Paper on Parables of the New Testament.

the Lord. And he shall send Jesus Christ, which before was preached unto you." In the revised version this is changed into: "Repent ye therefore, and turn again, that your sins may be blotted out, that so there may come seasons of refreshing from the presence of the Lord: and that he may send the Christ who hath been appointed for you, even Jesus." Between these two renderings there is a distinct difference of meaning. According to the older version the duty of repentance is enjoined as a means towards a desired end in the indefinite future: "When the times of refreshing shall come from the presence of the Lord." But, according to the newer version, repentance is enjoined for the sake of immediate forgiveness, and both seasons of refreshment and a blessed reception of Christ are indicated as subsequent boons that will accompany or flow from conversion. This particular rendering by the revisers, too, is no novelty, for although it does not occur in any of the principal versions of the English Bible, it was given long ago in some of the private translations to which reference has been made in this chapter. Both in Doddridge's translation and in Thomson's translation, the new rendering is given almost *ipsissimis verbis*.[1] Another passage in the Acts of the Apostles that has, by a new translation, received a new meaning in the revised version, is the saying recorded by Agrippa in the 28th verse of the 26th chapter. In the King's translation we read: "Agrippa said unto Paul, Almost thou persuadest me to be a Christian,"—as if Agrippa had felt the weight of the Apostle's argument, and was at the point of embracing the Christian faith. A very different statement is imputed to Agrippa in the recent revision. He is there represented as having said to Paul: "With but little persuasion thou would'st fain make me a Christian," as if the King had treated the Apostle's reasoning with contempt,

---

[1] Another verse in which the revisers' rendering has been anticipated by Dr. Doddridge is Mat. xii. 15. Following the Bishops' Bible, and disregarding the Rhemes Testament, the King's translators have rendered the opening words of that verse, "*When* Jesus knew," as if Jesus for a time did not know. This is clearly a very unorthodox statement, but it has now been corrected by a more literal translation, "Jesus perceiving it, withdrew."

and insinuated that the Apostle's reference to the prophets was beside the question. In none of the early principal versions of the English Testament does the revisers' rendering of this passage occur, nor does it occur in either Thomson's or Doddridge's translation. But it was not unknown a hundred and fifty years ago as a possible rendering of the verse. Doddridge refers to it as a very untenable rendering, but a rendering that scholastic ingenuity had broached nevertheless. "To interpret this as an irony," he writes, "as if Agrippa had said 'This is a very compendious way of persuading me to become a Christian,' is to suppose Agrippa very unreasonably and absurdly ludicrous." The ironical interpretation of Agrippa's words did not appear to the revisers so ludicrous as it did to the estimable Dr. Doddridge; and it is given by them not only as their rendering, but as a rendering that cannot be disputed. There is not even a marginal note to say that any other rendering is possible. And in this opinion they are at one with Mr. Conybeare, who translates Agrippa's exclamation: "Thou wilt soon persuade me to be a Christian!" and adds that "the words were doubtless spoken ironically and in contempt."[1] Another instance of corrected translation will be found in 1 Tim. vi. 5. In the authorised version, certain persons are there referred to, as "supposing that gain is godliness." And in all the earlier versions the same statement is made. But in the revised version there is a very different averment. It is there said that a mercantile spirit sometimes betrays itself in religious professions, and that some men of corrupt minds imagine "godliness to be a way of gain." Every one will see that if this rendering is faithful to the original, it should on grounds of common sense be hailed as very much preferable to the one it supersedes. And it is given by the revisers not on account of its intrinsic truthfulness, as a record of fact, but on account of its strict accordance with St. Paul's own words in the Greek. Nor is it altogether a modern

---

[1] In Conybeare and Howson's *Life and Epistles of St. Paul*. The revisers have adopted a slightly altered reading of this verse. They have substituted *poieesai*, "make," for "*genesthai*, "be."

rendering of the passage. It is found in Conybeare's free and paraphrastic translation, which is both translation and commentary combined, where it is happily expressed by the phrase, "think godliness a gainful trade," and it occurs also in Thomson's translation. The following note by Mr. Thomson, too, is as good as any that has since been written on the subject: "The rendering which I have given, viz., *who suppose godliness to be gain,* is more agreeable than the received rendering to the construction of the original words; for *eusebeia* (*godliness*) having the article before it is the subject, or thing affirmed of, and it is more agreeable to the truth."

One passage in which a very curious difference of rendering appears in the authorised and revised versions respectively, is 2 Tim. ii. 26. The authorised translation is, "That they may recover themselves out of the snare of the devil, who are taken captive by him at his will." The revised translation reads, "If peradventure . . . they may recover themselves out of the snare of the devil, having been taken captive by the Lord's servant unto the will of God." Between these two versions of St. Paul's statement, the discordance is so great that we may wonder whether they could have been drawn from the same Greek text. But, in the case of this verse, the revisers have not adopted any reading that was not in the Greek text used by the King's translators. The difference between the two versions is simply a difference of rendering. The literal translation of the passage is "that they may recover themselves out of the snare of the devil having been taken captive by *him unto the will of him.*" And a question arises who is the person referred to by the first and second *him* respectively. Is it for the devil or for the servant of the Lord that the first *him* stands? The King's translators thought one thing and the revisers another; and the revisers' view is confirmed by the fact that in the Greek the two words translated "him" are different, as if they referred to different persons.[1]

---

[1] The authorised rendering of this verse is found in nearly all the English translations of the Testament. In the first Geneva version (1557) of the Testament, however, the revisers' view was adopted :—" Being delivered out of the snare of the devil, may come to amendment and perform his will." In MacKnight's trans-

Many of the amended translations in the revised version of the New Testament have been occasioned by stricter regard to the grammatical construction of the Greek language. In Greek the article is a very important part of speech, and it may be safely asserted that in the authorised and earlier English versions of the New Testament the Greek article was not translated with sufficient precision. In some cases it was over-looked, and in others it was over-emphasised. Scores of cases might be cited in which it is left untranslated in the authorised version, but the following corrected renderings in the revised version will suffice for examples: "In the resurrection, therefore, whose wife of them shall she be? for *the* seven had her to wife," Luke xx. 33; "And after *the* two days he went forth," John iv. 43; "As he reasoned of righteousness and temperance and *the* judgment to come," Acts xxiv. 25; "Distributing to the necessity of *the* saints," Romans xii. 13; "That no one of you be puffed up for *the* one against *the* other," 1 Cor. iv. 6. Sometimes, again, the article, although not altogether untranslated, is inadequately translated in the authorised version. The definite article is rendered indefinite, as in Mark iv. 21: "Is *a* candle brought to be put under *a* bushel, or under *a* bed, and not to be set on *a* candlestick?" The substitution of *the* for *a* all through the foregoing sentence gives realism to the picture, by setting before us the interior of a humble house in Israel, where the lamp, the bushel, the bed, and the lampstand were all specific and single articles of furniture. The English reader will see, too, that in the following passages the substitution of the definite for the indefinite article gives new

---

lation of the Epistles, the revised rendering is still more clearly anticipated; "Being caught alive by him out of the snare of the devil they may awake to do the will of God."

A similar instance of discrepancy between the authorised and revised renderings will be found in Acts xxvii. 40. In the older version, we read:—"When they had taken up the anchors, they *committed themselves*. unto the sea"; in the newer version—"Casting off the anchors, they *left them* in the sea."

It may be here mentioned also that the time honoured rendering "nothing doubting," Acts xi. 12, is by the revisers changed into "making no distinction," and the Greek word, Mat. iv. 24, that was literally translated by Tyndale *lunatic* and by Sir John Cheke *mooned* is now in the revised version altered into *epileptic*.

point and force to the translation: "Art thou *the* teacher of Israel, and knowest not these things?" John iii. 10; "*The* root of Jesse," Rom. xv. 12; "Wherefore, also, God hath highly exalted him, and given unto him *the* name which is above every name," Phil. ii. 9; "It will not be except *the* falling away come first," 2 Thess. ii. 3; "I have fought *the* good fight. I have finished *the* course. I have kept *the* faith," 2 Tim. iv. 7.[1] But while in some cases articles are in the authorised version omitted where they should be inserted, they are in other cases inserted where they should be omitted. In John i. 12 it is said: "To them gave he power to become *the* sons," instead of *sons* "of God"; in Acts i. 7, "It is not for you to know *the* times or *the* seasons," instead of *times or seasons;* in Rom. vi. 15, "We are not under *the* law," instead of *under law;* in Rom. xi. 19, "*The* branches," instead of *branches* "were broken off that I might be graffed in"; in 1 Cor. i. 23, "Christ crucified unto *the* Jews a stumbling block and unto *the* Gentiles foolishness," instead of *unto Jews a stumbling block and unto Gentiles foolishness*; and in Phil. iii. 5, "An Hebrew of *the* Hebrews," instead of *a Hebrew of Hebrews.* Sometimes, also, definite articles occur in the authorised version where there should be indefinite ones. Many an English reader, for instance, has stumbled at the statement, 1 Tim. vi. 10: "The love of money is *the* root of all evil." There is evidently much evil in the world that does not proceed from love of money. Insufficient regard for money is the cause of some evil. People were relieved, therefore, when they found it said in the revised version that the love of money is only "*a* root of all kinds of evil." And yet this was not a new account of the Apostle's statement, for although it is not to be found in any of the principal English versions of the New Testament, nor in Dr. Doddridge's Expositor, it is given both in Conybeare's and in Thomson's translation of the Epistles. Indeed, the wonder is that the rendering in the authorised version ever was made by

---

[1] So also:—"He himself was in the stern, asleep on *the* cushion," Mark iv. 38; "Then he poureth water into *the* bason," John xiii. 5; "There sat in *the* window," Acts xx. 9; "Say *the* amen at thy giving of thanks," 1 Cor. xiv. 16.

any translator. It is neither a right rendering nor a true statement of fact. But in the authorised version there are many places in which the same form of mis-translation occurs. And, as was shown in a previous chapter, there are instances not a few in the King's translation where the article is unduly emphasised, and is even transformed into a demonstrative pronoun, as in 1 Cor. x. 4, "*That* rock was Christ"; and in 1 Cor. x. 17, " We are all partakers of *that* one bread." In these and other cases the revisers, in their zeal for scholastic accuracy, have displaced the demonstrative pronoun, and substituted the definite article in its room.

It may be asked whether it is either absolutely necessary or beneficial that, in an English version of the New Testament, the Greek articles in the original text should be uniformly and literally rendered. It can scarcely be said so. The revisers state in their preface that in using the definite article "it was necessary to consider the peculiarities of English idiom, as well as the general tenor of each passage. Sometimes they felt it enough to prefix the article to the first of a series of words to all of which it is prefixed in the Greek, and thus, as it were, to impart the idea of definiteness to the whole series without running the risk of overloading the sentence. Sometimes, conversely, they had to tolerate the presence of the definite article in their version when it is absent in the Greek . . .: simply because English idiom would not allow the noun to stand alone. . . In a word, they were careful to observe the use of the article, wherever it seemed to be idiomatically possible : where it did not seem to be possible they yielded to necessity." In the translation of the Greek article, therefore, some freedom and discretion are allowed. How much should be, is a question on which there may be difference of opinion. Some eminent scholars have, on scholastic grounds, objected to the literalness with which the Greek article is, in many cases, translated by the revisers. Dean Burgon, for instance, takes exception to the following and other renderings as unidiomatic English : "greater than *the* herbs," Mat. xiii. 32 ; " Did not I choose you *the* twelve," John vi. 70 ; " for *the* joy that a man is born into the world," John xvi. 21 ; "*the* lust when it hath conceived beareth sin," James i. 15. The revisers themselves, too, have not been absolutely consistent in their treatment of the Greek article. The same Greek words are in one place translated "serpents," and in another "the serpents"; "Be wise as serpents," Mat. x. 16 ; " Perished by *the* serpents," 1 Cor. x. 9. One verse in the translation of which the revisers have played fast and loose is 1 Tim. iii. 2 : " *The* Bishop must be without reproach, *the* husband of one wife." The first article in this sentence has its counterpart in the original text, but the second has not. If the verse were translated literally throughout, it might read : " *The* Bishop must be . . . *a* husband of one wife." Such a rendering, however, would present unutterable horrors to the episcopal mind. While forbidding the bishop to indulge in the pleasures of polygamy, it would give, or seem to give, Scripture sanction for his wife's luxuriating in the barbaric dignity of polyandrism! For the bishop's sake, therefore, the revisers, like all previous translators, made the rules of grammar, in this instance, succumb to the dictates of sober theology.[1] And seeing that the revisers in translating the Greek article have given some consideration to "the peculiarities of English idiom, and the general tenor of each passage," it may be questioned whether they would not have done well to have gone a little further in that direction than they have done. The following passages are not improvements on the authorised renderings : " The city was filled with *the* confusion," Acts xix. 29 ; "Where then is *the* glorying," Rom. iii. 27 ; " Peradventure for *the* good man some one would even dare to die," Rom. v. 7.

Of other small particles more correctly translated in the revised than in the authorised version of the New Testament, prepositions may be instanced.[2] In the authorised version we read, 2 Thess. ii. 1 ; " Now, we beseech you, brethren, *by* the

---

[1] Mr. Conybeare, in a note, remarks that the Greek words *ton episkopon* in this verse are " rightly translated in the authorised version, ' A Bishop,' not *the bishop*, in spite of the article." The phrase " *in spite of the article* " is good.

[2] In Young's Analytical Concordance it is shewn that in the authorised version the English prepositions *in* and *of* each represent 14 different Greek particles ; *with* and *for* 13 each ; and *at* and *by* 11 each.

coming of our Lord Jesus Christ, and by our gathering together unto him, that ye be not soon shaken in mind or be troubled, neither by spirit, nor by word, nor by letter, as that the day of Christ is at hand." From this translation we might imagine that the Apostle was here adjuring his Thessalonian converts by their belief in Christ's second coming, and by all the terrors and blessings of that great event, not to let their minds be disturbed by any of the current mistakes about the near approach of their Lord's return. And it is expressly said in some popular commentaries that this is really what the Apostle was doing. It would have been a pointless argument, however, and it does not express the Apostle's meaning. That meaning is brought out very plainly by the revisers who, for the italicised preposition *by* have substituted the word *touching*, and made the verse read : "Now, we beseech you, brethren, *touching* the coming of our Lord Jesus Christ, and our gathering together unto him : to the end that ye be not quickly shaken from your mind, nor yet be troubled . . . as that the day of the Lord is now present."[1] And this is neither a fantastical nor a modern rendering, but one that is to be found in the writings of such popular commentators as Dr. Doddridge and Mr. Conybeare. Another instance of prepositional mistranslation in the authorised version is Luke xxiii. 42, "Lord, remember me when thou comest *into* thy kingdom." It is stated, in the margin of the revised version, that some ancient authorities give a reading in the original which would warrant that translation. But the text from which the revised version is taken, and the text which is presumed to underlie the authorised version should be rendered, "*in* thy kingdom." In respect of letters this is a very slight alteration, but it makes a great change on the meaning of the prayer. And there are scores of passages in the revised version where, by similarly slight prepositional changes, the diction of the authorised trans-

---

[1] One verse in the authorised translation that is much obscured by the use of the word *by* is 1 Cor. iv. 4. The substitution of *against* for *by* in that verse has virtually to common readers unacquainted with the archaic meanings of *by*, thrown new light on the apostle's argument :—" I know nothing *against* myself, yet am I not hereby justified."

lation has been much improved. The following cases will show the kind of improvement that by this means has been effected[1]:

AUTHORISED VERSION.	REVISED VERSION.
Rom. v. 12.—As *by* one man sin entered into the world, and death *by* sin: and so death passed *upon* all men, for that all have sinned.	Rom. v. 12.—As *through* one man sin entered into the world, and death *through* sin: and so death passed *unto* all men, for that all sinned.
Gal. iii. 19.—It was ordained *by* angels *in* the hand of a mediator.	Gal. iii. 19.—It was ordained *through* angels *by* the hand of a mediator.
Heb. vi. 7.—Bringeth forth herbs meet for them *by* whom it is dressed.	Heb. vi. 7. — Bringeth forth herbs meet for them *for whose sake* it is also tilled.
Jas. iii. 4.—Behold also the ships, which though they be so great and are driven *of* fierce winds, yet are they turned about *with* a very small helm.	Jas. iii. 4.—Behold, the ships also, though they are so great, and are driven *by* rough winds, are yet turned about *by* a very small rudder.

The point, however, to which the New Testament revisers devoted most particular attention was the correct rendering of the Greek verb, and accuracy in this matter is not so easily attained as the English reader uninitiated in the mysteries of the Greek tongue may imagine. The inflections of the Greek and English verb are altogether different. It is very difficult, therefore, to express in English the precise shade of meaning that is conveyed in a particular tense, mood, and voice of the Greek verb for which there is no English equivalent. The revisers have with much pains done their best in this matter, and the English reader must accept their translations in faith and trust, as scholastic dicta which it is beyond his province to dispute.[2]

---

[1] The correct translation of the prepositions in the Greek Testament was a point on which Mr. Thomson laid much stress. In his "Preliminary Observations," he says:—" In my opinion the most numerous and the greatest faults in the common version, and in other versions, have arisen from a mistranslation of the prepositions." Mr. Thomson has, in many instances, anticipated the translations of the prepositions that now appear in the revised version: as in Mat. xxviii. 19, " Baptizing them *into* the name of the Father, etc." ; John xi. 38, "a stone lay *against* it" ; Rom. xi. 32, " God hath shut them all up *unto* disobedience " ; 1 Cor. xii. 8, "to one indeed is given *through* the spirit the word of wisdom ; and to another the word of knowledge, *according* to the same spirit "; 1 Cor. xv. 5, " he appeared *to* Cephas, then *to* the twelve " ; Gal. i. 12, " neither did I receive it *from* man, nor was I taught it, but *through* a revelation of Jesus Christ.

[2] They are disputed, however, by some learned critics. See Burgon's *Revision Revised.*

Sometimes the mind is strained with noting the little distinctions of tense and mood that the revisers have introduced into the Scripture narrative; but there are at least many cases in which we can see that from a literary point of view the changes are improvements. The following passages which contain translations of different tenses of the Greek verb will shew how far correct tensing goes to make statements accurate and arguments cogent.

AUTHORISED VERSION.	REVISED VERSION.
Luke i. 59.—They called him Zacharias.	Luke i. 59.—They *would have* called him Zacharias.
Luke xvi. 1.—Was accused unto him that he had wasted his goods.	Luke xvi. 1.—Was accused unto him that he *was wasting* his goods.
Luke xxi. 31.—When ye see these things come to pass, know ye that the kingdom of God is nigh at hand.	Luke xxi. 31.—When ye see these things *coming* to pass, know ye that the kingdom of God is nigh.
Luke xxii. 31.—Simon, Simon, behold, Satan *hath* desired to have you . . . but I *have prayed* for thee that thy faith fail not.	Luke xxii. 31.—Simon, Simon, behold Satan *asked* to have you . . . but I *made* supplication for thee, that thy faith fail not.
Luke xxiv. 37.—They were terrified and affrighted, and supposed that they *had seen* a spirit.	Luke xxiv. 37.—They were terrified and affrighted, and supposed that they *beheld* a spirit.
John i. 3.—Without him was not any thing made that *was* made.	John i. 3.—Without him was not anything made that *hath been* made.
John iv. 1.—That Jesus made and baptised more disciples than John.	John iv. 1.—That Jesus *was making* and *baptizing* more disciples than John.
1 Cor. iii. 6.—I *have* planted, Apollos watered, but God gave the increase.	1 Cor. iii. 6.—I *planted*, Apollos watered, but God gave the increase.
2 Cor. vii. 8.—Though I made you sorry with a letter, I do not repent. For I perceive that the same Epistle *hath made* you sorry, though it were but for a season. *v.* 13.—Therefore we *were* comforted in your comfort, yea and exceedingly the more joyed we for the joy of Titus, because his spirit *was* refreshed by you all.	2 Cor. vii. 8.—Though I made you sorry with my epistle, I do not regret it, though I did regret : for I see that that epistle *made* you sorry, though but for a season. *v.* 13.—Therefore we *have been* comforted ; and in our joy we joyed the more exceedingly for the joy of Titus ; because his spirit *hath been* refreshed by you all.
2 Cor. xi. 4.—If he that cometh preacheth another Jesus whom we *have not preached*, or if ye receive another spirit which ye *have not received*, or another gospel which ye *have not accepted*, ye might well bear with him.	2 Cor. xi. 4.—If he that cometh preacheth another Jesus, whom ye *did not preach ;* or if ye receive a different spirit, which ye *did not receive ;* or a different gospel, which ye *did not accept*, ye do well to bear with him.
Gal. i. 6.—I marvel that you are so soon *removed* from him that called you into the grace of Christ.	Gal. i. 6.—I marvel that ye are so quickly *removing* from him that called you in the grace of Christ.
Gal. iii. 1.—O foolish Galatians, who *hath bewitched* you, that you should not obey the truth, before whose eyes Jesus Christ *hath been* evidently set forth, crucified among you.	Gal. iii. 1.—O foolish Galatians, who *did* bewitch you, before whose eyes Jesus Christ *was* openly set forth crucified ?
2 Thess. ii. 13.—God *hath* from the beginning *chosen* you to salvation.[1]	2 Thess. ii. 13.—God *chose* you from the beginning unto salvation.

---

[1] The question of *shall* or *will* is involved in the rendering of the Greek verb,

One point on which the New Testament revisers declared themselves at issue with the King's translators is the importance of uniformity in the rendering of words and phrases. This is a species of literary bondage to which the King's translators would not submit. "We cannot," they said, "follow a better pattern for elocution than God himself: therefore, he using divers words in his holy writ, and indifferently, for one thing in nature, we, if we will not be superstitious, may use the same liberty in our English versions." The revisers contend that this liberty was carried too far by the King's translators, " and that their studied avoidance of uniformity in the rendering of the same words, even when occurring in the same context, is one of the blemishes in their work." For instance, we read in the authorised version, Phil. i. 4, "always in every *prayer* of mine for you all making *request* with joy." It is the same Greek word that is here variously translated *prayer* and *request*. And in Phil. iv. 6, it is translated *supplication*. The revisers shew scholastic consistency, therefore, by rendering the word

and of the Hebrew verb also; but it is one on which it would be presumptuous for Scotsmen to express an opinion. They may modestly take note, however, of the contentions of Englishmen on the subject. There are more than a score of cases in which the revisers have substituted their *will* for the *shall* of King James's divines, or *vice versa*. The reason why, and the nature of the change thereby made on the meaning of some passages of Scripture, will be apparent to those that have eyes to see. For other people the following quotations may furnish food for reflection :—

AUTHORISED VERSION.	REVISED VERSION.
Ps. xvii. 15.—As for me, I *will* behold thy face in righteousness.	Ps. xvii. 15.—As for me, I *shall* behold thy face in righteousness.
Ps. xxxii. 7.—Thou *shalt* preserve me from trouble; thou *shalt*, etc.	Ps. xxxii. 7.—Thou *wilt* preserve me from trouble; thou *wilt*, etc.
Amos i. 2.—And he said, The Lord *will* roar from Zion.	Amos i. 2.—And he said, The Lord *shall* roar from Zion.
Mark ii. 20.—The bridegroom shall be taken away from them, and then *shall* they fast in those days.	Mark ii. 20.—The bridegroom shall be taken away from them, and then *will* they fast in those days.
1 Cor. xiv. 11.—If I know not the meaning of the voice I shall be unto him that speaketh a barbarian, and he that speaketh *shall* be a barbarian unto me.	1 Cor. xiv. 11.—If then I know not the meaning of the voice, I shall be to him that speaketh a barbarian, and he that speaketh *will* be a barbarian unto me.
2 Tim. iv. 18.—The Lord *shall* deliver me from every evil work, and *will* preserve me unto his heavenly kingdom.	2 Tim. iv. 8.—The Lord *will* deliver me from every evil work, and *will* save me unto his heavenly kingdom.

"supplication," in all the three places.[1] In the authorised version, again, we read, 1 Pet. i. 19, that men have been redeemed by the precious blood of Christ "as of a lamb *without blemish* and without spot." The word rendered in this sentence, "without blemish," in distinction from "without spot," is in Heb. ix. 14, translated *without spot*, and in Jude 24, *faultless*. On the other hand, the English word *blameless* is used by the King's translators to represent no fewer than five different Greek words. It may be conceded, therefore, that the received renderings in the New Testament required some revision, and it can scarcely be disputed that the revisers, by adhering to the principle of uniform translation, have in many cases improved the English text of the Bible.[2]

---

[1] The following are other instances in which the revisers have curtailed the diversity of renderings found in the authorised translation : *agora*, market, Acts xvii. 17 ; *street*, Mark vi. 56 :—*aulee*, court, Rev. xi. 2 ; *hall*, Mark xv. 16 ; *palace*, Mark xiv. 54 :—*gnomee*, mind, Rev. xvii. 13 ; *will*, Rev. xvii. 17 ; *agree*, Rev. xvii. 17 ; judgment, 1 Cor. vii. 25 ; *advice*, 2 Cor. viii. 10 :—*diabolos*, devil, Mat. iv. 1 ; slanderer, 1 Tim. iii. 11 ; *false accuser*, 2 Tim. iii. 3 :—*zeelos*, zeal, Rom. x. 2 ; *fervent mind*, 2 Cor. vii. 7 ; jealousy, 2 Cor. xi. 2 ; *emulation*, Gal. v. 20 ; *envy*, Acts xiii. 45 ; *envying*, 1 Cor. iii. 3 :—*kleesis*, calling, 2 Tim. i. 9 ; *vocation*, Eph. iv. 1 :—*mneema*, tomb, Luke viii. 27 ; *sepulchre*, Luke xxiii. 53 ; *grave*, Rev. xi. 9 :—*patheema*, suffering, 1 Peter v. 1 ; *affliction*, 1 Peter v. 9 ; passion, Gal. v. 24 (margin) ; *affection*, Gal. v. 24 ; *motion*, Rom. vii. 5 :—*paraiteomai*, entreat, Heb. xii. 19 ; make excuse, Luke xiv. 18 ; refuse, 1 Tim. iv. 7 ; *avoid*, 2 Tim. ii. 23 ; *reject*, Tit. iii. 10 :—*tasso*, ordain, Rom. xiii. 1 ; set, Luke vii. 8 ; *addict*, 1 Cor. xvi. 15 ; appoint, Acts xxviii. 23 ; *determine*, Acts, xv. 2 :—*hubris* (injury, Rev. Version), *reproach*, 2 Cor. xii. 10 ; *hurt*, Acts xxvii. 10.

[2] Following out this principle, the revisers have translated some verses much more accurately than the King's translators have. For instance, in the Greek text of Eph. iii. 6, there are three compound words with the same prefix. There is an idea, therefore, conveyed by each of these words in common, which the Apostle wishes to bring home to the minds of his readers. The idea is fellowship, and the fellowship extends to three particulars. How much more cogently the Apostle's argument in that passage is stated in the revised than in the authorised version will be seen by a comparison of the two translations side by side.

REVISED VERSION.	AUTHORISED VERSION.
Eph. iii. 6.—That the Gentiles are *fellow-heirs*, and *fellow-members of the body*, and *fellow-partakers of the promise* in Christ Jesus through the gospel.	Eph. iii. 6.—That the Gentiles should be fellow-heirs, and of the same body, and partakers of his promise in Christ by the gospel.

The rendering in the Rhemes Testament is :—"The Gentils to be *coheires*, and *concorporat*, and *comparticipant*, of his promise in Christ Jesus by the gospel."

At the same time, that principle, while sound enough in a general way, may be carried out too rigidly. Almost every word has more meanings or more shades of meaning than one; and it is reasonable to expect that many words in the original Scriptures must, in order to be fully and accurately translated, be differently Englished in different places.[1] And the revisers have paid rather little attention to this fact. There is, for instance, in the Greek language, a small particle *oun*, whose meanings, as given in the Dictionary, are "(1) *then*, denoting the mere *sequence* of one clause upon another; (2) *therefore, accordingly, consequently*, to denote the *consequence* of one clause upon another." This particle is not invariably, but it is too frequently, translated *therefore* by the revisers. In the eighteenth chapter of St. John's Gospel it occurs at least twenty times. In seventeen out of these twenty times it is translated *therefore*; in two it is translated *so*; and once it is rendered *then*.[2] In many of the cases where it is rendered *therefore* there is plainly no *consequence* or *causation* intended to be expressed, and the text is accordingly made by the revisers to read very unnaturally, as the following passage will shew:—

Verse 23-28. Jesus answered him, If I have spoken evil, bear witness of the evil; but if well, why smitest thou me? Annas *therefore* sent him bound unto Caiaphas, the high-priest. Now Simon Peter was standing and warming himself. They said *therefore* unto him, Art thou also one of his disciples? He denied and said I am not. One of the servants of the high-priest, being a kinsman of him whose ear Peter cut off, saith, Did not I see thee in the garden with him? Peter *therefore* denied again; and straightway the cock crew. They lead Jesus *therefore* from Caiaphas into the palace; and it was early."

---

[1] The following words in the Greek Testament have more meanings than one, widely apart from each other, and their different meanings are exhibited in the revised as well as in the authorised version:—*Agoraios*, of the baser sort (A. V.), of the rabble (R. V.), Acts xvii. 5; the law (A. V.), the court (R. V.), Acts xix. 38; *therapeia*, healing, Luke ix. 11, household, Luke xii. 42; *kosmos*, world, 1 Pet. i. 20, adorning, 1 Pet. iii. 3; *meros*, part, John xiii. 8, Acts xxiii. 6, respect, Col. ii. 16; coast (A. V.), country (R. V.), Acts xix. 1; craft (A. V.), trade (R. V.), Acts xix. 27.

[2] The word *oun* occurs unemphasised more than 450 times in the Greek Testament. In 245 places, the King's translators have rendered it *therefore*; in 192, *then*; in 11, *so*; in 7, *now*; and in other places, *wherefore, and, but*, etc.—Young's *Analytical Concordance*.

In the varieties of rendering that appear in the authorised version of the New Testament, the revisers profess to have discriminated between those "which were compatible with fidelity to the true meaning of the text, and those which involved inconsistency and were suggestive of differences that had no existence in the Greek. . . . If the meaning was fairly expressed by the word or phrase that was before them in the authorised version they made no change, even where rigid adherence to the rule of translating, as far as possible, the same Greek word by the same English word might have prescribed some modification." There are, therefore, to be found varieties of rendering in the revised as well as in the authorised version. [1] Indeed, there are cases in which the revisers have broken up the uniformity of rendering which they found in the authorised version, and, for reasons of their own, have introduced variety. The words *apistia* and *makarismos*, for instance, have in the authorised version only one rendering respectively, but in the revised version *apistia* is in one passage, Heb. iii. 12, translated *unbelief*, and in another, Rom. iii. 3, *want of faith;* while *makarismos* is, in Rom. iv. 9, translated *blessing*, and in Gal. iv. 15, *gratulation*. Both in 1 Cor. i. 8, and in 1 Tim. iii. 10, again, the word *anengkleetos* is, in the authorised version, translated *blameless*, but in the revised version it is in the one verse rendered *blameless* and in the other, *unreprovable*. The word *splanchna* is, in like manner, variously rendered by the revisers, "bowels," Acts i. 18; "heart," Philemon 12; "compassion," 1 John iii. 17; "affections," 2 Cor. vi. 12; "tender

---

[1] For instance, *himatismos* is translated *raiment* (Luke ix. 29), *vesture* (John xix. 24), and *apparel* (Acts xx. 33); *kosmeo*, *trim* (Mat. xxv. 7), *garnish* (Mat. xxiii. 29), and *adorn* (1 Tim. ii. 9); *misthos*, *hire* (Luke x. 7), *wages* (John iv. 36), and *reward* (Luke vi. 23); *synoche*, *anguish* (2 Cor. ii. 4), and *distress* (Luke xxi. 25); *biblion*, *scroll* (Rev. vi. 14), *book* (Rev. i. 11), and *bill* (Mark x. 4); *didaskalos*, *teacher* (John iii. 2), *doctor* (Luke ii. 46), and *master* (John i. 38); *therapeuo*, *heal* (Luke iv. 23), and *cure* (Luke ix. 1); *kurios*, *lord* (Mat. viii. 8), *sir* (Mat. xiii. 27), *master* (Mat. vi. 24), and *owner* (Luke xix. 33); *parakleesis*, *comfort* (2 Cor. i. 4), *consolation* (Acts xv. 31), *encouragement* (Heb. vi. 18), *exhortation* (Heb. xii. 5), *entreaty* (2 Cor. viii. 4); and *prosōpon*, *face* (Mat. vi. 17), *countenance* (Luke ix. 27), *fashion* (Jas. i. 11), *appearance* (2 Cor. v. 12), *presence* (2 Cor. x. 1), *person* (Mat. xxii. 16).

mercies," Phil. i. 8.[1] On the other hand, *splanchna* is in the authorised version almost uniformly rendered *bowels*, and the changes made on that fleshly rendering by the revisers are as grateful as they are varied. There are other cases in which the revisers might, with much advantage, have studied a similar variety of expression. From a mistaken resolution to translate two different parts of one Greek verb by the same English word, they have made their rendering of 2 Cor. x. 2, very feeble and pointless: " I beseech you, that I may not when present shew courage with the confidence wherewith I *count* to be bold against some, which *count* of us as if we walked according to the flesh." The repetition of the word *count*, which many people will think not a well-chosen word, grates on the ear; and in the Greek there is no such grating, because the two words translated *count* (logizomai and logizomenous), although parts of one verb, have very dissimilar endings. A like remark may be made regarding the revised version of 1 Cor. xiii. 8: " Love never faileth : but whether there be prophecies, they shall *be done away* : whether there be tongues, they shall cease: whether there be knowledge, it shall *be done away*." The authorised translation of this verse, however, although sonorous enough, is not very felicitous either; the word *fail* as applied to prophecy being capable of a false meaning, and the statement that knowledge shall vanish being of doubtful truth and orthodoxy. If we wish to find an admirable rendering of this noble verse we have only to turn to Mr. Conybeare's translation, where, untrammelled by the bonds of soulless literalism, the sense and spirit of the original are exhibited in simple and vigorous English : " Love shall never pass away : though the gift of prophecy shall vanish, and the gift of tongues shall cease, and the gift of knowledge shall come to nought."

In respect of diction, that is wording and phrasing, the revised

---

[1] The word *anengkleetos* is in one passage (Col. i. 22) of the authorised version rendered *unreprovable*; *splanchna* is in one passage (2 Cor. vii. 15) rendered *inward affection*, and in another (Luke i. 78) *tender*. In all these cases the authorised rendering has been retained by the revisers.

version of the New Testament has been subjected to severe criticism, and certainly there could easily be culled from its pages a ghastly array of most unfamiliar expressions. The excessive eagerness of the revisers to bring out the full significance of the Greek article has led them to coin phrases, which plain people may be excused for refusing, notwithstanding epistles of commendation from learned men, to pass as Queen's English. One verse that has been much lauded by scholastic admirers for its precision of statement, but which, from the frequent iteration of the definite article, strains and perplexes the untutored intellect of the common reader and throws him into acrobatic attitudes of imagination which are too much for him, is Rom. v. 15 : "Not as *the* trespass so also is *the* free gift. For if by *the* trespass of *the* one *the* many died, much more did *the* grace of God, and *the* gift by *the* grace of *the* one man, Jesus Christ, abound unto *the* many." A phrase that would need, but is not likely, to be well bushed is, " *the* weeping and gnashing of teeth." In their zeal, again, to present literally the exact significance of every tense in the Greek verb, the revisers have occasionally introduced forms of expression that are little better than conundrums.[1] We have been accustomed to read in Heb. xi. 5: "Before his translation he (Enoch) had this testimony that he pleased God." This plain and easily comprehended statement has been changed by the revisers into the following grammatical and historical puzzle : " Before his translation he *hath had* witness borne to him that he *had* been well pleasing unto God."[2] And passing on to changes on single words, it

---

[1] " The difference between the A. V. and the R. V. seems to ourselves," writes Dean Burgon, "to be simply this, that the renderings in the former are the idiomatic English of certain well understood Greek tenses, while the substitutes are nothing else but the pedantic efforts of mere grammarians to reproduce in another language idioms which it abhors."—p. 158.

[2] Among other cases of infelicitous expression in the revised New Testament, the following may be given as specimens :—"Glorify thy Son that the son may glorify thee ; even as thou gavest him authority over all flesh, that *whatsoever* thou hast given him, to them he should give eternal life," John xvii. 1, 2 ; " *Thy much learning doth turn thee to madness*," Acts xxvi. 24 ; " The mystery which hath been kept *in silence through times eternal*," Rom. xvi. 25 ; " Being in the form of God, counted it not a *prize* to be on an equality with God, but *emptied himself*," Phil. ii. 7 ; "Turned about by a very small rudder, whither the *impulse* of the steersman willeth," Jas. iii. 4.

may be said confidently that few people will think it an improvement that the revisers have made on the translation of Mat. xii. 43, by substituting *waterless* for *dry:* "The unclean spirit, when he is gone out of the man, passeth through *waterless* places seeking rest, and findeth it not." The *bowls* of wrath are not a happy substitute either, Rev. xvi. 1, for vials of wrath;[1] and there is nothing gained in accuracy, but a good deal lost in dignity, by the substitution, Mat. ix. 23, of *flute-players* for minstrels. A word that has been much praised as an improvement on what it has been made to supersede is "advanced" for *profited*, in Gal. i. 14. It is far, however, from being the right word in the right place, for it leaves the reader doubtful whether St. Paul means to say that he made proficiency in the knowledge of the Jewish religion, made religious progress according to Judaistic standards of religion, or gained notoriety and distinction for his zeal in upholding and defending the Jewish system of religion. Far more again is lost than gained by the crude literalism of such expressions, as: "Love our Lord Jesus Christ in *uncorruptness*," Eph. vi. 24; "God sendeth them a *working of error* that they should believe a lie," 2 Thess. ii. 11; and "Pray for us, that the word of the Lord may *run* and be glorified," 2 Thess. iii. 1. The adoption of a new Greek reading in Heb. xii. 7, by the substitution of *eis* for *ei*, makes a verse that was clear and relevant before well nigh incomprehensible now: "*It is for chastening that ye endure:* God dealeth with you as with sons." But although these, and "baskets full" of other similar expressions, may be quoted as samples of infelicitous rendering by the revisers of the New Testament, and may be held as going far to shew that the revised version of the Bible needs to be revised again, the text of the English Scriptures has still, from a literary point of view, been very greatly changed for the better by the revisers.

---

[1] The word vial or vials appears in the authorised version of the New Testament only in the Revelation of John, and it is uniformly changed by the revisers into bowl or bowls. It appears in the authorised version of the Old Testament only once, 1 Sam. x. 1, and it is there left unchanged by the revisers. The Greek word for vial in Revelation is *phiale*, and the Greek word in the Septuagint version of the Old Testament for vial, 1 Sam. x. 1, is *phakos*.

Clearer, terser, more graphic, and more correct phraseology is on almost every page substituted for what is found in the authorised version. "Lord it over them," Mark x. 42, is terser English than *exercise lordship over them;* "He was minded to go forth into Galilee," John i. 43, is more explicit than *he would go forth;* "When men have drunk freely," John ii. 10, is a better phrase than *when men have well drunk;* and less open to misconstruction, by Scotsmen at least, is the statement, Heb. xii. 17, "He desired to inherit the blessing," than *he would have inherited the blessing.* It accords much more with our notions of divine majesty, again, that God should be represented, Acts xvii. 30, as *overlooking,* than as *winking at,* the times of ignorance; "Persuasive words of wisdom," 1 Cor. ii. 4, is a choicer expression than *enticing words of man's wisdom;* "Preached to you the gospel of God for nought," 2 Cor. xi. 7, has not the ambiguity of *preached the gospel of God freely;* "Before whose eyes Jesus Christ was openly set forth, Gal. iii. 1, is a clearer statement than *Christ was evidently set forth;* "They that have served well as deacons gain to themselves a good standing," 1 Tim. iii. 13, is a better specimen of literary art than *they that have used the office of a deacon well purchase to themselves a good degree;* "We make known to you the grace of God, 2 Cor. viii. 1, is a more direct and simple form of writing than *we do you to wit of the grace of God;* "Not a hearer that forgetteth, but a doer that worketh," James i. 25, is in point both of precision and of antithetical force a happier phrase than the time honoured one, *not a forgetful hearer, but a doer of the work.* And scores of other passages might be adduced in which the revisers have made an equally great improvement on the diction of the authorised version of the New Testament.[1] The following cases will serve for illustration :—

---

[1] The revisers, like the King's translators, sometimes use *which* where modern writers (Dean Alford excepted) would use *who*; as in Mat. vi. 9, "Our father, *which* art in heaven"; 1 Thess. i. 10, "Even Jesus, *which* delivereth us from the wrath to come." The revisers, also, do not always, any more than the King's translators, use *which* and *that* in the distinctive senses that some modern grammarians assign to these relative pronouns. In the revised version we read, "All they *which* dwelt in Asia," Acts xix. 10; "They are not all Israel

AUTHORISED VERSION.	REVISED VERSION.
Mat. xxiv. 25.—Behold, I have told you before.	Mat. xxiv. 25.—Behold, I have told you *beforehand*.
Luke xxiii. 48.—And all the people that came together to that sight, beholding the things which were done, *smote their breasts, and returned*.	Luke xxiii. 48.—And all the multitudes that came together to this sight, when they beheld the things that were done, *returned smiting* their breasts.
Acts xii. 13.—And as Peter knocked at the door of the gate, a damsel came to *hearken*, named Rhoda.	Acts xii. 13.—And when he knocked at the door of the gate, a maid came to *answer*, named Rhoda.
Acts. xix. 7.—And *all the men were about twelve*.	Acts xix. 7.—And they were *in all* about twelve men.
Acts xxiii. 27.—This man was *taken of* the Jews, and *should have been* killed of them : Then came I with an *army*, and rescued him, having *understood* that he was a Roman.	Acts xxiii. 27.—This man was *seized by* the Jews, and *was about to be* slain of them, when I came upon them with *the soldiers*, and rescued him, having *learned* that he was a Roman.
Acts xxv. 20.—Because I *doubted of such manner of questions*, I asked him whether he would go to Jerusalem, and there be judged of these matters.	Acts xxv. 20.—I, *being perplexed how to enquire concerning these things*, asked whether he would go to Jerusalem, and there be judged of these matters.
Rom. iii. 3.—For what if some did not believe? shall their unbelief make the *faith* of God without effect?	Rom. iii. 3.—For what if some were *without faith*? shall *their want of faith* make of none effect *the faithfulness* of God?
Rom. vi. 17.—But God be thanked, *that ye were the servants of sin ;* but ye have obeyed from the heart that form of doctrine which was delivered you.	Rom. vi. 17.—But thanks be to God, that *whereas* ye were servants of sin, ye *became* obedient from the heart to that form of teaching whereunto ye were delivered.
1 Cor. vii. 28.—Such (as marry) shall have trouble in the flesh : but I spare you.	1 Cor. vii. 28.—Such (as marry) shall have tribulation in the flesh : and I *would spare* you.
1 Cor. ix. 5.—Have we not power to lead about *a sister a wife* as well as other Apostles?	1 Cor. ix. 5.—Have we no right to lead about *a wife that is a believer* even as the rest of the apostles?
1 Cor. xii. 27.—Now ye are the body of Christ, and members in particular.	1 Cor. xii. 27.—Now ye are the body of Christ, and *severally* members thereof.
1 Cor. xvi. 15.—They have *addicted themselves to the ministry* of the saints.	1 Cor. xvi. 15.—They have *set themselves to minister* unto the saints.
2 Cor. v. 21.—He hath made him to be sin for *us, who* knew no sin.	2 Cor. v. 21.—Him who knew no sin he made to be sin on our behalf.
2 Cor. viii. 20-21.—Avoiding this, that no man should blame us in this abundance which is administered by us. Providing for honest things, not only in the sight of the Lord, but in the sight of men.	2 Cor. viii. 20-21.—Avoiding this that any man should blame us in *the matter of this bounty which is ministered by us ; for we take thought for* things honourable, not only in the sight of the Lord, but also in the sight of men.
Col. iv. 3.—Praying also for us, that God would open unto us *a door of utterance*, to speak the mystery of Christ.	Col. iv. 3.—Praying for us also, that God may open unto us *a door for the word*, to speak the mystery of Christ.
1 Tim. i. 16.—I obtained mercy, that in me *first* Jesus Christ might shew forth	1 Tim. i. 16.—I obtained mercy, that in me *as chief* might Jesus Christ shew

---

which are of Israel," Rom. ix. 6 ; and " It is God *which* worketh in you both to will and to work, for his good pleasure," Phil. ii. 13. As a rule, however, the revisers correct the improper use of *which* for *that* in the authorised version, as in Luke vi. 27-28, Rom. xii. 14, Rev. xxii. 11, etc., etc.

all longsuffering for a *pattern* to them that should hereafter believe.	forth all *his* longsuffering, for an *example* to them which should hereafter believe.
1 Tim. vi. 2.—And they that have believing masters, let them not despise them because they are brethren: but rather do them service because they are faithful and beloved.	1 Tim. vi. 2.—And they that have believing masters, let them not despise them, because they are brethren: but *let them serve them the rather, because they that partake of the benefit are believing and beloved.*
Titus i. 12.—The Cretians are alway liars, evil beasts, *slow bellies*.	Titus i. 12.—Cretans are alway liars, evil beasts, *idle gluttons*.
Heb. ix. 5. — Cherubims of glory *shadowing* the Mercy-seat.	Heb. ix. 5.—Cherubim of glory *overshadowing* the mercy-seat.
Heb. xi. 26.—He *had respect unto* the recompense of the reward.[1]	Heb. xi. 26.—He *looked* unto the recompense of reward.
Heb. xiii. 5.—Let your *conversation be without covetousness*.	Heb. xiii. 5.—Be ye free from the love of money.

Turning now to the Old Testament, we find that, in determining the text of this part of the original Scriptures, the revisers had a comparatively simple task to perform. They were not embarassed with a multitude of discordant manuscripts. "The Received, or, as it is commonly called, the Massoretic Text of the Old Testament Scriptures has come down to us in manuscripts which are of no very great antiquity,[2] and which all belong to the same family or recension." And although it is admitted to be probable that other recensions were at one time in existence, the revisers considered that "the state of knowledge on the subject is not at present such as to justify any attempt at an entire reconstruction of the text." . . They accordingly deemed it "most prudent to adopt the Massoretic Text as the basis of their work, and to depart from it, as the authorised translators had done, only in exceptional cases. . . In some few instances of extreme difficulty, a reading has been adopted on the authority of the ancient versions, and the departure from the Massoretic Text recorded in the margin. In other cases, where the versions appeared to supply a very probable, though not so necessary, a correction of the text, the text has been left, and the variation indicated in the margin only."

---

[1] The phrase, *he had respect unto*, is a phrase that has come from Tyndale, and has evidently been inspired by the Latin version of Erasmus:—" Respectum enim habebat remunerationis." In the Vulgate, we read, "aspiciebat enim"; and in Beza "intuebatur enim."

[2] Preface.

On the margin of the revised version of the old Testament, therefore, a number of alternative readings are indicated. Sometimes, a note states " another reading " (which means another reading in the Massoretic text) is so and so ; at other times, the note states that "according to some ancient versions," (that is according to some other text than the Massoretic) the passage should read thus and thus. In many cases, where alternative readings are presented on the margin, the revisers have adopted the same reading as appears in the authorised translation. Their version of Deut. xxviii. 22, for instance, is: " The Lord shall smite thee with consumption . . . and with the sword, and with blasting, and with mildew." A marginal note, however, states that " according to some ancient versions, *drought*" should be substituted for *sword.* If we turn to the authorised translation we shall find that the reading adopted there is not the one that the revisers have relegated to the margin but the one that they have embodied in the text of Scripture. So also in Josh. vii. 17, Judges viii. 16, 1 Sam. ii. 3, Psalms ii. 12, Hos. vii. 6. In other cases where alternative readings are noted in the revised translation, the one that appears on the margin is the one that is given in the text of the authorised version. In these cases the revised version deviates from the authorised, and the deviation is caused not by a different rendering of the same Hebrew words, but by the adoption of a different, and presumably more authentic Hebrew text. As specimens of these textual variations the following passages may be cited.

REVISED VERSION, 1885.

Ex. xxxi. 10.—The finely wrought garments.
Lev. x. 6.—Let not the hair of your heads go loose, neither rend your clothes.
Josh. iii. 16. — The waters . . . rose up in one heap, a great way off, at Adam, the city that is beside Zarethan.
2 Sam. xvi. 10.—What have I to do with you, ye sons of Zeruiah? Because he curseth and, etc.
Job. iii. 6.—As for that night . . . let it not rejoice among the days of the year.
Ps. c. 3.—It is he that hath made us, and we are his.

AUTHORISED VERSION. 1611.

Ex. xxxi. 10.—The cloths of service.
Lev. x. 6.—Uncover not your heads, neither rend your clothes.
Josh. iii. 16.—The waters . . . rose up upon an heap very far from the city Adam, that is beside Zaretan.
2 Sam. xvi. 10.—What have I to do with you, ye sons of Zeruiah? so let him curse, etc.
Job. iii. 6.—As for that night . . . let it not be joined unto the days of the year.
Ps. c. 3.—It is he that hath made us, and not we ourselves.

Is. ix. 3.—Thou hast multiplied the nation, thou hast increased their joy.	Is. ix. 3.—Thou hast multiplied the nation, and not increased the joy.
Amos iii. 12.—That sit in Samaria in the corner of a couch, and on the silken cushions of a bed.	Amos iii. 12.—That dwell in Samaria in the corner of a bed, and in Damascus in a couch.
Amos v. 26.—Ye have borne Siccuth your king, and Chiun your images.	Amos v. 26.—Ye have borne the tabernacle of your Moloch, and Chiun your images.
Micah i. 10,—At Beth-le-Aphrah have I rolled myself in the dust.	Micah i. 10.—In the house of Aphrah roll thyself in the dust.

We have seen that in a large number of cases in which the revisers have departed from the text believed to underlie the authorised version of the *New* Testament they have adopted readings that Catholics have all along maintained to be the true letter of Scripture. It is not a little strange, therefore, that out of all the foregoing passages from the *Old* Testament, there is not one in which the new readings adopted by the revisers correspond with the text of either the Vulgate (Clementine) or Douay Bible.

In respect of its renderings, the revised version of the Old Testament has provoked very little hostile criticism. The revisers have, in the Old Testament, been content to adhere to the established forms of speech. Some of their renderings, however, will scarcely commend themselves to English readers. One verse, for instance, to which they have given a singularly feeble ending is Jonah iv. 6: "The Lord God prepared a gourd, and made it to come up over Jonah, that it might be a shadow over his head, to deliver him from *his evil case.*" A well-known verse, again, that they have robbed of soul, if not of sense, is Jer. xvii. 9: "The heart is deceitful above all things, and it is desperately *sick*: who can know it?" For the clear, simple statement attributed to the perverse man, Deut. xxix. 19, "I shall have peace, though I walk in the imagination of mine heart, to add drunkenness to thirst," they have substituted the dark saying: "I shall have peace, though I walk in the stubbornness of mine heart, *to destroy the moist with the dry.*" The fine religious phrase, "vexation of spirit," they have, from some scruple of scholastic conscience, perverted into "striving after wind." But for every instance in which the revisers have enfeebled or impaired, there are ten and more than ten instances in which they have strengthened and improved the English of the Old Testament. A very inconsequent statement in the authorised version is: "*Though* thy people Israel be as the sand of the sea, *yet* a remnant of them shall return," Is. x. 22. This reads like a declaration of mercy and not of judgment. But by the substitution of *only* for *yet*, the revisers have thrown on this prophetic utterance a new light, and its meaning is now quite apparent to the most cursory reader: "Though thy people Israel be as the sand of the sea, *only* a remnant of them shall return: a consumption is determined, overflowing with righteousness." Another sentence in the old version that may well perplex plain people is Is. xvi. 6: "We have heard of the pride of Moab: he is very proud: even of his haughtiness, and his pride, and his wrath: *but his lies shall not be so.*" For the words italicised the revisers substitute "his boastings are nought," and by this change they divest the passage of all obscurity.[1] One verse that has a new antithetical force imparted to it by the revisers is Hos. xii. 3: "In the womb he took his brother by the heel: and in his manhood he had power with God." And many are the verses that in the authorised translation are clear and explicit enough, but are made in the revision to read more smoothly or more forcibly by a slight transposition or inversion of words, as Prov. viii. 2: "In the top of high places by the way, where the paths meet, *she standeth*"; Is. ix. 4; "For the yoke of his burden, and the staff of his shoulder, the rod of his oppressor, *thou hast broken.*"

To show as briefly as possible, however, what amendments

---

[1] To make language so plain that it cannot be misunderstood is impossible. A countryman (five and thirty years ago) once confessed to me that he was sorely exercised over Job ix. 25, "My days are swifter than a *post.*" A post, he said, has neither swiftness nor motion. It is a thing that stands still for people to hang gates on, or tie horses to! Another countryman confessed to me that he was as sorely exercised over Ps. cvii. 23, "They that go down *to* the sea in *ships.*" People, he said, go down to the sea in carts, and go into ships when they come to the sea! On asking a class of grown-up lads in a small landward parish the meaning of the word "trance" in Acts x. 10, "Peter went up upon the housetop to pray, . . . and he fell into a *trance,*" I was told it was a "passage" or "lobby"! and at this answer no one present evinced the slightest sign of either amazement or amusement.

have been made by the revisers on the diction of the English version of the Old Testament, a few selected verses from the authorised and revised translations respectively may, without comment, be submitted for comparison in parallel columns :

AUTHORISED VERSION.	REVISED VERSION.
Job xv. 29.—He shall not be rich, neither shall his substance continue, neither shall *he prolong the perfection thereof upon* the earth.	Job xv. 29.—He shall not be rich, neither shall his substance continue, neither shall *their produce bend* to the earth.
Ps. xvi. 2.—Thou art my Lord ; *my goodness extendeth not to thee ; but* to the saints that are in the earth, *and to* the excellent, in whom is all my delight.	Ps. xvi. 2.—Thou art my Lord : *I have no good beyond thee. As for* the saints that are in the earth, *they are* the excellent, in whom is all my delight.
Ps. xlv. 13.—The King's daughter is all glorious *within*.	Ps. xlv. 13.—The King's daughter *within the palace* is all glorious.
Ps. lxxxviii. 5.—*Free* among the dead, like the slain that lie in the grave, whom thou rememberest no more.	Ps. lxxxviii. 5.—*Cast off* among the dead, like the slain that lie in the grave, whom thou rememberest no more.
Ps. cxxxvii. 7.—Remember, O Lord, the children of Edom in the day of Jerusalem.	Ps. cxxxvii. 7.—Remember, O Lord, against the children of Edom the day of Jerusalem.
Ps. cxli. 5.—Let the righteous smite me : it shall be a kindness ; and let him reprove me : it shall be *an excellent oil which shall not break my head.*	Ps. cxli. 5.—Let the righteous smite me, it shall be a kindness ; and let him reprove me, it shall be *as oil upon the head : let not my head refuse it.*
Prov. viii. 26.—While as yet he had not made the earth, nor the fields, nor the *highest part* of the dust of the world.	Prov. viii. 26.—While as yet he had not made the earth, nor the fields, nor the *beginning* of the dust of the world.
Prov. xiii. 23.—Much food is in the tillage of the poor ; but there is that is destroyed *for want of judgment.*	Prov. xiii. 23.—Much food is in the tillage of the poor ; but there is that is destroyed *by reason of injustice.*
Prov. xix. 14.—House and riches are the inheritance *of* fathers : *and* a prudent wife is from the Lord.	Prov. xix. 14.—House and riches are an inheritance *from* fathers, *but* a prudent wife is from the Lord.
Eccles. viii. 8. — Neither hath he power *in* the day of death.	Eccles. viii. 8. — Neither hath he power *over* the day of death.
Eccles. xi. 5.—As thou knowest not what is the way of the *spirit*, . . . even so thou knowest not.	Eccles. xi. 5.—As thou knowest not what is the way of the *wind*, . . . even so thou knowest not.
Is. ix. 1.—Nevertheless the dimness shall not be such as was in her vexation, when at the first he lightly afflicted the land of Zebulun, and the land of Napthali, and afterwards did more grievously afflict her by the way of the sea, beyond Jordan, in Galilee of the nations.	Is. ix. 1.—But *there shall be no gloom to her that was in anguish. In the former time he brought into contempt* the land of Zebulun, and the land of Napthali, but *in the latter time hath he made it glorious*, by the way of the sea, beyond Jordan, Galilee of the nations.
Is. xxix. 16.—*Surely your turning of things upside down shall be esteemed as the potter's clay ;* for shall the work say of him that made it, He made me not.	Is. xxix. 16.—*Ye turn things upside down !* Shall the potter be counted as clay ; that the thing made should say of him that made it, He made me not.
Is. lvii. 2.—They shall *rest in their beds, each one walking in his uprightness.*	Is. lvii. 2.—They rest in their beds, each one that walketh in his uprightness.
Is. lxv. 11.—But ye are they that forsake the Lord, that forget my holy mountain, that prepare a table for *that*	Is. lxv. 11.—But ye that forsake the Lord, that forget my holy mountain, that prepare a table for *Fortune*, and

troop, and that furnish the drink offering unto *that number*.

Jer. xxxi. 35.—Which *divideth the sea when the waves thereof roar*.

Jer. xlvi. 7.—Who is this that *cometh up as a flood, whose waters are moved* as the rivers?

Jer. xlviii. 12.—Behold, the days come, saith the Lord, that I will send unto him *wanderers*, that shall *cause him to wander*, and shall empty his vessels, and break their bottles.

Jer. xlviii. 27.—Was not Israel a derision unto thee? was he found among thieves? for since thou speakest of him, *thou skippedst for joy*.

Ezek. vii. 7.—*The morning* is come unto thee, O thou that dwellest in the land: the time is come, the day of trouble is near, and not the *sounding again of the mountains*.

Micah ii. 11.—If a man walking in *the spirit* and falsehood do lie, saying, I will prophesy to thee of wine and of strong drink.

Zeph. iii. 3.—Her princes within her are roaring lions; her judges are evening wolves; *they gnaw not the bones till the morrow*.

Dan. viii. 17.—*At the time of the end shall be* the vision.

Dan. viii. 25.—He shall magnify himself in his heart, and *by peace* shall destroy many.

that fill up mingled wine unto *Destiny*.

Jer. xxxi. 35.—Which *stirreth up the sea, that the waves thereof roar*.

Jer. xlvi. 7.—Who is this that *riseth up like the Nile, whose waters toss themselves* like the rivers?

Jer. xlviii. 12.—Behold, the days come, saith the Lord, that I will send unto him *them that pour off*, and they shall empty his vessels, and break their bottles in pieces.

Jer. xlviii. 27.—Was not Israel a derision unto thee? was he found among thieves? for as often as thou speakest of him, *thou waggest the head*.

Ezek. vii. 7.—*Thy doom* is come unto thee, Oh inhabitant of the land; the time is come, the day is near; a day of tumult and not *of joyful shouting upon the mountains*.

Micah ii. 11.—If a man walking in *wind* and falsehood, do lie, saying, I will prophesy unto thee of wine and of strong drink.

Zeph. iii. 3.—Her princes in the midst of her are roaring lions; her judges are evening wolves; *they leave nothing till the morrow*.

Dan. viii. 17.—The vision *belongeth to the time of the end*.

Dan. viii. 25.—He shall magnify himself in his heart, and *in their security* shall he destroy many.

Out of the dissimilar English readings in the authorised and revised versions of the Old Testament an interesting chapter of curious information might be compiled.[1] In some cases the readings in the two versions are as nearly as possible the opposite of each other. In the one version we read, Prov. xxv. 23, that "the north wind driveth away rain," and in the other that "the north wind bringeth forth rain." In the one version we are told, Ex. xxxiv. 33, that Moses put a veil on his face "*till* he had done speaking with the Israelites," in the other that he put on the veil "*when* he had done speaking." In the one version the prophet is represented as saying, Hos. viii. 5, "Thy calf, O Samaria, hath cast thee off," in the other, "He hath cast

---

[1] The term "readings" is here used to signify *the English words found in the two translations*, whether the difference of wording in the two versions arises from the adoption of a different Hebrew text, or from a different rendering of the same Hebrew text.

off thy calf, O Samaria." The blessing pronounced on Reuben in the one version, Deut. xxxiii. 6, " Let Reuben live and not die ; and *let not* his men be few," is in the other version so minimised as to look like an imprecation rather than a benediction, " Let Reuben live and not die ; yet *let* his men be few." The " handful of corn " on the top of the mountains that in the one version is predicted, Ps. lxxii. 16, for Israel during the benignant reign of Solomon, is in the other version magnified into "abundance of corn, the fruit whereof shall shake like Lebanon." Of Immanuel the child of hope, it is said in the one version, Is. vii. 15, " Butter and honey shall he eat *that he may know* to refuse the evil and choose the good." The enigma of this statement is in the other version removed by converting the words "that he may know" into "when he knoweth." Of the man, again, that has begotten an hundred children and seen many days on earth it is in the one version said sorrowfully, Eccles. vi. 4, that " an untimely birth is better than he ; for *he* cometh in with vanity and departeth in darkness, and *his* name shall be covered with darkness." In the other version it is not the rich and prosperous man but the untimely birth that is declared to be the subject of this oblivion. " *It* cometh in with vanity and departeth in darkness. . . . moreover *it* hath not seen nor known the sun." [1]

In order to give complete expression to their renderings, the King's translators introduced into their version of the Bible many English words for which there are no counter-parts in the original. And, that no misapprehension might arise from this paraphrastic mode of translation, the added words were printed in italic characters. In the revised version also, there are interpolated words printed in a similarly distinctive manner.

---

[1] The following may be cited as curious readings in the revised version of the Old Testament :—" And he (Ishmael) shall be *as a wild ass* among men," Gen. xvi. 12 ; " Abraham said unto his servant, *the elder of his house*, that ruled over all that he had, etc.," Gen. xxiv. 2 ; " I asked her and said, Whose daughter art thou? And she said, The daughter of Bethuel : and I *put the ring upon her nose*," Gen. xxiv. 47. A phrase that is shewn by the revisers to be of far greater antiquity than many people suppose, is " worth one's salt." The authorised rendering of Ezra iv. 14, "We have *maintenance* from the king's palace," is changed on principles of literalism into, " We eat the *salt* of the palace."

It is clear, however, that by interpolations of this kind the Scriptures might be twisted ever so far from their true meanings. In the new version of the nineteenth Psalm, for instance, it is said of the heavens which declare the glory of God, and of the firmament which showeth his handiwork: " There is no speech nor language; their voice cannot be heard." But by inserting the word *where*, the King's translators have in the old version given a very different representation of the Psalmist's statement. Instead of making the Psalmist describe the hosts of heaven as dumb and voiceless, they make him say: " There is no speech nor language, *where* their voice is not heard." In the following verses will be found other instances in which the meaning of Old Testament Scripture has been affected by interpolations.[1]

AUTHORISED VERSION.	REVISED VERSION.
Ps. xxxvii. 8.—Fret not thyself in any wise to do evil.	Ps. xxxvii. 8.—Fret not thyself, *it tendeth* only to evil doing.
Ps. lx. 9-10.—Who will lead me into Edom? *Wilt* not thou, O God, *which* hadst cast us off? and *thou*, O God, *which* didst not go out with our armies?	Ps. lx. 9-10.—Who hath led me unto Edom? Hast not thou, O God, cast us off? and thou goest not forth, O God, with our hosts.
Job. xi. 20.—Their hope shall be *as* the giving up of the ghost.	Job. xi. 20.—Their hope shall be the giving up of the ghost.
2 Sam. i. 18.—He bade them teach the children of Judah *the use of* the bow.[2]	2 Sam. i. 18.—He bade them teach the children of Judah *the song of* the bow.

It is astonishing to find how much the revisers have changed the meaning of some verses, by the alteration of a single word, sometimes an apparently unimportant word. The following passages will speak for themselves, the distinctive words being

---

[1] In the New Testament, also, the meaning of some passages has been affected by the revisers' interpolations. A new light, for instance, is thrown on Mark vii. 19, by the interpolation of the words "this he said."

AUTHORISED VERSION.	REVISED VERSION.
Mark vii. 18-19.—Whatsoever thing from without entereth into the man, it cannot defile him, because it entereth not into his heart, but into the belly, and goeth out into the draught, purging all meats.	Mark vii. 18-19.—Whatsoever from without goeth into the man, it cannot defile him: because it goeth not into his heart, but into his belly, and goeth out into the draught. *This he said*, making all meats clean.

[2] Two passages previously quoted, namely, Is. x. 22, and Is. xvi. 6, are also cases in point.

italicised, and all other words, whether interpolated or not, being printed in common type.

AUTHORISED VERSION.	REVISED VERSION.
Ps. xvi. 11.—*At* thy right hand there are pleasures for evermore.	Ps. xvi. 11.—*In* thy right hand there are pleasures for evermore.
Ps. xxvii. 3.—Though war should rise against me, *in this* will I be confident.	Ps. xxvii. 3.—Though war should rise against me, *even then* will I be confident.
Ps. lxix. 5.—When the iniquity *of* my heels shall compass me about.	Ps. xlix. 5.—When iniquity *at* my heels compasseth me about.
Ps. li. 12.—Uphold me with *thy* free spirit.	Ps. li. 12.—Uphold me with *a* free spirit.
Ps. lx. 2.—Thou hast made the *earth* to tremble.	Ps. lx. 2.—Thou hast made the *land* to tremble.
Ps. lxxiii. 8-9.—They speak loftily. They set their mouth *against* the heavens; and their tongue walketh through the earth.	Ps. lxxiii. 8-9.—They speak loftily. They have set their mouth *in* the heavens, and their tongue walketh through the earth.
Ps. lxxvi. 4.—Thou art *more* glorious and excellent *than* the mountains of prey.	Ps. lxxvi. 4.—Glorious art thou and excellent *from* the mountains of prey.
Ps. lxxxvii. 4.—I will make mention of Rahab and Babylon *to* them that know me.	Ps. lxxxvii. 4.—I will make mention of Rahab and Babylon *as among* them that know me.

In a very considerable number of instances, the revisers have inverted the authorised renderings, so as to make the predicate of a sentence the subject, and the subject the predicate. This is particularly noticeable in the book of Proverbs, as will appear from the following examples :—

AUTHORISED VERSION.	REVISED VERSION.
Prov. xi. 12.—He that is void of wisdom despiseth his neighbour.	Prov. xi. 12.—He that despiseth his neighbour is void of wisdom.
Prov. xi. 30.—He that winneth souls is wise.	Prov. xi. 30.—He that is wise winneth souls.
Prov. xii. 27.—The substance of a diligent man is precious.	Prov. xii. 27.—The precious substance of men is to the diligent.
Prov. xiv. 31.—He that honoureth his Maker hath mercy on the poor.	Prov. xiv. 31.—He that hath mercy on the needy honoureth his Maker.
Prov. xvii. 27.—He that hath knowledge spareth his words, and a man of understanding is of an excellent spirit.	Prov. xvii. 27.—He that spareth his words hath knowledge, and he that is of a cool spirit is a man of understanding.

The most remarkable thing however, about some of the revised readings is that they have no apparent point of either resemblance or contrast to those they have superseded. They have seemingly no more in common with the authorised readings than the clusters of Eshcol had with the sword of Gideon. For instance, the nation described in the authorised version, Is. xviii. 2, as "scattered and peeled," is, by the revisers, renovated into "tall and smooth"; the man that by the King's translators, was designated "a quiet prince," Jer. li. 59, is transformed into "chief chamberlain" or "quarter-master"; and those of the uncircumcision formerly particularised, Jer. ix. 26, as inhabiting "the utmost corners,"[1] are now specified as the men of peculiar customs, who "have the corners of their hair polled." To the delectation doubtless of modern Rechabites, "flagons of wine" have several times over been changed into "cakes of raisins"; and these innocent materials of refection are set forth, Is. xvi. 7, as what were anciently reckoned the "foundations" of Kir-hareseth. In like manner, "linen yarn" is commuted, 1 Kings x. 28, into "droves of horses"; "mules" are metamorphosed, Gen. xxxvi. 24, into "hot springs"; "musical instruments" are abandoned, Eccles. ii. 8, for "concubines"; and "the pen of the writer" is exchanged, Judges v. 14, for "the marshall's staff." Among other substitutions, too, may be mentioned "sheep-folds" for "two burdens," Gen. xlix. 14; "seamew" for "cuckoo," Lev. xi. 16; "submit themselves" for "be found liars," Deut. xxxiii. 29;[2] "porcupine" for "bittern," Is. xiv. 23; "them that are lusty" for "desolate places," Is. lix. 10; "enlargest thine eyes" for "rentest thy face," Jer. iv. 30; "break bread" for "tear themselves," Jer. xvi. 7; "desolations" for "Sabbaths," Lam. i. 7; "eminency among them" for "wailing for them," Ez. vii. 11; "spears" for "fir-trees," Nahum ii. 3; "pledges" for "thick clay," Hab. ii. 6; and "mantles" for "hats," Dan. iii. 21.

Not a few notable words and phrases in the authorised version, too, have been excluded from the revised. Conspicuous among these are some terms that were regarded as designations of Christ. The proclamation, " I will raise up for them a

---

[1] The revised renderings of Jer. ix. 26, and Jer. li. 59, are given as alternative renderings on the margin of the authorised version.

[2] The zoological nomenclature in the authorised version has undergone much change in the recent revision. One verse will suffice for an example :—

AUTHORISED VERSION.	REVISED VERSION.
Lev. xi. 30.—And the ferret and the chameleon, and the lizard and the snail and the mole.	Lev. xi. 30.—And the gecko, and the land-crocodile, and the lizard, and the sand-lizard, and the chameleon.

plant of renown," Ez. xxxiv. 29, is changed into, "I will raise up unto them *a plantation for renown*"; the word "Messiah," Dan. ix. 25, is turned into "the anointed one"; and the expression "desire of all nations," Hag. ii. 7, is transmuted into "the desirable things of all nations." In these changes, however, there is nothing to cause uneasiness, as if modern scholarship were abstracting from holy Scripture its true spiritual meaning. There was a tendency in divines of the old school to strain the language of the Bible, and to bring out Messianic references where none really existed.[2]

Many passages, also, are made to read differently in the old and new versions according as certain words in the original text have been considered common or proper nouns. The following will serve as instances:—

AUTHORISED VERSION.	REVISED VERSION.
Gen. xxxiii. 18.—And Jacob came to *Shalem*, a city of Shechem.	Gen. xxxiii. 18.—And Jacob came *in peace* to the city of Shechem.
Deut. ii. 23.—The Avims which dwelt in Hazerim even unto Azzah.	Deut. ii. 23.—The Avvim which dwelt *in villages* as far as Gaza.
Judges viii. 13.—Gideon returned from battle *before the sun was up*.	Judges viii. 13.—Gideon returned from the battle from the ascent of Heres.
1 Kings v. 18.—Hiram's builders did hew them, and the *stone squarers*.	1 Kings v. 18.—Hiram's builders and the *Gebalites* did fashion them.
Is. xv. 5.—My heart shall cry out for Moab: his fugitives shall flee unto Zoar, *an heifer of three years old*.	Is. xv. 5.—My heart crieth out for Moab: her nobles flee unto Zoar, to *Eglath-shelishiyah*.
Is. xxiii. 11.—The Lord hath given a commandment against the *merchant city*, to destroy the strongholds thereof.	Is. xxiii. 11.—The Lord hath given commandment concerning *Canaan*, to destroy the strongholds thereof.
Is. xxx. 7.—For the Egyptians shall help in vain, and to no purpose: therefore have I cried concerning this. *Their strength* is to sit still.	Is. xxx. 7.—For Egypt helpeth in vain and to no purpose; therefore have I called her *Rahab*, that sitteth still.
Jer. li. 1.—Behold, I will raise up against Babylon, and against them that dwell in the *midst of them that rise up against me*, a destroying wind.	Jer. li. 1.—Behold, I will raise up against Babylon, and against them that dwell in *Leb-kamai* a destroying wind.

---

[2] For instance, Jer. xi. 19 is in the revised (and, barring a slight variation, in the authorised) version rendered:—"I was like a gentle lamb that is led to the slaughter, and I knew not that they had devised devices against me, saying, *let us destroy the tree with the fruit thereof*, and let us cut him off from the land of the living that his name be no more remembered." These words are by all Protestants considered as referring to the prophet himself. But Catholics contend that they are spoken of Jesus, and in Catholic Bibles the passage italicised above is made to read, "Let us cast wood on his bread," which by St. Jerome is fancifully interpreted to mean, let us cast the cross on the body of our Saviour.—See *Fulke's Defence*, etc., chap. xvii. sec. 18.

Authorised Version	Revised Version
Ezek. xxvii. 6.—The *company of the Ashurites* have made thy benches of ivory, brought out of the isles of Chittim.	Ezek. xxvii. 6.—They have made thy benches of ivory *inlaid in boxwood*, from the isles of Kittim.
Zech. vii. 2.—When they had sent *unto the house of God* Sherezer and Regem-melech, and their men, to pray before the Lord.	Zech. vii. 2.—Now they *of Bethel* had sent Sherezer and Regem-melech, and their men, to entreat the favour of the Lord.

By a change of spelling, too, the revisers have, in some instances, thrown light on the meaning of a verse in which a proper name occurs. In the authorised translation, Joshua, the servant of Moses, is referred to in Acts vii. 45 and Heb. iv. 8, under the name of *Jesus;* and the English reader who does not happen to have a Bible with marginal notes, or does not consult the marginal notes, is very apt to imagine that the person there called *Jesus* is the Saviour of sinners, who died on the cross. By printing the name *Joshua*, the revisers have removed this source of misapprehension; and it is interesting to note that in this orthographic change they have simply reverted to the old spelling of the word, as given in Tyndale's Testament.

As further specimens of dissimilar English readings in the authorised and revised translations of the Old Testament, the following verses may be adduced:—

Authorised Version.	Revised Version.
Job v. 24.—Thou shalt visit thy habitation, and shalt not sin.	Job. v. 24.—Thou shalt visit thy fold, and shalt miss nothing.
Job xi. 6.—That he would shew thee the secrets of wisdom, that they are double to that which is.	Job. xi. 6.—That he would shew thee the secrets of wisdom, that it is manifold in effectual working.
Job xvii. 6.—Aforetime I was as a tabret.	Job. xvii. 6.—I am become an open abhorring.
Ps. x. 4.—God is not in all his thoughts.	Ps. x. 4.—All his thoughts are. There is no God.
Ps. lxviii. 4.—Extol him that rideth upon the heavens, by his name Jah.	Ps. lxviii. 4.—Cast up a highway for him that rideth through the deserts; his name is Jah.
Ps. lxviii. 19.—Blessed be the Lord, who daily loadeth us with benefits.	Ps. lxviii. 19.—Blessed be the Lord, who daily beareth our burden.
Prov. v. 16.—Let thy fountains be dispersed abroad, and rivers of waters in the streets.	Prov. v. 16.—Should thy springs be dispersed abroad, and rivers of water in the streets?
Prov. xviii. 24.—A man that hath friends must shew himself friendly.	Prov. xviii. 24.—He that maketh many friends doeth it to his own destruction.
Eccles. x. 11.—Surely the serpent will bite without enchantment, and a babbler is no better.	Eccles. x. 11.—If the serpent bite before it be charmed, then there is no advantage in the charmer.
Is. xix. 10.—And they shall be broken in the purposes thereof, all that make sluices and ponds for fish.	Is. xix. 10.—And her pillars shall be broken in pieces, all they that work for hire shall be grieved in soul.

Is. xxvii. 8.—He stayeth his rough wind in the day of the east wind.	Is. xxvii. 8.—He hath removed her with his rough blast in the day of the east wind.
Is. lix. 19.—When the enemy shall come in like a flood, the Spirit of the Lord shall lift up a standard against him.	Is. lix. 19.—For he shall come as a rushing stream, which the breath of the Lord driveth.
Jer. vi. 2.—I have likened the daughter of Zion to a comely and delicate woman.	Jer. vi. 2.—The comely and delicate one, the daughter of Zion, will I cut off.
Jer. xviii. 14.—Will a man leave the snow of Lebanon, which cometh from the rock of the field?	Jer. xviii. 14.—Shall the snow of Lebanon fail from the rock of the field?
Ezek. xi. 3.—Which say, It is not near: let us build houses.	Ezek. xi. 3.—Which say, The time is not near to build houses.
Hos. xiii. 9.—O Israel, thou hast destroyed thyself, but in me is thine help.	Hos. xiii. 9.—It is thy destruction, O Israel, that thou art against me, against thy help.
Hab. ii. 5.—Yea, also, because he transgresseth by wine, he is a proud man, neither keepeth at home, who enlargeth his desire as hell, and is as death and cannot be satisfied.	Hab. ii. 5.—Yea, moreover, wine is a treacherous dealer, a haughty man, and that keepeth not at home: who enlargeth his desire as hell, and he is as death, and cannot be satisfied.
Mal. i. 10.—Who is there even among you that would shut the doors for nought? neither do you kindle fire on mine altar for nought.	Mal. i. 10.—Oh that there were one among you that would shut the doors, that ye might not kindle fire on mine altar in vain.

One of the rules laid down to the revisers was to introduce into the new version of the Bible " as few alterations as possible, consistent with faithfulness." The revisers admit that, in the application of this conservative principle to the numerous and intricate details of their work, they found themselves " constrained by faithfulness to introduce changes which might not at first sight appear to be included under the rule." There are, for instance, many words in the authorised version that are either never used in modern English, or are used in a sense widely different from what they were by the King's translators two hundred and eighty years ago. The revisers had to consider what should be done with these words, whether they should be retained or changed. The result is that some of them have been changed, and others have been kept as they were. "We have never," say the revisers of the New Testament, " removed any archaisms, whether in structure or in words, except where we were persuaded either that the meaning of the words was not generally understood, or that the nature of the expression led to some misconception of the true sense of the passage." The revisers of the Old Testament make a similar declaration in their preface. Unless words were both unintelligible and obsolete they have been retained, but when they were both obsolete and unintelligible they have been changed. The word "earing," in the phrase "earing and harvest," has been changed into its equivalent, *ploughing;* because, not only was the true meaning of *earing* unknown to most readers, but a positively erroneous meaning was generally attached to the word. On the other hand, the term "bolled," applied to flax when in pod, has been retained, Ex. ix. 31 ; because, although obsolete, it is not associated with a wrong meaning. The consequence is that, in the revised version of the Bible, there are to be found a great many archaic words, which some people may possibly consider should have been displaced by words that are less antiquated. In the Old Testament we still find *ark* for basket ; *bravery* for beauty ; *chargers* for platters ; *chapmen* for traders ; *clouted* for patched ; *cunning* for skill ; *desired* for regretted ; *dukes* for chiefs ; *eminent* for projecting ; *fats* for vats ; *fine* for refine ; *fray* for frighten ; *imperfect* for unformed ; *mount* for mound ; *neesings* for sneezings ; *occurrent* for opponent ; *peculiar* for own ; *prevent* for anticipate ; *several* house for separate house ; *seethe* for boil ; *sith* for since ; *stomacher* for robe ; *tabering* for beating ; *withs* for twigs, etc., etc. In the New Testament, we find *fulfilled* for "made full" (John iii. 29) ; *hale* for drag : *honestly* for honourably, and also for becomingly ; *instant* for urgent ; *listed* for desired ; *mortify* for put to death ; *perfected* for ended ; *reprobate* for cannot stand the test ; *wot* and *wist* for know and knew.[1] It is a matter of opinion whether all or any of these old fashioned words should have been extruded by more modern terms. The line must be drawn somewhere ; and very few of those who think that the diction of the Bible might have been more modernised by the revisers, will go the length of approving the transatlantic suggestion that the "ladder" of Jacob's dream should be changed into "staircase." But whether the revisers

---

[1] Besides these, the most of the words given in last chapter, pages 319-20, as specimens of words used in an archaic or peculiar sense in the authorised version of the Bible have been retained by the revisers of 1881 and 1885.

have, or have not, gone as far as they might in purifying the diction of the Bible, it must be conceded that they have gone a considerable length. The curse on Cain no longer reads "a fugitive and a *vagabond* shalt thou be," but "a fugitive and a *wanderer*." The reproach of Asher is no longer that he "continued on the sea shore, and abode in his *breaches*," when the trumpet sounded to battle, but that "he sat still at the haven of the sea, and abode in his *creeks*." In the New Testament, too, there are many passages that the revisers have made much plainer to the English reader, by the removal of words that had grown out of their original meaning. Very hazy must have been the notion in some minds of what was meant by the exhortation, Luke xiv. 8, "when thou art bidden of any man to a wedding, sit not down in the *highest room*." The revisers have made the exhortation plain, by modernising the expression "highest room" into *chief seat*. It may be questioned, again, if in these latter days many people have been able, unaided, to find out what is meant by the statement, Gal. iv. 17: "They zealously *affect* you, but not well: yea they would *exclude* you, that you might *affect* them." But no one needs to ask the meaning of the revisers' rendering of the verse: "They zealously *seek* you in no good way: nay, they desire to shut you out, that ye may *seek* them." Even in passages that did not require explanation or clearing, the revisers have greatly improved the text of the English Testament by removing uncouth and archaic words, and setting in their place simple terms in current use. In the story of the woman who touched the garment of Jesus, it is said in the authorised version, Mark v. 30, that Jesus, "knowing in himself that *virtue* had gone out of him, turned him about in the *press*, and said, who touched my clothes?" Possibly no reader misapprehends this statement, but every one will, nevertheless, admit that the revisers have made it more explicit by changing the words *virtue* and *press* into *power* and *crowd*.[1]

---

[1] An archaic phrase in the Old Testament, which has been modernised by the revisers, is:—"They should heat the furnace *one* seven times more than it was wont to be heated," Daniel iii. 19. Another archaic phrase in the authorised ver-

It may now be asked what good, if any, has been got from the recent revision of the English version of the Bible. Much good has doubtless been got, and in more ways than one. For twenty years before the issue of the revised version of the New Testament, people had been hearing so much said about the wrong readings and the wrong renderings in the authorised translation of the Scriptures that many persons were wondering if the true Bible was altogether different from the book hitherto received in this country under that designation. The alleged wrong readings and wrong renderings have now been subjected to careful scrutiny, and been by a large body of competent scholars rectified, where correction was needed; and as the result of this scrutiny and rectification we have now a Bible that in every point of practical significance is the same as we had before.[1] Suspicions have thus been laid to rest. And besides allaying suspicions the revisers have supplied us with a noble work. Their emendations, although for the most part minute, are numerous, and they have done much to elucidate the Scriptures to English readers. But to say that the revision is perfect would be to say of it what cannot be said of any work that the head and hand of man ever executed. Like all previous versions of the Bible in English, it has faults of both omission and commission, and it is not unlikely that many persons are alive to-day that shall live to see the issue of another and still better revision of the "dearworth" book.

---

sion of the Old Testament, which has been retained in the revised, is :—"They made ready the present *against* Joseph came at noon," Gen. xliii. 25. Of archaic phrases in the New Testament which have been modernised by the revisers may be mentioned, "About *an* eight days after these sayings," Luke ix. 28, and "by and by" in the sense of *immediately* or *at once*, as in Mark vi. 25, Luke xvii. 7, etc.

[1] How much some persons endeavour to make of small matters may be inferred from the following remarks by Dean Burgon. "We entirely miss (in the revised version of the Testament) many a solemn utterance of the Spirit, as when we are assured that verses 44 and 46 of Mark ix. are omitted by the best authorities," p. 510. The two verses here referred to are :—"Where their worm dieth not, and the fire is not quenched," and they are the same as verse 48, which is retained in the revised as well as in the authorised version.

APPENDIX.

A

EARLY SCOTTISH RENDERINGS OF SCRIPTURE.

In the month of March, 1542 (1543 modern reckoning) an Act was passed by the Parliament of Scotland declaring it "lefull to all our souirane ladyis lieges to haif the haly write, baith the new testament and the auld, in the vulgar toung, in Inglis or Scottis of ane gude and trew translation, and (that) thei sall incur na crimes for the hesing or reding of the samin, providing alwayis that na man despute or hald oppinzeones under the panis contenit in the Act of parliament."

Dr. Eadie says that by the word "Scottis" in this Act is meant Gaelic. Before accepting that opinion we would need to see evidence in support of it.[1] In the sixteenth century Gaelic was in Scotland called Irish. In 1595 a preacher was presented to the parish of Callander, but found himself "not meet for that congregation in respect he wants the Irish language"; and in 1598 another presented to the same parish was found by the Presbytery unfit for the charge "in respect he knaws not the Irish language quhilk is maist commonlie usit be the saids parochiners" (Scott's Fasti). On the other hand "Scottis" was the term applied in the sixteenth century to the dialect of English that was then spoken in Scotland. In a letter addressed to John Knox, on the 27th October, 1563, Ninian Winzet says:—"Gif ye, throu curiositie of nouationis, hes forzet our auld plane

---

[1] "Among the means used for the reformation of the Highlands, it is proper to mention the translation of Knox's Liturgy into Gaelic, by John Carswell, Superintendent of the West, and Bishop of the Isles, printed at Edinburgh, in 1567. . . . I have little doubt that the Highlanders had the Psalms in their own language during the Sixteenth Century. A Gaelic translation of the first fifty Psalms was published by the Synod of Argyll in the year 1650, most probably made from the newly authorised version in English."—M'Crie's *Life of Melville* (sec. edition) ii. p. 91-92, note.

Scottis quhilk your mother lerit you, in tymes cuming I sall wryte to zou my mynd in Latin, for I am nocht acquyntit with zour Southeroun."[1] It seems clear, therefore, that the vulgar tongue referred to in the foregoing Act, 1543, was English in its two forms, as spoken in England and as spoken in Scotland. But although permission was granted to the Queen's lieges to possess and read a translation of the Bible in Scottis, no such translation was then, or ever afterwards, published.

In the works of some Scottish authors, however, there are to be found renderings of particular verses of Scripture in the writers' own vernacular, and a comparison of these renderings with their counterparts in the English translations of corresponding date will shew what difference there was between "auld plane Scottis" and fashionable "Southeroun."

The first printed exposition in Scottis of the Protestant doctrine is a treatise that was published by John Gau in 1533. This treatise is now ascertained to be a translation of a work by a Continental Protestant named Christiern Pedersen. A comparison of Scripture quotations in this work of Gau's, with the renderings in Tyndale's first version of the Scriptures, will indicate how far the "Inglis" of 1526, and the "Scottis" of 1534, differed both in their vocabulary and pronunciation.

GAU, 1533.	TYNDALE, 1526.
Mat. ix. 12.—Thay quhilk ar hail thay mister notht ane lech bot yay quhilk ar seik. P. 62.	Mat. ix. 12.—The whole neade not the visicion but they thatt are sicke.
Mat. xii. 40.—Siclik as he wesz iii dais and iii nichtis in the weyme of ane quhail sua sal the sone of man be iii dais and iii nichtis in the hart of the zeird. P. 46.	Mat. xii. 40.—For as jonas was thre days and thre nyghtes in the whales belly, soo shall the sone of man be thre days and thre nyghtes in the hert of the erth.

---

[1] Archbishop Hamilton's Catechism is in like manner described in an Act of Provincial Council, Jan., 1551 (1552), as a certain book written in the vulgar and Scottish dialect:—"librum quendam vulgari et Scotico idiomate conscriptum." —M'Crie's *Life of Knox*, vol. i. p. 411. As specimens of Scottish renderings of Scripture in Hamilton's Catechism, the following verses may be submitted :—

Ex. xx. 2-5.—I am ye Lord thi God, quhilk hais brocht ye fra the land of Egypt, fra the house of bondage. Thow sall haif na other goddis but me, thou sal nocht mak to thee ony grauit ymage, nother ony similitude of ony thing that is in the heuin abone, or in ye erd beneth, nor of ony thing yat is in the watter under the erd. Thow sal nocht adorne yame, nor worschip yame.

Hos. xiii. 14.—O dede I sal be thi dede, O hel I sal byte the. (Morsus tuus ero.—*Vulgate*. I will be thy bite.—*Douay Trans*.

Mat. xviii. 17.—Gif he will nocht heir the kirk, lat him be to the as ane infidele, unchristinit, and ane publican.

Mat. xvi. 18.—Thow art Peter, and apone this steyne I sal big my kirk. P. 61.	Mat. xvi. 18.—Thou arte Peter, and apon this roocke I wyll bylde my congregacion.
Mat. xviii. 28.—Thane he twik hime be the halsz and said pay quhat thou aw to me. P. 60.	Mat. xviii. 28.—And toke hym by the throote sainge, paye that thou owest.
Mat. xviii. 32-34.—Thow vikkit seruand, I forgaif ze al thy det quhen thow desirit of me, suld thow noth siclik be marciful to thy marow and forgiff hime his dettes as I forgaff ze thyne? yane he vesz crabit [1] and deliuerit hime to ye tormentours. P. 60.	Mat. xviii. 32-34.—O evyll servaunt, y forgave the all thatt dett, because thou praydest me. Was it not mete also that thou shuldest have had compassion on thy folow even as y had pitie on the? And his lord was wrooth and delyvered hym to the ioylers.
Mat. xxv. 34.—Cum ze quhilk ar ye blist barnis of my fader and possess ye euerlastand kingdome quhilk is graith to zow or ye beginning of ye vardil. p. 72.	Mat. xxv. 34.—Come ye blessed chyldren of my father, inheret ye the kyngdom prepared for you from the beginninge of the worlde.
Mat. xxvii. 29-34.—Crounit with ane croune of thorne and be claischit apone his chekis and they suld cast cauels apone his kot and giff to hime vinaker. P. 41.	Mat. xxvii. 29-34.—Platted a croune of thornes and putt uppon hys heed, and smoote hym on the heed, they parted his garments and did cast lotts, and they gave hym veneger to drynke.
Mark ix. 23-24.—Cane thow trow, for al thing is possibil to hime that trowis, thane he criit and grat and said Lord I trow. P. 76.	Mark ix. 23-24.—Yf thou couldest beleve all thynges are possyble to hym that belevith. And streygthwaye the father off the chylde cryed with teares saying, Lorde I beleve.
John v. 14.—Nou thow art hail tak tent that thow sine na mair, sua yat it happine noth ye var. P. 65.	John v. 14.—Beholde thou arte made whole se thou synne no moore, lest a worsse thinge happen unto the.
Rom. viii. 17.—Giff we be the barnis of God thane ar we alsua heritours zei heritours of God and heritours with Christ. P. 38.	Rom. viii. 17.—Yf we be the sonnes we are also the heyres (the heyres I meane of God) and heyres anexed with Christ.
1 Cor. ii. 9.—The E [2] of man hes noth seine, na the eir of man hes noth hard.	1 Cor. ii. 9.—The eye hath not sene and the eare hath not herde.
1 Cor. xv. 18.—Haid he notht rissine up fra deid thane we haid beine tint and zeit in our sinnes. P. 69.	1 Cor. xv. 18.—Yf it be so thatt Christ rose not, then is youre fayth in vayne, and yetare ye in youre synnes.
1 Cor. xv. 55.—O deid quhair is thy brod? P. 70.	1 Cor. xv. 55.—Deeth where is thy stynge?

---

[1] Dr. M'Crie remarks (*Knox*, vol. i., note *N*.) that in a printed edition of Knox's Treatise on Prayer, the word "crabbid" occurs in the quotation of two verses of Scripture where in the Reformer's manuscript "angrie" is used. "Thou art crabbid, O Lord," Is. lxiv. 5, and in *v*. 9, "Be not crabbid, O Lord." This word, says Dr. M'Crie, I have never met in any old version of the Bible. It occurs, however, as we see in Gau's rendering of Mat. xviii. 34.

[2] Wyclif's (or rather Purvey's) translation of this verse is given in a footnote, p. 32, as "I saie not," and a remark is made that the transcriber or printer must have made a mistake in representing *eye* by *I*. It may seem that the capital I in this case is not more strange than capital E in Gau's treatise. As a matter of fact, *e* and *ee* are given in Middle-English Dictionaries as spellings of *eye*, but *I* is not. The quotation on page 32 was taken from Bagster's Hexapla. In Forshall and Madden's edition of Wyclif's Bible the words are printed, (1st version, 1380) *yze syz not*, (2nd version, 1388) *ize say not*.

Col. ii. 9.—Al the fouth of God ramanis verale in hime. P. 37.
Jas. ii. 19.—The dewillis trowis and trimlis. P. 29.

Col. ii. 9.—In him dwelleth all the fulnes of the godheed boddyly.
Jas. ii. 19.—The devyls also beleve and tremble.

A few specimens of Scripture renderings may now be taken from Winzet's Tractates, 1562-5, and placed alongside of the corresponding passages as printed in the first edition of the Geneva Bible. This will help to shew wherein Scottis differed from Southeroun in 1560.

WINZET, 1562-63.	GENEVA BIBLE 1560.
Ezek. xxii. 28.—Bot the prophetes of it, spargeonit thaim with untemperit morter, seing vaniteis and propheciing leis unto thaim. P. 14. (Hewison's edition).	Ezek. xxii. 28.—Her prophetes haue dawbed them with untempered morter, seeing vanities, and diuining lies unto them.
Ezek. xxii. 30.—I socht of thaim ane man that wald mak vp the haige, and set hymself in the slope before me in the landis behaif, that I suld not vterlie destroy it; bot I could fynd naine. P. 14.	Ezek. xxii. 30.—I soght for a man among them, that shulde mak up the hedge, and stand in the gap before me for the lande, that I shulde not destroy it, but I founde none.
Joel ii. 12.—Turn to me in all your hert, in fasting, sobing, and greting. P. 105.	Joel ii. 12.—Turne you unto me with all your heart, and with fasting, and with weping, and with mourning.
Luke x. 2.—That the Lorde of the winezarde send us lauchfull treu workmen thairto. P. 45.	Luke x. 2.—Pray therefore the Lord of the haruest to send forth laborers into his harvest.
Ps. lxxx. 13.—(A reference rather than a quotation). To schute oute the unclene baris, and to schut out, or cut of, alsua the wyld sangleris.[1] P. 45.	Ps. lxxx. 13.—The wilde bore out of the wood hath destroyed it, and the wilde beastes of the fielde haue eaten it up.
Acts vii. 51.—Ze haif ay gainstand the Haly spirit. P. 130.	Acts vii. 51.—Ye haue alwayes resisted the holie Gost.
1 Cor. xv. 41-42.—As a sterne differis fra an wther sterne in brychtnes, sua sall be the resurrection of the deid. P. 122.	1 Cor. xv. 41-42.—One starre differeth from another starre in glory. So also is the resurrection of the dead.
2 Cor. ix. 6.—Quha sawis scairslie sall scheir scairslie. P. 122.	2 Cor. ix. 6.—He which soweth sparingly shall reape also sparingly.
Heb. iv. 12.—Quhais Worde is mair peirceand than ony twa aigeit sworde. P. 37.	Heb. iv. 12.—The worde of God is sharper than anie two edged sworde.
Rev. iii. 15—Nother haet nor cauld. P. 26.	Rev. iii. 15—Nether colde not (nor) hote.

In chap. iv. it is stated that the Geneva Bible was the version of the Scriptures that was used by Knox and the Scottish Reformers. That statement must of course be limited to the period subsequent to 1560, when the Geneva Bible was first published. But some of Knox's writings pertain to a date previous to 1560, and in these early writings

---

[1] Exterminavit eam aper de silva : et *singularis ferus* depastus est eam, *Vulgate*. The words italicised are both in Wyclif's Bible and the Douay Bible imperfectly translated *a singular wild beast*. The Greek word in the Septuagint is *monios*.

of Knox's there are many quotations of Scripture to be found. As a rule these quotations are not drawn word for word from any English version of the Bible, but are free renderings or paraphrases of Knox's own. Occasionally a word appears that seems to have been taken from Coverdale's version, 1535; at other times a word or phrase indicates that Knox preferred the rendering in the Great Bible to what is given in Coverdale's original translation. For instance, in his denunciation of the mass, 1550, Knox uses the expression, "Who slayeth a scheip *choketh* a dog." This is Coverdale's rendering of Is. lxvi. 3, and the amendment made on it in the Great Bible is "knetcheth a dog." On the other hand, in a quotation of Gen. xlix. 6, which is given in a letter of date 1553, Knox evidently adopts the Great Bible version in preference to Coverdale's original one, and instead of saying they "houghed an ox," he says they "destroyit the citie." As has already been stated, however, the quotations of Scripture that are found in Knox's early writings are generally paraphrastic, and not taken verbatim from any version of the Bible in English. They are expressed in "auld plane Scottis," moreover, and not in an unknown "Southeroun" tongue, as the following examples will shew.

Knox's Writings prior to 1560.	Great Bible (Edition, Nov. 1541).
Deut. iv. 7.—Thair is no natioun that have thair Godis so adherent or neir unto thame as oure God, whilk is present at all oure prayeris. (On Prayer, 1554.)	Deut. iv. 7.—What other nacyon is so great that Goddes come so nye unto, as the Lorde oure God is nye unto us in all thynges as ofte as we call unto him.
Deut. vi. 6-9.—Theis wordis whilk I command the this day salbe in thi hart, and thou sal exerceis thi children in thame, thou sal talk of thame when thou art at home in thi hous, and as thou walkest be the way, and when thou lyis doun, and when thou rysis up, and thou sall bind thame for a signe upon thi hand, and they salbe paperis of remembrance[1] betwene thi eis, and thou sall wryt thame upon the postis of thy hous, and upon thi gatis. (Letter to Protestants of Scotland, 1557.	Deut. vi. 6-9.—These wordes whiche I commaund the this day shalbe in thyne hart and thou shall shewe them unto thy chyldren and shalte talke of them when thou arte at home in thyne house and as thou walkest by the waye and when thou lyest downe, and when thou rysest up, and thou shalt bynde them for a sygne upon thyne hande. And they shalbe warnynges betwene thyne eyes, and thou shalt wryte them upon the postes of thy house and upon thy gates.
Rom. vii. 24.—O unhappie man that I am, wha sal delyver me fra this bodie of syn. (Letter, 1553).	Rom. vii. 24.—O wretched man that I am, who shal delyuer me from this body subdued unto death.
Rom. viii. 26. — Mychtelie making intercessioun for us with incessibill	Rom. viii. 26.—The sprete maketh intercessyon for u,s with gronynges

---

[1] "A token of remembraunce."—*Coverdale*.

groanis whilk cannot be expressit with toung.[1] (On Prayer, 1554).

Rom. xiv. 20.—Yf a man eat with offence he synneth.[2] (Mass, 1550).

Heb. ix. 12.—By his awn blude hath he anis enterit into the halie place. (Mass, 1550).

Heb. x. 18.—Remissioun of synnis anis gotten, thair resteth na mair sacrifice. (Mass, 1550).

whyche cannot be expressed.

Rom. xiv. 20.—It is euell for that man whych eateth wyth hurte of conseyence.

Heb. ix. 12.—By hys owne bloud he entred in once into the holy place.

Heb. x. 18.—Where remissyon of these thinges is there is no more offering for synne.

A good illustration of what Winzet means by auld plane Scottis as opposed to Southeroun will be found in the published Sermons (1599) of Robert Rollock, Principal of the University, and minister of Greyfriars' Church, Edinburgh. Rollock's texts are taken from the Geneva version (Tomson's revision) of the New Testament, but the words are changed from their English into a Scottish form, as the subjoined specimens will indicate.[3]

GENEVA VERSION (Tomson's).

1 Cor. ii. 11.—For what man knoweth the things of a man, saue the spirit of a man, which is in him? euen so the things of God knoweth no man but the Spirit of God.

2 Cor. v. 5-6.—God, who also hath giuen unto us the earnest of the Spirit, therefore we are alway bold, though we know that whiles wee are at home in the body, we are absent from the Lord.

2 Cor. x. 4.—For the weapons of our warfarre are not carnall, but mightie through God to cast down holdes.

Titus iii. 5.—Not by the workes of righteousnesse, which we had done, but according to his mercie he saued us, by the washing of the new birth, and the renewing of the holy Ghost.

ROLLOCK'S TEXTS.

1 Cor. ii. 11.—For quhat man knaws the thingis of man, saue the spreit of a man, quhilk is in him? euen sa the thingis of God knawis na man, bot the Spreit of God.

2 Cor. v. 5-6.—God, quha also hes giuen unto us the arlis of the Spreit, thairfoir we ar alwayis bauld, thocht we knaw that quhylis we ar at hame in the body we ar absent from the Lord.

2 Cor. x. 4.—For the weapons of our weirfair ar not carnall, bot michtie throuch God to cast down haldis.

Titus iii. 5.—Not be the warkis of richteousnes quhilk we had done, bot according to his mercie he saued us, by the wasching of the new birth, and the renewing of the halie Gaist.

---

[1] "The sprete maketh intercession mightely for us with gronynges which cannot be expressid with tonge."—*Tyndale*.

[2] "It is euill for the man which eateth with offence."—*Geneva*, 1560.

[3] As a sample of this learned dignitary's diction, the following sentences (p. 18) may be quoted:—"It is the violent that enters in heuin, Mat. xi. 12, as ze will see ane man violentlie thring in at ane zet. Thou that wald gang to heuin, make thee for thringing throw quhill all thy guttis be almaist thrustit out."

B

MODERN SCOTCH VERSIONS OF SCRIPTURE.

WITHIN the last fifty years there have issued from the press several booklets purporting to be Scottish versions of parts of Scripture. These versions however were not called for, in order to meet any real want, and they have not served any practical purpose. They can be regarded only as literary exercises, written for the writers' amusement and put into print for the reader's entertainment; and very little entertainment some of them are fitted to give.

In 1862, there was published a Scottish version of the Gospel by St. Matthew. It was a work of neither merit nor originality. It was simply a travesty of the authorised English version, in bad spelling, which was meant to indicate Scottish pronunciation, with a vulgar Scotticism here and there from the language of low life in the north. Its diction is as unlike the Scotch of Gau and Winzet as affectation is unlike reality. The following passage will give the reader a fair notion of the style of this version:—

Chapter viii. 28-34: "An' whan he was come til the ither side intil the kintra o' the Gergesenes, there met him twa possesset wi' deevils comin' out o' the tombs, unco fierce, sae that nae man micht gang by that road. An', behald, they cried out, sayin, What hae we to do wi' thee, Jesus, thou son o' God? Art thou come here to torment us afore the time? An' there was a guid way aff frae them a hirsel o' mony swine feedin'. Sae the deevils besoucht him, sayin', Gif thou cast us out, let us gae intil the hirsel o' swine. An' he said until them, gae. An' whan they were come out, they gaed intil the hirsel o' swine: an', behald, the hale hirsel o' swine ran headlang doun a heugh intil the sea, an' perishet in the waters. An' they wha herdet them fled, an' gaed their gate intil the toun, an' tauld ilka thing, an' what was befa'en to the possesset o' the deevils. An', behald, the hale toun cam' out to meet Jesus, an' whan they saw him they besoucht him that he wad gang awa out o' their marches."

Of a considerably higher literary character than this prosaic version of St. Matthew's gospel is the Scotch version of the Psalms by the Rev. P. Hately Waddell, LL.D., which was published in 1871. In Dr. Waddell's work there is no lack of either originality or vivacity. There is rather much of both of these qualities. The translation is accordingly not a faithful representation of the original. It is a paraphrase, some would say a burlesque, of David's Psalms and sentiments: such as a woman like Mause Headrigg would be likely to give in her higher moments. There is a gusty inflation in the language as if the writer had fairly lost command of himself, and were carried away by his own verbosity. Sometimes, too, there is an assumption of familiarity with the Deity, like what we find in persons of the Mause Headrigg type, but which nevertheless is very unlike the reverential tone of the Psalms themselves. Where for instance in the authorised English version we read, Ps. xxii. 2, "O my God, I cry in the day time, but thou hearest not," it is said in Dr. Waddell's Scotch version, "My God, I hae skreight the lee-lang day, bot ye mind me nane."

As specimens of Dr. Waddell's vigorous Scotch the two following verses may be quoted:—

Ps. xxii. 12, Droves o' nowt hae rinket me roun: stoor stirks o' Bashan hae fankit me about.

Ps. cxviii. 12, They byket about me, like bees: they gaed down like a bleeze o' thorns: i' the name o' the Lord, I maun sned them by.

Not only is Dr. Waddell's language generally rhythmical, but it often runs into rhyme, sometimes for an instant in a single clause, and sometimes for a longer period in several successive sentences. The statement, "They that sow in tears shall reap in joy," reads in Dr. Waddell's version, "Wha saw wi' a tear, wi' a sang they shall shear." Of longer and more elaborate rhymes, the following will furnish favourable specimens of Dr. Waddell's peculiar paraphrase:

PSALMS XXVII. 5, 6.

For mysel in his howff he sal hap, i' the day o' dule an' dree;
He sal biel' me ben i' his biggin *then*; on a craig he sal set me hie.
Syne sae sall my head, abune my faes, be lifted fu' heigh roun' a';
An' gifts o' glee in his house I maun gie; till the Lord I maun lilt and blaw.

PSALMS XXXVII. 23-24.

Frae the Lord, the wide yett o' the mighty man's sett:
An he fuhres on his gate fu' blythe:
Tho' he stacher *a wee*, he sal nane down gae:
For the Lord hauds his han' fu' stythe.

PSALMS CV. 34, 35 . . . 40, 41.

He spak, an' the locust scho cam:
An' the worm (an' that ayont count) on the swaird:
An' they glaum'd a' the green on their grun':
An' they sorn'd on the frute o' their yaird.
They sought, an' he airtit them quails:
An' he stegh't them wi' bread frae the lift:
He racket the craig, an' the waters cam but:
They gae'd i' the wust, *like* a drift.

C

THEOCRACY IN GENEVA AND SCOTLAND.

THE statement on page 187, in regard to the Theocracy established by Calvin at Geneva, is open to misconstruction, particularly in so far as it may seem to imply that the sole authority exercised in that city and state was ecclesiastical.

The theory of Government held by the Reformers at Geneva was much the same as that preached by the Reformers in Scotland. The tenor of the Scottish theory, gathered from historical documents, may be stated in the following propositions :

I. *Civil government is authorised and ordained by God.* In the Confession of Faith, drawn up by the Scottish Reformers, and ratified by the Scottish Parliament, 1560, it is said in chapter xxiv. : " We confess and acknowledge impyres, kingdoms, dominions, and citeis, to be distructed and ordeaned by God, and the powers and authorities in the same . . . to be God's holie ordinance. . . . So that whosoever goeth about to tak away, or to confound the whole state of civill policeis now long established, we affirm the same men not onlie to be enemeis to mankinde, but also wickedlie to fight against God his expressed will (Calderwood's History, II., page 35).

II. *A hereditary monarchy established by popular consent, and a supreme magistracy and council periodically elected by the people are each agreeable to the ordinance of God.* In Geneva, in the days of Calvin, the civil Government was republican. All legislative and executive power was vested in certain Councils popularly elected for limited periods. In Scotland, the government from time immemorial till the rebellion in 1652, was monarchical. In Buchanan's treatise *De jure regni apud Scotos*, the question is asked : " By what name shall we qualify him who shall perform the part of physician to the body politic ? " The answer returned is : " About the name I am not very anxious ; but such a personage, whatever his name may be, I hold to be of the first excellence. . . . Much forecast seems discovered in the wisdom of our ancestors, who distinguished an office so honourable in its own nature by a very splendid name, King." Further on it is asked, "if the people, from a dislike to an ambitious canvass every year, should choose to elect as king an individual not possessed indeed of every regal virtue, but still eminent for nobility, etc. . . . might not he with the greatest justice be deemed a king?" And the answer to this is, " undoubtedly ; for the people have a right of investing whom they please with the sovereign power." So also Samuel Rutherford in his *Lex. Rex.*, chapter xliv., quest. 4 and 5, says that nature has not determined whether there should be one supreme ruler or many rulers in a free community, but that every free community has in it a supremacy of majesty, which it may formally place in one person or in many persons.

III. *In every Christian country, the word of God as contained in the Scriptures of the Old and New Testaments must be the fundamental law of the State, and everything inconsistent with the said word of God be held illegal.* In the first Parliament of King James VI. it was statute and ordained, "That all Kings, Princes or Magistrates whatsoever . . . which hereafter shall happen in any time to raign and beare rule over this realm . . . shall make their faithful promise by oath in the presence of the eternall God that during the whole course of their lives, they shall . . . rule the people committed to their charge according to the will and command of God revealed in his word." Rutherford accordingly says in his preface to *Lex. Rex.*, No. 29, "What civil laws parliaments make against God's word, they (Assemblies of the Church) may authoritatively declare them to be unlawful, as though an emperor (Acts xv.) had commanded fornication and eating of blood."

IV. *All civil magistrates, from the King downwards, are accordingly only vicegerents and ministers of God.* So far from having absolute and unlimited power to rule as he pleases, the King is bound to rule in accordance with God's laws, and is, as Andrew Melville told James VI., only "*God's sillie vassal.*" Many other statements in corroboration of this account of the Reformers' doctrines might be quoted, but the following will suffice. In the General Assembly's seasonable and necessary warning, 1649, it is said that "as Magistrates and their power is ordained of God, so are they in the exercise thereof, not to walke according to their own will, but according to the law of equity and righteousness, as being the ministers of God for the safety of his people: Therefore a boundless and illimitted power is to be acknowledged in no King nor Magistrate." At the coronation of King Charles II. at Scone, on the 1st January 1651, a sermon on the functions and duties of kings was preached by Robert Douglas. In the course of this sermon, Douglas said that "Kings not only have their crowns from God, but must reign according to his will. They are called *Ministers of God:* they are God's servants."

V. *Along with a civil government in the State, God has also appointed an ecclesiastical government in the Church; and within the same realm these two governments are in their respective spheres distinct, independent, and supreme.* One document in which this doctrine is clearly declared is the General Assembly's Answer to the Profession, etc., made by the Marquis of Hamilton, his Majesty's High Commissioner to the said Assembly in 1638. It is there stated that: "The Acts of the Assembly and the book of policie in the first and tenth chapters, putteth clear merches betwixt civill and ecclesiasticall jurisdiction: making every one independent in matters properly belonging to their owne judicatorie, and every one subject to the other in matters properly belonging to that other; so that as the Assembly cannot make civill laws nor repeal them, nor imped the Parliament from making or repealing civill laws, no more can the Parliament make ecclesiasticall laws originally, nor repeal or hinder the lawful Assemblies to repeal the same. For albeit Acts of the Assembly are and may be ratified in Parliament, that is only that the civill sanction may concur with the ecclesiasticall constitution, but will not stop the Assembly to recall their own act,[1] which being adnulled by them the civill ratification and sanction falls *ex consequenti.*" (Large Declaration, by the King, 1639, p. 349.) By Act of Parliament, 1570. "The jurisdiction granted to the Kirk was declared to stand in preaching of the word, ministratioun of the sacraments, and correctioun of maners." (Calderwood iii. 460.) How the freedom of action claimed for the Church within this jurisdiction was abused by injudicious preachers, who converted their pulpits into privileged sanctuaries where they asserted their right to libell and lampoon whom they pleased without interference from the civil magistrates is known to all readers of Scottish history. Notwithstanding what was declared by churchmen, therefore, we may safely say that the "merches between civil and ecclesiastical jurisdiction" were not put clear for the first hundred years after the Reformation.

---

[1] " They (Churchmen) allege that they meddle only in ecclesiastical causes . . but by ecclesiastical they mean, as their practice sheweth, any thing which is *in ordine ad ecclesiastica,* nay more, *in ordine ad spiritualia,* whatsoever may be thought conducible to the good of the Church, or to any spiritual good, and yet more vastly to the glorie of God : by which latitude of the word, *ecclesiastical,* we would know what they have left out of the compasse of their cognisance. Just nothing. For in this sense they may set the price on victuals, they may censure the actions of all men in what kind soever, because St. Paul biddeth us, '*whether we eate or drinke, or whatsoever we doe, doe it all to the glory of God.*"—(*Large Declaration,* p. 415.)

VI. *While it was declared that the word of God contains the fundamental laws of the land according to which the civil magistrate is to exercise his government, the Church claimed the right to interpret and teach the word of God to the magistrate.* In the second book of discipline it is said : " The ministeris exerce not the civill jurisdiction, bot teich the magistrat how it sould be exercit according to the word." In the contentions between civil and ecclesiastical authority during the time of the troubles in Scotland, we thus read a great deal about what is termed the Church's right of " antecedent judgment." There were ever so many cases, it was alleged, in which the magistrate had no right to take action till " an antecedent judgment " on the premises was pronounced by the Church.[1] And this claim that was made by the Church was often submitted to by the State, when the State and Church happened to be on affectionate terms. In 1641, the Parliament deputed certain of its members to wait on the General Assembly, and crave from that reverend court its judgment on the lawfulness of a certain engagement subscribed by Montrose and others. Here, says Baillie, " great wisdom was requisite." But the Assembly was equal to the occasion, and a Committee appointed to consider the question " drew up their wise answer penned by the Moderator, making that band to be unlawful and not obligatory of any." What are known as the Public Resolutions of 1651, were in like manner submitted to the Commission of Assembly for " antecedent judgment," before the King and his Ministers ventured to proclaim them.

VII. *The Church claimed the right also of calling upon and requiring the civil power to enforce her orders.* In the second book of discipline it is declared that while " the civill power sould command the spiritual to exercise and doe their office according to the word of God, the spiritual rewlaris sould requyre the Christian magistrate to minister justice and punish vice and maintaine the libertie and quietness of the kirk within their boundis." How far the Church was in this matter alleged to have pressed her authority on the State may be conjectured

---

[1] In the General Assembly of 1639 a small passage of arms took place between the King's Commissioner and the Moderator. " How farr the constitutions of the Kirk will warrand you to go on in censuring such thinges I know not," said the Commissioner, " but I believe you intend not to exclude the civile magistrat from punishing of such thinges." To this the Moderator replied with more wit and humour than might have been expected of a Churchman, " We are so farr from that, that we are content to be the *first* tryers of those thinges, that we may make schorte worke for the civile magistrat."

from the King's complaint in 1639: "If we or our Commissioner sitting in Assembly shall denie our voice to any thing which to us appeareth to be unjust, and repugnant to our laws, yet if that shall be concluded by most voices of the Assemblie, that then we are bound *jure divino* to see all these conclusions made in despight of us obeyed by all our subjects, and by our authoritie to inforce obedience to these acts; and if our Councillors or judges shall refuse to do the like, then they shall be lyable to the sentence of excommunication, and so be deprived not only of their places but of their estates " (Large Declaration, p. 411).

VIII. *While, in things civil, ecclesiastical rulers were submissive to the Magistrate; the Magistrate was required, in things spiritual, to be as submissive to the Church.* This is expressly stated in the first chapter of the second book of discipline. And very submissive high potentates sometimes were to ecclesiastical rule. King James openly declared his willingness to listen to public rebuke, if private remonstrance were adopted first, and found to fail. On the 25th March, 1596, he was present in the General Assembly, and heard ominous references to a proposal "concernyng the purgatione of the Kirk." Every estate in the realm was alleged to have "its owne gross sins," and it was whispered that even in his Majesties house there were some "offences." It behoved the church, accordingly, to do her duty to all her members. The King thereupon rose and "granted he was a sinner, as other men were, but not infected, he trusted, with anie sinne that could be called gross: and he therefore requyred that no preacher would inveygh against him or his counsell publictlie, but to come to him or them privile, and tell what is the offence; and as for himself, if he mended not, in cace he were guiltie, they might deale publictlie; his chamber doore sould be made patent to the meanest minister in Scotland, there sould not be anie meane gentleman in Scotland more subject to the good order and discipline of the Kirk than he would be." (Calderwood, v. 397.)

IX. *It was the duty of the civil and ecclesiastical powers to co-operate, and work to each other's hands for the glory of God and the welfare of men.* "They be both of God, and tend to one end, if they be rightly usit, *to wit*, to advance the glorie of God and to have godlie and gud subjectis." (Sec. Bk. of Discip.) This conviction of duty led to alliance in different forms. There was concurrent legislation. The Church drew up ecclesiastical constitutions and to these the State gave civil sanction. The State framed what at the present day would be called "bills," and the Church pronounced on these bills a favourable "antecedent judgment," which armed the State with the authority of public opinion to pass them into statutes, and enforce their observance. Local authorities, too, were ingeniously constructed out of combined civil and ecclesiastical elements. In Geneva there was a consistorial court. "It was constituted by the five pastors of the city parishes and twelve elders. These elders were selected from the two representative councils of the city, two from the Council of Sixty and the remainder from the Council of Two Hundred." (Tulloch's Leaders of Reformation.) Although an ecclesiastical court, therefore, the majority of its members were laymen and nominees of the State councils. This arrangement enlisted the interest of the State in Church affairs, and gave churchmen a certain amount of indirect influence on the councils of the city. Although ecclesiastical in name, too, the consistorial court "extended its jurisdiction over all social usages, as well as offences against morality and religion. It was a court of practical ethics in the widest sense of the term." And while its only direct weapon of authority was excommunication, if this was unavailing, offenders were transmitted to the council where they were dealt with as criminals and punished with fines or imprisonment. In Scotland there was in every Parish a Kirk-Session not unlike the consistorial court in Geneva. It had lay as well as clerical members, and the lay members outnumbered the clerical. Not a few of the ruling elders in it, too, were men of good social position. It was a court of strict inquisition, and took cognizance of every form of offence from murder to gossip, and from blasphemy to "science falsely so called." Its own censures were merely spiritual, but like the consistorial court in Geneva it brought offences formally under the notice of the magistrates. And to facilitate business it was usually arranged to have a magistrate in the Session, who sat at meetings of Session in both an ecclesiastical and a civil capacity. When a "delinquent" was found guilty in the Session of a sin that was also an offence at law punishable by a fixed penalty, he was first dealt with by the Court for his scandal and then by the Session-Bailie for his crime.

It will thus be seen that both in Geneva, in the days of Calvin, and in Scotland from the days of Queen Mary to those of Charles II. the form of government was practically theocratic. The laws in force were the laws of God: the rulers, civil and ecclesiastical, were regarded as Ministers of God: the church by her right of "antecedent judgment" had a large say in the affairs of state: and by her courts of discipline, she wielded over the community a power that was practically both spiritual and temporal. In a small state like Geneva this distribution of power made a man like Calvin virtually dictator.

At the present day, Scotsmen are content to say that Presbytery is "agreeable to the word of God," and they sneer at the pretensions of Anglicans who claim for prelatic government in the Church a *jus divinum*. At one time it was the Presbyterians that were pretentious, and the Prelatists that were modest. In their answer to the Declaration of the Parliament of England, the General Assembly, 1642, wrote that "although the Reformed Kirks do hold, without doubting, their Kirk-officers and Kirk-government by Assemblies higher and lower, in their strong and beautiful subordination, to be *jure divino* and perpetuall; yet Prelacie, as it differeth from the office of a Pastor, is almost universally acknowledged by the Prelates themselves, and their adherents, to be but an humane ordinance, introduced by humane reason, and settled by humane law and custome for supposed conveniencie." These old prelates were right. Whatever form of church-government is agreeable to Scripture, and most convenient for the people, is the one that has the best *raison d'être*, whether it be Presbytery, as in Scotland, or Prelacy, as in England.

D

THE WORD "MASS."

IN the note on page 216 it is said: "The words *Missa* and *Mass* are not Hebrew words at all. They are derived from the Latin formula, *ite, missa est.*"

The account thus given of the etymology of the Church terms *Missa* and *Mass* is quite correct;[1] but there, nevertheless, are Hebrew words that might in Roman characters be printed *Missah* and *Mas*. The latter word *Mas* occurs frequently in the Hebrew Scriptures. In the first chapter of Judges it occurs four times, and is translated in one place *tribute* and in three places *tributaries*. In the fifth chapter of the first book of Kings it occurs three times, and is there translated

---

[1] While by some authorities no doubt is expressed on this point, Prof. Skeat cautiously remarks, "*Mass*, usually said to be from the phrase, *ite missa est* (go, the congregation is dismissed), used at the end of the service: in any case, the derivation is from Latin *missus*, pp. of *mittere*, to send away."

levy. The word *Missah* on the other hand occurs once, and apparently only once, in the Hebrew Bible; and it is in Deut. xvi. 10, where it is translated *tribute*. This word *Missah*, therefore, and not *Matstsah* *(unleavened bread)*, as conjectured in the note on page 216, is evidently the word referred to by Winzet in the eleventh of his Four Score questions. The ingenuity of Winzet in connecting the Church term *Mass* or *Missa* with the Hebrew word *Missah* in Deut. xvi. 10, will appear if we read the verse as given in the authorised English translation: "Thou shalt keep the feast of weeks unto the Lord thy God with a *tribute (Missah)* of a free-will-offering of thine hand which thou shalt give." The verse, as will be seen, would read sensibly enough if the word *mass* were substituted for *tribute*, but a false meaning of the verse, and a wrong etymology of the word *mass*, would be suggested to the reader.

INDEX.

Aelfric, Abbot of Peterborough, 2, 3
Ainsworth, Dr. H., ... 331-2
Aldhelm, Bishop of Sherborne, 2
Aldred of Holy Isle, ... 2
Alford, Dean, ... 366
Alfred, King, ... 2
Allen, Cardinal, ... 237
Anderson, Mrs., ... 298
Anne of Bohemia, ... 8
Anne Boleyn, ... 114
Arbuthnot, Alexander, 152, 153
Arius, ... 261
Arundel, Archbishop, ... 8
Augustine, St., ... 276, 284, 292

Baber, Rev. Henry, ... 1
Bagster, S., 1, 9, 49, 72, 73, 100, 124, 140, 218, 234, 286, 296, 298, 387
Baillie, Robert, ... 396
Bain, Prof., ... 317
Balfour, Sir James, ... 152
Barker, Christopher, 140, 155, 191, 197, 232
Bassandyne, Thomas, ... 152, 153
Becke, Edmund, ... 122, 123
Bede, ... 2
Bellarmin, ... 240
Bergen-op-Zoom, Marquis of, ... 69
Beza, Theodore, 13, 144-7, 156-7, 159, 161-2, 164-6, 179, 180, 183, 215, 217-8, 222, 250-1, 344, 347, 368
Blayney, Dr., ... 296
Bloomfield, Dr., 78, 85, 97, 258, 337
Bodleigh, John, ... 194
Bonar, Rev. Andrew, ... 151
Bonner, Bishop, ... 122
Bristow, Richard, ... 237
Broughton, Hugh, ... 198, 327
Buchanan, George, ... 393
Burgon, Dean, 338, 342, 344, 354, 357, 364, 383
Burleigh, *See* Cecil.
Burnet, Bishop, ... 204

Calderwood, David, 151, 393, 395, 397
Calvin, John, 144, 157-8, 165-6, 180, 185-6, 251, 260-1, 393, 398-9
Carlyle, Thomas, ... 335
Caryl, Joseph, ... 329
Carmarden, Richard, ... 122

Carswell, John, Superintendent of the West of Scotland, ... 385
Catharine of Arragon, ... 142
Cecil, Lord Burleigh, ... 194-5, 199
Challoner, Dr. 234, 272, 275, 278, 283
Charles II., ... 106, 288, 394, 398
Cheke, Sir John, ... 140-3, 352
Clarke, Dr. Adam, 1, 3, 4, 9, 122, 133, 135, 171
Clement VIII., ... 240
Cochlaeus, John, ... 56-7
Conybeare, Rev. W. J., 95, 350-1, 353, 355-6, 363
Cook, Dr. John, ... 27
Cotton, Dr., ... 197
Coverdale, Miles, 77, 83, 86, 97, 100-117, 120-3, 125-9, 131-140, 142-3, 148-9, 168-9, 171, 175, 179, 215, 269, 291, 300, 308, 310-12, 314-17, 340, 319, 321, 389
Cowan, James, ... 323
Cowper, Bishop of Galloway, ... 151
Coyne, Richard, ... 234, 279, 282
Cranmer, Archbishop, 27, 47, 115, 119, 120, 140, 143, 182, 191, 200, 229
Cromwell, Oliver, ... 171
Cromwell, Thomas, 63, 65-6, 69, 115, 119, 121-2, 150, 191
Cudworth, Dr. Ralph, ... 329
Cumming, Dr., ... 331

Daye, John, ... 123
Demaus, Rev. R., 53, 56-59, 64, 66, 69, 70
Denham, Henry, ... 232
Dickson, David, ... 151
Dobson, W. T., ... 153, 298
Doddridge, Philip, 85, 332-4, 349-50, 353, 356
Donne, Gabriel, ... 67-8
Douglas, Robert, ... 394
Dudley, Earl of Leicester, ... 195

Eadie, Dr. John, 7, 8, 70, 101, 118, 122, 124, 197, 224, 297, 316, 385
Edward VI., ...139, 287
Egenolph of Frankfort, ... 101
Elizabeth of England, 176, 193, 195, 236
Ellicott, Bishop, ... 331

Elyot, Sir Thomas, ... 67
Elzevir, ... 344
Erasmus, 59, 70, 71, 80, 110, 111, 158,
179, 257, 283, 344, 368
Euing, William (Glasgow), ... 123
Eusebius, ... 142
Eutyches, ... 261

Facciolatus, Jacobus, ... 28, 269
Forshall, Rev. Josiah, ... 1, 9, 387
Foxe, John, ... 52, 68
Froschover, Christopher, ... 101
Fry, F., ... 49, 73
Fulke, Dr. William, 155, 187, 191, 197,
232-3, 249, 250, 253, 258, 378

Gammack, Dr. James, ... 154
Gardiner, Bishop, ... 241
Gau, John, 209, 255, 317, 386-7, 391
Gaunt, John of, ... 4
Geddes, Dr. Alexander, ... 313
Gell, Dr. Robert, ... 330
Gilby, Anthony, ... 149, 165
Gillespie, George, ... 27, 299
Ginsburg, Dr., ... 113
Gipps, Rev. Thomas, ... 298
Goodwin, Dr. Thomas, ... 329
Grafton, Richard, ... 100, 120, 124
Gratius, Ortuinus, ... 235
Gregory, St., ... 284
Griesbach, J. J., ... 336
Grindal, Bishop of London, ... 204
Guildford, Sir Henry, ... 54

Hamilton, Archbishop, ... 386
Hamilton, Marquis of, ... 395
Hart, Andro, ... 154
Heath, Bishop of Rochester, ... 124
Henderson, Alexander, ... 151
Henry VIII., 65-6, 114, 119, 136, 176, 287
Henry, Matthew, ... 78, 132, 211
Hereford, Nicholas de, 1, 6, 8-11, 19,
25, 155, 311
Horne, Bishop of Winchester, 202, 204
Hort, Dr., ... 344
Howson, Dr., ... 350

James VI. of Scotland 1st of
England, 32, 153-4, 187, 286-292,
295, 300, 348, 359, 394, 397
Jerome, St., 27, 29, 34, 250, 271, 347
Joye, George, ... 72
Jude, Leo., ... 165-6
Jugge, Richard, ... 191
Junius, Francis, ... 185

Kenrick, Bishop, ... 279
Knox, John, 22, 144, 149, 151, 204,
229, 385-9

Laud, Archbishop, ... 36, 295
Lee, Principal, ... 154
Leicester, Earl of. See Dudley.
L'Estrange, Roger, ... 36
Lewis, Rev. John, 100, 122, 194, 198,
278, 286, 327-332
Lewis, M., ... 155
Lightfoot, Bishop, ... 331
Lloyd, Bishop, ... 296
Luther, Martin, 53, 56-7, 60, 62, 70-1,
110-113, 165, 261
Lowth, Bishop, ... 330
Lymburn, James, ... 123

Macedonius, ... 261
Madden, Sir Frederick, 1, 9, 387
Mahomet, ... 46
Malan, Mr., ... 331
Marsh, Bishop, ... 330
Martin, Gregory, 78, 155, 232, 237-8,
249, 250, 252
Mary of England, ... 139, 142
Mary of Scotland, ... 398
Matthew, Thomas. See also
John Rogers, 100, 102, 114-5, 117,
119, 122-4, 127-9, 143, 150, 291, 300
M'Caul, Dr., ... 331
M'Crie, Dr., ... 149, 204, 229, 385-7
M'Knight, Dr. James, 334-5, 351
M'Mahon, Rev. Bernard, ... 278
Melville, Andrew, 22, 151, 186, 385, 394
Melville, James, ... 27
Menander, ... 333
Meteren, Jacob van, ... 101
Mill, John, ... 336
Mitchell, Prof. A. F., ... 255
Mombert, Dr., 6, 59, 70, 79, 101, 117-8,
124, 196, 232, 240, 297, 339
Monmouth, Humphrey, ... 55, 56
Montrose, Marquis of, ... 396
More, Sir Thomas, 9, 52-3, 60, 62-67,
79, 80
Moulton, Prof., 8, 113, 145, 197, 199,
200, 213, 238, 277
Munster, S., ... 128, 165, 166
Nary, Cornelius, ... 278
Nestorius, ... 261
Newcome, Archbishop, ... 330

Offer, Mr., ... 53
Orm or Ormin, ... 3
Orme, William, ... 335
Owen, Dr. John, ... 329

Packington, Augustine, ... 61, 62
Pagninus, 112-3, 145, 165-6, 174, 176, 269
Parker, Archbishop of Canterbury, ... 193-5, 198-9

Index. 403

Patmore, Thomas, ... 59
Pedersen, Christiern, ... 386
Philips, Henry,... 67-68
Plumptre, Dean, ... 71, 117, 198
Purvey, John, 1, 4, 6, 8-18, 20, 22-4, 26-7, 31-4, 36, 50, 155, 311, 314, 387

Rogers, John, (*see also* Thomas Matthew), 115, 116, 118, 122, 139, 143
Rolle, Richard, of Hampole, ... 3
Roye, Father, ... 72
Rollock, Robert, ... 390
Rutherford, Samuel, ... 151, 394
Row, Prof., ... 329
Row, John, of Carnock, ... 329

Sampson, Thomas, ... 149, 165
Scapula, J., ... 244
Scattergood, Dr., ... 296
Scholefield, Prof., ... 330
Scott, Dr. Hew, ... 385
Scrivener, Dr., ... 53, 331, 344
Secker, Archbishop, ... 330
Selden, John, ... 293, 328
Selwyn, Prof., ... 330-1
Shakespeare, ... 16, 102
Sixtus V., ... 239, 240
Skeat, Prof., ... 16, 17, 209, 399
Smith, Dr. Miles, ... 291-4
Smith, Dr. William, ... 8, 240
Smyth, J. Paterson, ... 59
Stephens, Robert, ... 144, 344, 347
Strype, Rev. John, ... 204
Stunica, ... 344
Symonds, Prof. John, ... 330

Taverner, Richard, 100, 102, 117-8, 120, 122-3, 129, 140, 160
Thomson, Rev. W., 335-7, 349-51, 357
Todd, Rev. H. J., ... 331

Tomson, Laurence, 140, 149, 154-5, 162-4, 184-5, 297
Trench, Archbishop of Dublin, 319, 330-1
Troy, Archbishop (Cath.) of Dublin, ... 278-9
Tulloch, Principal, ... 398
Tunstall, Bishop of London, 54-5, 59, 61-2, 124
Tyndale, John, ... 59
Tyndale, William, 27, 32, 46-7, 51-101, 103, 105, 107-111, 115, 118, 119, 123, 125-7, 139-143, 145-7, 156, 158, 165, 177-183, 186, 214-5, 238, 246, 248, 257, 291, 295, 297, 300, 308-10, 312-13, 315-7, 340, 352, 368, 379, 386, 390

Vaughan, Stephen, ... 65, 66

Waddell, Rev. P. H. 391-2
Walsh, Sir John, ... 51-54
Walsingham, Sir Francis, ... 149
Watkins, Richard, ... 232
Watson, James, ... 298
Westcott, Dr., 113, 118, 124, 128, 197, 213, 240, 295, 327, 344
Wetstein, Prof., ... 336
Whitchurch, Edward, ... 300
Whittingham, William, 144-150, 155-6, 165-6, 179-181
Winzet, Ninian, 215, 385, 388, 391
Wiseman, Cardinal, 228, 279, 283, 348
Wolsey, Cardinal, ... 58
Wordsworth, Bishop of Lincoln, 344
Wyclif, John, 1 to 48, 50-1, 69, 74-5, 77-8, 86, 89, 103, 141, 155, 160, 179, 188, 237, 243, 246, 260, 263-4, 308, 310-12, 314-5, 387-8

Young, Dr. Robert, ... 355, 361

www.ingramcontent.com/pod-product-compliance
Lightning Source LLC
Chambersburg PA
CBHW050846300426
44111CB00010B/1152